"Preece, Sharp & Rogers have become a recognized brand name trusted by students, design practitioners in an increasingly diverse field across user experience design, ubiq informatics, and mobile applications. The 4th edition refreshes this foundational textbook that continues to provide a comprehensive, current, and compelling coverage of concepts, methods, and cases of interaction design. Informed by the combined wisdom and thought leadership of these three senior academics, the book is a trusted source of applied knowledge grounded and refined by years of experience."

Professor Marcus Foth, Director, Urban Informatics Research Lab Interactive & Visual Design, School of Design, Queensland University of Technology Brisbane, Australia

"The authors of this book have succeeded! Again! This new edition reflects in full richness what constitutes modern interaction design. While being the most comprehensive and authoritative source in the field it is also amazingly accessible and a pleasure to read."

Dr. Erik Stolterman, Professor in Informatics, School of Informatics and Computing, Indiana University, Bloomington, USA

"The speed of change in ICT is both the cause and the consequence of new ways to view, design and support human interactions with digital technology. Keeping a textbook up-to-date in HCI is therefore a major challenge. Thanks to the authors' firm commitment to education and outstanding capacity to combine, in every new edition, an account of the deep foundations of the field with a broad selection of advanced topics, the complete set of all four editions of this book testifies to the remarkable evolution of HCI as a discipline. *Interaction Design* is thus not only a first-class textbook for HCI education but also an insightful depiction of how the discipline has grown and contributed to the pervasiveness of digital technology in everyday life."

Clarisse Sieckenius de Souza, Departamento de Informática, PUC-Rio, Brazil

"I've loved *Interaction Design* in the past, as it provided a contemporary line of sight between theory and practice. Its style encouraged interaction, especially for readers where English is not their first language, by capturing the wisdom in engagingly readable ways. This *4th edition* updates what is already wholesome and good, to deliver more, especially with the e-text version. I'd say this latest revision not only gives its readers the best chance to know where their learning journey ought to start, it takes them well down the track to understanding this important field with a much more critical lens."

Patrick O'Brien, Managing Director, The Amanuenses Network Pte Ltd, Singapore

"*Interaction Design* has been my textbook of choice for generalist and introductory HCI courses ever since the first edition. It is well written, with great use of examples and supplementary resources. It is authoritative and has excellent coverage. The latest edition brings the material up-to-date. Importantly, it is also an engaging read."

Ann Blandford, Professor of Human-Computer Interaction, University College London, UK

"*Interaction Design* by Preece, Sharp and Rogers offers an engaging excursion through the world of interaction design. The new edition offers a view on a broad range of topics needed for students in the field of interaction design, human-computer interaction, information design, web design or ubiquitous computing. The book should be one of the things every student should have in their backpack. It guides one through the jungle of information in our digital age. The online resources are a great help to create good classes my students and remove some weight from my backpack."

Johannes Schöning, Professor of Computer Science, Hasselt University, Belgium

"*Interaction Design* has been one of the textbooks of reference at the University of Castilla – La Mancha (Spain) for several years. It covers the main topics in Human Computer Interaction offering a comprehensive equilibrium between theoretical and practical approaches to the discipline. The new chapter about 'Interaction Design in Practice' and the remarkable updates in some chapters, with new case studies and examples, allow the user to explore the book from different perspectives and facilitate its use as a textbook in different subjects."

Professor Manuel Ortega, CHICO Group (Computer Human Interaction and Collaboration), University of Castilla - La Mancha, Spain

"*Interaction Design* is an excellent textbook for general HCI courses that covers topics from the essential theoretical and methodological knowledge to the state-of-the-art practical knowledge in HCI and interaction design.

The fourth edition again maintains this book's position as a must-have book for all HCI and interaction design students."

Youn-kyung Lim, Department of Industrial Design, KAIST, Korea

"For years this book has been my recommendation for a general introduction to Human–Computer Interaction. What I particularly admire is the combination of theoretical content exploring human understanding and behaviour, along with practical content on designing, developing, and evaluating interaction systems – all with references to the literature. The new edition updates existing content, and adds important material on recent developments, for example touch-interaction on smartphones and tablets."

Robert Biddle, Professor of Human–Computer Interaction, Carleton University, Ottawa, Canada

"This new edition provides another wonderful opportunity to reflect on the core issues of Interaction Design and their ongoing definition and redefinition in changing contexts. It's great to see the maker community welcomed into the new edition along with all the other updated material. I am confident I can continue to set this book as the basic text for my classes and for those wishing to learn more about Interaction design and related areas."

Toni Robertson, Professor of Interaction Design, University of Technology, Sydney, Australia

"This book teaches interaction design by motivating and activating the student, and there really is no other way."

Dr. Albert Ali Salah, Boğaziçi University, Turkey

"I picked up the first edition of *Interaction Design* when I started learning about HCI and interaction design and haven't left it since. Now I use the latest edition to introduce the subject to both undergraduate and research students because the book provides a truly multidisciplinary overview of IxD, doing justice to the natures of the discipline. It offers an excellent balance: from general concepts, to design, prototyping and evaluation methodology and, importantly, to plenty of colourful and inspiring examples. The new section on IxD practice is a much needed addition, as the industry keeps growing and reaches maturity."

Enrico Costanza, Electronics and Computer Science, The University of Southampton, UK

"This fourth edition is going to continue to be the Interaction Design reference book for academics and students. Our work in communication sciences and technologies will continue to find many enlightening pathways and references within the traditional human-centric approach but also deeper into social and emotional interaction issues. The updates to this edition are of utmost relevance and also underline very well the strategic relation with industry's use of HCI R&D methods and techniques nowadays."

Oscar Mealha, Department of Communication and Art, University of Aveiro, Portugal

"I have used all editions of the book in my courses. I love how each new edition continues to be relevant, vibrant and central for educating interaction designers, and keeping them up to date with the changes in the field. Thumbs up for the fourth edition, too!"

Alma Leora Culén, Design of Information Systems, University of Oslo, Norway

"The book is great. Now, I have very good resources to support me teaching my undergraduate HCI course. I really liked how the information is presented in the book; an excellent blend of theories, concepts, examples, and case studies. Moreover, I would like to use the book as one of my resources in research on HCI education. I would highly recommend this book for HCI instructors and students."

Dr. Harry B. Santoso, Instructor of Interaction System (HCI) course at Faculty of Computer Science, Universitas Indonesia, Indonesia

"For many years, *Interaction Design: Beyond Human–Computer Interaction* has been used as a major textbook or reference book for human–computer interaction (HCI) related courses for undergraduate and postgraduate students in computer science, design and industrial engineering in Chinese universities. I especially appreciate its focus on HCI design, instead of just focusing on those technological aspects of HCI. This gives students a basic but very important body of knowledge and skills in the user-centered design approach for developing usable and enjoyable products in industry settings or conducting HCI research in an academic context. The timely four revisions of the book in the past years have always kept it well updated to the newest developments in the field."

Zhengjie Liu, Professor, Director, Sino-European Usability Center, Dalian Maritime University, P.R. China

INTERACTION DESIGN
beyond human–computer interaction

Fourth Edition

PREECE · ROGERS · SHARP ·

WILEY

Contents

What's Inside

Welcome to the fourth edition of *Interaction Design: Beyond Human–Computer Interaction*, and our interactive website at **www.id-book.com**. Building on the success of the previous editions, we have substantially updated and streamlined the material to provide a comprehensive introduction to the fast-growing and multidisciplinary field of interaction design. But rather than let the book expand, we have again made a conscious effort to reduce its size – with a little help from our publisher.

Our textbook is aimed primarily at undergraduate, masters, and doctoral students from a range of backgrounds studying introductory classes in human–computer interaction, interaction design, web design, software engineering, digital media, information systems, and information studies. It will also appeal to a wide range of professionals and technology users who can dip into it and learn about a specific approach, interface, or topic.

It is called *Interaction Design: Beyond Human–Computer Interaction* because interaction design is concerned with a broader scope of issues, topics, and methods than was traditionally the scope of human–computer interaction (HCI), with a focus on the diversity of design and evaluation processes involved. We define interaction design as

> *designing interactive products to support the way people communicate and interact in their everyday and working lives.*

This relies on an understanding of the capabilities and desires of people and on the kinds of technology available to interaction designers, together with a knowledge of how to identify requirements and develop them into a suitable design. Our textbook provides an introduction to all of these areas, teaching practical techniques to support development as well as discussing possible technologies and design alternatives.

The number of different types of interface available to today's interaction designers continues to increase steadily so our textbook, likewise, has been expanded to cover this. For example, we discuss and provide examples of brain, mobile, robotic, wearable, shareable, mixed reality, and multimodel interfaces as well as more traditional desktop, multimedia, and web interfaces.

The book has 15 chapters and includes discussion of the wide range of interfaces that are now available, how cognitive, social, and affective issues apply to interaction design, and how to gather, analyze, and present data for interaction design. A central theme is that design and evaluation are interleaving, highly iterative processes, with some roots in theory but which rely strongly on good practice to create usable products. The book has a hands-on orientation and explains how to carry out a variety of techniques used to design and evaluate the wide range of applications coming onto the market. It also has a strong pedagogical design and includes many activities (with detailed comments), assignments, and the special pedagogic features discussed below.

TASTERS

We address topics and questions about the what, why, and how of interaction design. These include:

- Why some interfaces are good and others are poor
- Whether people can really multitask
- How technology is transforming the way people communicate with one another
- What users' needs are and how we can design for them
- How interfaces can be designed to change people's behavior
- How to choose between the many different kinds of interactions that are now available (e.g. talking, touching, wearing)
- What it means to design truly accessible interfaces
- The pros and cons of carrying out studies in the lab versus in the wild
- When to use qualitative versus quantitative methods
- How to construct informed consent forms
- How the detail of interview questions affects the conclusions that can safely be drawn
- How to move from a set of scenarios, personas, and use cases to initial low-fidelity prototypes
- How to represent the results of data analysis clearly
- Why it is that what people say can be different from what they do
- The ethics of monitoring and recording people's activities
- What are Agile UX and Lean UX and how do they relate to interaction design? ∎

The style of writing throughout the book is intended to be accessible to students, as well as professionals and general readers. It is largely conversational in nature and includes anecdotes, cartoons, and case studies. Many of the examples are intended to relate to readers' own experiences. The book and the associated website are also intended to encourage readers to be active when reading and to think about seminal issues. For example, a popular feature that we have included throughout is the dilemma, where a controversial topic is aired. The aim is for readers to understand that much of interaction design needs consideration of the issues, and that they need to learn to weigh up the pros and cons and be prepared to make trade-offs. We particularly want readers to realize that there is rarely a right or wrong answer, although there is a world of difference between a good design and a poor design. This book is accompanied by a website (**www.id-book.com**), which provides a variety of resources, including slides for each chapter, comments on chapter activities, and a number of in-depth case studies written by researchers and designers. Pointers to respected blogs, online tutorials, and other useful materials are provided.

Changes from Previous Editions

New to this edition is an e-text version. Publishing technology has matured considerably in recent years, to the extent that it is possible to create an interactive textbook. Our e-text version is in full color and supports note sharing, annotating, contextualized navigating, powerful search features, inserted videos, links, and quizzes. To reflect the dynamic nature of the field, the fourth edition has been thoroughly updated and new examples, images, case studies, dilemmas, and so on have been included to illustrate the changes. A brand new Chapter 12 has been included called 'Interaction design in practice,' which covers how practical UX methods, such as Agile UX and Lean UX, have become increasingly popularized and more widely used in the world of commerce and business. Old examples and methods no longer used in the field have been removed to make way for the new material (some of which can now be found on www.id-book.com). The former Chapter 12 has been removed (but is still available on the website), making the evaluation section three compact chapters. Some chapters have been completely rewritten whilst others have been extensively revised. For example, Chapters 4 and 5 have been substantially updated to reflect new developments in social media and emotional interaction, while also covering the new interaction design issues they raise, such as privacy and addiction. Many examples of new interfaces and technologies have been added to Chapter 6. Chapters 7 and 8 on data collection and analysis have also been substantially updated. We have updated our interviews with leading figures involved in innovative research, state-of-the-art design, and contemporary practice (with the exception of Gary Marsden who, we are sorry to report, died unexpectedly at the end of 2013).

Acknowledgments

Many people have helped us over the years in writing the four editions. We have benefited from the advice and support of our many professional colleagues across the world, our students, friends, and families. We especially would like to thank everyone who generously contributed their ideas and time to help make all the editions successful.

These include our colleagues and students at the College of Information Studies – 'Maryland's iSchool' – University of Maryland, and the Human–Computer Interaction Laboratory (HCIL) and Center for the Advanced Study of Communities and Information (CASCI), the Open University, University College London, and Indiana University. We would especially like to thank (in alphabetical first name order) all of the following who have helped us over the years:

Alex Quinn, Alice Robbin, Alice Siempelkamp, Alina Goldman, Allison Druin, Anijo Mathew, Ann Blandford, Ann Jones, Anne Adams, Ben Bederson, Ben Shneiderman, Carol Boston, Connie Golsteijn, Dan Green, Dana Rotman, danah boyd, Debbie Stone, Derek Hansen, Duncan Brown,

Edwin Blake, Eva Hornecker, Gill Clough, Harry Brignull, Janet van der Linden, Jennifer Ferreira, Jennifer Golbeck, Jeff Rick, Joh Hunt, Johannes Schöning, Jon Bird, Jonathan Lazar, Judith Segal, Julia Galliers, Kent Norman, Laura Plonka, Leeann Brumby, Mark Woodroffe, Michael Wood, Nadia Pantidi, Nick Dalton, Nicolai Marquardt, Paul Marshall, Philip 'Fei' Wu, Rachael Bradley, Rafael Cronin, Richard Morris, Richie Hazlewood, Rob Jacob, Rose Johnson, Stefan Kreitmayer, Stephanie Wilson, Tammy Toscos, Tina Fuchs, Tom Hume, Tom Ventsias, Toni Robertson and Youn-kyung Lim.

We are particularly grateful to Nadia Pantidi and Mara Balestrini for filming, editing, and compiling a series of on the spot 'talking heads' videos, where they posed probing questions to the diverse set of attendees at CHI'11 and CHI'14, including a variety of CHI people from across the globe. The questions included asking about the future of interaction design and whether HCI has gone too wild. There are about 50 of them – which can be viewed on our website. We are also indebted to danah boyd, Harry Brignull, Leah Beuchley, Kees Dorst, Ellen Gottesdiener, and the late Gary Marsden for generously contributing in-depth text-based interviews in the book.

Finally, we would like to thank our editor and the production team at Wiley who once more have been very supportive and encouraging throughout the process of developing this fourth edition: Georgia King, Deborah Egleton and Juliet Booker.

About the Authors

The authors are senior academics with a background in teaching, researching, and consulting in the UK, USA, Canada, Australia, and Europe. Having worked together on three previous editions of this book, and an earlier textbook on Human–Computer Interaction, they bring considerable experience in curriculum development, using a variety of media for distance learning as well as face-to-face teaching. They have considerable knowledge of creating learning texts and websites that motivate and support learning for a range of students. All three are specialists in interaction design and human–computer interaction (HCI). In addition they bring skills from other disciplines. Yvonne Rogers started off as a cognitive scientist, Helen Sharp is a software engineer, and Jenny Preece works in information systems. Their complementary knowledge and skills enable them to cover the breadth of concepts in interaction design and HCI to produce an interdisciplinary text and website.

Jennifer Preece is Professor and Dean in the College of Information Studies – Maryland's iSchool – at the University of Maryland. Jenny's research focuses at the intersection of information, community, and technology. She is particularly interested in community participation on- and offline. She has researched ways to support empathy and social support online, patterns of online participation, reasons for not participating (i.e. lurking), strategies for supporting online communication, development of norms, and the attributes of successful technology-supported communities. Currently Jenny is researching how technology can be used to educate and motivate citizens to contribute quality data to citizen science projects. This research contributes to the broader need for the collection of data about the world's flora and fauna at a time when many species are in rapid decline due to habitat loss, pollution, and climate change. She was author of one of the first books on online communities: *Online Communities: Designing Usability, Supporting Sociability* (2000) published by John Wiley & Sons Ltd. Jenny is widely published, a regular keynote speaker, and a member of the ACM's CHI Academy.

Helen Sharp is Professor of Software Engineering and Associate Dean in the Faculty of Mathematics, Computing and Technology at the Open University. Originally trained as a software engineer, it was watching the frustration of users and the clever 'work-arounds' they developed that inspired her to investigate HCI, user-centered design, and the other related disciplines that now underpin the field of interaction design. Her research focuses on the study of professional software practice and the effect of human and social aspects on software development, leveraging her expertise in the intersection between interaction design and software engineering, and working closely with practitioners to support practical impact. She is very active in both the software engineering and CHI communities and has had a long association with practitioner-related conferences. Helen is on the editorial board of several software engineering journals including IEEE's *Transactions on Software Engineering*, and is a regular invited speaker at academic and practitioner venues.

Yvonne Rogers is the Director of the Interaction Centre at University College London and a Professor of Interaction Design. She is internationally renowned for her work in HCI and ubiquitous computing and, in particular, for her pioneering approach to innovation and ubiquitous learning. She was awarded a prestigious EPSRC dream fellowship to rethink the relationship between ageing, computing, and creativity. Yvonne is widely published and the author of two recent books: *The Secrets of Creative People* (2014, Belmont Press) and *HCI Theory: Classical, Modern and Contemporary* (2012, Morgan Claypool). She is also a regular keynote speaker. Former positions include: Professor of Interaction Design at the Open University (2006–2011), Professor of Human-Computer Interaction at the School of Informatics and Computing at Indiana University (2003–2006), and Professor in the former School of Cognitive and Computing Sciences at Sussex University (1992–2003). She has also been a Visiting Professor at University of Cape Town, Melbourne University, Stanford, Apple, Queensland University, and UCSD. She is a Fellow of the British Computer Society and the ACM's CHI Academy.

Chapter 1

WHAT IS INTERACTION DESIGN?

Objectives

The main aims of this chapter are to:

- Explain the difference between good and poor interaction design.
- Describe what interaction design is and how it relates to human–computer interaction and other fields.
- Explain the relationship between the user experience and usability.
- Describe what and who is involved in the process of interaction design.
- Outline the different forms of guidance used in interaction design.
- Enable you to evaluate an interactive product and explain what is good and bad about it in terms of the goals and core principles of interaction design.

1.1 Introduction

How many interactive products are there in everyday use? Think for a minute about what you use in a typical day: smartphone, tablet, computer, remote control, coffee machine, ATM, ticket machine, printer, iPod, GPS, e-reader, TV, electric toothbrush, radio, games console . . . the list is endless. Now think for a minute about how usable they are. How many are actually easy, effortless, and enjoyable to use? Some, like the iPod, are a joy to use. Others, like a ticket machine, can be very frustrating. Why is there a difference?

Many products that require users to interact with them, such as smartphones and social networking sites, have been designed primarily with the user in mind. They are generally easy and enjoyable to use. Others, such as switching from viewing a rented movie on your smart TV to watching a sports channel, or setting the alarm on a digital clock, have not necessarily been designed with the users in mind, but have been engineered primarily as systems to perform set functions. While they may work effectively, it can be at the expense of how they will be used by real people.

One main aim of interaction design is to reduce the negative aspects (e.g. frustration, annoyance) of the user experience while enhancing the positive ones (e.g. enjoyment, engagement). In essence, it is about developing interactive products[1] that are easy, effective, and pleasurable to use – from the users' perspective. In this chapter we begin by examining what interaction design is. We look at the difference between good and poor design, highlighting how products can differ radically in how usable and enjoyable they are. We then describe what and who is involved in the process of interaction design. The user experience, which is a central concern of interaction design, is then introduced. Finally, we outline how to characterize the user experience in terms of usability goals, user experience goals, and design principles. An assignment is presented at the end of the chapter in which you have the opportunity to put into practice what you have read by evaluating the design of an interactive product.

1.2   Good and Poor Design

A central concern of interaction design is to develop interactive products that are usable. By this is generally meant easy to learn, effective to use, and providing an enjoyable user experience. A good place to start thinking about how to design usable interactive products is to compare examples of well- and poorly-designed ones. Through identifying the specific weaknesses and strengths of different interactive products, we can begin to understand what it means for something to be usable or not. Here, we describe two examples of poorly designed products – a voice mail system used in hotels and the ubiquitous remote control device – and contrast these with two well-designed examples of products that perform the same function.

(1) Voice Mail System

Imagine the following scenario. You are staying at a hotel for a week while on a business trip. You discover you have left your cell phone at home so you have to rely on the hotel's facilities. The hotel has a voice mail system for each room. To find out if you have a message, you pick up the handset and listen to the tone. If it goes 'beep, beep, beep' there is a message. To find out how to access the message you have to read a set of instructions next to the phone. You read and follow the first step:

'1. Touch 41.'
The system responds: 'You have reached the Sunny Hotel voice message center. Please enter the room number for which you would like to leave a message.'

You wait to hear how to listen to a recorded message. But there are no further instructions from the phone. You look down at the instruction sheet again and read:

---

[1]We use the term interactive products generically to refer to all classes of interactive systems, technologies, environments, tools, applications, services, and devices.

'2. Touch*, your room number, and #.'
You do so and the system replies: 'You have reached the mailbox for room 106. To leave a message, type in your password.'

You type in the room number again and the system replies: 'Please enter room number again and then your password.'

You don't know what your password is. You thought it was the same as your room number, but clearly it's not. At this point you give up and call reception for help. The person at the desk explains the correct procedure for recording and listening to messages. This involves typing in, at the appropriate times, the room number and the extension number of the phone (the latter is the password, which is different from the room number). Moreover, it takes six steps to access a message and five steps to leave a message. You go out and buy a new cell phone.

What is problematic with this voice mail system?

- It is infuriating.
- It is confusing.
- It is inefficient, requiring you to carry out a number of steps for basic tasks.
- It is difficult to use.
- It has no means of letting you know at a glance whether any messages have been left or how many there are. You have to pick up the handset to find out and then go through a series of steps to listen to them.
- It is not obvious what to do: the instructions are provided partially by the system and partially by a card beside the phone.

Now consider the following phone answering machine. Figure 1.1 shows two small sketches of an answering machine phone. Incoming messages are represented using physical marbles. The number of marbles that have moved into the pinball-like chute indicates the number of messages. Dropping one of these marbles into a slot in the machine causes the recorded message to play. Dropping the same marble into another slot on the phone dials the caller who left the message.

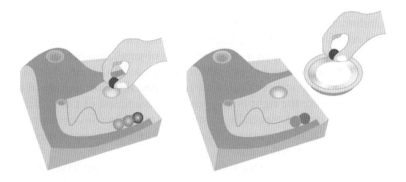

Figure 1.1 The marble answering machine

Source: Adapted from Gillian Crampton Smith: "The Hand that Rocks the Cradle" *ID Magazine*, May/June 1995, pp. 60–65.

How does the marble answering machine differ from the voice mail system?

- It uses familiar physical objects that indicate visually at a glance how many messages have been left.
- It is aesthetically pleasing and enjoyable to use.
- It only requires one-step actions to perform core tasks.
- It is a simple but elegant design.
- It offers less functionality and allows anyone to listen to any of the messages.

The marble answering machine is considered a design classic and was designed by Durrell Bishop while he was a student at the Royal College of Art in London (described by Crampton Smith, 1995). One of his goals was to design a messaging system that represented its basic functionality in terms of the behavior of everyday objects. To do this, he capitalized on people's everyday knowledge of how the physical world works. In particular, he made use of the ubiquitous everyday action of picking up a physical object and putting it down in another place. This is an example of an interactive product designed with the users in mind. The focus is on providing them with an enjoyable experience but one that also makes efficient the activity of receiving messages. However, it is important to note that although the marble answering machine is a very elegant and usable design, it would not be practical in a hotel setting. One of the main reasons is that it is not robust enough to be used in public places: for instance, the marbles could easily get lost or be taken as souvenirs. Also, the need to identify the user before allowing the messages to be played is essential in a hotel setting. When considering the design of an interactive product, therefore, it is important to take into account where it is going to be used and who is going to use it. The marble answering machine would be more suited in a home setting – provided there were no children who might be tempted to play with the marbles!

> **Video** of Durrell Bishop's answering machine at **http://vimeo.com/19930744**

(2) Remote Control Device

Every home entertainment system, be it the TV, cable, smart TV, music system, and so forth, comes with its own remote control device. Each one is different in terms of how it looks and works. Many have been designed with a dizzying array of small, multicolored, and double-labeled buttons (one on the button and one above or below it) that often seem arbitrarily positioned in relation to one another. Many viewers, especially when sitting in their living room, find it difficult to locate the right ones, even for the simplest of tasks, like pausing or finding the main menu. It can be especially frustrating for those who need to put on their reading glasses each time to read the buttons. The remote control device appears to have been put together very much as an afterthought.

In contrast, much effort and thought went into the design of the TiVo remote control. The buttons were large, clearly labeled, and logically arranged, making them easy to locate and use in conjunction with the menu interface that appears on the TV monitor. In terms of its physical form, the remote device was designed to fit into the palm of a hand, having a peanut shape. It also has a playful look and feel about it: colorful buttons and cartoon icons were used that are very distinctive, making it easy to identify them in the dark and without having to put reading glasses on.

How was it possible to create such a usable and appealing remote device where so many others have failed? The answer is simple: TiVo invested the time and effort to follow a user-centered design process. Specifically, TiVo's director of product design at the time involved potential users in the design process, getting their feedback on everything from the feel of the device in the hand to where best to place the batteries – making them easy to replace but not prone to falling out. He and his design team also resisted the trap of 'buttonitis' – to which so many other remote controls have fallen victim – where buttons breed like rabbits, one for every new function. They did this by restricting the number of control buttons embedded in the device to the essential ones. Other functions were then represented as part of the menu options and dialog boxes displayed on the TV screen, which could be selected via the core set of physical control buttons. The result was a highly usable and pleasing device that has received much praise and numerous design awards.

DILEMMA

What is the best way to interact with a smart TV?

A challenge facing Smart TV providers is how to enable users to interact with online content such that it can still be as easy and enjoyable to do as it was with previous generations of TV, with a remote control device. Viewers can now select a whole range of content via their TV screens, but it also involves having to type in passwords and search terms, while scrolling through lots of menus, etc. In many ways it has become more like a computer than a TV. This raises the question of whether the remote control is the best input device to use for someone who is sat on a sofa or chair that is some distance from the TV wide screen. Another possibility is to add a keyboard and touch pad to the remote for menu/icon selection and text input. However, this can be clunky and awkward to use, especially with only one hand. An alternative is to provide an on-screen keyboard and number pad – as Apple TV has done (see Figure 1.2). It has designed a slimline remote device that controls the cursor on the TV screen. However, to type requires pecking at a grid of alphanumeric letters/numbers that is not the same as the conventional QWERTY keyboard on phones and computers. This style of interaction can be painstakingly slow; it is also easy to overshoot and select the wrong letter or number. Another option is to download an app onto a smartphone and interact with the keypad as if texting. But the app has to be opened each time to act as 'a remote' and is only as good as the person whose smartphone it is.

Might there be a better way to choose between thousands of films or send an email whilst sat on the sofa using the TV?

One innovative solution is Minuum's new keyboard that works a bit like a Wii remote, except that you point at an online staggered line keyboard to select characters. This layout seems more intuitive and faster to use on a small device, especially with one hand. ∎

(Continued)

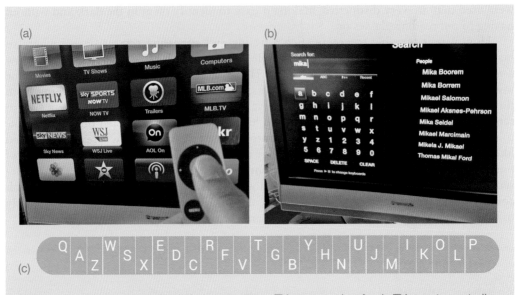

Figure 1.2 (a) Interacting with digital content on a TV screen using Apple TV remote controller (b) The online table of letters and numbers that the user has to select by pressing one button on the remote (c) Minuum's small staggered keyboard

Source: Image (c) Courtesy of Whirlscape http://minuum.com/.

Link to a more in-depth discussion of the ins and outs of the different kinds of remote physical and digital input devices, at **http://minuum.com/who-forgot-the-smart-tv/**

1.2.1 What to Design

Designing interactive products requires considering who is going to be using them, how they are going to be used, and where they are going to be used. Another key concern is to understand the kind of activities people are doing when interacting with the products. The appropriateness of different kinds of interfaces and arrangements of input and output devices depends on what kinds of activities are to be supported. For example, if the activity is to enable people to bank online, then an interface that is secure, trustworthy, and easy to navigate is essential. In addition, an interface that allows the user to find out new information about the services offered by the bank without it being intrusive would be useful.

The world is becoming suffused with technologies that support increasingly diverse activities. Just think for a minute what you can currently do using computer-based systems: send messages, gather information, write essays, control power plants, program, draw, plan,

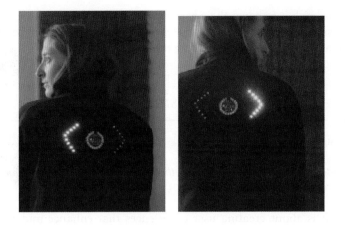

Figure 1.3 Turn signal biking jacket using e-textiles developed by Leah Beuchley
Source: Photos courtesy of Leah Buechley.

calculate, monitor others, play games – to name but a few. Now think about the types of interfaces and interactive devices that are available. They, too, are equally diverse: multi-touch displays, speech-based systems, handheld devices, and large interactive displays – to name but a few. There are also many ways of designing how users can interact with a system, e.g. via the use of menus, commands, forms, icons, gestures, etc. Furthermore, ever more innovative everyday artifacts are being created, using novel materials, such as e-textiles and wearables (see Figure 1.3).

The interfaces for everyday consumer items, like cameras, microwave ovens, and wash-ing machines, that used to be physical and the realm of product design, are now predomi-nantly digitally based, requiring interaction design (called consumer electronics). The move towards transforming human–human transactions into solely interface-based ones has also introduced a new kind of customer interaction. Self-checkouts at grocery stores, airports, and libraries are becoming the norm where customers themselves have to check in their own goods, luggage, or books. Instead of a friendly face helping them out, interfaces bark orders at them. While more cost-effective, it puts the onus on the users to interact with the system. Accidentally pressing the wrong button can result in a frustrating, and sometimes mortifying, experience, especially for first-time users.

What this all amounts to is a multitude of choices and decisions that interaction designers have to make for an ever-increasing range of products. A key question for interaction design is: how do you optimize the users' interactions with a system, environment, or product, so that they support and extend the users' activities in effective, useful, and usable ways? One could use intuition and hope for the best. Alternatively, one can be more principled in decid-ing which choices to make by basing them on an understanding of the users. This involves:

- Taking into account what people are good and bad at.
- Considering what might help people with the way they currently do things.
- Thinking through what might provide quality user experiences.
- Listening to what people want and getting them involved in the design.
- Using tried and tested user-based techniques during the design process.

The aim of this book is to cover these aspects with the goal of teaching you how to carry out interaction design. In particular, it focuses on how to identify users' needs and the context of their activities, and from this understanding move to designing usable, useful, and pleasurable interactive products.

1.3   What Is Interaction Design?

By interaction design, we mean

> *designing interactive products to support the way people communicate and interact in their everyday and working lives.*

Put another way, it is about creating user experiences that enhance and augment the way people work, communicate, and interact. More generally, Winograd describes it as "designing spaces for human communication and interaction" (1997, p. 160). Thackara views it as "the why as well as the how of our daily interactions using computers" (2001, p. 50) while Saffer emphasizes its artistic aspects: "the art of facilitating interactions between humans through products and services" (2010, p. 4).

A number of terms have been used to emphasize different aspects of what is being designed, including user interface design, software design, user-centered design, product design, web design, experience design, and interactive system design. Interaction design is increasingly being accepted as the umbrella term, covering all of these aspects. Indeed, many practitioners and designers, who in the 1990s would have described what they were doing as interface design or interactive system design, now promote what they are doing as interaction design.

The focus of interaction design is very much concerned with practice, i.e. how to design user experiences. It is not wedded to a particular way of doing design, but is more eclectic, promoting the use of a range of methods, techniques, and frameworks. Which is given prominence or is currently in vogue will very much depend on the time and context (Lowgren and Stolterman, 2004; Saffer, 2010).

How does interaction design differ from other approaches to the design of computer-based systems, such as software engineering? A simple analogy to another profession, concerned with creating buildings, may clarify this difference. In his account of interaction design, Winograd (1997) asks how architects and civil engineers differ when faced with the problem of building a house. Architects are concerned with the people and their interactions with each other and with the house being built. For example, is there the right mix of family and private spaces? Are the spaces for cooking and eating in close proximity? Will people live in the space being designed in the way it was intended to be used? In contrast, engineers are interested in issues to do with realizing the project. These include practical concerns like cost, durability, structural aspects, environmental aspects, fire regulations, and construction methods. Just as there is a difference between designing and building a house, so too is there a distinction between designing an interactive product and engineering the software for it.

1.3.1   The Components of Interaction Design
We view interaction design as fundamental to all disciplines, fields, and approaches that are concerned with researching and designing computer-based systems for people (see Figure 1.4).

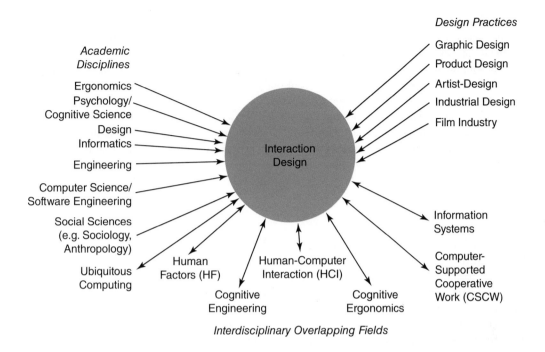

Figure 1.4 Relationship among contributing academic disciplines, design practices, and interdisciplinary fields concerned with interaction design (double-headed arrows mean overlapping)

Why are there so many and what do they all do? Furthermore, how do the various disciplines, fields, and design approaches differ from one another?

We have already described the distinction between interaction design and software engineering. The differences between interaction design and the other approaches referred to in the figure are largely down to which methods, philosophies, and lenses they use to study, analyze, and design computers. Another way they vary is in terms of the scope and problems they address. For example, Information Systems is concerned with the application of computing technology in domains like business, health, and education, whereas Computer-Supported Cooperative Work (CSCW) is concerned with the need also to support multiple people working together using computer systems (Greif, 1988).

BOX 1.1

Is interaction design beyond HCI?

We see the main difference between Interaction Design (ID) and Human–Computer Interaction (HCI) as one of scope. ID has cast its net much wider, being concerned with the theory, research, and practice of designing user experiences for all manner of technologies, systems,

(Continued)

and products, whereas HCI has traditionally had a narrower focus, being "concerned with the design, evaluation, and implementation of interactive computing systems for human use and with the study of major phenomena surrounding them" (ACM SIGCHI, 1992, p. 6). That is one of the reasons why we chose to call our book *Interaction Design: Beyond Human–Computer Interaction*, to reflect the wider scope.

What about Human Factors and Ergonomics? We see Ergonomics and Human Factors as having closely overlapping goals with HCI, being concerned with understanding the interactions among humans and other aspects of a system in order to optimize human well-being and overall system performance. ∎

1.3.2   Who Is Involved in Interaction Design?

From Figure 1.4 it can also be seen that many people are involved, ranging from social scientists to movie-makers. This is not surprising given that technology has become such a pervasive part of our lives. But it can all seem rather bewildering to the onlooker. How does the mix of players work together?

Designers need to know many different things about users, technologies, and interactions between them in order to create effective user experiences. At the very least, they need to understand how people act and react to events and how they communicate and interact with each other. To be able to create engaging user experiences, they also need to understand how emotions work, what is meant by aesthetics, desirability, and the role of narrative in human experience. Developers also need to understand the business side, the technical side, the manufacturing side, and the marketing side. Clearly, it is difficult for one person to be well versed in all of these diverse areas and also know how to apply the different forms of knowledge to the process of interaction design. Interaction design is mostly carried out by multidisciplinary teams, where the skill sets of engineers, designers, programmers, psychologists, anthropologists, sociologists, artists, toy makers, and others are drawn upon. It is rarely the case, however, that a design team would have all of these professionals working together. Who to include in a team will depend on a number of factors, including a company's design philosophy, its size, purpose, and product line.

One of the benefits of bringing together people with different backgrounds and training is the potential of many more ideas being generated, new methods developed, and more creative and original designs being produced. However, the downside is the costs involved. The more people there are with different backgrounds in a design team, the more difficult it can be to communicate and make progress forward with the designs being generated. Why? People with different backgrounds have different perspectives and ways of seeing and talking about the world. What one person values as important others may not even see (Kim, 1990). Similarly, a computer scientist's understanding of the term 'representation' is often very different from a graphic designer's or a psychologist's.

What this means in practice is that confusion, misunderstanding, and communication breakdowns can surface in a team. The various team members may have different ways of talking about design and may use the same terms to mean quite different things. Other problems can arise when a group of people who have not previously worked as a team is thrown together. For example, Philips found that its multidisciplinary teams that were responsible for developing ideas and products for the future experienced a number of difficulties, namely that project team members did not always have a clear idea of who needed what information, when, and in what form (Lambourne *et al*, 1997).

ACTIVITY 1.1

In practice, the makeup of a given design team depends on the kind of interactive product being built. Who do you think should be involved in developing:
1. A public kiosk providing information about the exhibits available in a science museum?
2. An interactive educational website to accompany a TV series?

Comment
Ideally, each team will have a number of different people with different skill sets. For example, the first interactive product would include:
- Graphic and interaction designers, museum curators, educational advisers, software engineers, software designers, ergonomists.

The second project would include:
- TV producers, graphic and interaction designers, teachers, video experts, software engineers, software designers.

In addition, as both systems are being developed for use by the general public, representative users, such as school children and parents, should be involved.

In practice, design teams often end up being quite large, especially if they are working on a big project to meet a fixed deadline. For example, it is common to find teams of 15 people or more working on a website project for an extensive period of time, like six months. This means that a number of people from each area of expertise are likely to be working as part of the project team. ■

1.3.3 Interaction Design Consultants

Interaction design is now widespread in product development. In particular, website consultants, global corporations, and the computing industries have all realized its pivotal role in successful interactive products. The presence or absence of good interaction design can make or break a company. To get noticed in the highly competitive field of web products requires standing out. Being able to say that your product is easy, effective, and engaging to use is seen as central to this. Marketing departments are also realizing how branding, the number of hits, customer return rate, and customer satisfaction are greatly affected by the usability of a website.

There are many interaction design consultancies now. These include established companies, such as Cooper, NielsenNorman Group, and IDEO, and more recent ones that specialize in a particular area, such as job board software (e.g. Madgex) or mobile design (e.g. CXpartners). IDEO is a large global enterprise, with branches across the world and 30 years of experience in the area. They design products, services, and environments for other companies,

Figure 1.5 An innovative product developed by IDEO: wireless cell phones for Telespree. The phones were designed to be inexpensive, playful, and very simple to use, employing voice recognition for driving the interaction and only one button, for turning them on and off

Source: IDEO, http://www.ideo.com/.

pioneering new user experiences (Spreenberg *et al*, 1995). They have developed thousands of products for numerous clients, each time following their particular brand of interaction design (see Figure 1.5). Some of their most famous designs include the first mouse used by Apple, the Palm V and mMode, the integrated service platform for AT&T cell phones. They were also involved in the design of the TiVo system. More recently, they have focused on designing solutions with climate change at the forefront. Their approach emphasizes design thinking and lies at the intersection of insight and inspiration, informed by business, technology, and culture.

1.4 The User Experience

The user experience (UX) is central to interaction design. By this it is meant how a product behaves and is used by people in the real world. Nielsen and Norman (2014) define it as encompassing "all aspects of the end-user's interaction with the company, its services, and its products." As stressed by Garrett (2010, p. 10), "every product that is used by someone has a user experience: newspapers, ketchup bottles, reclining armchairs, cardigan sweaters." More specifically, it is about how people feel about a product and their pleasure and satisfaction when using it, looking at it, holding it, and opening or closing it. It includes their overall impression of how good it is to use, right down to the sensual effect small details have on them, such as how smoothly a switch rotates or the sound of a click and the touch of a button when pressing it. An important aspect is the quality of the experience someone has, be it a quick one, such as topping up a cell phone, a leisurely one, such as playing with an interactive toy, or an integrated one, such as visiting a museum (Law *et al*, 2009).

It is important to point out that one cannot design a user experience, only design for a user experience. In particular, one cannot design a sensual experience, but only create the design features that can evoke it. For example, the outside case of a cell phone can be designed to be smooth, silky, and fit in the palm of a hand; when held, touched, looked at, and interacted with, that can provoke a sensual and satisfying user experience. Conversely, if it is designed to be heavy and awkward to hold, it is much more likely to end up providing a poor user experience, one that is uncomfortable and unpleasant.

Designers sometimes refer to UX as UXD. The addition of the D to UX is meant to encourage design thinking that focuses on the quality of the user experience rather than on the set of design methods to use (Allanwood and Beare, 2014). As Norman (2004) has stressed for many years, "It is not enough that we build products that function, that are understandable and usable, we also need to build joy and excitement, pleasure and fun, and yes, beauty to people's lives."

ACTIVITY 1.2

The iPod phenomenon

Apple's classic (and subsequent) generations of iPods (e.g. Touch, Nano, Shuffle) have been a phenomenal success. How do you think this happened?

Comment

Apple realized early on that successful interaction design involves creating interactive products that have a quality user experience. The sleek appearance of the iPod music player (see Figure 1.6), its simplicity of use, its elegance in style, its distinct family of rainbow colors, a novel interaction style that many people discovered was a sheer pleasure to learn and use, the catchy naming of its product and content (iTunes, iPod), among many other design features, led to it becoming one of the greatest of its kind and a must-have fashion item for teenagers, students, and others alike. While there were many competing players on the market at the time – some with more powerful functionality, others that were cheaper and easier to use, or with bigger screens and more memory, and so on – the quality of the overall user experience paled in comparison with that provided by the iPod. ■

Figure 1.6 The iPod Nano Touch

Source: ©Press Association, reproduced with permission.

There are many aspects of the user experience that can be considered and ways of taking them into account when designing interactive products. Of central importance are the usability, the functionality, the aesthetics, the content, the look and feel, and the sensual and emotional appeal. In addition, Carroll (2004) stresses other wide-reaching aspects, including fun, health, social capital (the social resources that develop and are maintained through social networks, shared values, goals, and norms), and cultural identity, e.g. age, ethnicity, race, disability, family status, occupation, education. At a more subjective level, McCarthy and Wright (2004) discuss the importance of people's expectations and the way they make sense of their experiences when using technology.

How realistic is it for interaction designers to take all of these factors (and potentially many others) into account and, moreover, be able to translate and combine them to produce quality user experiences? Put frankly, there is no magic formula to help them. As of yet, there isn't a unifying theory or framework that can be readily applied by interaction designers. However, there are numerous conceptual frameworks, tried and tested design methods, guidelines, and many relevant research findings – these are described throughout the book. Here, we begin by outlining the process and goals of interaction design.

More generally, McCarthy and Wright's (2004) *Technology as Experience* framework accounts for the user experience largely in terms of how it is felt by the user. They recognize that defining experience is incredibly difficult because it is so nebulous and ever-present to us, just as swimming in water is to a fish. Nevertheless, they have tried to capture the essence of human experience by describing it in both holistic and metaphorical terms. These comprise a balance of sensual, cerebral, and emotional threads. Their framework draws heavily from the philosophical writings of Dewey and Pragmatism, which focus on the sense-making aspects of human experience. As Dewey (1934) points out: "Emotion is the moving and cementing force. It selects what is congruous and dyes what is selected with its color, thereby giving qualitative unity to materials externally disparate and dissimilar. It thus provides unity in and through the varied parts of experience."

McCarthy and Wright propose four core threads that make up our holistic experiences: sensual, emotional, compositional, and spatio-temporal:

- *The sensual thread.* This is concerned with our sensory engagement with a situation and is similar to the visceral level of Norman's model. It can be equated with the level of absorption people have with various technological devices and applications, most notable being computer games, smartphones, and chat rooms, where users can be highly absorbed in their interactions at a sensory level. These can involve thrill, fear, pain, and comfort.

- *The emotional thread.* Common examples of emotions that spring to mind are sorrow, anger, joy, and happiness. In addition, the framework points out how emotions are intertwined with the situation in which they arise – e.g. a person becomes angry with a computer because it does not work properly. Emotions also involve making judgments of value. For example, when purchasing a new cell phone, people may be drawn to the ones that are most cool-looking but be in an emotional turmoil because they are the most expensive. They can't really afford them but they really would like one of them.

- *The compositional thread.* This is concerned with the narrative part of an experience, as it unfolds, and the way a person makes sense of it. For example, when shopping online, the options laid out to people can lead them in a coherent way to making a desired purchase or they can lead to frustrating experiences resulting in no purchase being made. When in this situation, people ask themselves questions such as: What is this about? Where am I? What has happened? What is going to happen next? What would happen if . . . ? The compositional thread is the internal thinking we do during our experiences.

- *The spatio-temporal thread*. This refers to the space and time in which our experiences take place and their effect upon those experiences. There are many ways of thinking about space and time and their relationship with one another: for example, we talk of time speeding up, standing still, and slowing down, while we talk of space in terms of public and personal places, and needing one's own space.

The threads are meant as ideas to help designers think and talk more clearly and concretely about the relationship between technology and experience. By describing an experience in terms of its interconnected aspects, the framework can aid thinking about the whole experience of a technology rather than as fragmented aspects, e.g. its usability, its marketability, or its utility. For example, when buying clothes online, the framework can be used to capture the whole gamut of experiences, including: the fear or joy of needing to buy a new outfit; the time and place where it can be purchased, e.g. online stores or shopping mall; the tensions of how to engage with the vendor, e.g. the pushy sales assistant or an anonymous website; the value judgment involved in contemplating the cost and how much one is prepared to spend; the internal monologue that goes on where questions are asked such as will it look good on me, what size should I buy, do I have shoes to match, do I need to try it on, how easy will it be to wash, will I need to iron it each time, and how often will I be able to wear it? All of these aspects can be described in terms of the four threads and in so doing highlight which aspects are more important for a given product. For example, if you were to do this exercise when buying a new car versus a domestic energy-saving device, you would find you would get quite different descriptions.

1.5   The Process of Interaction Design

The process of interaction design involves four basic activities:

1. Establishing requirements
2. Designing alternatives
3. Prototyping
4. Evaluating.

These activities are intended to inform one another and to be repeated. For example, measuring the usability of what has been built in terms of whether it is easy to use provides feedback that certain changes must be made or that certain requirements have not yet been met. Eliciting responses from potential users about what they think and feel about what has been designed, in terms of its appeal, touch, engagement, usefulness, and so on, can help explicate the nature of the user experience that the product evokes.

Evaluating what has been built is very much at the heart of interaction design. Its focus is on ensuring that the product is appropriate. It is usually addressed through a user-centered approach to design, which, as the name suggests, seeks to involve users throughout the design process. There are many different ways of achieving this: for example, through observing users, talking to them, interviewing them, modeling their performance, asking them to fill in questionnaires, and even asking them to become co-designers. The findings from the different ways of engaging and eliciting knowledge from users are then interpreted with respect to ongoing design activities (we give more detail about all these aspects of evaluation in Chapters 13 to 15).

Equally important as involving users when evaluating an interactive product is understanding what people do. Chapters 3, 4, and 5 explain in detail how people act and interact with one another, with information, and with various technologies, together with describing their abilities, emotions, needs, desires, and what causes them to get annoyed, frustrated, lose patience, and get bored. Such knowledge can greatly help designers determine which solutions to choose from the many design alternatives available, and how to develop and test these further. Chapter 10 describes how an understanding of people and what they do can be translated to requirements, while Chapters 9 and 11 discuss how to involve users effectively in the design process.

A main reason for having a better understanding of people in the contexts in which they live, work, and learn is that it can help designers understand how to design interactive products that will fit those niches. A collaborative planning tool for a space mission, intended to be used by teams of scientists working in different parts of the world, will have quite different needs from one targeted at customer and sales agents, to be used in a furniture store to draw up kitchen layout plans. Understanding the differences between people can also help designers appreciate that one size does not fit all; what works for one user group may be totally inappropriate for another. For example, children have different expectations than adults about how they want to learn or play. They may find having interactive quizzes and cartoon characters helping them along to be highly motivating, whereas most adults find them annoying. Conversely, adults often like talking-heads discussions about topics, but children find them boring. Just as everyday objects like clothes, food, and games are designed differently for children, teenagers, and adults, so interactive products should be designed for different kinds of user.

Learning more about people and what they do can also reveal incorrect assumptions that designers may have about particular user groups and what they need. For example, it is often assumed that because of deteriorating vision and dexterity, old people want things to be big – be it text or graphical elements appearing on a screen or the physical controls, like dials and switches, used to control devices. This may be true for some old people, but studies have shown that many people in their 70s, 80s, and older are perfectly capable of interacting with standard-size information and even small interfaces, e.g. cell phones, just as well as those in their teens and 20s, even though, initially, some might think they will find it difficult (Siek *et al*, 2005). It is increasingly the case that as people get older, they do not like to consider themselves as lacking in cognitive and manual skills. Being aware of people's sensitivities is as important as knowing how to design for their capabilities.

Being aware of cultural differences is also an important concern for interaction design, particularly for products intended for a diverse range of user groups from different countries. An example of a cultural difference is the dates and times used in different countries. In the USA, for example, the date is written as month, day, year (e.g. 05/21/15) whereas in other countries it is written in the sequence of day, month, year (e.g. 21/05/15). This can cause problems to designers when deciding on the format of online forms, especially if intended for global use. It is also a concern for products that have time as a function, e.g. operating systems, digital clocks, car dashboards. Which cultural group do they give preference to? How do they alert users to the format that is set as default? This raises the question of how easily an interface designed for one user group can be used and accepted by another (Callahan, 2005). Moreover, why is it that certain products, like the iPod, are universally accepted by people from all parts of the world, whereas websites are designed differently and reacted to differently by people from different cultures?

As well as there being standard differences in the way cultures communicate and represent information, designers from different cultures (that can be cross- or within-country) will often use different form factors, images, and graphical elements when creating products and dialog features for an interface. This can take the form of contrasting designs, where different colors, types of images, and structuring of information are used to appeal to people in different countries (see Figure 1.7).

Figure 1.7 Anna the online sales agent, designed to be subtly different for UK and US customers. What are the differences and which is which? What should Anna's appearance be like for other countries, like India, South Africa, or China?

Source: Reproduced with permission from IKEA Ltd.

BOX 1.2

Accessibility

Accessibility refers to the degree to which an interactive product is accessible by as many people as possible. A focus is on people with disabilities.[2]

But what does it mean to be disabled? Definitions vary, but the following captures the main points. People are considered to be disabled if:

- They have a mental or physical impairment.
- The impairment has an adverse effect on their ability to carry out normal day-to-day activities.
- The adverse effect is substantial and long term (meaning it has lasted for 12 months, or is likely to last for more than 12 months or for the rest of their life).

Whether or not a person is considered to be disabled changes over time with age, or as recovery from an accident progresses. In addition, the severity and impact of an impairment can vary over the course of a day or in different environmental conditions.

It is quite common, when people first consider the topic of accessibility and interaction design, to consider it largely in terms of a specific physical disability, such as the inability to walk or being visually impaired. However, it can often be the case that a person will have more than one disability. There is a wide range of disabilities including:

- Color-blindness: The inability to distinguish between two colors affects approximately 1 in 10 men and 1 in 200 women. This has an impact on the use of color for highlighting or distinguishing interface elements.
- Dyslexia: Although usually associated with difficulties in reading and writing, there are many different forms of dyslexia, some of which affect the way in which people comprehend the totality of concepts. A relatively simple interaction design decision that can cause difficulties for people with dyslexia is the contrast between foreground and background text or images.
- Physical impairments: These range from conditions such as tremor or shaking, weakness, pain, reduced control of limbs, inability to sit upright, to short or missing limbs.

Quesenbery (2009) comments on how accessibility is often considered as making sure there aren't any barriers to access for assistive technologies but without regard to usability, while usability usually targets everyone who uses a site or product, without considering people who have disabilities. The challenge is to create a good user experience for people with disabilities that is both accessible and usable. ■

---

[2] The accepted terminology when discussing disabilities varies between countries. For example, people with disabilities is preferred in the US, while disabled people is preferred in the UK. In this book we have followed the publisher's policy of using the USA terminology.

1.6 Interaction Design and the User Experience

Part of the process of understanding users is to be clear about the primary objective of developing an interactive product for them. Is it to design an efficient system that will allow them to be highly productive in their work, or is it to design a learning tool that will be challenging and motivating, or is it something else? To help identify the objectives we suggest classifying them in terms of usability and user experience goals. Traditionally, usability goals have been viewed as being concerned with meeting specific usability criteria, e.g. efficiency, whereas, more recently, user experience goals have been concerned with explicating the nature of the user experience, e.g. to be aesthetically pleasing. It is important to note, however, that the distinction between the two types of goal is not clear-cut, since usability is fundamental to the quality of the user experience and, conversely, aspects of the user experience, such as how it feels and looks, are inextricably linked with how usable the product is. We distinguish between them here to help clarify their roles but stress the importance of considering them together when designing for a user experience. Also, historically, HCI was concerned primarily with usability (known as usability engineering) but has since become concerned with understanding, designing for, and evaluating a wider range of user experience aspects.

1.6.1 Usability Goals

Usability refers to ensuring that interactive products are easy to learn, effective to use, and enjoyable from the user's perspective. It involves optimizing the interactions people have with interactive products to enable them to carry out their activities at work, at school, and in their everyday lives. More specifically, usability is broken down into the following goals:

- effective to use (effectiveness)
- efficient to use (efficiency)
- safe to use (safety)
- having good utility (utility)
- easy to learn (learnability)
- easy to remember how to use (memorability).

Usability goals are typically operationalized as questions. The purpose is to provide the interaction designer with a concrete means of assessing various aspects of an interactive product and the user experience. Through answering the questions, designers can be alerted very early on in the design process to potential design problems and conflicts that they might not have considered. However, simply asking 'is the system easy to learn?' is not going to be very helpful. Asking about the usability of a product in a more detailed way – for example, 'how long will it take a user to figure out how to use the most basic functions for a new smartwatch; how much can they capitalize on from their prior experience; and how long would it take a user to learn the whole set of functions?' – will elicit far more information. Below we give a description of each goal and a question for each one.

- Effectiveness is a very general goal and refers to how good a product is at doing what it is supposed to do.

Question: Is the product capable of allowing people to learn, carry out their work efficiently, access the information they need, or buy the goods they want?

- Efficiency refers to the way a product supports users in carrying out their tasks. The marble answering machine described at the beginning of this chapter was considered efficient in that it let the user carry out common tasks, e.g. listening to messages, through a minimal number of steps. In contrast, the voice mail system was considered inefficient because it required the user to carry out many steps and learn an arbitrary set of sequences for the same common task. This implies that an efficient way of supporting common tasks is to let the user use single button or key presses. An example of where this kind of efficiency mechanism has been employed effectively is in online shopping. Once users have entered all the necessary personal details in an online form to make a purchase, they can let the web-site save all their personal details. Then, if they want to make another purchase at that site, they don't have to re-enter all their personal details again. A highly successful mechanism patented by Amazon.com is the one-click option, which requires users only to click a single button when they want to make another purchase.

Question: Once users have learned how to use a product to carry out their tasks, can they sustain a high level of productivity?

- Safety involves protecting the user from dangerous conditions and undesirable situations. In relation to the first ergonomic aspect, it refers to the external conditions where people work. For example, where there are hazardous conditions – such as X-ray machines or toxic chemicals – operators should be able to interact with and control computer-based systems remotely. The second aspect refers to helping any kind of user in any kind of situation avoid the dangers of carrying out unwanted actions accidentally. It also refers to the perceived fears users might have of the consequences of making errors and how this affects their behavior. To make interactive products safer in this sense involves (i) preventing the user from making serious errors by reducing the risk of wrong keys/buttons being mistakenly activated (an example is not placing the quit or delete-file command right next to the save command on a menu) and (ii) providing users with various means of recovery should they make errors. Safe interactive systems should engender confidence and allow the user the opportunity to explore the interface to try out new operations (see Figure 1.8a). Other safety mechanisms include undo facilities and confirmatory dialog boxes that give users another chance to consider their intentions (a well-known example is the appearance of a dialog box, after issuing the command to delete everything in the trashcan, saying: 'Are you sure you want to remove all the items in the Trash permanently?' – see Figure 1.8b).

Question: What is the range of errors that are possible using the product and what measures are there to permit users to recover easily from them?

- Utility refers to the extent to which the product provides the right kind of functionality so that users can do what they need or want to do. An example of a product with high utility is an accounting software package that provides a powerful computational tool that accountants can use to work out tax returns. An example of a product with low utility is a software drawing tool that does not allow users to draw freehand but forces them to use a mouse to create their drawings, using only polygon shapes.

Question: Does the product provide an appropriate set of functions that will enable users to carry out all their tasks in the way they want to do them?

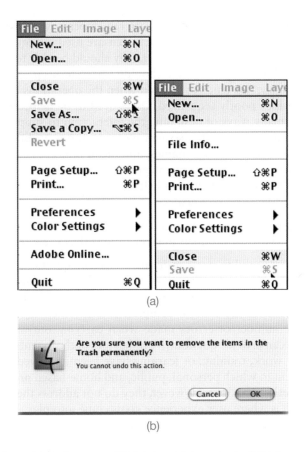

Figure 1.8 (a) A safe and unsafe menu. Which is which and why? (b) A warning dialog box for Mac OS X

- Learnability refers to how easy a system is to learn to use. It is well known that people don't like spending a long time learning how to use a system. They want to get started straight away and become competent at carrying out tasks without too much effort. This is especially so for interactive products intended for everyday use (e.g. social media, email, GPS) and those used only infrequently (e.g. online tax forms). To a certain extent, people are prepared to spend longer learning more complex systems that provide a wider range of functionality, like web authoring tools. In these situations, pop-up tutorials can help by providing contextualized step-by-step material with hands-on exercises. A key concern is determining how much time users are prepared to spend learning a product. It seems a waste if a product provides a range of functionality that the majority of users are unable or not prepared to spend time learning how to use.

Question: Is it possible for the user to work out how to use the product by exploring the interface and trying out certain actions? How hard will it be to learn the whole set of functions in this way?

- Memorability refers to how easy a product is to remember how to use, once learned. This is especially important for interactive products that are used infrequently. If users haven't used an operation for a few months or longer, they should be able to remember or at least rapidly be reminded how to use it. Users shouldn't have to keep relearning how to carry out tasks. Unfortunately, this tends to happen when the operations required to be learned are obscure, illogical, or poorly sequenced. Users need to be helped to remember how to do tasks. There are many ways of designing the interaction to support this. For example, users can be helped to remember the sequence of operations at different stages of a task through meaningful icons, command names, and menu options. Also, structuring options and icons so they are placed in relevant categories of options, e.g. placing all the drawing tools in the same place on the screen, can help the user remember where to look to find a particular tool at a given stage of a task.

Question: What kinds of interface support have been provided to help users remember how to carry out tasks, especially for products and operations they use infrequently?

As well as couching usability goals in terms of specific questions, they are turned into usability criteria. These are specific objectives that enable the usability of a product to be assessed in terms of how it can improve (or not) a user's performance. Examples of commonly used usability criteria are time to complete a task (efficiency), time to learn a task (learnability), and the number of errors made when carrying out a given task over time (memorability). These can provide quantitative indicators of the extent to which productivity has increased, or how work, training, or learning have been improved. They are also useful for measuring the extent to which personal, public, and home-based products support leisure and information-gathering activities. However, they do not address the overall quality of the user experience, which is where user experience goals come into play.

1.6.2   User Experience Goals

A diversity of user experience goals has been articulated in interaction design, which cover a range of emotions and felt experiences. These include desirable and undesirable ones, as shown in Table 1.1.

Desirable aspects		
Satisfying	Helpful	Fun
Enjoyable	Motivating	Provocative
Engaging	Challenging	Surprising
Pleasurable	Enhancing sociability	Rewarding
Exciting	Supporting creativity	Emotionally fulfilling
Entertaining	Cognitively stimulating	
Undesirable aspects		
Boring	Unpleasant	
Frustrating	Patronizing	
Making one feel guilty	Making one feel stupid	
Annoying	Cutesy	
Childish	Gimmicky	

Table 1.1 Desirable and undesirable aspects of the user experience

Many of these are subjective qualities and are concerned with how a system feels to a user. They differ from the more objective usability goals in that they are concerned with how users experience an interactive product from their perspective, rather than assessing how useful or productive a system is from its own perspective. Whereas the terms used to describe usability goals comprise a small distinct set, many more terms are used to describe the multifaceted nature of the user experience. They also overlap with what they are referring to. In so doing, they offer subtly different options for expressing the way an experience varies for the same activity over time, technology, and place. For example, we may describe listening to music in the shower as highly pleasurable, but consider it more apt to describe listening to music in the car as enjoyable. Similarly, listening to music on a high-end powerful music system may invoke exciting and emotionally fulfilling feelings, while listening to it on an iPod Shuffle may be serendipitously enjoyable, especially not knowing what tune is next. The process of selecting terms that best convey a user's feelings, state of being, emotions, sensations, and so forth when using or interacting with a product at a given time and place can help designers understand the multifaceted and changing nature of the user experience.

ACTIVITY 1.3

There are more desirable than undesirable aspects of the user experience listed in Table 1.1. Why do you think this is so?

Comment

The two lists we have come up with are not meant to be exhaustive. There are likely to be more – both desirable and undesirable – as new products surface. The reason for there being more of the former is that a primary goal of interaction design is to create positive experiences. There are many ways of achieving this.

Similar to usability goals, user experience concepts are most useful when turned into specific questions. For example, when considering how engaging an interactive virtual agent is for an online store, one can ask:

How long do users interact with the virtual sales agent? Do they suspend their disbelief when typing in questions?

To consider the effect of its appeal one can ask:

What is the user's immediate response to the agent's appearance? Is it one of mockery, dismay, or enjoyment? Do they smile, laugh, or scoff?

The concepts can be further defined in terms of elements that contribute to making a user experience pleasurable, fun, exciting, etc. They include attention, pace, play, interactivity, conscious and unconscious control, style of narrative, and flow. The concept of flow (Csikszentmihalyi, 1997) is popular in interaction design for informing the design of user experiences for

(Continued)

websites, video games, and other interactive products. It refers to a state of intense emotional involvement that comes from being completely involved in an activity, like playing music, and where time flies. Instead of designing web interfaces to cater for visitors who know what they want, they can be designed to induce a state of flow, leading the visitor to some unexpected place, where they become completely absorbed. In an interview with *Wired* magazine, Csik-szentmihalyi (1996) uses the analogy of a gourmet meal to describe how a user experience can be designed to be engrossing, "starting off with the appetizers, moving on to the salads and entrées, and building toward dessert and not knowing what will follow."

Those working in the computer games industry have acknowledged for a long time that there is an important relationship between pleasure and usability. Counter-intuitively, they also realized it can work in a negative direction. Many gamers enjoy and find most challenging non-easy video games, which contravene usability goals (Frohlich and Murphy, 1999). Banging a plastic hammer to hit a virtual nail represented on the computer screen, compared with using a more efficient way to do the same thing, e.g. selecting an option using command keys, may require more effort and be more error-prone but can result in a much more enjoyable and fun experience.

Not all usability and user experience goals will be relevant to the design and evaluation of an interactive product being developed. Some combinations will also be incompatible. For example, it may not be possible or desirable to design a process control system that is both safe and fun. Recognizing and understanding the nature of the relationship between usability and other user experience goals is central to interaction design. It enables designers to become aware of the consequences of pursuing different combinations when designing products and highlight potential trade-offs and conflicts. As suggested by Carroll (2004), articulating the interactions of the various components of the user's experience can lead to a deeper and more significant interpretation of the role of each component. ■

BOX 1.3
Beyond usability: designing to persuade

Schaffer (2009) argues that we should be focusing more on the user experience and less on usability. He points out how many websites are designed to persuade or influence rather than enable users to perform their tasks in an efficient manner. For example, many online shopping sites are in the business of selling services and products, where a core strategy is to entice people to buy what they might not have thought they needed. Online shopping experiences are increasingly about persuading people to buy rather than being designed to make shopping easy. This involves designing for persuasion, emotion, and trust – which may or may not be compatible with usability goals.

This entails determining what customers will do, whether it is to make a donation, buy a product, or renew a membership and involves encouraging, suggesting, or reminding the user of things they might like or need. Many online travel sites try to lure visitors to purchase additional items (such as hotels, insurance, car rental, car parking, day trips) besides the flight they went to book originally and will add a list full of tempting graphics to the visitor's booking form, which they have to scroll through before being able to complete their transaction. These persuasion opportunities need to be designed to be eye-catching and enjoyable – in the same way an array of products are attractively laid out in the aisles of a grocery store that one is required to walk past before reaching one's desired product. Some online sites, however, have gone too far; for example, adding items to the customer's shopping basket (e.g. insurance, special delivery) that the shopper has to deselect if not wanted. This sneaky add-on approach can often result in a negative experience. More generally, this deceptive approach to UX has been described by Harry Brignull as 'dark patterns' (see http://darkpatterns.org/). Shoppers often become annoyed if they notice decisions, that cost money, have been made on their behalf without them even being asked (see Figure 1.9). The key is to nudge people in subtle and pleasant ways that they can trust and feel comfortable with. ■

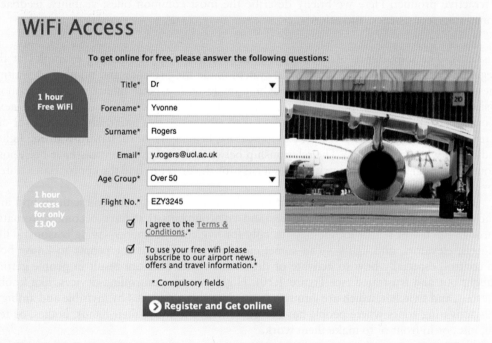

Figure 1.9 Dark pattern. In order to get free WiFi at this airport, you have to subscribe to news, offers, and travel information. The box is already checked and you cannot uncheck it

1.6.3   Design Principles

Design principles are used by interaction designers to aid their thinking when designing for the user experience. These are generalizable abstractions intended to orient designers towards thinking about different aspects of their designs. A well-known example is feedback: products should be designed to provide adequate feedback to the users to ensure they know what to do next in their tasks. Another one that has become increasingly important is findability (Morville, 2005). This refers to the degree to which a particular object is easy to discover or locate – be it navigating a website, moving through a building, or finding the delete image option on a digital camera.

Design principles are derived from a mix of theory-based knowledge, experience, and common sense. They tend to be written in a prescriptive manner, suggesting to designers what to provide and what to avoid at the interface – if you like, the dos and don'ts of interaction design. More specifically, they are intended to help designers explain and improve their designs (Thimbleby, 1990). However, they are not intended to specify how to design an actual interface, e.g. telling the designer how to design a particular icon or how to structure a web portal, but act more like triggers to designers, ensuring that they have provided certain features at an interface.

A number of design principles have been promoted. The best known are concerned with how to determine what users should see and do when carrying out their tasks using an interactive product. Here we briefly describe the most common ones: visibility, feedback, constraints, consistency, and affordance.

Visibility. The importance of visibility is exemplified by our contrasting examples at the beginning of the chapter. The voice mail system made the presence and number of waiting messages invisible, while the answer machine made both aspects highly visible. The more visible functions are, the more likely it is that users will be able to know what to do next. Norman (1988) describes the controls of a car to emphasize this point. The controls for different operations are clearly visible, e.g. indicators, headlights, horn, hazard warning lights, indicating what can be done. The relationship between the way the controls have been positioned in the car and what they do makes it easy for the driver to find the appropriate control for the task at hand.

In contrast, when functions are out of sight, it makes them more difficult to find and know how to use. For example, devices and environments that have become automated through the use of sensor technology (usually for hygiene and energy-saving reasons) – like faucets, elevators, and lights – can sometimes be more difficult for people to know how to control, especially how to activate or deactivate them. This can result in people getting caught out and frustrated (see Figure 1.10). Highly visible controlling devices, like knobs, buttons, and switches, which are intuitive to use, have been replaced by invisible and ambiguous activating zones where people have to guess where to move their hands, bodies, or feet on, into, or in front of to make them work.

Feedback. Related to the concept of visibility is feedback. This is best illustrated by an analogy to what everyday life would be like without it. Imagine trying to play a guitar, slice bread using a knife, or write using a pen if none of the actions produced any effect for several seconds. There would be an unbearable delay before the music was produced, the bread was cut, or the words appeared on the paper, making it almost impossible for the person to continue with the next strum, cut, or stroke.

Feedback involves sending back information about what action has been done and what has been accomplished, allowing the person to continue with the activity. Various kinds of

Figure 1.10 A sign in the restrooms at Cincinnati airport. Because it is not visible to the user as to what to do to turn the faucet (tap) on and off, a sign has been added to explain what is normally an everyday and well-learned activity. It does not explain, however, what to do if you are wearing black clothing

feedback are available for interaction design – audio, tactile, verbal, visual, and combinations of these. Deciding which combinations are appropriate for different kinds of activities and interactivities is central. Using feedback in the right way can also provide the necessary visibility for user interaction.

Constraints. The design concept of constraining refers to determining ways of restricting the kinds of user interaction that can take place at a given moment. There are various ways this can be achieved. A common design practice in graphical user interfaces is to deactivate certain menu options by shading them gray, thereby restricting the user only to actions permissible at that stage of the activity (see Figure 1.11). One of the advantages of this form of constraining is that it prevents the user from selecting incorrect options and thereby reduces the chance of making a mistake. The use of different kinds of graphical representations can also constrain a person's interpretation of a problem or information space. For example,

Figure 1.11 A menu showing restricted availability of options as an example of logical constraining. Shaded areas indicate deactivated options

Source: Adobe product box shot reprinted with permission from Adobe Systems Incorporated.

flow chart diagrams show which objects are related to which, thereby constraining the way the information can be perceived. The physical design of a device can also constrain how it is used; for example, the external slots in a computer have been designed to only allow a cable or card to be inserted in a certain way. Sometimes, however, the physical constraint is ambiguous, as shown in Figure 1.12.

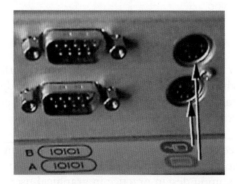

Figure 1.12 Where do you plug in the mouse and keyboard? This figure shows part of the back of a computer. There are two sets of connectors; the two on the right are for a mouse and a keyboard. They look identical and are physically constrained in the same way. How do you know which is which? Do the labels help?

Source: Photograph courtesy of Baddesigns.com.

Consistency. This refers to designing interfaces to have similar operations and use similar elements for achieving similar tasks. In particular, a consistent interface is one that follows rules, such as using the same operation to select all objects. For example, a consistent operation is using the same input action to highlight any graphical object at the interface, such as always clicking the left mouse button. Inconsistent interfaces, on the other hand, allow exceptions to a rule. An example is where certain graphical objects (e.g. email messages presented in a table) can be highlighted only by using the right mouse button, while all other operations are highlighted using the left button. A problem with this kind of inconsistency is that it is quite arbitrary, making it difficult for users to remember and making the users more prone to mistakes.

One of the benefits of consistent interfaces, therefore, is that they are easier to learn and use. Users have to learn only a single mode of operation that is applicable to all objects. This principle works well for simple interfaces with limited operations, such as a portable radio with a small number of operations mapped onto separate buttons. Here, all the user has to do is learn what each button represents and select accordingly. However, it can be more problematic to apply the concept of consistency to more complex interfaces, especially when many different operations need to be designed for. For example, consider how to design an interface for an application that offers hundreds of operations, e.g. a word-processing application. There is simply not enough space for a thousand buttons, each of which maps onto an individual operation. Even if there were, it would be extremely difficult and time-consuming for the user to search through them all to find the desired operation. A much more effective design solution is to create categories of commands that can be mapped into subsets of operations.

Affordance. This is a term used to refer to an attribute of an object that allows people to know how to use it. For example, a mouse button invites pushing (in so doing activating clicking) by the way it is physically constrained in its plastic shell. At a simple level, to afford means 'to give a clue' (Norman, 1988). When the affordances of a physical object are perceptually obvious, it is easy to know how to interact with it. For example, a door handle affords pulling, a cup handle affords grasping, and a mouse button affords pushing. The term has since been much popularized in interaction design, being used to describe how interfaces should make it obvious as to what can be done at them. For example, graphical elements like buttons, icons, links, and scrollbars are talked about with respect to how to make it appear obvious how they should be used: icons should be designed to afford clicking, scrollbars to afford moving up and down, buttons to afford pushing.

Norman (1999) suggests that there are two kinds of affordance: perceived and real. Physical objects are said to have real affordances, like grasping, that are perceptually obvious and do not have to be learned. In contrast, user interfaces that are screen-based are virtual and do not have these kinds of real affordances. Using this distinction, he argues that it does not make sense to try to design for real affordances at the interface – except when designing physical devices, like control consoles, where affordances like pulling and pressing are helpful in guiding the user to know what to do. Alternatively, screen-based interfaces are better conceptualized as perceived affordances, which are essentially learned conventions.

There are numerous websites and guidebooks that provide more exhaustive sets of design principles that we have just touched upon here, with specific examples for designing for the web,

GUIs, and, more generally, interaction design. A well-known resource is Tog's First Principles of Interaction Design (asktog.com).

Applying Design Principles in Practice

One of the problems of applying more than one of the design principles in interaction design is that trade-offs can arise between them. For example, the more you try to constrain an interface, the less visible information becomes. The same can also happen when trying to apply a single design principle. For example, the more an interface is designed to afford through trying to resemble the way physical objects look, the more it can become cluttered and difficult to use. Consistency can be a problematic design principle; trying to design an interface to be consistent with something can make it inconsistent with something else. Furthermore, sometimes inconsistent interfaces are actually easier to use than consistent interfaces. This is illustrated by Grudin's (1989) use of the analogy of where knives are stored in a house. Knives come in a variety of forms, e.g. butter knives, steak knives, table knives, fish knives. An easy place to put them all and subsequently locate them is in the top drawer by the sink. This makes it easy for everyone to find them and follows a simple consistent rule. But what about the knives that don't fit or are too sharp to put in the drawer, like carving knives and bread knives? They are placed in a wooden block. And what about the best knives kept only for special occasions? They are placed in the cabinet in another room for safekeeping. And what about other knives like putty knives and paint-scraping knives used in home projects (kept in the garage) and jack-knives (kept in one's pockets or backpack)? Very quickly the consistency rule begins to break down.

Grudin notes how, in extending the number of places where knives are kept, inconsistency is introduced, which in turn increases the time needed to learn where they are all stored. However, the placement of the knives in different places often makes it easier to find them because they are at hand for the context in which they are used and are also next to the other objects used for a specific task, e.g. all the home project tools are stored together in a box in the garage. The same is true when designing interfaces: introducing inconsistency can make it more difficult to learn an interface but in the long run can make it easier to use.

ACTIVITY 1.4

One of the main design principles for website design is simplicity. Nielsen proposes that designers go through all of their design elements and remove them one by one. If a design works just as well without an element, then remove it. Do you think this is a good design principle? If you have your own website, try doing this and seeing what happens. At what point does the interaction break down?

Comment

Simplicity is certainly an important design principle. Many designers try to cram too much into a screenful of space, making it unwieldy for people to find what they are interested in.

Removing design elements to see what can be discarded without affecting the overall function of the website can be a salutary lesson. Unnecessary icons, buttons, boxes, lines, graphics, shading, and text can be stripped, leaving a cleaner, crisper, and easier-to-navigate website. However, graphics, shading, coloring, and formatting can make a site aesthetically pleasing and enjoyable to use. Plain vanilla sites with just lists of text and a few links may not be as appealing and may put certain visitors off returning. Good interaction design involves getting the right balance between aesthetic appeal and the optimal amount and kind of information per page. ■

Assignment

This assignment is intended for you to put into practice what you have read about in this chapter. Specifically, the objective is to enable you to define usability and user experience goals and to transform these and other design principles into specific questions to help evaluate an interactive product.

Find an everyday handheld device, e.g. remote control, digital camera, smartphone, and examine how it has been designed, paying particular attention to how the user is meant to interact with it.

(a) From your first impressions, write down what first comes to mind as to what is good and bad about the way the device works.

(b) Give a description of the user experience resulting from interacting with it.

(c) Based on your reading of this chapter and any other material you have come across, compile a set of usability and user experience goals that you think will be most relevant in evaluating the device. Decide which are the most important ones and explain why.

(d) Translate each of your sets of usability and user experience goals into two or three specific questions. Then use them to assess how well your device fares.

(e) Repeat (c) and (d) but this time using the design principles outlined in the chapter.

(f) Finally, discuss possible improvements to the interface based on the answers obtained for (d) and (e).

Summary

In this chapter we have looked at what interaction design is and its importance when developing apps, products, services, and systems. To begin, a number of good and bad designs were presented to illustrate how interaction design can make a difference. We described who and what is involved in interaction design, and the core set of design processes that need to be followed. We explained in detail what usability and user experience are and how they have been characterized, and how to operationalize them in order to assess the quality of a user experience resulting from interacting with an interactive product. The increasing emphasis on designing for the user experience and not just products that are usable was stressed. A number of core design principles were also introduced that provide guidance for helping to inform the interaction design process.

Key points:
- Interaction design is concerned with designing interactive products to support the way people communicate and interact in their everyday and working lives.
- Interaction design is multidisciplinary, involving many inputs from wide-ranging disciplines and fields.
- The notion of the user experience is central to interaction design.
- Optimizing the interaction between users and interactive products requires taking into account a number of interdependent factors, including context of use, types of activity, accessibility, cultural differences, and user groups.
- Identifying and specifying relevant usability and user experience goals can help lead to the design of good interactive products.
- Design principles, such as feedback and simplicity, are useful heuristics for analyzing and evaluating aspects of an interactive product.

Further Reading

Here we recommend a few seminal readings on interaction design and the user experience (in alphabetical order). A more comprehensive list of useful books, articles, websites, videos, and other material can be found at our website.

COOPER, A., REIMANN, R., CRONIN, D. and NOESSEL, C. (2014) *About Face: The essentials of interaction design* (4th edn). John Wiley & Sons Inc. This fourth edition of *About Face* provides an updated overview of what is involved in interaction design and is written in a personable style that appeals to practitioners and students alike.

GARRETT, J. J. (2010) *The Elements of User Experience: User-centered design for the web and beyond* (2nd edn). New Riders Press. This is the second edition of the very popular coffee-table introductory book to interaction design. It focuses on how to ask the right questions when designing for a user experience. It emphasizes the importance of understanding how products work on the outside, i.e. when a person comes into contact with those products and tries to work with them. It also takes into account a business perspective.

LIDWELL, W., HOLDEN, K. and BUTLER, J. (2003) *Universal Principles of Design*. Rockport Publishers, Inc. This book presents over 100 design principles that include consistency, accessibility, and visibility but also some lesser-known ones, such as constancy, chunking, and symmetry. They are alphabetically ordered (for easy reference) with a diversity of examples to illustrate how they work and can be used.

NORMAN, D.A. (2013) *The Design of Everyday Things: Revised and Expanded Edition*. MIT Press. This book was first published in 1988 and became an international best seller, introducing the world of technology to the importance of design and psychology. It covers the design of everyday things, such as fridges and thermostats, providing much food for thought in relation to how to design interfaces. This latest edition is comprehensively revised showing how principles from psychology apply to a diversity of old and new technologies. The book is highly accessible with many illustrative examples.

SAFFER, D. (2010) *Designing for Interaction* (2nd edn). New Riders Press. This is a thought-provoking introduction to the practice of interaction design using examples from a diversity of up-to-date interactive products.

INTERVIEW
with Harry Brignull

Harry Brignull is a User Experience Consultant based in Brighton, UK. He has a PhD in Cognitive Science and his work involves building better experiences by blending user research and interaction design. In previous roles, Harry has consulted for The Telegraph, Lloyds, British Airways, Vodafone, and various others. In his spare time, Harry also runs a blog on interaction design that has attracted a lot of eyeballs. It is called 90percentofeverything .com and well worth checking out.

What are the characteristics of a good interaction designer?
A good interaction designer has a very malleable set of skills. Each project you work on is like a lock without a key. You have a team with certain skills, and there are certain problems that need to be solved – although at the outset, the nature of the problems is unknown. As the interaction designer, it's up to you to apply your skills in a way that matches the gaps in the team's skill set, and matches the challenges. In that sense, you have to adjust the shape of the skills you apply, to make up the right shaped 'key' for the project.

For example, if you find yourself paired up with an excellent front-end developer who is also a great visual designer, you'll find you won't need to create detailed mock-ups or prototypes yourself – you can spend more time doing user research and sketching ideas in front of a whiteboard. Alternatively, if the project involves optimizing a digital product, you might find yourself needing to brush off your analytics and conversion-rate optimization skills. On one project I worked on recently, we started out with a brief to design a customer management system and ended up spending a lot of time analyzing and restructuring the company's internal workflow. This isn't interaction design but it's a different part of the same problem. Interaction design problems do not have tidy edges – they spill over into all disciplines and as an interaction designer you need to be comfortable with that.

How has interaction design changed in the past few years?
Well the obvious answer here is gestural touch interfaces and application ecosystems. Smartphones and tablets are such a big part of product strategy that it no longer makes sense to put them in a separate box called 'mobile strategy' – if anything, it's the other way around. As an interaction designer this means you need to know iOS and Android intimately. It's all changing so quickly that you have to get used to looking forward (i.e. "What's coming next and what interaction design opportunities will it give me?") rather than reflecting on what you can do today. For example, what does it mean if your product is spread across different user interfaces in a client's life – their tablet, their watch, their games console, and so on? And what if you had fine-grained indoor location awareness, giving you a

measure of proximity to other devices and objects in the world?

Prototyping gestural interfaces is not as easy as old-school point-and-click web UIs. With touch you need to consider a full suite of gestures and subtle UI animations. This massively limits the utility of wireframe prototyping tools like Axure and Omnigraffle.

What projects are you working on now?
I'm working on a suite of apps for a large UK news organization. There's a lot of subtlety needed in designing reading experiences and I'm really enjoying focusing on the tiny details that differentiate, say, a magazine-style reading experience from a newspaper reading experience in a gestural interface.

What would you say are the biggest challenges facing you and other consultants doing interaction design these days?
A career in interaction design is one of continual education and training. The biggest challenge is to keep this going. Even if you feel that you're at the peak of your skills, the technology landscape will be shifting under your feet and you need to keep an eye on what's coming next so you don't get left behind. In fact, things move so quickly in interaction design that by the time you read this interview, it will already be dated.

If you ever find yourself in a 'comfortable' role doing the exact same thing every day, then beware – you're doing yourself a disservice. Get out there, stretch yourself, and make sure you spend some time every week outside your comfort zone.

If you're asked to evaluate a prototype service or product and you discover it is really bad, how do you break the news?
It depends what your goal is. If you want to just deliver the bad news and leave then by all means be totally brutal and don't pull any punches. But if you want to build a relationship with the client, you're going to need to help them work out how to move forward. This isn't just a question of design decisions ("Don't make mistakes like this in the future and you'll be fine"), it's a question of finding out why the organization is prone to making these sorts of mistakes. Chances are there are some problems with their design process, with their team structures and competencies, and with the way decisions are made within the organization. If it's a big organization, this can take a long time to fix.

Remember, when you deliver bad news to a client, you're basically explaining to them that they're in a dark place and it's their fault. It can be quite embarrassing and depressing for them. It can drive stakeholders apart when really you need to bring them together and give them a shared vision to work towards. Always pair an observation of bad design with a recommendation for how to improve. ∎

Chapter 2

UNDERSTANDING AND CONCEPTUALIZING INTERACTION

Objectives

The main aims of this chapter are to:

- Explain what is meant by the problem space.
- Explain how to conceptualize interaction.
- Describe what a conceptual model is and how to begin to formulate one.
- Discuss the use of interface metaphors as part of a conceptual model.
- Outline the core interaction types for informing the development of a conceptual model.
- Introduce paradigms, visions, theories, models, and frameworks informing interaction design.

2.1 Introduction

Imagine you have been asked to design an application to enable people to share their photos, movies, music, chats, documents, and so on in an efficient, safe, and enjoyable way. What would you do? How would you start? Would you begin by sketching out how the interface might look, work out how the system architecture should be structured, or start coding? Or, would you start by asking users about their current experiences of sharing files and look at existing tools, e.g. Dropbox, and, based on this, begin thinking about why and how you were going to design the application?

It depends on what you are designing or building. Traditionally, interaction designers begin by doing user research and then sketching their ideas. In AgileUX (see Chapter 12), ideas are often expressed in code early in the design process. It is important to realize that having a clear understanding of why and how you are going to design something can save enormous amounts of time, effort, and money later on in the design process. Ill-thought-out ideas, and incompatible and unusable designs can be refined while it is relatively easy to do so. Such preliminary thinking through of ideas about the user experience and what kinds of designs might be appropriate is, however, a skill that needs to be learned. It is not something that can be done overnight by following a checklist, but requires practice in learning to identify, understand, and examine the issues. In this chapter we describe the steps involved. In particular, we focus on what it takes to understand and conceptualize interaction.

2.2 Understanding the Problem Space and Conceptualizing Interaction

In the process of creating an interactive product, it can be tempting to begin at the nuts and bolts level of design. By this we mean working out how to design the physical interface and what technologies and interaction styles to use, e.g. whether to use multitouch, speech, graphical user interface, head-up display, augmented reality, gesture-based, etc. The problem with starting here is that usability and user experience goals (which we describe in Chapter 1) can be overlooked. For example, consider the possibility of designing an integrated in-car entertainment, phone, and navigation system that allows drivers to follow directions, find nearby eating places, watch TV (already possible in Korea – see Figure 2.1a), and read their email. Such a gadget might seem attractive to some, offering drivers more choice: they can keep an eye on live sports games, find if there is a Cozy Coffee Shop in the next town, and

(a)   (b)

Figure 2.1 (a) Combined GPS and TV system available in Korea and (b) A screen shot taken from HP's vision of the future, CoolTown. In this hypothetical scenario, digital information about the vehicle's state and the driver's navigation plans is projected onto the windshield. A multimodal voice browsing interface is proposed that allows the driver to control interactions with the vehicle when driving. How safe do you think this would be?

Source: (b) http://www.ibiblio.org/jlillie/cooltown/lillie.htm.

so on. However, you might already be thinking 'How distracting is that?' Now imagine how new projection technology could be used as part of the system – instead of displaying the different kinds of information all on one small display that has to be toggled through, it could be displayed throughout the vehicle, on the dashboard, the rear-view mirror, and the windshield (see Figure 2.1b). However, this is likely to be even more dangerous – it could easily distract drivers, encouraging them to switch their attention from the road to the various images being projected.

While it is certainly necessary at some point to choose which technology to employ and decide how to design the physical aspects, it is better to make these kinds of decisions after articulating the nature of the problem space. By this we mean understanding and conceptualizing what is currently the user experience/product and how this is going to be improved or changed. This requires a design team thinking through how their ideas will support or extend the way people communicate and interact in their everyday activities. In the above example, it involves finding out what is problematic with existing forms of navigating while driving, e.g. trying to read maps while moving the steering wheel or looking at a small GPS display mounted on the dashboard when approaching a roundabout, and how to ensure that drivers can continue to drive safely without being distracted.

As emphasized in Chapter 1, identifying usability and user experience goals is a prerequisite to understanding the problem space. Another important consideration is to make explicit underlying assumptions and claims. By an assumption is meant taking something for granted when it needs further investigation, e.g. people will want to watch TV while driving. By a claim is meant stating something to be true when it is still open to question, e.g. a multimodal style of interaction for controlling a car navigation system – one that involves speaking while driving – is perfectly safe. Writing down your assumptions and claims and then trying to defend and support them can highlight those that are vague or wanting. In so doing, poorly constructed design ideas can be reformulated. In many projects, this process involves identifying human activities and interactivities that are problematic and working out how they might be improved through being supported with a different set of functions. In others, it can be more speculative, requiring thinking through what to design for an engaging user experience that does not exist.

The process of articulating the problem space is typically done as a team effort. Invariably, team members will have differing perspectives on the problem space. For example, a project manager is likely to be concerned about a proposed solution in terms of budgets, timelines, and staffing costs, whereas a software engineer will be thinking about breaking it down into specific technical concepts. It is important that the implications of pursuing each perspective are considered in relation to one another. Although time-consuming and sometimes resulting in disagreements among the team, the benefits of this process can far outweigh the associated costs: there will be much less chance of incorrect assumptions and unsupported claims creeping into a design solution that later turn out to be unusable or unwanted. Furthermore, spending time enumerating and reflecting upon ideas during the early stages of the design process enables more options and possibilities to be considered. Box 2.1 presents a hypothetical scenario of a team working through their assumptions and claims, showing how, in so doing, problems are explicated and explored, leading to a specific avenue of investigation agreed on by the team.

Explicating people's assumptions and claims about why they think something might be a good idea (or not) enables the design team as a whole to view multiple perspectives on

BOX 2.1

A hypothetical scenario of early design highlighting the assumptions and claims (*italicized*) made by different members of a design team

A large software company has decided it needs to develop an upgrade of its web browser for smartphones because its marketing team has discovered that many of the company's customers have switched over to using another mobile browser. The marketing people *assume* something is wrong with their browser and that their rivals have a better product. But they don't know what the problem is with theirs. The design team put in charge of this project *assume* they need to improve the usability of a number of the browser's functions. They *claim* that this will win back users by making features of the interface simpler, more attractive, and more flexible to use.

The user experience researchers on the design team conduct an initial user study investigating how people use the company's web browser on a variety of smartphones. They also look at other mobile web browsers on the market and compare their functionality and usability. They observe and talk to many different users. They discover several things about the usability of their web browser, some of which they were not expecting. One revelation is that many of their customers have never actually used the bookmarking tool. They present their findings to the rest of the team and have a long discussion about why each of them thinks it is not being used. One member *claims* that the web browser's function for organizing bookmarks is fiddly and error-prone and *assumes* this is the reason why many users do not use it. Another member backs her up, saying how awkward it is to use this method when wanting to move bookmarks between folders. One of the user experience architects agrees, noting how several of the users he talked to mentioned how difficult and time-consuming they found it when trying to move bookmarks between folders and how they often ended up accidentally putting them into the wrong folders.

A software engineer reflects on what has been said, and makes the *claim* that the bookmark function is no longer needed since he *assumes* that most people do what he does, which is to revisit a website by flicking through their history list of previously visited pages. Another member of the team disagrees with him, *claiming* that many users do not like to leave a trail of the sites they have visited and would prefer to be able to save only sites they think they might want to revisit. The bookmark function provides them with this option. Another option discussed is whether to include most-frequently visited sites as thumbnail images or as tabs. The software engineer agrees that providing all options could be a solution but worries how this might clutter the small screen interface.

After much discussion on the pros and cons of bookmarking versus history lists, the team decides to investigate further how to support effectively the saving, ordering, and retrieving of websites using a mobile web browser. All agree that the format of the existing web browser's structure is too rigid and that one of their priorities is to see how they can create a simpler way of revisiting websites on the smartphone. ■

the problem space and, in so doing, reveal conflicting and problematic ones. The following framework is intended to provide a set of core questions to aid design teams in this process:

- Are there problems with an existing product or user experience? If so, what are they?
- Why do you think there are problems?
- How do you think your proposed design ideas might overcome these?
- If you have not identified any problems and instead are designing for a new user experience, how do you think your proposed design ideas support, change, or extend current ways of doing things?

ACTIVITY 2.1

Use the framework in the above list to explicate the main assumptions and claims behind 3D TV. Then do the same for curved TV screens. Are the assumptions similar?

Comment

3D TV went on sale in 2010 and curved TV in 2014. There was much hype and fanfare about the enhanced user experience they would offer, especially when watching movies, sports events, and dramas. An *assumption* for 3D TV was that people would not mind wearing the glasses that were needed to see in 3D, nor would they mind paying a lot more for a new 3D-enabled TV screen. A *claim* was that people would really enjoy the enhanced clarity and color detail provided by 3D, based on the favorable feedback received worldwide when viewing 3D films, such as *Avatar*, at a cinema. An *assumption* for curved TV was that it would provide more flexibility for viewers to optimize the viewing angle for someone's living room. But the unanswered question for both was: Could the enhanced cinema viewing experience that both claim become an actual desired living room experience? There is no existing problem to overcome – what is being proposed is a new way of experiencing TV. Were people

Figure 2.2 A family watching 3D TV
Source: Andrey Popov/Shutterstock.com.

prepared to pay more money for a new TV because of this enhancement? A number of people did. However, a fundamental usability problem was overlooked: many people complained of motion sickness. The glasses were also easily lost, slipping down the back of the sofa. And wearing them made it difficult to do other things like flicking through multiple channels, texting, and tweeting (many people simultaneously use second devices, such as smartphones and tablets, while watching TV). Most people who bought 3D TVs stopped watching them after a while because of the usability problems. While curved TV doesn't require viewers to wear special glasses, it is not clear whether the claim about the enhanced viewing experience warrants the extra cost of buying a new TV. ■

Having a good understanding of the problem space greatly helps design teams to then be able to conceptualize the design space. Primarily this involves articulating the proposed system and the user experience. The benefits of conceptualizing the design space early on are:

- Orientation – enabling the design team to ask specific kinds of questions about how the conceptual model will be understood by the targeted users.
- Open-mindedness – preventing the design team from becoming narrowly focused early on.
- Common ground – allowing the design team to establish a set of common terms that all can understand and agree upon, reducing the chance of misunderstandings and confusion arising later on.

Once formulated and agreed upon, a conceptual model can then become a shared blueprint. This can be represented as a textual description and/or in a diagrammatic form, depending on the preferred lingua franca used by the design team. The conceptual model is used by the design team as the basis from which to develop more detailed and concrete aspects of the design. In doing so, it can produce simpler designs that match with users' tasks, allow for faster development time, result in improved customer uptake, and need less training and customer support (Johnson and Henderson, 2012).

2.3 Conceptual Models

How do you develop a conceptual model and how do you know you have a good one? We begin to address these questions here by drawing on Johnson and Henderson's (2002) account of a conceptual model. They describe one as "a high-level description of how a system is organized and operates" (Johnson and Henderson, 2002, p. 26). In this sense, it is an abstraction outlining what people can do with a product and what concepts are needed to understand how to interact with it. A key benefit of conceptualizing a design at this level is that it enables "designers to straighten out their thinking before they start laying out their widgets" (Johnson and Henderson, 2002, p. 28).

In a nutshell, a conceptual model provides a working strategy and a framework of general concepts and their interrelations. The core components are:

- Metaphors and analogies that convey to people how to understand what a product is for and how to use it for an activity (e.g. browsing, bookmarking).

- The concepts that people are exposed to through the product, including the task–domain objects they create and manipulate, their attributes, and the operations that can be performed on them (e.g. saving, revisiting, organizing).
- The relationships between those concepts (e.g. whether one object contains another, the relative importance of actions to others, and whether an object is part of another).
- The mappings between the concepts and the user experience the product is designed to support or invoke (e.g. one can revisit through looking at a list of visited sites, most-frequently visited, or saved websites).

How the various metaphors, concepts, and their relationships are organized determines the user experience. By explicating these, the design team can debate the merits of providing different methods and how they support the main concepts, e.g. saving, revisiting, categorizing, reorganizing, and their mapping to the task domain. They can also begin discussing whether a new overall metaphor may be preferable that combines the activities of browsing, searching, and revisiting. In turn, this can lead the design team to articulate the kinds of relationships between them, such as containership. For example, what is the best way to sort and revisit saved pages and how many and what types of containers should be used (e.g. folders, bars, panes)? The same enumeration of concepts can be repeated for other functions of the web browser – both current and new. In so doing, the design team can begin to systematically work out what will be the most simple, effective, and memorable way of supporting users while browsing the Internet.

The best conceptual models are those that appear obvious; the operations they support being intuitive to use. However, sometimes applications can end up being based on overly complex conceptual models, especially if they are the result of a series of upgrades, where more and more functions and ways of doing something are added to the original conceptual model. Whereas in the first version of the software there may have been one way of doing something, later versions are often designed to allow several ways of performing the same operation. For example, operating systems and word processors now make it possible for the user to carry out the same activity in a number of different ways, e.g. to delete a file the user can press the function Ctrl and D keys, speak to the computer by saying 'delete file,' or drag an icon of the file to the recycle bin. Users have to learn each of the different styles to decide which they prefer. Many users prefer to stick to the methods they have always used and trusted and, not surprisingly, become annoyed when they find a simple way of doing something has been changed, albeit more flexibly, now allowing them to do it in three or more different ways. The benefits of providing multiple ways of carrying out the same operation need to be weighed against a constrained interface that offers only one way of performing an operation.

Most interface applications are actually based on well-established conceptual models. For example, a conceptual model based on the core aspects of the customer experience when at a shopping mall underlies most online shopping websites. These include the placement of items a customer wishes to purchase into a shopping cart or basket and proceeding to checkout when ready to make the purchase. A variation – which is also based on what happens in a physical store – is making a booking, where new items are added, before proceeding to pay. Collections of patterns are now readily available to help design the interface for these core transactional processes – together with many other aspects of a user experience – meaning interaction designers do not have to start from scratch every time they design or

BOX 2.2

Design concept (Hazlewood *et al*, 2010)

Another term that is sometimes used is a design concept – essentially it is a set of ideas for a design. Typically, it comprises scenarios, images, mood boards, or text-based documents. For example, Figure 2.3 shows the first page of a design concept developed for an ambient display that was aimed at changing people's behavior in a building. Part of the design concept was envisioned as an animated pattern of twinkly lights that would be embedded in the carpet near the entrance of the building with the intention of luring people towards the stairs (Hazlewood *et al*, 2010). ■

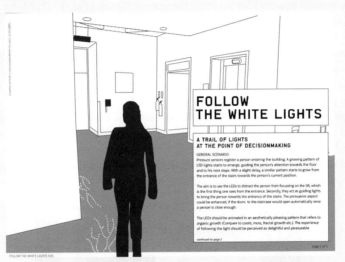

Figure 2.3 The first page of a design concept for an ambient display

redesign an application. Examples include patterns for online forms and navigation on mobiles (for more on these, see Chapter 12).

Hence, it is rare for completely new conceptual models to emerge that transform the way we carry out our everyday and work activities when using a computer. The classics include the desktop (developed by Xerox in the late 1970s), the spreadsheet (developed by Bricklin and Frankston in the late 1970s), and the web (developed by Berners Lee in the early 1980s). All have made what was previously limited to a few skilled people accessible to all, while greatly expanding what is possible. The first dramatically changed how office tasks can be performed (including creating, editing, and printing documents); the second made accounting highly flexible and easier to accomplish, enabling a diversity of new computations to be performed simply through filling in interactive boxes; and the third allowed anyone to remotely browse a network of information. More recently, e-readers and tablets have introduced a new way of reading, supporting associated activities such as annotating, highlighting, commenting, copying, and tracking. Importantly, all of these conceptual models were based on familiar activities that have greatly transformed them.

BOX 2.3

A classic conceptual model: the Star (Hazlewood *et al*, 2010)

The Star interface, developed by Xerox back in 1981 (see Figure 2.4), revolutionized the way interfaces were designed for personal computing (Smith *et al*, 1982; Miller and Johnson, 1996). It was designed as an office system, targeted at workers not interested in computing per se, and was based on a conceptual model that included the familiar knowledge of an office. Paper, folders, filing cabinets, and mailboxes were represented as icons on the screen and were designed to possess some of the properties of their physical counterparts. Dragging a document icon across the desktop screen was seen as equivalent to picking up a piece of paper in the physical world and moving it (but this, of course, is a very different action). Similarly, dragging an electronic document onto an electronic folder was seen as being analogous to placing a physical document into a physical cabinet. In addition, new concepts that were incorporated as part of the desktop metaphor were operations that could not be performed in the physical world. For example, electronic files could be placed onto an icon of a printer on the desktop, resulting in the computer printing them out. ■

Figure 2.4 The Xerox Star
Source: Courtesy of Xerox.

Video of the history of the Xerox Star at **http://youtu.be/Cn4vC80Pv6Q**

2.4 Interface Metaphors

As mentioned earlier, metaphors are considered to be a central component of a conceptual model. They provide a structure that is similar in some way to aspects of a familiar entity (or entities) but also have their own behaviors and properties. More specifically, an interface metaphor is one that is instantiated in some way as part of the user interface: for example, the desktop metaphor. Another well-known one is the search engine. This term was originally coined in the early 1990s to refer to a software tool that indexed and retrieved files remotely from the Internet, using various algorithms to match terms selected by the user. The metaphor invites comparisons between a mechanical engine, which has several parts working, and the everyday action of looking in different places to find something. The functions supported by a search engine also include other features besides those belonging to an engine that searches, such as listing and prioritizing the results of a search. It also does these actions in quite different ways from how a mechanical engine works or how a human being might search a library for books on a given topic. The similarities implied by the use of the term search engine, therefore, are at a general level. They are meant to conjure up the essence of the process of finding relevant information, enabling the user to link these to less familiar aspects of the functionality provided.

ACTIVITY 2.2

Go to a few online stores and see how the interface has been designed to enable the customer to order and pay for an item. How many use the 'add to shopping cart/trolley/basket' followed by the 'checkout' metaphor? Does this make it straightforward and intuitive to make a purchase?

Comment

Making a purchase online is an undertaking with risks and people want to feel they are making the right choice. Designing the interface to have a familiar metaphor (with an icon of a shopping cart/basket – although not a cash register) makes it easier for people to know what to do at the different stages of making a purchase. Importantly, placing an item in the basket does not commit the customer to purchase it there and then. It also enables them to browse further and select other items – as they might in a physical store. ∎

Interface metaphors are intended to provide familiar entities that enable people to readily understand the underlying conceptual model and know what to do at an interface. However, they can also contravene people's expectations about how things should be, such as the recycle bin (trashcan) that used to sit on the desktop. Logically and culturally (i.e. in the real world) it should have been placed under the desk. But users would not have been able to see it because it would be occluded by the desktop surface. So it needed to go on the desktop. Some users found this irksome but most did not find it to be a problem. Once they understood why the bin icon was on the desktop they simply accepted it being there.

BOX 2.4

Material metaphors (Hazlewood *et al*, 2010)

An interface metaphor that has become pervasive in the last few years is the card. Many of the social media apps, such as Facebook, Twitter, and Pinterest, started presenting their content on cards. Cards have a very familiar form factor – having been around for a long time. Just think of how many kinds there are: playing cards, business cards, birthday cards, credit cards, driving cards, postcards, red cards – to name a few. They have strong associations, providing an intuitive way of organizing limited content that is 'card size.' They can be easily flicked through, sorted, and themed.

There has also been a move towards adding material properties to the underlying conceptual model. By this is meant giving the appearance and physical behavior of real-world objects. Google, for example, launched Material Design in 2014 to provide a new kind of UI framework for all of its devices, including smartwatches, phones, and tablets. It uses the metaphor of the surface of paper. So, for example, their Google Now Card (that provides short snippets of useful information) appears on and moves across a smartphone screen in the way people would expect a real card to do – in a lightweight, paper-based sort of way. ■

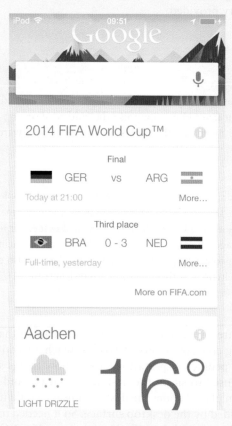

Figure 2.5 Google Now Card

Source: Google and the Google logo are registered trademarks of Google Inc., used with permission.
http://www.google.com/design/spec/material-design/introduction.html

In many cases, new interface metaphors rapidly become integrated into common par-
lance, as witnessed by the way people talk about them. For example, parents talk about how
much screen time children are allowed each day in the same way they talk more generally
about spending time. As such, the interface metaphors are no longer talked about as familiar
terms to describe less familiar computer-based actions; they have become everyday terms in
their own right. Moreover, it is hard not to use metaphorical terms when talking about technology use, as they have become so ingrained in the language we use to express ourselves.
Just ask yourself or someone else to describe Twitter and Facebook and how people use them.
Then try doing it without using a single metaphor.

BOX 2.5

Why are metaphors so popular? (Hazlewood *et al*, 2010)

People frequently use metaphors and analogies (here we use the terms interchangeably) as
a source of inspiration for understanding and explaining to others what they are doing, or
trying to do, in terms that are familiar to them. They are an integral part of human language
(Lakoff and Johnson, 1980). Metaphors are commonly used to explain something that is unfamiliar or hard to grasp by way of comparison with something that is familiar and easy to
grasp. For example, they are commonly employed in education, where teachers use them to
introduce something new to students by comparing the new material with something they already understand. An example is the comparison of human evolution with a game. We are all
familiar with the properties of a game: there are rules, each player has a goal to win (or lose),
there are heuristics to deal with situations where there are no rules, there is the propensity
to cheat when the other players are not looking, and so on. By conjuring up these properties,
the analogy helps us begin to understand the more difficult concept of evolution – how it
happens, what rules govern it, who cheats, and so on.

It is not surprising, therefore, to see how widely metaphors have been used in interaction
design to conceptualize abstract, hard to imagine, and difficult to articulate computer-based
concepts and interactions in more concrete and familiar terms and as graphical visualizations
at the interface. Metaphors and analogies are used in three main ways:

1. As a way of conceptualizing what we are doing (e.g. surfing the web).
2. As a conceptual model instantiated at the interface (e.g. the card metaphor).
3. As a way of visualizing an operation (e.g. an icon of a shopping cart into which we place
   items we wish to purchase on an online shopping site). ∎

2.5   Interaction Types

Another way of conceptualizing the design space is in terms of the interaction types that will
underlie the user experience. Essentially, these are the ways a person interacts with a product
or application. We propose that there are four main types: instructing, conversing, manipulating, and exploring. Deciding upon which of these to use, and why, can help designers

formulate a conceptual model before committing to a particular interface in which to implement them, e.g. speech-based, gesture-based, touch-based, menu-based, and so on. Note that we are distinguishing here between interaction types (which we discuss in this section) and interface types (which are discussed in Chapter 6). While cost and other product constraints will often dictate which interface style can be used for a given application, considering the interaction type that will best support a user experience can highlight the potential trade-offs, dilemmas, and pros and cons.

Consider the following problem description: a company has been asked to design a computer-based system that will encourage autistic children to communicate and express themselves better. What type of interaction would be appropriate to use at the interface for this particular user group? It is known that autistic children find it difficult to express what they are feeling or thinking through talking and are more expressive when using their bodies and limbs. Clearly an interaction style based on talking would not be effective, but one that involves the children interacting with a system by moving in a physical and/or digital space would seem a more promising starting point.

Below we describe in more detail each of the four types of interaction. It should be noted that they are not meant to be mutually exclusive (e.g. someone can interact with a system based on different kinds of activities); nor are they meant to be definitive.

1. Instructing – where users issue instructions to a system. This can be done in a number of ways, including: typing in commands, selecting options from menus in a windows environment or on a multitouch screen, speaking aloud commands, gesturing, pressing buttons, or using a combination of function keys.
2. Conversing – where users have a dialog with a system. Users can speak via an interface or type in questions to which the system replies via text or speech output.
3. Manipulating – where users interact with objects in a virtual or physical space by manipulating them (e.g. opening, holding, closing, placing). Users can hone their familiar knowledge of how to interact with objects.
4. Exploring – where users move through a virtual environment or a physical space. Virtual environments include 3D worlds, and augmented and virtual reality systems. They enable users to hone their familiar knowledge of physically moving around. Physical spaces that use sensor-based technologies include smart rooms and ambient environments, also enabling people to capitalize on familiarity.

Besides these core activities of instructing, conversing, manipulating, and exploring, it is possible to describe the specific domain and context-based activities users engage in, such as learning, working, socializing, playing, browsing, writing, problem-solving, decision making, and information searching – to name but a few. McCullough (2004) suggests describing them as situated activities, organized by: work (e.g. presenting to groups), home (e.g. resting), in town (e.g. eating), and on the road (e.g. walking). The rationale is to help designers be less ad hoc and more systematic when thinking about the usability of technology-modified places in the environment. Below we illustrate in more detail our four core interaction types and how to design applications for them.

2.5.1 Instructing

This type of interaction describes how users carry out their tasks by telling the system what to do. Examples include giving instructions to a system to perform operations such as tell the time, print a file, and remind the user of an appointment. A diverse range of products has been designed based on this model, including home entertainment systems, consumer electronics, and computers. The way in which the user issues instructions can vary from pressing buttons to typing in strings of characters. Many activities are readily supported by giving instructions.

In Windows and other GUI-based systems, control keys or the selection of menu options via a mouse, touch pad, or touch screen are used. Typically, a wide range of functions are provided from which users have to select when they want to do something to the object on which they are working. For example, a user writing a report using a word processor will want to format the document, count the number of words typed, and check the spelling. The user instructs the system to do these operations by issuing appropriate commands. Typically, commands are carried out in a sequence, with the system responding appropriately (or not) as instructed.

One of the main benefits of designing an interaction based on issuing instructions is that the interaction is quick and efficient. It is particularly fitting where there is a need to frequently repeat actions performed on multiple objects. Examples include the repetitive actions of saving, deleting, and organizing files.

ACTIVITY 2.3

There are many different kinds of vending machines in the world. Each offers a range of goods, requiring the user initially to part with some money. Figure 2.6 shows photos of two different vending machines, one that provides soft drinks and the other a range of snacks. Both use an instructional mode of interaction. However, the way they do so is quite different.

Figure 2.6 Two different types of vending machine

(*Continued*)

What instructions must be issued to obtain a soda from the first machine and a bar of chocolate from the second? Why has it been necessary to design a more complex mode of interaction for the second vending machine? What problems can arise with this mode of interaction?

Comment
The first vending machine has been designed using simple instructions. There are a small number of drinks to choose from and each is represented by a large button displaying the label of each drink. The user simply has to press one button and this should have the effect of returning the selected drink. The second machine is more complex, offering a wider range of snacks. The trade-off for providing more options, however, is that the user can no longer instruct the machine by using a simple one-press action but is required to use a more complex process, involving (i) reading off the code (e.g. C12) under the item chosen, then (ii) keying this into the number pad adjacent to the displayed items, and (iii) checking the price of the selected option and ensuring that the amount of money inserted is the same or greater (depending on whether or not the machine provides change). Problems that can arise from this type of interaction are the customer misreading the code and/or miskeying the code, resulting in the machine not issuing the snack or providing the wrong item.

A better way of designing an interface for a large number of options of variable cost might be to continue to use direct mapping, but use buttons that show miniature versions of the snacks placed in a large matrix (rather than showing actual versions). This would use the available space at the front of the vending machine more economically. The customer would need only to press the button of the object chosen and put in the correct amount of money. There is less chance of error resulting from pressing the wrong code or keys. The trade-off for the vending company, however, is that the machine is less flexible in terms of which snacks it can sell. If a new product line comes out, they will also need to replace part of the physical interface to the machine – which would be costly. ∎

2.5.2   Conversing

This form of interaction is based on the idea of a person having a conversation with a system, where the system acts as a dialog partner. In particular, the system is designed to respond in a way another human being might when having a conversation. It differs from the activity of instructing insofar as it encompasses a two-way communication process, with the system acting like a partner rather than a machine that obeys orders. It has been most commonly used for applications where the user needs to find out specific kinds of information or wants to discuss issues. Examples include advisory systems, help facilities, and search engines.

The kinds of conversation that are currently supported range from simple voice-recognition, menu-driven systems that are interacted with via phones, to more complex natural language-based systems that involve the system parsing and responding to queries typed in by the user. Examples of the former include banking, ticket booking, and train-time inquiries, where the user talks to the system in single-word phrases and numbers – e.g. yes, no, three – in response to prompts from the system. Examples of the latter include help systems, where the user types in a specific query – e.g. 'how do I change the margin widths?' – to which the system responds by giving various answers.

Figure 2.7 Siri's response to the question "Do I need an umbrella?"

A main benefit of developing a conceptual model that uses a conversational style of interaction is that it allows people to interact with a system in a way that is familiar to them. For example, Apple's speech system, Siri, lets you talk to it as if it were another person. You can ask it to do tasks for you, such as make a phone call, schedule a meeting, or send a message. You can also ask it indirect questions that it knows how to answer, such as "Do I need an umbrella today?" It will look up the weather for where you are and then answer with something like, "I don't believe it is raining" while also providing a weather forecast (see Figure 2.7).

A problem that can arise from using a conversational-based interaction type is that certain kinds of tasks are transformed into cumbersome and one-sided interactions. This is especially true for automated phone-based systems that use auditory menus to advance the interaction. Users have to listen to a voice providing several options, then make a selection, and repeat through further layers of menus before accomplishing their goal, e.g. reaching a real human or paying a bill. Here is the beginning of a dialog between a user who wants to find out about car insurance and an insurance company's reception system:

<user dials an insurance company>

'Welcome to St. Paul's Insurance Company. Press 1 if you are a new customer; 2 if you are an existing customer.'

'Thank you for calling St. Paul's Insurance Company. If you require house insurance press 1, car insurance press 2, travel insurance press 3, health insurance press 4, other press 5.'

<user presses 2>

'You have reached the car insurance division. If you require information about fully comprehensive insurance press 1, third-party insurance press 2 . . .'

"If you'd like to press 1, press 3.
If you'd like to press 3, press 8.
If you'd like to press 8, press 5..."

2.5.3   Manipulating

This form of interaction involves manipulating objects and capitalizes on users' knowledge of how they do so in the physical world. For example, digital objects can be manipulated by moving, selecting, opening, and closing. Extensions to these actions include zooming in and out, stretching, and shrinking – actions that are not possible with objects in the real world. Human actions can be imitated through the use of physical controllers (e.g. Wii) or gestures made in the air (e.g. Kinect) to control the movements of an on-screen avatar. Physical toys and robots have also been embedded with computation and capability that enable them to act and react in programmable ways depending on whether they are squeezed, touched, sensed, or moved. Tagged physical objects (e.g. balls, bricks, blocks) that are manipulated in a physical world (e.g. placed on a surface) can result in other physical and digital events occurring, such as a lever moving or a sound or animation being played.

A framework that has been highly influential in informing the design of GUI applications is direct manipulation (Shneiderman, 1983). It proposes that digital objects be designed at the interface so that they can be interacted with in ways that are analogous to how physical objects in the physical world are manipulated. In so doing, direct manipulation interfaces are assumed to enable users to feel that they are directly controlling the digital objects represented by the computer. The three core principles are:

1. continuous representation of the objects and actions of interest;
2. rapid reversible incremental actions with immediate feedback about the object of interest;
3. physical actions and button pressing instead of issuing commands with complex syntax.

According to these principles, an object on the screen remains visible while a user performs physical actions on it and any actions performed on it are immediately visible. For example, a user can move a file by dragging an icon that represents it from one part of the desktop to another. The benefits of direct manipulation include:

- helping beginners learn basic functionality rapidly;
- enabling experienced users to work rapidly on a wide range of tasks;
- allowing infrequent users to remember how to carry out operations over time;
- preventing the need for error messages, except very rarely;
- showing users immediately how their actions are furthering their goals;
- reducing users' experiences of anxiety;
- helping users gain confidence and mastery and feel in control.

Many apps have been developed based on some form of direct manipulation, including word processors, video games, learning tools, and image editing tools. However, while direct manipulation interfaces provide a very versatile mode of interaction, they do have their drawbacks. In particular, not all tasks can be described by objects and not all actions can be undertaken directly. Some tasks are also better achieved through issuing commands. For example, consider how you edit an essay using a word processor. Suppose you had referenced work by Ben Shneiderman but had spelled his name as 'Schneiderman' throughout the essay. How would you correct this error using a direct manipulation interface? You would need to read through your essay and manually select the 'c' in every 'Schneiderman,' highlighting and then deleting it. This would be very tedious and it would be easy to miss one or two. By contrast, this operation is relatively effortless and also likely to be more accurate when using a command-based interaction. All you need to do is instruct the word processor to find every 'Schneiderman' and replace it with 'Shneiderman.' This can be done through selecting a menu option or using a combination of command keys and then typing the changes required into the dialog box that pops up.

2.5.4 Exploring

This mode of interaction involves users moving through virtual or physical environments. For example, users can explore aspects of a virtual 3D environment, such as the interior of a building. Physical environments can also be embedded with sensing technologies that, when they detect the presence of someone or certain body movements, respond by triggering certain digital or physical events. The basic idea is to enable people to explore and interact with an environment, be it physical or digital, by exploiting their knowledge of how they move and navigate through existing spaces.

Many 3D virtual environments have been built that include virtual worlds designed for people to move between various spaces to learn (e.g. virtual universities) and fantasy worlds where people wander around different places to socialize (e.g. virtual parties) or play games (e.g. Minecraft). Numerous virtual landscapes depicting cities, parks, buildings, rooms, and datasets have also been built, both realistic and abstract, that enable users to fly over them and zoom in and out of different parts. Other virtual environments that have been built include worlds that are larger than life, enabling users to move around them, experiencing things that are normally impossible or invisible to the eye (Figure 2.8a); highly realistic representations of architectural designs, allowing clients and customers to imagine how they will use and move through planned buildings and public spaces; and visualizations of complex datasets that scientists can virtually climb inside and experience (Figure 2.8b).

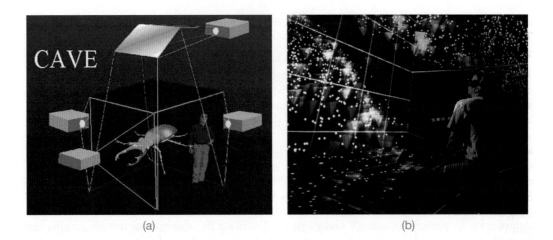

Figure 2.8 (a) A CAVE that enables the user to stand near a huge insect, e.g. a beetle, be swallowed, and end up in its abdomen; and (b) NCSA's CAVE being used by a scientist to move through 3D visualizations of the datasets

Source: (a) Reproduced with permission. http://home.comcast.net/~sharov/3d/cave.html (b) Image courtesy of Kalev Leetaru, National Center for Supercomputing Applications, University of Illinois.

A number of physical environments have been developed using embedded sensor technologies and other location-detection technologies. When the location and/or presence of people in the vicinity of a sensing device are detected, the environment decides which information to provide on a device (e.g. a nearby coffee bar where friends are meeting) or which action to perform (e.g. changing lights in a room) that is considered relevant or useful to the person at a particular time and place.

2.6   Paradigms, Visions, Theories, Models, and Frameworks

Other sources of inspiration and knowledge that are used to inform design and guide research are paradigms, visions, theories, models, and frameworks (Carroll, 2003). These vary in terms of their scale and specificity to a particular problem space. A paradigm refers to a general approach that has been adopted by a community of researchers and designers for carrying out their work, in terms of shared assumptions, concepts, values, and practices. A vision is a future scenario that frames research and development in interaction design – often depicted in the form of a film or a narrative. A theory is a well-substantiated explanation of some aspect of a phenomenon; for example, the theory of information processing that explains how the mind, or some aspect of it, is assumed to work. A model is a simplification of some aspect of human–computer interaction intended to make it easier for designers to predict and evaluate alternative designs. A framework is a set of interrelated concepts and/or a set of specific questions that are intended to inform a particular domain area (e.g. collaborative learning), online communities, or an analytic method (e.g. ethnographic studies).

2.6.1 Paradigms

To follow a particular paradigm means adopting a set of practices that a community has agreed upon. These include:

* the questions to be asked and how they should be framed;
* the phenomena to be observed;
* the way in which findings from studies are to be analyzed and interpreted (Kuhn, 1972).

In the 1980s, the prevailing paradigm in human–computer interaction was how to design user-centered applications for the desktop computer. Questions about what and how to design were framed in terms of specifying the requirements for a single user interacting with a screen-based interface. Task analytic and usability methods were developed based on an individual user's cognitive capabilities. The acronym WIMP was used as a way of characterizing the core features of an interface for a single user: this stood for Windows, Icons, Menus, and Pointer. This was later superseded by the GUI (graphical user interface), a term that has stuck with us ever since.

Within interaction design, many changes took place in the mid to late 1990s. The WIMP interface with its single thread, discrete event dialog was considered to be unnecessarily limiting (e.g. Jacob, 1996). Instead, many argued that a new paradigm was needed to enable more flexible forms of interaction to take place, having a higher degree of interactivity and parallel input/output exchanges. A shift in thinking, together with several technological advances, paved the way for a new method of conceptualizing human–computer interaction. The rhetoric 'beyond the desktop' became a pervasive starting point, resulting in many new challenges, questions, and phenomena being considered. New methods of designing, modeling, and analyzing came to the fore. At the same time, new theories, concepts, and ideas entered the stage. Turns to the social, the emotional, the environmental, and the wild began shaping what was studied, how it was studied, and ultimately what was designed. Significantly, one of the main frames of reference – the single user – was replaced by context.

A big influence in the more recent paradigmatic changes was Weiser's (1991) vision of ubiquitous technology. He proposed that computers would become part of the environment, embedded in a variety of everyday objects, devices, and displays. He envisioned a world of serenity, comfort, and awareness, where people were kept perpetually informed of what was happening around them, what was going to happen, and what had just happened. Ubiquitous computing devices would enter a person's center of attention when needed and move to the periphery of their attention when not, enabling the person to switch calmly and effortlessly between activities without having to figure out how to use a computer when performing their tasks. In essence, the technology would be unobtrusive and largely disappear into the background. People would be able to get on with their everyday and working lives, interacting with information and communicating and collaborating with others without being distracted or becoming frustrated with technology.

Since the late 1990s, many researchers have been concerned with how to embed and augment the environment with various computational resources to provide information and services, when and where desired. An assortment of sensors have been experimented with in our homes, hospitals, public buildings, physical environments, and even our bodies to detect trends and anomalies, providing a huge array of data about our health and movements, and changes in the environment. Algorithms have been developed to analyze the data in order for inferences to be drawn about what actions to take for people. In addition, sensed data are increasingly being used to automate mundane operations and actions that we would have done in our everyday worlds using conventional knobs, buttons, and other physical controls.

2.6.2   Visions

Visions of the future are another driving force that frame research and development in interaction design. A number of tech companies have produced videos about the future of technology and society, inviting audiences to imagine what life will be like in 10, 15, or 20 years' time. One of the most well known is Apple's 1987 Knowledge Navigator, which presented a scenario of a professor using a touch-screen tablet with a speech-based intelligent assistant reminding him of what he needed to do that day while answering the phone and helping him prepare his lectures. It was 25 years ahead of its time - set in 2011 – the actual year that Apple launched its speech system, Siri. It was much viewed and talked about, arguably inspiring much research into and development of future interfaces.

A current vision that is driving much future technology development is the Internet of Things (IoT). By this is meant a scenario where people, objects, and animals are all connected through the Internet by having their own unique identifier. The assumed benefits of this kind of 'everything and everyone' connecting include improved services, up-to-date information and energy-saving utilities. An early example that has been much talked about is the smart home. Imagine your day starts with the heating/cooling silently turning on (and then off) to provide the perfect temperature for you while in the bathroom, followed by your alarm clock gently waking you up at the exact time you need to get up, while at the same time 'talking' to your coffee machine to start making the perfect cup of coffee at the time you want to drink it. Meanwhile, your fridge has sensed that you are running low on milk and fresh berries and has already sent an alert to your smartphone shopping app. As you walk into the bathroom, your smart mirror reveals how long each member of your family has cleaned their teeth for in the last week. You smile to see your son is cleaning his teeth regularly and for longer than all of you. Then you glance at the cat dashboard that shows a vizualization of where your cat has been prowling the night before in the neighbourhood. And so on.

These kinds of future visions provide concrete scenarios of how society can use the next generation of imagined technologies to make their lives more safe, comfortable, informative, and efficient. But they also, importantly, raise many questions concerning privacy, trust, and what we want as a society. They provide much food for thought for researchers, policy makers, and developers, challenging them to consider both positive and negative implications.

Video of Apple Knowledge Navigator at **http://youtu.be/HGYFEI6uLy0**

Video of IBM's Internet of Things at **http://youtu.be/sfEbMV295Kk**

Many new challenges, themes, and questions have been articulated through these visions (e.g. Rogers, 2006; Harper *et al*, 2008), including:

- How to enable people to access and interact with information in their work, social, and everyday lives, using an assortment of technologies.
- How to design user experiences for people using interfaces that are part of the environment but where there are no obvious controlling devices.
- How and in what form to provide contextually relevant information to people at appropriate times and places to support them while on the move.
- How to ensure that information that is passed around via interconnected displays, devices, and objects is secure and trustworthy.

2.6.3   Theories

Over the past 30 years, numerous theories have been imported into human–computer interaction, providing a means of analyzing and predicting the performance of users carrying out tasks for specific kinds of computer interfaces and systems (Rogers, 2012). These have been primarily cognitive, social, and organizational in origin. For example, cognitive theories about human memory were used in the 1980s to determine the best ways of representing operations, given people's memory limitations. One of the main benefits of applying such theories in interaction design is to help identify factors (cognitive, social, and affective) relevant to the design and evaluation of interactive products. Some of the most influential theories in HCI, including distributed cognition, will be covered in the next chapter.

2.6.4   Models

Models are typically abstracted from a theory coming from a contributing discipline, like psychology, that can be directly applied to interaction design. For example, Norman (1988) developed a number of models of user interaction based on theories of cognitive processing, arising out of cognitive science, that were intended to explain the way users interacted with interactive technologies. These include the seven stages of action model that describes how users move from their plans to executing physical actions they need to perform to achieve them, to evaluating the outcome of their actions with respect to their goals. Another highly influential model based on cognitive theory that made its mark in the 1980s was Card, Moran, and Newell's keystroke model. This was used by a number of researchers and designers as a predictive way of analyzing user performance for different interfaces to determine which would be the most effective. More recent models developed in interaction design are user models, which predict what information users want in their interactions, and models that characterize core components of the user experience, such as Norman's (2005) model of emotional design (Chapter 5).

2.6.5   Frameworks

Numerous frameworks have been introduced in interaction design to help designers constrain and scope the user experience for which they are designing. In contrast to a model – which is a simplification of a phenomenon – a framework offers advice to designers as to what to design or look for. This can come in a variety of forms, including steps, questions, concepts, challenges, principles, tactics, and dimensions. Frameworks, like models, have traditionally been based on theories of human behavior, but they are increasingly being developed from the experiences of actual design practice and the findings arising from user studies.

Many frameworks have been published in the HCI/interaction design literatures, covering different aspects of the user experience and a diversity of application areas. For example, there are frameworks for helping designers think about how to conceptualize learning, working, socializing, fun, emotion, and so on and others that focus on how to design particular kinds of technologies to evoke certain responses, e.g. persuasive technologies and pleasurable products (see Chapter 5).

A classic early example of a conceptual framework that has been highly influential in HCI is Norman's (1988) explication of the relationship between the design of a conceptual model and a user's understanding of it. The framework comprises three interacting components: the designer, the user, and the system. Behind each of these are:

- The designer's model – the model the designer has of how the system should work.
- The system image – how the system actually works is portrayed to the user through the interface, manuals, help facilities, and so on.
- The user's model – how the user understands how the system works.

The framework makes explicit the relationship between how a system should function, how it is presented to users, and how it is understood by them. In an ideal world, users should be able to carry out activities in the way intended by the designer by interacting with the system image that makes it obvious what to do. If the system image does not make the designer's model clear to the users, it is likely that they will end up with an incorrect understanding of the system, which in turn will increase the chances of their using the system ineffectively and making errors. This has been found to happen often in the real world. By drawing attention to this potential discrepancy, designers can be made aware of the importance of trying to bridge the gap more effectively.

In sum, paradigms, visions, theories, models, and frameworks are not mutually exclusive but overlap in their way of conceptualizing the problem and design space, varying in their level of rigor, abstraction, and purpose. Paradigms are overarching approaches that comprise a set of accepted practices and framing of questions and phenomena to observe; visions are scenarios of the future that set up challenges and questions for interaction design research and technology development; theories tend to be comprehensive, explaining human–computer interactions; models tend to simplify some aspect of human–computer interaction, providing a basis for designing and evaluating systems; and frameworks provide a set of core concepts, questions, or principles to consider when designing for a user experience.

DILEMMA

Who is in control?

A recurrent theme in interaction design is who should be in control at the interface. The different interaction types vary in terms of how much control a user has and how much the computer has. Whereas users are primarily in control for command-based and direct manipulation

interfaces, they are less so in sensor-based and context-aware environments, like the smart home. User-controlled interaction is based on the premise that people enjoy mastery and being in control. It assumes people like to know what is going on, be involved in the action, and have a sense of power over the computer.

In contrast, context-aware control assumes that having the environment monitor, recognize, and detect deviations in a person's behavior can enable timely, helpful, and even critical information to be provided when considered appropriate (Abowd and Mynatt, 2000). For example, elderly people's movements can be detected in the home and emergency or care services alerted if something untoward happens to them that might otherwise go unnoticed: for instance, if they fell over and broke a leg and were unable to get to a telephone. But what happens if a person chooses to take a rest in an unexpected area (on the carpet), which the system detects as a fall? Will the emergency services be called out unnecessarily and cause carers undue worry? Will the person who triggered the alarm be mortified at triggering a false alarm? And how will it affect their sense of privacy, knowing their every move is constantly being monitored?

Another concern is what happens when the locus of control switches between user and system. For example, consider who is in control when using a GPS for vehicle navigation. At the beginning the driver is very much in control, issuing instructions to the system as to where to go and what to include, e.g. highways, gas stations, traffic alerts. However, once on the road, the system takes over and is in control. People often find themselves slavishly following what the GPS tells them to do, even though common sense suggests otherwise.

To what extent do you need to be in control in your everyday and working life? Are you happy to let computing technology monitor and decide what you need or do you prefer to tell it what you want to do? How will it feel to step into an autonomous car that drives for you? While it might be safer and more fuel-efficient, will it take the pleasure out of driving? ■

Assignment

The aim of this assignment is for you to think about the appropriateness of different kinds of conceptual models that have been designed for similar physical and digital information artifacts;

Compare the following:

- a paperback book and an ebook;
- a paper-based map and a smartphone map.

What are the main concepts and metaphors that have been used for each (think about the way time is conceptualized for each of them)? How do they differ? What aspects of the paper-based artifact have informed the digital app? What is the new functionality? Are any aspects of the conceptual model confusing? What are the pros and cons?

Summary

This chapter has explained the importance of understanding and conceptualizing the problem and design space before trying to build anything. It has stressed throughout the need to be explicit about the claims and assumptions behind design decisions that are suggested. It described an approach to formulating a conceptual model and described the evolution of interface metaphors that have been designed as part of the conceptual model. Finally, it considered other ways of conceptualizing interaction, in terms of interaction types, paradigms, visions, theories, models, and frameworks.

Key points:

- It is important to have a good understanding of the problem space, specifying what it is you are doing, why, and how it will support users in the way intended.
- A fundamental aspect of interaction design is to develop a conceptual model.
- A conceptual model is a high-level description of a product in terms of what users can do with it and the concepts they need in order to understand how to interact with it.
- Decisions about conceptual design should be made before commencing physical design (e.g. choosing menus, icons, dialog boxes).
- Interface metaphors are commonly used as part of a conceptual model.
- Interaction types (e.g. conversing, instructing) provide a way of thinking about how best to support the activities users will be doing when using a product or service.
- Paradigms, visions, theories, models, and frameworks provide different ways of framing and informing design and research.

Further Reading

DOURISH, P. (2001) *Where the Action Is*. MIT Press. This book presents a new approach for thinking about the design of user interfaces and user experiences based on the notion of embodied interaction. The idea of embodied interaction reflects a number of trends that have emerged in HCI, offering new sorts of metaphors.

GREENFIELD, A. (2006) *Everyware: The dawning age of ubiquitous computing*. Easy Riders. This book provides a series of short essays that discuss seminal themes and topics in ubiquitous computing. The notion of everyware refers to how information will become accessible from just about anywhere at any time and accessed through a diversity of technologies, some visible and others not.

HARPER, R., RODDEN, T., ROGERS, Y. and SELLEN, A. (2008) *Being Human: HCI in the year 2020*. Microsoft (free copies from http://research.microsoft.com/en-us/um/cambridge/projects/hci2020/). This is a coffee table book that takes stock of the field of HCI and presents an overview of the new challenges and issues confronting HCI in the next 10 years. It focuses on the empirical, philosophical, and moral questions of our relationship with new technologies. It takes human values as a central concern.

JOHNSON, J. and HENDERSON, A. (2012) *Conceptual Models: Core to Good Design*. Morgan and Claypool Publishers. This short ebook, in the form of a lecture, provides a comprehensive overview of what a conceptual model is, with detailed examples. It outlines how to construct one and why it is necessary to do so. It is very cogently argued and shows how and where this design activity can be integrated into interaction design.

MCCULLOUGH, M. (2004) *Digital Ground: Architecture, pervasive computing and environmental knowing*. MIT Press. This book presents many ideas, concepts, and frameworks for designing pervasive technologies. In particular, it discusses in depth the many new challenges confronting interaction designers and architects when working out how to embed information technology into the ambient social complexities of the physical world.

ROGERS, Y. (2012) *HCI Theory: Classical, Modern, and Contemporary*. Morgan and Claypool Publishers. This short ebook, in the form of a lecture, charts the theoretical developments in HCI, both past and present, reflecting on how they have shaped the field. It explains how theory has been conceptualized, the different uses it has in HCI, and which has made the most impact.

INTERVIEW
with Kees Dorst

Kees Dorst is Professor of Design Innovation and Executive Director of the Design Innovation research centre at the University of Technology, Sydney, and Professor in Design Research at Eindhoven University of Technology. He works as a consultant and lectures at universities and design schools throughout the world. He has published numerous articles and five books – most recently the books *Understanding Design – 175 reflections on being a designer* (2006) and *Design Expertise* (2009) with Bryan Lawson.

Please would you tell me something about your background and your current passion?
I was trained as an Industrial Designer at Delft University of Technology. I also studied some Philosophy before moving into design practice – when I realized that I kept thinking about design too much. I took up a small research position at TUDelft to investigate the way designers reach integration in their projects. That project later turned into a bigger PhD study comparing the two paradigms we use to describe and think about design: Rational Problem Solving (in which design is seen as a search process from problem to solution) and Reflective Practice (in which design is seen as

a process of learning and reframing). In my thesis 'Describing Design' I use empirical data (protocol analysis) to argue that these two ways of looking at design are fundamentally incommensurable, as they are coming from very different philosophical roots. My design practice then moved into management and consultancy, as well as journalism. Currently I am working with a broad international network of researchers on the application of design thinking for organizational change.

Are there any particular findings or insights about the nature of design that stand out for you?
The work on design expertise has given me an idea of the impressive breadth of activities that we so conveniently label design: there are many different kinds and layers of design activities. I find it exciting that we are now at the point of understanding these much more deeply. That deeper understanding allows us to create a level of discussion that is much more precise, and also to transport/transpose practices that are traditionally part of the designing disciplines to other fields. I am convinced that the introduction of elements of creative thought and action that have been professionalized within the design disciplines will

revolutionize the way we create solutions to the problems we face in many different professional fields.

Can you give me an example of this?
We live in an increasingly complex and dynamic world, where traditional forms of problem solving are showing unforeseen limitations. Let me explain. Recent technological developments have landed humanity in a state of hyper-connectedness, where we find ourselves linked to innumerable other people. While we are living in this brave new networked society, we are now beginning to realize that the problems we face have become networked, too – to the point where the most important issues we face have become so complicated that they seem impervious to solution. Governments, institutions, and companies alike are struggling to come up with answers and are forced to reconsider their old problem-solving strategies. They used to abstract from the details of the concrete problem situation, decompose and analyze it, and reach a conclusion in due course. But this strategy will not work at all for today's problems: a tangle of relationships within complex and overlapping networks. Problems are intimately related to each other and are so dynamic that the world will have moved on by the time the formal analysis is completed. You can see this happen all the time: governments in particular are used to a hierarchical and purely analysis-based way of problem solving, and they seem powerless to deal with the complex issues we are facing today.

More and more, people are turning towards the field of design for help. Designers have been dealing with complex, networked problems that involve multiple stakeholders for many years. And they somehow have been able to come up with creative solutions that satisfy many of the relevant parties: they do not solve the problem as it has been defined, they innovate by proposing frames and ideas in a solution-focused manner, and test these proposals through experiments. This is a radically solution-focused strategy, as opposed to the problem-focused approaches that are the basis for conventional problem solving.

Are there any tools or techniques for developing alternative or innovative designs that you've found to be particularly successful?
This is hard to say . . . What I have found in studying the way design expertise develops, is that experienced designers work very differently from novices. That has alerted me to the fundamental problem that severely limits the usefulness of many tools and techniques: while these tools and techniques are normally developed to support the professional designer, they tend to be rule-based – and experienced designers do not work in a rule-based manner. Thus professional designers tend to see the tools and techniques as alien and disturbing to their natural design process (cumbersome, wordy, bureaucratic). And they are absolutely right. Rule-based tools and techniques would be particularly useful in education and in the early stages of a design career, but not much beyond that. I think this is a real challenge for the academic community: we need to conceive of support for designers that is appropriate for their level of expertise and doesn't unnecessarily disturb the natural flow of their design activities. What would such a non-rule-based tool or technique look like? This requires tool builders to be clearer on what qualities their tools or techniques

aim to achieve, what the scope of their applicability is, and demonstrate to the intended users that they are constructed with a close knowledge of the processes they are supposed to support.

What is the hardest part of designing?

For me, the hardest part of designing is dealing with its fundamentally dual nature: it is an open process of creation, that is also goal-directed . . . In practice this means that the designer, at any point in the project, has the choice of either a problem-solving approach or a solution-focused approach. Choosing a problem-solving approach might lead to unnecessarily limiting the scope of possible solutions; choosing a solution-focused approach might lead to a process that just spins out of control. The wisdom to choose well in a particular design situation comes with a lot of experience.

What does all this mean for interaction design?

Interaction designers can play a key role in the developments that are sketched above. Of all design disciplines, they may be the closest to having the skills and knowledge to deal with the dynamic and complex problems that we are confronted with. After all, interaction designers have always been used to dealing with dynamic relationships and complex scenarios – in contrast to, for instance, industrial designers, who have tended to focus more on the physical design outcome. This ability to describe, understand, explore, and create new frameworks and relationships is the key strength of design into the future.

The challenge for interaction designers will be to look beyond the current borders of their discipline, and re-contextualize their current abilities to meet these bigger challenges. In some of the leading companies and institutions (especially service providers, like banks and cultural institutions), we already see interaction designers moving into very strategic management roles where their core skills and knowledge are applied far beyond the reaches of the interaction design profession. ∎

Chapter 3

COGNITIVE ASPECTS

Objectives

The main aims of this chapter are to:

- Explain what cognition is and why it is important for interaction design.
- Discuss what attention is and its effects on our ability to multitask.
- Describe how memory can be enhanced through technology aids.
- Explain what mental models are.
- Show the difference between classic internal cognitive frameworks (e.g. mental models) and more recent external cognitive approaches (e.g. distributed cognition) that have been applied to HCI.
- Enable you to try to elicit a mental model and be able to understand what it means.

3.1 Introduction

Imagine it is late in the evening and you are sitting in front of your computer. You have an assignment to complete by tomorrow morning – a 3000 word essay on how natural are natural user interfaces – but you are not getting very far with it. You begin to panic and start biting your nails. You see two text messages flash up on your smartphone. You instantly abandon your essay and cradle your smartphone to read them. One is from your mother and the other from your friend asking if you want to go out for a drink. You reply straight away to them both. Before you know it you're back on Facebook to see if any of your friends have posted anything about the party you wanted to go to but had to say no. FaceTime rings and you see it is your dad calling. You answer it and he asks if you have been watching the football game. You say you are too busy working toward your deadline and he tells you your team has just scored. You chat with him and then say you have to get back to work. You realize 30 minutes has passed and you return your attention to the essay title. You type 'Natural User Interface' into Google Scholar and click on the top article. You click on the PDF icon for the article and it takes you to another page that requires a login and password. You don't have them for that publisher. You go back to Google Scholar and click on the next link. This time it takes you to the ACM digital library that your university has access to. But before you realize it you have clicked on the BBC Sports site to check the latest score for the football game. Your team has just scored again. Your phone starts buzzing. Two new WhatsApp messages are waiting for you. One is from your dad and another one from your girlfriend. You reply to both and within seconds they text back.

And on it goes. You glance at the time on your computer. It is 3.00 a.m. You really are in a panic now and finally switch everything off except your word processor.

In the past 10 to 15 years it has become increasingly common for people to be always switching their attention between multiple tasks. At its most extreme form, such behavior has been found to be highly addictive: instead of focusing on our work we're really waiting for the next hit – be it a new email, text, Facebook posting, news feed, tweet, and so forth. For some, such chronic media multitasking can be debilitating as they are unable to focus their attention on a single task for very long. For others, they have become very adept at using multiple sources of information to perform multiple tasks.

The study of human cognition can help us understand these and other new kinds of computer-augmented behaviors by examining humans' abilities and limitations when interacting with technologies. In this chapter we examine cognitive aspects of interaction design. Specifically, we consider what humans are good and bad at and show how this knowledge can be used to inform the design of technologies that both extend human capabilities and compensate for their weaknesses. We also look at some of the influential cognitive-based conceptual frameworks that have been developed for explaining the way humans interact with technology. (Other ways of conceptualizing human behavior that focus on the social and emotional aspects of interaction are presented in the following two chapters.)

3.2   What Is Cognition?

There are many different kinds of cognition, such as thinking, remembering, learning, daydreaming, decision making, seeing, reading, writing, and talking. Norman (1993) distinguishes between two general modes: experiential and reflective cognition. Kahneman (2011) describes them in terms of fast and slow thinking. The former is a state of mind in which we perceive, act, and react to events around us intuitively and effortlessly. It requires reaching a certain level of expertise and engagement. Examples include driving a car, reading a book, having a conversation, and playing a video game. In contrast, reflective cognition and slow thinking involve mental effort, attention, judgment, and decision making. This kind of cognition is what leads to new ideas and creativity. Examples include designing, learning, and writing a book. Both modes are essential for everyday life. It is useful to think of how the mind works in this way as it provides a basis from which to consider how each can be supported by different kinds of technologies.

Other ways of describing cognition are in terms of the context in which it takes place, the tools that are employed, the artifacts and interfaces that are used, and the people involved. Depending on when, where, and how it happens, cognition can be distributed, situated, extended, and embodied. Cognition has also been described in terms of specific kinds of processes. These include:

- attention
- perception
- memory
- learning
- reading, speaking, and listening
- problem solving, planning, reasoning, and decision making.

It is important to note that many of these cognitive processes are interdependent: several may be involved for a given activity. It is rare for one to occur in isolation. For example, when you try to learn material for an exam, you need to attend to the material, perceive and recognize it, read it, think about it, and try to remember it. Below we describe these various kinds of cognitive processes in more detail, followed by a summary box highlighting core design implications for each. Most relevant for interaction design are attention and memory, which we describe in greatest detail.

3.2.1   Attention

This is the process of selecting things to concentrate on, at a point in time, from the range of possibilities available. Attention involves our auditory and/or visual senses. An example of auditory attention is waiting in the dentist's waiting room for our name to be called out to know when it is our time to go in. An example of visual attention is scanning the football results as they appear online via a live feed, checking to see whether our team is winning. Attention allows us to focus on information that is relevant to what we are doing. The extent to which this process is easy or difficult depends on (i) whether we have clear goals and (ii) whether the information we need is salient in the environment.

(1) Our Goals

If we know exactly what we want to find out, we try to match this with the information that is available. For example, if we have just landed at an airport after a long flight and want to find out who has won the World Cup, we might scan the headlines at the newspaper stand, find the results on our smartphone, call a friend, or ask someone in the street. When we are not sure exactly what we are looking for, we may browse through information, allowing it to guide our attention to interesting or salient items. For example, when we go to a restaurant we may have the general goal of eating a meal but only a vague idea of what we want to eat. We peruse the menu to find things that whet our appetite, letting our attention be drawn to the imaginative descriptions of various dishes. After scanning through the possibilities and imagining what each dish might be like (plus taking into account other factors, such as cost, who we are with, what the specials are, what the waiter recommends, whether we want a two- or three-course meal, and so on), we may then make a decision.

(2) Information Presentation

The way information is displayed can also greatly influence how easy or difficult it is to attend to appropriate pieces of information. Look at Figure 3.1 and try the activity (based on Tullis, 1997). Here, the information-searching tasks are very precise, requiring specific answers.

South Carolina

City	Motel/Hotel	Area code	Phone	Rates Single	Double
Charleston	Best Western	803	747-0961	$126	$130
Charleston	Days Inn	803	881-1000	$118	$124
Charleston	Holiday Inn N	803	744-1621	$136	$146
Charleston	Holiday Inn SW	803	556-7100	$133	$147
Charleston	Howard Johnsons	803	524-4148	$131	$136
Charleston	Ramada Inn	803	774-8281	$133	$140
Charleston	Sheraton Inn	803	744-2401	$134	$142
Columbia	Best Western	803	796-9400	$129	$134
Columbia	Carolina Inn	803	799-8200	$142	$148
Columbia	Days Inn	803	736-0000	$123	$127
Columbia	Holiday Inn NW	803	794-9440	$132	$139
Columbia	Howard Johnsons	803	772-7200	$125	$127
Columbia	Quality Inn	803	772-0270	$134	$141
Columbia	Ramada Inn	803	796-2700	$136	$144
Columbia	Vagabond Inn	803	796-6240	$127	$130

(a)

Pennsylvania
Bedford Motel/Hotel: Crinaline Courts
   (814) 623-9511   S: $118 D: $120
Bedford Motel/Hotel: Holiday Inn
   (814) 623-9006 S: $129 D: $136
Bedford Motel/Hotel: Midway
   (814) 623-8107 S: $121 D: $126
Bedford Motel/Hotel: Penn Manor
   (814) 623-8177 S: $119 D: $125
Bedford Motel/Hotel: Quality Inn
   (814) 623-5189 S: $123 D: $128
Bedford Motel/Hotel: Terrace
   (814) 623-5111 S: $122 D: $124
Bradley Motel/Hotel: De Soto
   (814) 362-3567 S: $120 D: $124
Bradley Motel/Hotel: Holiday House
   (814) 362-4511 S: $122 D: $125
Bradley Motel/Hotel: Holiday Inn
   (814) 362-4501 S: $132 D: $140
Breezewood Motel/Hotel: Best Western Plaza
   (814) 735-4352 S: $120 D: $127
Breezewood Motel/Hotel: Motel 70
   (814) 735-4385 S: $116 D: $118

(b)

Figure 3.1 Two different ways of structuring the same information at the interface: one makes it much easier to find information than the other

Source: Reproduced by permission of Dr. Tom Tullis.

ACTIVITY 3.1

Look at the top screen of Figure 3.1 and (i) find the price for a double room at the Quality Inn in Columbia, and (ii) find the phone number of the Days Inn in Charleston. Then look at the bottom screen in Figure 3.1 and (i) find the price of a double room at the Holiday Inn in Bradley, and (ii) find the phone number of the Quality Inn in Bedford. Which took longer to do?

In an early study, Tullis found that the two screens produced quite different results: it took an average of 3.2 seconds to search the top screen and 5.5 seconds to find the same kind of information in the bottom screen. Why is this so, considering that both displays have the same density of information (31%)?

Comment
The primary reason is the way the characters are grouped in the display. In the top screen, they are grouped into vertical categories of information – i.e. place, kind of accommodation, phone number, and rates – that have columns of space between them. In the bottom screen, the information is bunched up together, making it much harder to search through. ■

Multitasking and Attention

Many of us now spend a large proportion of our time staring at a screen, be it a smartphone, laptop, TV, or tablet. As mentioned in the introduction, while focusing on one task at a screen, we switch constantly between others. For example, every 5 or 10 minutes while writing this chapter, I check my email, breaking off sometimes in mid-sentence to see who has sent me a message and then finding myself diverted to looking at the latest news item or URL recommended to me by a colleague. Like nearly everyone else, I am addicted; I can't stop myself from looking.

But is it possible for us to perform multiple tasks without one or more of them being detrimentally affected? Consider the following. While attending a talk at a conference I watched a student volunteer in front of me deftly switch between four ongoing instant message chats (one at the conference, one at school, one with friends, one at her part-time job), read, answer, delete, and place all new messages in various folders of her two email accounts, check and scan Facebook and her Twitter feeds – while appearing to listen to the talk, take some notes, Google the speaker's background, and open up his publications. When she had a spare moment she played a game of patience. I must say, I felt quite exhausted just watching her for a few minutes. It was as if she were capable of living in multiple worlds, all at the same time, while not letting a moment go to waste. But how much did she take in of the talk?

There has been much research on the effects of multitasking on memory and attention. A main finding is that it depends on the nature of the tasks and how much attention each demands. For example, listening to gentle music while working can help people tune out background noise, such as traffic or other people talking, and help them concentrate on what they are doing. However, if the music is loud, like Drum and Bass, it can be very distracting. Individual differences have also been found. For example, the results of a series of experiments comparing heavy with light multitaskers showed that heavy media multitaskers (such as the one described above) were more prone to being distracted by the multiple streams of media they are looking at than those who infrequently multitask. The latter were found to be better at allocating their attention when faced with competing distractions (Ophir *et al*, 2009). This suggests that people who are heavy multitaskers are likely to be those who are easily distracted and find it difficult to filter out irrelevant information.

"This project calls for real concentration. Are you still able to monotask?"

Design implications

Attention

- Make information salient when it needs attending to at a given stage of a task.
- Use techniques like animated graphics, color, underlining, ordering of items, sequencing of different information, and spacing of items to achieve this.
- Avoid cluttering the interface with too much information. This especially applies to the use of color, sound, and graphics: it is tempting to use lots, resulting in a mishmash of media that is distracting and annoying rather than helping the user attend to relevant information.
- Search engines and form fill-ins that have simple and clean interfaces are easier to use. ■

3.2.2   Perception

Perception refers to how information is acquired from the environment via the different sense organs – eyes, ears, fingers – and transformed into experiences of objects, events, sounds, and tastes (Roth, 1986). It is complex, involving other cognitive processes such as memory, attention, and language. Vision is the most dominant sense for sighted individuals, followed by hearing and touch. With respect to interaction design it is important to present information in a way that can be readily perceived in the manner intended.

As was demonstrated in Activity 3.1, grouping items together and leaving spaces between them can aid attention. In addition, many web designers recommend using blank space (more commonly known as white space) when grouping objects together on a screen as it helps users to perceive and locate items more easily and quickly. However, some researchers suggest that too much white space can be detrimental, making it sometimes harder to find information (Spool *et al*, 1997). In a study comparing web pages displaying the same amount of information, but which were structured using different graphical methods, it was found that people took less time to locate items from information that was grouped using a border than when using color contrast (Weller, 2004; see Figure 3.2). The findings suggest that using contrasting color is not a good way to group information on a screen and that using borders is more effective (Galitz, 1997).

Design implications
Perception

Representations of information need to be designed to be perceptible and recognizable across different media:

- Icons and other graphical representations should enable users to readily distinguish their meaning.
- Bordering and spacing are effective visual ways of grouping information that makes it easier to perceive and locate items.
- Sounds should be audible and distinguishable so users understand what they represent.
- Speech output should enable users to distinguish between the set of spoken words and also be able to understand their meaning.
- Text should be legible and distinguishable from the background (e.g. it is okay to use yellow text on a black or blue background but not on a white or green background).
- Tactile feedback used in virtual environments should allow users to recognize the meaning of the various touch sensations being emulated. The feedback should be distinguishable so that, for example, the sensation of squeezing is represented in a tactile form that is different from the sensation of pushing. ■

3.2.3 Memory

Memory involves recalling various kinds of knowledge that allow us to act appropriately. It is very versatile, enabling us to do many things. For example, it allows us to recognize someone's face, remember someone's name, recall when we last met them, and know what we said to them last.

It is not possible for us to remember everything that we see, hear, taste, smell, or touch, nor would we want to, as our brains would get completely overloaded. A filtering process is used to decide what information gets further processed and memorized. This filtering process, however, is not without its problems. Often we forget things we would dearly love to remember and conversely remember things we would love to forget. For example, we may find it difficult to remember everyday things like people's names and phone numbers, or scientific knowledge such as mathematical formulae. On the other hand, we may effortlessly remember trivia or tunes that cycle endlessly through our heads.

Black Hills Forest | Peters Landing | Jefferson Farms | Devlin Hall
Cheyenne River | Public Health | Psychophysics | Positions
Social Science | San Bernardino | Political Science | Hubard Hall
South San Jose | Moreno Valley | Game Schedule | Fernadino Beach
Badlands Park | Altamonte Springs | South Addision | Council Bluffs
Juvenile Justice | Peach Tree City | Cherry Hills Village | Classical Lit

Results and Stats | Highland Park | Creative Writing | Sociology
Thousand Oaks | Machesney Park | Lake Havasu City | Greek
Promotions | Vallecito Mts. | Engineering Bldg | Wallace Hall
North Palermo | Rock Falls | Sports Studies | Concert Tickets
Credit Union | Freeport | Lakewood Village | Public Radio FM
Wilner Hall | Slaughter Beach | Rock Island | Children's Museum

Performing Arts | Rocky Mountains | Deerfield Beach | Writing Center
Italian | Latin | Arlington Hill | Theater Auditions
Coaches | Pleasant Hills | Preview Game | Delaware City
Mckees Rocks | Observatory | Richland Hills | Scholarships
Glenwood Springs | Public Affairs | Experts Guids | Hendricksville
Urban Affairs | Heskett Center | Neff Hall | Knights Landing

McLeansboro | Brunswick | Grand Wash Cliffs | Modern Literature
Experimental Links | East Millinocket | Indian Well Valley | Studio Arts
Graduation | Women's Studies | Online Courses | Hugher Complex
Emory Lindquist | Vacant | Lindquist Hall | Cumberland Flats
Clinton Hall | News Theatre | Fisk Hall | Central Village
San Luis Obispo | Candlewood Isle | Los Padres Forest | Hoffman Estates

---

Webmaster | Curriculum | Student Life | Dance
Russian | Emergency (EMS) | Accountancy | Gerontloge
Athletics | Statistics | Mc Knight Center | Marketing
Go Shockers | Award Documents | Council of Women | College Bylaws
Degree Options | Language Center | Commute | Why Wichita?
Newsletter | Future Shockers | Small Business | Tickets

Gelogy | Intercollegiate | Thinker & Movers | Career Services
Manufacturing | Bowling | Alumni | Doers & Shockers
Management | Wichita Gateway | Foundations | Core Values
UCATS | Transfer Day | Corbin Center | Grace Wilkie Hall
Alumni News | Job Openings | Jardine Hall | Strategic Plan
Saso | Live Radio | Hugo Wall School | Medical Tech

Educational Map | Beta Alpha Psi | Staff | Softball, Men's
Physical Plant | Liberal Arts | Aerospace | McKinley Hall
Graphic Design | Counseling | Choral Dept. | Email
Non Credit Class | Biological Science | Alberg Hall | Dental Hygiene
Media Relations | Duerksen Fine Art | French | Tenure
Advertising | EMT Program | Spanish | Personnel Policies

English | Religion | Parents | Instrmental
Graduate Complex | Art Composition | Wrestling | Nrsing
Music Education | Physics | Philosopy | Opera
Advising Center | Entrepreneurship | Wichita Lyceum | Sports History
Medical School | Koch Arena | Fairmount Center | Athletic Dept.
Levitt Arena | Roster | Women's Museum | Health Plan

Figure 3.2 Two ways of structuring information on a web page. It takes more time for people to find a named item in the top one than in the bottom one, suggesting that using bordering as a grouping method helps searching while using contrasting color hinders it

Source: Reproduced with permission from D. Weller: "The Effects of Contrast and Density on Visual Web Search" from *Usability News 6.2*, 2004.

How does this filtering process work? Initially, encoding takes place, determining which information is attended to in the environment and how it is interpreted. The extent to which it takes place affects our ability to recall that information later. The more attention that is paid to something and the more it is processed in terms of thinking about it and comparing it with other knowledge, the more likely it is to be remembered. For example, when learning about a topic it is much better to reflect upon it, carry out exercises, have discussions with others about it, and write notes than just passively read a book or watch a video about it. Thus, how information is interpreted when it is encountered greatly affects how it is represented in memory and how easy it is to retrieve subsequently.

Another factor that affects the extent to which information can be subsequently retrieved is the context in which it is encoded. One outcome is that sometimes it can be difficult for people to recall information that was encoded in a different context from the one they are currently in. Consider the following scenario:

> *You are on a train and someone comes up to you and says hello. You don't recognize him for a few moments but then realize it is one of your neighbors. You are only used to seeing your neighbor in the hallway of your apartment block and seeing him out of context makes him difficult to recognize initially.*

Another well-known memory phenomenon is that people are much better at recognizing things than recalling things. Furthermore, certain kinds of information are easier to recognize than others. In particular, people are very good at recognizing thousands of pictures even if they have only seen them briefly before. In contrast, we are not as good at remembering details about the things we take photos of when visiting places, such as museums. It seems we remember less about objects when we have photographed them than when we observe them just with the naked eye (Henkel, 2014). The reason for this difference in our ability to remember details about objects is that people don't process as much information about an object when taking photos of it compared with when they are actually looking at it – and hence are not able to remember as much about it later.

ACTIVITY 3.2

Try to remember the dates of all the members of your family's and your closest friends' birthdays. How many can you remember? Then try to describe the image/graphic of the latest app you downloaded.

Comment

It is likely that you remembered much better the image, the colors, and the name of the app you downloaded than the birthdays of your family and friends (which most people now rely on Facebook or other online app to remind them of). People are very good at remembering visual cues about things, for example the color of items, the location of objects (e.g. a book being on the top shelf), and marks on an object (e.g. a scratch on a watch, a chip on a cup). In contrast, people find other kinds of information persistently difficult to learn and remember, especially arbitrary material like birthdays and phone numbers. ■

Memory and Search

The number of documents created, images, music files, and videoclips downloaded, emails and attachments saved, URLs bookmarked, and so on increases every day. Increasingly, people are saving their digital content to the Cloud so that it can be accessed from multiple platforms, but it still needs to be organized in a way that can be easily searched. For example, do they place items in folders or albums or lists? Many people use proprietary storage facilities, such as iCloud, Vimeo, Pinterest, and Flickr, to save their content. A challenge facing these companies is providing interfaces that will enable their users to store their content so they can readily access specific items at a later date, for example a particular image, video, or document. This can be challenging, especially if they have uploaded thousands of them. How do you find that photo you took of your dog spectacularly jumping into the sea to chase a seagull, which you think was taken two or three years ago? It can take ages wading through the hundreds of folders you have, catalogued by date, name, or tag. Do you start by homing in on folders for a given year, look for events, places, or faces, or type in a search term to find it again?

Naming is the most common means of encoding content, but trying to remember a name you created some time back can be very difficult, especially if you have tens of thousands of named files, images, videos, emails, etc. How might such a process be facilitated, taking into account people's memory abilities? Lansdale and Edmonds (1992) suggest that it is profitable to view this kind of remembering as involving two memory processes: recall-directed, followed by recognition-based scanning. The first refers to using memorized information about the required content to get as close to it as possible. The more exact this is, the more success the user will have in tracking down the desired content. The second happens when recall has failed to produce what a user wants and so requires reading through a list. To illustrate the difference between these two processes, consider the following scenario: a user is trying to access a couple of websites she visited the week before that compared the selling price of cars offered by different dealers. The user is able to recall the name of one website, autobargains.com. She types this in her web browser and the website appears. This is an example of successful recall-directed memory. However, the user is unable to remember the name of the second one. She vaguely remembers it was something like alwaysthecheapest.com, but typing this in proves unsuccessful. Instead, she switches to scanning her history list and selects the folder labeled more than six days ago. She notices two or three URLs that could be the one desired at the top of the list, and on the second attempt she finds the website she is looking for. In this situation, the user initially tries recall-directed memory and when this fails adopts the second strategy of recognition-based scanning – which takes longer but eventually results in success.

Digital content systems should be designed to optimize both kinds of memory processes. In particular, they should be designed to let people use whatever memory they have to limit the area being searched and then represent the information in this area of the interface so as to maximally assist them in finding what they need. The system should provide the user with a number of ways of encoding documents mnemonically, including time stamping, categorizing, tagging, and attribution (e.g. color, text, icon, sound, or image). Powerful search engines have gone a long way towards helping people track down the content they want. For example, various search and find tools, such as Android's Bravo SE and Apple's Spotlight, enable the user to type a full or partial name or even the first letter of a file that it then searches for in the entire system, including apps, games, emails, contacts, images, calendars, and applications. Figure 3.3

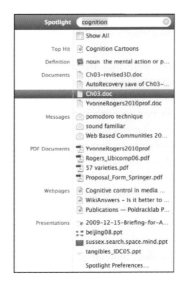

Figure 3.3 Apple's Spotlight search tool

shows part of a list of files that Spotlight matched to the phrase 'cognition', prioritized in terms of what I might be looking for, such as documents, web pages, and emails. The categories change depending on the words entered. For example, if someone's name is entered then images, contacts, and websites are prioritized.

BOX 3.1

The problem with the magical number seven, plus or minus two

Perhaps the best-known finding in psychology (certainly the one that nearly all students remember many years after they have finished their studies) is Miller's (1956) theory that seven, plus or minus two, chunks of information can be held in short-term memory at any one time. By short-term memory he meant a memory store in which information was assumed to be processed when first perceived. By chunks he meant a range of items like numbers, letters, or words. According to Miller's theory, therefore, people's immediate memory capacity is very limited. They are able to remember only a few words or numbers that they have heard or seen. If you are not familiar with this phenomenon, try out the following exercise: read the first set of numbers below (or get someone to read it to you), cover it up, and then try to recall as many of the items as possible. Repeat this for the other sets.

- 3, 12, 6, 20, 9, 4, 0, 1, 19, 8, 97, 13, 84
- cat, house, paper, laugh, people, red, yes, number, shadow, broom, rain, plant, lamp, chocolate, radio, one, coin, jet
- t, k, s, y, r, q, x, p, a, z, l, b, m, e

(Continued)

How many did you correctly remember for each set? Between five and nine, as suggested by Miller's theory?

Chunks can also be combined items that are meaningful. For example, it is possible to remember the same number of two-word phrases like hot chocolate, banana split, cream cracker, rock music, cheddar cheese, leather belt, laser printer, tree fern, fluffy duckling, cold rain. When these are all muddled up (i.e. split belt, fern crackers, banana laser, printer cream, cheddar tree, rain duckling, hot rock), however, it is much harder to remember as many chunks. This is mainly because the first set contains all meaningful two-word phrases that have been heard before and require less time to be processed in short-term memory, whereas the second set are completely novel phrases that don't exist in the real world. You need to spend time linking the two parts of the phrase together while trying to memorize them. This takes more time and effort to achieve. Of course, it is possible to do if you have time to spend rehearsing them, but if you are asked to do it having heard them only once in quick succession, it is most likely you will remember only a few.

By now, you may be thinking 'Okay, this is interesting, but what has it got to do with interaction design?' Well, not only does this classic theory have a special place in psychology, it has also made a big impression in HCI – unfortunately, however, for the wrong reasons. Many designers have heard or read about this phenomenon and think, 'Ah, here is a bit of psychology I can usefully apply to interface design.' Would you agree with them? If so, how might people's ability to only remember 7 ± 2 chunks that they have just read or heard be usefully applied to interaction design?

According to a survey by Bailey (2000), several designers have been led to believe the following guidelines and have even created interfaces based on them:

- Have only seven options on a menu.
- Display only seven icons on a menu bar.
- Never have more than seven bullets in a list.
- Place only seven tabs at the top of a website page.
- Place only seven items on a pull-down menu.

All of these are wrong. Why? The simple reason is that these are all items that can be scanned and rescanned visually and hence do *not* have to be recalled from short-term memory. They don't just flash up on the screen and disappear, requiring the user to remember them before deciding which one to select. If you were asked to find an item of food most people crave in the set of single words listed above, would you have any problem? No, you would just scan the list until you recognized the one (chocolate) that matched the task and then select it – just as people do when interacting with menus, lists, and tabs – regardless of whether they comprise three or 30 items. What the users are required to do here is not remember as many items as possible, having only heard or seen them once in a sequence, but instead scan through a set of items until they recognize the one they want. This is a quite different task. Furthermore, there is much more useful psychological research that can be profitably applied to interaction design. ■

Memory Load and Passwords

Phone banking has become increasingly popular in the past few years. It allows customers to carry out financial transactions, such as paying bills and checking the balance of their accounts, at their convenience. One of the problems confronting banks that provide this facility, however, is how to manage security concerns. Anyone can phone up a bank and pretend to be someone else. How do the banks prevent fraudulent transactions?

One solution has been to develop rigorous security measures whereby customers must provide various pieces of information before gaining access to their accounts. Typically, these include providing the answers to a combination of the following:

- their zip code or post code
- their mother's maiden name
- their birthplace
- the last school they attended
- the first school they attended
- a password of between five and ten letters
- a memorable address (not their home)
- a memorable date (not their birthday).

Many of these are relatively easy to remember and recall as they are very familiar. But consider the last two. How easy is it for someone to come up with such memorable information and then be able to recall it readily? Perhaps the customer can give the address and birthday of another member of their family as a memorable address and date. But what about the request for a password? Suppose a customer selects the word 'interaction' as a password – fairly easy to remember. The problem is that the bank operators do not ask for the full password, because of the danger that someone in the vicinity might overhear and write it down. Instead they are instructed to ask the customer to provide specific letters from it, like the seventh followed by the fifth. However, such information does not spring readily to mind. Instead, it requires mentally counting each letter of the password until the desired one is reached. How long does it take you to determine the seventh letter of the password 'interaction'? How did you do it?

To make things harder, banks also randomize the questions they ask. Again, this is to prevent someone who might be overhearing from memorizing the sequence of information. However, it also means that the customers themselves cannot learn the sequence of information required, meaning they have to generate different information every time they call up the bank.

This requirement to remember and recall such information puts a big memory load on customers. Some people find such a procedure quite nerve-racking and are prone to forget certain pieces of information. As a coping strategy they write down their details on a sheet of paper. Having such an external representation at hand makes it much easier for them to read off the necessary information rather than having to recall it from memory. However, it also makes them vulnerable to the very fraud the banks were trying to prevent, should anyone else get hold of that piece of paper!

ACTIVITY 3.3

How else might banks solve the problem of providing a secure system while making the memory load relatively easy for people wanting to use phone banking? How does phone banking compare with online banking?

(Continued)

Comment

An alternative approach is to provide the customers with a PIN and ask them to key this in on their phone keypad, followed by asking one or two questions like their zip or post code, as a backup. Online banking has similar security risks to phone banking, and hence this requires a number of security measures to be enforced. These include that the user sets up a nickname and a password. For example, some banks require answering a question only the user knows the answer to and then typing in three randomly selected letters from a password each time the user logs on. This is harder to do online than when asked over the phone, mainly because it interferes with the normally highly automated process of typing in a password. You really have to think about what letters and numbers are in your password – for example, has it got two letter 'f's after the number '6' or just one?

Researchers have also investigated whether images could be used instead of alpha- numerics for passwords. The idea is based on the principle that recognition is better than recall: users should be able to remember their passwords more accurately if they are required to recognize a set of images from a display that makes up their password than if they have to recall a sequence of alphanumerics. To this end, the graphical authentication approach has been developed, which asks people to select a series of images from different matrices of options. The images can be faces, cartoons, or photos of scenes or objects (e.g. sunset, dog, or even abstract images). To enable the process to be secure, however, requires people selecting a sequence of four to eight images and subsequently being able to recognize each item in the correct sequence. In other words, both recall (of the sequence) and recognition are involved. Studies have shown that while the graphical approach appears an attractive alternative, it has yet to demonstrate convincingly an advantage over the use of alphanumerics. Moreover, it takes much longer to create and subsequently select a sequence of images each time a person logs on than typing in a set of letters and numbers at a keyboard (De Angeli *et al*, 2005). ■

BOX 3.2

Digital forgetting

Much of the research on memory and interaction design has focused on developing cognitive aids that help people to remember; for example, reminders, to-do lists, and digital photo collections. However, there are times when we wish to forget a memory. For example, when someone breaks up with their partner, it can be emotionally painful to be reminded of them through shared digital images, videos, and Facebook friends. How can technology be designed to help people forget such memories? How could social media, such as Facebook, be designed to support this process?

Sas and Whittaker (2013) suggest designing new ways of harvesting digital materials con- nected to a broken relationship through using various automatic methods, such as face recog- nition, that dispose of them without the person needing to personally go through them and be confronted with painful memories. They also suggest that during a separation, people could create a collage of their digital content connected to the ex, so as to transform them into something more abstract, thereby providing a means for closure and helping with the process of moving on. ■

Computing Aids for Memory Loss

People suffering from memory impairments can find it difficult to complete common household tasks, like cooking and washing up, because they may forget a step or where they were. This can be exacerbated if the person gets interrupted (e.g. the phone rings), and they may end up not including an ingredient or adding the washing-up liquid twice. A prototype system called Cook's Collage was designed to provide surrogate memory support for general cooking tasks (Tran *et al*, 2005). Cameras were mounted underneath cabinets to capture still images of a cooking activity. These were then displayed as a series of images, in the form of a cartoon strip, on a flat-panel display mounted on an eye-level kitchen cabinet (see Figure 3.4). Preliminary evaluation of the prototype, being used by old people while cooking, showed them using it mainly as an aide-memoire, checking to see whether they had added certain ingredients after being distracted from the cooking task at hand.

Another computing technology that was used to help people suffering from memory loss (e.g. those with Alzheimer's disease) was the SenseCam, which was originally developed by Microsoft Research Labs in Cambridge (UK) to enable people to remember everyday events. This is a wearable camera (the predecessor of Autographer) that intermittently takes photos, without any user intervention, while it is being worn (see Figure 3.5). The camera can be

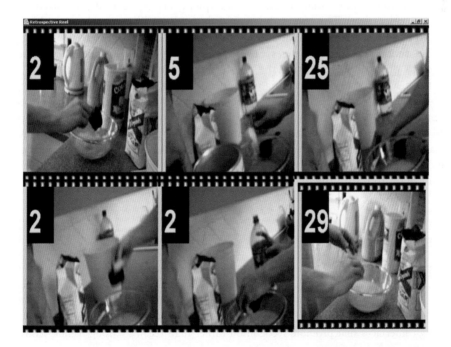

Figure 3.4 A screenshot of Cook's Collage showing images of a recent cooking activity. The strip is designed to be read backwards, starting with the highlighted image. This shows to the cook that he previously added the 29th scoop (!) of sugar and in the previous image two scoops of soda water

Source: Reproduced with permission from Elizabeth Mynatt, Everyday Computing Lab, Georgia Institute of Technology.

Figure 3.5 The SenseCam device and a digital image taken with it
Source: ©Microsoft Research Cambridge.

set to take pictures at particular times; for example, every 30 seconds, or based on what it senses (e.g. acceleration). The camera's lens is fish-eyed, enabling nearly everything in front of the wearer to be captured. The digital images for each day are stored, providing a record of the events that a person experiences. Several studies have been conducted on patients with various forms of memory loss using the device. For example, Hodges *et al* (2006) describe how a patient, Mrs B, who had amnesia was given a SenseCam to wear. The images that were collected were uploaded to a computer at the end of each day. For the next two weeks, Mrs B and her husband looked through these and talked about them. During this period, Mrs B's recall of an event nearly tripled, to a point where she could remember nearly everything about that event. Prior to using the SenseCam, Mrs B would have typically forgotten the little that she could initially remember about an event within a few days. It is not surprising that she did not want to return the device.

Design implications
Memory

- Do not overload users' memories with complicated procedures for carrying out tasks.
- Design interfaces that promote recognition rather than recall by using menus, icons, and consistently placed objects.
- Provide users with a variety of ways of encoding digital information (e.g. files, emails, images) to help them access them again easily, through the use of categories, color, tagging, time stamping, icons, etc. ■

3.2.4   Learning

It is well known that people find it hard to learn by following a set of instructions in a manual. Instead, they much prefer to learn through doing. GUIs and direct manipulation interfaces are good environments for supporting this kind of active learning by supporting exploratory interaction and, importantly, allowing users to undo their actions, i.e. return to a previous state if they make a mistake by clicking on the wrong option.

There have been numerous attempts to harness the capabilities of different technologies to help learners understand topics. One of the main benefits of interactive technologies, such as web-based learning, elearning, multimedia, and virtual reality, is that they provide alternative ways of representing and interacting with information that are not possible with traditional technologies, e.g. books. In so doing, they have the potential of offering learners the ability to explore ideas and concepts in different ways. For example, interactive multimedia simulations have been designed to help teach abstract concepts (e.g. mathematical formulae, notations, laws of physics) that students find difficult to grasp. Different representations of the same process (e.g. a graph, a formula, a sound, a simulation) are displayed and interacted with in ways that make their relationship with each other more explicit to the learner.

One form of interactivity that has been found to be highly effective is dynalinking (Rogers and Scaife, 1998). Abstract representations, such as diagrams, are linked together with a more concrete illustration of what they stand for, such as a simulation. Changes in one are matched by changes in the other, enabling a better understanding of what the abstraction means. An early example of its use was software developed for learning about ecological concepts, such as food webs (Rogers *et al*, 2003). A concrete simulation showed various organisms swimming and moving around and occasionally an event where one would eat another (e.g. a snail eating the weed). This was annotated and accompanied by various eating sounds, like chomping, to attract the children's attention. The children could also interact with the simulation. When an organism was clicked on, it would say what it was and what it ate (e.g. 'I am a weed. I make my own food'). The concrete simulation was dynalinked with other abstract representations of the pond ecosystem, including an abstract food web diagram (see Figure 3.6).

Dynalinking has been used in other domains to explicitly show relationships among multiple dimensions where the information to be understood or learned is complex (Sutcliffe,

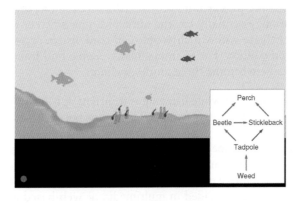

Figure 3.6 Dynalinking used in the Pondworld software

2002). For example, it can be useful for domains like economic forecasting, molecular modeling, and statistical analyses.

Increasingly, we rely on the Internet and our smartphones to act as cognitive prostheses in the way in which blind people use walking sticks. They have become a cognitive resource that we use in our daily lives as part of the extended mind. Sparrow *et al* (2011) showed how expecting to have Internet access reduces the need and hence the extent to which we attempt to remember the information itself, while enhancing our memory for knowing where to find it online. Many of us will whip out our smartphone to find out who acted in a film, what the name of a book is, what the word in another language is, and so on. Besides search engines, there are a number of other cognitive prosthetic apps that instantly help us find out or remember something, such as Shazam, the popular music recognition app. This has important implications for the design of technologies to support *how* future generations will learn, and *what* they learn.

Design implications
Learning

- Design interfaces that encourage exploration.
- Design interfaces that constrain and guide users to select appropriate actions when initially learning.
- Dynamically link concrete representations and abstract concepts to facilitate the learning of complex material. ∎

3.2.5   Reading, Speaking, and Listening

Reading, speaking, and listening are three forms of language processing that have similar and different properties. One similarity is that the meaning of sentences or phrases is the same regardless of the mode in which it is conveyed. For example, the sentence 'Computers are a wonderful invention' essentially has the same meaning whether one reads it, speaks it, or hears it. However, the ease with which people can read, listen, or speak differs depending on the person, task, and context. For example, many people find listening easier than reading. Specific differences between the three modes include:

- Written language is permanent while listening is transient. It is possible to re-read information if not understood the first time around. This is not possible with spoken information that is being broadcast.
- Reading can be quicker than speaking or listening, as written text can be rapidly scanned in ways not possible when listening to serially presented spoken words.
- Listening requires less cognitive effort than reading or speaking. Children, especially, often prefer to listen to narratives provided in multimedia or web-based learning material than to read the equivalent text online.

- Written language tends to be grammatical while spoken language is often ungrammatical. For example, people often start talking and stop in mid-sentence, letting someone else start speaking.
- Dyslexics have difficulties understanding and recognizing written words, making it hard for them to write grammatical sentences and spell correctly.

Many applications have been developed either to capitalize on people's reading, writing, and listening skills, or to support or replace them where they lack or have difficulty with them. These include:

- Interactive books and web-based materials that help people to read or learn foreign languages.
- Speech-recognition systems that allow users to interact with them by using spoken commands (e.g. word-processing dictation, Google Voice Search app, and home control devices that respond to vocalized requests).
- Speech-output systems that use artificially generated speech (e.g. written-text-to-speech systems for the blind).
- Natural-language systems that enable users to type in questions and give text-based responses (e.g. the Ask search engine).
- Cognitive aids that help people who find it difficult to read, write, and speak. Numerous special interfaces have been developed for people who have problems with reading, writing, and speaking (e.g. see Edwards, 1992).
- Customized input and output devices that allow people with various disabilities to have access to the web and use word processors and other software packages.
- Interaction techniques that allow blind people to read graphs and other visuals on the web through the use of auditory navigation and tactile diagrams (Petrie *et al*, 2002).

Design implications
Reading, speaking, and listening

- Keep the length of speech-based menus and instructions to a minimum. Research has shown that people find it hard to follow spoken menus with more than three or four options. Likewise, they are bad at remembering sets of instructions and directions that have more than a few parts.
- Accentuate the intonation of artificially generated speech voices, as they are harder to understand than human voices.
- Provide opportunities for making text large on a screen, without affecting the formatting, for people who find it hard to read small text. ■

3.2.6 Problem Solving, Planning, Reasoning, and Decision Making

Problem solving, planning, reasoning, and decision making are processes involving reflective cognition. They include thinking about what to do, what the options are, and what the consequences might be of carrying out a given action. They often involve conscious processes (being aware of what one is thinking about), discussion with others (or oneself), and the use of various kinds of artifacts (e.g. maps, books, pen and paper). For example, when planning the best route to get somewhere, say a foreign city, we may ask others, use a paper map, get directions from the web, or use a combination of these. Reasoning involves working through different scenarios and deciding which is the best option or solution to a given problem. In the route-planning activity we may be aware of alternative routes and reason through the advantages and disadvantages of each route before deciding on the best one. Many a family argument has come about because one member thinks he knows the best route while another thinks otherwise. Nowadays, many of us offload this kind of decision making (and the stress) onto technology, by simply following the instructions given by a car GPS or a smartphone map app. According to an internal survey carried out by YouGov in March 2014 in the UK, TomTom – which launched the first SatNav in 2004 – has helped 13 million couples avoid navigation arguments in the car!

There has been a growing interest in how people make decisions when confronted with information overload, such as when shopping on the web or at a store. How easy is it to make a decision when confronted with overwhelming choice? Classical rational theories of decision making (e.g. von Neumann and Morgenstern, 1944) posit that making a choice involves weighing up the costs and benefits of different courses of action. This is assumed to involve exhaustively processing the information and making trade-offs between features. Such strategies are very costly in computational and informational terms – not least because they require the decision-maker to find a way of comparing the different options. In contrast, research in cognitive psychology has shown how people tend to use simple heuristics when making decisions (Gigerenzer *et al*, 1999). A theoretical explanation is that human minds have evolved to act quickly, making just good enough decisions by using fast and frugal heuristics. We typically ignore most of the available information and rely only on a few important cues. For example, in the supermarket, shoppers make snap judgments based on a paucity of information, such as buying brands that they recognize, that are low-priced, or have attractive packaging – seldom reading other package information. This suggests that an effective design strategy is to follow the adage 'less is more' rather than 'more is more,' making key information about a product highly salient.

Thus, instead of providing ever more information to enable people to compare products when making a choice, a better strategy is to design technological interventions that provide just enough information, and in the right form, to facilitate good choices. One solution is to exploit new forms of augmented reality and wearable technology that enable information-frugal decision making and which have glanceable displays that can represent key information in an easy-to-digest form (Rogers, Payne and Todd, 2010).

DILEMMA

Can you make up your mind without an app?

Howard Gardner and Katie Davis (2013) in their book *The App Generation* note how the app mentality developing in the psyche of the younger generation is making it worse for them to make their own decisions because they are becoming more risk averse. By this they mean that young people are now depending on an increasing number of mobile apps that remove the risks of having to decide for themselves. They will first read what others have said on social media sites, blogs, and recommender apps before choosing where to eat, where to go, what to do, what to listen to, etc. But, relying on a multitude of apps means that young people are becoming increasingly more anxious about making decisions by themselves. For many, their first big decision is choosing which university to go to. This has become an agonizing and prolonged experience where both parents and apps play a central role in helping them out. They will read countless reviews, go on numerous visits to universities with their parents over several months, study the form of a number of league tables, read up on what others say on social networking sites, and so on. But in the end, was all that necessary? They may finally end up choosing where their friends are going or the one they liked the look of in the first place. Many will have spent hours, weeks, and even months talking about it, reading up on it, listening to lots of advice, and procrastinating right down to the wire. Compared to previous pre-Internet generations, they won't have made the decision by themselves. ∎

Design implications
Problem solving, planning, reasoning, and decision making

- Provide additional hidden information that is easy to access for users who wish to understand more about how to carry out an activity more effectively (e.g. web searching).
- Use simple and memorable functions at the interface for computational aids intended to support rapid decision making and planning that takes place while on the move. ∎

3.3 Cognitive Frameworks

A number of conceptual frameworks and theories have been developed to explain and predict user behavior based on theories of cognition. In this section, we outline three early internal frameworks that focus primarily on mental processes together with three more recent external ones that explain how humans interact and use technologies in the context in which they occur. These are:

Internal

1. Mental models
2. Gulfs of execution and evaluation
3. Information processing.

External

4. Distributed cognition
5. External cognition
6. Embodied interaction.

3.3.1   Mental Models

In Chapter 2 we pointed out that a successful system is one based on a conceptual model that enables users to readily learn that system and use it effectively. People primarily develop knowledge of how to interact with a system and, to a lesser extent, how that system works. In the 1980s and 1990s, these two kinds of knowledge were often referred to as a user's mental model.

It is assumed that mental models are used by people to reason about a system and, in particular, to try to fathom out what to do when something unexpected happens with the system or when encountering unfamiliar systems. The more someone learns about a system and how it functions, the more their mental model develops. For example, TV engineers have a deep mental model of how TVs work that allows them to work out how to set them up and fix them. In contrast, an average citizen is likely to have a reasonably good mental model of how to operate a TV but a shallow mental model of how it works.

Within cognitive psychology, mental models have been postulated as internal constructions of some aspect of the external world that are manipulated, enabling predictions and inferences to be made (Craik, 1943). This process is thought to involve the fleshing out and the running of a mental model (Johnson-Laird, 1983). This can involve both unconscious and conscious mental processes, where images and analogies are activated.

ACTIVITY 3.4

To illustrate how we use mental models in our everyday reasoning, imagine the following two scenarios:

1. You arrive home from a holiday on a cold winter's night to a cold house. You have a small baby and you need to get the house warm as quickly as possible. Your house is centrally heated. Do you set the thermostat as high as possible or turn it to the desired temperature (e.g. 70°F)?
2. You arrive home after being out all night and you're starving hungry. You look in the freezer and find all that is left is a frozen pizza. The instructions on the packet say heat the oven to 375°F and then place the pizza in the oven for 20 minutes. Your oven is electric. How do you heat it up? Do you turn it to the specified temperature or higher?

Comment

Most people when asked the first question imagine the scenario in terms of what they would do in their own house and choose the first option. A typical explanation is that setting the temperature to be as high as possible increases the rate at which the room warms up. While many people may believe this, it is incorrect. Thermostats work by switching on the heat and keeping it going at a constant speed until the desired set temperature is reached, at which point it cuts out. They cannot control the rate at which heat is given out from a heating system. Left at a given setting, thermostats will turn the heat on and off as necessary to maintain the desired temperature.

When asked the second question, most people say they would turn the oven to the specified temperature and put the pizza in when they think it is at the right temperature. Some people answer that they would turn the oven to a higher temperature in order to warm it up more quickly. Electric ovens work on the same principle as central heating, and so turning the heat up higher will not warm it up any quicker. There is also the problem of the pizza burning if the oven is too hot! ■

Why do people use erroneous mental models? It seems that in the above scenarios, they are running a mental model based on a general valve theory of the way something works (Kempton, 1986). This assumes the underlying principle of more is more: the more you turn or push something, the more it causes the desired effect. This principle holds for a range of physical devices, such as faucets and radio controls, where the more you turn them, the more water or volume comes out. However, it does not hold for thermostats, which instead function based on the principle of an on–off switch. What seems to happen is that in everyday life, people develop a core set of abstractions about how things work, and apply these to a range of devices, irrespective of whether they are appropriate.

Using incorrect mental models to guide behavior is surprisingly common. Just watch people at a pedestrian crossing or waiting for an elevator. How many times do they press the button? A lot of people will press it at least twice. When asked why, a common reason given is that they think it will make the lights change faster or ensure the elevator arrives. This seems to be another example of following the 'more is more' philosophy: it is believed that the more times you press the button, the more likely it is to result in the desired effect.

Many people's understanding of how technologies and services (e.g. the Internet, wireless networking, broadband, search engines, and computer viruses) work is poor. Their mental models are often incomplete, easily confusable, and based on inappropriate analogies and superstition (Norman, 1983). As a consequence, they find it difficult to identify, describe, or solve a problem, and lack the words or concepts to explain what is happening.

If people could develop better mental models of interactive systems, they would be in a better position to know how to carry out their tasks efficiently, and know what to do if a system started malfunctioning. Ideally, they should be able to develop a mental model that matches the conceptual model. But to what extent is this realistic, given that most people are resistant to spending much time learning about how things work, especially if it involves reading manuals or other documentation? Alternatively, if interactive technologies could be designed to be more transparent, then it might be easier to understand them in terms of how they work and what to do when they don't. Transparency involves including:

* useful feedback in response to user input; and
* easy-to-understand and intuitive ways of interacting with the system.

In addition, it requires providing the right kind and level of information, in the form of:

- clear and easy-to-follow instructions;
- appropriate online help and tutorials; and
- context-sensitive guidance for users, set at their level of experience, explaining how to proceed when they are not sure what to do at a given stage of a task.

DILEMMA

How much transparency?

How much and what kind of transparency do you think a designer should provide in an interactive product? This is not a straightforward question to answer and depends a lot on the requirements of the targeted user groups. Some users simply want to get on with their tasks and don't want to have to learn about how the thing they are using works. In this situation, the interface should be designed to make it obvious what to do and how to use it. Functions that are difficult to learn can be off-putting. Users simply won't bother to make the extra effort, meaning that many of the functions provided are never used. Other users like to understand how the device they are using works in order to make informed decisions about how to carry out their tasks, especially if there are numerous ways of doing something. Some search engines have been designed with this in mind: they provide background information on how they work and how to improve one's searching techniques. ■

3.3.2   Gulfs of Execution and Evaluation

The gulf of execution and the gulf of evaluation describe the gaps that exist between the user and the interface (Norman, 1986; Hutchins *et al*, 1986). They are intended to show how to design the latter to enable the user to cope with them. The first one – the gulf of execution – describes the distance from the user to the physical system while the second one – the gulf of evaluation – is the distance from the physical system to the user (see Figure 3.7). Norman and his colleagues suggest that designers and users need to concern themselves with how to bridge the gulfs in order to reduce the cognitive effort required to perform a task. This can be achieved, on the one hand, by designing usable interfaces that match the psychological characteristics of the user (e.g. taking into account their memory limitations) and, on the other hand, by the user learning to create goals, plans, and action sequences that fit with how the interface works.

3.3.3.   Information Processing

Another classic approach to conceptualizing how the mind works has been to use metaphors and analogies. Numerous comparisons have been made, including conceptualizing the mind as a reservoir, a telephone network, and a digital computer. One prevalent metaphor from cognitive

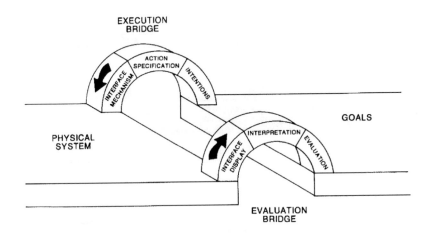

Figure 3.7 Bridging the gulfs of execution and evaluation

Source: User centered system design: new perspectives on human-computer interaction by D Norman. Copyright 1986 by Taylor & Francis Group LLC - Books. Reproduced with permission of Taylor & Francis Group LLC.

psychology is the idea that the mind is an information processor. Information is thought to enter and exit the mind through a series of ordered processing stages (see Figure 3.8). Within these stages, various processes are assumed to act upon mental representations. Processes include comparing and matching. Mental representations are assumed to comprise images, mental models, rules, and other forms of knowledge.

The information processing model provides a basis from which to make predictions about human performance. Hypotheses can be made about how long someone will take to perceive and respond to a stimulus (also known as reaction time) and what bottlenecks occur if a person is overloaded with too much information. One of the first HCI models to be derived from the information processing theory was the human processor model, which modeled the cognitive processes of a user interacting with a computer (Card *et al*, 1983). Cognition was conceptualized as a series of processing stages, where perceptual, cognitive, and motor processors are organized in relation to one another (see Figure 3.9). The model predicts which cognitive processes are involved when a user interacts with a computer, enabling calculations to be made of how long a user will take to carry out various tasks.

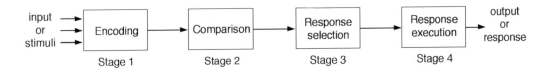

Figure 3.8 Human information processing model

Source: Reproduced with permission from P. Barber: *Applied Cognitive Psychology* 1998 Methuen, London.

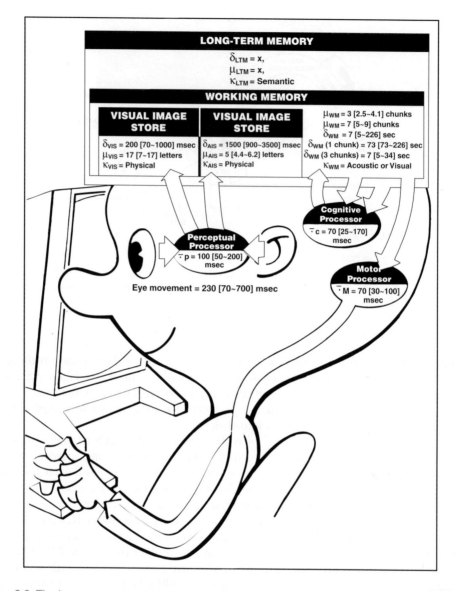

Figure 3.9 The human processor model

Source: The psychology of human-computer interaction by S. Card, T. Moran and A. Newell. Copyright 1983 by Taylor & Francis Group LLC - Books. Reproduced with permission of Taylor & Francis Group LLC.

In the 1980s, it was found to be a useful tool for comparing different word processors for a range of editing tasks.

The information processing approach was based on modeling mental activities that happen exclusively inside the head. Many have argued, however, that they do not adequately account for how people interact with computers and other devices, for example:

> *The traditional approach to the study of cognition is to look at the pure intellect, isolated from distractions and from artificial aids. Experiments are performed in closed, isolated rooms, with a minimum of distracting lights or sounds, no other people to assist with the task, and no aids to memory or thought. The tasks are arbitrary ones, invented by the researcher. Model builders build simulations and descriptions of these isolated situations. The theoretical analyses are self-contained little structures, isolated from the world, isolated from any other knowledge or abilities of the person.* (Norman, 1990, p. 5)

Instead, there has been an increasing trend to study cognitive activities in the context in which they occur, analyzing cognition as it happens in the wild (Hutchins, 1995). A central goal has been to look at how structures in the environment can both aid human cognition and reduce cognitive load. The three external approaches we consider next are distributed cognition, external cognition, and embodied cognition.

3.3.4 Distributed Cognition

Most cognitive activities involve people interacting with external kinds of representations, like books, documents, and computers – not to mention one another. For example, when we go home from wherever we have been, we do not need to remember the details of the route because we rely on cues in the environment (e.g. we know to turn left at the red house, right when the road comes to a T-junction, and so on). Similarly, when we are at home we do not have to remember where everything is because information is out there. We decide what to eat and drink by scanning the items in the fridge, find out whether any messages have been left by glancing at the answering machine to see if there is a flashing light, and so on. Likewise, we are always creating external representations for a number of reasons, not only to help reduce memory load and the cognitive cost of computational tasks, but also, importantly, to extend what we can do and allow us to think more powerfully (Kirsh, 2010).

The distributed cognition approach studies the nature of cognitive phenomena across individuals, artifacts, and internal and external representations (Hutchins, 1995). Typically, it involves describing a cognitive system, which entails interactions among people, the artifacts they use, and the environment they are working in (see Figure 3.10). An example of a cognitive system is an airline cockpit, where a top-level goal is to fly the plane. This involves:

- the pilot, captain, and air traffic controller interacting with one another;
- the pilot and captain interacting with the instruments in the cockpit; and
- the pilot and captain interacting with the environment in which the plane is flying (i.e. sky, runway).

A primary objective of the distributed cognition approach is to describe these interactions in terms of how information is propagated through different media. By this is meant how information is represented and re-represented as it moves across individuals and through the array of artifacts that are used (e.g. maps, instrument readings, scribbles, spoken word) during activities. These transformations of information are referred to as changes in representational state.

This way of describing and analyzing a cognitive activity contrasts with other cognitive approaches, such as the information processing model, in that it focuses not on what

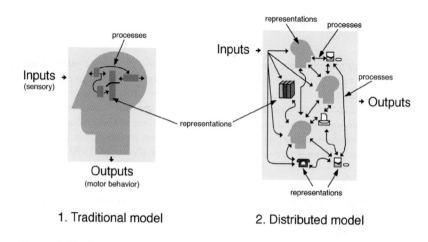

Figure 3.10 Comparison of traditional and distributed cognition approaches

is happening inside the head of an individual, but on what is happening across a system of individuals and artifacts. For example, in the cognitive system of the cockpit, a number of people and artifacts are involved in the activity of flying to a higher altitude. The air traffic controller initially tells the pilot when it is safe to fly to a higher altitude. The pilot then alerts the captain, who is flying the plane, by moving a knob on the instrument panel in front of them, indicating that it is now safe to fly (see Figure 3.11). Hence, the information concerning this activity is transformed through different media (over the radio, through the pilot, and via a change in the position of an instrument).

A distributed cognition analysis typically involves examining:

- The distributed problem solving that takes place (including the way people work together to solve a problem).
- The role of verbal and non-verbal behavior (including what is said, what is implied by glances, winks, and the like, and what is not said).
- The various coordinating mechanisms that are used (e.g. rules, procedures).
- The various ways communication takes place as the collaborative activity progresses.
- How knowledge is shared and accessed.

3.3.5   External Cognition

People interact with or create information through using a variety of external representations, including books, multimedia, newspapers, web pages, maps, diagrams, notes, drawings, and so on. Furthermore, an impressive range of tools has been developed throughout history to aid cognition, including pens, calculators, and computer-based technologies. The combination of external representations and physical tools has greatly extended and supported people's ability to carry out cognitive activities (Norman, 2013). Indeed, they are such an integral part that it is difficult to imagine how we would go about much of our everyday life without them.

External cognition is concerned with explaining the cognitive processes involved when we interact with different external representations (Scaife and Rogers, 1996). A main goal

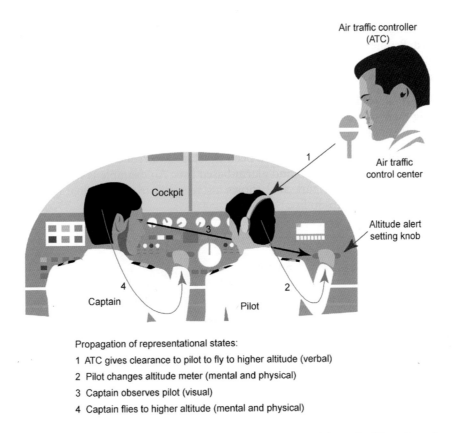

Propagation of representational states:
1 ATC gives clearance to pilot to fly to higher altitude (verbal)
2 Pilot changes altitude meter (mental and physical)
3 Captain observes pilot (visual)
4 Captain flies to higher altitude (mental and physical)

Figure 3.11 A cognitive system in which information is propagated through different media

Source: Preece, J. and Keller, L. (1994) *Human-Computer Interaction*, Figure 3.5 (p. 70) Addison Wesley, 1994.

is to explicate the cognitive benefits of using different representations for different cognitive activities and the processes involved. The main ones include:

1. Externalizing to reduce memory load
2. Computational offloading
3. Annotating and cognitive tracing.

(1) Externalizing to Reduce Memory Load

Numerous strategies have been developed for transforming knowledge into external representations to reduce memory load. One such strategy is externalizing things we find difficult to remember, such as birthdays, appointments, and addresses. Diaries, personal reminders, and calendars are examples of cognitive artifacts that are commonly used for this purpose, acting as external reminders of what we need to do at a given time, like buy a card for a relative's birthday.

Other kinds of external representations that people frequently employ are notes, like sticky notes, shopping lists, and to-do lists. Where these are placed in the environment can also be crucial. For example, people often place notes in prominent positions, such as on walls, on the side of computer monitors, by the front door, and sometimes even on their hands, in a deliberate attempt to ensure they do remind them of what needs to be done or remembered. People also place things in piles in their offices and by the front door, indicating what needs to be done urgently and what can wait for a while.

Externalizing, therefore, can help reduce people's memory burden by:

- reminding them to do something (e.g. get something for mother's birthday);
- reminding them of what to do (e.g. buy a card); and
- reminding them of when to do something (e.g. send it by a certain date).

A number of smartphone apps have been developed to reduce the burden on people to remember things, including to-do and alarm-based lists. An example is Memory Aid, developed by Jason Blackwood. Figure 3.12 shows a screenshot from it of floating bubbles with keywords that relate to a to-do list.

Figure 3.12 A screenshot from a smartphone app for reminding users what to do

Source: Memory Aid developed by Jason Blackwood.

(2) Computational Offloading

Computational offloading occurs when we use a tool or device in conjunction with an external representation to help us carry out a computation. An example is using pen and paper to solve a math problem.

ACTIVITY 3.5

1. Multiply 2 by 3 in your head. Easy. Now try multiplying 234 by 456 in your head. Not as easy. Try doing the sum using a pen and paper. Then try again with a calculator. Why is it easier to do the calculation with pen and paper and even easier with a calculator?
2. Try doing the same two sums using Roman numerals.

Comment

1. Carrying out the sum using pen and paper is easier than doing it in your head because you offload some of the computation by writing down partial results and using them to continue with the calculation. Doing the same sum with a calculator is even easier, because it requires only eight simple key presses. Even more of the computation has been offloaded onto the tool. You need only follow a simple internalized procedure (key in first number, then the multiplier sign, then next number, and finally the equals sign) and then read off the result from the external display.
2. Using Roman numerals to do the same sum is much harder: 2 times 3 becomes II × III, and 234 times 456 becomes CCXXXIV × CDLVI. The first calculation may be possible to do in your head or on a bit of paper, but the second is incredibly difficult to do in your head or even on a piece of paper (unless you are an expert in using Roman numerals or you cheat and transform it into Arabic numerals). Calculators do not have Roman numerals so it would be impossible to do on a calculator.

   Hence, it is much harder to perform the calculations using Roman numerals than Arabic numerals – even though the problem is equivalent in both conditions. The reason for this is that the two kinds of representation transform the task into one that is easy and one that is more difficult, respectively. The kind of tool used also can change the nature of the task to being more or less easy. ∎

(3) Annotating and Cognitive Tracing

Another way in which we externalize our cognition is by modifying representations to reflect changes that are taking place that we wish to mark. For example, people often cross things off in a to-do list to show that they have been completed. They may also reorder objects in the environment by creating different piles as the nature of the work to be done changes. These two kinds of modification are called annotating and cognitive tracing:

• Annotating involves modifying external representations, such as crossing off or underlining items.
• Cognitive tracing involves externally manipulating items into different orders or structures.

Annotating is often used when people go shopping. People usually begin their shopping by planning what they are going to buy. This often involves looking in their cupboards and fridge to see what needs stocking up. However, many people are aware that they won't remember all this in their heads and so often externalize it as a written shopping list. The act of writing may also remind them of other items that they need to buy, which they may not have noticed when looking through the cupboards. When they actually go shopping at the store, they may cross off items on the shopping list as they are placed in the shopping basket or cart. This provides them with an annotated externalization, allowing them to see at a glance what items are still left on the list that need to be bought. Some displays (e.g. tablet PCs, large interactive displays, and iPads) enable users to physically annotate documents, such as circling data or writing notes using styluses or their fingertips (see Chapter 6). The annotations can be stored with the document, enabling the users to revisit theirs or others' externalizations at a later date.

Cognitive tracing is useful in situations where the current state of play is in a state of flux and the person is trying to optimize her position. This typically happens when playing games, such as:

- In a card game, when the continuous rearrangement of a hand of cards into suits, in ascending order, or collecting same numbers together helps to determine what cards to keep and which to play as the game progresses and tactics change.
- In Scrabble, where shuffling around letters in the tray helps a person work out the best word given the set of letters (Maglio *et al*, 1999).

Cognitive tracing has also been used as an interactive function: for example, letting students know what they have studied in an online elearning package. An interactive diagram can be used to highlight all the nodes visited, exercises completed, and units still to study.

A general cognitive principle for interaction design based on the external cognition approach is to provide external representations at an interface that reduce memory load and facilitate computational offloading. Different kinds of information visualizations can be developed that reduce the amount of effort required to make inferences about a given topic (e.g. financial forecasting, identifying programming bugs). In so doing, they can extend or amplify cognition, allowing people to perceive and do activities that they couldn't do otherwise. For example, information visualizations (see Chapter 6) represent masses of data in a visual form that can make it easier to make cross-comparisons across dimensions. GUIs are also able to reduce memory load significantly through providing external representations, e.g. Wizards and dialog boxes that guide users through their interactions.

3.3.6   Embodied Interaction

The concept of embodied interaction has become popular in interaction design and HCI since the publication of Dourish's (2001) book *Where the Action Is*. It is about understanding interaction in terms of practical engagement with the social and physical environment. HCI, which grew out of collaborations between computer scientists and psychologists, initially adopted an information processing perspective. Dourish and others before him, such as Winograd and Flores (1986) and Suchman (1987), criticized this view of cognition as failing to account for the ways that people get things done in real situations. It provides a framing and organizing principle to help researchers uncover issues in the design and use of existing technologies and in the design of new systems.

It has been applied quite broadly to HCI, including work that focuses on the emotional quality of interaction with technology (Höök, 2008), on publicly available actions in physically shared spaces (Robertson, 1997), and on the role of the body in mediating our interaction with technology (Klemmer *et al*, 2006). Others have looked at how to apply a new generation of cognitive theories in interaction design (e.g. Antle *et al*, 2009; Hurtienne, 2009). These theories of embodied cognition are more grounded in the ways that people experience the world through physical interaction, but still emphasize the value of using abstraction from particular contexts.

Assignment

The aim of this assignment is for you to elicit mental models from people. In particular, the goal is for you to understand the nature of people's knowledge about an interactive product in terms of how to use it and how it works.

(a) First, elicit your own mental model. Write down how you think contactless cards (Figure 3.13) work – where customers 'wave' their debit or credit card over a card reader instead of typing in a PIN. Then answer the following questions:

Figure 3.13 A contactless debit card indicated by symbol

- What information is sent between the card and the card reader when it is waved in front of it?
- What is the maximum amount you can pay for something using a contactless card?
- How many times can you use a contactless card in a day?
- Can you use your smartphone to pay in the same way? If so, how is that possible?
- What happens if you have two contactless cards in the same wallet/purse?
- What happens when your contactless card is stolen and you report it to the bank? What does the bank do?

(Continued)

Next, ask two other people the same set of questions.

(b) Now analyze your answers. Do you get the same or different explanations? What do the findings indicate? How accurate are people's mental models of the way contactless cards work?

(c) What other ways might there be for paying for purchases instead of using cash, debit, or credit cards?

(d) Finally, how might you design a better conceptual model that would allow users to develop a better mental model of contactless cards (assuming this is a desirable goal)?

Summary

This chapter has explained the importance of understanding users, especially their cognitive aspects. It has described relevant findings and theories about how people carry out their everyday activities and how to learn from these when designing interactive products. It has provided illustrations of what happens when you design systems with the user in mind and what happens when you don't. It has also presented a number of conceptual frameworks that allow ideas about cognition to be generalized across different situations.

Key points
- Cognition comprises many processes, including thinking, attention, learning, memory, perception, decision making, planning, reading, speaking, and listening.
- The way an interface is designed can greatly affect how well people can perceive, attend, learn, and remember how to carry out their tasks.
- The main benefits of conceptual frameworks and cognitive theories are that they can explain user interaction, inform design, and predict user performance.

Further Reading

CLARK, A. (2003) *Natural Born Cyborgs: Minds, technologies, and the future of human intelligence.* Oxford University Press. This book eloquently outlines the extended mind theory, explaining how human nature is integrally shaped by technology and culture. Andy Clark explores ways, and provides many examples, of how we have adapted our lives to make use of technology as well as ways in which technologies can be designed to adapt to us. A particular thesis that runs through the book is as we move into an era of ubiquitous computing, the line between users and their tools becomes less clear by the day. What this means for interaction design has deep ramifications.

ERICKSON, T. D. and MCDONALD, D. W. (2008) *HCI Remixed: Reflections on works that have influenced the HCI community.* MIT Press. This collection of essays from over 50 leading HCI researchers describes in accessible prose papers, books, and software that influenced their approach to HCI and shaped its history. They include some of the classic papers on cognitive theories, including the psychology of HCI and the power of external representations.

GIGERENZER, G. (2008) *Gut Feelings.* Penguin. This provocative paperback is written by a psychologist and behavioral expert in decision making. When confronted with choice in a variety of contexts, he explains how often 'less is more.' He explains why this is so in terms of how people rely on fast and frugal heuristics when making decisions, which are often unconscious rather than rational. These revelations have huge implications for interaction design that are only just beginning to be explored.

JACKO, J. (ed.) (2012) *The Human–Computer Interaction Handbook: Fundamentals, evolving technologies and emerging applications* (3rd edn). CRC Press. Part 1 is about human aspects of HCI and includes in-depth chapters on information processing, mental models, decision making, and perceptual motor interaction.

KAHNEMAN, D. (2011) *Thinking, fast and slow.* Penguin. This bestseller presents an overview of how the mind works, drawing on aspects of cognitive and social psychology. The focus is on how we make judgments and choices. It proposes we use two ways of thinking: one that is quick and based on intuition and one that is slow and more deliberate and effortful. The book explores the many facets of life and how and when we use each.

Chapter 4

SOCIAL INTERACTION

Objectives

The main aims of this chapter are to:

- Explain what is meant by social interaction.
- Describe the social mechanisms that are used by people when communicating and collaborating.
- Discuss how social media have changed the ways in which we keep in touch, make contact, and manage our social and working lives.
- Explain what is meant by telepresence.
- Give an overview of shareable technologies and some of the studies showing how they can facilitate collaboration and group participation.

4.1 Introduction

Imagine not having access to your smartphone or the Internet for a week. How would you cope? Would you get bored, start twitching, or even go stir crazy? Would you feel isolated and be constantly wondering what is happening in your online social network? Many people now cannot go for very long without checking for messages, the latest tweets, Facebook updates, emails, etc. – even when on vacation. For many, checking their phone is the first thing they do when waking up. It has become a daily routine and an integral part of their social lives. This is not surprising given that humans are inherently social: they live together, work together, learn together, play together, interact and talk with each other, and socialize.

There are many kinds of sociality and many ways of studying it. In this chapter our focus is on how people communicate and collaborate in their social, work, and everyday lives. We examine how the emergence of a diversity of communication technologies has changed the way people live – the way they keep in touch, make friends, and coordinate their social and work networks. We look at the conversation mechanisms that have conventionally been used in face-to-face interactions and examine how these have changed for the various kinds of computer-based conversations that take place at a distance. We describe the idea of telepresence, where novel technologies have been designed to allow a person to feel as if they are present or to give the appearance of being present at another location. We also outline some technologies that have been developed to enable new forms of interaction, focusing on how shareable technologies can facilitate and support collocated collaboration.

4.2 Being Social

A fundamental aspect of everyday life is being social – interacting with each other. We continuously update each other about news, changes, and developments on a given project, activity, person, or event. For example, friends and families keep each other posted on what's happening at work, at school, at the pub, at the club, next door, in soap operas, and in the news. Similarly, people who work together keep each other informed about their social lives and everyday happenings, as well as what is happening at work, for instance when a project is about to be completed, plans for a new project, problems with meeting deadlines, rumors about closures, and so on.

While face-to-face conversations remain central to many of our social interactions, the use of social media has dramatically increased. Many of us now routinely spend several hours a day communicating online – texting, emailing, tweeting, Facebooking, Skyping, using Yammer, instant messaging, and so on. The almost universal uptake of social media in mainstream life has resulted in many people now being connected in multiple ways over time and space – in ways unimaginable 25 or even 10 years ago. For example, the average number of friends adults have on Facebook was 338 in 2014 (Pew Research), while many people have over 500 or more work connections in LinkedIn – many more than those made through face-to-face networking. The way we make contact, how we stay in touch, who we connect to, and how we maintain our social networks and family ties have irrevocably changed.

A key question this raises is how do we cope with the dramatic increase in networking in our daily lives? Are the ways we live and interact with one another changing? Have the conventions, norms, and rules established in face-to-face interactions to maintain social order been adopted in social media interactions? Or have new norms emerged? In particular, are the established conversational rules and etiquette – whose function it is to let people know how they should behave in social groups – also applicable to online social behavior? Or, have new conversational mechanisms evolved for the various kinds of social media? For example, do people greet each other in the same way, depending on whether they are chatting online, Skyping, or at a party? Do people take turns when online chatting in the way they do when talking with each other face-to-face? How do people choose which technology or app to use from the diversity available today for their various work and social activities; for example,

SnapChat, WhatsApp, text message, Skype, or phone call? In order to answer these questions we next describe the core social mechanisms that exist in face-to-face interactions, followed by a discussion of the extent to which they remain or have been replaced with other mechanisms in online interactions.

4.3 Face-to-Face Conversations

Talking is something that is effortless and comes naturally to most people. And yet holding a conversation is a highly skilled collaborative achievement, having many of the qualities of a musical ensemble. Below we examine what makes up a conversation. We begin by examining what happens at the beginning:

A: Hi there.

B: Hi!

C: Hi.

A: All right?

C: Good. How's it going?

A: Fine, how are you?

C: Good.

B: OK. How's life treating you?

Such mutual greetings are typical. A dialog may then ensue in which the participants take turns asking questions, giving replies, and making statements. Then when one or more of the participants wants to draw the conversation to a close, they do so by using either implicit or explicit cues. An example of an implicit cue is when a participant looks at his watch, signaling indirectly to the other participants that he wants the conversation to draw to a close. The other participants may choose to acknowledge this cue or carry on and ignore it. Either way, the first participant may then offer an explicit signal, by saying, 'Well, I must be off now. Got work to do' or, 'Oh dear, look at the time. Must dash. Have to meet someone.' Following the acknowledgment by the other participants of such implicit and explicit signals, the conversation draws to a close, with a farewell ritual. The different participants take turns saying, 'Bye,' 'Bye then,' 'See you,' repeating themselves several times, until they finally separate.

ACTIVITY 4.1

How do you start and end a conversation when (i) talking on a phone and (ii) chatting online?

Comment
The person answering the call will initiate the conversation by saying 'hello' or, more formally, the name of their company/department (and sometimes the phone number being called). Most

phones (landline and smart) have the facility to display the name of the caller so the receiver can be more personal when answering, e.g. 'Hello John. How are you doing?' Phone conversations usually start with a mutual greeting and end with a mutual farewell. In contrast, conversations that take place via online chatting have evolved new conventions. The use of opening and ending greetings when joining and leaving is rare; instead most people simply start their message with what they want to talk about, and then stop when they have got an answer, as if in the middle of a conversation. ▪

These conversational mechanisms enable people to coordinate their talk with one another, allowing them to know how to start and stop. Throughout a conversation further turn-taking rules are followed, enabling people to know when to listen, when it is their cue to speak, and when it is time for them to stop again to allow the others to speak. Sacks *et al* (1978) – who are famous for their work on conversation analysis – describe these in terms of three basic rules:

- Rule 1: the current speaker chooses the next speaker by asking a question, inviting an opinion, or making a request.
- Rule 2: another person decides to start speaking.
- Rule 3: the current speaker continues talking.

The rules are assumed to be applied in the above order, so that whenever there is an opportunity for a change of speaker to occur, e.g. someone comes to the end of a sentence, rule 1 is applied. If the listener to whom the question or request is addressed does not accept the offer to take the floor, the second rule is applied, and someone else taking part in the conversation may take up the opportunity and offer a view on the matter. If this does not happen then the third rule is applied and the current speaker continues talking. The rules are cycled through recursively until someone speaks again.

To facilitate rule following, people use various ways of indicating how long they are going to talk and on what topic. For example, a speaker might say right at the beginning of his turn in the conversation that he has three things to say. A speaker may also explicitly request a change in speaker by saying to the listeners, 'OK, that's all I want to say on that matter. So, what do you think?' More subtle cues to let others know that their turn in the conversation is coming to an end include the lowering or raising of the voice to indicate the end of a question or the use of phrases like 'You know what I mean?' or, simply, 'OK?' Back channeling (uhhuh, mmm), body orientation (e.g. moving away from or closer to someone), gaze (staring straight at someone or glancing away), and gesture (e.g. raising of arms), are also used in different combinations when talking, to signal to others when someone wants to hand over or take up a turn in the conversation.

Another way in which conversations are coordinated and given coherence is through the use of adjacency pairs (Schegloff and Sacks, 1973). Utterances are assumed to come in pairs in which the first part sets up an expectation of what is to come next and directs the way in which what does come next is heard. For example, A may ask a question to which B responds appropriately:

A: So shall we meet at 8:00?

B: Um, can we make it a bit later, say 8:30?

Sometimes adjacency pairs get embedded in each other, so it may take some time for a person to get a reply to their initial request or statement:

A: So shall we meet at 8:00?

B: Wow, look at him.

A: Yes, what a funny hairdo!

B: Um, can we make it a bit later, say 8:30?

For the most part people are not aware of following conversational mechanisms, and would be hard pressed to articulate how they can carry on a conversation. Furthermore, people don't necessarily abide by the rules all the time. They may interrupt each other or talk over each other, even when the current speaker has clearly indicated a desire to hold the floor for the next two minutes to finish an argument. Alternatively, a listener may not take up a cue from a speaker to answer a question or take over the conversation, but instead continue to say nothing even though the speaker may be making it glaringly obvious it is the listener's turn to say something. Often times a teacher will try to hand over the conversation to a student in a seminar, by staring at her and asking a specific question, only to see the student look at the floor and say nothing. The outcome is an embarrassing silence, followed by either the teacher or another student picking up the conversation again.

Other kinds of breakdowns in conversation arise when someone says something that is ambiguous and the interlocutor misinterprets it to mean something else. In such situations the participants will collaborate to overcome the misunderstanding by using repair mechanisms. Consider the following snippet of conversation between two people:

A: Can you tell me the way to get to the Multiplex Ranger cinema?

B: Yes, you go down here for two blocks and then take a right [pointing to the right], go on till you get to the lights and then it's on the left.

A: Oh, so I go along here for a couple of blocks and then take a right and the cinema is at the lights [pointing ahead of him]?

B: No, you go on *this* street for a couple of blocks [gesturing more vigorously than before to the street to the right of him while emphasizing the word this].

A: Ahhhh! I thought you meant *that* one: so it's *this* one [pointing in the same direction as the other person].

B: Uh-hum, yes that's right: *this* one.

Detecting breakdowns in conversation requires the speaker and listener to be attending to what the other says (or does not say). Once they have understood the nature of the failure, they can then go about repairing it. As shown in the above example, when the listener misunderstands what has been communicated, the speaker repeats what she said earlier, using a stronger voice intonation and more exaggerated gestures. This allows the speaker to repair the mistake and be more explicit to the listener, allowing her to understand and follow better what they are saying. Listeners may also signal when they don't understand something or want further clarification by using various tokens, like 'Huh?' or 'What?' (Schegloff, 1981), together with giving a puzzled look (usually frowning). This is especially the case when the speaker says something that is vague. For example, he might say 'I want it' to his partner, without saying what *it* he wants. The partner may reply using a token or, alternatively, explicitly ask, 'What do you mean by *it*?' Non-verbal communication also plays an important role in augmenting face-to-face conversation, involving the use of facial expressions, back channeling (aha and umm), voice intonation, gesturing, and other kinds of body language.

Taking turns also provides opportunities for the listener to initiate repair or request clarification, or for the speaker to detect that there is a problem and initiate repair. The listener will usually wait for the next turn in the conversation before interrupting the speaker, to give the speaker the chance to clarify what is being said by completing the utterance (Suchman, 1987).

ACTIVITY 4.2

How do people repair breakdowns in conversations when using a phone or email?

Comment
In these settings people usually cannot see each other and so have to rely on other means of repairing their conversations. Furthermore, there are more opportunities for breakdowns to occur and fewer mechanisms available for repair. When a breakdown occurs over the phone, people will often shout louder, repeating what they said several times, and use stronger intonation. When a breakdown occurs via email, people may literally spell out what they meant, making things much more explicit in a subsequent email, using capitals, emoticons, exclamations, bold, highlighting, and so on. If the message is beyond repair, they may resort to another mode of communication that allows greater flexibility of expression, either telephoning or speaking to the recipient face-to-face. ■

BOX 4.1
SnapChat – ephemeral messaging

According to Forbes, over 50 million people were using SnapChat worldwide in 2014, of which most were teenagers. One of the reasons for its mass appeal is it is quick, fun, and easy to use. Another is that it is ephemeral. Teenagers like using the messaging app as it doesn't leave a digital trace, allowing them to express themselves in personal ways without fear it will get into the hands of their prying parents or future employers. Users simply take a photo or video, annotate it, and then decide how long the intended recipient has to look at it by selecting from a dial of 1–10 seconds. The recipient then has up to the allocated time set to view it before it disappears. Whether a sender chooses to assign a mere 2 or 3 seconds or a high 8 or 9 seconds to their SnapChat adds a bit of intrigue – the recipient can try to fathom out why so little or so much value was placed on that particular image. ■

(Continued)

Figure 4.1 A screenshot of my SnapChat (deleted after 8 seconds when sent to the recipient)

4.4 Remote Conversations

The telephone was invented back in the nineteenth century by Alexander Graham Bell, enabling two people to talk to one another at a distance. A number of other technologies have since been developed that support synchronous remote conversations, including videophones (see Figure 4.2) videochat, and VoIP (Voice over Internet Protocol). In the late 1980s and 1990s, new generations of media spaces were experimented with. The aim was to see whether it was possible for people, distributed over space and time, to communicate and interact with one another as if they were actually physically present. Audio, video, and computer systems were combined to extend the world of desks, chairs, walls, and ceilings (Harrison, 2009).

An early example was Xerox's Media Space that was designed to support the informal types of communication that occur in hallways and at water coolers, providing opportunities

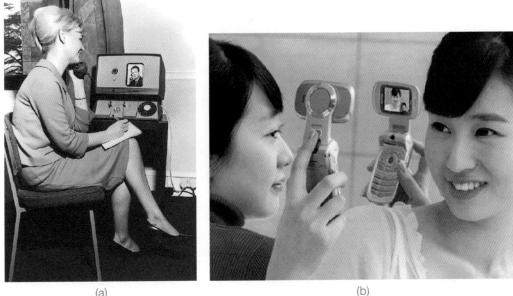

Figure 4.2 (a) One of British Telecom's early videophones and (b) an early mobile visualphone developed in Japan

Source: (a) ©British Telecommunications Plc. Reproduced with permission (b) Reproduced by permission of Kyocera Corporation.

for people in the company, located in different offices, to engage in social chat while at their desks (Mackay, 1999). Other media spaces include Cruiser, Hydra (see Figure 4.3), and VideoWindow (see Figure 4.4). Cruiser consisted of audio and video equipment on a person's desktop that allowed those connected to 'glance' at who was in their office and whether they wanted to talk or have coffee (Fish, 1989). The idea was to allow people to interact with each other via the video technology in a similar way to how they do when walking down a physical hallway. Hydra used spatialized audio-video to enhance communication with a group of colleagues – separate units were placed at different places on someone's desk, one assigned to each person connected to the system (Sellen *et al*, 1992). VideoWindow was built at Bellcore in 1989 as a shared space that allowed people in different locations to carry on a conversation as they would do if drinking coffee together in the same room. Two lounge areas that were 50 miles apart were connected by a 3 foot by 5 foot picture-window onto which video images of each location were projected. The large size enabled viewers to see a room of people roughly the same size as themselves. A study of its use showed that many of the conversations that took place between the remote conversants were indeed indistinguishable from similar face-to-face interactions – with the exception that they spoke a bit louder and constantly talked about the video system (Kraut *et al*, 1990).

Since this early research, there are now many technologies and messaging apps that are used worldwide for synchronous and asynchronous communication, including videoconferencing, texting, and chat groups. However, despite the increasing ubiquity and popularity of online conversations (via phone, texting, chatting, and/or video-conferencing), they have yet

Figure 4.3 The Hydra system: Each hydra unit consists of a camera, monitor, and speaker and is meant to act as a surrogate for a person in a different space. The design is intended to preserve the personal space that people have in face-to-face meetings, simulating where they would sit in the physical space if they were physically present

Source: A. Sellen, W. Buxton and J. Arnott: Using Spayial Cues to Improve Videoconferencing. ©1992 Association for Computing Machinery, Inc. Reprinted by permission.

to match the richness afforded by face-to-face conversations. To compensate for not being there, people have adapted the way they hold conversations to fit in with the constraints of the respective technologies. For example, they tend to shout more when misunderstood over the phone. They also tend to speak more loudly when talking on the phone, since they can't monitor how well the person can hear them at the other end of the connection. Likewise, people tend to project themselves more when taking part in a videoconference. They also

Figure 4.4 Diagram of VideoWindow system in use

Source: Kraut *et al.* (1990) Informal communications in organizations: Form, function and technology. In S. Oskamp and S. Krug (eds) *Don't Make Me Think.* New Riders/Peachpit.

take longer conversational turns and interrupt each other less (O'Connaill *et al*, 1993), while turn-taking appears to be much more explicit and greetings and farewells more ritualized.

Conversations via social media apps, including Twitter, WhatsApp, and Facebook, have also evolved their own particular style of interaction. Posting a status update and tweeting encourage a one-to-many broadcasting conversation, where people update their multiple friends and followers, respectively, while keeping abreast of what they are doing. They can also be one-sided, where some people don't post much about themselves, but are keen observers, avidly following and looking at their friends' latest whereabouts, activities, photos posted, and so on. Online chatting and instant messaging have also evolved their own forms of expressions that compensate for the constraints of the medium, such as the frequent use of shorthand, abbreviations, emoticons (humorous facial expression such as a smiley ;-) that emerged through people using ASCII symbols tipped sideways in their email), and emojis (invented by Shigetaka Kurita in 1995 as a set of small pictorial icons, now widely used on smartphone apps that are often country-specific).

Given the numerous ways of communicating now, how do people decide which one to use and when? In general, people move effortlessly between them, texting when wanting to send only a short message, emailing when wanting to send a longer message or other content, and chatting when online with a group of friends. However, now that many people have a number of messaging apps on their smartphone, it can sometimes be confusing to remember which one they are in or which group they are talking with. A mistake can easily be made, where someone fires off a message or sends a picture to the wrong person or group, not looking closely at who it is addressed to as they think they are still in conversation with someone else.

When planning and coordinating social activities, groups often switch from one mode to another. Most people send texts in preference to calling someone up, but may switch to phone calling or mobile group messaging (such as WhatsApp, GroupMe) at different stages of the planning (Schuler *et al,* 2014). However, there can be a cost as conversations about what to do, where to meet, and who to invite multiply across people. Some people might get left off or others might not reply, and much time can be spent to-ing and fro-ing across the different apps and threads. Conversational overload can develop where the number of people involved in coordinating, the time over which it happens, and the unknowns that are not resolved all get out of hand. This is compounded by the fact that often people don't want to commit until close to the time of the event – in case an invitation to do something from another friend appears that is more interesting to them. Teenagers, especially, often leave it until the last minute to micro-coordinate their arrangements with their friends before deciding on what to do. They will wait and see if a better offers comes their way rather than making a decision for themselves a week in advance, say, to see a movie with a friend and sticking to it. This can make it very frustrating for those who initiate the planning and are waiting to book tickets before they sell out.

The speed of knowledge dissemination via digital volunteers during unexpected events and disasters can also have an immediate impact. For example, while writing this chapter there was a massive thunderstorm overhead which was very dramatic. I checked out the Twitter hashtag #hove (the place I was at in the UK) and found hundreds of people had uploaded photos of the hailstones (that made it look like the road was covered in snow in the middle of summer!), the flooding, and minute-by-minute updates of how public transport and traffic were being affected. It was easy to get a sense of the scale of the storm before it was picked up by the official media channels – which then used some of the photos and quotes from Twitter in their coverage (see Figure 4.5). Likewise, when word came of a huge explosion in

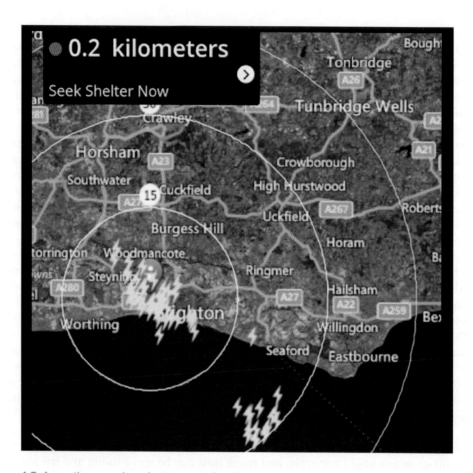

Figure 4.5 A weather warning photo tweeted and retweeted about a severe storm in Hove, UK

San Bruno, California, in 2010, the chief of the Federal Emergency Management Agency in the US logged on to Twitter and searched for the word 'explosion'. Based on the tweets coming from that area, he was able to discern that the gas explosion and ensuing fire was a localized event that would not spread to other communities. He noted how he got better situational awareness and more quickly from reading Twitter than hearing about it from official sources.

There is much potential for harnessing the power and immediacy of Twitter in this way, providing first responders and those living in the affected areas with up-to-the-minute information about how a wildfire, storm, or gas plume is spreading. However, the reliability of the tweeted information can sometimes be a problem. For example, some people end up obsessively checking and posting, and sometimes without realizing can start or fuel rumors by adding news that is old or incorrect. Regulars can go into a feeding frenzy, constantly adding new tweets about an event, as witnessed when an impending flood was announced (Starbird et al, 2010). While such citizen-led dissemination and retweeting of information from disparate sources is well intentioned, it can also flood the Twitter streams, making it difficult to know what is old, actual, or hearsay.

ACTIVITY 4.3

How do you represent yourself online? What image and names do you use?

Comment

Many people choose photos of themselves in a pose that they or others think best conveys their character for their online profiles – be it Skype, Facebook, or other social media site. Others choose to upload pictures of their pets, children, or a favorite cartoon character, while some prefer to remain enigmatic, appearing in shadow, revealing only part of their face or simply using the default anonymous person icon. Likewise, the names people choose for their online profiles, such as their avatars and Twitter handles, are often based on their real name, company name, nickname, or some jokey reference, such as one of their favorite characters in Star Trek or a movie/TV series. Some people use the same name across different social media while other have separate identities. ■

ACTIVITY 4.4

What would you expect the most retweeted selfie to be? Why do we send so many selfies?

Comment

In 2014, the most retweeted selfie was one taken by Ellen DeGeneres at the Oscar Academy Awards of her in front of a star-studded, smiling group of actors and friends. It was retweeted over 2 million times (over three quarters of a million in the first half hour of being tweeted) – far exceeding the one taken by Barack Obama at Nelson Mandela's funeral the previous year. There is something magical about the moment this particular selfie captures. Check it out and see for yourself. One of the main reasons why sending selfies has become so popular is that it is an instant and fun means of keeping in touch with others that speaks volumes. By pointing our phone camera at ourselves – wherever we are and whoever we are with – lets others know that we are thinking about them and shows what we are doing and feeling at that time. While it might appear vain, a picture in this context can indeed paint a 1000 words. ■

Social media has led to new ways of communicating and keeping in touch remotely. Another area of research where computer tools and services have been developed to support people who cannot be physically present during a meeting or social gathering is telepresence.

4.5 Telepresence

It is without question that face-to-face conversations with work colleagues, relations, and friends will continue to be preferable for many interactions, such as family occasions, work meetings, and simply going out partying. However, there will always be times when it is not possible for people to be physically together for such events, much as they would like to be, and this concern has been the driving force behind much of the research into the design of telepresence technologies. These have been designed to allow a person to feel as if they were present or to give the appearance that they were present in the other location by projecting their body movements, actions, voice, and facial expressions to the other location or person.

One line of research has been to superimpose images of the other person on a workspace. For example, ClearBoard was designed to enable facial expressions of participants to be made visible to others by using a transparent board that showed their face to the others (Ishii *et al*, 1993). Remote gesturing can also help people perform tasks more easily. The presence of a remote instructor's hands as shadows overlaying the physical hands of a student in a workspace have been found to be effective at guiding them in assembling physical parts of a system (Kirk *et al*, 2007). Another telepresence system, HyperMirror, synthesized and projected mirror reflections of people in different places onto a single screen, so that they appeared side by side in the same virtual space (Morikawa and Maesako, 1998). Observations of people using the system showed how quickly they adapted to perceiving themselves and others in this way. For example, participants quickly became sensitized to the importance of virtual personal space, moving out of the way if they perceived they were overlapping someone else on the screen (see Figure 4.6).

(a)   (b)

(c)

Figure 4.6 Hypermirror in action, showing perception of virtual personal space. (a) A woman is in one room (indicated by the arrow on the screen), (b) while a man and another woman are in the other room chatting to each other. They move apart when they notice they are 'overlapping' her and (c) virtual personal space is established

Source: Reproduced with permission http://staff.aist.go.jp/morikawa.osamu/soft/int01.htm.

(a)   (b)

(c)   (d)

Figure 4.7 BiReality: (a) a surrogate robot at a meeting 'sitting' between two physically present people; (b) the remote user's view of the meeting while controlling the surrogate; (c) an early version of the surrogate on the move; and (d) a second-generation surrogate designed to preserve the height and sitting/standing posture of the user (Jouppi, 2002). See also www.hpl.hp.com/personal/ Norman_Jouppi/BiReality240x180v1.3.mov

Source: N. P. Jouppie (2002) "First steps towards mutually-immersive mobile telepresence". In: *Proceedings of the 2002 ACM Conference on Computer Supported Cooperative Work, CSCW '02*. pp. 354–363 ©2002 Association for Computing Machinery, Inc. Reprinted by permission.

One of the most innovative prototypes was BiReality (see Figure 4.7), which used a tele-operated mobile robotic surrogate to visit remote locations as a substitute for physical travel (Jouppi *et al*, 2004). Much attention was paid to its design. An underlying principle was to make it seem like the person was actually there by making the surrogate look and sound like the remote person. Specifically, the robot had a life-size head shaped as a cube, with each side displaying a view of the remote person's face. The head sat on a human-shaped body base that

Figure 4.8 A telepresence room
Source: Cisco Systems, Inc with permission.

was colored blue to match the color of business clothing. Multichannel bidirectional audio was also used to project the remote person's voice. To move in the physical space, the remote person would steer their surrogate using a console from inside their home linked into the remote meeting room. The real people in the meeting room would leave a gap at the table for the surrogate to sit with them.

To what extent do you think this kind of telepresence is compelling and could really enhance the conversation? How does it compare with high-quality videoconferencing systems, already now commercially available, called telepresence rooms (see Figure 4.8)? In these settings, remote people appear life-like, which is made possible by using multiple high-definition cameras with eye-tracking features and directional microphones. Unfortunately, there have not yet been any user studies published to evaluate BiReality so it is difficult to tell if there is any significant difference in quality of conversation or perceived presence – from the point of view of both the surrogate and those physically at a meeting.

> **Video** of BiReality at
> **http://www.hpl.hp.com/research/mmsl/demonstrations/etravel.html**

More recently, at the ACM CHI 2014 conference, one of the registered attendees was present virtually, via a tablet that was placed on a stick and wheels to make it mobile and have the height of a person (see Figure 4.9). Developed by Chelsea Barabas and Nathan Mathias, The People's Bot allows people to attend and report on events where they are not physically present. Although a little wobbly on its wheels when moving through the conference auditorium, the image and height of the virtual attendee has more presence than a videoconference app appearing on a stationary screen on a phone or desktop. However, where it did not work well was when everyone left during the coffee break to socialize. It was left stranded owing to some technical difficulties.

Figure 4.9 The People's Bot attending CHI 2014

Audio about the People's Bot at **http://youtu.be/Lwr-81whEvk**

BOX 4.2

Beyond Facebook: The ultimate social experience?

Instead of looking down at a mobile 2D screen all the time when using Facebook, SnapChat, Twitter, and so on, the future of social networking could soon become 3D, where we interact with our friends in the here and now, wearing 3D goggles. Rather than perpetually flicking through text and images on these apps, we will take part in a form of socializing that overlays the virtual and physical environments so as to make them appear seamless, where digital

(Continued)

avatars and objects populate a world of real people and objects (see Figure 4.10). And if we suspend our disbelief, we will find it difficult to know what is actual and what is digital.

To enable a truly immersive social telepresence experience to happen, Will Steptoe and colleagues (Steptoe *et al*, 2014) have been experimenting with overlaying webcams on the Oculus Rift headset to fuse virtual and video spaces into one. In doing so, they hope to blur the lines between what is real and what is virtual. But could an immersive Facebook truly enhance our experience of how we interact and communicate with people remotely? How many of us would put on a pair of goggles, 10 or more times a day (the average number of times someone looks at Facebook on their phone each day is 14), in order to teleport to a friend's party, go for a walk in the park, or just hang out, without ever leaving our living room? While there have been numerous attempts over the last 30 years to create such virtual social spaces, notably Second Life, the Oculus Rift may just have that specialness to make it happen – provided it can overcome the perennial problems of lag and motion sickness. ■

FIGURE 4.10 Oculus Rift: The overlaying of virtual and physical objects to make them appear seamless to the user

Source: Courtesy of Will Steptoe.

Video about adaption of Oculus Rift describing the merging of immersive video and augmented reality at
http://willsteptoe.com/post/66968953089/ar-rift-part-1

BOX 4.3

Communicating via virtual hugging

Another approach to increasing the sense of presence and togetherness for people who are at a distance is the development of wearable devices that send hugs between them. An early example was CuteCircuit's Hug Shirt shown in Figure 4.11. Embedded in the shirt are sensors that detect the strength of the wearer's skin warmth and heart rate and actuators that recreate the sensation of a hug through being buzzed on various parts of the body. More recently, Huggy Pajama (2009) was designed as a prototype system to promote physical interaction between a parent and child who are apart (see Figure 4.12). When the parent wants to send

Figure 4.11 CuteCircuit's Hug Shirt

Source: ©2010 CuteCircuit. Reproduced with permission.

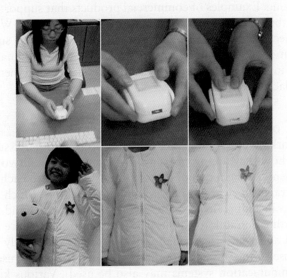

Figure 4.12 Huggy Pajama with mother squeezing the remote device and child being correspondingly squeezed

Source: Huggy Pajama reproduced from http://youtu.be/hQ6usrx-GPM.

(Continued)

a hug to their child, they interact with a sensing device that they hold. The child feels the hug through wearing a customized haptic jacket that uses air pressure actuation: as the parent presses the lower part of the body of the device, the lower part of the child is squeezed by the haptic pajama jacket.

To what extent do you think these kinds of novel wearable communication devices actually emulate a real hug? Would you rather receive a text on your cell phone from your partner or parent saying 'missing you' or a buzz or a squeeze on your stomach? ■

Video of Huggy Pajama at **http://youtu.be/hQ6usrx-GPM**

4.6   Co-presence

Alongside telepresence there has been much interest in co-presence. Numerous shareable interfaces have been developed to enable more than one person to use them at the same time. The motivation is to enable co-located groups to collaborate more effectively when working, learning, and socializing. Examples of commercial products that support this kind of parallel interaction are Smartboards and Surfaces, which use multitouch, and Wii and Kinect, which use gesture and object recognition. To understand how these can support and enhance co-located collaboration and gaming, we first consider the coordinating and awareness mechanisms already in use by people in face-to-face interaction and then see how these have been adapted or replaced.

4.6.1   Physical Coordination

When people are working closely together they talk to each other, issuing commands and letting others know how they are progressing. For example, when two or more people are collaborating, as when moving a piano, they shout instructions to each other, like 'Down a bit, left a bit, now straight forward,' to coordinate their actions. Much non-verbal communication is also used – including nods, shakes, winks, glances, and hand-raising – in combination with such coordination talk to emphasize and sometimes replace it.

For time-critical and routinized collaborative activities, especially where it is difficult to hear others because of the physical conditions, people frequently use gestures (although radio-controlled communication systems may also be used). Various kinds of hand signals have evolved, with their own set of standardized syntax and semantics. For example, the arm and baton movements of a conductor coordinate the different players in an orchestra, while the arm and baton movements of a ground marshal at an airport signal to a pilot how to bring the plane into its allocated gate. Universal gestures, such as beckoning, waving and halting hand movement, are also used by people in their everyday settings.

The use of physical objects, such as wands and batons, can also facilitate coordination. Group members can use them as external thinking props to explain a principle, an idea, or a plan to the others (Brereton and McGarry, 2000). In particular, the act of waving or holding up a physical object in front of others is very effective at commanding attention. The persistence and ability to manipulate physical artifacts may also result in more options being explored in a group setting (Fernaeus and Tholander, 2006). They can help collaborators gain a better overview of the group activity and increase awareness of others' activities.

4.6.2   Awareness

Awareness involves knowing who is around, what is happening, and who is talking with whom (Dourish and Bly, 1992). For example, when we are at a party, we move around the physical space, observing what is going on and who is talking to whom, eavesdropping on others' conversations, and passing on gossip to others. A specific kind of awareness is peripheral awareness. This refers to a person's ability to maintain and constantly update a sense of what is going on in the physical and social context, through keeping an eye on what is happening in the periphery of their vision. This might include noting whether people are in a good or bad mood by the way they are talking, how fast the drink and food is being consumed, who has entered or left the room, how long someone has been absent, and whether the lonely guy in the corner is finally talking to someone – all while we are having a conversation with someone else. The combination of direct observations and peripheral monitoring keeps people informed and updated on what is happening in the world.

Another form that has been studied is situational awareness. This refers to being aware of what is happening around you in order to understand how information, events, and your own actions will affect ongoing and future events. Having good situational awareness is critical in technology-rich work domains, such as air traffic control or an operating theater, where it is necessary to keep abreast of complex and continuously changing information. Within CSCW workspace, awareness has been described as "the up-to-the-moment understanding of another person's interaction with the shared workspace" (Gutwin and Greenberg, 2002). This concept was specifically developed to inform the design of technologies that can support the opportunistic ways co-located groups move between working by themselves and then closely together on a shared activity, such as programming or project work.

People who work closely together also develop various strategies for coordinating their work, based on an up-to-date awareness of what the others are doing. This is especially so for interdependent tasks, where the outcome of one person's activity is needed for others to be able to carry out their tasks. For example, when putting on a show, the performers will constantly monitor what each other is doing in order to coordinate their performance efficiently. The metaphorical expression *close-knit teams* exemplifies this way of collaborating. People become highly skilled in reading and tracking what others are doing and the information they are attending to. A classic study of this phenomenon is of two controllers working together in a control room in the London Underground subway system (Heath and Luff, 1992). An overriding observation was that the actions of one controller were tied very closely to what the other was doing. One of the controllers (controller A) was responsible for the movement of trains on the line while the other (controller B) was responsible for providing information to passengers about the current service. In many instances, it was found that controller B overheard what controller A was saying and doing, and acted accordingly – even though controller A had not said anything explicitly to him. For example, on overhearing controller A discussing a problem with a train driver over the in-cab intercom system, controller B inferred from the conversation that there was going to be a disruption to the service and so started announcing this to the passengers on the platform before controller A had even finished talking with the train driver. At other times, the two controllers keep a lookout for each other, monitoring the environment for actions and events that they might not have noticed but which may be important for them to know about so that they can act appropriately.

ACTIVITY 4.5

What do you think happens when one person in a close-knit team does not see or hear something, or misunderstands what has been said, while the others in the group assume that person has seen, heard, or understood what has been said?

Comment
In such circumstances, the person is likely to carry on as normal. In some cases this will result in inappropriate behavior. Repair mechanisms will then need to be set in motion. The knowledgeable participants may notice that the other person has not acted in the manner expected. They may then use one of a number of subtle repair mechanisms, say coughing or glancing at something that needs attending to. If this doesn't work, they may then resort to explicitly stating aloud what had previously been signaled implicitly. Conversely, the unaware participant may wonder why the event hasn't happened and, likewise, look over at the other people, cough to get their attention, or explicitly ask them a question. The kind of repair mechanism employed at a given moment will depend on a number of factors, including the relationship among the participants, e.g. whether one is more senior than the others – this determines who can ask what, the perceived fault or responsibility for the breakdown, and the severity of the outcome of not acting there and then on the new information. ■

4.6.3   Shareable Interfaces

How might shareable technologies be designed to exploit existing forms of coordination and awareness mechanisms? Several studies have been carried out investigating whether different arrangements of shared technologies can help co-located people work together better (e.g. Müller-Tomfelde, 2010). An assumption is that shareable interfaces provide more opportunities for flexible kinds of collaboration compared with single-user PCs, through enabling co-located users to simultaneously interact with digital content. Fingertip actions are highly visible and hence observable by others, increasing opportunities for building situational and peripheral awareness. The sharable surfaces are also considered to be more natural than other technologies, enticing people to touch them without feeling intimidated or embarrassed by the consequences of their actions. For example, small groups found it more comfortable working together around a tabletop compared with sitting in front of a PC or standing in a line in front of a vertical display (Rogers and Lindley, 2004).

BOX 4.4

Collaborative expression through the Reactable Experience

The Reactable Experience (2010) was designed for groups of children, families, or adults to create music together in public spaces and institutions, such as museums and science centers. Based on the original Reactable (Jordà *et al*, 2005), colorful tangible pucks are moved and rotated on the surface of a translucent tabletop, which results in various digital annotations appearing and connecting them. A synthesizer creates immediate sounds in response to the various tabletop interactions. One of the main ideas behind the design was to enable groups to create music together on the fly. This is achieved through making visible everyone's interactions at the tabletop surface and by providing real-time feedback about what is currently happening (see Figure 4.13). ■

Figure 4.13 Two girls interacting with the Reactable Experience
Source: Courtesy of Yamaguchi Center for Arts and Media [YCAM]. Photo by Ryuichi Maruo [YCAM].

Video of Reactable Experience at **http://youtu.be/IA29AE6O69k**
Website at
http://reactable.com/products/experience/experience-for-museums/

One area of research has been to investigate whether group collaboration can result in more equitable interaction around a tabletop surface. This will depend on how obvious it is to the group members what to do at the interface and how to take turns to progress with the task. Of primary importance is whether the interface invites people to select, add, manipulate, or remove digital content from the displays and devices. A study by Rogers *et al* (2009) showed that a tabletop that allowed group members to add digital content by using physical tokens, using an RFID (radio-frequency identification) reader, resulted in more equitable participation than if only digital input was allowed via icons and menus at the tabletop. This suggests that it was easier for people who are normally shy in groups to make a contribution to the task. Moreover, people who spoke the least were found to make the biggest contribution to the design task at the tabletop – in terms of selecting, adding, moving, and removing options. This reveals how changing the way people can interact with a shareable surface can have an impact on group participation. It shows that it is possible for more reticent members to make a contribution without feeling under pressure to have to speak more.

Other studies have also shown that under-participators tend not to increase their level of verbal contribution in small group meetings when provided with various kinds of support, such as awareness visualizations displaying who is contributing over time (Norton *et al*, 2004). Real-time feedback presented via ambient displays has also been experimented with to provide a new form of awareness for co-located groups. LEDs glowing in tabletops and abstract visualizations on handheld and wall displays have been designed to represent how different group members are performing, such as turn-taking. The assumption is that this kind of real-time feedback can promote self and group regulation and in so doing modify group members' contributions to make them more equitable. For example, the Reflect Table was designed based on this assumption (Bachour *et al*, 2008). The table monitors and analyzes ongoing conversations using embedded microphones in front of each person and represents this in the form of increasing numbers of colored LEDs (see Figure 4.14). A study investigated whether students became more aware of how much they were speaking during a group meeting when their relative levels of talk were displayed in this manner and, if so, whether they regulated their levels of participation more effectively. In other words, would the girl in the bottom right reduce her contributions (as she clearly has been talking the most) while the boy in the bottom left increase his (as he has been talking the least)? The findings were mixed: some participants changed their level to match the levels of others while others became frustrated and chose simply to ignore the LEDs. Specifically, those who spoke the most changed their behavior the most (i.e. reduced their level) while those who spoke the least changed theirs the least (i.e. did not increase their level). Another finding was that participants who believed it was beneficial to contribute equally to the conversation took more notice of the LEDs and regulated their conversation level accordingly. For example, one participant said that she "refrained from talking to avoid having a lot more lights than the others" (Bachour *et al*, 2010). Conversely, participants who thought it was not important took less notice. How do you think you would react?

Figure 4.14 The Reflect Table
Source: Reproduced with permission from Pierre Dillenbourg.

An implication from the various user studies on co-located collaboration around tabletops is that designing shareable interfaces to encourage more equitable participation isn't straightforward. Providing explicit real-time feedback on how much someone is speaking in a group may be a good way of showing everyone who is talking too much but it may be intimidating for those who are talking too little. Allowing discreet and accessible ways for adding and manipulating content to an ongoing collaborative task at a shareable surface may be more effective at encouraging greater participation from people who normally find it difficult or who are simply unable to verbally contribute to group settings (e.g. those on the autistic spectrum, those who stutter, or those who are shy or are non-native speakers).

How best to represent the activity of online social networks in terms of who is taking part has also been the subject of much research. A design principle that has been influential is social translucence (Erickson and Kellogg, 2000). This refers to the importance of designing communication systems to enable participants and their activities to be visible to one another. This idea was very much behind the early communication tool, Babble, developed at IBM by David Smith (Erickson *et al*, 1999), which provided a dynamic visualization of the participants in an ongoing chat room. A large 2D circle was depicted using colored marbles on each user's monitor. Marbles inside the circle conveyed those individuals active in the current conversation. Marbles outside the circle showed users involved in other conversations. The more active a participant was in the conversation, the more the corresponding marble moved towards the center of the circle. Conversely, the less engaged a person was in the ongoing conversation, the more the marble moved towards the periphery of the circle.

Since this early work on visualizing social interactions, there have been a number of virtual spaces developed that provide awareness about what people are doing, where they are, and their availability, with the aim of helping them feel more connected. Working in remote teams can be isolating, especially if you are part of a virtual team and rarely get to see your colleagues face to face. Also, you miss out on the office gossip and coffee room chats, where great ideas often start. There are various communication services that have been designed to make people feel more connected. One is the virtual office system, Sococo, that uses the spatial metaphor of a floor plan of an office to show where people are, who is in a meeting, and who is chatting with whom (see Figure 4.15). It provides a bird's-eye view of each floor so that everyone connected can see where everyone is at any given time. It also makes it easy to pop in and say hello to someone – in the same way office workers might do if they were in the same building. You simply click on a room and virtually pop your head round the door and start talking with the person inside. Or you can shut your door and that lets others know you are busy and not to be disturbed. Before entering a meeting, you can see who is already there by the presence of their avatar icon. There are also 'water cooler' and lobby areas where users can jump over just for a spontaneous conversation with someone.

Software tools are available that visualize social networks using social media (e.g. tweets) or data collected about a group or a community that is entered into a spreadsheet. For example, NodeXL (Hansen *et al*, 2011) provides an easy way of showing relationships between people or topics that interest them. More generally, social network analysis (SNA) can be used to analyze big data in a social context, enabling researchers to visualize the impact a person has in a given social network, showing who they are talking to and what hot topics are being talked about.

Figure 4.15 Sococo floor plan of a virtual office, showing who is where and who is meeting with whom https://www.sococo.com/

Source: Courtesy of Leeann Brumby.

BOX 4.5

Can technologies be designed to help people break the ice and socialize?

Have you ever found yourself at a party, wedding, conference, or other social gathering, standing awkwardly by yourself, not knowing who to talk to or what to talk about? Social embarrassment and self-consciousness affect most of us at such moments and such feelings are most acute when one is a newcomer and by oneself, such as a first-time attendee at a conference. How can we help make conversation initiation easier and less awkward among people who do not know each other?

A number of mechanisms have been employed by organizers of social events, such as asking old-timers to act as mentors and the holding of various kinds of ice-breaking activities. Badge-wearing, the plying of alcohol and food, and introductions by others are also common ploys. While many of these methods can help, engaging in ice-breaking activities requires people to act in a way that is different to the way they normally socialize and which they may find equally uncomfortable or painful to do. They often require people to agree to join in a collaborative game, which they can find embarrassing. This can be exacerbated by the fact that once people have agreed to take part it is difficult for them to drop out, because of the perceived consequences it will have for the others and themselves, (e.g. being seen by the others as a spoilsport or party-pooper). Having had one such embarrassing experience, most people will shy away from any further kinds of ice-breaking activities.

How might less intrusive mechanisms be developed using collaborative technologies? One line of research has investigated how computer-based matchmaking techniques can be used, based on algorithms that determine which preferences and views shared among people would make them suitable conversational partners. The profiles of like-minded people are revealed to one other when in close proximity via LCD name tags that light up (Borovoy *et al*, 1998) or as icons that appear on a person's cell phone display (Burak and Sharon, 2004). While such explicit revelations of what is normally hidden and discreet can be entertaining for some, for others it can feel invasive and an unnatural way of meeting someone.

An alternative approach is to design a physical space where people can enter and exit a conversation with a stranger in more subtle ways, i.e. one where people do not feel threatened or embarrassed, and which does not require a high level of commitment. The Opinionizer system was designed along these lines, with the aim of encouraging people in an informal gathering to share their opinions visually and anonymously (Brignull and Rogers, 2003). The collective creation of opinions via a public display was intended to provide a talking point for the people standing beside it. Users submitted their opinions by typing them in at a public keyboard. To add color and personality to their opinions, a selection of small cartoon avatars and speech bubbles were available. The screen was also divided into four labeled quadrants representing different backgrounds, e.g. techie, softie, designer, or student, to provide a factor on which people could comment (see Figure 4.16).

When the Opinionizer was placed in various social gatherings, a honey-pot effect was observed: as the number of people in the immediate vicinity of the Opinionizer increased, a sociable buzz was created in the area. By standing in this space and showing an interest, e.g. visibly facing the screen or reading the text, people gave off a tacit signal to others that they were open to discussion and interested in meeting new people. ∎

Figure 4.16 The Opinionizer interface and a photo of it being used at a book launch party

Figure 4.17 The Dynamo system in use at a sixth form college in the UK. The student with the spiky blond hair is showing various media he has created to the girl sitting next to him. Others sitting around the display are drawn into his show and subsequently hold a conversation about it

Source: H. Brignull, S. Izadi, G. Fitzpatrick, Y. Rogers and T. Rodden: The introduction of a shared interface surface into a communal space. In: *Proceedings of the Conference on Computer Supported Cooperative Work, CSCW '04,* ACM Press, New York, pp. 49–58 ©2004 Association for Computing Machinery, Inc. Reprinted with permission.

Interactive shared displays have been placed in various public spaces, e.g. hallways, reception areas, and shopping malls, with the aim of encouraging people to meet, interact with each other, and socialize. Early systems were designed for people to send notes, news items, and other materials from the PCs in their offices to a large public display: e.g. the Notification Collage system (Greenberg and Rounding, 2001) and the Plasma Posters (Churchill *et al*, 2003). The Dynamo system went one step further by enabling communities to readily share and exchange a variety of media on a large shared display by hooking up their memory sticks, laptops, cameras, and other devices in the vicinity of the display (Izadi *et al*, 2003). A study of its deployment in a sixth form common room in the UK (see Figure 4.17) showed how students often used it as a conversational prop while displaying and manipulating media on the shared display, which in turn led to impromptu conversations between those sitting in the room (Brignull *et al*, 2004).

Besides offering a compelling form of advertising, interactive digital displays are now commonplace in urban spaces. Some have been used to encourage various forms of public engagement. For example, the BBC Big Screens Public Space Broadcasting project installed a number of big (5 meters by 5 meters) screens outdoors in British cities. A collaborative application developed for it was called the Red Nose Game. The game starts with red blobs splattered on the screen. The objective of the game is for passers-by to push the blobs together by using their bodies, which are tracked by a live camera feed embedded in the display. When the camera image of a player touches a red nose blob, it enables that person to push it around the screen towards other blobs. The game ends when all the small blobs become one large blob. A study conducted by O'Hara *et al* (2008) showed that people were reluctant to play in case they made a fool of themselves in front of the other members of the public. It often required a compère to cajole people into playing the game. However, once in the game, people worked closely together as groups, developing effective strategies to move their blobs together, such as linking arms and sweeping the blobs together across the screen.

A range of technological interventions have been developed and placed in physical work settings with the aim of encouraging people to socialize and talk more with each other. For example, the Break-Time Barometer was designed to persuade people to come out of their offices for a break to meet others they might not talk with otherwise (Kirkham *et al*, 2013). An ambient display, based on a clock metaphor, shows how many people are currently in the common room; if there are people present, it also sends an alert that it would be a good time to join them for a break. While the system nudged some people to go for a break in the staff room, it also had the opposite effect on others who used it to determine when breaks weren't happening so that they could take a break without their colleagues being around for company.

DILEMMA
Mindless versus mindful interaction

We are increasingly living in our own digital bubbles. Even when physically together – as families and friends in our living rooms, outdoors, and in public places – we have our eyes glued to our own phones, tablets, and laptops, sometimes oblivious to our family, friends, and colleagues who we might be sitting with, eating with or traveling with. Teenagers have become 'screenagers.' Young kids are having their screen time rationed. Many of us are lost without our smartphones, constantly flipping them out of our pockets and purses to catch up on the latest gossip, news, or snap – at the expense of appearing rude to those around us. The new generation of 'all about me' health and fitness gadgets, which is becoming more mainstream, is making this phenomenon worse. Do we really need smart shoes that tell us when we are being lazy and glasses that tell us what we can and cannot eat? Is this what we want from technology – ever more forms of mindless interaction and data addiction? By mindless is meant indifferent to, unaware of, and blind to what is going on around us. How can we begin to rethink our relationship with future digital technologies that is more mindful? By this is meant being alive and aware or conscious of someone or something. It could be through thinking more about how we can do things together using shared devices, tools, and data – technology that encourages us to be more thoughtful of each other and our surrounding environments. ∎

(Continued)

Video that went viral showing mindless smartphone use at 'I Forgot My Phone' **http://youtu.be/OINa46HeWg8**

Figure 4.18 A family all in their own digital bubbles, including the dog!

Assignment

The aim of this activity is to analyze how collaboration, coordination and communication are supported in massively multiplayer online games (MMOGs).

Visit an MMOG (e.g. World of Warcraft, Eve, NeverWinter) and answer the following:

(a) General social issues
- What is the purpose of the MMOG?
- What kinds of conversations are supported?
- How is awareness supported of the others in the MMOG?
- What kinds of social protocols and conventions are used?
- What kinds of awareness information are provided?

- Does the mode of communication and interaction seem natural or awkward?
- How do players coordinate their actions in the game?

(b) Specific interaction design issues
- What form of interaction and communication is supported, e.g. text/audio/video?
- What other visualizations are included? What information do they convey?
- How do users switch between different modes of interaction, e.g. exploring and chatting? Is the switch seamless?
- Are there any social phenomena that occur specific to the context of the MMOG that wouldn't happen in face-to-face settings?

(c) Design issues
- What other features might you include in the MMOG to improve communication, coordination and collaboration?

Summary

Human beings are inherently social; people will always need to collaborate, coordinate, and communicate with one another, and the diverse range of applications, web-based services, and technologies that have emerged are enabling them to do so in more extensive and diverse ways. In this chapter we have looked at some core aspects of sociality, namely communication and collaboration. We examined the main social mechanisms that people use in different conversational settings when interacting face-to-face and at a distance. A number of collaborative and telepresence technologies designed to support and extend these mechanisms were discussed, highlighting core interaction design concerns.

Key points
- Social interaction is central to our everyday life.
- Social mechanisms have evolved in face-to-face and remote contexts to facilitate conversation, coordination, and awareness.
- Talk and the way it is managed are integral to coordinating social interaction.
- Many kinds of computer-mediated communication systems have been developed to enable people to communicate with one another when in physically different locations.
- Keeping aware of what others are doing and letting others know what you are doing are important aspects of collaboration and socializing.
- Social media have brought about significant changes in the way people keep in touch and manage their social lives.

Further Reading

BOYD, D. (2014) *It's Complicated: the social lives of networked teens*. Yale. Based on a series of in-depth interviews with a number of teenagers, boyd offers new insights into how teenagers across the US, who have only ever grown up in a world of apps and media, navigate, use, and appropriate them to grow up and develop their identities. A number of topics are covered that are central to what it means to grow up in a networked world, including bullying, addiction, expressiveness, privacy, and inequality. It is insightful, up to date, and covers much ground.

CRUMLISH, C. and MALONE, E. (2009) *Designing Social Interfaces*. O'Reilly. This is a collection of design patterns, principles, and advice for designing social websites, such as online communities.

GARDNER, H. and DAVIS, K. (2013) *The App Generation: how today's youth navigate identity, intimacy, and imagination in a digital world*. Yale. This book explores the impact of new technologies (especially the millions of apps available today) on the young generation, examining how they affect their identity, intimacy, and imagination. It focuses on what it means to be app-dependent versus app-empowered.

HARRISON, S. (ed.) (2009) *Media Space 20 + Years of Mediated Life*. Springer. This collection gives a historical overview of many of the developments in media spaces, such as telepresence, together with reflections on future developments and technologies by researchers in the field.

ROBINSON, S., MARSDEN, G. and JONES, M. (2015) *There's Not An App For That: Mobile user experience design for life*. Elsevier. This book offers a fresh and exciting approach for designers, students, and researchers to dare to think differently by moving away from the default framing of technological design in terms of yet another 'looking down' app. It asks the reader to instead look up and around them – to be inspired by how we actually live our lives when 'out there' app-less. They also explore what it means to design technologies to be more mindful.

Chapter 5

EMOTIONAL INTERACTION

Objectives

The main aims of this chapter are to:

- Explain how our emotions relate to behavior and user experience.
- Provide examples of interfaces that are both pleasurable and usable.
- Explain what expressive and annoying interfaces are and the effects they can have on people.
- Introduce the area of automatic emotion recognition and emotional technologies.
- Describe how technologies can be designed to change people's attitudes and behavior.
- Give an overview on how anthropomorphism has been applied in interaction design.
- Enable you to critique the persuasive impact of an online agent on customers.

5.1   Introduction

An overarching goal of interaction design is to develop products that elicit positive responses from users, such as feeling at ease, being comfortable, and enjoying the experience of using them – be it a washing machine or a flight deck. Designers are also concerned with how to create interactive products that elicit specific kinds of emotional responses in users, such as motivating them to learn, play, or be creative or social. There has also been much interest in designing websites and apps that people can trust, and that make them feel comfortable about divulging personal information when making a purchase or giving feedback.

Taken together, we refer to this emerging area as emotional interaction. In this chapter we look at how and why the design of interactive products may cause certain kinds of emotional responses in people. We begin by explaining what emotions are and how they shape our behavior and everyday experiences. We then look at expressive interfaces, examining the role of an interface's appearance to users and how it affects usability and the user experience. We then consider how products elicit positive effects, e.g. pleasure, or negative responses, e.g. frustration. We introduce technological approaches to sensing people's emotions and how these are being used to inform the design of new kinds of emotional technology. The ways technologies are being designed and used to persuade people to change their behavior and attitudes are then covered. We look, in particular, at ubiquitous technology interventions that are being designed to improve health and well-being and reduce domestic energy and water consumption. Following this, we show how anthropomorphism has been used in interaction design and the implications of designing applications that have human-like qualities. To illustrate this approach, virtual characters and robot pets are described that have been developed to motivate people to learn, buy, and listen.

5.2   Emotions and the User Experience

Emotional interaction is concerned with how we feel and react when interacting with technology. It covers different aspects of the user experience, from how we feel when first finding out about a new product to getting rid of it. It also looks at why people become emotionally attached to certain products (e.g. virtual pets), how social robots might help reduce loneliness, and how to change human behavior through the use of emotive feedback.

Consider the different emotions you experience for a common everyday activity – shopping online for a product, such as a new smartphone, a washing machine, or a vacation. Firstly, there is the realization of needing or wanting it, and then the desire and anticipation of purchasing it. This is followed by the joy or frustration of finding out more about what products are available and deciding which to choose from potentially hundreds or even thousands (by visiting numerous websites, such as comparison sites, reviews, recommendations, and social media sites). This entails matching what is available with what you like or need and whether you can afford it. The thrill of deciding on a purchase may be quickly followed by the shock of how much it costs and the disappointment that you can't afford it. The process of having to decide again may be accompanied by annoyance as you can't find one that is as good as your first choice. You think about other options, such as seeking advice from an expert in a shopping mall, but you have an aversion to sales assistants and don't trust their advice, because you think they have their own interests (making money), rather than yours, at heart. So you carry on looking, getting more tired and frustrated. When you do make a decision, you experience a sense of relief. You click merrily though the various options (such as color, size, warranty) and then the dreaded online payment form pops up. You type in all your details and press the final payment button. A window then appears saying that your credit card number is incorrect. So you type it in again very slowly. And you notice you need to type the three-number security code in again. Finally, when all is done you let out a big sigh. But as you walk away from your computer, doubts start to form in your mind – maybe you should have bought the other one . . .

This rollercoaster set of emotions is what many of us experience when shopping online, especially for expensive products, where there is a myriad of options to choose from and where we want to be sure that we make the right choice.

ACTIVITY 5.1

Wufoo is a company specializing in building online forms, with the intention of transforming what are usually boring and tedious tasks into more fun activities. How do the forms in Figure 5.1 compare with others you have had to fill in?

Comment

One difference with these forms is the way minimalism, balance, and aesthetics have been used in the design. As commented by one of Wufoo's creators, Kevin Hale: "The inspiration for our color palette came from our competitors. It was really depressing to see so much software designed to remind people they're making databases in a windowless office and so we immediately knew we wanted to go in the opposite direction. My goal was to design Wufoo to feel like something Fisher-Price would make. We were determined to make sure Wufoo was fun." ■

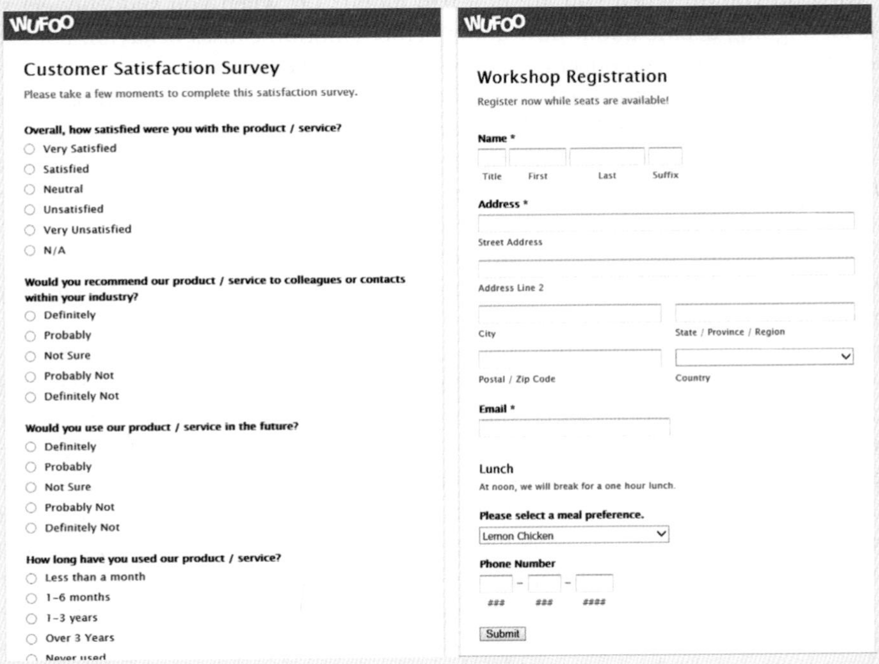

WUFOO

Customer Satisfaction Survey

Please take a few moments to complete this satisfaction survey.

Overall, how satisfied were you with the product / service?

- Very Satisfied
- Satisfied
- Neutral
- Unsatisfied
- Very Unsatisfied
- N/A

Would you recommend our product / service to colleagues or contacts within your industry?

- Definitely
- Probably
- Not Sure
- Probably Not
- Definitely Not

Would you use our product / service in the future?

- Definitely
- Probably
- Not Sure
- Probably Not
- Definitely Not

How long have you used our product / service?

- Less than a month
- 1-6 months
- 1-3 years
- Over 3 Years
- Never used

WUFOO

Workshop Registration

Register now while seats are available!

Name *

Title First Last Suffix

Address *

Street Address

Address Line 2

City State / Province / Region

Postal / Zip Code Country

Email *

Lunch

At noon, we will break for a one hour lunch.

Please select a meal preference.

Lemon Chicken

Phone Number

- ### -

Submit

Figure 5.1 Examples of Wufoo's online forms

Source: Reproduced with permission from Wufoo.com. http://wufoo.com/examples/#survey.

Emotional interaction is about considering what makes us happy, sad, annoyed, anxious, frustrated, motivated, delirious, and so on, and using this knowledge to inform the design of different aspects of the user experience, from when we first want something to when we no longer interact with it or need to replace it. However, it is not straightforward to achieve as people's moods and feelings are constantly changing. There are also many reasons that might cause someone to be happy or sad, such as the sun shining or someone else winning a game.

A good place to start understanding how emotions affect behavior and how behavior affects emotions is to examine how people express themselves and read each other's expressions. These include understanding the relationship between facial expressions, body language, gestures, and tone of voice. For example, when people are happy they typically smile, laugh, and open their bodies up. When they are angry they shout, gesticulate, and screw up their face. A person's expressions can trigger emotional responses in others. So when someone smiles it can cause others to feel good and smile back. Emotional skills, especially the ability to express and recognize emotions, are central to human communication. Most of us are highly skilled at detecting when someone is angry, happy, sad, or bored by recognizing their facial expressions, way of speaking, and other body signals. We are also very good at knowing what emotions to express in a given situation. For example, when someone has just heard he has failed an exam, we know it is not a good time to smile and be happy. Instead we try to empathize.

So what do you do when you are in a bad mood? Or when you suddenly get scared? There is an ongoing debate about how and whether emotion causes behavior. For example, does being angry make you concentrate better? Or does being happy make you take more risks, such as spending too much money? Or vice versa? Or neither? It could be that we can just be happy, sad, or angry and that this does not affect our behavior. Many theorists argue that emotions cause behavior, for example the 'fear brings flight and anger brings fight' perspective. When we are frightened or angry, the emotional response is to focus on the problem at hand and try to overcome or resolve the perceived danger. Our bodies will respond by tensing our muscles and sweating. In contrast, when we are very happy, such as watching our team win the last game of the championship, the emotional response is to laugh, cheer, and jump about. The body relaxes.

Baumeister *et al* (2007) argue that the role of emotion is more complicated than a simple cause and effect model; emotions can be both simple and short-lived or complex and long-lasting. For example, someone can become startled by a sudden, unexpected loud noise or remain annoyed for hours when staying in a hotel room that has a noisy air conditioning unit. To distinguish between these types of emotions and their effect on behavior, automatic responses (e.g. being startled) are called affect. They can happen rapidly, typically within a fraction of a second and, likewise, may dissipate just as quickly. Conscious emotions, on the other hand, tend to be slow to develop and equally slow to dissipate, and are often the result of a conscious cognitive behavior, such as weighing up the odds, reflecting, or contemplating. They require our attention and underlie our ability to learn and adapt our behavior. For example, someone might drink too much when out at a bar one night with a friend, causing them to become rowdy, which the next morning makes them feel guilty and embarrassed. These subequent feelings make them reflect on their behavior, such that they realize they have behaved inappropriately. This could then lead them to think about how to deal with such a situation in the future, which might be to have only non-alcoholic drinks when going to the pub with this friend.

Understanding how emotions work provides a way of considering how to design interfaces and apps that can trigger affect or reflection in the user. For example, Norman (2005) suggests that being in a positive state of mind can enable us to be more creative as we are less focused. Designers, therefore, might consider how to design products that can make people feel happy, assuming it will then make them creative. He also suggests that when people are happy, they are more likely to overlook and cope with minor problems they are experiencing with a device. In contrast, when someone is anxious or angry, they are more likely to be less tolerant. So if the product is intended to be used during leisure time and is meant to be fun and enjoyable to use, designers "can get away with more" and not be too worried about how the information appears at the interface. On the other hand, he says that for serious tasks, such as monitoring a process control plant or driving a car, designers need to pay special attention to all the information required to do the task at hand and that the interface should be visible with clear and unambiguous feedback. The bottom line is "things intended to be used under stressful situations require a lot more care, with much more attention to detail" (Norman, 2005, p. 26).

ACTIVITY 5.2

Do you feel more creative when you are in a happy mood? Do you get less work done when you are feeling stressed?

Comment
Many people are more open to new ideas when they are happy. When they are worrying about something that has annoyed them recently, it can distract them, preventing them from being productive. ∎

> **Video** of Kia Höök talking about affective interaction in a series of videos that consider emotion in terms of how it is constructed in interaction with technology and people is available at
> **www.interaction-design.org/encyclopedia/affective_computing.html**

BOX 5.1
A model of emotional design

Ortony *et al*'s (2005) model of emotion and behavior is couched in terms of different levels of the brain. At the lowest level are parts of the brain that are pre-wired to automatically respond to events happening in the physical world. This is called the visceral level. At the next level are the brain processes that control our everyday behavior. This is called the behavioral level. At the highest level are brain processes that contemplate. This is called the reflective level (Figure 5.2). The visceral level responds rapidly, making judgments about what is good or bad,

(Continued)

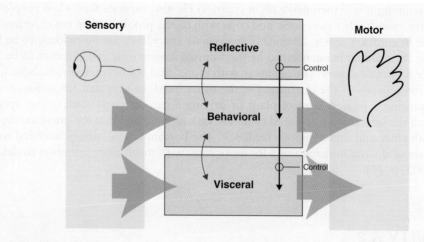

Figure 5.2 Ortony *et al*'s (2005) model of emotional design showing three levels: visceral, behavioral, and reflective

Source: The illustration and text are from Figure 1.1 of Norman, D. A. (2004). *Emotional Design: We love (or hate) everyday things*. New York: Basic Books. Reprinted with permission of the author.

safe or dangerous, pleasurable or abhorrent. It also triggers the emotional responses to stimuli (e.g. fear, joy, anger, and sadness) that are expressed through a combination of physiological and behavioral responses. For example, on seeing a very large hairy spider running across the floor of the bathroom, many people will experience fear, causing them to scream and run away. The behavioral level is the site where most human activities occur; examples include well-learned routine operations such as talking, typing, and driving. The reflective level entails conscious thought where people generalize across events or step back from the routine and the immediate. An example is switching between thinking about the narrative structure and special effects used in a Harry Potter movie and becoming scared at the visceral level when watching the movie. ■

One way of using the model is to think about how to design products in terms of the three levels. Visceral design refers to making products look, feel, and sound good. Behavioral design is about use and equates with the traditional values of usability. Reflective design is about taking into account the meaning and personal value of a product in a particular culture. For example, the design of a Swatch watch focuses on reflective aspects, where the aesthetics and the use of cultural images and graphical elements are central. Brilliant colors, wild designs, and art are very much part of the Swatch trademark and are what draw people to buy and wear their watches.

Figure 5.3 A Swatch watch called Dip in Color

Source: With permission from The Swatch Group (UK) Limited.
http://store.swatch.com/suop103-dip-in-color.html

"it's a very user-friendly model."

5.3   Expressive Interfaces

Expressive forms like emoticons, sounds, icons, and virtual agents have been used at the interface to (i) convey emotional states and/or (ii) elicit certain kinds of emotional responses in users, such as feeling at ease, comfort, and happiness. Icons and animations have been used to indicate the current state of a computer or a phone, notably when it is waking up or being rebooted. A classic from the 1980s and 1990s was the happy Mac icon that appeared on the screen of the Apple computer whenever the machine was booted (see Figure 5.4). The smiling icon conveyed a sense of friendliness, inviting the user to feel at ease and even smile back. The appearance of the icon on the screen was also very reassuring to users, indicating that their computer was working correctly. This was especially true for situations where users had to reboot their computer after it had crashed, and where previous attempts to reboot had failed (usually indicated by a sad icon face – see Figure 5.4). After nearly 20 years, the happy Mac icon was laid to rest. The sad Mac icon lasted a bit longer, showing its face on an iPod when its software needed restoring. Apple has since switched to the use of more abstract icons to indicate starting up and busy with a process, showing a swirling clock or a colorful beach ball. Android has a lime-green robot icon on its start-up page, suggesting something between being techno-like and human-like.

Other ways of conveying the status of a system are through the use of:

- Dynamic icons (e.g. a recycle bin expanding when a file is placed in it and paper disappearing in a puff when emptied).
- Animations (e.g. a beach ball whirling to say the computer is busy).
- Spoken messages, using various kinds of voices, telling the user what needs to be done (e.g. GPS navigation system instructing you politely where to go after having taken a wrong turn).
- Various sonifications indicating actions and events (e.g. whoosh for window closing, schlook for a file being dragged, ding for new email arriving).
- Vibrotactile feedback, such as distinct smartphone buzzes that specifically represent special messages from friends and family.

The style of an interface, in terms of the shapes, fonts, colors, balance, white space, and graphical elements that are used and the way they are combined, can also influence its emotional impact. Use of imagery at the interface can result in more engaging and enjoyable experiences (Mullet and Sano, 1995). A designer can use a number of aesthetic techniques such as clean lines, balance, simplicity, and texture. The iPod, featured in Chapter 1, exemplifies this approach.

The design of aesthetically pleasing interfaces has become of central concern to interaction design. Empirical studies have shown that the aesthetics of an interface can have a positive effect on people's perception of the system's usability (e.g. Tractinsky, 1997). When the

Figure 5.4 Smiling and sad Apple icons for the classic Mac

look and feel of an interface is pleasing and pleasurable – e.g. beautiful graphics, nice feel to the way the elements have been put together, well-designed fonts, elegant use of images and color, a good sense of balance – users are likely to be more tolerant, e.g. they may be prepared to wait a few more seconds for a website to download. Furthermore, good-looking interfaces are often more satisfying and pleasurable to use. A key concern, therefore, is to strike a balance between designing aesthetic versus usable interfaces (Tractinsky *et al*, 2000) and pleasurable versus useful ones (Jordan, 2000).

BOX 5.2

A new breed of home technology: The NEST and Sproutling interfaces

There is an assortment of technologies on the market now that can track, aggregate, and visualize our every behavior – from toothbrushes that check whether you and your family are brushing your teeth correctly to devices that monitor how well a baby is sleeping and what it is feeling when awake. Two that stand out in terms of their appearance are the Nest (nest.com) and the Sproutling (sproutling.com). The designs are simple, round, and use bright colors – this makes them cute and aesthetically pleasing to the eye. The Nest thermostat provides an intelligent way of controlling how your house is heated or cooled. The Sproutling is a band that is wrapped around a baby's ankle that senses heart rate, skin temperature, motion, and position. It communicates with a smartphone app to let parents know if their baby is sleeping soundly or if something is wrong – using cute baby emoticons. These are examples of products designed for families to use in the home and via their smartphones. Both were designed by ex-Apple employees. Do you think their focus on the design aesthetic enhances the user experience and usability? ■

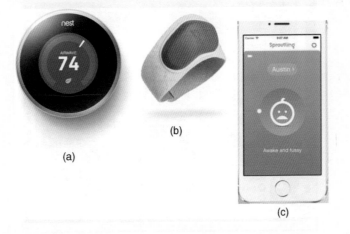

(b)

(a)

(c)

Figure 5.5 (a) The Nest, (b) the Sproutling anklet band (c) the Sproutling smartphone app
Source: With permission from NestLabs.com and sproutling.com.

5.4 Annoying Interfaces

In many situations, computer interfaces may inadvertently elicit negative emotional responses such as anger and disgust. This typically happens when something that should be simple to use or set turns out to be complex. The most common examples are remote controls, printers, digital alarm clocks, and digital TV systems. Getting a printer to work with a new digital camera, trying to switch from watching a DVD to the TV, and changing the time on a digital alarm clock in a hotel can be very trying. Also, fiddly actions that have to be done every day, such as attaching the ends of USB cables between smartphones, laptops, and fit bands, can be irksome, especially if it is not easy to see which way up to insert them.

This does not mean that developers are unaware of such usability problems. Several methods have been devised to help the novice user get set up and become familiarized with a technology. However, these have sometimes backfired, since the design solution itself has ironically become a source of annoyance and frustration. For example, one technique that was popularized in the 1990s was the use of friendly agents at the interface. The assumption was that novices would feel more at ease with a companion and would be encouraged to try things out after listening, watching, following, and interacting with it. Microsoft pioneered a class of agent-based software, Bob, aimed at new computer users (many of whom were viewed as computer-phobic). The agents were presented as friendly characters, including a pet dog and a cute bunny. An underlying assumption was that having these kinds of agents on the screen would make users feel more comfortable with using the software. An interface metaphor of a warm, cozy living room, replete with fire and furniture, was also provided (see Figure 5.6) – again intended to convey a comfortable feeling. However, Bob never became a commercial product. Why do you think not?

Figure 5.6 'At home with Bob' software developed for Windows 95. Although now defunct, it has been resurrected affectionately to run on a Virtual PC platform

Source: Microsoft product screenshot reproduced with permission from Microsoft Corporation.

Figure 5.7 Microsoft's agent Clippy

Source: Microsoft product screenshot reproduced with permission from Microsoft Corporation.

Contrary to the designers' expectations, many people did not like the idea of Bob at all, finding the interface too cute and childish. However, Microsoft did not give up on the idea of making their interfaces more friendly and developed other kinds of agents, including the infamous Clippy (a paper clip that has human-like qualities), as part of their Windows 98 operating environment. Clippy typically appeared at the bottom of a user's screen whenever the system thought the user needed help carrying out a particular task (see Figure 5.7). It, too, was depicted as a cartoon character, with a warm personality. This time, Clippy was released as a commercial product but it was not a success. Many Microsoft users found it very trying and intrusive, distracting them from their work. When it was finally retired, numerous websites posted jokes and witty comments, celebrating its demise.

Interfaces, if designed poorly, can make people look stupid, or feel insulted or threatened. The effect can be to make them annoyed to the point of losing their temper. There are many situations that cause such emotional responses. These include:

- When an application doesn't work properly or crashes.
- When a system doesn't do what the user wants it to do.
- When a user's expectations are not met.
- When a system does not provide sufficient information to let the user know what to do.
- When error messages pop up that are vague or obtuse.
- When the appearance of an interface is too noisy, garish, gimmicky, or patronizing.
- When a system requires users to carry out too many steps to perform a task, only to discover a mistake was made somewhere along the line and they need to start all over again.
- Websites that are overloaded with text and graphics, making it difficult to find the information desired and making them slow to access.
- Flashing animations, especially flashing banner ads and pop-up ads that cover what the user is looking at and which require them to actively click on a check box to close them.
- The over-use of sound effects and music, especially when selecting options, carrying out actions, running tutorials, or watching website demos.

- Featuritis – an excessive number of operations, such as the array of buttons on remote controls.
- Poorly laid out keyboards, pads, control panels, and other input devices that cause users to persistently press the wrong keys or buttons.

ACTIVITY 5.3

Most of us are familiar with the '404 error' message that pops up now and again when our computer doesn't upload the web page we're trying to view. But what does it mean and why the number 404? How does it make you feel when you see it and what do you do next? Is there a better way of letting users know when they or the computer have made an error?

Comment

The main reasons for this error message appearing are: (i) you have typed in the URL incorrectly, (ii) you have followed an old link that is now broken, or (iii) you have tried to access a page that is blocked by an ISP. The number 404 comes from the HTML language. The first 4 indicates a client error. The server is telling you that you've done something wrong, such as misspelt the URL or requested a page that no longer exists. The middle 0 refers to a general syntax error, such as a spelling mistake. The last 4 indicates the specific nature of the error. For the user, however, it is an arbitrary number. It might even suggest that there are 400 other errors they could make! ∎

Some systems are very emotive in the way they let you know you have made an error. Figure 5.8 shows one such example, where bold letters (that used to be in red) and an exclamation mark are used to alert the user to the severity of the error. The effect can cause a user to become quite anxious, making them panic, especially if subsequently given only two chances to rectify the situation, as is often the case after typing in a password incorrectly. Is it really necessary to be so shouty? Would it not be more pleasant if the message suggested that the user try again? Some companies have started using more polite and useful error messages, such as this one provided for a user who could not log in to his Wallet using the Android app, "Greetings. We're having a problem. We can't show the info you requested. Sorry about this. It appears we're having an unexpected problem getting you what you need. Try again."

FLPPS009

Error!

___

Your login information is incorrect...

Please verify that you typed in your Last Name, NSF ID, and Password correctly. If you still cannot login, please contact the Administrator regarding your access rights.

Return To Previous Page

Figure 5.8 An error message that appears if a user types in his or her personal details for accessing the protected website incorrectly

DILEMMA
Should computers say they're sorry?

A provocative idea is that computers should apologize when they make a mistake. Reeves and Nass (1996), for example, argue that they should be polite and courteous in the same way that people are to one another. While apologizing is normal social etiquette in human behavior, especially when someone makes a mistake, would you agree that computers should be made to behave in the same way? Would users be as forgiving of computers as they are of one another? For example, what would most users think if, after their computer had crashed, it came up with a spoken or written apology such as, "I am really sorry I crashed. I'll try not to do it again"? Would they think that it was being sincere? Would the apology make them forgive the computer in the way they forgive other people, after receiving such an apology? Or would it have no effect at all? Worse still, would users perceive such messages as vacuous statements and regard them simply as condescending, thereby increasing their level of frustration? It seems people would rather a computer said sorry. An empirical study comparing error messages that apologized versus those that did not were perceived by users to be less frustrating (Park *et al*, 2012). ■

5.5 Detecting Emotions and Emotional Technology

The approach called affective computing develops computer-based systems that try to recognize and express emotions in the same way humans do (Picard, 1998). A long-standing area of research in artificial intelligence and artificial life has been the creation of intelligent robots that are designed to behave like humans and other creatures. An early classic was COG, where a group of researchers attempted to build an artificial two-year-old. An offspring of COG was Kismet (Breazeal, 1999), which was designed to engage in meaningful social interactions with humans.

More recently, an area of research that has become of interest to interaction design is automatic emotion analysis. A number of sensing technologies are now used to automatically measure and analyze users' emotions and, from the data collected, predict aspects of their behavior – for example, what is someone most likely to buy online when feeling sad, bored, or happy. The main techniques and technologies used are: cameras for measuring facial expressions; bio-sensors placed on fingers or palms of the hands to measure galvanic skin response (which is used to infer how anxious or nervous someone is as indicated by an increase in their sweat); and body movement and gestures as detected by motion capture systems or accelerometer sensors placed on various parts of the body. Emotion assessing technology, such as automated facial coding, is gaining popularity in commercial settings, especially in marketing and e-commerce. For example, Affdex® emotion analytics and insights software from Affectiva® employs advanced computer vision and machine-learning algorithms to catalog a user's emotion reactions to digital content, as captured through a standard webcam, to analyze how engaged the user is with movies, online shopping sites, and ads. Six fundamental emotions are classified based on the face expressions Affdex collects (see Figure 5.9). These are sadness, happiness, disgust, fear, surprise, and anger. If a user screws up their face when an ad pops up,

Figure 5.9 A screen shot showing facial coding from Affdex software
Source: Courtesy of Affectiva, Inc.

that suggests they feel disgust, whereas if they start smiling, it suggests they are feeling happy. The website can then adapt its ad, movie storyline, or content to what it perceives the person needs at that point in their emotional state.

Other indirect methods that are used to reveal the emotional state of someone include eye-tracking, finger pulse, speech, and the words/phrases they use when tweeting, chatting online, or posting to Facebook (van den Broek, 2013). The level of affect expressed by users, the language they use, and the frequency with which they express themselves when using social media can all indicate their mental state, well-being, and aspects of their personality (e.g. whether they are extrovert or an introvert, neurotic or calm). Some companies may try to use a combination of these measures, such as facial expression and the language they use when online, while others may focus on just one, such as the tone of their voice, when answering questions over the phone. This kind of indirect emotion detection is beginning to be used to help infer or predict someone's behavior; for example, determining their suitability for a job, or how they will vote at an election.

DILEMMA

Is it OK for technology to work out how you are feeling?

Do you think it is creepy that technology is trying to read your emotions from your facial expressions or from what you write in your tweets and, based on its analysis, filter the online content you are browsing, such as ads, the news, or a movie, to match your mood?

Human beings will suggest things to each other, often based on what they think the other is feeling. For example, they might suggest a walk in the park to cheer them up. They might also suggest a book to read or a movie to watch. However, many people don't like the idea that a technology might do the same but at a finer level of granularity; for example, suggesting what you might like to eat, watch, or buy, based on how it analyzes your feelings. ▧

An example of a more benign emotional technology is 'Moon Phrases' – an app that has been developed to help people reflect upon their emotional well-being (de Choudhury *et al*, 2013). The app allows people to think about their emotional states and feelings via analyzing what they say in their postings on Twitter. The aim is to help them cope better with stress and anxiety by recognizing the triggers that cause them to occur. The tool works by analyzing the way users express themselves in social media – through the types of words, mood hashtags, emoticons, and expressions used and their frequency. It then visualizes this data in terms of a series of moon icons conveying positive and negative affect, representing each day for a period of several months; full moons indicate positivity, while half or quarter moons reflect more negativity. By looking back at their history of moons, users can start to identify patterns that could help them understand more about themselves and what might be causing their mood swings.

BOX 5.3

How much do you touch?

As well as expressing our emotions through facial, vocal, gesture, and body movements, we also use touch. For example, when someone touches our shoulder or strokes our arm during a conversation, they are often conveying affection towards us. Conversely, when someone shakes or squeezes our arms, they are more likely to be expressing anger or fear. The type of touch, how much pressure is applied, and where on the body it happens can provide clues as to the emotion being experienced by the person who is touching. HCI researchers are investigating how to develop 'touch profiles' based on measuring how users touch screens and consoles when playing video games (e.g. Gao *et al*, 2012). However, there is not a straightforward mapping between one kind of touch and one type of emotion (they can overlap), and current research tries to model and infer the range of someone's emotional experiences over time. These profiles can then provide information about how they feel without interrupting their user experience – which is very valuable feedback for game designers when thinking of how to design engrossing and gripping games. ■

5.6   Persuasive Technologies and Behavioral Change

A diversity of technologies is increasingly being used to draw people's attention to certain kinds of information in an attempt to change what they do or think. Pop-up ads, warning messages, reminders, prompts, personalized messages, and recommendations are some of the methods that are being deployed on computer screens. Fogg (2003) has labeled this phenomenon persuasive technology; interactive computing systems are deliberately designed to change people's attitudes and behaviors. Traditionally, media such as magazines, newspapers, pamphlets, radio, and TV have been used to persuade people to join a good cause, give up a bad habit, donate money, or buy a product. For example, a picture of a starving child with big round eyes staring out at the reader on the front of a newspaper is commonly used by charities. The effect is to pull at the readers' heartstrings, inducing feelings of guilt and, in so doing, spur them on to sending money.

More recently, interactive techniques have been used to entice, cajole, and persuade people to do something they might not have otherwise done. Successful examples include Amazon's one-click mechanism that makes it so easy and tempting to buy something at their online store, and recommender systems that suggest specific books, hotels, restaurants, etc a reader might want to try based on their previous purchases, choices, and taste. Splash pages to online shopping sites and color images of gorgeous-looking beach and mountain scenes on travel sites are designed to lure people into making impulse purchases.

In addition to using interactive technologies as a more targeted and personalized form of advertising, they can be used to change people's behaviors in non-commercial domains, such as safety, preventative healthcare, fitness, personal relationships, energy consumption, and learning. Here, the emphasis is on changing habits or doing something that will improve an individual's well-being through monitoring their behavior. An early example was Nintendo's Pokémon Pikachu with pedometer attached that was designed to motivate children into being more physically active on a consistent basis. The owner of the digital pet that lives in the device was required to walk, run, or jump each day to keep it alive. The wearer received credits with each step taken – the currency being watts that could be used to buy Pikachu presents. Twenty steps on the pedometer rewarded the player with one watt. If the owner did not exercise for a week, the virtual pet became angry and refused to play anymore. This use of positive rewarding and sulking can be a powerful means of persuasion, given that children often become emotionally attached to their virtual pets, especially when they start to care for them.

Similarly, the WaterBot system was developed using a special monitoring and feedback device, but for adults as a way of reducing their usage of water in their homes (Arroyo *et al*, 2005). There is much evidence to suggest that people are wasteful with water, often leaving the tap running continuously for long periods of time while cleaning their teeth or washing. The research team thought that the use of monitoring technology could help persuade householders to change their behavior to be more conservative in their water usage. To this end, they used the theory of positive reinforcement to inform their design, which states that activities are likely to be repeated if some kind of reward is given occasionally and randomly (similar to the reward system used in slot machines). A sensor-based system was developed where positive auditory messages and chimes were sounded when the tap was turned off. The water was also lit with a random pattern of color as a reward for consistent water-saving behavior. Two illuminated bar graphs were also presented alongside the tap, showing how much water a person had used relative to others in the household. Here, the idea was to encourage peer pressure and for the members of the household to talk to each other about their water usage. Informal feedback of the prototype system in a small number of people's homes suggested that the most effective method of persuasion was the constantly changing bar graph. It drew people's attention to the tap, leading them to make quick comparisons between their and the others' water consumption. The rewards of chimes and colored water had less impact, especially as their novelty wore off.

ACTIVITY 5.4

Watch the two videos:

(i) The Piano Staircase http://youtu.be/2lXh2n0aPyw
(ii) The Outdoor Bin http://youtu.be/cbEKAwCoCKw

Do you think such playful methods are effective at changing people's behavior?

Comment
Volkswagen sponsored an open competition, called the fun theory, asking people to transform mundane artifacts into novel enjoyable user experiences in an attempt to change people's behavior for the better (www.thefuntheory.com). The idea was to encourage a desired behavior through making it more fun. The Piano Staircase and the Outdoor Bin are the most well known examples; the stairs sounded like piano keys being played when walked on while the bin sounded like a well echoing when something was thrown into it. ■

HAPIfork is a device intended to help someone monitor and track their eating habits (see Figure 5.10). If it detects they are eating too quickly, it will vibrate (similar to the way

Figure 5.10 A friend using the HAPIfork in a restaurant when eating a cake

ACTIVITY 5.5

What do you think might be problematic when using this kind of dieting device in a restaurant?

Comment

The photo shows a friend using the device to eat a cake in a restaurant. He first commented on the fork being awkward to hold. He also felt self-conscious using a brightly coloured fork in a public setting that was very different from what everyone else was using to eat their food. The waiters also gave him funny looks when using it. He said it might be fun to try once but not to use for every meal and that he could not see himself or anyone else he knew using it in public. ∎

a smartphone does when on silent mode) and an ambient light will appear at the end of the fork, providing the eater with real-time feedback intended to slow them down. The assumption is that eating too fast results in poor digestion and poor weight control, and that making people aware that they are gobbling their food down can help them think about how to eat more slowly at a conscious level. Other data is collected about how long it took them to finish their meal, the amount of fork servings per minute, and the time between them. These are turned into a dashboard of graphs and statistics so the user can see each week whether their fork behavior is improving.

Nowadays, there are a number of mobile apps and personal tracking devices on the market that are designed to help people monitor various behaviors and then change their behavior based on the data collected and represented back to them. These include fitness and sleep bands, such as FitBit and Jawbone Up, and weight trackers such as smart scales. Similar to HAPIfork, these devices and apps are designed to encourage people to change their behavior by providing them with dashboards of statistics and graphs that show how much exercise, sleep, or food/drink they have had over a day, week, or longer period, compared with what they have done in the previous day/week/month. This can also be compared, through online leaderboards and charts, with how well they have done in relation to their peers and friends. A survey of how people use such devices in their everyday lives revealed that often people bought them to simply try them out – rather than specifically to change a particular behavior (Rooksby et al, 2014). How, what, and when they tracked depended on their interests and lifestyles; some used them as a way of showing how fast they could run during a marathon or cycle on a track, or how they could change their lifestyle to sleep or eat better.

Video of BBC News item showing smart scales being demonstrated at
http://www.bbc.co.uk/news/technology-24184634

An alternative approach to automatically collecting quantified data about a behavior is to ask people to write down manually how they are feeling now or to rate their mood, and to then reflect upon how they felt about themselves in the past. A mobile app called Echo, for example, asks people to write a subject line, rate their happiness at that moment, and add a description, photos, and/or videos if they want to (Isaacs *et al*, 2013). Sporadically, the app then asks them to reflect on previous entries. An assumption is that this kind of technology-mediated reflection can increase well-being and happiness. Each reflection is shown as a stacked card with the time and a smiley happiness rating. People who used Echo reported on the many postive effects of doing so, including reliving positive experiences and overcoming negative experiences, by writing them down. The double act of recording and reflecting enabled them to generalize from the positive experiences and draw positive lessons from negative ones.

ACTIVITY 5.6

The photo on the left in Figure 5.11 is of a banner placed in downtown LA, in an attempt to encourage the general public to take the stairs instead of the elevator, asking people to climb stairs on a certain day. The two photos on the right are of ambient displays (see also Chapter 2) designed to do the same thing but using more subtle and interactive methods: (i) lights that twinkled when people approach them, intended to lure them to take the stairs and (ii) clouds of different colored spheres that move up and down depending on how many people have taken the stairs or the elevator for a given period of time (gray represents elevator). The higher the orange cloud is relative to the gray one, the more people are taking the stairs than the elevator (Rogers, Hazlewood, Marshall *et al*, 2010). Which representation do you think is the most effective?

Comment
The banner on the left uses a striking slogan that metaphorically points a finger at you. Some people might find this amusing or a challenge. Others, however, are likely to find it

Figure 5.11 Stairs versus elevators: static sign versus ambient persuasive displays. Which is most persuasive?

(Continued)

offensive and even insulting and ignore it. The extent to which it will change behavior is debatable. In contrast, the ambient displays shown in the other images are meant to be much more subtle and aesthetic. They are assumed to work by raising people's awareness of a behavior that they normally overlook or try not to think about and nudge them at the point of decision making (Thaler and Sunstein, 2008). An in-the-wild study conducted when they were embedded in a building showed a significant increase in stair taking. Interestingly, the majority of people, when asked, were not aware of changing their behavior in response to noticing them. This suggests that ambient displays can influence at an unconscious level, and they can be used to encourage people to adhere to certain kinds of desired behaviors, where there is a choice, such as washing hands or not, eating healthy or unhealthy snacks, taking one route or another through a building, switching off the lights or leaving them on. ■

The global concern about climate change has led a number of HCI researchers to design and evaluate various energy sensing devices that display real-time feedback. A goal is to find ways of helping people reduce their energy consumption (and is part of a larger research agenda called sustainable HCI: see Mankoff *et al*, 2008; DiSalvo *et al*, 2010; Hazas *et al*, 2012). A focus is on persuading people to change their everyday habits with respect to environmental concerns, such as reducing their own carbon footprint, their community's (e.g. school, workplace), or an even larger organization's (e.g. street, town, country). Two early products were the Power Aware Cord and the Waatson (see Figure 5.12).

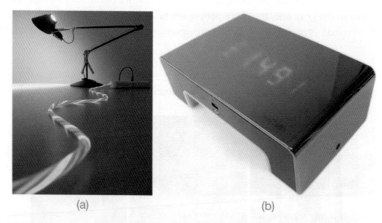

(a)   (b)

Figure 5.12 (a) The Power Aware Cord consists of an electrical power strip in which the cord is designed to visualize the energy rather than hiding it. Increase and decrease in use is conveyed through showing glowing pulses, flow, and intensity of light. (b) The Waatson (now a commercial product available in many countries) measures in watts or cost how much electricity someone is using in their home at any moment. This is conveyed in LEDs on the top side. On the underside are colored lights: when they glow blue it shows you are using less than normal; when it changes to purple it indicates that your usage is average: and when it is red it indicates you are using more than normal

Source: (a) Photo taken from the Interactive Institute's research program "Static!" and reproduced with permission. (b) Reproduced with permission from DIY Kyoto Ltd. www.diykyoto.com.

Extensive research has shown that domestic energy usage can be reduced by providing households with feedback on their consumption (Froehlich *et al*, 2010). But what are the properties that make real-time feedback effective? One dimension is frequency of feedback; continuous or daily feedback of energy consumption has been found to give higher saving results than monthly feedback. Another is the type of representation used. If it is too obvious and explicit, it may be perceived as too personal, blunt, or in your face, resulting in people objecting to it. In contrast, simple representations that are more anonymous but striking and whose function is to lure people's attention may be more effective. They may encourage people to reflect more on their energy use and even promote public debate about what is represented and how it affects them. However, if a representation is too abstract and implicit, it may be attributed other meanings, such as simply being an art piece, resulting in people ignoring it. The ideal may be somewhere in between. Peer pressure can also be effective, where peers, parents, or children chide or encourage one another to turn lights off, take a shower instead of a bath, and so on.

Another influencing factor is social norms. In a study by Schultz *et al* (2007), households were shown how their energy consumption compared with their neighborhood average. Households above the average tended to decrease their consumption but those using less electricity than average tended to increase their consumption. The study found that this 'boomerang' effect could be counteracted by providing households with an emoticon along with the numerical information about their energy usage: households using less energy than average continued to do so if they received a smiley icon; households using more than average decreased their consumption more if they were given a sad icon.

In contrast to the Schultz study, where each household's energy consumption was kept private, the Tidy Street project (Bird and Rogers, 2010) that was run in Brighton in the UK created a large-scale visualization of the street's electricity usage by spraying a stenciled display on the road surface using chalk (see Figure 5.13). The public display was updated each day to represent how the average electricity usage of the street compared to the city of Brighton's average. The aim was to provide real-time feedback that all the householders and the general public could see change each day over a period of three weeks. The street graph also proved to be very effective at getting people who lived in Tidy Street to talk to each other about their electricity consumption and habits. It also encouraged them to talk with the many passers-by who walked up and down the street. The outcome was to reduce electricity consumption in the street by 15%, which was considerably more than other eco projects have been able to achieve.

Figure 5.13 Looking down at the Tidy Street public electricity graph from a bedroom window

BOX 5.4

The darker side: deceptive technology

Technology is increasingly being used to deceive people into parting with their personal details that allow Internet fraudsters to access their bank accounts and draw money from them. Authentic-looking letters, appearing to be sent from eBay, PayPal, and various leading banks, are spammed across the world, ending up in people's email boxes with messages such as 'During our regular verification of accounts, we couldn't verify your information. Please click here to update and verify your information.' Given that many people have an account with one of these corporations, there is a chance that they will be misled and unwittingly follow what is being asked of them, only to discover a few days later they are several thousand dollars worse off. Similarly, letters from supposedly super-rich individuals in far-away countries, offering a share of their assets if the recipient of the email provides them with his bank details, have been persistently spammed worldwide. While many people are becoming increasingly wary of what are known as phishing scams, there are still many vulnerable people who are gullible to such tactics. (Note: The term phishing is a play on the term fishing that refers to the sophisticated way of luring users' financial information and passwords.) Moreover, Internet fraudsters are becoming smarter and are always changing their tactics. While the art of deception is centuries old, the increasing, pervasive, and often ingenious use of the web to trick people into divulging personal information may have catastrophic effects on society. ■

5.7   Anthropomorphism and Zoomorphism

Anthropomorphism is the propensity people have to attribute human qualities to animals and objects while zoomorphism is the shaping of an object or design in animal form. For example, people sometimes talk to their computers as if they were humans, treat their robot cleaners as if they were their pets, and give all manner of cute names to their mobile devices, routers, and so on. Advertisers are well aware of these phenomena and often create human-like and animal-like characters out of inanimate objects to promote their products. For example, breakfast cereals, butter, and fruit drinks have all been transmogrified into characters with human qualities (they move, talk, have personalities, and show emotions), enticing the viewer to buy them. Children are especially susceptible to this kind of magic, as witnessed by their love of cartoons, where all manner of inanimate objects are brought to life with human-like qualities.

The finding that people, especially children, have a propensity to accept and enjoy objects that have been given human-like qualities has led many designers to capitalize on it, most notably in the design of human–computer dialogs modeled on how humans talk to each other. It is now possible to have conversations and interact with various screen characters, such as agents, tutors, and virtual pets, as if they were human.

Anthropomorphism has also been exploited in the development of computer-based cuddly toys that are embedded with various sensors. Early commercial products like ActiMates™ were designed to encourage children to learn through playing with them. Barney (a bear), for example, attempted to motivate play in children by using human-based speech and movement (Strommen, 1998). The toys were programmed to react to the child and make comments while watching TV together or working together on a computer-based task. In particular, Barney was programmed to congratulate the child whenever she produced a right answer and also to react to the content on screen with appropriate emotions, e.g. cheering at good news and expressing concern at bad news. Interactive dolls have been designed to talk, sense, and understand the world around them, using sensor-based technologies, speech recognition, and various mechanical protractors embedded in their bodies. For example, Amazing Amanda was able to exhibit a number of facial expressions to convey her feelings. If she was offered something to eat she did not want, e.g. a piece of plastic pizza embedded with an RFID tag that when placed near her mouth was read by a tag reader hidden in her neck, she would contort her face and say 'I don't want that.'

Video of Amazing Amanda in Action at **http://youtu.be/1gJA3NkmlUY**

Furnishing technologies with personalities and other human-like attributes makes them more enjoyable and fun to interact with. They can also motivate people to carry out various activities, such as learning. Being addressed in the first person (e.g. 'Hello Chris! Nice to see you again. Welcome back. Now what were we doing last time? Oh yes, exercise 5. Let's start again') is much more appealing than being addressed in the impersonal third person ('User 24, commence exercise 5'), especially for children. It can make them feel more at ease and reduce their anxiety. Similarly, interacting with screen characters like tutors and wizards can be much more pleasant than interacting with a cold dialog box or blinking cursor on a blank screen.

However, virtual agents, robots, and toys can also be patronizing and annoying in certain contexts. They also do not have the range of emotional intelligence to respond in the nuanced ways humans do with each other. Nevertheless much effort has gone into designing interface agents to be life-like, exhibiting realistic human movements, like walking and running, and having distinct personalities and traits. The design of the characters' appearance, their facial expressions, and how their lips move when talking are all considered important interface design concerns. This has included modeling various conversational mechanisms such as:

- Recognizing and responding to verbal and non-verbal input.
- Generating verbal and non-verbal output.
- Coping with breakdowns, turn-taking, and other conversational mechanisms.
- Giving signals that indicate the state of the conversation as well as contributing new suggestions for the dialog (Cassell, 2000).

ACTIVITY 5.7

A robot or a cuddly pet?

Early robot pets, such as Sony's AIBO and QRIO, were made of metal and looked like robots. In contrast, a more recent trend has been to make robot pets feel and look more like real pets by covering them in fur (e.g. squirrels, cats, rabbits) and making them behave in more cute pet-like ways. Two contrasting examples are presented in Figure 5.14. Which do you prefer and why?

Comment

Most people like stroking pets and cuddly toys and so will likely want to stroke pet robots. However, because they look and feel like the real thing some people may find them a bit creepy. A motivation for making robot pets cuddly is to enhance the emotional experience people have through using their sense of touch. For example, the Haptic Creature on the right is a robot that mimics a pet that might sit in your lap, such as a cat or a rabbit (Yohanan and MacLean, 2008). It is made up of a body, head, and two ears, as well as mechanisms that simulate breathing, a vibrating purr, and the warmth of a living creature. The robot 'detects' the way it is touched by means of an array of (roughly 60) touch sensors laid out across its whole body and an accelerometer. When the Haptic Creature is stroked, it responds accordingly, using the ears, breathing, and purring to communicate its emotional state through touch. On the other hand, the sensors are also used by the robot to detect the human's emotional state through touch. Note how the robot has no eyes, nose, or mouth. Facial expressions are the most common way humans communicate emotional states. Since the Haptic Creature communicates and senses emotional states solely through touch, the face was deliberately left off to prevent people trying to 'read' emotion from it. ■

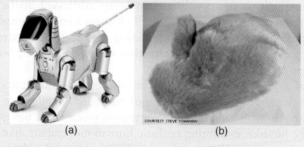

(a)   (b)

Figure 5.14 Two kinds of robot pets

Source: (a) Courtesy of Sony Corporation, (b) Reproduced with permission of Steve Yohanan. Photo: Martin Dee.

Audio of a radio show recorded in 2014 about emotions and emotional technology with interaction designers Jennifer Dunnam, Don Norman, and Elizabeth Churchill at
http://www.cbc.ca/spark/blog/2014/06/08/emotional-tech/

Assignment

This assignment requires you to write a critique of the persuasive impact of a virtual agent by considering what it would take for a virtual agent to be believable, trustworthy, and convincing.

(a) Look at a website that has a virtual assistant, e.g. Anna at Ikea.com, Jenn at Alaskaair.com and answer the following:

- What does the virtual agent do?
- What type of agent is it?
- Does it elicit an emotional response from you? If so, what kind?
- What kind of personality does it have?
- How is this expressed?
- What kinds of behavior does it exhibit?
- What are its facial expressions like?
- What is its appearance like? Is it realistic or cartoon-like?
- Where does it appear on the screen?
- How does it communicate with the user (text or speech)?
- Is the level of discourse patronizing or at the right level?
- Is the agent helpful in guiding the user towards making a purchase or finding out something?
- Is it too pushy?
- What gender is it? Do you think this makes a difference?
- Would you trust the agent to the extent that you would be happy to buy a product from it or follow its guidance? If not, why not?
- What else would it take to make the agent persuasive?

(b) Next, look at an equivalent website that does not include an agent but is based on a conceptual model of browsing, e.g. Amazon.com. How does it compare with the agent-based site you have just looked at?

- Is it easy to find information?
- What kind of mechanism does the site use to make recommendations and guide the user in making a purchase or finding out information?
- Is any kind of personalization used at the interface to make the user feel welcome or special?
- Would the site be improved by having an agent? Explain your reasons either way.

(c) Finally, discuss which site you would trust most and give your reasons for this.

Summary

This chapter has described the different ways interactive products can be designed (both deliberately and inadvertently) to make people respond in certain ways. The extent to which users will learn, buy a product online, quit a bad habit, or chat with others depends on how convincing the interface is, how comfortable they feel when using a product, or how much they can trust it. If the interactive product is frustrating to use, annoying, or patronizing, users will easily become angry and despondent, and often stop using it. If, on the other hand, the product is pleasurable, enjoyable to use, and makes people feel comfortable and at ease, then they will continue to use it, make a purchase, return to the website, or continue to learn. This chapter has described various interaction mechanisms that can be used to elicit positive emotional responses in users and ways of avoiding negative ones.

Key points

- Emotional aspects of interaction design are concerned with how to facilitate certain states (e.g. pleasure) or avoid certain reactions (e.g. frustration) in user experiences.
- Well-designed interfaces can elicit good feelings in people.
- Aesthetically pleasing interfaces can be a pleasure to use.
- Expressive interfaces can provide reassuring feedback to users as well as be informative and fun.
- Badly designed interfaces often make people frustrated, annoyed, or angry.
- Emotional technologies can be designed to persuade people to change their behaviors or attitudes.
- Anthropomorphism is the attribution of human qualities to objects.
- Virtual agents and robot pets have been developed to make people feel motivated, reassured, and in a good mood.

Further Reading

FOGG, B. J. (2003) *Persuasive Technology: Using computers to change what we think and do*. Morgan Kaufmann. This is a very readable and provocative book, explaining how a diversity of technologies can and have been designed to persuade people to change their behavior and attitudes. It presents a conceptual framework of the different types and a host of examples, together with discussing social, ethical, and credibility issues to do with using persuasive technologies.

JORDAN, P. W. (2000) *Designing Pleasurable Products*. Taylor & Francis. This book was written primarily for a product design audience to consider as part of the human factors. However, its applicability to interaction design has meant that it has become a popular book for those wanting to understand more about the relationship between usability and pleasure. It provides many illuminating case studies of the design of products, such as cars, cameras, and clocks. It also provides detailed product benefits specifications that are a form of guidance on how to design and evaluate pleasurable aspects.

LEDOUX, J. E. (1998) *The Emotional Brain: The mysterious underpinnings of emotional life*. Simon & Schuster. This book explains what causes us to feel fear, love, hate, anger, and joy and explores whether we control our emotions versus them controlling us. The book also covers the origins of human emotions and explains that many evolved to enable us to survive.

NORMAN, D. (2005) *Emotional Design: Why we love (or hate) everyday things.* Basic Books. This book is an easy read while at the same time being thought-provoking. We get to see inside Dan Norman's kitchen and learn about the design aesthetics of his collection of teapots. The book also includes essays on the emotional aspects of robots, computer games, and a host of other pleasurable interfaces.

WALTER, A. (2011) *A Book Apart: Designing for Emotion.* Zeldman, Jeffrey. This short book is targeted at web designers who want to understand how to design websites that users will enjoy and want to come back to. It covers the classic literature on emotions and proposes practical approaches to emotional web design.

Chapter 6

INTERFACES

Objectives

The main aims of this chapter are to:

- Provide an overview of the many different kinds of interfaces.
- Highlight the main design and research issues for each of the interfaces.
- Discuss the difference between graphical (GUIs) and natural user interfaces (NUIs).
- Consider which interface is best for a given application or activity.

6.1 Introduction

Until the mid-1990s, interaction designers concerned themselves largely with developing efficient and effective user interfaces for desktop computers aimed at the single user. This involved working out how best to present information on a screen such that users would be able to perform their tasks, including determining how to structure menus to make options easy to navigate, designing icons and other graphical elements to be easily recognized and distinguished from one another, and developing logical dialog boxes that are easy to fill in. Advances in graphical interfaces, speech, gesture and handwriting recognition, together with the arrival of the Internet, smartphones, wireless networks, sensor technologies, and an assortment of other new technologies providing large and small displays, have changed the face of human–computer interaction. During the last decade, designers have had many more opportunities for designing user experiences. The range of technological developments has encouraged different ways of thinking about interaction design and an expansion of research in the field. For example, innovative ways of controlling and interacting with digital information have been developed that include gesture-based, touch-based, and even brain–computer interaction. Researchers and developers have combined the physical and digital in novel ways, resulting in mixed realities, augmented realities, tangible interfaces, and wearable computing. A major thrust has been to design new interfaces that extend beyond the individual user: supporting small- and large-scale social interactions for people on the move, at home, and at work.

There is now a diversity of interfaces. The goal of this chapter is to consider how to design interfaces for different environments, people, places, and activities. We present a catalog of

20 interface types, starting with command-based and ending with brain–computer. For each one, we present an overview and outline the key research and design concerns. Some are only briefly touched upon while others – that are more established in interaction design – are described in more depth. It should be stressed that the chapter is not meant to be read from beginning to end but dipped into to find out about a particular type of interface.

6.2   Interface Types

Numerous adjectives have been used to describe the different kinds of interfaces that have been developed, including graphical, command, speech, multimodal, invisible, ambient, affective, mobile, intelligent, adaptive, smart, tangible, touchless, and natural. Some of the interface types are primarily concerned with a function (e.g. to be intelligent, to be adaptive, to be ambient, to be smart), while others focus on the interaction style used (e.g. command, graphical, multimedia), the input/output device used (e.g. pen-based, speech-based, gesture-based), or the platform being designed for (e.g. tablet, mobile, PC, wearable). Rather than cover every possible type that has been developed or described, we have chosen to select the main types that have emerged over the last 40 years. The interface types are loosely ordered in terms of when they were developed. They are numbered to make it easier to find a particular one (see Table 6.1 for complete set). It should be noted, however, that this classification is for convenience. The interface entries are not mutually exclusive since some products can appear in two categories. For example, a smartphone can be considered to have either a mobile or touch interface. Table 6.1 suggests which interfaces are related or have design issues in common.

Interface type	See also
1. Command-based	
2. WIMP and GUI	
3. Multimedia	WIMP and web
4. Virtual reality	Augmented and mixed reality
5. Information visualization and dashboards	Multimedia
6. Web	Mobile and multimedia
7. Consumer electronics and appliances	Mobile
8. Mobile	Augmented and mixed reality
9. Speech	
10. Pen	Shareable, touch
11. Touch	Shareable, air-based gesture
12. Air-based gesture	Tangible
13. Haptic	Multimodal
14. Multimodal	Speech, pen, touch, gesture, and haptic
15. Shareable	Touch
16. Tangible	
17. Augmented and mixed reality	Virtual reality
18. Wearable	
19. Robots and drones	
20. Brain–computer interaction (BCI)	

Table 6.1   The types of interfaces covered in this chapter

1. **The Sketchpad** – Ivan Sutherland (1963) describes the first interactive graphical interface
   http://youtu.be/USyoT_Ha_bA
2. **The Mother of All Demos** – Douglas Engelbart (1968) describes the first WIMP.
   http://youtu.be/yJDv-zdhzMY
3. **Put that there** (1979) – A short video from MIT demonstrating the first speech and
   gesture interface
   http://youtu.be/RyBEUyEtxQo
4. **Unveiling the genius of multi-touch interface design** – Jeff Han's TED talk (2007)
   http://youtu.be/ac0E6deG4AU
5. **Intel's Future Technology Vision** (2012)
   http://youtu.be/g_cauM3kccI

Table 6.2 A selection of classic HCI videos on the Internet that demonstrate pioneering interfaces

6.2.1   Command-Based

Early interfaces required the user to type in commands that were typically abbreviations (e.g. ls) at the prompt symbol appearing on the computer display, which the system responded to (e.g. by listing current files using a keyboard). Another way of issuing commands is through pressing certain combinations of keys (e.g. Shift + Alt + Ctrl). Some commands are also a fixed part of the keyboard, such as delete, enter, and undo, while other function keys can be programmed by the user as specific commands (e.g. F11 standing for print).

Command line interfaces have been largely superseded by graphical interfaces that incorporate commands such as menus, icons, keyboard shortcuts, and pop-up/predictable text commands as part of an application. Where command line interfaces continue to have an advantage is when users find them easier and faster to use than equivalent menu-based systems (Raskin, 2000) and for performing certain operations as part of a complex software package, such as for CAD environments, (e.g. Rhino3D and AutoCAD), to enable expert designers to be able to interact rapidly and precisely with the software. They also provide scripting for batch operations and are being increasingly used on the web, where the search bar acts as a general-purpose command line facility, e.g. www.yubnub.org. They have also been developed for visually impaired people to enable them to interact in virtual worlds, such as Second Life (see Box 6.1).

BOX 6.1

Command-based interfaces for virtual worlds

Virtual worlds such as Second Life have become popular places for learning and socializing. Unfortunately people who are visually impaired cannot join in. A command-based interface, called TextSL, was developed to enable them to participate by using a screen reader (Folmer *et al*, 2009). Commands can be issued to enable the user to move their avatar around, interact with others, and find out about the environment they are in. Figure 6.1 shows that the user has issued the command for their avatar to smile and say hello to other avatars sitting by a log fire. ■

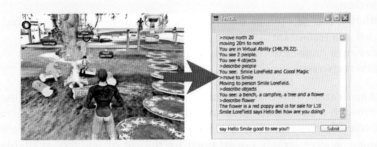

Figure 6.1 Second Life command-based interface for visually impaired users
Source: Reproduced with permission from http://www.eelke.com/images/textsl.jpg.

Research and design issues

In the 1980s, much research investigated ways of optimizing command-based interfaces. The form of the commands (e.g. use of abbreviations, full names, familiar names), syntax (e.g. how best to combine different commands), and organization (e.g. how to structure options) are examples of some of the main areas that have been investigated (Shneiderman, 1998). A further concern was which names to use as commands that would be the easiest to remember. A number of variables were tested, including how familiar users were with the chosen names. Findings from a number of studies, however, were inconclusive; some found specific names were better remembered than general ones (Barnard *et al*, 1982), others showed names selected by users themselves were preferable (e.g. Ledgard *et al*, 1981; Scapin, 1981), while yet others demonstrated that high-frequency words were better remembered than low-frequency ones (Gunther *et al*, 1986).

The most relevant design principle is consistency (see Chapter 1). The method used for labeling/naming the commands should be chosen to be as consistent as possible, e.g. always use first letters of operation when using abbreviations. ■

6.2.2 WIMP and GUI

The Xerox Star interface (described in Chapter 2) led to the birth of the WIMP and subsequently the GUI, opening up new possibilities for users to interact with a system and for information to be presented and represented at the interface. Specifically, new ways of visually designing the interface became possible, which included the use of color, typography, and imagery (Mullet and Sano, 1995). The original WIMP comprises:

- Windows (that could be scrolled, stretched, overlapped, opened, closed, and moved around the screen using the mouse).
- Icons (to represent applications, objects, commands, and tools that were opened or activated when clicked on).
- Menus (offering lists of options that could be scrolled through and selected in the way a menu is used in a restaurant).
- Pointing device (a mouse controlling the cursor as a point of entry to the windows, menus, and icons on the screen).

The first generation of WIMP interfaces was primarily boxy in design; user interaction took place through a combination of windows, scroll bars, checkboxes, panels, palettes, and dialog boxes that appeared on the screen in various forms (see Figure 6.2). Application programmers were largely constrained by the set of widgets available to them, of which the dialog box was most prominent. (A widget is a standardized display representation of a control, like a button or scroll bar, that can be manipulated by the user.) The challenge for software developers today is to design GUIs that are best suited for tablet, smartphone, and smartwatch interfaces. Instead of using a mouse and keyboard as input,

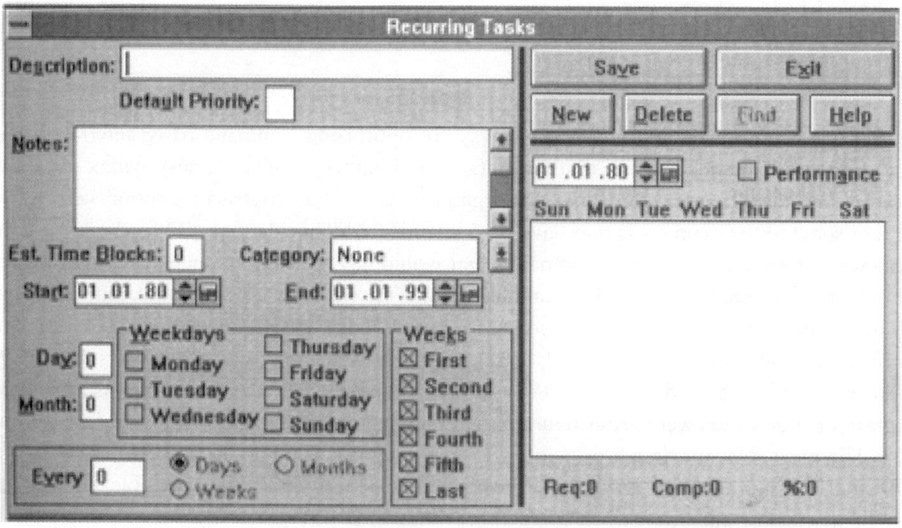

Figure 6.2 The boxy look of the first generation of GUIs. The window presents several check boxes, notes boxes, and options as square buttons

Source: Mullet, Kevin; Sano, Darrell, *Designing Visual Interfaces: Communication Oriented Techniques*, 1st, © 1995. Reproduced by permission of Pearson Education, Inc., Upper Saddle River, New Jersey.

the default for most users is to swipe and touch using a single finger when browsing and interacting with digital content (for more on this see sections on touch and mobile interfaces).

The basic building blocks of the WIMP are still part of the modern GUI used as part of a computer display, but have evolved into a number of different forms and types. For example, there are now many different types of icons and menus, including audio icons and audio menus, 3D animated icons, and 2D icon-based menus. Windows have also greatly expanded in terms of how they are used and what they are used for; for example, a variety of dialog boxes, interactive forms, and feedback/error message boxes have become pervasive. In addition, a number of graphical elements that were not part of the WIMP interface have been incorporated into the GUI. These include toolbars and docks (a row or column of available applications and icons of other objects such as open files) and rollovers (where text labels appear next to an icon or part of the screen as the mouse is rolled over it). Here, we give an overview of the design issues concerning the basic building blocks of the WIMP/GUI: windows, menus, and icons.

Window design. Windows were invented to overcome the physical constraints of a computer display, enabling more information to be viewed and tasks to be performed at the same screen. Multiple windows can be opened at any one time, e.g. web pages and word processor documents, enabling the user to switch between them when needing to look or work on different documents, files, and applications. Scrolling bars within windows also enable more information to be viewed than is possible on one screen. Scroll bars can be placed vertically and horizontally in windows to enable upwards, downwards, and sideways movements through a document.

One of the disadvantages of having multiple windows open is that it can be difficult to find specific ones. Various techniques have been developed to help users locate a particular window, a common one being to provide a list as part of an application menu. Mac OS also provides a function that shrinks all windows that are open so they can be seen side by side on one screen. The user needs only to press one function key and then move the cursor over each one to see what they are called. This technique enables users to see at a glance what they have in their workspace and also enables them to easily select one to come to the forefront. Another option is to display all the windows open for a particular application, e.g. Word. The web browser, Safari, has an option of showing 12 shrunken web pages that you have recently visited (history) or most commonly visited (top sites) as a window pane that enables quick scanning (see Figure 6.3).

A particular kind of window that is commonly used in GUIs is the dialog box. Confirmations, error messages, checklists, and forms are presented through them. Information in the dialog boxes is often designed to guide user interaction, with the user following the sequence of options provided. Examples include a sequenced series of forms (i.e. Wizards) presenting the necessary and optional choices that need to be filled in when choosing a PowerPoint presentation or an Excel spreadsheet. The downside of this style of interaction is that there can be a tendency to cram too much information or data entry fields into one box, making the interface confusing, crowded, and difficult to read (Mullet and Sano, 1995).

Figure 6.3 A window management technique provided in Safari: pressing the 4 × 3 icon in the top left corner of the bookmarks bar displays the 12 top sites visited, by shrinking them and placing them side by side. This enables the user to see them all at a glance and be able to rapidly switch between them

BOX 6.2

The joys of filling in forms on the web

For many of us, shopping on the Internet is generally an enjoyable experience. For example, choosing a book on Amazon or flowers from Interflora can be done at our leisure and convenience. The part we don't enjoy, however, is filling in the online form to give the company the necessary details to pay for the selected items. This can often be a frustrating and time-consuming experience. It starts with having to create an account and a new password. Once past this hurdle, a new interactive form pops up for the delivery address and credit card details. The standard online form has a fixed format, making it cumbersome and annoying to fill in, especially for people whose address does not fit within its constraints. Typically, boxes are provided (asterisked for where they must be filled in) for: address line 1 and address line 2, providing no extra lines for addresses that have more than two lines; a line for the town/city; and a line for the zip code (if the site is based in the USA) or other postal code (if based in another country). The format for the codes is different, making it difficult for non-US residents (and US residents for other country sites) to fill in this part. Further boxes are provided for home, work, and cell phone number, and email address (is it really necessary to provide all of these?) and credit card type, name of the owner, and credit card number.

One of the biggest gripes about online registration forms is the country of residence box that opens up as a never-ending menu, listing all of the countries in the world in alphabetical order. Instead of typing in the country they live in, users are forced to select the one they are from, which is fine if they happen to live in Australia or Austria but not if they live in Venezuela or Zambia. Some menus place the host site country first, but this can be easily overlooked if the user is primed to look for the letter of their country (see Figure 6.4).

Figure 6.4 A scrolling menu

Source: Screenshot of Camino browser, ©The Camino Project.

This is an example of where the design principle of recognition over recall (see Chapter 3) does not apply and where the converse is true. A better design might be to have a predictive text option, where users need only to type in the first two or so letters of the country they are from to cause a narrowed-down list of choices to appear that they can then select from at the interface. ∎

ACTIVITY 6.1

Go to the Interflora site (known as FTD in the US) and click on the international delivery option (its location varies across countries). How are the countries ordered? Is it an improvement to the scrolling pop-up menu?

Comment

Earlier versions such as shown in Figure 6.4 for interflora.co.uk listed eight countries at the top starting with the United Kingdom, then the USA, France, Germany, Italy, Switzerland, Austria, and Spain. This was followed by the remaining set of countries listed in alphabetical order. The reason for having this particular ordering is likely to have been because the top eight are the countries that have most customers, with the UK residents using the service the most. The website has changed to using a table format, grouping all the countries in alphabetical order using four columns across the page (see Figure 6.5). Do you think this is an improvement? It took me about 8 seconds to select Ireland, having overshot the target the

(Continued)

F	G	H	I	J
Fiji	Gabon	Haiti	Iceland	Jamaica
Finland	Germany	Holland	India	Japan
France	Gibraltar	Honduras	Indonesia	Jordan
French Guyana	Greece	Hong Kong	Iran	
French Polynesia	Greenland	Hungary	Ireland	
	Guadeloupe		Israel	
	Guam		Italy	
	Guatemala		Ivory Coast	

Figure 6.5 An excerpt of the listing of countries in alphabetical order from interflora.co.uk
Source: www.interflora.co.uk. Reproduced with permission.

first time I scrolled through, and 4 seconds to scroll through the more recent table using the web browser scroll bar. The use of letter headings and shading also makes searching quicker. In the US version they are simply listed alphabetically in four columns but using a tiny font that is hard to read. ∎

Research and design issues

A key research concern is window management – finding ways of enabling users to move fluidly between different windows (and monitors) and to be able to rapidly switch their attention between them to find the information they need or to work on the document/task within each of them – without getting distracted. Studies of how people use windows and multiple monitors have shown that window activation time (i.e. the time a window is open and interacted with) is relatively short, an average of 20 seconds, suggesting that people switch frequently between different documents and applications (Hutchings *et al*, 2004). Widgets like the taskbar and Jump List (see Figure 6.8) in the Windows environment are used as the main method of switching between windows.

To increase the legibility and ease of use of information presented in windows, the design principles of spacing, grouping, and simplicity should be used (discussed in Chapter 3). An early overview of window interfaces – that is still highly relevant today – is Myers's taxonomy of window manager interfaces (Myers, 1988). ∎

Menu design. Just like restaurant menus, interface menus offer users a structured way of choosing from the available set of options. Headings are used as part of the menu to make it easier for the user to scan through them and find what they want. Figure 6.6 presents two different styles of restaurant menu, designed to appeal to different cultures: Jamie's Italian one is organized into a number of categories including antipasti and sides, pasta, mains, and desserts, while the Japanese is presented in sequential categories: sushi and sashimi, sushi

(a)

(b)

Figure 6.6 Two different menu layouts

Source: (a) http://www.jamieoliver.com/italian/menu
(b) http://www.tonysasianfusion.com/japanesemenu.html.

entrée, Japanese entrée platters, and Asian fusion chef speciality. Jamie's Italian menu uses enticing images to depict each category, while the Japanese menu uses a combination of text descriptions for the different choices and one photo of a representative dish for each category. Jamie's Italian requires you to select a category to find out more about the dishes available and their price, whereas the Japanese provides all the information you need to know to make an order.

Interface menu designs have employed similar methods of categorizing and illustrating options available that have been adapted to the medium of the GUI. A difference is that interface menus are typically ordered across the top row or down the side of a screen using category headers as part of a menu bar. The contents of the menus are also for the large part invisible, only dropping down when the header is selected or rolled over with a mouse. The various options under each menu are typically ordered from top to bottom in terms of most frequently used options and grouped in terms of their similarity with one another, e.g. all formatting commands are placed together.

There are numerous menu interface styles, including flat lists, drop-down, pop-up, contextual, and expanding ones, e.g. scrolling and cascading. Flat menus are good at displaying a small number of options at the same time or where the size of the display is small, e.g. cell phones, cameras, MP3 players, smartwatches. However, they often have to nest the lists of options within each, requiring several steps to be taken by a user to get to the list with the desired option. Once deep down in a nested menu, the user then has to take the same number of steps to get back to the top of the menu. Moving through previous screens can be tedious.

Expanding menus enable more options to be shown on a single screen than is possible with a single flat menu list. This makes navigation more flexible, allowing for the selection of options to be done in the same window. However, as highlighted in Figure 6.4 it can be frustrating having to scroll through tens or even hundreds of options. To improve navigation through scrolling menus, a number of novel controls have been devised. For example, the original iPod provided a physical scrollpad that allows for clockwise and anti-clockwise movement, enabling long lists of tunes or artists to be rapidly scrolled through.

The most common type of expanding menu used as part of the PC interface is the cascading one (see Figure 6.7), which provides secondary and even tertiary menus to appear alongside the primary active drop-down menu, enabling further related options to be selected, e.g. selecting track changes from the tools menu leads to a secondary menu of three options by which to track changes in a Word document. The downside of using expanding menus, however, is that they require precise mouse control. Users can often end up making errors, namely overshooting or selecting the wrong options. In particular, cascading menus require users to move their mouse over the menu item, while holding the mouse pad or button down, and then when the cascading menu appears on the screen to move their cursor over to the next menu list and select the desired option. Most of us have experienced the frustration of under- or over-shooting a menu option that leads to the desired cascading menu and worse, losing it as we try to maneuver the mouse onto the secondary or tertiary menu. It is even worse for people who have poor motor control and find controlling a mouse difficult. Menus that are interacted with on smart TVs can also be difficult to navigate because the user has to use a remote button while sitting several feet away from the screen.

Figure 6.7 A cascading menu

It is easy to overshoot a letter when trying to type the name of a movie in a search box. Contextual menus provide access to often-used commands associated with a particular item, e.g. an icon. They provide appropriate commands that make sense in the context of a current task. They appear when the user presses the Control key while clicking on an interface element. For example, clicking on a photo in a website together with holding down the Control key results in a small set of relevant menu options appearing in an overlapping window, such as open it in a new window, save it, or copy it. The advantage of contextual menus is that they provide a limited number of options associated with an interface element, overcoming some of the navigation problems associated with cascading and expanding menus. Figure 6.8 shows another kind of contextual window that jumps up as a list.

Figure 6.8 Windows jump list
Source: http://windows.microsoft.com/en-US/windows7/products/features/jump-lists.

ACTIVITY 6.2

Open an application that you use frequently (e.g. word processor, email, web browser) on a PC/laptop or tablet and look at the menu header names (but do not open them just yet). For each one (e.g. File, Edit, Tools) write down what options you think are listed under each. Then look at the contents under each header. How many options were you able to remember and how many did you put in the wrong category? Now try to select the correct menu header for the following options (assuming they are included in the application): replace, save, spelling, and sort. Did you select the correct header each time or did you have to browse through a number of them?

Comment

Popular everyday applications, like word processors, have grown enormously in terms of the functions they now offer. The current version of Microsoft Word, for example, has 12 menu headers and 18 toolbars. Under each menu header there are on average 15 options, some of which are hidden under subheadings and only appear when they are rolled over with the mouse. Likewise, for each toolbar there is a set of tools that is available, be it for drawing, formatting, web, table, or borders. Remembering the location of frequently used commands like spelling and replace is often achieved by remembering their spatial location. For infrequently used commands, like sorting a list of references into alphabetical order, users can spend time flicking through the menus to find the command sort. It is difficult to remember that the command 'sort' should be under the table heading since what they are doing is not a table operation but using a tool to organize a section of their document. It would be more intuitive if the command was under the tool header along with similar tools like spelling. What this example illustrates is just how difficult it can be to group menu options into clearly defined and obvious categories. Some fit into several categories, while it can be difficult to group others. The placement of options in menus can also change between different versions of an application as more functions are added. ■

Research and design issues

Similar to command names, it is important to decide which are the best terms to use for menu options. Short phrases like 'bring all to front' can be more informative than single words like 'front.' However, the space for listing menu items is often restricted, such that menu names need to be short. They also need to be distinguishable, i.e. not easily confused with one another so that the user does not choose the wrong one by mistake. Operations such as quit and save should also be clearly separated to avoid the accidental loss of work.

The choice of which type of menu to use will often be determined by the application and type of system. Which is best will depend on the number of options that are on offer and the size of the display to present them in. Flat menus are best for displaying a small number of options at one time, while expanding menus are good for showing a large number of options, such as those available in file and document creation/editing applications. ■

Icon design. The appearance of icons at the interface came about following the Xerox Star project. They were used to represent objects as part of the desktop metaphor, namely folders, documents, trashcans, and in- and out-trays. An assumption behind using icons instead of text labels is that they are easier to learn and remember, especially for non-expert computer users. They can also be designed to be compact and variably positioned on a screen.

Icons have become a pervasive feature of the interface. They now populate every application and operating system, and are used for all manner of functions besides representing desktop objects. These include depicting tools (e.g. paintbrush), applications (e.g. web browser), and a diversity of abstract operations (e.g. cut, paste, next, accept, change). They have also gone through many changes in their look and feel: black and white, color, shadowing, photorealistic images, 3D rendering, and animation have all been used.

While there was a period from the late 1980s into the early 1990s when it was easy to find poorly designed icons at the interface (see Figure 6.9), icon design has now come of age. Interface icons look quite different; many have been designed to be very detailed and animated, making them both visually attractive and informative. The result is the design of GUIs that are highly inviting and emotionally appealing, and that feel alive. For example, Figure 6.10

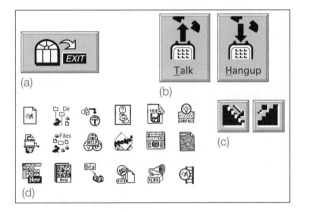

Figure 6.9 Poor icon set from the early 1990s. What do you think they mean and why are they so bad?

Source: K. Mullet and D. Sano: "Designing Visual Interfaces" Pearson 1995, reproduced with permission of Pearson Education.

Figure 6.10 Early and more recent Mac icon designs for the TextEdit application

contrasts the simple and jaggy Mac icon designs of the early 1990s with those that were developed as part of the Aqua range for Mac OS X. Whereas early icon designers were constrained by the graphical display technology of the day, they now have more flexibility. For example, the use of anti-aliasing techniques enables curves and non-rectilinear lines to be drawn, enabling more photo-illustrative styles to be developed (anti-aliasing means adding pixels around a jagged border of an object to visually smooth its outline).

Icons can be designed to represent objects and operations at the interface using concrete objects and/or abstract symbols. The mapping between the representation and underlying referent can be similar (e.g. a picture of a file to represent the object file), analogical (e.g. a picture of a pair of scissors to represent cut), or arbitrary (e.g. the use of an X to represent delete). The most effective icons are generally those that are isomorphic since they have direct mapping between what is being represented and how it is represented. Many operations at the interface, however, are of actions to be performed on objects, making it more difficult to represent them using direct mapping. Instead, an effective technique is to use a combination of objects and symbols that capture the salient part of an action through using analogy, association, or convention (Rogers, 1989). For example, using a picture of a pair of scissors to represent cut in a word-processing application provides sufficient clues as long as the user understands the convention of cut for deleting text.

The greater flexibility offered by current GUI interfaces has enabled developers to create icon sets that are distinguishable, identifiable, and memorable. For example, different graphical genres have been used to group and identify different categories of icons. Figure 6.11 shows how colorful photo-realistic images have been used, each slanting slightly to the left, for the category of *user* applications (e.g. email) whereas monochrome straight on and simple images have been used for the class of *utility* applications (e.g. printer setup). The former have a fun feel to them, whereas the latter have a more serious look about them.

Another approach that many smartphone designers use is flat 2D icons. These are very simple and use strong colors and pictograms or symbols. The effect is to make them easily recognizable and distinctive. Examples shown in Figure 6.12 include the white ghost on a yellow background (Snapchat), a white line bubble with a solid white phone handset on a lime-green background (WhatsApp), and the sun next to a cloud (weather).

Icons that appear in toolbars or palettes as part of an application or presented on small device displays (e.g. digital cameras, smartwatches) have much less screen real estate

Figure 6.11 Contrasting genres of Aqua icons used for the Mac. The top row of icons have been designed for user applications and the bottom row for utility applications

Figure 6.12 Flat 2D icons designed for smartphone apps

available. Because of this, they have been designed to be simple, emphasizing the outline form of an object or symbol and using only grayscale or one or two colors. They tend to convey the tool and action performed on them using a combination of concrete objects and abstract symbols, e.g. a blank piece of paper with a plus sign representing a new blank document, an open envelope with an arrow coming out of it indicating a new message has arrived.

ACTIVITY 6.3

Sketch simple icons to represent the following operations to appear on a digital camera screen:

- Turn image 90 degrees sideways.
- Auto-enhance the image.
- Fix red-eye.
- Crop the image.

Show them to someone else, tell them that they are icons for a new digital camera intended to be really simple to use, and see if they can understand what each represents.

Comment
Figure 6.13 shows the basic Edit Photo icons on an iPhone that appear at the bottom of the screen when a user selects the edit function. The box with an arrow represents 'move image 90 degrees to the side', the wand means 'auto-enhance', the three overlapping translucent circles represent 'different lenses' that can be used, the eye with a line through it represents the red-eye function, and the square with extended lines is the icon for cropping an image. A key design issue is to make the icons easy to recognize and be distinctive from one another. ∎

(*Continued*)

Figure 6.13 The basic Edit Photo icons that appear on an iPhone

Research and design issues

There are many icon libraries available that developers can download for free. Various online tutorials and books on how to design icons are also available (e.g. Hicks, 2012) together with sets of proprietary guidelines and style guides. For example, Apple provides its developers with style guides, explaining why certain designs are preferable to others and how to design icon sets. On its developers' website (developer.apple.com), advice is given on how and why certain graphical elements should be used when developing different types of icon. Among the various guidelines, it suggests that different categories of application (e.g. user, utility) should be represented by a different genre and recommends displaying a tool to communicate the nature of a task, e.g. a magnifying glass for searching, a camera for a photo editing tool. Microsoft also provides extensive guidance and step-by-step procedures on how to design icons for its applications on its website.

To help disambiguate the meaning of icons, text labels can be used under, above, or to the side of their icons. This method is effective for toolbars that have small icon sets, e.g. those appearing as part of a web browser, but is not as good for applications that have large icon sets, e.g. photo editing or word processing, since the screen can get very cluttered and busy making it sometimes harder and longer to find an icon. To prevent text/icon clutter at the interface, a rollover function can be used, where a text label appears adjacent to or above an icon after one second of the user holding the cursor over it and for as long as the user keeps the cursor on it. This method allows identifying information to be temporarily displayed when needed. ■

6.2.3   Multimedia

Multimedia, as the name implies, combines different media within a single interface, namely, graphics, text, video, sound, and animations, and links them with various forms of interactivity. It differs from previous forms of combined media, e.g. TV, in that the different media are interactive (Chapman and Chapman, 2004). Users can click on hotspots or links in an image or text appearing on one screen that leads them to another part of the program where, say, an animation or a video clip is played. From there they can return to where they were previously or move on to another place.

Many multimedia narratives and games have been developed that are designed to encourage users to explore different parts of the game or story by clicking on different parts of the screen. An assumption is that a combination of media and interactivity can provide better ways of presenting information than can either one alone. There is a general belief that more is more and the whole is greater than the sum of the parts (Lopuck, 1996). In addition, the added value assumed from being able to interact with multimedia in ways not possible with single media (i.e. books, audio, video) is easier learning, better understanding, more engagement, and more pleasure (see Scaife and Rogers, 1996).

One of the distinctive features of multimedia is its ability to facilitate rapid access to multiple representations of information. Many multimedia encyclopedias and digital libraries have been designed based on this multiplicity principle, providing an assortment of audio and visual materials on a given topic. For example, if you want to find out about the heart, a typical multimedia-based encyclopedia will provide you with:

- One or two video clips of a real live heart pumping and possibly a heart transplant operation.
- Audio recordings of the heart beating and perhaps an eminent physician talking about the cause of heart disease.
- Static diagrams and animations of the circulatory system, sometimes with narration.
- Several columns of hypertext, describing the structure and function of the heart.

Hands-on interactive simulations have also been incorporated as part of multimedia learning environments. An early example was the Cardiac Tutor, developed to teach students about cardiac resuscitation, that required students to save patients by selecting the correct

Figure 6.14 Screen dump from the multimedia environment BioBLAST
Source: Screenshot from BioBlast, ©Wheeling Jesuit University.

set of procedures in the correct order from various options displayed on the computer screen (Eliot and Woolf, 1994). Several educational websites now provide multimedia educational content. For example, NASA has a multimedia section that provides simulation models based on their research to enable students to develop and test their own designs for a life support system for use on the Moon (see Figure 6.14). The learning environment provides a range of simulators that are combined with online resources.

Multimedia has largely been developed for training, educational, and entertainment purposes. It is generally assumed that learning (e.g. reading and scientific inquiry skills) and playing can be enhanced through interacting with engaging multimedia interfaces. But what actually happens when users are given unlimited, easy access to multiple media and simulations? Do they systematically switch between the various media and 'read' all the multiple representations on a particular subject? Or, are they more selective in what they look at and listen to?

ACTIVITY 6.4

Watch the video of Don Norman appearing in his first multimedia CD-ROM book (1994), where he pops up every now and again in boxes or at the side of the page to illustrate the points being discussed on that page: http://vimeo.com/18687931

What do you think should be included in a modern-day interactive e-textbook? Do you think that as e-textbooks replace paper-based books, students will be tempted to jump to the interactivities – watching the videos, listening to the audios, doing the quizzes, and playing the animations – and maybe not even reading the text?

Comment

Anyone who has interacted with educational multimedia knows just how tempting it is to play the video clips and animations, while skimming through accompanying text or static diagrams. The former are dynamic, easy and enjoyable to watch, while the latter are viewed as static, boring, and difficult to read from the screen. For example, in an evaluation of Voyager's "First Person: Donald Norman, Defending Human Attributes in the Age of the Machine", students consistently admitted to ignoring the text at the interface in search of clickable icons of the author, which when selected would present an animated video of him explaining some aspect of design (Rogers and Aldrich, 1996). Given the choice to explore multimedia material in numerous ways, ironically, users tend to be highly selective as to what they actually attend to, adopting a channel-hopping mode of interaction. While enabling the users to select for themselves the information they want to view or features to explore, there is the danger that multimedia environments may in fact promote fragmented interactions where only part of the media is ever viewed. This may be acceptable for certain kinds of activities, e.g. browsing, but less optimal for others, e.g. learning about a topic. One way to encourage more systematic and extensive interactions (when it is considered important for the activity at hand) is to require certain activities to be completed that entail the reading of accompanying text, before the user is allowed to move on to the next level or task. ■

BOX 6.3

Accessible interactive TV services for all

TV now provides many digital channels, of which sports, news, and movie channels are very popular. In addition, a range of interactive TV services are being offered that enable users to browse the web, customize their viewing choices, play interactive games, do their banking and shopping, and take an active part in a number of broadcast shows, e.g. voting. Besides offering a wide diversity of choices to the general public, there is much potential for empowering disabled and elderly users, by enabling them to access the services from the comfort of their own armchair. But it requires a sensitivity to interactive design, taking into account specific usability issues for those with impaired motor control, poor vision, and hearing difficulties (Newell, 2003). For example, remote controls need to be designed that can be manipulated with poor dexterity, text/icons need to be readable for those with poor eyesight, while navigation methods need to be straightforward for viewers who are not experienced with multimedia-based interfaces. ■

Research and design issues

A key research question is how to design multimedia to help users explore, keep track of, and integrate the multiple representations of information provided, be it a digital library, a game, or learning material. As mentioned above, one technique is to provide hands-on interactivities and simulations at the interface that require the user to complete a task, solve a problem, or explore different aspects of a topic. Specific examples include electronic notebooks that are integrated as part of the interface, where users can copy, download, or type in their own material; multiple-choice quizzes that give feedback about how well the user has done; interactive puzzles where the user has to select and position different pieces in the right combination; and simulation-type games where the user has to follow a set of procedures to achieve some goal for a given scenario. Another approach is to employ dynalinking, where information depicted in one window explicitly changes in relation to what happens in another. This can help users keep track of multiple representations and see the relationship between them (Scaife and Rogers, 1996).

Specific guidelines are available that recommend how best to combine multiple media in relation to different kinds of task, e.g. when to use audio with graphics, sound with animations, and so on for different learning tasks. For example, Alty (1991) suggests that audio information is good for stimulating imagination, movies for action information, text for conveying details, whilst diagrams are good at conveying ideas. From such generalizations it is possible to devise a presentation strategy for learning. This can be along the lines of: first, stimulate the imagination through playing an audio clip; then, present an idea in diagrammatic form; then, display further details about the concept through hypertext. ■

6.2.4 Virtual Reality

Virtual reality (VR) uses computer-generated graphical simulations to create "the illusion of participation in a synthetic environment rather than external observation of such an environment" (Gigante, 1993, p. 3). VR is a generic term that refers to the experience of interacting with an artificial environment, which makes it feel virtually real. The term virtual environment (VE) is used more specifically to describe what has been generated using computer technology (although both terms are used interchangeably). Images are displayed stereoscopically to the users – most commonly through shutter glasses – and objects within the field of vision can be interacted with via an input device like a joystick. The 3D graphics can be projected onto CAVE (Cave Automatic Virtual Environment) floor and wall surfaces, desktops, 3D TV, or large shared displays, e.g. IMAX screens. An early example of VR was the Virtual Zoo project. Allison *et al* (1997) found that people were highly engaged and very much enjoyed the experience of adopting the role of a gorilla, navigating the environment, and watching other gorillas respond to their movements and presence.

One of the main attractions of VR is that it can provide opportunities for new kinds of immersive experience, enabling users to interact with objects and navigate in 3D space in ways not possible in the physical world or a 2D graphical interface. The resulting user experience can be highly engaging; it can feel as if one really is flying around a virtual world. People can become completely absorbed by the experience (Kalawsky, 1993). The sense of presence can make the virtual setting seem convincing. By presence is meant "a state of consciousness, the (psychological) sense of being in the virtual environment" (Slater and Wilbur, 1997, p. 605), where someone behaves in a similar way to how they would if at an equivalent real event.

One of the advantages of VR is that simulations of the world can be constructed to have a higher level of fidelity with the objects they represent compared with other forms of graphical interface, e.g. multimedia. The illusion afforded by the technology can make virtual objects appear to be very life-like and behave according to the laws of physics. For example, landing and take-off terrains developed for flight simulators can appear to be very realistic. Moreover, it is assumed that learning and training applications can be improved through having a greater fidelity with the represented world.

Another distinguishing feature of VR is the different viewpoints it can offer. Players can have a first-person perspective, where their view of the game or environment is through their own eyes, or a third-person perspective, where they see the world through an avatar visually represented on the screen. An example of a first-person perspective is that experienced in first-person shooter games such as DOOM, where the player moves through the environment without seeing a representation of themselves. It requires the user to imagine what he might look like and decide how best to move around. An example of a third-person perspective is that experienced in Tomb Raider, where the player sees the virtual world above and behind the avatar of Lara Croft. The user controls Lara's interactions with the environment by controlling her movements, e.g. making her jump, run, or crouch. Avatars can be represented from behind or from the front, depending on how the user controls its movements. First-person perspectives are typically used for flying/driving simulations and games, e.g. car racing, where it is important to have direct and immediate control to steer the virtual vehicle. Third-person perspectives are more commonly used in games, learning environments, and simulations, where it is important to see a representation of self with respect to the environment and others in it. In some virtual environments it is possible to switch between the two perspectives, enabling the user to experience different viewpoints on the same game or training environment.

Early VR was developed using head-mounted displays. However, they were found to be uncomfortable to wear, sometimes causing motion sickness and disorientation. They were also expensive and difficult to program and maintain. VR technology has advanced considerably since the 1990s, with more affordable and comfortable VR headsets (e.g. Oculus Rift) that have more accurate head tracking that allows developers to create more compelling games, movies, and virtual environments (see Figure 4.10).

3D software toolkits are also available that make it much easier to program a virtual environment, e.g. Alice (www.alice.org/). Instead of moving in a physical space with a head-mounted display, users interact with a desktop virtual environment – as they would any other desktop application – using mice, keyboards, or joysticks as input devices. The desktop virtual environment can also be programmed to present a more realistic 3D effect (similar to that achieved in 3D movies shown at IMAX cinemas), requiring users to wear a pair of shutter glasses.

Research and design issues

VR has been developed to support learning and training for numerous skills. Researchers have designed applications to help people learn to drive a vehicle, fly a plane, and perform delicate surgical operations – where it is very expensive and potentially dangerous to start learning with the real thing. Others have investigated whether people can learn to find their way around a real building/place before visiting it by first navigating a virtual representation of it, e.g. Gabrielli *et al* (2000). VEs have also been designed to help people practice social and speaking skills, and confront their social phobias, e.g. Cobb *et al* (2002) and Slater *et al* (1999). An underlying assumption is that the environment can be designed as a safe place to help people gently overcome their fears (e.g. spiders, talking in public) by confronting them through different levels of closeness and unpleasantness (e.g. seeing a small virtual spider move far away, seeing a medium one sitting nearby, and then finally touching a large one). Studies have shown that people can readily suspend their disbelief, imagining a virtual spider to be a real one or a virtual audience to be a real audience. For example, Slater *et al* (1999) found that people rated themselves as being less anxious after speaking to a virtual audience that was programmed to respond to them in a positive fashion than after speaking to virtual audiences programmed to respond to them negatively.

Core design issues that need to be considered when developing virtual environments are: how to prevent users experiencing nausea; determining the most effective ways of enabling users to navigate through them, e.g. first versus third person; how to control their interactions and movements, e.g. use of head and body movements; how best to enable them to interact with information in them, e.g. use of keypads, pointing, joystick buttons; and how to enable users to collaborate and communicate with others in the virtual environment. A central concern is the level of realism to aim for. Is it necessary to design avatars and the environments they inhabit to be life-like, using rich graphics, or can simpler and more abstract forms be used, but which nonetheless are equally capable of engendering a sense of presence? For more on this topic see the dilemma box below. ■

DILEMMA

Realism versus abstraction?

One of the challenges facing interaction designers is whether to use realism or abstraction when designing an interface. This means designing objects either to (i) give the illusion of behaving and looking like real-world counterparts or (ii) appear as abstractions of the objects being represented. This concern is particularly relevant when implementing conceptual models that are deliberately based on an analogy with some aspect of the real world.

For example, is it preferable to design a desktop to look like a real desktop, a virtual house to look like a real house, or a virtual terrain to look like a real terrain? Or, alternatively, is it more effective to design representations as simple abstract renditions, depicting only a few salient features?

One of the main benefits of using realism at the interface is that it can enable people to feel more comfortable when first learning an application. The rationale behind this is that such representations can readily tap into people's understanding of the physical world. Hence, realistic interfaces can help users initially understand the underlying conceptual model. In contrast, overly schematic and abstract representations can appear to be off-putting to the newcomer. The advantage of more abstract interfaces, however, is that they can be more efficient to use. Furthermore, the more experienced users become, the more they may find comfortable interfaces no longer to their liking. A dilemma facing designers, therefore, is deciding between creating interfaces to make novice users feel comfortable (but experienced users are less comfortable) and designing interfaces to be effective for more experienced users (but maybe harder to learn by novices).

Mullet and Sano (1995) pointed out how early 3D graphical renditions of objects such as a desk suffered from both an unnatural point of view and an awkward rendering style. One reason for this is that these kinds of 3D depictions conflict with the effective use of display space, especially when 2D editing tasks need to be performed. As can be seen in Figure 6.15, these kinds of task were represented as flat buttons that appear to be floating in front of the desk, e.g. mail, program manager, task manager.

Figure 6.15 Magic Cap's 3D desktop interface
Source: Reprinted by permission of General Magic Inc.

For certain kinds of applications, using realism can be very effective for both novices and experienced users. Computer-based games fall into this category, especially those where users have to react rapidly to dynamic events that happen in a virtual world in real time, say flying a plane or playing a game of virtual football. Making the characters in the game resemble humans in the way they look, move, dress, and behave also makes them seem more convincing and lifelike, enhancing the enjoyment and fun factor. ■

ACTIVITY 6.5

Many games have been ported from the PC platform to cell and smartphones. Because of the screen size, however, they tend to be simpler and sometimes more abstract. To what extent does this adaptation of the interface affect the experience of playing the same game?

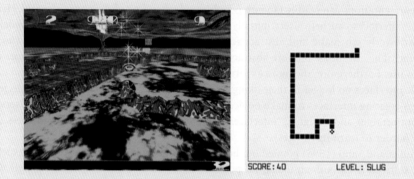

SCORE: 40   LEVEL: SLUG

Figure 6.16 Two screenshots from the game Snake – the one on the left is played on a PC and the one on the right on a cell phone. In both games, the goal is to move the snake (the blue thing and the black squares, respectively) towards targets that pop up on the screen (e.g. the bridge, the star) and to avoid obstacles (e.g. a flower, the end of the snake's tail). When a player successfully moves his snake head over or under a target, the snake increases its length by one blob or block. The longer the snake gets, the harder it is to avoid obstacles. If the snake hits an obstacle, the game is over. On the PC version there are lots of extra features that make the game more complicated, including more obstacles and ways of moving. The cell phone version has a simple 2D bird's eye representation, whereas the PC version adopts a 3D third-person avatar perspective

Comment

The most effective games that have been ported over to the cell and smartphone are highly addictive games that use simple graphics and do not require the user to navigate between different windows. Examples are Snake (see Figure 6.16), Tetris, and Snood, where the goal of the game is to move an object (e.g. a snake, abstract shapes, a shooter) small distances in order to eat food, fill a container, or delete shapes. More complex games like World of Warcraft – which are very popular on the PC platform – would not port over nearly as well. It is simply too difficult to navigate and engage in the same level of interaction that makes the game enjoyable and addictive when played on a PC. ■

6.2.5　Information Visualization and Dashboards

Information visualizations (infoviz) are computer-generated graphics of complex data that are typically interactive and dynamic. The goal is to amplify human cognition, enabling users to see patterns, trends, and anomalies in the visualization and from this to gain insight (Card *et al*, 1999). Specific objectives are to enhance discovery, decision-making, and explanation of phenomena. Most interactive visualizations have been developed for use by experts to enable them to understand and make sense of vast amounts of dynamically changing domain data or information, e.g. satellite images or research findings, that take much longer to achieve if using only text-based information.

Common techniques that are used for depicting information and data are 3D interactive maps that can be zoomed in and out of and which present data via webs, trees, clusters, scatterplot diagrams, and interconnected nodes (Bederson and Shneiderman, 2003; Chen, 2004). Hierarchical and networked structures, color, labeling, tiling, and stacking are also used to convey different features and their spatial relationships. Figure 6.17 shows a typical treemap, called MillionVis, that depicts one million items all on one screen using the graphical techniques of 2D stacking, tiling, and color (Fekete and Plaisant, 2002). The idea is that viewers can zoom in to parts of the visualization to find out more about certain data points, while also being able to see the overall structure of an entire data set. The treemap (Shneiderman, 1992) has been used to visualize file systems, enabling users to understand why they are running out of disk space, how much space different applications are using, and also for viewing

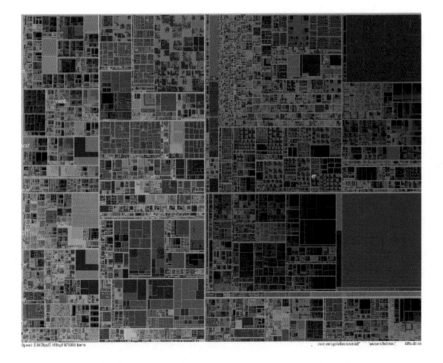

Figure 6.17 An info visualization, using flat colored blocks

Source: Reproduced with permission from Fekete, J.D., Plaisant, C., Interactive Information Visualization of a Million Items, Proc. IEEE Symposium on Information Visualization (2002), 117–124. www.cs.umd.edu/hcil/millionvis.

large image repositories that contain terabytes of satellite images. Similar visualizations have been used to represent changes in stocks and shares over time, using rollovers to show additional information, e.g. Marketmap on SmartMoney.com.

Dashboards have become an increasingly popular form of visualizing information. They show screenshots of data updated over periods of time, intended to be read at a glance. Unlike other kinds of information visualizations, they tend not to be interactive; the slices of data are intended to depict the current state of a system or process. However, many commercial dashboards have been constructed with poor visual design by software vendors who "focus their marketing efforts on dazzle that subverts the goals of clear communication" (Few, 2013, p. 2). The result can be a hotch-potch of dials, gauges, and graphs, making it difficult to know where to find something or how to compare data over time or across dimensions. Dashboards should be designed to provide digestible and legible information so that users can home in on what is important to them. This requires considering how best to design the spatial layout of a dashboard so that it is intuitive to read when first looking at it. It also needs to be designed in order to direct a user's attention to anomalies or unexpected deviations. This involves working out how best to combine and contrast different elements.

ACTIVITY 6.6

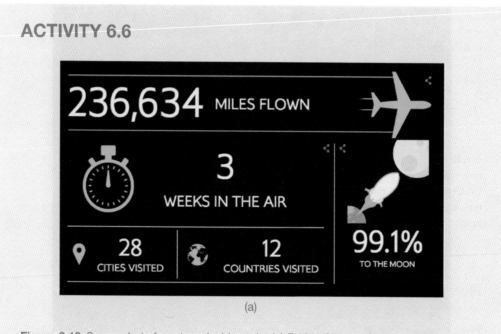

(a)

Figure 6.18 Screenshots from two dashboards: (a) British Airways frequent flier club that shows how much a member has flown since joining them, and (b) London City that provides various information feeds. Which is the easier to read and most informative?

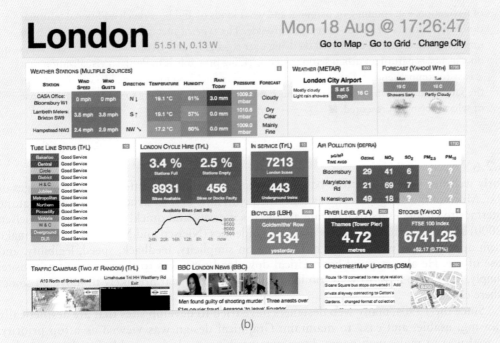

(b)

Comment

Much thought has gone into the visual design of the BA dashboard – the pictograms are simple and colorful, and draw the reader's attention. The first thing that grabs your attention is that the flier has flown an enormous number of miles that is equivalent to three weeks in the air! This factoid is striking and stands out. The piece of information in the lower right-hand corner also adds a bit of humor. The London dashboard, on the other hand, is incredibly busy, visually, and requires the viewer to spend time scanning it to find some relevant information. The individual graphics and text used are relatively simple and easy to understand. It also provides much more information than the British Airways dashboard about transport, the level of service on London Underground lines, the weather, news headlines, cycle hire capacity, weather forcast, and air pollution. After a few times glancing at it, the viewer can learn where to look to see the feeds that interest them; for example, how bad the traffic is, or what the air pollution is in Bloomsbury.

Research and design issues

Key design issues include whether to use animation and/or interactivity, what form of coding to use, e.g. color or text labels, whether to use a 2D or 3D representational format, what forms

(Continued)

of navigation, e.g. zooming or panning, and what kinds of and how much additional information, e.g. rollovers or tables of text, to provide. The type of metaphor to be used is also an important concern, e.g. one based on flying over a geographical terrain or one that represents documents as part of an urban setting. An overriding principle is to design a visualization that is easy to comprehend and easy to make inferences from. If too many variables are depicted in the same visualization, it can make it much more difficult for viewers to read and make sense of what is being represented. ■

6.2.6   Web

Early websites were largely text-based, providing hyperlinks to different places or pages of text. Much of the design effort was concerned with how best to structure information at the interface to enable users to navigate and access it easily and quickly. For example, Nielsen (2000) adapted his and Mohlich's usability guidelines (Nielsen and Mohlich, 1990) to make them applicable to website design, focusing on simplicity, feedback, speed, legibility, and ease of use. He also stressed how critical download time was to the success of a website. Simply, users who have to wait too long for a page to appear are likely to move on somewhere else.

Since the 1990s, many web designers have tried to develop sites that are aesthetically pleasing, usable, and easy to maintain. Graphical design was viewed as a top priority. A goal was to make web pages distinctive, striking, and pleasurable for the user when they first view them and also to make them readily recognizable on their return. Sometimes, they were able to meet all three criteria while at other times they have managed to make a website look good but terrible to navigate and even worse to update content. Other times, they managed to design easy to navigate sites that looked dreadful. Krug (2014) characterized the debate on usability versus attractiveness in terms of the difference between how designers create websites and how users actually view them. He argues that web designers create sites as if the user was going to pore over each page, reading the finely crafted text word for word, looking at the use of images, color, icons, etc., examining how the various items have been organized on the site, and then contemplating their options before they finally select a link. Users, however, often behave quite differently. They will glance at a new page, scan part of it, and click on the first link that catches their interest or looks like it might lead them to what they want. Much of the content on a web page is not read. In his words, web designers are "thinking great literature" (or at least "product brochure") while the user's reality is much closer to a "billboard going by at 60 miles an hour" (Krug, 2014, p. 21). While somewhat of a caricature of web designers and users, his depiction highlights the discrepancy between the meticulous ways designers create their websites and the rapid and less than systematic approach that users take to look at them.

Website design took off in a big way in the early 2000s when user-centered editing tools (e.g. Dreamweaver) and programming languages (e.g. php, Flash and XML) emerged, providing opportunities for both designers and the general public to create websites to look and behave more like multimedia environments. HTML5 and web development techniques, such as Ajax, enable applications to be built that are largely executed on a user's computer, allowing the development of web applications that mimic desktop apps. Wikis and blogs also became very popular, enabling any number of interlinked web pages to be created and edited easily. WordPress then became very popular, with an easy-to-use interface that provided over 200 free themes (i.e. templates) for users to get started creating their own blog or website. Customized web pages started to be developed for smartphone browsers that listlinked (i.e. provided scrolling lists of articles, games, tunes that could be clicked on) rather than hyperlinked pages.

Swiping became the new form of interaction that very young children learn as naturally as clicking on buttons and turning dials. To the extent sometimes that they think that is how you interact with the real world as the video below suggests!

Video of 'A Magazine Is an iPad That Does Not Work' at **http://youtu.be/aXV-yaFmQNk**

With the universal uptake of tablet computers in the late 2000s, web traffic shot up and began to overtake that of smartphones. Web designers started to rethink how to design web browsers and websites – not just for PC/laptops and small displays – but for touch-screen tablets. More and more people were looking at online content by scrolling and flicking through it with their fingers rather than using a mouse. The standard desktop interface was found to not work as well on a tablet. In particular, the typical fonts, buttons, and menu tabs were too small and fiddly to select when using a finger. Instead of double-clicking on interface elements – as users do with a mouse or trackpad – tablet screens afford finger tapping. The main ways of navigating are by swiping and pinching. A new style of website emerged that mapped better onto this kind of interaction style but which could also be interacted with easily when using a mouse and trackpad. Responsive websites were developed that change their layout, graphic design, font and appearance depending on the screen size (smartphone, tablet, PC) it was being displayed on.

If you look at the design of many websites, you will see that the front page presents a banner at the top, a short promotional video about the company/product/service, arrows to the left or right to indicate where to flick to move through pages and further details appearing beneath the home page that the user can scroll through. Navigation is largely done through swiping of pages from left to right (and right to left) or scrolling up and down.

Link to some tips on designing websites for tablets at
http://css-tricks.com/a-couple-of-best-practices-for-tablet-friendly-design/
http://webdesign.tutsplus.com/articles/how-the-ipad-and-tablets-are-driving-new-web-design-trends--webdesign-2428

BOX 6.4

In-your-face web ads

Web advertising has become pervasive and invasive. Advertisers realized how effective flashing and animated ads were for promoting their products, taking inspiration from the animated neon light adverts used in city centers, such as London's Piccadilly Circus. But since the banner ads emerged in the 1990s, they have become even more cunning and aggressive in their tactics. In addition to designing even flashier banner ads, more intrusive kinds of web ads have begun to appear on our screens. Short movies and garish cartoon animations – often with sound – now pop up in floating windows that zoom into view or are tagged on at the front end of an online newspaper or magazine news videoclip. Moreover, this new breed of in-your-face web ads often requires the user to either wait till it ends or find a check box to close the window down. This can be really annoying, especially when multiple ad windows open up. Sites that provide free services, such as Facebook, YouTube, and Gmail, have also become populated with web ads. Many people choose to ignore them or simply put up with them. However, as advertisers get even more aggressive in their tactics there will be a point where that will become harder to do. The problem is that advertisers pay significant revenues to online companies to have their adverts placed on their websites, entitling them to say where, what, and how they should appear. ■

Research and design issues

There are numerous classic books on web design and usability that have been updated as new editions (e.g. Krug (2014); Cooper *et al* (2014)). In addition, there are many good online sites offering guidelines and tips, together with pointers to examples of bad websites. Key design issues for websites are captured very well by three questions proposed by Keith Instone (quoted in Veen, 2001): Where am I? What's here? Where can I go?

These three fundamental questions are still very relevant for today's websites. Web Content Accessibility Guidelines (WCAG) are available to enable developers to know how to design websites that are inclusive. The latest version, WCAG 2.0, is available at http://www.w3.org/WAI/intro/wcag. These guidelines include designing websites for:

- Users who may not be able to see, hear, or move, or may not be able to process some types of information easily or at all.
- Users who have difficulty reading or comprehending text.
- Users who may not have or be able to use a keyboard or mouse.
- Users who may have a text-only screen, a small screen, or a slow Internet connection.

Website content also needs to be designed for:

- Users who may not speak or understand fluently the language in which the document is written.
- Users who are in a setting where their eyes, ears, or hands are busy or interfered with, e.g. driving to work.
- Users who may have an early version of a browser, a different browser entirely, a voice browser, or a different operating system. ■

ACTIVITY 6.7

Look at a fashion brand's website, such as Nike or Levi's, and describe the kind of interface used. How does it contravene the design principles outlined by Veen? Does it matter? What kind of user experience is it providing for? What was your experience of engaging with it?

Comment

Fashion companies' sites, like Nike's or Levi's, are often designed to be more like a cinematic experience and use rich multimedia elements, e.g. videos, sounds, music, animations, and interactivity. Branding is central. In this sense, it is a far cry from a conventional website and contravenes many of the usability guidelines. Specifically, the site has been designed to entice the visitor to enter the virtual store and watch high-quality and innovative movies that show cool dudes wearing their products. Often multimedia interactivities are embedded into the sites to help the viewer move to other parts of the site, e.g. clicking on parts of an image or animation. Screen widgets are also provided, e.g. menus, skip over, and next buttons. It is easy to become immersed in the experience and forget it is a commercial store. It is also easy to get lost and to not know: Where am I? What's here? Where can I go? But this is precisely what companies such as Nike and Levi's want their visitors to do and to enjoy the experience. ■

6.2.7 Consumer Electronics and Appliances

Consumer electronics and appliances include machines for everyday use in the home, public place, or car (e.g. washing machines, DVD players, vending machines, remotes, photocopiers, printers, and navigation systems) and personal devices (e.g. MP3 player, digital clock, and digital camera). What they have in common is that most people using them will be trying to get something specific done in a short period of time, such as putting the washing on, watching a program, buying a ticket, changing the time, or taking a snapshot. They are unlikely to be interested in spending time exploring the interface or spending time looking through a manual to see how to use the appliance.

Research and design issues

Cooper *et al* (2014) suggest that appliance interfaces require the designer to view them as transient interfaces, where the interaction is short. All too often, however, designers provide full-screen control panels or an unnecessary array of physical buttons that serve to frustrate and confuse the user and where only a few in a structured way would be much better. Here, the two fundamental design principles of simplicity and visibility are paramount. Status information, such as what the photocopier is doing, what the ticket machine is doing, and how much longer the washing is going to take should be provided in a very simple form and at a prominent place on the interface. A key design question is: as soft displays, e.g. LCD and touch screens, increasingly become part of an appliance interface, what are the trade-offs with replacing the traditional physical controls, e.g. dials, buttons, knobs? ∎

ACTIVITY 6.8

Look at the controls on your toaster (or the one in Figure 6.19 if you don't have one nearby) and describe what each does. Consider how these might be replaced with an LCD screen. What would be gained and lost from changing the interface in this way?

Comment

Standard toasters have two main controls, the lever to press down to start the toasting and a knob to set the amount of time for the toasting. Many now come with a small eject button intended to be pressed if the toast starts to burn. In Figure 6.19 it is to the left of the timer knob. Some also come with a range of settings for different ways of toasting (e.g. one side, frozen), selected by moving a dial or pressing buttons.

Figure 6.19 A typical toaster with basic physical controls

To design the controls to appear on an LCD screen would enable more information and options to be provided, e.g. only toast one slice, keep the toast warm, automatically pop up when the toast is burning. It would also allow precise timing of the toasting in minutes and seconds. However, as has happened with the design evolution of microwave ovens, a downside is that it is likely to increase the complexity of what previously was a set of logical and very simple actions – placing something in an oven and heating it up – making it more difficult to use. ■

6.2.8 Mobile

Mobile devices have become pervasive, with people increasingly using them in all aspects of their everyday and working lives. They have become business tools to clinch important deals; a remote control for the real world, helping people cope with daily travel delay frustrations; and a relationship appliance to say goodnight to loved ones when away from home (Jones and Marsden, 2006). The Android app, Locket, monitored how many times its 150,000 users checked their phone and found during a six-month period in 2013 that the average person checks their phone 110 times a day. This varies greatly across the day, but they also found it increases considerably in the evening. How does this compare with your usage?

Handheld devices, such as smartphones and iPods, differ from PCs and laptops, in terms of their size, portability, and interaction style. They can be kept in someone's pocket or purse. Early cell phones provided hard-wired small physical keyboards, where letters were pressed. Most smartphones are now touch based, with virtual keyboards that pop up when needed, and are interacted with by finger and thumb tapping. They are increasingly being used by people in mobile settings where they need access to real-time data or information whilst walking around. For example, they are now commonly used in restaurants to take orders, car rentals to check in car returns, supermarkets for checking stock, and on the streets for multiplayer gaming. Tablets are also being used in work settings. For example, many airlines provide their flight attendants with one so they can use their customized flight apps while airborne and at airports; sales and marketing people also use them to demonstrate their goods or collect public opinions. Tablets and smartphones are also being increasingly used in classrooms.

The introduction of Apple's iPhone in 2008 introduced the world to the app – a new user experience that was designed primarily for people to enjoy. There are now over one million apps available with many new ones appearing each day for many different categories, including games, entertainment, social networking, music, productivity, lifestyle, travel, and navigation. Healthy lifestyle and well-being apps (e.g. FitBit, Jawbone Up), which combine a wearable device such as a wristband or headband with a smartphone mobile app (see Chapter 5), are becoming more popular. These can be used on the go and while asleep to monitor and track someone's behaviors and bodily functions. They make use of sensors embedded in the wearable device, such as an accelerometer to detect movement, a thermometer to measure temperature, and galvanic skin response to measure changes in sweat level on someone's skin. Other apps may not be designed for any need, want, or use but purely for idle moments to have some fun. An example of an early highly successful fun app was iBeer (see Figure 6.20), developed by magician Steve Sheraton. Within months of release, hundreds of thousands of people had downloaded the app, then showed their friends who also then downloaded it and

Figure 6.20 The iBeer smartphone app

Source: iBeer™ Photo ©2010 HOTTRIX® Reproduced with permission.

showed it to their friends. It became an instant hit, a must have, a party piece – quite unlike any other kind of software. Moreover, a magician created it – rather than an interaction designer – who really understood what captivates people. Part of its success was due to the ingenious use of the accelerometer that is inside the phone. It detects the tilting of the iPhone and uses this information to mimic a glass of beer being drunk. The graphics and sounds are also very enticing; the color of the beer together with frothy bubbles and accompanying sound effects give the illusion of virtual beer being swished around a virtual glass. The beer can be drained if the phone is tilted enough, followed by a belch sound when it has been finished.

Smartphones can also be used to download contextual information by scanning barcodes in the physical world. Consumers can instantly download product information by scanning barcodes using their iPhone when walking around a supermarket, including allergens, such as nuts, gluten, and dairy. For example, the GoodGuide app enables shoppers to scan products in a store by taking a photo of their barcode to see how they rate for healthiness and impact on the environment. Another method that provides quick access to relevant information is the use of QR (quick response) codes that store URLs and look like black and white chequered squares. They can appear in magazines (see Figure 6.21), on billboards, business cards, clothing, food and drink packaging, trains, and so on. They work by people taking a picture using

Figure 6.21 QR code appearing on a magazine page

their camera phone which then instantly takes them to a particular website. However, despite their universal appeal to companies as a way of providing additional information or special offers, not many people actually use them in practice. One of the reasons is that they can be slow, fiddly, and cumbersome to use in situ. People have to download a QR reader app first, open it, and then try to hold it over the QR code to take a photo that can take time to open up a webpage (if the WiFi reception is poor).

Research and design issues

Mobile interfaces typically have a small screen and limited control space. Designers have to think carefully about what type of dedicated controls (i.e. hard wired) to include, where to place them on the device, and then how to map them onto the software. Applications designed for mobile interfaces need to take into account that navigation will be restricted and text input entry slow, whether using touch, pen, or keypad input. The use of vertical and horizontal scrolling provides a rapid way of scanning though images, menus, and lists. A number of mobile browsers have also been developed that allow users to view and navigate the Internet, magazines, or other media, in a more streamlined way. For example, Edge Browser was one of the first cell phone browser apps to not have an address bar or navigation buttons. The trade-off, however, is it makes it less obvious how to perform the functions that are no longer visible on the screen. A key concern is the hit area. This is an area on the phone display that the user touches to make something happen, such as a key, an icon, a button, or an app. The space needs to be big enough for fat fingers to accurately press. If the space is too small, the user may accidentally press the wrong key, which can be very annoying. The average fingertip is between one and two centimeters wide. Apple, Nokia, and Microsoft each recommend slightly different sizes to accommodate these hit areas to account for the nature of their touch screens (see Chapter 15 for more about how to determine the best size and location of buttons and touch area).

A number of guidelines exist providing advice on how to design interfaces for mobile devices (e.g. Weiss, 2002). Android, Windows Phone, and Apple also provide extensive guidelines for developing smartphone interfaces and apps. Case study 11.1 describes how prototyping can be used for developing mobile interfaces, while case study 11.2 explores the effect of different form factors. ■

Link to website where Elaine McVicar has provided a number of online easy-to-read and nicely illustrated tutorials as part of the UX Booth for mobile interaction design that include 1) information architecture and 2) interaction techniques, including logging on, page flipping, swiping, pinching, and form design, which can be found at
1) **http://tinyurl.com/cmw54vj**
2) **http://tinyurl.com/c32ns6d**

6.2.9   Speech

A speech or voice user interface is where a person talks with a system that has a spoken language application, like a train timetable, a travel planner, or a phone service. It is most commonly used for inquiring about specific information (e.g. flight times) or to perform a transaction (e.g. buy a ticket or top up a smartphone account). It is a specific form of natural language interaction that is based on the interaction type of conversing (see Chapter 2), where users speak and listen to an interface. There are many commercially available speech-based applications that are now being used by corporations, especially for offering their services over the phone. Speech-to-text systems have also become popular, such as Dragon Dictate. Speech technology has also advanced applications that can be used by people with disabilities, including speech recognition word processors, page scanners, web readers, and speech recognition software for operating home control systems, including lights, TV, stereo, and other home appliances.

Technically, speech interfaces have come of age, being much more sophisticated and accurate than the first generation of speech systems in the early 1990s, which earned a reputation for *mis*hearing all too often what a person said (see cartoon). Actors are increasingly used to record the messages and prompts provided that are much friendlier, more convincing, and pleasant than the artificially sounding synthesized speech that was typically used in the early systems.

One of the most popular applications of speech technology is call routing, where companies use an automated speech system to enable users to reach one of their services. Many companies are replacing the frustrating and unwieldy touchtone technology for navigating their services (which was restricted to 10 numbers and the # and * symbols) with the use of caller-led speech. Callers can now state their needs in their own words (rather than pressing a series of arbitrary numbers); for example, 'I'm having problems with my voice mail,' and in response are automatically forwarded to the appropriate service (Cohen *et al*, 2004).

In human conversations we often interrupt each other, especially if we know what we want, rather than waiting for someone to go through a series of options. For example, at a restaurant we may stop the waitress in mid-flow when describing the specials if we know what we want rather than let her go through the whole list. Similarly, speech technology has been designed with a feature called barge-in that allows callers to interrupt a system message and provide their request or response before the message has finished playing. This can be very useful if the system has numerous options for the caller to choose from and the chooser knows already what he wants.

There are several ways a dialog can be structured. The most common is a directed dialog where the system is in control of the conversation, asking specific questions and requiring specific responses, similar to filling in a form (Cohen *et al*, 2004):

System: Which city do you want to fly to?

Caller: London

System: Which airport – Gatwick, Heathrow, Luton, Stansted, or City?

Caller: Gatwick

System: What day do you want to depart?

Caller: Monday week

System: Is that Monday 5th May?

Caller: Yes

Other systems are more flexible, allowing the user to take more initiative and specify more information in one sentence (e.g. 'I'd like to go to Paris next Monday for two weeks'). The problem with this approach is that there is more chance of error, since the caller might assume that the system can follow all of her needs in one go as a real travel agent can (e.g. 'I'd like to go to Paris next Monday for two weeks and would like the cheapest possible flight, preferably leaving Stansted airport and definitely no stop-overs . . .'). The list is simply too long and would overwhelm the system's parser. Carefully guided prompts can be used to get callers back on track and help them speak appropriately (e.g. 'Sorry, I did not get all that. Did you say you wanted to fly next Monday?').

A number of speech-based phone apps exist that enable people to use them while mobile, making them more convenient to use than text-based entry. For example, people can speak their queries into their phone using Google Voice or Apple Siri rather than entering text manually. Mobile translators are also coming into their own, allowing people to communicate in real time with others who speak a different language, by letting a software app on their phone do the talking (e.g. Google translate). People speak in their own language using their own phone while the software translates what each person is saying into the language of the other one. Potentially, that means people from all over the world (there are over 6000 languages) can talk to one another without ever having to learn another language.

Research and design issues

Key research questions are concerned with how to design systems that can recognize speech and keep the conversation on track. Some researchers focus on making it appear natural (i.e. like human conversations) while others are concerned more with how to help people navigate efficiently through a menu system, by enabling them to recover easily from errors (their own or the system's), be able to escape and go back to the main menu (cf. to the undo

(Continued)

button of a GUI), and to guide those who are vague or ambiguous in their requests for information or services using prompts. The type of voice actor, e.g. male, female, neutral, or dialect and form of pronunciation are also topics of research. Do people prefer to listen to and are more patient with a female or male voice? What about one that is jolly or one that is serious?

Cohen *et al* (2004) discuss the pros and cons of using different techniques for structuring the dialog and managing the flow of voice interactions, the different ways of expressing errors, and the use of conversational etiquette. A number of commercial guidelines are available for voice interfaces and for the visually impaired. ■

6.2.10   Pen

Pen-based devices enable people to write, draw, select, and move objects at an interface using lightpens or styluses that capitalize on the well-honed drawing and writing skills that are developed from childhood. They have been used to interact with tablets and large displays, instead of mouse or keyboard input, for selecting items and supporting freehand sketching. Digital ink, such as Anoto, uses a combination of an ordinary ink pen with a digital camera that digitally records everything written with the pen on special paper. The pen works by recognizing a special non-repeating dot pattern that is printed on the paper. The non-repeating nature of the pattern means that the pen is able to determine which page is being written on, and where on the page the pen is. When writing on the digital paper with a digital pen, infrared light from the pen illuminates the dot pattern, which is then picked up by a tiny sensor. The pen decodes the

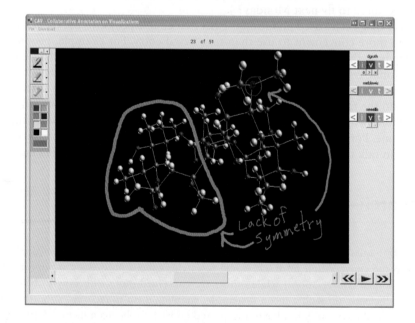

Figure 6.22 Microsoft's digital ink in action showing how it can be used to annotate a scientific diagram

Source: Reproduced by permission of Dennis Groth.

dot pattern as the pen moves across the paper and stores the data temporarily in the pen. The digital pen can transfer data that has been stored in the pen via Bluetooth or USB port to a PC. Handwritten notes can also be converted and saved as standard typeface text.

Another advantage of digital pens is that they allow users to quickly and easily annotate existing documents, such as spreadsheets, presentations, and diagrams (see Figure 6.22) – in a similar way to how they would do when using paper-based versions. A number of usability studies have been carried out comparing different ways of entering text using pen input, for children and adults. For example, a study by Read (2005) compared three methods for text input using digital ink technologies; handwriting with a stylus on a Tablet PC, handwriting with a graphics tablet and pen on a standard PC, and handwriting with a digital pen on digital paper. The user group was made up of children aged between 7 and 8, and 12 and 13. The findings showed that the older children were able to use the digital pens best but that both sets of children were able to use the stylus with the Tablet PC without making many errors.

A problem with using pen-based interactions on small screens, such as PDAs, is that sometimes it can be difficult to see options on the screen because a user's hand can occlude part of it when writing.

BOX 6.5

Electronic ink

Digital ink is not to be confused with the term electronic ink (or e-ink). Electronic ink is a display technology designed to mimic the appearance of ordinary ink on paper used in e-readers. The display used reflects light like ordinary paper. ∎

6.2.11 Touch

Touch screens, such as walk-up kiosks (e.g. ticket machines, museum guides), ATMs, and till machines (e.g. restaurants), have been around for some time. They work by detecting the presence and location of a person's touch on the display; options are selected by tapping on the screen. More recently, multitouch surfaces have been developed as the interface for tabletops and smartphones that support a range of more dynamic finger tip actions, such as swiping, flicking, pinching, pushing, and tapping. These have been mapped onto specific kinds of operations, e.g. zooming in and out of maps, moving photos, selecting letters from a virtual keyboard when writing, and scrolling through lists. Two hands can also be used together to stretch and move objects on a tabletop surface, similar to how both hands are used to stretch an elastic band or scoop together a set of objects.

The flexibility of interacting with digital content afforded by finger gestures has resulted in new ways of experiencing digital content. Most notable are the richer ways of reading, scanning, and searching interactive magazines and books on tablets. *Wired* magazine, for example, was the first to enhance reading through accompanied experiencing of its online version. Similar to the idea behind multimedia, the idea is to enable the reader to readily switch between reading about something (e.g. the history of Mars landings) and experiencing it (e.g. by exploring a virtual simulation of the planet) – only rather than through mouse clicking on hyperlinks, to do it by deft finger movements. A new conceptual model has also been used; content is organized using cards, carousels, and stacks to support rapid finger-flicking navigation, allowing readers to go directly to specific stories while still maintaining a sense of place.

Research and design issues

A research question is whether finger-flicking, swiping, stroking, and touching a screen rather than pointing, dragging, and clicking with a mouse will result in new ways of consuming, reading, creating, and searching digital content. On the one hand, it can be much faster to scroll through wheels, carousels, and bars of thumbnail images or lists of options by finger flicking. On the other, it can be more cumbersome, error-prone, and slower to type using a virtual keyboard on a touch display than using a physical keyboard. A novel typing method that has been developed for touch displays is to allow people to swipe their fingers across a virtual keyboard rather than tap at it, such as Swype (see Figure 6.23 and video). Swyping allows the user to move their finger from letter to letter on a virtual keyboard without lifting it. The software senses which are the intended letters by where the user pauses and changes direction.

Figure 6.23 The Swype interface developed for mobile touch displays

Source: Reproduced from http://www.geek.com/articles/mobile/nuances-t9-trace-virtual-keyboard-allows-you-to-swipe-rather-than-type-20100323/technology/.

One of the benefits of typing by sliding your fingers across a screen rather than pecking at the keys is that it can make typing faster while also reducing error rate. Another approach, mentioned in Chapter 1, is Minuum's new keyboard that provides a staggered line keyboard for selecting characters. This layout provides a way of fanning out the alphanumeric characters, thereby expanding the hit area. This can be effective for small devices, such as smartwatches, where the screen is relatively small. ■

Video of Swype demo at **http://youtu.be/2xA64e3Txe8**

6.2.12 Air-Based Gestures

Camera capture, sensor, and computer vision techniques have advanced such that it is now possible to fairly accurately recognize people's body, arm, and hand gestures in a room. An early commercial application that used gesture interaction was Sony's EyeToy, which used a motion-sensitive camera that sat on top of a TV monitor and plugged into the back of a Sony PlayStation. It could be used to play various video games. The camera filmed the player when standing in front of the TV, projected her image onto the screen, and made her the central character of the video game. The game could be played by anyone, regardless of age or computer experience, simply by moving her legs, arms, head, or any part of the body.

Sony then introduced a motion-sensing wand, called the Move, that uses the Playstation Eye camera to track players' movements using light recognition technology. Nintendo's Wii gaming console also introduced the Wii Remote (Wiimote) controller as a novel input device. It uses accelerometers for gesture recognition. The sensors enable the player to directly input by waving the controller in front of a display, such as the TV. The movements are mapped onto a variety of gaming motions, such as swinging, bowling, hitting, and punching. The player is represented on the screen as an avatar that shows him hitting the ball or swinging the bat against the backdrop of a tennis court, bowling alley, or boxing ring. Like Sony's EyeToy, it was designed to appeal to anyone, from young children to grandparents, and from professional gamers to technophobes, to play games such as tennis or golf, together in their living room. The Wiimote also plays sound and has force feedback, allowing the player to experience rumbles that are meant to enhance the experience when playing the game. The Nunchuk controller can also be used in conjunction with the Wiimote to provide further input control. The analog stick can be held in one hand to move an avatar or characters on the screen while the Wiimote is held in the other to perform a specific action, such as throwing a pass in football.

In late 2010, Microsoft introduced another gesture-based gaming input system for the Xbox: the Kinect (see Figure 6.24). It is more similar to the EyeToy than the Wii in that it does not use a sensor-controller for gesture recognition but camera technology together with

Figure 6.24 Microsoft's Xbox Kinect comprising an RGB camera for facial recognition plus video capturing, a depth sensor (an infrared projector paired with a monochrome camera) for movement tracking, and downward-facing mics for voice recognition
Source: ©PA Images.

a depth sensor and a multi-array microphone (this enables speech commands). An RGB camera sits on the TV, and works by looking for your body; on finding it, it locks onto it, and measures the three-dimensional positioning of the key joints in your body. The feedback provided on the TV screen in response to the various air-gestures has proven to be remarkably effective. Many people readily see themselves as the avatar and learn how to play games in this more physical manner. However, sometimes the gesture/body tracking can misinterpret a player's movements, and make the ball or bat move in the wrong direction. This can be disconcerting, especially for expert gamers.

A number of air-based gesture systems were developed for controlling home appliances. Early systems used computer vision techniques to detect certain gesture types (e.g. location of hand, movement of arm) that were then converted into system commands. Other systems then began using sensor technologies to detect touch, bend, and speed of movement of the hand and/or arm. Ubi-Finger was developed to allow users to point at an object, e.g. a switch, using his/her index finger and then control it by an appropriate gesture, e.g. pushing the finger down as if flicking on the switch (Tsukada and Yasumura, 2002). Sign language applications have also been built to enable hearing-impaired people to communicate with others without needing a sign language interpreter (Sagawa *et al*, 1997).

A recent application of air-based gesture interaction is in the operating theater. Surgeons need to keep their hands sterile during operations but also need to be able to look at X-rays and scans during an operation. However, after being scrubbed and gloved, they need to avoid touching any keyboards, phones, and other non-sterile surfaces. A far from ideal workaround is to pull their surgical gown over their hands and manipulate a mouse through the gown. As an alternative, O'Hara *et al* (2013) have developed a touchless gesture-based system, using

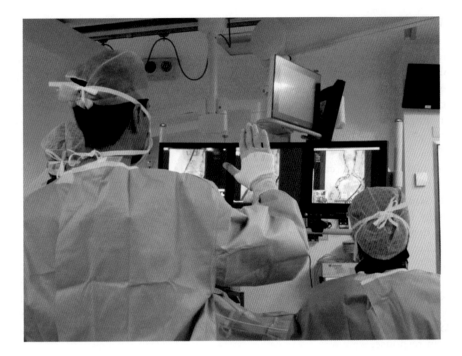

Figure 6.25 Touchless gesturing in the operating theater
Source: Courtesy of Kenton O'Hara, Microsoft.

Microsoft's Kinect technology, which can recognize a range of gestures that surgeons can use to interact with and manipulate MRI or CT images, including single-handed gestures for moving forward or backward through images, and two-handed gestures for zooming and panning.

Research and design issues

A key design concern for using air-based gestural input is to consider how a computer system recognizes and delineates the user's gestures. In particular, how does it determine the start and end point of a hand or arm movement and how does it know the difference between a deictic gesture (a deliberate pointing movement) and hand waving (an unconscious gesticulation) that is used to emphasize what is being said verbally? Another key design issue is whether holding a control device feels more intuitive for the game or other activity than controller-free gestures. Sometimes it clearly is better to be holding something – when for example, hitting a ball with a bat. Other times it may be better hands-free such as when dancing or doing aerobics. ■

6.2.13   Haptic

Haptic interfaces provide tactile feedback, by applying vibration and forces to the person, using actuators that are embedded in their clothing or a device they are carrying, such as a smartphone or smartwatch. We have already mentioned above how the Wiimote provides rumbles as a form of haptic feedback. Other gaming consoles have also employed vibration to enrich the experience. For example, car steering wheels that are used with driving simulators can vibrate in various ways to provide a feel of the road. As the driver makes a turn, the steering wheel can be programmed to feel like it is resisting – in the way a real steering wheel does.

Vibrotactile feedback can also be used to simulate the sense of touch between remote people who want to communicate. Actuators embedded in clothing can be designed to recreate the sensation of a hug or a stroke through being buzzed on various parts of the body (see Huggy Pajama in Chapter 4). Another use of haptics is to provide feedback to guide people when learning a musical instrument, such as a violin or drums. For example, the MusicJacket (van der Linden *et al*, 2011) was developed to help novice violin players learn how to hold their instrument correctly and develop good bowing action. Vibrotactile feedback is provided via the jacket to give nudges at key places on the arm and torso to inform the student when either they are holding their violin incorrectly or their bowing trajectory has deviated from a desired path (see Figure 6.26). A user study with novice players showed that players were able to react to the vibrotactile feedback, and adjust their bowing or their posture in response.

Figure 6.26 The MusicJacket prototype with embedded actuators that nudge the player

Research and design issues

Haptics are now commonly used in gaming consoles and controllers to heighten the experience. Haptic feedback is also being developed in clothing and other wearables as a way of simulating being touched, stroked, prodded, or buzzed. A promising application area is sensory-motor skills, such as in sports training and learning to play a musical instrument. For example, patterns of vibrations have been placed across snowboarders' bodies to indicate which moves to take whilst snowboarding. A study reported faster reaction times than when the same instructions were given verbally (Spelmezan *et al*, 2009). A key design question is where best to place the actuators on the body, whether to use a single or a sequence of touches, when to activate, and at what intensity and how often to use them to make the feeling of being touched convincing (e.g. Jones and Sarter, 2008). Providing continuous haptic feedback would be simply too annoying. People would also habituate too quickly to the feedback. Intermittent buzzes can be effective at key moments when a person needs to attend to something but not necessarily tell them what to do. For example, a study by Johnson *et al* (2010) of a commercially available haptic device, intended to improve posture through giving people a vibrotactile buzz whenever they slouched, found that while the buzzing did not show them how to improve their posture it did improve their body awareness. Different kinds of buzzes can also be used to indicate different tactile experiences that map onto events; for example, a smartphone could transmit feelings of slow tapping to feel like water dropping, which is meant to indicate it is about to rain, and transmit the sensation of heavy tapping to indicate a thunderstorm is looming. ∎

6.2.14 Multimodal

Multimodal interfaces are intended to provide enriched and complex user experiences by multiplying the way information is experienced and controlled at the interface through using different modalities, i.e. touch, sight, sound, speech (Bouchet and Nigay, 2004). Interface techniques that have been combined for this purpose include speech and gesture, eye-gaze and gesture, and pen input and speech (Dumas *et al*, 2009). An assumption is that multimodal interfaces can support more flexible, efficient, and expressive means of human–computer interaction, that are more akin to the multimodal experiences humans experience in the physical world (Oviatt, 2002). Different input/outputs may be used at the same time, e.g. using voice commands and gestures simultaneously to move through a virtual environment, or alternately using speech commands followed by gesturing. The most common combination of technologies used for multimodal interfaces is speech and vision processing (Deng and Huang, 2004), such as used by Microsoft's Kinect.

Speech-based mobile devices that allow people to interact with information via a combination of speech and touch are beginning to emerge. An example is SpeechWork's multimodal interface developed for one of Ford's SUV concept cars, which allows the occupants to operate on-board systems including entertainment, navigation, cell phone, and climate control by speech.

Research and design issues

Multimodal systems rely on recognizing aspects of a user's behavior – be it her handwriting, speech, gestures, eye movements, or other body movements. In many ways, this is much harder to accomplish and calibrate than single modality systems that are programmed to recognize one aspect of a user's behavior. The most researched modes of interaction are speech, gesture, and eye-gaze tracking. A key research question is what is actually gained from combining different input and outputs and whether talking and gesturing as humans do with other humans is a natural way of interacting with a computer (see Chapter 4). Guidelines for multimodal design can be found in Reeves *et al* (2004). ■

6.2.15   Shareable

Shareable interfaces are designed for more than one person to use. Unlike PCs, laptops, and mobile devices – that are aimed at single users – they typically provide multiple inputs and sometimes allow simultaneous input by collocated groups. These include large wall displays, e.g. SmartBoards (see Figure 6.27a), where people use their own pens or gestures, and interactive tabletops, where small groups can interact with information being displayed on the surface using their fingertips. Examples of interactive tabletops include Microsoft's Surface, Smart's SmartTable, and Circle Twelve's DiamondTouch (Dietz and Leigh, 2001, see Figure 6.27b). The DiamondTouch tabletop is unique in that it can distinguish between different users touching the surface concurrently. An array of antennae is embedded in the touch surface and each one transmits a unique signal. Each user has their own receiver embedded in a mat they stand on or a chair they sit on. When a user touches the tabletop, very small signals are sent through the user's body to their receiver, which identifies which antenna has been touched and sends this to the computer. Multiple users can touch the screen at the same time.

Video of 'Circle Twelve's' demonstration of Diamond Touch tabletop at
http://youtu.be/S9QRdXITndU

An advantage of shareable interfaces is that they provide a large interactional space that can support flexible group working, enabling groups to create content together at the same time. Compared with a collocated group trying to work around a single-user PC or laptop – where typically one person takes control, making it more difficult for others to take part – large displays have the potential of being interacted with by multiple users, who can point to and touch the information being displayed, while simultaneously viewing the interactions and having the same shared point of reference (Rogers *et al*, 2009).

Roomware designed a number of integrated interactive furniture pieces, including walls, table, and chairs, that can be networked and positioned together so they can be used in unison

(a)

(b)

Figure 6.27 (a) A SmartBoard in use during a meeting and (b) Mitsubishi's interactive tabletop interface, where collocated users can interact simultaneously with digital content using their fingertips

Source: (a) ©2006 SMART Technologies Inc. Used with permission. (b) Image courtesy of Mitsubishi Electric Research Labs.

to augment and complement existing ways of collaborating (see Figure 6.28). An underlying premise is that the natural way people work together is by congregating around tables, huddling, and chatting besides walls and around tables. The Roomware furniture was designed to augment these kinds of informal collaborative activities, allowing people to engage with digital content that is pervasively embedded at these different locations.

Figure 6.28 Roomware furniture

Source: By permission of AMBIENTE.

Research and design issues

Early research on shareable interfaces focused largely on interactional issues, such as how to support electronically based handwriting and drawing, and the selecting and moving of objects around the display (Elrod *et al*, 1992). The PARCTAB system (Schilit *et al*, 1993) investigated how information could be communicated between palm-sized, A4-sized, and whiteboard-sized displays using shared software tools, such as Tivoli (Rønby-Pedersen *et al*, 1993). Another concern was how to develop fluid and direct styles of interaction with large displays, both wall-based and tabletop, involving freehand and pen-based gestures (e.g. Shen *et al*, 2003). Ecologies of devices have been developed where groups can share and create content across multiple devices, such as tabletops and wall displays.

A key research issue is whether shareable surfaces can facilitate new and enhanced forms of collaborative interaction compared with what is possible when groups work together using their own devices, like laptops and PCs (see Chapter 4). One benefit is easier sharing and more equitable participation. For example, tabletops have been designed to support more effective joint browsing, sharing, and manipulation of images during decision-making and design activities (Shen *et al*, 2002; Yuill and Rogers, 2012). Core design concerns include whether size, orientation, and shape of the display have an effect on collaboration. User studies have shown that horizontal surfaces compared with vertical ones support more turn-taking and collaborative working in collocated groups (Rogers and Lindley, 2004), while providing larger-sized tabletops does not necessarily improve group working but can encourage more division of labor (Ryall *et al*, 2004). The need for both personal and shared spaces has been investigated to see how best to enable users to move between working on their own and together as a group. Several researchers have begun to investigate the pros and cons of providing users with complementary devices, such as iPods, digital pens, and other wall displays that are used in conjunction with the shareable surface. Tangible devices (see Section 6.2.16), such as blocks, pucks, and paper models, have also been designed to be used in conjunction with tabletops. An example of this mixed form of interface (described in Chapter 4) is the Reactable, which is an interactive tool for computer music performers. Design guidelines and summaries of empirical research on tabletops and multitouch can be found in Scott *et al* (2003), O'Hara *et al* (2003), and Müller-Tomfelde (2010). ∎

6.2.16 Tangible

Tangible interfaces use sensor-based interaction, where physical objects, e.g. bricks, balls, and cubes, are coupled with digital representations (Ishii and Ullmer, 1997). When a person manipulates the physical object(s), it is detected by a computer system via the sensing mechanism embedded in the physical object, causing a digital effect to occur, such as a sound, animation, or vibration (Fishkin, 2004). The digital effects can take place in a number of media and places, or they can be embedded in the physical object itself. For example, Zuckerman and Resnick's (2005) Flow Blocks depict changing numbers and lights that are embedded in the blocks, depending on how they are connected together. The flow blocks are designed to simulate real-life dynamic behavior and react when arranged in certain sequences. Another type of tangible interface is where a physical model, e.g. a puck, a piece of clay, or a model, is superimposed on a digital desktop. Moving one of the physical pieces around the tabletop causes digital events to take place on the tabletop. For example, one of the earliest tangible interfaces, called Urp, was built to facilitate urban planning; miniature physical models of buildings could be moved around on the tabletop and used in combination with tokens for wind and shadow-generating tools, causing digital shadows surrounding them to change over time and visualizations of airflow to vary.

The technologies that have been used to create tangibles include RFID tags and sensors embedded in physical objects and digital tabletops that sense the movements of objects and subsequently provide visualizations surrounding the physical objects. Many tangible systems have been built with the aim of encouraging learning, design activities, playfulness, and collaboration. These include planning tools for landscape and urban planning (e.g. Hornecker, 2005; Underkoffler and Ishii, 1998). Another example is Tinkersheets, which combines tangible models of shelving with paper forms for exploring and solving warehouse logistics problems (Zufferey *et al*, 2009). The underlying simulation allows students to set parameters by placing small magnets on the form.

Tangible computing (Dourish, 2001) has been described as having no single locus of control or interaction. Instead of just one input device such as a mouse, there is a coordinated interplay of different devices and objects. There is also no enforced sequencing of actions and no modal interaction. Moreover, the design of the interface objects exploits their affordances to guide the user in how to interact with them. Tangible interfaces differ from the other approaches insofar as the representations are artifacts in their own right that the user can directly act upon, lift up, rearrange, sort, and manipulate.

What are the benefits of using tangible interfaces compared with other interfaces, like GUI, gesture, or pen-based? One advantage is that physical objects and digital representations can be positioned, combined, and explored in creative ways, enabling dynamic information to be presented in different ways. Physical objects can also be held in both hands and combined and manipulated in ways not possible using other interfaces. This allows for more than one person to explore the interface together and for objects to be placed on top of each other, beside each other, and inside each other; the different configurations encourage different ways of representing and exploring a problem space. In so doing, people are able to see and understand situations differently, which can lead to greater insight, learning, and problem-solving than with other kinds of interfaces (Marshall *et al*, 2003).

BOX 6.6

VoxBox – a tangible questionnaire machine

Traditional methods for gathering public opinions, such as surveys, involve approaching people in situ but can disrupt the positive experience they are having. VoxBox is a tangible system

Figure 6.29 VoxBox – Front and back of the tangible machine questionnaire

Source: Golsteijn, C., Gallacher, S., Koeman, L., Wall, L., Andberg, S., Rogers, Y. and Capra, L. (2015) VoxBox: a Tangible Machine that Gathers Opinions from the Public at Events. In *Proc. of TEI' 2015.* ACM.

designed to gather opinions on a range of topics in situ at an event through playful and engaging interaction (Golsteijn *et al*, 2015). It is intended to encourage wider participation by grouping similar questions, encouraging completion, gathering answers to open and closed questions, and connecting answers and results. It was designed as a large physical system that provides a range of tangible input mechanisms through which people give their opinions, instead of using, for example, text messages or social media input. The various input mechanisms include sliders, buttons, knobs, and spinners – which people are all familiar with. In addition, the system has a transparent tube at the side that drops a ball step by step as sets of questions are completed – to act as an incentive for completion and as a progress indicator. The results of the selections are aggregated and presented as simple digital visualizations on the other side (e.g. 95% are engaged; 5% are bored). VoxBox has been used at a number of events drawing in the crowds, who become completely absorbed in answering questions in this tangible format. ■

Research and design issues

Because tangible interfaces are quite different from GUI-based ones, researchers have developed alternative conceptual frameworks that identify their novel and specific features, e.g. Fishkin (2004) and Ullmar *et al* (2005). A key design concern is what kind of coupling to use between the physical action and effect. This includes determining where the digital feedback is provided in relation to the physical artifact that has been manipulated: for example, should it appear on top of the object, beside it, or some other place. The type and placement of the digital media will depend to a large extent on the purpose of using a tangible interface. If it is to support learning then an explicit mapping between action and effect is critical. In contrast, if it is for entertainment purposes, e.g. playing music or storytelling, then it may be better to design them to be more implicit and unexpected. Another key design question is what kind of physical artifact to use to enable the user to carry out an activity in a natural way. Bricks, cubes, and other component sets are most commonly used because of their flexibility and simplicity, enabling people to hold them in both hands and to construct new structures that can be easily added to or changed. Sticky notes and cardboard tokens can also be used for placing material onto a surface that is transformed or attached to digital content, e.g. Klemmer *et al* (2001) and Rogers *et al* (2006). An extensive overview about tangible user interfaces, outlining the important research and design questions, has been written by Shaer and Hornecker (2010). ■

6.2.17 Augmented and Mixed Reality

Other ways that the physical and digital worlds have been bridged include augmented reality, where virtual representations are superimposed on physical devices and objects, and mixed reality, where views of the real world are combined with views of a virtual environment (Drascic and Milgram, 1996). One of the precursors of this work was the Digital Desk

(Wellner, 1993). Physical office tools, like books, documents, and paper, were integrated with virtual representations, using projectors and video cameras. Both virtual and real documents were combined.

To begin with, augmented reality was mostly experimented with in medicine, where virtual objects, e.g. X-rays and scans, were overlaid on part of a patient's body to aid the physician's understanding of what was being examined or operated on. It was then used to aid controllers and operators in rapid decision-making. One example is air traffic control, where controllers are provided with dynamic information about the aircraft in their section that is overlaid on a video screen showing the real planes landing, taking off, and taxiing. The additional information enables the controllers to easily identify planes that are difficult to make out – something especially useful in poor weather conditions. Similarly, head-up displays (HUDs) are used in military and civil planes to aid pilots when landing during poor weather conditions. A HUD provides electronic directional markers on a fold-down display that appears directly in the field of view of the pilot. Instructions for building or repairing complex equipment, such as photocopiers and car engines, have also been designed to replace paper-based manuals, where drawings are superimposed upon the machinery itself, telling the mechanic what to do and where to do it.

Everyday graphical representations, e.g. maps, can be overlaid with additional dynamic information. Such augmentations can complement the properties of the printed information in that they enable the user to interact with embedded information in novel ways. An early application is the augmentation of paper-based maps with photographs and video footage to enable emergency workers to assess the effects of flooding and traffic (Reitmayr *et al*, 2005). A camera mounted above the map tracks the map's locations on the surface while a projector augments the maps with projected information from overhead. Figure 6.30 shows areas of flooding that have been superimposed on a map of Cambridge (UK), together with images of the city center captured by cameras.

There are many augmented reality apps available now for a range of contexts, from education to car navigation, where digital content is overlaid on geographic locations and

Figure 6.30 An augmented map showing the flooded areas at high water level overlaid on the paper map. The handheld device is used to interact with entities referenced on the map
Source: Reproduced with permission.

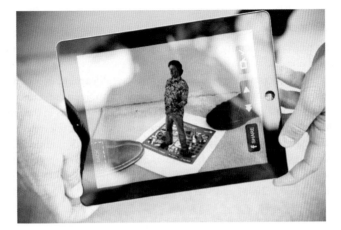

Figure 6.31 James May appearing in 3D Augmented Reality

Source: http://www.wired.com/2012/04/top-gear-host-narrates-museum-exhibits-as-augmented-reality-avatar/. Roberto Baldwin/Wired/©Conde Nast

objects. To reveal the digital information, users open the AR app on a smartphone or tablet and the content appears superimposed on what is viewed through the screen. An example is of Top Gear presenter, James May, appearing as a 3D character (see Figure 6.31) to act as personal tour guide at the Science Museum in London. Other AR apps have been developed to aid people walking in a city or town. Directions (in the form of a pointing hand or arrow) and local information (e.g. the nearest McDonald's) are overlaid on a picture of the street the person holding the phone is walking in. Real-estate apps have also been developed that combine an image of a residential property with its price per square meter. The directions and information change as the person walks or drives up the street.

> **Link** to app of James May, appearing as a 3D character to act as personal tour guide at the Science Museum in London, can be seen at
> **http://www.sciencemuseum.org.uk/visitmuseum_old/jamesmay.aspx**

Research and design issues

A key research concern when designing mixed reality environments and augmented reality is what form the digital augmentation should take and when and where it should appear in the physical environment (Rogers *et al*, 2005). The information needs to stand out but not distract the person from his ongoing activity in the physical world. For example, ambient sounds need to be designed to be distinct from naturally occurring sounds so that they draw a person's attention without distracting him and then allow him to return to what he was doing.

(Continued)

Information that is superimposed on the physical world, e.g. digital information overlaying video footage of a runway to identify vehicles and planes, needs to be simple and easy to align with the real-world objects.

It is important to understand how designing for playful learning experiences is very different from designing for military or medical applications. Ambiguity and uncertainty may be exploited to good effect in mixed reality games but could be disastrous in the latter categories. The type of technology will also determine what guidance will be of relevance. A guideline for the use of an optical see-through display, e.g. shutter glasses or head-mounted display, may not be relevant for a video see-through display. Likewise, a guideline for a mobile augmented reality solution may not be relevant for a fixed display application. Published design guidelines include Cawood and Fiala (2008) and Wetzel *et al* (2008). ∎

6.2.18   Wearables

Imagine being at a party and being able to access the Facebook of a person whom you have just met, while or after talking to her, to find out more about her. The possibility of having instant information before one's very own eyes that is contextually relevant to an ongoing activity and that can be viewed surreptitiously (i.e. without having to physically pull out a smartphone) is very appealing. Since the early experimental days of wearable computing, where Steve Mann (1997) donned head and eye cameras to enable him to record what he saw while also accessing digital information on the move, there have been many innovations and inventions including the latest Google Glass.

DILEMMA

Google Glass: Seeing too much?

Google Glass is a wearable that went on sale in 2014 in various fashion styles (see Figure 6.32). It was designed to look like a pair of glasses, but with one lens of the glass being an interactive display with an embedded camera that can be controlled with speech input. It allows the wearer to take photos and video on the move and look at digital content, such as emails, texts, and maps. The wearer can also search the web using voice commands and the results come back on the screen. A number of applications have been developed besides everyday use, including WatchMeTalk that provides live captions that help the hearing-impaired in their day-to-day conversations and Preview for Glass that enables a wearer to watch a movie trailer the moment they look at a movie poster.

Video of 'London through Google Glass' at **http://youtu.be/Z3AIdnzZUsE**

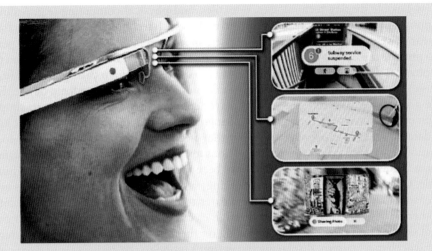

Figure 6.32 Google Glass

Source: https://www.google.co.uk/intl/en/glass/start/.
Google and the Google logo are registered trademarks of Google Inc., used with permission.

However, it can be slightly unnerving when in the company of someone wearing Google Glass as they look up and to the right to view what is on the glass screen rather than at you and into your eyes. As a result, you might see more of the whites of their eyes than the usual interested dilated pupils. Could this be the end of eye contact as we know it? One of the criticisms of early wearers of Google Glass was that it made them appear to be staring into the distance.

Others are worried that those wearing Google Glass are recording everything that is happening in front of them. As a reaction, a number of bars and restaurants in San Francisco and other cities have implemented a 'no Glass' policy to prevent customers from recording other patrons. There has also been much debate in the press about the latest developments in facial recognition. There are apps developed for Google Glass that take a picture of the person you are talking with and then check their online profile, providing a cloud of personal information about them, presumably mined from Facebook and other social media apps. So you can find out more about someone on the go while talking to them – for example, what music they like, what films they have just seen, where they have just been on vacation, and so on – all in a digestible précis surrounded by a halo of photos. One could imagine that if this way of meeting up with others actually takes off, we might find ourselves in the situation where we won't need to talk to each other anymore. Just as text messaging has largely taken over from making phone calls for many people, 'cloud talk' could start taking over our initial encounters with people when we meet them at parties, at conferences, on trains, etc. We might nod and smile in acknowledgement of each other but we won't ever have to have those awkward conversations anymore, such as about where you come from or what you do for work. A panacea for the shy? But how will we know what each other is looking at? You might think I am reading your blog or tweets when in your presence, but really I might just be watching the latest updates of the football results and pretending to 'meet you'. ■

New flexible display technologies, e-textiles, and physical computing (e.g. Arduino) pro-vide opportunities for thinking about how to embed such technologies on people in the clothes they wear. Jewelry, head-mounted caps, glasses, shoes, and jackets have all been experimented with to provide the user with a means of interacting with digital information while on the move in the physical world. An early motivation was to enable people to carry out tasks (e.g. select-ing music) while moving without having to take out and control a handheld device. Examples include a ski jacket with integrated MP3 player controls that enable wearers to simply touch a button on their arm with their glove to change a track and automatic diaries that keep users up-to-date on what is happening and what they need to do throughout the day. More recent applications have focused on embedding various textile, display, and haptic technologies to pro-mote new forms of communication and have been motivated by aesthetics and playfulness. For example, CuteCircuit develops fashion clothing, such as the KineticDress, which is embedded with sensors that follow the body of the wearer to capture their movements and interaction with others. These are then displayed through electroluminescent embroidery that covers the external skirt section of the dress. Depending on the amount and speed of the wearer's move-ment it will change pattern, displaying the wearer's mood to the audience and creating a magic halo around her. CuteCircuit also developed the Hug Shirt (see Chapter 4).

Video of the 'Talking Shoe' concept at **http://youtu.be/VcaSwxbRkcE**

Research and design issues

A core design concern – that is specific to wearable interfaces – is comfort. Users need to feel comfortable wearing clothing that is embedded with technology. It needs to be light, small, not get in the way, fashionable, and (with the exception of the displays) preferably hidden in the clothing. Another related issue is hygiene – is it possible to wash or clean the clothing once worn? How easy is it to remove the electronic gadgetry and replace it? Where are the batteries going to be placed and how long is their lifetime? A key usability concern is how does the user control the devices that are embedded in his clothing – is touch, speech, or more conventional buttons and dials preferable? ■

ACTIVITY 6.9

Smartwatches, such those made by Android, Apple, Pebble, and Samsung, have become popu-lar wearables, providing a multitude of functions including fitness tracking and beaming out messages, Facebook updates, and the latest tweets. Samsung's even has a fingerprint scanner to enable payments to be made simply by touching the watch. Smartwatches are also context and location aware. On detecting the wearer's presence, promotional offers may be pinged to a person wearing a smartwatch from nearby stores, tempting them in to buy. How do you feel about this?

Comment

Smartwatches are similar to smartphones in that they, too, get pinged with promotions and ads for nearby restaurants and stores. However, the main difference is that smartwatches when worn on a wrist are ever-present to look at; the user only needs to glance down at it to notice a new notification, whereas they have to take out their phones from their pockets and purses to see what new item has been pinged (although some people have their smartphone permanently held in their hand). This means that they may be always looking and more prone to being nudged to spend money. While some people might like to get 10% off a coffee if they walk into the cafe that has just sent them a digital voucher, for others it may be very annoying to be constantly bombarded with this kind of promotional material. Worse still, it could tempt children and vulnerable people who are wearing such a watch to spend money when perhaps they shouldn't or to nag their parents or carers to buy it for them. ■

6.2.19   Robots and Drones

Robots have been with us for some time, most notably as characters in science fiction movies, but also playing an important role as part of manufacturing assembly lines, as remote investigators of hazardous locations (e.g. nuclear power stations and bomb disposal), and as search and rescue helpers in disasters (e.g. fires) or far-away places (e.g. Mars). Console interfaces have been developed to enable humans to control and navigate robots in remote terrains, using a combination of joysticks and keyboard controls together with camera and sensor-based interactions (Baker *et al*, 2004). The focus has been on designing interfaces that enable users to effectively steer and move a remote robot with the aid of live video and dynamic maps.

Domestic robots that help with the cleaning and gardening have become popular. Robots are also being developed to help the elderly and disabled with certain activities, such as picking up objects and cooking meals. Pet robots, in the guise of human companions, are being commercialized. A somewhat controversial idea is that sociable robots should be able to collaborate with humans and socialize with them – as if they were our peers (Breazeal, 2005).

Several research teams have taken the 'cute and cuddly' approach to designing robots, signaling to humans that the robots are more pet-like than human-like. For example, Mitsubishi has developed Mel the penguin (Sidner and Lee, 2005) whose role is to host events, while the Japanese inventor Takanori Shibata developed Paro in 2004, a baby harp seal that looks like a cute furry cartoon animal, and whose role was as a companion (see Figure 6.33). Sensors have been embedded in the pet robots, enabling them to detect certain human behaviors and respond accordingly. For example, they can open, close, and move their eyes, giggle, and raise their flippers. The robots afford cuddling and talking to – as if they were pets or

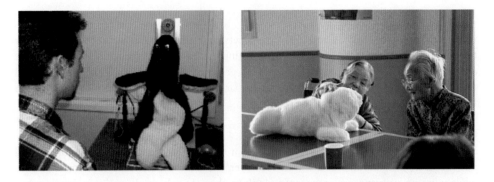

Figure 6.33 Left: Mel, the penguin robot, designed to host activities; right: Japan's Paro, an interactive seal, designed as a companion, primarily for the elderly and sick children

Source: (left) Image courtesy of Mitsubishi Electric Research Labs. (right) Courtesy of Parorobots.com.

animals. The appeal of pet robots is thought to be partially due to their therapeutic qualities, being able to reduce stress and loneliness among the elderly and infirm (see Chapter 5 for more on cuddly robot pets). Paro has since been used in the UK to help patients with dementia to make them feel more at ease and comforted (Griffiths, 2014). Specifically, it has been used to encourage social behavior amongst patients who often anthropomorphize it. For example, they might say as a joke "it's farted on me!", which makes them and others around them laugh, leading to further laughter and joking. This form of encouraging of social interaction is thought to be therapeutic.

> **Video** of 'Robot Pets of the Future' at **http://youtu.be/wBFws1lhuv0**

Drones are a form of unmanned aircraft that are controlled remotely. They were first used by hobbyists and then by the military. Since, they have become more affordable, accessible, and easier to fly, and as a result have begun to be used in a wider range of contexts. These include entertainment, such as carrying drinks and food to people at festivals and parties; agricultural applications, such as flying them over vineyards and fields to collect data that is useful to farmers; and helping to track poachers in wildlife parks in Africa. Compared with other forms of data collecting, they can fly low and stream photos to a ground station, where the images can be stitched together into maps and then used to determine the health of a crop or when it is the best time to harvest the crop.

> **Video** of OppiKoppi, a drone that drops beer to festival goers at
> **http://youtu.be/janur7RJwm0**

Figure 6.34 A drone being used to survey the state of a vineyard

Source: Courtesy of Discover Sonoma County Wine
http://www.latimes.com/business/la-fi-drones-agriculture-20140913-story.html#page=1.

Research and design issues

An ethical concern is whether it is acceptable to create robots that exhibit behaviors that humans will consider to be human- or animal-like. While this form of attribution also occurs for PC-based agent interfaces (see Chapter 2), having a physical embodiment – as robots do – can make people suspend their disbelief even more, viewing the robots as pets or humans. This raises the moral question as to whether such anthropomorphism should be encouraged. Should robots be designed to be as human-like as possible, looking like us with human features, e.g. eyes and mouth, behaving like us, communicating like us, and emotionally responding like us? Or should they be designed to look like robots and behave like robots, e.g. vacuum cleaner robots that serve a clearly defined purpose? Likewise, should the interaction be designed to enable people to interact with the robot as if it were another human being, e.g. talking, gesturing, holding its hand, and smiling at it, or should the interaction be designed to be more like human–computer interaction, e.g. pressing buttons, knobs, and dials to issue commands?

For many people, the cute pet approach to robotic interfaces seems preferable to one that aims to design them to be more like fully fledged human beings. Humans know where they stand with pets and are less likely to be unnerved by them and, paradoxically, are more likely to suspend their disbelief in the companionship they provide.

Another ethical concern is whether it is acceptable to use unmanned drones to take a series of images or videos of fields, towns, and private property without permission or people knowing what is happening. ∎

"Frankly, I'm not sure this whole idea-sharing thing is working."

6.2.20 Brain–Computer Interfaces

Brain–computer interfaces (BCI) provide a communication pathway between a person's brain waves and an external device, such as a cursor on a screen or a tangible puck that moves via airflow). The person is trained to concentrate on the task (e.g. moving the cursor or the puck). Several research projects have investigated how this technique can be used to assist and augment human cognitive or sensory-motor functions. The way BCIs work is through detecting changes in the neural functioning in the brain. Our brains are filled with neurons that comprise individual nerve cells connected to one another by dendrites and axons. Every time we think, move, feel, or remember something, these neurons become active. Small electric signals rapidly move from neuron to neuron – that can to a certain extent be detected by electrodes that are placed on a person's scalp. The electrodes are embedded in specialized headsets, hairnets, or caps (see Figure 6.35). Tan Le, in her 2010 TED talk, demonstrated how it is possible, using the Emotiv Systems headset, for a participant to move virtual objects, such as a cube, on a screen.

Figure 6.35 The Brainball game using a brain–computer interface
Source: "Brainball" from The Interactive Institute. Reproduced with permission.

> **Video** demonstrating brain–computer interaction at
> **www.ted.com/talks/tan_le_a_headset_that_reads_your_brainwaves.html**

Brain–computer interfaces have also been developed to control various games. For example, Brainball was developed as a game to be controlled by players' brain waves in which they compete to control a ball's movement across a table by becoming more relaxed and focused.

Other possibilities include controlling a robot and being able to fly a virtual plane by thinking of lifting the mind.

Pioneering medical research conducted by the BrainGate research group at Brown University has started using brain–computer interfaces to enable people who are paralyzed to control robots. For example, a robotic arm controlled by a tethered BCI has enabled patients who are paralyzed to feed themselves (see video).

> **Video** of a woman who is paralyzed moving a robot with her mind at
> **http://youtu.be/ogBX18maUiM**

6.3 Natural User Interfaces and Beyond

As we have seen, there are many kinds of interface that can be used to design for user experiences. The staple for many years was the GUI (graphical user interface), which without doubt has been very versatile in supporting all manner of computer-based activities, from sending email to managing process control plants. But is its time up? Will NUIs (short for natural user interfaces) begin to overtake them?

But what exactly are NUIs? A NUI is one that enables people to interact with a computer in the same ways they interact with the physical world, through using their voice, hands, and bodies. Instead of using a keyboard and a mouse (as is the case with GUIs), a natural user interface allows users to speak to machines, stroke their surfaces, gesture at them in the air, dance on mats that detect feet movements, smile at them to get a reaction, and so on. The naturalness refers to the way they exploit the everyday skills we have learned, such as talking, writing, gesturing, walking, and picking up objects. In theory, they should be easier to learn and map more readily onto how people interact with the world than compared with learning to use a GUI. For example, as Steve Ballmer, a former CEO of Microsoft, noted when the idea of NUIs first came to the fore:

> *I believe we will look back on 2010 as the year we expanded beyond the mouse and keyboard and started incorporating more natural forms of interaction such as touch, speech, gestures, handwriting, and vision – what computer scientists call the 'NUI' or natural user interface.* (Ballmer, 2010)

Instead of having to remember which function keys to press to open a file, a NUI means a person only has to raise their arm or say 'open'. But how natural are NUIs? Is it more natural to say 'open' than to flick a switch when wanting to open a door? And is it more natural to raise both arms to change a channel on the TV than to press a button on the remote? Whether a NUI is more natural than a GUI will depend on a number of factors, including how much learning is required, the complexity of the application/device's interface, and whether accuracy and speed are needed (Norman, 2010). Sometimes a gesture is worth a thousand words. Other times, a word is worth a thousand gestures. It depends on how many functions the system supports.

Consider the sensor-based faucets that were described in Chapter 1. The gesture-based interface works mostly (with the exception of people wearing black clothing that cannot be detected) because there are only two functions: (i) turning on by waving one's hands under the tap, and (ii) turning off by removing them from the sink. Now think about other functions that faucets usually provide, such as controlling water temperature and flow. What kind of a gesture would be most appropriate for changing the temperature and then the flow? Would one decide on the temperature first by raising one's left hand and the flow by raising one's right hand? How would we know when to stop raising our hand to get the right temperature? We would need to put a hand under the tap to check. If we put our right hand under that might have the effect of decreasing the flow. And when does the system know that the desired temperature and flow has been reached? Would it require having both hands suspended in mid-air for a few seconds to register that was the desired state? We would all need to become water conductors. It is hardly surprising that such a system of control does not exist – since it simply would not work. Hence, the reason why sensor-based faucets in public toilets all have their temperature and flow set to a default.

This caricature illustrates how it can be more difficult to design even a small set of gestures to map onto a set of control functions, which can be accurately recognized by the system while also readily learned and remembered by the general public. It also highlights how gestural, speech, and other kinds of NUIs will not replace GUIs as the new face of interaction design. However, it does not mean they will not be useful. They are proving to be effective and enjoyable to use when controlling and manipulating digital content in a number of tasks and activities. For example, using gestures and whole body movement has proven to be highly enjoyable as a form of input for many computer games and physical exercises, such as those that have been developed for the Wii and Kinect systems. Furthermore, new kinds of gesture, speech, and touch interfaces have proven to be very empowering for people who are visually impaired and who have previously had to use specialized tools to interface with GUIs. For example, the iPhone's VoiceOver control features enable visually impaired people to send email, use the web, play music, and so on, without having to buy an expensive customized phone or screen reader. Moreover, being able to purchase a regular phone means not being singled out for special treatment. And while some gestures may feel cumbersome for sighted people to learn and use, they may not be for blind or visually impaired people. The VoiceOver press and guess feature that reads out what you tap on the screen (e.g. 'messages,' 'calendar,' 'mail: 5 new items') can open up new ways of exploring an application while a three-finger tap can become a natural way to turn the screen off.

An emerging class of human–computer interfaces are those that rely largely on subtle, gradual, continuous changes triggered by information obtained implicitly from the user. They are connected with lightweight, ambient, context aware, affective, and augmented cognition interfaces and are especially found in high-performance tasks such as gaming apps (Solovey *et al*, 2014). Using brain, body, behavioral, and environmental sensors, it is now possible to capture subtle changes in people's cognitive and emotional states in real time. This opens up new doors in human–computer interaction. In particular, it allows for information to be used as both continuous and discrete input, potentially enabling new outputs to match and be updated with what people might want and need at any given time. However, brain, body, and other sensor data are different from GUIs. Future research needs to consider how best to exploit this more subtle class of input in order to achieve new interfaces.

6.4 Which Interface?

In this chapter we have given an overview of the diversity of interfaces that is now available or currently being researched. There are many opportunities to design for user experiences that are a far cry from those originally developed using command-based interfaces in the 1980s. An obvious question this raises is: but which one and how do you design it? In many contexts, the requirements for the user experience that have been identified during the design process will determine what kind of interface might be appropriate and what features to include. For example, if a healthcare application is being developed to enable patients to monitor their dietary intake, then a mobile device – that has the ability to scan barcodes and/or take pictures of food items that can be compared with a database – would appear to be a good interface to use, enabling mobility, effective object recognition, and ease of use. If the goal is to design a work environment to support collocated group decision-making activities then combining shareable technologies and personal devices that enable people to move fluidly between them would be a good choice.

But how do we decide which interface is preferable for a given task or activity? For example, is multimedia better than tangible interfaces for learning? Is speech effective as a command-based interface? Is a multimodal interface more effective than a single media interface? Are wearable interfaces better than mobile interfaces for helping people find information in foreign cities? Are virtual environments the ultimate interface for playing games? Or will mixed reality or tangible environments prove to be more challenging and captivating? Will shareable interfaces, such as interactive furniture, be better at supporting communication and collaboration compared with using networked desktop technologies? And so forth. These questions are currently being researched. In practice, which interface is most appropriate, most useful, most efficient, most engaging, most supportive, etc., will depend on the interplay of a number of factors, including reliability, social acceptability, privacy, ethical, and location concerns.

Assignment

In Activity 6.4 we asked you to compare the experience of playing the game of Snake on a PC with playing on a cell/smart phone. For this assignment, we want you to consider the pros and cons of playing the same game using different interfaces. Select three interfaces, other than the GUI and mobile ones (e.g. tangible, wearable, and shareable) and describe how the game could be redesigned for each of these, taking into account the user group being targeted. For example, the tangible game could be designed for young children, the wearable interface for young adults, and the shareable interface for elderly people.

(a) Go through the research and design issues for each interface and consider whether they are relevant for the game setting and what issues they raise. For the wearable interface, issues to do with comfort and hygiene are important when designing the game.

(b) Describe a hypothetical scenario of how the game would be played for each of the three interfaces.

(c) Consider specific design issues that will need to be addressed. For example, for the shareable surface would it be best to have a tabletop or a wall-based surface? How will the users interact with the snake for each of the different interfaces; by using a pen, fingertips, or other input device? Is it best to have a representation of a snake for each player or one they take turns to play with? If multiple snakes are used, what will happen if one person tries to move another person's snake? Would you add any other rules? And so on.

(d) Compare the pros and cons of designing the Snake game using the three different interfaces with respect to how it is played on the cell phone and the PC.

Summary

This chapter has given an overview of the diversity of interfaces that can be designed for user experiences, identifying key design issues and research questions that need to be addressed. It has highlighted the opportunities and challenges that lie ahead for designers and researchers who are experimenting with and developing innovative interfaces. It has also explicated some of the assumptions behind the benefits of different interfaces – some that are supported, others that are still unsubstantiated. It has presented a number of interaction techniques that are particularly suited (or not) for a given interface type. It has also discussed the dilemmas facing designers when using a particular kind of interface, e.g. abstract versus realism, menu selection versus free-form text input, human-like versus non-human-like. Finally, it has presented pointers to specific design guidelines and exemplary systems that have been designed using a given interface.

Key points
• Many interfaces have emerged post the WIMP/GUI era, including speech, wearable, mobile, tangible, brain–computer, robots, and drones.
• A range of design and research questions need to be considered when deciding which interface to use and what features to include.

- So-called natural user interfaces may not be as natural as graphical user interfaces – it depends on the task, user, and context.
- An important concern that underlies the design of any kind of interface is how information is represented to the user (be it speech, multimedia, virtual reality, augmented reality), so that they can make sense of it with respect to their ongoing activity, e.g. playing a game, shopping online, or interacting with a pet robot.
- Increasingly, new interfaces that are context-aware or monitor people raise ethical issues concerned with what data is being collected and what it is used for.

Further Reading

Many of the best books on designing interfaces have been developed for the practitioner market. They are often written in a humorous and highly accessible way, replete with cartoons, worldly prescriptions, and figures. They also use modern fonts that make the text very appealing. We recommend:

GOOGLE (2014) *Material Design* http://www.google.com/design/spec/material-design/introduction.html. This online resource provides a living online document that visually illustrates essential interface design principles. It is beautifully laid out and very informative to click through all the interactive examples it provides. It shows how to add some physical properties to the digital world to make it feel more intuitive to use across platforms.

JOHNSON, J. (2007) *GUI Bloopers. 2.0: Common user interface design don'ts and dos*, (2nd edn). Morgan Kaufmann. This second edition of a classic has been updated to reflect the bloopers that are common across the design of a range of interfaces. It is full of the author's amusing anecdotes and other designer howlers.

There are also many good practical guides on web usability and interaction design that have been published by New Riders. Some are updated on a regular basis while others are new. These include:

KRUG, S. (2014) *Don't Make Me Think!* (3rd edn). New Riders Press.

NIELSEN, J. and LORANGER, H. (2006) *Prioritizing Web Usability*. New Riders Press.

VEEN, J. (2001) *The Art and Science of Web Design*. New Riders Press.

And finally, a thought-provoking essay that everyone should read (a shorter version is also available on Don Norman's website):

NORMAN, D. (2010) Natural interfaces are not natural, *interactions*, May/June, 6–10.

INTERVIEW
with Leah Beuchley

Leah Buechley is an independent designer, engineer, and educator. She has a PhD in Computer Science and a degree in physics. She began her studies as a dance major and has also been deeply engaged in theater, art, and design over the years. She was the founder and director of the high-low tech group at the MIT media lab from 2009 to 2014. She has always blended the sciences and the arts in her education and her career – as witnessed by her current work, comprising computer science, industrial design, interaction design, art, and electrical engineering.

Why did you call your MIT media lab research group high-low tech?
Technology is made from a limited palette of physical materials, designed and built by a small subset of people, and interacted with in a very constrained manner. The name high-low tech is meant to evoke an alternate vision of technology – technology that is handcrafted by different people to fit their own personal needs. More specifically, I was interested in expanding the technology space to encompass a broader palette of materials (including materials like fabrics, ceramics, paper, and wood), a more diverse group of designers and engineers, and an expanded conception of interface.

Can you give me some examples of how you mesh the digital with physical materials?
I've been working on a project called LilyPad Arduino (or LilyPad) for almost 10 years. LilyPad is a construction kit that enables people to embed computers and electronics into their clothes. It's a set of sewable electronic pieces – including microcontrollers, sensors, and LEDs – that are stitched together with conductive thread. People can use the kit to make singing pillows, glow in the dark handbags, and interactive ball gowns. I recently co-authored a book with my former student Kanjun Qiu, *Sew Electric*, that introduces electronics and programming via LilyPad.

Another example is the work my former students and I have done in paper-based computing. My former student Jie Qi just developed a kit called 'circuit stickers' that lets you build interactive paper-based projects. Based on her years of research in high-low tech, the kit is a set of flexible peel-and-stick electronic stickers. You can connect ultra-thin LEDs, microcontrollers, and sensors with conductive ink, tape, or thread to quickly make beautiful electronic sketches.

Why would anyone want to wear a computer in their clothing?
Computers open up new creative possibilities for designers. Computers are simply a new tool, albeit an especially powerful one, in a designer's toolbox. They allow clothing designers to make garments that are dynamic and interactive. Clothing that can, for example, change color in response to pollution levels, sparkle when a loved one calls you on the phone,

or notify you when your blood pressure increases.

How do you involve people in your research?

I engage with people in a few different ways. First, I design hardware and software tools to help people build new and different kinds of technology. The LilyPad is a good example of this kind of work. I hone these designs by teaching workshops to different groups of people, and once a tool is stable, I work hard to disseminate it to users in the real world. The LilyPad has been commercially available since 2007 and it has been fascinating and exciting to see how a group of real-world designers – who are predominantly female – is using it to build things like smart sportswear, plush video game controllers, soft robots, and interactive embroideries.

I also strive to be as open as possible with my own design and engineering explorations. I document and publish as much information as I can about the materials, tools, and processes I use. I apply an open source approach not only to the software and hardware I create but, as much as I can, to the entire creative process. I develop and share tutorials, classroom and workshop curricula, materials references, and engineering techniques.

What excites you most about your work?

I am infatuated with materials. There is nothing more inspiring than a sheet of heavy paper, a length of wool felt, a rough block of wood, or a box of old motors. My thinking about design and technology is largely driven by explorations of materials and their affordances. So materials are always delightful. But the real-world adoption of tools I've designed and the prospect this presents for changing technology culture is perhaps what's most exciting. My most dearly held goal is to expand and diversify technology culture and it's tremendously rewarding to see evidence that my work is starting to do that. ▪

Chapter 7

DATA GATHERING

Objectives

The main aims of the chapter are to:

- Discuss how to plan and run a successful data gathering program.
- Enable you to plan and run an interview.
- Enable you to design a simple questionnaire.
- Enable you to plan and carry out an observation.

7.1 Introduction

This chapter presents some techniques for data gathering which are commonly used in inter-action design activities. In particular, data gathering is a central part of establishing require-ments, and of evaluation. Within the requirements activity, the purpose of data gathering is to collect sufficient, accurate, and relevant data so that a set of stable requirements can be produced; within evaluation, data gathering is needed in order to capture users' reactions and performance with a system or prototype.

In this chapter we introduce three main techniques for gathering data: interviews, ques-tionnaires, and observation. In the next chapter we discuss how to analyze and interpret the data collected. Interviews involve an interviewer asking one or more interviewees a set of ques-tions, which may be highly structured or unstructured; interviews are usually synchronous and are often face-to-face, but they don't have to be. Questionnaires are a series of questions designed to be answered asynchronously, i.e. without the presence of the investigator; these may be on paper, or online. Observation may be direct or indirect. Direct observation involves spending time with individuals observing activity as it happens. Indirect observation involves making a record of the user's activity as it happens to be studied at a later date. All three techniques may be used to collect qualitative or quantitative data.

Although this is a small set of basic techniques, they are flexible and can be combined and extended in many ways. Indeed it is important not to focus on just one data gathering technique but to use them flexibly and in combination so as to avoid biases which are inherent in any one approach. The way in which each technique is used varies, depending on the interaction design activity being undertaken. More detailed descriptions of how they are used and additional techniques relevant only to specific activities of the lifecycle are given in later chapters (Chapter 10 for requirements, and Chapters 13–15 for evaluation).

7.2   Five Key Issues

Data gathering sessions need to be planned and carried out carefully. Specific issues relating to the three data gathering techniques are discussed in the following sections, but first we consider five key issues that require attention for any data gathering session to be successful: goal setting, identifying participants, the relationship between the data collector and the data provider, triangulation, and pilot studies.

7.2.1   Setting Goals

The main reason for gathering data at all is to glean information about something. For example, you might want to understand how technology fits into normal family life, or you might want to identify which of two icons representing 'send message' is easier to use, or you might want to find out whether the redesign you are planning for a hand-held meter reader is along the right lines. There are many different reasons for gathering data, and before beginning it is important to identify specific goals for the study. The goals that are set will influence the nature of the data gathering sessions, the data gathering techniques to be used, and also the analysis to be performed. Once the goals have been set, you can concentrate on what data to look for and what to do with it once it is gathered.

The goals may be expressed more or less formally, e.g. using some structured or even mathematical format, or using a simple description such as the ones in the previous paragraph, but whatever the format they should be clear and concise. In interaction design it is more usual to express goals for data gathering informally.

7.2.2   Identifying Participants

The goals you develop for your data gathering session will indicate the kind of people you want to gather data from. Those people who fit this profile are called the population. In some cases, the people you need to gather data from may be clearly identifiable – maybe because there is a small group of users and you have access to each one. However, it is more likely that you will need to choose the participants to include in your data gathering, and this is called sampling. The situation where you have access to all members of your target population is called saturation sampling, but this is quite rare. Assuming that you will be choosing to involve a proportion of your population in data gathering, then you have two options: probability sampling or non-probability sampling. In the former case, the most commonly used approaches are simple random sampling or stratified sampling; in the latter the most common are convenience sampling or volunteer panels.

Random sampling can be achieved by using a random number generator or by choosing every *n*th person in a list. Stratified sampling relies on being able to divide the population into groups (e.g. classes in a secondary school), and then applying random sampling. Both convenience sampling and volunteer panels rely less on you choosing the participants and more on participants being prepared to take part. The term convenience sampling is used to describe a situation where the sample includes those who were available rather than those specifically selected.

The crucial difference between probability and non-probability methods is that in the former you can apply statistical tests and generalize to the whole population, while in the latter such generalizations are not robust. Using statistics also requires having a sufficient number of participants. What exactly 'sufficient' means will depend on the type of data being collected and the kind of statistical tests that need to be applied. This can be a complex issue so if not confident with statistics, it is best to consult with a someone who knows about them. See Sue and Ritter (2012) for a more detailed treatment of sampling.

7.2.3   Relationship with Participants

One significant aspect of any data gathering is the relationship between the person (people) doing the gathering and the person (people) providing the data. Making sure that this relationship is clear and professional will help to clarify the nature of the study. One way in which this can be achieved is to ask participants to sign an informed consent form. The details of this form will vary, but it usually asks the participants to confirm that the purpose of the data gathering and how the data will be used have been explained to them and that they are happy to continue. It also often includes a statement that participants may withdraw at any time, and that in this case none of their data will be used in the study.

It is common practice in many countries to use an informed consent form when running evaluation sessions, particularly where the participants are members of the public, or are volunteers in a research project. The informed consent form is intended to protect the interests of both the data gatherer and the data provider (see Chapter 13). The gatherer wants to know that the data she collects can be used in her analysis, presented to interested parties, and published in reports (as appropriate). The data provider wants reassurance that the information he gives will not be used for other purposes, or in any context that would be detrimental to him. For example, he wants to be sure that personal contact information and other personal details are not made public. This is especially true when people with disabilities or children are being interviewed. In the case of children, using an informed consent form reassures parents that their children will not be asked threatening, inappropriate, or embarrassing questions, or be asked to look at disturbing or violent images. In these cases, parents are asked to sign the form. Figure 7.1 shows an example of a typical informed consent form.

However, this kind of consent is not generally required when collecting data for the requirements activity where a contract usually exists in some form between the data collector and the data provider. For example, consider the situation where a consultant is hired to gather data from a company in order to establish a set of requirements for a new interactive system to support timesheet entry. The employees of this company would be the users of the system, and the consultant would therefore expect to have access to the employees to gather data about the timesheet activity. In addition, the company would expect its employees to cooperate in this exercise. In this case, there is already a contract in place which covers the data gathering activity, and therefore an informed consent form is less likely to be required. As with most ethical

---

Crowdsourcing Design for Citizen Science Organizations

SHORT VERSION OF CONSENT FORM for participants at the University of Maryland – 18 YEARS AND OLDER

You are invited to participate in a research project being conducted by the researchers listed on the bottom of the page. In order for us to be allowed to use any data you wish to provide, we must have your consent.

In simplest terms, we hope you will use the mobile phone, tabletop, and project website at the University of Maryland to

- Take pictures
- Share observations about the sights you see on campus
- Share ideas that you have to improve the design of the phone or tabletop application or website
- Comment on pictures, observations, and design ideas of others

The researchers and others using CampusNet will be able to look at your comments and pictures on the tabletop and/or website, and we may ask if you are willing to answer a few more questions (either on paper, by phone, or face-to-face) about your whole experience. You may stop participating at any time.

A long version of this consent form is available for your review and signature, or you may opt to sign this shorter one by *checking off all the boxes that reflect your wishes and signing and dating the form below.*

___I agree that any photos I take using the CampusNet application may be uploaded to the tabletop at the University of Maryland and/or a website now under development.

___I agree to allow any comments, observations, and profile information that I choose to share with others via the online application to be visible to others who use the application at the same time or after me.

___I agree to be videotaped/audiotaped during my participation in this study.

___I agree to complete a short questionnaire during or after my participation in this study.

NAME [Please print]	
SIGNATURE	
DATE	

[Contact information of Senior Researcher responsible for the project]

Figure 7.1 Example of an informed consent form

issues, the important thing is to consider the situation carefully and make a judgment based on the specific circumstances. Increasingly, projects that involve collecting data from humans are being reviewed to ensure that participants' personal information is protected.

Incentives for completing a questionnaire might be needed in some circumstances because there is no clear and direct advantage to the respondents, but in other circumstances, respondents may see it as part of their job to complete the questionnaire. For example, if the questionnaires form part of the requirements activity for a new mobile sales application to support sales executives, then it is likely that sales executives will complete a questionnaire about their job if they are told that the new device will impact their day-to-day lives. In this case, the motivation for providing the required information is clear. However, if you are collecting data to understand how appealing a new interactive website is for school children, different incentives would be appropriate. Here, the advantage for the individuals to complete a questionnaire is not so obvious.

7.2.4   Triangulation

Triangulation is a term used to refer to the investigation of a phenomenon from (at least) two different perspectives (Denzin, 2006; Jupp, 2006). Four types of triangulation have been defined (Jupp, 2006):

1. Triangulation of data means that data is drawn from different sources at different times, in different places, or from different people (possibly by using a different sampling technique).
2. Investigator triangulation means that different researchers (observers, interviewers, etc.) have been used to collect and interpret the data.
3. Triangulation of theories means the use of different theoretical frameworks through which to view the data or findings.
4. Methodological triangulation means to employ different data gathering techniques.

The last of these is the most common form of triangulation. One application of triangulation (and again the most common) is to validate the results of some inquiry by pointing to similar results yielded through the use of different perspectives. However, validation through triangulation is difficult to achieve. Different data gathering methods result in different kinds of data, which may or may not be compatible. Using different theoretical frameworks may or may not result in complementary findings, but to achieve theoretical triangulation would require the theories to have similar philosophical underpinnings. Using more than one data gathering technique, and more than one data analysis approach, is good practice, but achieving true triangulation is rare.

7.2.5   Pilot Studies

A pilot study is a small trial run of the main study. The aim is to make sure that the proposed method is viable before embarking on the real study. Data gathering participants can be (and usually are) very unpredictable, even when a lot of time and effort has been spent carefully planning the data gathering session. Plans should be tested by doing a pilot study before launching into the main study. For example, the equipment and instructions that are to be used can be checked, the questions for an interview or in a questionnaire can be tested for clarity, and an experimental procedure can be confirmed as viable. Potential problems can be identified in advance so that they can be corrected. Distributing 500 questionnaires and then being told that two of the questions were very confusing wastes time, annoys participants, and is an expensive error that could have been avoided by doing a pilot study.

If it is difficult to find people to participate or if access to participants is limited, colleagues or peers can be asked to comment. Getting comments from peers is quick and inexpensive and can be a substitute for a pilot study. It is important to note that anyone involved in a pilot study cannot be involved in the main study. Why? Because they will know more about the study and this can distort the results.

BOX 7.1

Data, information, and conclusions

There is an important difference between raw data, information, and conclusions. Data is what you collect; this is then analyzed and interpreted and conclusions drawn. Information is gained from analyzing and interpreting the data and conclusions represent the actions to be taken based on the information. For example, you might want to know whether a particular screen layout has improved the user's understanding of the application. In this case, the raw data collected might include the time it takes for a set of users to perform a particular task, the users' comments regarding their use of the application, biometric readings about the users' heart rates while using the application, and so on. At this stage, the data is raw. Information will emerge once this raw data has been analyzed and the results interpreted. For example, you may find after analyzing the data that people with more than 5 years' experience find the new design frustrating and take longer to achieve their goals, while those with less than 2 years' experience find the design helpful and complete tasks more quickly. Your interpretation may be that the new layout has improved novices' understanding but has irritated more experienced users, and you may conclude that the layout needs to be redesigned. ■

7.3 Data Recording

Capturing data is necessary so that the results of a data gathering session may be taken away and analyzed. Some forms of data gathering such as questionnaires, diaries, interaction logging, and collecting work artifacts are self-documenting and no further recording is necessary, but for other techniques there is a choice of recording approaches. The most common of these are taking notes, audio recording, taking photographs, and video recording. These may be used individually or in combination. For example, an interview may be audio recorded and then to help the interviewer in later analysis, a photograph of the interviewee may be taken.

Which data recording approaches are used will depend on the context, time and resources available, and the sensitivity of the situation; the choice of data recording approach will affect the level of detail collected, and how intrusive the data gathering will be. In most settings, audio recording, photographs, and notes will be sufficient. In others it is essential to collect video data so as to record in detail the intricacies of the activity and its context. Three common data recording approaches are discussed below.

7.3.1 Notes Plus Photographs

Taking notes (by hand or by typing) is the least technical and most flexible way of recording data. Handwritten notes may be transcribed, in whole or in part. While this may seem tedious, it is usually the first step in the analysis, and this activity gives the analyst a good overview of the quality and contents of the data collected. Even though tools exist for supporting data collection and analysis, the advantages of handwritten notes include that pen and paper are much less intrusive than a keyboard, and they are extremely flexible. Disadvantages with notes include that it can be difficult and tiring to write (or type) and listen or observe at the same time, it is easy to lose concentration, biases creep in, handwriting can be difficult to decipher, and the speed of writing (or typing) is limited. However, working with another person solves some of these problems and provides another perspective.

If appropriate, photograph(s) and short videos, captured via smartphones or other hand-held devices, of artifacts, events, and the environment can be used to supplement notes and hand-drawn sketches, provided permission has been given.

7.3.2   Audio Plus Photographs

Audio recording can be a useful alternative to note taking and is less intrusive than video. In observation, it allows observers to focus on the activity rather than trying to capture every spoken word. In an interview, it allows the interviewer to pay more attention to the interviewee rather than try to take notes as well as listen, but transcribing a lot of audio data is time-consuming. However, it isn't always necessary to transcribe all of it – often only sections are needed, depending on why the data was collected. Many studies do not need a great level of detail, and instead, recordings are used as a reminder and as a source of anecdotes for reports. It is also surprising how evocative it can be to hear audio recordings of people or places from when you collected the data. If you are using audio recording as the main or only data collection technique then it is important that the quality is good and it is advisable to check this before starting your data collection.

Audio recording can be supplemented with photographs, as mentioned above.

7.3.3   Video

Video has the advantage of capturing both visual and audio data but video recording has some additional planning issues that need to be addressed, and it can be intrusive (no matter how well you plan it) (Denzin and Lincoln, 2011). Heath *et al* (2010) identify several of these issues including:

- Deciding whether to fix the camera's position or use a roving recorder. This decision depends on the activity being recorded and the purpose to which the video data will be put – e.g. for illustrative purposes only or for detailed data analysis. In some cases, such as pervasive games, a roving camera is the only way to capture the required action.
- Deciding where to point the camera in order to capture what is required. Heath and his colleagues suggest carrying out fieldwork for a short time before starting to video record in order to become familiar with the environment and be able to identify suitable recording locations. Involving the participants themselves in deciding what and where to record also helps to capture relevant action.
- Understanding the impact of the recording on participants. It is often assumed that video recording will have an impact on participants and their behavior but Heath *et al* (2010) suggest taking an empirical approach to the question and examining the data itself to see whether there is any evidence of behavior orienting to the camera.

ACTIVITY 7.1

Imagine you are a consultant who is employed to help develop a new computerized garden planning tool to be used by amateur and professional garden designers. Your goal is to find out how garden designers use an early prototype as they walk around their clients' gardens sketching design ideas, taking notes, and asking the clients about what they like and how they and their families use the garden. What are the advantages and disadvantages of the three approaches to data recording discussed above, in this environment?

Comment

Handwritten notes do not require specialist equipment. They are unobtrusive and very flexible but difficult to do while walking around a garden. If it starts to rain, there is no equipment to get wet, but notes may get soggy and difficult to read (and write!). Video captures more information, e.g. the landscape, where the designers are looking, sketches, comments, etc., but it is more intrusive and you must hold the camera. Video may also be tricky to capture if it starts to rain. Short video sequences captured on a smartphone are easier to collect and tend to be less obtrusive. Audio may be a good compromise, but integrating sketches and other artifacts later can be more difficult.

Garden planning is a highly visual, aesthetic activity, so it would be important to supplement note taking and audio recording with photographs captured using either a digital camera or a smartphone. ■

7.4 Interviews

Interviews can be thought of as a "conversation with a purpose" (Kahn and Cannell, 1957). How like an ordinary conversation the interview can be depends on the type of interview method used. There are four main types of interviews: open-ended or unstructured, structured, semi-structured, and group interviews (Fontana and Frey, 2005). The first three types are named according to how much control the interviewer imposes on the conversation by following a predetermined set of questions. The fourth involves a small group guided by a facilitator.

The most appropriate approach to interviewing depends on the purpose of the interview, the questions to be addressed, and the stage in the lifecycle. For example, if the goal is to gain first impressions about how users react to a new design idea, such as an interactive sign, then an informal, open-ended interview is often the best approach. But if the goal is to get feedback about a particular design feature, such as the layout of a new web browser, then a structured interview or questionnaire is often better. This is because the goals and questions are more specific in the latter case.

7.4.1 Unstructured Interviews

Open-ended or unstructured interviews are at one end of a spectrum of how much control the interviewer has over the interview process. They are exploratory and are more like conversations around a particular topic; they often go into considerable depth. Questions posed by the interviewer are open, meaning that there is no particular expectation about the format or content of answers. For example, the first question asked of all participants might be: 'What are the advantages of using a touch screen?' Here, the interviewee is free to answer as fully or as briefly as she wishes and both interviewer and interviewee can steer the interview. For example, often the interviewer will say: "Can you tell me a bit more about . . ." This is referred to as probing.

Despite being unstructured and open, it is always advisable for the interviewer to have a plan of the main topics to be covered, so that she can make sure that all the topics of interest are included. Going into an interview without an agenda should not be confused with being open to hearing new ideas (see Section 7.4.5 on planning an interview). One of the skills necessary for conducting an unstructured interview is getting the balance right between making sure that answers to relevant questions are obtained, while at the same time being prepared to follow new lines of enquiry that were not anticipated.

A benefit of unstructured interviews is that they generate rich data that is often interrelated and complex, i.e. data that gives a deep understanding of the topic. In addition, interviewees may mention issues that the interviewer has not considered. A lot of unstructured data is generated and the interviews will not be consistent across participants since each interview takes on its own format. Unstructured interviews can therefore be time-consuming to analyze, although themes can often be identified across interviews using techniques from grounded theory and other approaches discussed in Chapter 8. These characteristics need to be taken into account when deciding which type of interview to choose.

7.4.2   Structured Interviews

In structured interviews, the interviewer asks predetermined questions similar to those in a questionnaire (see Section 7.5), and the same questions are used with each participant so the study is standardized. The questions need to be short and clearly worded, and they are typically closed questions, which means that they require an answer from a predetermined set of alternatives (this may include an 'other' option, but ideally this would not be chosen very often). Closed questions work well if the range of possible answers is known, and when participants are in a rush. Structured interviews are only really useful when the goals are clearly understood and specific questions can be identified. Example questions for a structured interview might be:

- Which of the following websites do you visit most frequently: amazon.com, google.com, msn.com?
- How often do you visit this website: every day, once a week, once a month, less often than once a month?
- Do you ever purchase anything online: yes/no? If your answer is yes, how often do you purchase things online: every day, once a week, once a month, less frequently than once a month?

Questions in a structured interview should be worded exactly the same for each participant, and they should be asked in the same order.

7.4.3   Semi-structured Interviews

Semi-structured interviews combine features of structured and unstructured interviews and use both closed and open questions. The interviewer has a basic script for guidance, so that the same topics are covered with each interviewee. The interviewer starts with preplanned questions and then probes the interviewee to say more until no new relevant information is forthcoming. For example:

> *Which music websites do you visit most frequently?* <Answer: mentions several but stresses that she prefers hottestmusic.com>
> *Why?* <Answer: says that she likes the site layout>
> *Tell me more about the site layout* <Silence, followed by an answer describing the site's layout>
> *Anything else that you like about the site?* <Answer: describes the animations>
> *Thanks. Are there any other reasons for visiting this site so often that you haven't mentioned?*

It is important not to pre-empt an answer by phrasing a question to suggest that a particular answer is expected. For example, 'You seemed to like this use of color . . .' assumes that this is the case and will probably encourage the interviewee to answer that this is true so as not to offend the interviewer. Children are particularly prone to behave in this way (see Box 7.2 for more on data gathering with children). The body language of the interviewer, for example whether she is smiling, scowling, looking disapproving, etc., can have a strong influence on whether the interviewee will agree with a question, and the interviewee needs to have time to speak and not be moved on too quickly.

Probes are a useful device for getting more information, especially neutral probes such as 'Do you want to tell me anything else?', and prompts which remind interviewees if they forget terms or names help to move the interview along. Semi-structured interviews are intended to be broadly replicable, so probing and prompting should aim to help the interview along without introducing bias.

BOX 7.2

Working with children

Children think and react to situations differently from adults. Therefore, if children are to be included in data gathering sessions, then child-friendly methods are needed to make them feel at ease so that they will communicate with you. For example, for very young children of pre-reading or early reading age, data gathering sessions need to rely on images and chat rather than written instructions or questionnaires. Many researchers who work with children have developed sets of 'smileys', such as those shown in Figure 7.2, so that children can select the one that most closely represents their feelings (e.g. Read *et al*, 2002).

Awful   Not very good   Good   Really good   Brilliant

Figure 7.2 A smileyometer gauge for early readers

Source: Figure 2, Janet Read, Stuart MacFarlane and Chris Casey "Endurability, Engagement and Expectations: Measuring Children's Fun" Department of Computing, University of Central Lancashire. Reproduced with permission.

(Continued)

Several other techniques for data gathering with children have been developed. For example, in KidReporter (Bekker *et al*, 2003) children are asked to produce newspaper articles on the topic being investigated, while the Mission from Mars approach (Dindler *et al*, 2005) involves children explaining everyday experiences over an audio connection to a researcher pretending to be a Martian.

Druin (2002) identifies four roles for children in the design of technology (particularly for learning): user, tester, informant, and design partner. In the role of user children use the technology while adults observe, as tester children test prototypes of technology, as informant children take part in the design process at various stages, and as design partner children are equal stakeholders throughout the design process.

Guha *et al* (2013) work with children as technology design partners. They have found that unexpected innovations result when working as an intergenerational team, i.e. adults and children working together. The method they use is called cooperative inquiry (Druin, 2002; Guha *et al*, 2013), based on Scandinavian cooperative design practices, participatory design, and contextual inquiry. Many techniques can be used in cooperative inquiry, such as sketching ideas and brainstorming, and observational research.

Researchers also use a variety of participatory design methods in design-based research (DBR), a methodology that is common in the fields of learning sciences and interaction design for children. In DBR, researchers design theory-driven learning environments, test these designs in authentic educational contexts, and then use the resulting research findings to inform further iterative cycles of design and testing. Yip *et al* (2013) employ these methodologies in designing educational environments and technologies for children's science learning. They find that children play very different design roles based on their prior knowledge. Children who had experience in the learning environment often were able to improve the practical and pragmatic aspects of technology designed for those environments. On the other hand, children who had explicit design experience were more able to generate open and unconstrained ideas regarding aesthetics, features, and novel ideas related to technology.

Ahn *et al* (2014) and Clegg *et al* (2014) also used participatory design and DBR methods to create a social media application called ScienceKit (see Figure 7.3), where children can share aspects of their daily lives via mechanisms commonly seen in popular apps such as Instagram, but in the process engage in scientific inquiry in everyday life. Their studies illuminate how combining design activities with children with focused studies of their technology use helps researchers to understand: (i) how children learn with social media, as their design ideas and use of technologies directly inform what kind of learning behavior is possible with new tools, (ii) how iterative implementation of the designed technologies with children yield further insights that can be fed back into additional design iterations, and (iii) result in technologies that are usable and engaging, but also theoretically informed to positively benefit children cognitively and socially. By enacting cycles of participatory design, studies of learning, and implementation, research studies can yield deeper insights about both child–computer interaction and issues of children's social and cognitive development.

Duveskog *et al* (2009) designed a story-based interactive digital platform to educate children about HIV and AIDS in southern Tanzania. They included secondary school children, university counseling students, HIV counseling experts, and experts in ICT in their team; groups were involved at different times through the design process. For example, before the implementation, interviews were conducted with secondary school children to elicit stories of their HIV and AIDS experiences. Other students produced drawings to illustrate their stories.

Figure 7.3 Children using the ScienceKit app which was developed as part of a design-based research project.

Source: Ahn *et al*, Seeing the Unseen Learner: Designing and Using Social Media to Recognize Children's Science Dispositions in Action. 2014. Reproduced with permission of Taylor and Francis Group LLC.

Later in development, students in a local drama group recorded voices for the characters in the stories, and once a pilot system was developed, counseling students tested the platform. Using these different forms of communication helped the students to think about and communicate their ideas and feelings. ■

What the examples in Box 7.2 demonstrate is that technology developers have to be prepared to adapt their data collection techniques to suit the participants with whom they work – in those cases, children. Similarly, different approaches are needed when working with users from different cultures. Winschiers-Theophilus *et al* (2012) comment that: "Many attempts have been made to adapt participatory and user-centered design methods to specific regions by localizing usability measures or incorporating cultural models of people's interpersonal interactions and communicative habits into analytic tools. However, our failure to successfully apply user-centered methods, evaluations, or benchmarks in developing regions, or to assess the efficacy of cross-cultural projects according to 'universally valid' a priori measures calls for the reframing of relationships between cultural contexts and meaning in design" p. 90. In their work with local communities in Namibia they had to find ways of involving the local participants, which included developing a variety of visual and other techniques to communicate ideas and capture the collective understanding and feelings inherent in the local cultures of the people with whom they worked. (See also Winschiers-Theophilus and Bidwell (2013) and Case Study 11.3.)

7.4.4 Focus Groups

Interviews are often conducted with one interviewer and one interviewee, but it is also common to interview people in groups. One form of group interview that is frequently used in marketing, political campaigning, and social sciences research is the focus group. Normally three to ten people are involved, and the discussion is led by a trained facilitator. Participants are selected to provide a representative sample of the target population. For example, in an evaluation of a university website, a group of administrators, faculty, and students may form three separate focus groups because they use the web for different purposes. In requirements activities it is quite common to hold a focus group in order to identify conflicts in terminology or expectations from different sections within one department or organization.

The benefit of a focus group is that it allows diverse or sensitive issues to be raised that might otherwise be missed. The method assumes that individuals develop opinions within a social context by talking with others, which means that this approach is more appropriate for investigating community issues rather than individual experiences. Focus groups aim to enable people to put forward their own opinions in a supportive environment. A preset agenda is developed to guide the discussion, but there is sufficient flexibility for the facilitator to follow unanticipated issues as they are raised. The facilitator guides and prompts discussion and skillfully encourages quiet people to participate and stops verbose ones from dominating the discussion. The discussion is usually recorded for later analysis and participants may be invited to explain their comments more fully at a later date.

The focus group hated it. So he
showed it to an out-of-focus group.

7.4.5   Planning and Conducting an Interview

Planning an interview involves developing the set of questions or topics to be covered, collating any documentation to give to the interviewee (such as consent form or project description), checking that recording equipment works in advance and you know how to use it, working out the structure of the interview, and organizing a suitable time and place.

Developing Interview Questions

Questions for an interview may be open or closed. Open questions are best suited where the goal of the session is exploratory; closed questions can only be used where the possible

DILEMMA
What they say and what they do

What users say isn't always what they do. When asked a question, people sometimes give the answers that they think show them in the best light, or they may just forget what happened, or they may want to please the interviewer by answering in the way they anticipate will satisfy the interviewer. For example, in a study looking at the maintenance of telecommunications software, the developers stated that most of their job involved reading documentation, but when observed, it was found that searching and looking at source code was much more common than looking at documentation (Singer *et al*, 1997).

So, can interviewers believe all the responses they get? Are the respondents telling the truth or are they simply giving the answers that they think the interviewer wants to hear?

It isn't possible to avoid this behavior, but it is important to be aware of it and to reduce such biases by choosing questions carefully, getting a large number of participants, or by using a combination of data gathering techniques. ■

answers are known in advance. An unstructured interview will usually consist entirely of open questions, while a structured interview will usually consist of closed questions. A semi-structured interview may use a combination of both types.

The following guidelines for developing interview questions are derived from Robson (2011):

- Compound sentences can be confusing, so split them into two separate questions. For example, instead of, 'How do you like this smartphone app compared with previous ones that you have owned?' say, 'How do you like this smartphone app?' 'Have you owned other smartphone apps?' If so, 'How did you like them?' This is easier for the interviewee to respond to and easier for the interviewer to record.
- Interviewees may not understand jargon or complex language and might be too embarrassed to admit it, so explain things to them in layman's terms.
- Try to keep questions neutral. For example, if you ask 'Why do you like this style of interaction?' this question assumes that the person does like it and will discourage some interviewees from stating their real feelings.

ACTIVITY 7.2

Several e-readers for reading ebooks, watching movies, and browsing photographs are available on the market (see Figure 7.4). These devices are thin and lightweight and are ideally designed for reading books, newspapers, and magazines. The exact design differs between

(Continued)

Figure 7.4 (a) Sony's e-reader, (b) Amazon's Kindle, and (c) Apple's iPad
Source: (a) Courtesy of Sony Europe Limited, (b) and (c) ©PA Images.

makes and models, but they all support book reading that is intended to be as comfortable as reading a paper book.

The developers of a new e-reader want to find out how appealing it will be to young people under 18 years of age. To this end, they have asked you to conduct some interviews for them.

1. What is the goal of your data gathering session?
2. Suggest ways of recording the interview data.
3. Suggest a set of questions that are suitable for use in an unstructured interview that seek opinions about e-readers and their appeal to the under-18s.
4. Based on the results of the unstructured interviews, the developers of the new e-reader have found that two important acceptance factors are whether the device can be handled easily and whether the typeface and appearance can be altered. Write a set of semi-structured interview questions to evaluate these two aspects. If you have an e-reader available, show it to two of your peers and ask them to comment on your questions. Refine the questions based on their comments.

Comment

1. The goal is to seek opinions about whether e-readers would be appealing to people under 18.
2. Taking notes might be cumbersome and distracting to the interviewee, and it would be easy to miss important points. An alternative is to audio record the session. Video recording is not needed as it isn't necessary to see the interviewee. However, it would be useful to have a camera at hand to take photographs of any aspects of the device referred to by the interviewee.
3. Possible questions include: Do you find reading a book on the e-reader comfortable? Do you know how to turn the page in an ebook? In what way(s) does the e-reader affect your ability to become engrossed in the story you are reading?
4. Semi-structured interview questions may be open or closed. Some closed questions that you might ask include:
   - Have you used an e-reader before?
   - Would you like to read a book using an e-reader?
   - In your opinion, is the e-reader easy to handle?
   Some open questions, with follow-on probes, include:
   - What do you like most about the e-reader? Why?
   - What do you like least about the e-reader? Why?
   - Please give me an example where the e-reader was uncomfortable or difficult to use. ∎

It is helpful when collecting answers to list the possible responses together with boxes that can just be checked (i.e. ticked). Here's how we could convert some of the questions from Activity 7.2.

1. Have you used an e-reader before? (Explore previous knowledge)
   Interviewer checks box   ☐ *Yes*   ☐ *No*   ☐ *Don't remember/know*
2. Would you like to read a book using an e-reader? (Explore initial reaction, then explore the response)
   Interviewer checks box   ☐ *Yes*   ☐ *No*   ☐ *Don't know*
3. Why?
   If response is 'Yes' or 'No,' interviewer says, 'Which of the following statements represents your feelings best?'
   For 'Yes,' interviewer checks the box
   ☐ *I don't like carrying heavy books*
   ☐ *This is fun/cool*
   ☐ *My friend told me they are great*
   ☐ *It's the way of the future*
   ☐ *Another reason (interviewer notes the reason)*
   For 'No,' interviewer checks the box
   ☐ *I don't like using gadgets if I can avoid it*
   ☐ *I can't read the screen clearly*
   ☐ *I prefer the feel of paper*
   ☐ *Another reason (interviewer notes the reason)*

4. In your opinion, is an e-reader easy to handle or cumbersome?
   Interviewer checks box
   ☐ *Easy to handle*
   ☐ *Cumbersome*
   ☐ *Neither*

Running the Interview

Before starting, make sure that the aims of the interview have been communicated to and understood by the interviewees, and they feel comfortable. Some simple techniques can help here, such as finding out about their world before the interview so that you can dress, act, and speak in a manner that will be familiar. This is particularly important when working with children, seniors, people from different ethnic and cultural groups, people who have disabilities, and seriously ill patients.

   During the interview, it is better to listen more than to talk, to respond with sympathy but without bias, and to appear to enjoy the interview (Robson, 2011). Robson suggests the following steps for conducting an interview:

1. An introduction in which the interviewer introduces herself and explains why she is doing the interview, reassures interviewees regarding any ethical issues, and asks if they mind being recorded, if appropriate. This should be exactly the same for each interviewee.
2. A warm-up session where easy, non-threatening questions come first. These may include questions about demographic information, such as 'What area of the country do you live in?'
3. A main session in which the questions are presented in a logical sequence, with the more probing ones at the end. In a semi-structured interview the order of questions may vary between participants, depending on the course of the conversation, how much probing is done, and what seems more natural.
4. A cool-off period consisting of a few easy questions (to defuse any tension that may have arisen).
5. A closing session in which the interviewer thanks the interviewee and switches off the recorder or puts her notebook away, signaling that the interview has ended.

7.4.6   Other Forms of Interview

Conducting face-to-face interviews and focus groups can sometimes be impractical, especially when the participants live in different geographical areas. Skype, email, and phone-based interactions, sometimes with screen-sharing software, are therefore increasing in popularity. These are carried out similarly to face-to-face sessions, although such issues as dropped Skype connections and insufficient Internet bandwidth for reliable video can be a challenge to conducting them. However, there are some advantages to remote focus groups and interviews, especially when done through audio-only channels. For example, the participants are in their own environment and are more relaxed, participants don't have to worry about what they wear, who other people are, or interact in an unnatural environment surrounded by strangers; for interviews that involve sensitive issues, interviewees may prefer to be anonymous. In addition, participants can leave the conversation whenever they want to by just putting down the phone, which adds to their sense of security. While it is questionable whether data collected face-to-face can be compared directly with data collected remotely, it seems that remote phone-based group or individual interviews are preferable at least in some circumstances.

Figure 7.5 Enriching a focus group with prototypes. Here storyboards are displayed on the wall for all participants to see

> **Link** to more information on telephone focus groups, at
> **http://mnav.com/shocking-truth/**
> and for some interesting thoughts on remote usability testing, see
> **http://www.uxbooth.com/articles/hidden-benefits-remote-research/**

Retrospective interviews, i.e. interviews which reflect on an activity or a data gathering session in the recent past, may be conducted with participants to check that the interviewer has correctly understood what was happening.

7.4.7 Enriching the Interview Experience

Face-to-face interviews often take place in a neutral environment, e.g. a meeting room away from the interviewee's normal place of work or their home. In such situations the interview location provides an artificial context that is different from the interviewee's normal tasks. In these circumstances it can be difficult for interviewees to give full answers to the questions posed. To help combat this, interviews can be enriched by using props such as prototypes or work artifacts that the interviewee or interviewer brings along, or descriptions of common tasks (examples of these kinds of props are scenarios and prototypes, which are covered in Chapters 10 and 11). These props can be used to provide context for the interviewees and help to ground the data in a real setting. Figure 7.5 illustrates the use of prototypes in a focus group setting.

For example, Jones *et al* (2004) used diaries as a basis for interviews. They performed a study to probe the extent to which certain places are associated with particular activities and information needs. Each participant was asked to keep a diary in which they entered information about where they were and what they were doing at 30 minute intervals. The interview questions were then based around their diary entries.

7.5   Questionnaires

Questionnaires are a well-established technique for collecting demographic data and users' opinions. They are similar to interviews in that they can have closed or open questions but they can be distributed to a larger number of participants so more data can be collected than would normally be possible in an interview study. Furthermore, the issues of involving people who are located in remote locations or cannot attend an interview at a particular time can be dealt with more conveniently. Often a message is sent electronically to potential participants to direct them to an online questionnaire.

Effort and skill are needed to ensure that questions are clearly worded and the data collected can be analyzed efficiently. Well-designed questionnaires are good at getting answers to specific questions from a large group of people. Questionnaires can be used on their own or in conjunction with other methods to clarify or deepen understanding. For example, information obtained through interviews with a small selection of interviewees might be corroborated by sending a questionnaire to a wider group to confirm the conclusions.

Questionnaire questions and structured interview questions are similar, so how do you know when to use which technique? Essentially, the difference lies in the motivation of the respondent to answer the questions. If you think that this motivation is high enough to complete a questionnaire without anyone else present, then a questionnaire will be appropriate. On the other hand, if the respondents need some persuasion to answer the questions, it would be better to use an interview format and ask the questions face-to-face through a structured interview. For example, structured interviews are easier and quicker to conduct in situations in which people will not stop to complete a questionnaire, such as at a train station or while walking to their next meeting.

It can be harder to develop good questionnaire questions compared with structured interview questions because the interviewer is not available to explain them or to clarify any ambiguities. Because of this, it is important that questions are specific; when possible, closed questions should be asked and a range of answers offered, including a 'no opinion' or 'none of these' option. Finally, negative questions can be confusing and may lead to the respondents giving false information, although some questionnaire designers use a mixture of negative and positive questions deliberately because it helps to check the users' intentions.

7.5.1   Questionnaire Structure

Many questionnaires start by asking for basic demographic information (gender, age, place of birth) and details of relevant experience (the time or number of years spent using computers, or the level of expertise within the domain under study, etc.). This background information is useful for putting the questionnaire responses into context. For example, if two respondents conflict, these different perspectives may be due to their level of experience – a group of people who are using a social networking site for the first time are likely to express different opinions to another group with five years' experience of such sites. However, only contextual information that is relevant to the study goal needs to be collected. In the example above, it is unlikely that the person's shoe size will provide relevant context to their responses!

Specific questions that contribute to the data gathering goal usually follow these more general questions. If the questionnaire is long, the questions may be subdivided into related topics to make it easier and more logical to complete.

The following is a checklist of general advice for designing a questionnaire:

- Think about the ordering of questions. The impact of a question can be influenced by question order.
- Consider whether you need different versions of the questionnaire for different populations.
- Provide clear instructions on how to complete the questionnaire. For example, if only one of the boxes needs to be checked, then say so. Questionnaires can make their message clear with careful wording and good typography.
- A balance must be struck between using white space and the need to keep the questionnaire as compact as possible.

7.5.2   Question and Response Format

Different formats of question and response can be chosen. For example, with a closed question, it may be appropriate to indicate only one response, or it may be appropriate to indicate several. Sometimes it is better to ask users to locate their answer within a range. Selecting the most appropriate question and response format makes it easier for respondents to answer clearly. Some commonly used formats are described below.

Check Boxes and Ranges

The range of answers to demographic questionnaires is predictable. Gender, for example, has two options, male or female, so providing the two options and asking respondents to circle a response makes sense for collecting this information. A similar approach can be adopted if details of age are needed. But since some people do not like to give their exact age, many questionnaires ask respondents to specify their age as a range. A common design error arises when the ranges overlap. For example, specifying two ranges as 15–20, 20–25 will cause confusion: which box do people who are 20 years old check? Making the ranges 14–19, 20–24 avoids this problem.

A frequently asked question about ranges is whether the interval must be equal in all cases. The answer is no – it depends on what you want to know. For example, if you want to identify people who might use a website about life insurance, you will most likely be interested in people with jobs who are 21–65 years old. You could, therefore, have just three ranges: under 21, 21–65, and over 65. In contrast, if you wanted to see how the population's political views varied across the generations, you might be interested in looking at 10-year cohort groups for people over 21, in which case the following ranges would be appropriate: under 21, 22–31, 32–41, etc.

Rating Scales

There are a number of different types of rating scales that can be used, each with its own purpose (see Oppenheim, 1998). Here we describe two commonly used scales: the Likert and semantic differential scales. The purpose of these is to elicit a range of responses to a question that can be compared across respondents. They are good for getting people to make judgments about things, e.g. how easy, how usable, and the like.

The success of Likert scales relies on identifying a set of statements representing a range of possible opinions, while semantic differential scales rely on choosing pairs of words that represent the range of possible opinions. Likert scales are more commonly used because identifying suitable statements that respondents will understand is easier than identifying semantic pairs that respondents interpret as intended.

Likert scales. Likert scales are used for measuring opinions, attitudes, and beliefs, and consequently they are widely used for evaluating user satisfaction with products. For example, users' opinions about the use of color in a website could be evaluated with a Likert scale using a range of numbers, as in (1), or with words as in (2):

(1) The use of color is excellent (where 1 represents strongly agree and 5 represents strongly disagree):

    1   2   3   4   5
    □   □   □   □   □

(2) The use of color is excellent:

    strongly agree   agree   OK   disagree   strongly disagree
        □   □   □   □   □

In both cases, respondents could be asked to tick or ring the right box, number or phrase. Designing a Likert scale involves the following three steps:

1. Gather a pool of short statements about the subject to be investigated. For example, 'This control panel is clear' or 'The procedure for checking credit rating is too complex.' A brainstorming session with peers in which you identify key aspects to be investigated is a good way of doing this.
2. Decide on the scale. There are three main issues to be addressed here: How many points does the scale need? Should the scale be discrete or continuous? How to represent the scale? See Box 7.3 for more on this topic.
3. Select items for the final questionnaire and reword as necessary to make them clear.

In the first example above, the scale is arranged with 1 as the highest choice on the left and 5 as the lowest choice on the right. While there is no absolute right or wrong way of ordering the numbers, some researchers prefer to have 1 as the higher rating on the left and 5 as the lowest rating on the right. The logic for this is that first is the best place to be in a race and fifth would be the worst. Other researchers prefer to arrange the scales the other way around with 1 as the lowest on the left and 5 as the highest on the right. They argue that intuitively the higher number suggests the best choice and the lowest number suggests the worst choice. Another reason for going from lowest to highest is that when the results are reported, it is more intuitive for readers to see high numbers representing the best choices. The important things to remember are to decide which way around you will apply the scales, make sure your participants know, and then apply your scales consistently throughout your questionnaire.

Semantic differential scales. Semantic differential scales explore a range of bipolar attitudes about a particular item. Each pair of attitudes is represented as a pair of adjectives. The participant is asked to place a cross in one of a number of positions between the two extremes to indicate agreement with the poles, as shown in Figure 7.6. The score for the investigation is found by summing the scores for each bipolar pair. Scores can then be computed across groups of participants. Notice that in this example the poles are mixed, so that good and bad features are distributed on the right and the left. In this example there are seven positions on the scale.

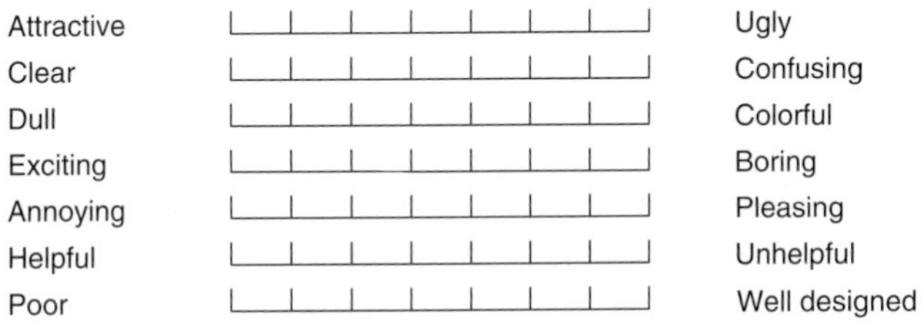

Attractive	└─┴─┴─┴─┴─┴─┴─┘	Ugly
Clear	└─┴─┴─┴─┴─┴─┴─┘	Confusing
Dull	└─┴─┴─┴─┴─┴─┴─┘	Colorful
Exciting	└─┴─┴─┴─┴─┴─┴─┘	Boring
Annoying	└─┴─┴─┴─┴─┴─┴─┘	Pleasing
Helpful	└─┴─┴─┴─┴─┴─┴─┘	Unhelpful
Poor	└─┴─┴─┴─┴─┴─┴─┘	Well designed

Figure 7.6 An example of a semantic differential scale

BOX 7.3

What scales to use: three, five, seven, or more?

When designing Likert and semantic differential scales, issues that need to be addressed include: how many points are needed on the scale, how should they be presented, and in what form?

Many questionnaires use seven- or five-point scales and there are also three-point scales. Some even use 9-point scales. Arguments for the number of points go both ways. Advocates of long scales argue that they help to show discrimination. Rating features on an interface is more difficult for most people than, say, selecting among different flavors of ice cream, and when the task is difficult there is evidence to show that people 'hedge their bets.' Rather than selecting the poles of the scales if there is no right or wrong, respondents tend to select values nearer the center. The counter-argument is that people cannot be expected to discern accurately among points on a large scale, so any scale of more than five points is unnecessarily difficult to use.

Another aspect to consider is whether the scale should have an even or odd number of points. An odd number provides a clear central point. On the other hand, an even number forces participants to make a decision and prevents them from sitting on the fence.

We suggest the following guidelines:

How many points on the scale?

Use a small number, e.g. three, when the possibilities are very limited, as in yes/no type answers:

☐   ☐   ☐

yes   don't know   no

Use a medium-sized range, e.g. five, when making judgments that involve like/dislike, agree/disagree statements:

strongly agree	agree	OK	disagree	strongly disagree
☐	☐	☐	☐	☐

Use a longer range, e.g. seven or nine, when asking respondents to make subtle judgments. For example, when asking about a user experience dimension such as 'level of appeal' of a character in a video game:

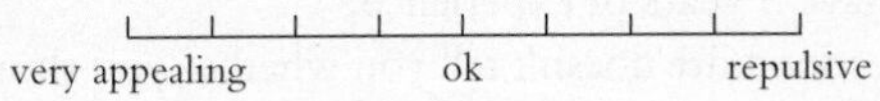

└─┴─┴─┴─┴─┴─┴─┘

very appealing   ok   repulsive

(Continued)

Discrete or continuous?
Use boxes for discrete choices and scales for finer judgments.
What order?
Decide which way you will order your scale and be consistent. For example, some people like to go from the strongest agreement to the weakest because they find it intuitive to order the scale that way:

— strongly agree
— slightly agree
— agree
— slightly disagree
— strongly disagree. ■

ACTIVITY 7.3

Spot four poorly designed features in the questionnaire in Figure 7.7.

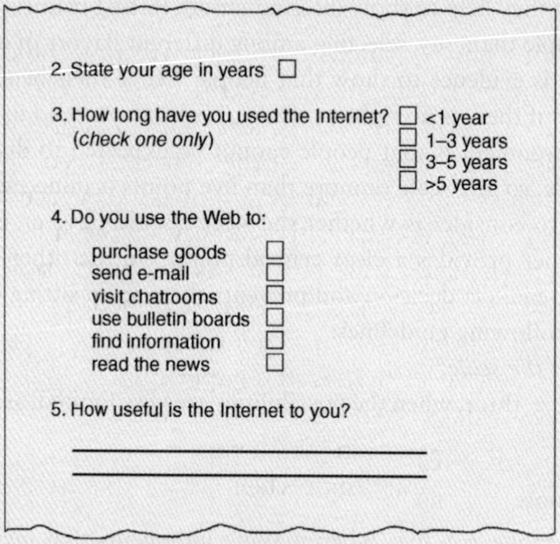

2. State your age in years ☐

3. How long have you used the Internet? (*check one only*)
☐ <1 year
☐ 1–3 years
☐ 3–5 years
☐ >5 years

4. Do you use the Web to:
purchase goods ☐
send e-mail ☐
visit chatrooms ☐
use bulletin boards ☐
find information ☐
read the news ☐

5. How useful is the Internet to you?

Figure 7.7 A questionnaire with poorly designed features

Comment

Some of the features that could be improved include:

- Question 2 requests exact age. Many people prefer not to give this information and would rather position themselves in a range.
- In question 3, years of experience is indicated with overlapping scales, i.e. 1–3, 3–5. How do you answer if you have 3 years of experience?
- For question 4, the questionnaire doesn't tell you whether you should check one, two, or as many boxes as you wish.

- The space left for people to answer the open-ended question 5 is too small, which will annoy some people and deter them from giving their opinions.

Many online survey tools have the added advantage that they prevent users from making some of these design errors. But it is important to be aware of such things because paper is still sometimes used! ■

7.5.3 Administering Questionnaires

Two important issues when using questionnaires are reaching a representative sample of participants and ensuring a reasonable response rate. For large surveys, potential respondents need to be selected using a sampling technique. However, interaction designers commonly use small numbers of participants, often fewer than 20 users. 100% completion rates are often achieved with these small samples, but with larger or more remote populations, ensuring that surveys are returned is a well-known problem. 40% return is generally acceptable for many surveys, but much lower rates are common. Depending on your audience you might want to consider offering incentives (see Section 7.2.3).

While questionnaires are often web-based, paper questionnaires are used in situations where participants do not have Internet access, such as in airplanes, airports where people are on the move, and in remote areas of the world where the Internet is either not available or very expensive to use. Occasionally, short questionnaires are sent within the body of an email, but more often the advantages of the data being compiled and either partly or fully analyzed make web-based questionnaires attractive. In a recent study by Diaz de Rada and Dominguez-Alvarez (2014), in which the quality of the information collected from a survey given to citizens of Andalusia in Spain was analyzed, several advantages of using web-based versus paper-based questionnaires were identified. These included: a low number of unanswered questions, more detailed answers to open questions, and longer answers to questions in the web questionnaires than in the paper questionnaires. In the five open questions, respondents wrote 63 characters more on the web-based questionnaires than on the paper questionnaires. For the questions in which participants had to select from a drop-down menu, there was a better response rate than when the selection was presented on paper with blank spaces.

Web-based questionnaires are interactive and can include check boxes, radio buttons, pull-down and pop-up menus, help screens, graphics or videos, e.g. Figure 7.8. They can also provide immediate data validation, e.g. the entry must be a number between 1 and 20, and automatically skip questions that are irrelevant to some respondents, e.g. questions only aimed at teenagers. Other advantages of web-based questionnaires include faster response rates and automatic transfer of responses into a database for analysis (Sue and Ritter, 2012).

The main problem with web-based questionnaires is the difficulty of obtaining a random sample of respondents; web-based questionnaires usually rely on convenience sampling and hence their results cannot be generalized. In some countries, web- and smartphone-based questions are used in conjunction with television to elicit viewers' opinions of programs and political events, e.g. the television program Big Brother.

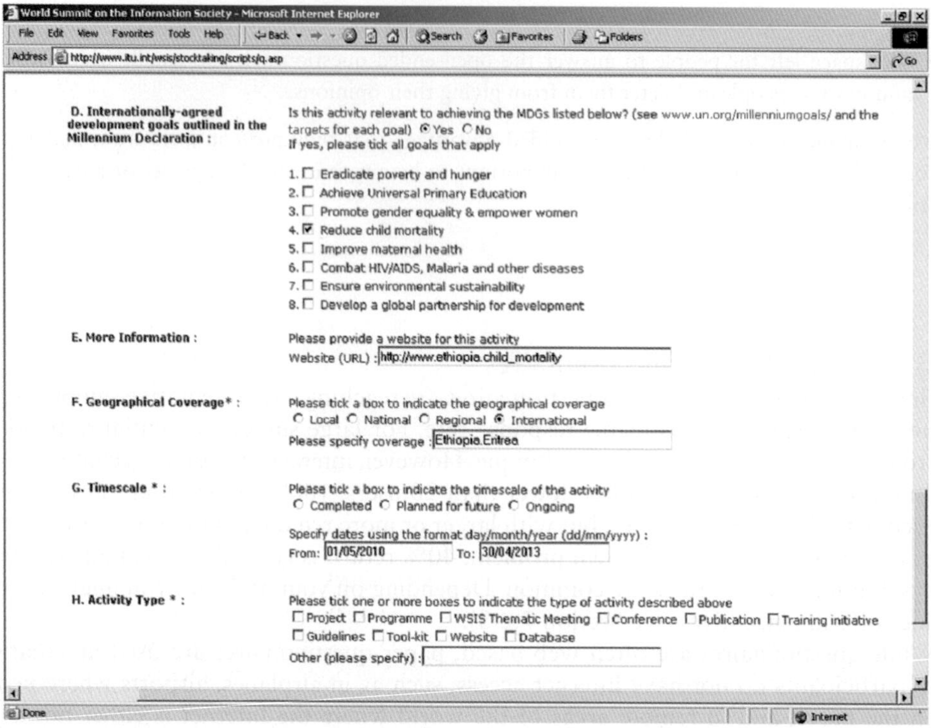

Figure 7.8 An excerpt from a web-based questionnaire showing check boxes, radio buttons, and pull-down menus

Deploying a web-based questionnaire involves the following steps (Andrews *et al*, 2003):

1. Design and implement an error-free interactive electronic questionnaire. It may be useful to embed feedback and pop-up help within the questionnaire.

2. Make sure information identifying each respondent can be captured and stored confidentially because the same person may submit several completed surveys. This can be done by recording the Internet domain name or the IP address of the respondent, which can then be transferred directly to a database. However, this action could infringe people's privacy and the legal situation should be checked. Another way is to access the transfer and referrer logs from the web server, which provide information about the domains from which the web-based questionnaire was accessed. Unfortunately, people can still send from different accounts with different IP addresses, so additional identifying information may also be needed.

3. Thoroughly pilot test the questionnaire. This may be achieved in four stages: the survey is reviewed by knowledgeable analysts; typical participants complete the survey using a think-aloud protocol (see below); a small version of the study is attempted; a final check to catch small errors is conducted.

There are many online questionnaire templates available on the web that provide a range of options, including different question types (e.g. open, multiple choice), rating scales (e.g. Likert, semantic differential), and answer types (e.g. radio buttons, check boxes, drop-down menus). The following activity asks you to make use of one of these templates to design a questionnaire for the web.

ACTIVITY 7.4

Go to questionpro.com or surveymonkey.com, or a similar survey site that allows you to design your own questionnaire using their set of widgets for a free trial period.

    Create a web-based questionnaire for the set of questions you developed for Activity 7.2. For each question produce two different designs, for example radio buttons and drop-down menus for one question; for another question provide a ten-point semantic differential scale and a five-point scale.

    What differences (if any) do you think your two designs will have on a respondent's behavior? Ask a number of people to answer one or other of your questions and see if the answers differ for the two designs.

Comment

You may have found that respondents use the response types in different ways. For example, they may select the end options more often from a drop-down menu than from a list of options that are chosen via radio buttons. Alternatively, you may find no difference and that people's opinions are not affected by the widget style used at the interface. Any differences found, of course, may be due to the variation between individual responses rather than being caused by features in the questionnaire design. To tease the effects apart you would need to ask a large number of participants (e.g. in the range 50–100) to respond to the questions for each design. ∎

BOX 7.4

Do people answer online questionnaires differently to paper and pencil? If so, why?

There has been much research examining how people respond to surveys when using a computer compared with the traditional paper and pencil method. Some studies suggest that people are more revealing and consistent in their responses when using a computer to report their habits and behaviors, such as eating, drinking, and amount of exercise, e.g. Luce *et al* (2003). Students have also been found to rate their instructors less favorably when online (Chang, 2004). One reason for this is that students may feel less social pressure when filling in a questionnaire at a computer and hence freer to write the truth than when sitting in a classroom, with others around them, filling out a paper-based version.

    Another factor that can influence how people answer questions is the way the information is structured, such as the use of headers, the ordering, and the placement of questions. But the potential may be greater for web-based questionnaires since they provide more opportunities than paper ones for manipulating information (Smyth *et al*, 2004).

For example, the use of drop-down menus, radio buttons, and jump-to options may influence how people read and navigate a questionnaire. But do these issues affect respondents' answers? Smyth *et al* (2005) have found that providing forced choice formats results in more options being selected. Another example is provided by Funcke *et al* (2011), who found that continuous sliders enabled researchers to collect more accurate data because they support continuous rather than discrete scales. They also encouraged higher response rates, but they were more challenging for participants who had not encountered continuous scales before and found the concept difficult to understand. ■

7.6   Observation

Observation is a useful data gathering technique at any stage during product development. Early in design, observation helps designers understand the users' context, tasks, and goals. Observation conducted later in development, e.g. in evaluation, may be used to investigate how well the developing prototype supports these tasks and goals.

Users may be observed directly by the investigator as they perform their activities, or indirectly through records of the activity that are studied afterwards. Observation may also take place in the field, or in a controlled environment. In the former case, individuals are observed as they go about their day-to-day tasks in the natural setting. In the latter case, individuals are observed performing specified tasks within a controlled environment such as a usability laboratory.

ACTIVITY 7.5

To appreciate the different merits of observation in the field and observation in a controlled environment, read the scenarios below and answer the questions that follow.

Scenario 1. A usability consultant joins a group of tourists who have been given a wearable navigation device that fits onto a wrist strap to test on a visit to Stockholm. After sightseeing for the day, they use the device to find a list of restaurants within a two-kilometer radius of their current position. Several are listed and they find the telephone numbers of a couple, call them to ask about their menus, select one, make a booking, and head off to the restaurant. The usability consultant observes some difficulty operating the device, especially on the move. Discussion with the group supports the evaluator's impression that there are problems with the interface, but on balance the device is useful and the group is pleased to get a table at a good restaurant nearby.

Scenario 2. A usability consultant observes how participants perform a pre-planned task using the wearable navigation device in a usability laboratory. The task requires the participants to find the telephone number of a restaurant called Matisse. It takes them several minutes to do this and they appear to have problems. The video recording and interaction log suggest that the interface is very fiddly and the audio interaction is of poor quality, and this is supported by participants' answers on a user satisfaction questionnaire.

1. What are the advantages and disadvantages of these two types of observation?
2. When might each type of observation be useful?

Comment

1. The advantages of the field study are that the observer saw how the device could be used in a real situation to solve a real problem. She experienced the delight expressed with the overall concept and the frustration with the interface. By watching how the group used the device on the move, she gained an understanding of what they liked and what was lacking. The disadvantage is that the observer was an insider in the group, so how objective could she be? The data is qualitative and while anecdotes can be very persuasive, how useful are they? Maybe she was having such a good time that her judgment was clouded and she missed hearing negative comments and didn't notice some people's annoyance. Another study could be done to find out more, but it is not possible to replicate the exact conditions of this study. The advantages of the laboratory study are that it is easier to replicate, so several users could perform the same task, specific usability problems can be identified, users' performance can be compared, and averages for such measures as the time it took to do a specific task and the number of errors can be calculated. The observer could also be more objective because she was an outsider. The disadvantage is that the study is artificial and says nothing about how the device would be used in the real environment.

2. Both types of study have merits. Which is better depends on the goals of the study. The laboratory study is useful for examining details of the interaction style to make sure that usability problems with the interface and button design are diagnosed and corrected. The field study reveals how the navigation device is used in a real-world context and how it integrates with or changes users' behavior. Without this study, it is possible that developers might not have discovered the enthusiasm for the device because the reward for doing laboratory tasks is not as compelling as a good meal! In fact, according to Kjeldskov and Skov (2014), there is no definitive answer to which kind of study is preferable for mobile devices. They suggest that the real question is when and how to engage with in the wild longitudinal studies. ■

7.6.1 Direct Observation in the Field

It can be very difficult for people to explain what they do or to even describe accurately how they achieve a task. So it is very unlikely that an interaction designer will get a full and true story by using interviews or questionnaires. Observation in the field can help fill in details about how users behave and use the technology, and nuances that are not elicited from the other forms of investigation may be observed. This understanding about the context for tasks provides important information about why activities happen the way they do. However, observation in the field can be complicated, and much more difficult to do well than at first appreciated. Observation can also result in a lot of data that is tedious to analyze and not very relevant, especially if the observation is not planned and carried out carefully.

All data gathering should have a clearly stated goal, but it is particularly important to have a focus for an observation session because there is always so much going on. On the other hand, it is also important to be able to respond to changing circumstances: for example, you may have planned one day to observe a particular person performing a task, but you are invited to an unexpected meeting which is relevant to your observation goal, and so it makes sense to attend the meeting instead. In observation there is a careful balance between being guided by goals and being open to modifying, shaping, or refocusing the study as you learn about the situation. Being able to keep this balance is a skill that develops with experience.

Structuring Frameworks for Observation in the Field

During an observation, events can be complex and rapidly changing. There is a lot for observers to think about, so many experts have a framework to structure and focus their observation. The framework can be quite simple. For example, this is a practitioner's framework for use in evaluation studies that focuses on just three easy-to-remember items to look for:

- The person: Who is using the technology at any particular time?
- The place: Where are they using it?
- The thing: What are they doing with it?

Even a simple framework such as this one based on who, where, and what can be surprisingly effective to help observers keep their goals and questions in sight. Experienced observers may, however, prefer more detailed frameworks, such as the one suggested by Robson (2011) which encourages observers to pay greater attention to the context of the activity:

- Space: What is the physical space like and how is it laid out?
- Actors: What are the names and relevant details of the people involved?
- Activities: What are the actors doing and why?
- Objects: What physical objects are present, such as furniture?
- Acts: What are specific individual actions?
- Events: Is what you observe part of a special event?
- Time: What is the sequence of events?
- Goals: What are the actors trying to accomplish?
- Feelings: What is the mood of the group and of individuals?

   This framework was devised for any type of observation, so when used in the context of interaction design, it might need to be modified slightly. For example, if the focus is going to be on how some technology is used, the framework could be modified to ask:

- Objects: What physical objects, in addition to the technology being studied, are present, and do they impact on the technology use?

   Other modifications might also be useful.

ACTIVITY 7.6

1. Find a small group of people who are using any kind of technology, e.g. computers, household or entertainment appliances, and try to answer the question, 'What are these people doing?' Watch for three to five minutes and write down what you observe. When you have finished, note down how you felt doing this, and any reactions in the group of people you observed.
2. If you were to observe the group again, how would you change what you did the first time?
3. Observe this group again for about 10 minutes using Robson's framework.

Comment

1. What problems did you encounter doing this exercise? Was it hard to watch everything and remember what happened? How do you think the people being watched felt? Did they know they were being watched? Perhaps some of them objected and walked away. If you didn't tell them, do you think you should have?

2. The initial goal of the observation, i.e. to find out what the people are doing, was vague, and the chances are that it was quite a frustrating experience not knowing what was significant for answering your question and what could be ignored. The questions used to guide observation need to be more focused. For example, you might ask: What are the people doing with the technology? Is everyone in the group using it? Are they looking pleased, frustrated, serious, happy? Does the technology appear to be central to the users' goals?

3. Hopefully you will have felt more confident this second time, partly because it is the second time you've done some observation, and partly because the framework provided you with a structure for what to look at. ■

Both of the frameworks introduced above are relatively general and could be used in many different types of study, and as a basis for developing your own frameworks.

Degree of Participation

Depending on the type of study, the degree of participation within the study environment varies across a spectrum, which can be characterized as insider at one end and outsider at the other. Where a particular study falls along this spectrum depends on its goal and on the practical and ethical issues that constrain and shape it.

An observer who adopts an approach right at the outsider end of the spectrum is called a passive observer and she will not take any part in the study environment at all. It is difficult to be a truly passive observer if you are in the field, simply because you can't avoid interacting with the activities happening around you. Passive observation is more appropriate in laboratory studies.

An observer who adopts an approach at the insider end of this spectrum is called a participant observer. This means that he attempts, at various levels depending on the type of study, to become a member of the group he is studying. This can be a difficult role to play since being an observer also requires a certain level of detachment, while being a participant assumes a different role. As a participant observer it is important to keep the two roles clear and separate, so that observation notes are objective, while participation is also maintained. It may not be possible to take a full participant observer approach, for other reasons. For example, you may not be skilled enough in the task at hand, the organization/group may not be prepared for you to take part in their activities, or the timescale may not provide sufficient opportunity to become familiar enough with the task to participate fully. Similarly, if you wish to observe activity in a private place such as the home, full participation would be difficult. Bell, for example, emphasizes the importance of spending time with families and using a range of data gathering including observation (Bell, 2003; Bell *et al*, 2005).

Planning and Conducting an Observation in the Field

The frameworks introduced in the previous section are useful not only for providing focus but also for organizing the observation and data gathering activity. But although choosing a framework is important, it is only one aspect of planning an observation. Other decisions include: the level of participation to adopt; how to make a record of the data; how to gain acceptance in the group being studied; how to handle sensitive issues such as cultural differences or access to private spaces; and how to ensure that the study uses different perspectives (people, activities, job roles, etc.). One way to achieve this last point is to work as a team. This can have several benefits: each person can agree to focus on different people or different parts of the context, thereby covering more ground; observation and reflection can be interweaved more easily when there is more than one observer; more reliable data is likely to be generated because observations can be compared; and results will reflect different perspectives.

Once in the throes of an observation, there are other issues that need to be considered. For example, it will be easier to relate to some people than others and it will be tempting to pay attention to those who receive you well, but everyone in the group needs to be attended to. Observation is a fluid activity, and the study will need refocusing as you reflect upon what has been seen. Having observed for a while, interesting phenomena that seem relevant will start to emerge. Gradually ideas will sharpen into questions that guide further observation.

Observing is an intense and tiring activity, but however tired you are, it is important to check the notes and other records and to write up experiences and observations at the end of each day. If this is not done, then valuable information may be lost as the next day's events override your previous day's impressions. Writing a diary or private blog is one way of achieving this. Any documents or other artifacts that are collected or copied (e.g. minutes of a meeting, or discussion items) should be annotated, describing how they are used and at what stage of the activity. Some observers conducting an observation over several days or weeks take time out of each day to go through their notes and other records.

As notes are reviewed, personal opinion should be separated from observation of what happened, and suggestions of issues for further investigation should be clearly marked. It is also a good idea to check observations with an informant or members of the group to ensure that you have understood what is happening and that your interpretations are accurate.

DILEMMA

When should I stop observing?

Knowing when to stop doing any type of data gathering can be difficult for novices, but it is particularly tricky in observational studies because there is no obvious ending. Schedules often dictate when your study ends. Otherwise, stop when you stop learning new things. Two indications of having done enough are when you start to see similar patterns of behavior being repeated, or when you have listened to all the main stakeholder groups and understand their perspectives. ∎

Ethnography

Ethnography has traditionally been used in the social sciences to uncover the social organization of activities, and hence to understand work. Since the early 1990s it has gained credibility in interaction design, and particularly in the design of collaborative systems: see Box 7.5 and Crabtree (2003). A large part of most ethnographic studies is direct observation,

BOX 7.5

Ethnography in requirements

The MERboard is a tool to support scientists and engineers display, capture, annotate, and share information to support the operation of two Mars Exploration Rovers (MERs) on the surface of Mars. The MER (see Figure 7.9) acts like a human geological explorer by collecting samples, analyzing them, and transmitting results back to the scientists on Earth. The scientists and engineers collaboratively analyze the data received, decide what to study next, create plans of action, and send commands to the robots on the surface of Mars.

The requirements for MERboard were identified partly through ethnographic fieldwork, observations, and analysis (Trimble *et al*, 2002). The team of scientists and engineers ran a series of field tests that simulated the process of receiving data, analyzing it, creating plans, and transmitting them to the MERs. The main problems they identified stemmed from the scientists' limitations in displaying, sharing, and storing information (see Figure 7.10a).

Figure 7.9 Mars Exploration Rover

Source: Reproduced by permission of NASA Jet Propulsion Laboratory (NASA-JPL).

(a)   (b)

Figure 7.10 (a) The situation before MERboard; (b) A scientist using MERboard to present information

Source: J. Trimble, R. Wales and R. Gossweiler (2002): "NASA position paper for the CSCW 2002 workshop on Public, Community and Situated Displays: Merboard".

(Continued)

These observations led to the development of MERboard (see Figure 7.10b), which contains four core applications: a whiteboard for brainstorming and sketching, a browser for displaying information from the web, the capability to display personal information and information across several screens, and a file storage space linked specifically to MERboard. ■

but interviews, questionnaires, and studying artifacts used in the activities also feature in many ethnographic studies. The main distinguishing feature of ethnographic studies compared with other approaches to data gathering is that the aim is to observe a situation without imposing any *a priori* structure or framework upon it, and to view everything as 'strange.'

Ethnography has become popular within interaction design because it allows designers to obtain a detailed and nuanced understanding of people's behavior and the use of technology that cannot be obtained by other methods of data gathering (Bell, 2001; Lazar *et al*, 2010a; Crabtree *et al*, 2009).

The observer in an ethnographic study adopts a participant observer (i.e. insider) role as much as possible (Fetterman, 2010). While participant observation is a hallmark of ethnographic studies, it can be used within other methodological frameworks as well such as within an action research program of study where one of the goals is to change and improve the situation.

Gathering ethnographic data is not hard. You gather what is available, what is 'ordinary,' what it is that people do, say, how they work. The data collected therefore has many forms: documents, notes of your own, pictures, room layout sketches. Notebook notes may include snippets of conversation and descriptions of rooms, meetings, what someone did, or how people reacted to a situation. Data gathering is opportunistic in that you collect what you can collect and make the most of opportunities as they present themselves. Often, interesting phenomena do not reveal themselves immediately but only later on, so it is important to gather as much as possible within the framework of observation. Initially, time should be spent getting to know the people in the workplace and bonding with them. It is critical, from the very beginning, that they understand why you are there, what you hope to achieve, and how long you plan to be there. Going to lunch with them, buying coffee, and bringing small gifts, e.g. cookies, can greatly help this socialization process. Moreover, it may be during one of the informal gatherings that key information is revealed.

Always show interest in the stories, gripes, and explanations that are provided but be prepared to step back if the phone rings or someone else enters the workspace. Most people will stop mid-sentence if their attention is required elsewhere. Hence, you need to be prepared to switch in and out of their work cycles, moving into the shadow if something happens that needs the person's immediate attention.

A good tactic is to explain to one of the participants during a quiet moment what you think is happening and then let her correct you. It is important not to appear overly keen or obtrusive. Asking too many questions, taking pictures of everything, showing off your knowledge, and getting in their way can be very off-putting. Putting up cameras on tripods on the first day is not a good idea. Listening and watching while sitting on the sidelines and occasionally asking questions is a much better approach. When you have gained the trust and respect of the participants you can then ask if they mind you setting up a video camera, taking pictures, or using a recorder. Even taking pictures with a smartphone can be obtrusive.

The following is an illustrative list of materials that might be recorded and collected during an ethnographic study (adapted from Crabtree, 2003, p. 53):

- Activity or job descriptions.
- Rules and procedures (and so on) said to govern particular activities.
- Descriptions of activities observed.
- Recordings of the talk taking place between parties involved in observed activities.
- Informal interviews with participants explaining the detail of observed activities.
- Diagrams of the physical layout, including the position of artifacts.
- Photographs of artifacts (documents, diagrams, forms, computers, etc.) used in the course of observed activities.
- Videos of artifacts as used in the course of observed activities.
- Descriptions of artifacts used in the course of observed activities.
- Workflow diagrams showing the sequential order of tasks involved in observed activities.
- Process maps showing connections between activities.

Traditionally, ethnographic studies in this field aim to understand what people do and how they organize action and interaction within a particular context of interest to designers. However, recently there has been a trend towards studies that draw more on ethnography's anthropological roots and the study of culture. This trend has been brought about by the perceived need to use different approaches because the computers and other digital technologies, especially mobile devices, are embedded in everyday activity, and not just in the workplace as in the 1990s. Crabtree *et al* (2009) warn that using ethnography to study cultural aspects of a situation requires a different set of approaches and contributes differently to design.

BOX 7.6

Doing ethnography online

As collaboration and social activity have moved to having a large online presence, ethnographers have adapted their approach to study social media and the various forms of computer mediated communication (Rotman *et al*, 2012, 2013). This practice has various names, the most common of which are: online ethnography (Rotman *et al*, 2012), virtual ethnography (Hine, 2000), or netnography (Kozinets, 2010). Where a community or activity has both an online and offline presence, it is usual to incorporate both online and offline techniques within the data gathering program. However, where the community or activities of interest exist almost exclusively online, then only online techniques are used and virtual ethnography becomes central.

Why, you may ask, is it necessary to distinguish between online and face-to-face ethnography? Well it is important because interaction online is different from interaction in person. For example, communication in person is richer (through gesture, facial expression, tone of

(*Continued*)

voice, and so on) than online communication, and anonymity is more easily achieved when communicating online. In addition, virtual worlds have a persistence, due to regular archiving, that does not typically occur in face-to-face situations. This makes characteristics of the communication different, which often includes how an ethnographer introduces herself to the community, how she acts within the community, and how she reports her findings.

For large social spaces such as digital libraries or Facebook, there are different ethical issues to consider. For example, it is probably unrealistic to ask everyone using a digital library to sign an informed consent form, yet you do need to make sure that participants understand your involvement in the study and the purpose of the study. Presentation of results will need to be modified too. Quotes from participants in the community, even if anonymized in the report, can easily be attributed by a simple search of the community archive or the IP address of the sender, so care is needed to protect their privacy. ■

7.6.2   Direct Observation in Controlled Environments

Observing users in a controlled environment may occur within a purpose-built usability laboratory, but portable laboratories that can be set up in any room are quite common and this avoids participants having to travel away from their normal environment, and reduces the expenses involved in creating and maintaining a purpose-built usability laboratory. Observation in a controlled environment inevitably takes on a more formal character than observation in the field, and the user is likely to feel apprehensive. As with interviews, discussed in Section 7.4, it is a good idea to prepare a script to guide how the participants will be greeted, be told about the goals of the study and how long it will last, and have their rights explained. Use of a script ensures that each participant will be treated in exactly the same way, which brings more credibility to the results obtained from the study.

The same basic data recording techniques are used for direct observation in the laboratory and field studies (i.e. capturing photographs, taking notes, collecting video, and so on), but the way in which these techniques are used is different. In the laboratory the emphasis is on the details of what individuals do, while in the field the context is important and the focus is on how people interact with each other, the technology, and their environment.

The arrangement of equipment with respect to the participant is important in a controlled study because details of the person's activity need to be captured. For example, one camera might record facial expressions, another might focus on mouse and keyboard activity, and another might record a broad view of the participant and capture body language. The stream of data from the cameras can be fed into a video editing and analysis suite where it is coordinated and time-stamped, annotated, and partially edited (see Chapters 13 and 14).

The Think-Aloud Technique

One of the problems with observation is that the observer doesn't know what users are thinking, and can only guess from what they see. Observation in the field should not be intrusive as this will disturb the very context you are trying to capture, so asking questions of the participant should be limited. However, in a controlled environment, the observer can afford to be a little more intrusive. The think-aloud technique is a useful way of understanding what is going on in a person's head.

Figure 7.11 Home page of Lycos search engine

Figure 7.12 The screen that appears in response to choosing 'child's phone'

Imagine observing someone who has been asked to evaluate the interface of the web search engine Lycos.com. The user, who does not have much experience of web searches, is told to look for a phone for a ten-year-old child. He is told to type 'www.lycos.com' and then proceed however he thinks best. He types the URL and gets a screen similar to the one in Figure 7.11.

Next he types 'child's phone' in the search box. He gets a screen similar to the one in Figure 7.12. He is silent. What is going on, you wonder? What is he thinking? One way around the problem of knowing what he is doing is to collect a think-aloud protocol, a technique developed by Erikson and Simon (1985) for examining people's problem-solving strategies. The technique requires people to say out loud everything that they are thinking and trying to do, so that their thought processes are externalized.

So, let's imagine an action replay of the situation just described, but this time the user has been instructed to think aloud:

> 'I'm typing in www.lycos.com, as you told me.' <types>
> 'Now I am typing 'child's phone' and then clicking on the search button.
> <pause and silence>
> 'It's taking a few seconds to respond.'
> 'Oh! Now I have a choice of other websites to go to. Hmm, I wonder which one I should select. Well, it's for a young child so I want "child safe phone".' <He clicks to select Smarter.com>
> 'Gosh, there's a lot more models to select from than I expected! Hmm, some of these are for older children. I wonder what I do next to find one for a ten-year-old.'
> <pauses and looks at the screen>
> 'I guess I should scroll through them and identify those that might be appropriate.'
> <silence . . .>

Now you know more about what the user is trying to achieve but he is silent again. You can see that he is looking at the screen. What you don't know is what he is thinking now or what he is looking at.

The occurrence of these silences is one of the biggest problems with the think-aloud technique.

ACTIVITY 7.7

Try a think-aloud exercise yourself. Go to a website, such as Amazon or eBay, and look for something that you want to buy. Think aloud as you search and notice how you feel and behave.

Afterwards, reflect on the experience. Did you find it difficult to keep speaking all the way through the task? Did you feel awkward? Did you stop when you got stuck?

Comment

You probably felt self-conscious and awkward doing this. Some people say they feel really embarrassed. At times you may also have started to forget to speak out loud. You may also have found it difficult to think aloud when the task got difficult. In fact, you probably stopped speaking when the task became demanding, and that is exactly the time when an observer is most eager to hear your comments.

If a user is silent during a think-aloud protocol, the observer could interrupt and remind him to think out loud, but that would be intrusive. Another solution is to have two people work together so that they talk to each other. Working with another person (called constructive interaction (Miyake, 1986)) is often more natural and revealing because participants talk in order to help each other along. This technique has been found particularly successful with children and it also avoids possible cultural influences on concurrent verbalization (Clemmensen et al, 2008). ∎

7.6.3   Indirect Observation: Tracking Users' Activities

Sometimes direct observation is not possible because it is obtrusive or observers cannot be present over the duration of the study, and so activities are tracked indirectly. Diaries and interaction logs are two techniques for doing this.

Diaries

Participants are asked to write a diary of their activities on a regular basis, e.g. what they did, when they did it, what they found hard or easy, and what their reactions were to the situation. For example, Sohn *et al* (2008) asked 20 participants to record their mobile information needs through text messages, and then to use these messages as prompts to help them answer six questions through a website at the end of each day. From the data collected, they identified 16 categories of mobile information needs, the most frequent of which was 'trivia.'

Diaries are useful when participants are scattered and unreachable in person, for example as in many web-based projects. Diaries have several advantages: they do not take up much researcher time to collect data; they do not require special equipment or expertise; and they are suitable for long-term studies. In addition, templates, like those used in open-ended online questionnaires, can be created online to standardize the data entry format so that the data can be entered directly into a database for analysis. However, diary studies rely on participants being reliable and remembering to complete them at the assigned time and as instructed, so incentives may be needed and the process has to be straightforward and quick. Furthermore, studies lasting longer than two weeks are less likely to be successful. Another problem is that the participants' memories of events are often exaggerated or detail is forgotten, e.g. remembering them as better or worse than they really were, or taking more or less time than they actually did take.

The use of multiple media in diaries (e.g. photographs including selfies, audio and video clips, and so on) has been explored by several researchers. Carter and Mankoff (2005) considered whether capturing events through pictures, audio, or artifacts related to the event affects the results of the diary study. They found that images resulted in more specific recall than other media, but audio was useful for capturing events when taking a picture was too awkward. Tangible artifacts, such as those in Figure 7.13, also encouraged discussion about wider beliefs and attitudes. Several researchers note that collecting diary data from mobile technology users can be particularly tricky when users are constantly on the move (Palen and Salzman, 2002).

The experience sampling method (ESM) is similar to a diary in that it relies on participants recording information about their everyday activities. However, it differs from more traditional diary studies because participants are prompted at random times using a pager, smartphone, or similar device to answer specific questions about their context, feelings, and actions (Hektner *et al*, 2006). These prompts have the benefit of encouraging immediate data capture. For example, Mancini *et al* (2009) used a combination of experience sampling and deferred contextual interviews when investigating mobile privacy. A simple multiple-choice questionnaire was sent electronically to the participants' smartphones, and participants also answered the questions through their smartphones. Interviews about the recorded events were based on the questionnaire answers given at the time.

Interaction Logs and Web Analytics

Interaction logging involves installing software on a device that is being used to record users' activity in a log that can be examined later. A variety of actions may be recorded, from key presses, and mouse or other device movements, to time spent searching a web page,

Figure 7.13 Some tangible objects collected by participants involved in a study about a jazz festival

Source: S. Carter and J. Mankoff (2005): "When participants do the capturing: the role of media in diary studies" CHI 2005 pp. 899–908 ©2005 Association for Computing Machinery, Inc. Reprinted by permission.

to looking at help systems, and task flow through software modules. If used in a usability evaluation, then gathering of the data is often synchronized with video and audio logs to help evaluators analyze users' behavior and understand how users worked on the tasks they set. Typically usability labs provide this facility.

A key advantage of logging activity is that it is unobtrusive provided system performance is not affected, but it also raises ethical concerns about observing participants if this is done without their knowledge (see the Dilemma box that follows). Another advantage is that large volumes of data can be logged automatically. However, visualization tools are needed to explore and analyze this data quantitatively and qualitatively. Examples of visualizations to help with data analysis and interpretation are in Figures 6.17, 6.18, 8.6, and 8.7.

Web analytics is one form of interaction logging that has become very popular. This involves collecting, analyzing, and reporting data that tracks a user's behavior when interacting with a website. Logging the number of visitors to a website has been common for many years. This kind of data can be used to monitor changes in the number of website visitors after making modifications. Web analytics data tracks users' behavior much more closely, such as how long people stay on a web page, where they spend most of their time, which other sites they came from, what adverts they looked at and for how long, and so on. Web analytics can be used to assess whether users' goals are being met, to support usability studies and to inform future design. They are a powerful tool for business and market research, and can benefit a range of projects. Khoo *et al* (2008) discuss the use of web metrics for digital libraries. They focus particularly on session length as a useful metric, but warn that it is important for any such metrics to be triangulated with other research. This project is discussed further in Box 8.5.

What Are Web Analytics Used for?

Web analytics are a system of tools and techniques for measuring, collecting, analyzing, and reporting web data to understand and optimize web usage. Web analytics help gauge traffic and popularity trends by providing information about the number of website visitors and number of page views. As well as measuring web traffic, analytics are used in business and market research to assess and improve website effectiveness. Web analytics can further help companies measure the result of print or media advertising campaigns by estimating how traffic to a site changes after launching a campaign.

There are two categories of web analytics: on-site and off-site analytics. On-site analytics are used by website owners to measure visitor behavior and the performance of their website in a commercial context. Data is compared against key performance indicators and used to improve a website or marketing campaign's audience response. Unlike on-site web analytics, off-site analytics measure the performance of a website's potential audience (opportunity), share of voice (visibility), and buzz (comments) on the Internet.

Historically, web analytics has referred to on-site visitor measurement, but in recent years the line between off-site and on-site analytics has blurred because vendors are producing tools spanning both categories. Additional data sources may be conjointly used to augment website behavior data. For instance, email and click-through rates, direct mail campaign data, sales, and history may be paired with web traffic data to provide further insights into user behavior.

Google Analytics is the most widely used on-site web analytics and statistics service, used by over 50% of the 10,000 most popular websites (Empson, 2012). The tool is designed to help Internet marketers and small business owners understand website traffic patterns, sources, and behaviors. The service tracks visitors from referring sites, search engines, social networks, and user visits, and tracks email marketing, pay-per-click networks, and display advertising.

Figure 7.14 shows segments from the Google Analytics dashboard for the accompanying website for this book, id-book.com, for a month in August–September 2014. The first segment shows information about who accessed the site and the second gives some information about the mobile devices used to view the website. These show only a fraction of the information that analytics packages like this can provide. Activity 7.8 asks you to investigate the information shown here.

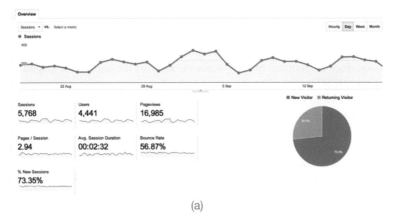

(a)

Figure 7.14 Segments of the Google Analytics dashboard for id-book.com in September 2014 (a) audience overview, (b) screen resolution of mobile devices used to view the website

	Screen Resolution	Acquisition			Behaviour		
		Sessions ↓	% New Sessions	New Users	Bounce Rate	Pages / Session	Avg. Session Duration
		688 % of Total 11.93% (5,768)	**74.27%** Site Avg: 73.35% (1.25%)	**511** % of Total 12.08% (4,231)	**68.46%** Site Avg: 56.87% (20.39%)	**2.32** Site Avg: 2.94 (-21.17%)	**00:01:47** Site Avg: 00:02:32 (-29.56%)
☐	1. 768x1024	173 (25.15%)	60.12%	104 (20.35%)	58.38%	2.66	00:02:17
☐	2. 320x568	137 (19.91%)	84.67%	116 (22.70%)	79.56%	1.53	00:00:45
☐	3. 360x640	40 (5.81%)	87.50%	35 (6.85%)	72.50%	2.00	00:01:50
☐	4. 320x480	34 (4.94%)	82.35%	28 (5.48%)	82.35%	1.35	00:00:07
☐	5. 360x592	19 (2.76%)	94.74%	18 (3.52%)	78.95%	1.68	00:00:13
☐	6. 480x800	19 (2.76%)	52.63%	10 (1.96%)	57.89%	7.05	00:06:24
☐	7. 720x1280	13 (1.89%)	69.23%	9 (1.76%)	69.23%	2.77	00:01:35
☐	8. 1366x768	10 (1.45%)	70.00%	7 (1.37%)	40.00%	4.20	00:05:52
☐	9. 1536x864	10 (1.45%)	50.00%	5 (0.98%)	30.00%	5.20	00:07:35
☐	10. 1280x800	9 (1.31%)	44.44%	4 (0.78%)	66.67%	2.00	00:02:23

(b)

Figure 7.14 Continued

ACTIVITY 7.8

Consider the two screenshot segments shown in Figure 7.14 from the Google Analytics for id-book.com. Study this information and answer the following questions.

1. How many people visited the site during this period?
2. What do you think someone might look at in 2.32 minutes (the average time they spent at the site)?
3. 'Bounce rate' refers to the percentage of visitors who view just one page of your site. What is the bounce rate for this period? Why do you think this might be a useful metric to capture for any website?
4. Which screen resolution has the highest bounce rate, and which has the lowest? Why do you think that might be?

Comment

1. 4441 users visited the site in this period. Notice that some users must have had more than one session since the number of users is not the same as the number of sessions.
2. The bounce rate is 56.87%. This is a useful metric because it represents a simple but significant characteristic of users' behavior. If the bounce rate is high (40–60% is about average while >65% is high and <35% is low), it deserves further investigation to see if there is a problem with the website.
3. The number of pages per session is about 3, so on average users looked at 3 pages in 2.32 minutes. In 2.32 minutes a user probably won't have played any of the videos on the site, nor read the case studies in any great detail. They may have downloaded PowerPoint slides, however, or looked at the additional resources and then moved on to one of the pointers given for extra information.

4. The highest bounce rate is 82.35% for screen resolutions of 320 × 480. The lowest bounce rate is 30% for screen resolutions of 1536 × 864. Visitors using a lower screen resolution tended to look at only one page on the website, hence they had a high bounce rate. On the other hand, visitors using high resolution screens viewed more pages. This may be because the site is difficult to read or navigate with a low resolution screen, or that the graphics are more appealing on a high resolution screen. ■

In President Obama's 2012 re-election campaign, quick and easy access to actionable data was essential to understanding and responding to voters. Nate Lubin, the Director of Digital Marketing for 'Obama for America', and his team used Google Analytics to inform them when making key decisions quickly during the re-election campaign. The ability to do rapid, real-time optimization, Lubin explained, was particularly important during the presidential debates. Research had shown that 64% of voters used the Internet to verify or 'fact check' a claim made by a candidate, and that voters researched issues discussed during presidential debates in real time. In order to speak to supporters and persuade voters who were researching online during debates, Lubin's team used real-time reports in Google Analytics to understand voters' questions and concerns, allowing them to deliver answers directly from the campaign.

You can view tutorials showing you how to install Google Analytics and more, as detailed below. You can also read a case study about how analytics were used in the wine trade in Chapter 15.

> Video on 'Google Analytics Tutorial – Install' to manually install Google Analytics 2013 on your website, at **http://youtu.be/P_l4oc6tbYk**

> Video on 'Google Analytics Tutorial Step-By-Step' for a comprehensive tutorial that describes the statistics included in Google Analytics, and provides insight into how the analytics may be used to improve user traffic, at **http://youtu.be/mm78xlsADgc**

For an overview of different dashboards that can be customized in Google Analytics, see Poulter, N. (2013), 6 Google Analytics Custom Dashboards to Save You Time NOW! Retrieved from http://www.stateofdigital.com/google-analytics-dashboards/.

BOX 7.7

Other analytics tools

As well as Google Analytics, new tools are emerging that provide additional layers of information, better access control options, and raw and real-time data collection.

- Moz Analytics – Tracks search marketing, social media marketing, brand activity, links and content marketing, and is particularly useful for link management and analysis: www.moz.com
- *TruSocialMetrics* – Tracks social media metrics and helps calculate social media marketing return on investment: www.truesocialmetrics.com
- *Clicky* – Comprehensive and real-time analytics tool that shows individual visitors and the actions they take, and helps define what people from different demographics find interesting: www.clicky.com
- *KISSmetrics* – Detailed analytics tool that displays what website visitors are doing on your website before, during, and after they buy: www.kissmetrics.com
- *Crazy Egg* – Tracks visitor clicks based on where they are specifically clicking, and creates click heat maps useful for website design, usability, and conversion: www.crazyegg.com
- *ClickTale* – Records website visitor actions and uses meta-statistics to create visual heat map reports on customer mouse movement, scrolling, and other visitor behaviors: www.clicktale.com ■

Link to more on this topic, described by Dubois (2014), 11 Best Web Analytics Tools at
http://www.inc.com/guides/12/2010/11-best-web-analytics-tools.html

DILEMMA

They don't know we are watching. Shall we tell them?

If you have appropriate algorithms and sufficient computer storage, large quantities of data about Internet usage can be collected and users need never know. This information could be very valuable for many different reasons. For example, Google, Facebook, Amazon, and other companies do this so that they can serve advertisements about products or services to their users at appropriate times. This enables the companies to sell more products and services directly or to collect more revenue from advertising companies. Have you ever wondered why, for instance, after searching for information about something recently, such as buying sports gear or a bike, other related products often appear at the side of a future search in the form of advertisements? Are these advertisements helpful or an annoying intrusion? Should users be told that their interactions online are being logged? Knowing this, users will likely change their behavior, which will make their logged data less useful to the company collecting it. What is reasonable? It depends on the context, how much personal information is collected, and how the information will be used. Many companies now tell you that your computer activity and phone calls may be logged for quality assurance and other purposes. Most people do not object to this practice. However, should we be concerned about logging personal information (e.g. discussions about health or financial information)? Should users be worried? How can we exploit the ability to log user behavior when visiting websites without overstepping a person's ethical and civil rights? Where should we draw the line? ■

7.7 Choosing and Combining Techniques

It is desirable to combine data gathering techniques for a single data gathering program; the benefit is to provide multiple perspectives. However, it can be time-consuming and costly. Choosing which data gathering techniques to use depends on a variety of factors related to your goals. There is no right technique or combination of techniques, but some will undoubtedly be more appropriate than others. The decision about which to use will need to be made after taking all the factors into account. Table 7.1 below provides some information to help you choose a set of techniques for a specific project. It lists the kind of information you can get (e.g. answers to specific questions) and the type of data it yields (e.g. mostly qualitative or mostly quantitative). It also includes some advantages and disadvantages for each technique (for a discussion of qualitative and quantitative data, see Section 8.2).

The Focus of the Study
The techniques used must be compatible with the goal of the study, i.e. they must be able to gather appropriate data. For example, the data to be collected may be implicit knowledge or it may be explicit, observable behavior; it may be opinion or it may be facts; it may be formal documented rules or it may be informal work-arounds and heuristics; it may be publicly accessible information or it may be confidential, and so on. The kind of data you want will probably be influenced by where you are in the development cycle. For example, at the beginning of the project you may not have any specific questions that need answering, so it is better to spend time exploring issues through interviews and observation rather than sending out questionnaires.

The activity being investigated will also have dimensions that influence the techniques to use. For example, Olson and Moran (1996) suggest a task can be characterized along three dimensions: (i) is it a set of sequential steps or a rapid overlapping series of subtasks; (ii) does it involve a lot of information and complex displays, or little information and simple representations; and (iii) is the task to be performed by a lay-person or by a trained professional?

Technique	Good for	Kind of data	Advantages	Disadvantages
Interviews	Exploring issues	Some quantitative but mostly qualitative	Interviewer can guide interviewee if necessary. Encourages contact between developers and users	Time-consuming. Artificial environment may intimidate interviewee
Focus groups	Collecting multiple viewpoints	Some quantitative but mostly qualitative	Highlights areas of consensus and conflict. Encourages contact between developers and users	Possibility of dominant characters
Questionnaires	Answering specific questions	Quantitative and qualitative	Can reach many people with low resource	The design is crucial. Response rates may be low. Unless carefully designed, the responses may not provide suitable data
Direct observation in the field	Understanding context of user activity	Mostly qualitative	Observing gives insights that other techniques don't give	Very time-consuming. Huge amounts of data are produced
Direct observation in a controlled environment	Capturing the detail of what individuals do	Quantitative and qualitative	Can focus on the details of a task without interruption	Results may have limited use in the normal environment because the conditions were artificial
Indirect observation	Observing users without disturbing their activity; data captured automatically	Quantitative (logging) and qualitative (diary)	User doesn't get distracted by the data gathering; automatic recording means that it can extend over long periods of time	A large amount of quantitative data needs tool support to analyze (logging); participants' memories may exaggerate (diary)

Table 7.1 Overview of data gathering techniques and their use

The Participants Involved

The characteristics of the target user group for the product will affect the kind of data gathering technique used. For example, techniques used for data gathering from young children may be very different from those used with adults (see Box 7.2). If the participants are in a hurry to catch a plane, they will not be receptive to a long interview; if their job involves interacting with people then they may be comfortable in a focus group, and so on.

The location and accessibility of participants also needs to be considered. It may be attractive to run a focus group for a large set of stakeholders, but if they are spread across a wide geographical area, a face-to-face meeting is unlikely to be practical. Similarly, the time participants need to give their undivided attention to the session is significant, e.g. an interview requires a higher level of active engagement while an observation allows the participant to continue with her normal activity.

Depending on what is motivating the participants to take part, it may be better to conduct interviews rather than to issue a questionnaire. It may also be better to conduct a focus group in order to widen consultation and participation, thereby enhancing feelings of ownership and expectations of the users.

The Nature of the Technique

We have already mentioned the issue of participants' time and the kind of data to be collected, but there is also the issue of whether the technique requires specialist equipment or training, and whether the available investigators have the appropriate knowledge and experience. For example, how experienced is the investigator at conducting ethnographic studies, or in handling video data?

Available Resources

The resources available will influence the choice of techniques, too. For example, sending out questionnaires nationwide requires sufficient time, money, and people to do a good design, pilot it, adapt the questionnaire based on the findings from the pilot study and distribute it, collate the data, and analyze them. If there is very little time and no one on the team has designed a questionnaire before, then the team may run into problems that result in poor data collection.

ACTIVITY 7.9

For each of the situations below, consider what kinds of data gathering would be appropriate and how you might use the different techniques introduced above. You should assume that you are at the beginning of product development and that you have sufficient time and resources to use any of the techniques.

1. You are developing a new software system to support a small organic produce shop. There is a system running already with which the users are reasonably happy, but it is looking dated and needs upgrading.
2. You are looking to develop an innovative device for diabetes sufferers to help them record and monitor their blood sugar levels. There are some products already on the market, but they tend to be a bit large and unwieldy. Many diabetes sufferers still rely on manual recording and monitoring methods involving a ritual with a needle or needle-like device, some chemicals, and a written or visual scale.
3. You are developing a website for a young persons' fashion e-commerce site.

Comment

1. As this is a small shop, there are likely to be few stakeholders. Some period of observation is always important to understand the context of the new and the old system. Interviewing the staff rather than giving them questionnaires is likely to be appropriate because there aren't very many of them, and this will yield richer data and give the developers a chance to meet the users. Organic produce is regulated by a variety of laws and so it is important to look at this documentation in order to understand any legal constraints that have to be taken into account. Therefore, we would suggest a series of interviews with the main users to understand the positive and negative features of the existing system, a short

observation session to understand the context of the system, and a study of documentation surrounding the regulations.

2. In this case, your user group is spread about, so talking to all of them is not feasible. However, it is important to interview some, possibly at a local diabetic clinic, making sure that you have a representative sample of potential users. And you would need to observe the existing manual operation to understand what is required. A further group of stakeholders would be those who use or have used the other products on the market. These stakeholders can be questioned to find out the problems with the existing devices so that the new device can improve on them. A questionnaire sent to a wider group in order to back up the findings from the interviews would be appropriate, as might a focus group where possible.

3. Again, you are not going to be able to interview all your users. In fact, the user group may not be very well defined. Interviews backed up by questionnaires and focus groups would be appropriate. In this case, identifying similar or competing sites and evaluating them will help provide information for an improved product. ■

Assignment

Part A

The aim of this assignment is for you to practice data gathering. Assume that you have been employed to improve an interactive product such as a smartphone app, an iPod, a DVD recorder, computer software, a photocopying machine, or some other type of technology that interests you. You may either redesign this product, or create a completely new product. To do the assignment you will need to find a group of people or a single individual prepared to be your user group. These could be your family, your friends, or people in your class or local community group.

For this assignment you should:

(a) Clarify the basic goal of improving the product by considering what this means in your circumstances.

(b) Watch the group (or person) casually to get an understanding of issues that might create challenges for you doing this assignment and get information that might enable you to refine your goals.

(c) Explain how you would use each of the three data gathering techniques: interview, questionnaire, and observation in your data gathering program. Explain how your plan takes account of triangulation.

(d) Consider your relationship with your user group and decide if an informed consent form is required (Figure 7.1 and Chapter 13 will help you to design your own if needed).

(e) Plan your data gathering program in detail:

- Decide what kind of interview you want to run, and design a set of interview questions for your study. Decide how you will record the data, then acquire and test any equipment needed and run a pilot study.

- Decide whether you want to include a questionnaire in your data gathering program, and design appropriate questions for it. Run a pilot study to check your questionnaire.

- Decide whether you want to use direct or indirect observation and where on the outsider–insider spectrum of observers you wish to be. Decide how you will record the data, then acquire and test any equipment needed and run a pilot study.

(f) Carry out your study but limit its scope. For example, only interview two or three people or plan only two half-hour observation periods.

(g) Reflect on your experience and suggest what you would do differently next time.

Keep the data you have gathered as this will form the basis of the assignment in Chapter 8.

Part B

This assignment (adapted from Golbeck, 2013) requires you to:

1. Go to https://wordpress.com/ and create a new blog.
2. On your new site, upload an original funny or interesting story, image, or video that you think others would be interested in viewing, making sure that your post does not violate a copyright.
3. Promote your site on social media outlets like Facebook and Twitter and encourage your peers and family to help you.
4. Each day at the same time (e.g. 10am), record the number of people who have visited your blog and the regions visitors came from. Make a chart that shows how these analytics changed over the 7-day period.
5. Analyze your success. How many users were you able to attract? What days attracted the most views? Where did your viewers come from? Based on the analytics data, think about what you could do in the future to attract more visitors.

Summary

This chapter has presented three main data gathering methods that are commonly used in interaction design: interviews, questionnaires, and observation. It has described in detail the planning and execution of each. In addition, five key issues of data gathering were presented, and how to record the data gathered was discussed.

Key points

- All data gathering sessions should have clear goals.
- Depending on the study you plan, you may need to develop an informed consent form and get other permissions to run the study.
- Each planned data gathering session should be tested by running a pilot study.
- Triangulation involves investigating a phenomenon from different perspectives.
- Data may be recorded using handwritten notes, audio or video recording, a camera, or any combination of these.
- There are three styles of interviews: structured, semi-structured, and unstructured.
- Questionnaires may be paper-based, email, or web-based.
- Questions for an interview or questionnaire can be open or closed. Closed questions require the interviewee to select from a limited range of options. Open questions accept a free-range response.

- Observation may be direct or indirect.
- In direct observation, the observer may adopt different levels of participation ranging from insider (participant observer) to outsider (passive observer).
- Choosing appropriate data gathering techniques depends on the focus of the study, the participants involved, the nature of the technique, and the resources available.

Further Reading

FETTERMAN, D. M. (2010). *Ethnography: Step by Step* (3rd edn) Applied Social Research Methods Series, Vol. 17. Sage. This book provides an introduction to the theory and practice of ethnography and is an excellent guide for beginners. It covers both data gathering and data analysis in the ethnographic tradition.

FULTON SURI, J. (2005) *Thoughtless Acts?* Chronicle Books, San Francisco. This intriguing little book invites you to consider how people react to their environment. It is a good introduction to the art of observation.

HEATH, C., HINDMARSH, J. and LUFF, P. (2010) *Video in Qualitative Research: Analyzing social interaction in everyday life*. Sage. This is an accessible book which provides practical advice and guidance about how to set up and perform data gathering using video recording. It also covers data analysis, presenting findings and potential implications from video research based on their own experience.

OLSON, J. S. and KELLOGG, W. A. (eds) (2014) *Ways of Knowing in HCI*. Springer. This edited collection contains useful chapters on a wide variety of data collection and analysis techniques. Some topics that are particularly relevant to this chapter include: ethnography, experimental design, log data collection and analysis, ethics in research, and more.

OPPENHEIM, A. N. (1998) *Questionnaire Design, Interviewing and Attitude Measurement*. Pinter Publishers. This text is now a classic but it is useful for reference. It provides a detailed account of all aspects of questionnaire design, illustrated with many examples. However, care will be needed in applying some of these suggestions to online questionnaires.

ROBSON, C. (2011) *Real World Research* (3rd edn). John Wiley & Sons. This book provides comprehensive coverage of data gathering and analysis techniques and how to use them. Early books and related books by Robson also address topics discussed in this chapter.

SUE, V. M. and RITTER, L. A. (2012) *Conducting Online Surveys*. Sage. This small book describes the process of conducting online surveys including how to set the survey goals, design the questions, implement the questionnaire, identify a suitable group of potential respondents, and analyze the results.

Chapter 8

DATA ANALYSIS, INTERPRETATION, AND PRESENTATION

Objectives

The main aims of this chapter are to:

- Discuss the difference between qualitative and quantitative data and analysis.
- Enable you to analyze data gathered from questionnaires.
- Enable you to analyze data gathered from interviews.
- Enable you to analyze data gathered from observation studies.
- Make you aware of software packages that are available to help your analysis.
- Identify some of the common pitfalls in data analysis, interpretation, and presentation.
- Enable you to be able to interpret and present your findings in a meaningful and appropriate manner.

8.1 Introduction

The kind of analysis that can be performed on a set of data will be influenced by the goals identified at the outset, and the data actually gathered. Broadly speaking, you may take a qualitative analysis approach or a quantitative analysis approach, or a combination of qualitative and quantitative. The last of these is very common as it provides a more comprehensive account of the behavior being observed or performance being measured.

Most analysis, whether it is quantitative or qualitative, begins with initial reactions or observations from the data. This might involve identifying patterns or calculating simple numerical values such as ratios, averages, or percentages. This initial analysis is followed by more detailed work using structured frameworks or theories to support the investigation.

Interpretation of the findings often proceeds in parallel with analysis, but there are different ways to interpret results and it is important to make sure that the data supports your conclusions. A common mistake is for the investigator's existing beliefs or biases to influence the interpretation of results. Imagine that through initial analysis of your data you have discovered a pattern of responses to customer care questionnaires which indicates that inquiries from customers that are routed through the Sydney office of an organization take longer to process than those routed through the Moscow office. This result can be interpreted in many different ways. Which do you choose? You may conclude that the customer care operatives in Sydney are less efficient, or you may conclude that the customer care operatives in Sydney provide more detailed responses, or you may conclude that the technology supporting the processing of inquiries needs to be updated in Sydney, or you may conclude that customers reaching the Sydney office demand a higher level of service, and so on. In order to determine which of these potential interpretations is more accurate, it would be appropriate to look at other data such as customer inquiry details, and maybe interviews with staff.

Another common mistake is to make claims that go beyond what the data can support. This is a matter of interpretation and of presentation. The words 'many' or 'often' or indeed 'all' need to be used very carefully when reporting conclusions. An investigator should remain as impartial and objective as possible if the conclusions are to be believed, and showing that your conclusions are supported by your results is an important skill to develop.

Finally, finding the best way to present your findings is equally skilled, and depends on your goals but also on the audience for whom the results were produced. For example, in the requirements activity you might choose to present your findings using a formal notation, while reporting the results of an evaluation to the team of developers might involve a summary of problems found, supported by video clips of users experiencing those problems.

In this chapter we will introduce a variety of methods and describe in more detail how to approach data analysis using some of the common approaches taken in interaction design.

8.2   Qualitative and Quantitative

Quantitative data is data that is in the form of numbers, or that can easily be translated into numbers. For example, the number of years' experience the interviewees have, the number of projects a department handles at a time, or the number of minutes it takes to perform a task. Qualitative data is not expressed in numerical terms. For example, qualitative data includes descriptions, quotes from interviewees, vignettes of activity, and images. It is possible to express qualitative data in numerical form, but it is not always meaningful to do so – see Box 8.1.

It is sometimes assumed that certain forms of data gathering can only result in quantitative data and others can only result in qualitative data. However, this is a fallacy. All the forms of data gathering discussed in the previous chapter may result in qualitative and quantitative data. For example, on a questionnaire, questions about the participant's age or number of software packages they use a day will result in quantitative data, while any comment fields will result in qualitative data. In an observation, quantitative data you may record includes the number of people involved in a project, or how many hours a participant spends trying to sort out a problem they encounter, while notes about the feelings of frustration, or the nature of interactions between team members, are qualitative data.

Quantitative analysis uses numerical methods to ascertain the magnitude, amount, or size of something; for example, the attributes, behavior, or opinions of the participants. For example, in describing a population, a quantitative analysis might conclude that the average person is 5 feet 11 inches tall, weighs 180 pounds, and is 45 years old. Qualitative analysis focuses on the nature of something and can be represented by themes, patterns, and stories. For example, in describing the same population, a qualitative analysis might conclude that the average person is tall, thin, and middle-aged.

BOX 8.1

Use and abuse of numbers

Numbers are infinitely malleable and can make a very convincing argument, but it is important to be clear why you are manipulating quantitative data, and what the implications will be. Before adding a set of numbers together, finding an average, calculating a percentage, or performing any other kind of numerical translation, consider whether the operation is meaningful in your context.

Qualitative data can also be turned into a set of numbers. Translating non-numerical data into a numerical or ordered scale is appropriate at times, and this is a common approach in interaction design. However, you need to be careful that this kind of translation is meaningful in the context of your study. For example, assume that you have collected a set of interviews from sales representatives regarding the use of a new mobile product for reporting sales queries. One way of turning this data into a numerical form would be to count the number of words uttered by each of your interviewees. You might then draw conclusions about how strongly the sales representatives feel about the mobile devices, e.g. the more they had to say about the product, the stronger they feel about it. But do you think this is a wise way to analyze the data? This set of quantitative data is unlikely to be of much use in answering your study questions.

Other, less obvious abuses include translating small population sizes into percentages. For example, saying that 50% of users take longer than 30 minutes to place an order through an e-commerce website carries a different meaning than saying that two out of four users had the same problem. It is better not to use percentages unless the number of data points is at least over 10, and even then it is appropriate to use both percentages and raw numbers, to make sure that your claim is not misunderstood.

It is possible to perform legitimate statistical calculations on a set of data and still to present misleading results by not making the context clear, or by choosing the particular calculation that gives the most favorable result (Huff, 1991). If you are not comfortable dealing with numbers, it is better to ask for help from someone who is, because it is easy to unintentionally misrepresent your data. ■

8.2.1   The First Steps in Analyzing Data

Having performed data gathering sessions, there is some initial processing of the data normally required before data analysis can begin in earnest. There are many different combinations of data, but here we discuss typical data collected through interviews, questionnaires, and observation sessions. This information is summarized in Table 8.1.

Interviews. Raw interview data is usually in the form of audio recordings and interviewer notes. The notes need to be written up and expanded as soon as possible after the interview has taken place so that the interviewer's memory is clear and fresh. The audio recording may be used to help in this process, or it may be transcribed for more detailed analysis. Transcription takes significant effort, as people talk more quickly than most people can type (or write), and the recording is not always clear. It is therefore worth considering whether or not to transcribe the whole interview, or just sections of it that are relevant to your investigation.

Interviews are sometimes video recorded, especially if the interviewee is given a task to perform or props are used to prompt discussion. The audio channel of the video data may also be transcribed.

	Usual raw data	Example qualitative data	Example quantitative data	Initial processing steps
Interviews	Audio recordings. Interviewer notes. Video recordings	Responses to open questions. Video pictures. Respondent's opinions	Age, job role, years of experience. Responses to closed questions	Transcription of recordings. Expansion of notes
Questionnaires	Written responses. Online database	Responses to open questions. Responses in 'further comments' fields. Respondent's opinions	Age, job role, years of experience. Responses to closed questions	Clean up data. Filter into different data sets
Observation	Observer's notes. Photographs. Audio and video recordings. Data logs. Think-aloud	Records of behavior. Description of a task as it is undertaken. Copies of informal procedures	Demographics of participants. Time spent on a task. The number of people involved in an activity	Expansion of notes. Transcription of recordings. Synchronization between data recordings

Table 8.1 Data gathered and typical initial processing steps for the main data gathering techniques

Closed questions are usually treated as quantitative data and analyzed using simple quantitative analysis (see below). For example, a question that asks for the respondent's age range can easily be analyzed to find out the percentage of respondents in each range. More complicated statistical techniques are needed to identify relationships between question responses that can be generalized, such as being able to say that men over the age of 35 all believe that buttons on cell phones are too small. Open questions typically result in qualitative data which might be searched for categories or patterns of response.

Questionnaires. Raw data from questionnaires consists of the respondents' answers to the questions, and these may be in written format, or for online surveys, the data is likely to be in a database. It may be necessary to clean up the data by removing entries where the respondent has misunderstood a question.

The data can be filtered according to respondent subpopulations, (e.g. everyone under 16) or according to a particular question (e.g. to understand respondents' reactions to color). This allows analyses to be conducted on subsets of the data, and hence to draw detailed conclusions for more specific goals. This is made easier by the use of a simple tool such as a spreadsheet, as discussed below.

As for interviews, closed questions are likely to be analyzed quantitatively and open questions qualitatively.

Observation. This kind of data gathering can result in a wide variety of raw data including observer's notes, photographs, data logs, think-aloud recordings (often called protocols), video and audio recordings. All this raw data presents a rich picture of the activity under observation, but it can also make it difficult to analyze unless a structured framework is adopted. Initial data processing here would include writing up and expanding notes, and transcribing elements of the audio and video recordings and the think-aloud protocols. For observation in a controlled environment, initial processing might also include synchronizing different data recordings.

Transcriptions and the observer's notes are most likely to be analyzed using qualitative approaches, while photographs provide contextual information. Data logs and some elements of the observer's notes would probably be analyzed quantitatively.

Throughout this initial processing, patterns and themes in the data may present themselves. It is useful to make a note of these initial impressions to use as a basis for further, more detailed analysis, but don't rely on these initial impressions alone as you may be unintentionally biased by them.

8.3 Simple Quantitative Analysis

Explaining statistical analysis requires a whole book on its own. We will not try to explain statistics in any detail, although some basic statistical terms and use of statistics are discussed further in Chapter 14. Here, we introduce some simple quantitative analysis techniques you can use effectively in an interaction design context. The techniques explored here are averages and percentages. Percentages are useful for standardizing the data, particularly if you want to compare two or more large sets of responses.

Averages and percentages are fairly well-known numerical measures. However, there are three different types of average and which one you use changes the meaning of your results. These three are: mean, median, and mode. Mean refers to the commonly understood interpretation of average: i.e. add together all the figures and divide by the number of figures you started with. Median and mode are less well-known but are very useful. The median is the middle value of the data when the numbers are ranked. The mode is the most commonly occurring number. For example, in a set of data (2, 3, 4, 6, 6, 7, 7, 7, 8), the median is 6 and the mode is 7, while the mean is $50/9 = 5.56$. In this case, the difference between the different averages is not that great. However, consider the set (2, 2, 2, 2, 450). Now the median is 2, the mode is 2, and the mean is $458/5 = 91.6$!

"Looks good. Let me run it past the
number-crunchers."

Use of simple averages can provide useful overview information, but they need to be used with caution. Karapanos *et al* (2009) go further and suggest that averaging treats diversity among participants as error and proposes the use of a multidimensional scaling approach instead.

Before any analysis can take place, the data needs to be collated into analyzable data sets. Quantitative data can usually be translated into rows and columns, where one row equals one record, e.g. respondent or interviewee. If these are entered into a spreadsheet such as Excel, this makes simple manipulations and data set filtering easier. Before entering data in this way, it is important to decide how you will represent the different possible answers. For example, 'don't know' represents a different response from no answer at all and they need to be distinguished, e.g. with separate columns in the spreadsheet. Also, if dealing with options from a closed question, such as job role, there are two different possible approaches which affect the analysis. One approach is to have a column headed Job role and to enter the job role as it is given to you by the respondent or interviewee. The alternative approach is to have a column for each possible answer. The latter approach lends itself more easily to automatic summaries. Note, however, that this option will only be open to you if the original question was designed to collect the appropriate data (see Box 8.2).

BOX 8.2

How question design affects data analysis

Activity 7.2 asked you to suggest some interview questions that you might ask a colleague to help evaluate e-readers. We shall use this example here to illustrate how different question designs affect the kinds of analysis that can be performed, and the kind of conclusions that can be drawn.

Assume that you have asked the question: 'How do you feel about e-readers?' Responses to this will be varied and may include that they are cool, lightweight, easy to carry, too expensive, difficult to use, technically complex, and so on. There are many possibilities, and the responses would need to be treated qualitatively. This means that analysis of the data must consider each individual response. If you have only 10 or so responses then this may not be too bad, but if you have many more then it becomes harder to process the information, and harder to summarize your findings. This is typical of open-ended questions – answers are not likely to be homogeneous and so will need to be treated individually. In contrast, answers to a closed question, which gives respondents a fixed set of alternatives to choose from, can be treated quantitatively. So, for example, instead of asking 'How do you feel about e-readers?' assume that you have asked 'In your opinion, are e-readers easy to use or tedious to use?' This clearly reduces the number of options and you would then record the response as 'easy to use,' 'tedious to use,' or 'neither.'

When entered in a spreadsheet, or a simple table, initial analysis of this data might look like the following:

Respondent	Easy to use	Tedious to use	Neither
A	1		
B		1	
C		1	
. . .			
Z			1
Total	14	5	7

Based on this, we can then say that 14 out of 26 (54%) of our respondents think e-readers are easy to use, 5 out of 26 (19%) think they are tedious to use, and 7 out of 26 (27%) think they are neither easy to use nor tedious. Note also that in the table, respondents' names are replaced by letters so that they are identifiable but anonymous to any onlookers. This strategy is important for protecting participants' privacy, which is usually assured in a consent form (see the example in Figure 7.1).

Another alternative that might be used in a questionnaire is to phrase the question in terms of a Likert scale, such as the one below. This again alters the kind of data and hence the kind of conclusions that can be drawn:

In your opinion, are e-readers easy to use:

strongly agree	agree	neither	disagree	strongly disagree
☐	☐	☐	☐	☐

(Continued)

Then the data could be analyzed using a simple spreadsheet or table:

Respondent	Strongly agree	Agree	Neither	Disagree	Strongly disagree
A		1			
B	1				
C				1	
...					
Z					1
Total	5	7	10	1	3

In this case we have changed the kind of data we are collecting, and cannot, based on this second set, say anything about whether respondents think e-readers are tedious to use, as we have not asked that question. We can only say that, for example, 4 out of 26 (15%) disagreed with the statement that e-readers are easy to use (and of those, 3 (11.5%) strongly disagreed). ■

For simple collation and analysis, spreadsheet software such as Excel is often used as it is commonly available, is well understood, and offers a variety of numerical manipulations and graphical representations. Initial analysis might involve finding out averages, and identifying any outliers, i.e. values that are significantly different from the others. Producing

	Internet use					
User	More than once a day	Once a day	Once a week	Two or three times a week	Once a month	Number of errors made
1		1				4
2	1					2
3			1			1
4	1					0
5				1		2
6		1				3
7	1					2
8		1				0
9					1	3
10	1					2
11				1		1
12			1			2
13		1				4
14		1				2
15						1
16				1		1
17		1			1	0
18		1				0
Totals	4	7	2	3	2	30
					Mean	1.67
						(to 2 decimal places)

Table 8.2 Data gathered during a study of a document sharing application

a graphical representation of the data helps to get an overall view of the data and any patterns it contains.

For example, consider the set of data shown in Table 8.2, which was collected during an evaluation study of a document sharing application. This data shows the experience of the users and the number of errors made while trying to complete a controlled task. It was captured automatically and recorded in a spreadsheet; then the totals and averages were calculated. The graphs in Figure 8.1 were generated using the spreadsheet package. They show an overall view of the data set. In particular, we can see that there are no significant outliers

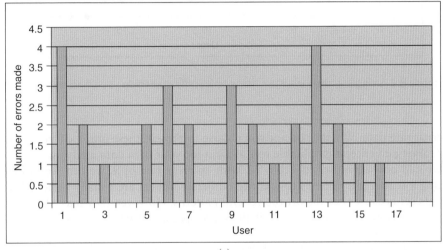

(a)

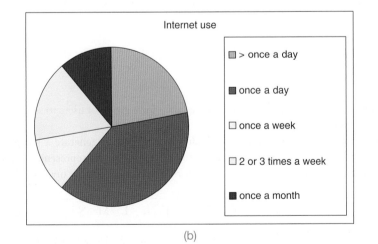

(b)

Figure 8.1 Graphical representations of the data in Table 8.2: (a) the distribution of errors made (take note of the scale used in these graphs, as seemingly large differences may be much smaller in reality), and (b) the spread of Internet experience within the participant group

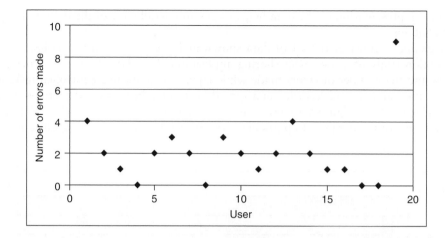

Figure 8.2 Using a scatter diagram helps to identify outliers in your data quite quickly

in the error rate data. Whether or not you choose to present these graphical representations to your target audience, it is valuable to use them for your own data analysis.

If we add one more user to Table 8.2 with an error rate of 9, we can see in Figure 8.2 how using a scatter graph helps to identify outliers. Outliers are usually removed from the larger data set because they distort the general patterns. However, they may also be interesting cases to investigate further to see if there are special circumstances surrounding those users and their session.

These initial investigations also help to identify other areas for further investigation. For example, is there something special about the users with error rate 0, or something distinctive about the performance of those who use the Internet only once a month?

ACTIVITY 8.1

The data in the table below represents the time taken for a group of users to select and buy an item from an online shopping website.

Using a spreadsheet application to which you have access, generate a bar graph and a scatter diagram to give you an overall view of the data. From this representation, make two initial observations about the data that might form the basis of further investigation.

User	A	B	C	D	E	F	G	H	I	J	K	L	M	N	O	P	Q	R	S
Time to complete (mins)	15	10	12	10	14	13	11	18	14	17	20	15	18	24	12	16	18	20	26

Comment

The bar graph and scatter diagram are shown below.

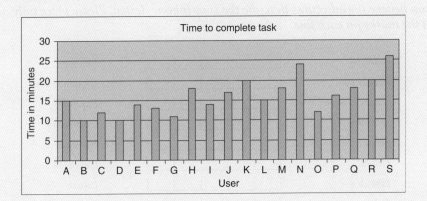

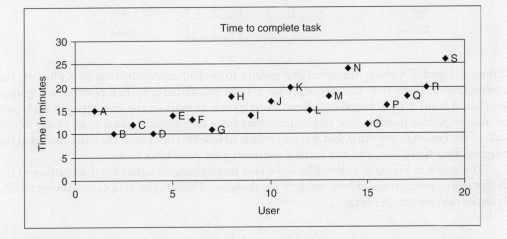

From these two diagrams there are two areas for further investigation. First of all, the values for user N (24) and user S (26) are higher than the others and could be looked at in more detail. In addition, there appears to be a trend that the users at the beginning of the testing time (particularly users B, C, D, E, F, and G) performed faster than those towards the end of the testing time. This is not a clear-cut situation, as O also performed well, and I, L, and P were almost as fast, but there may be something about this later testing time that has affected the results, and it is worth investigating further. ■

It is fairly straightforward to compare two sets of results, e.g. from the evaluation of two interactive products, using these kinds of graphical representations of the data. Semantic differential data can also be analyzed in this way and used to identify trends, provided the format of the question is appropriate. For example, the following question was asked in a questionnaire to evaluate two different smartphone designs:

For each pair of adjectives, place a cross at the point between them that reflects the extent to which you believe the adjectives describe the smartphone design. Please place only one cross between the marks on each line.

Annoying		*Pleasing*
Easy to use		*Difficult to use*
Value-for-money		*Expensive*
Attractive		*Unattractive*
Secure		*Not secure*
Helpful		*Unhelpful*
Hi-tech		*Lo-tech*
Robust		*Fragile*
Inefficient		*Efficient*
Modern		*Dated*

Tables 8.3 and 8.4 show the tabulated results from 100 respondents who replied to the questionnaire. Note that the responses have been translated into five possible categories, numbered from 1 to 5, based on where the respondent marked the line between each pair of adjectives. It is possible that respondents may have intentionally put a cross closer to one side of the box than the other, but it is acceptable to lose this nuance in the data, provided the original data is not lost, and any further analysis could refer back to it.

The graph in Figure 8.3 shows how the two smartphone designs varied according to the respondents' perceptions of how modern the design is. This graphical notation shows clearly how the two designs compare.

	1	2	3	4	5	
Annoying	35	20	18	15	12	Pleasing
Easy to use	20	28	21	13	18	Difficult to use
Value-for-money	15	30	22	27	6	Expensive
Attractive	37	22	32	6	3	Unattractive
Secure	52	29	12	4	3	Not secure
Helpful	33	21	32	12	2	Unhelpful
Hi-tech	12	24	36	12	16	Lo-tech
Robust	44	13	15	16	12	Fragile
Inefficient	28	23	25	12	12	Efficient
Modern	35	27	20	11	7	Dated

Table 8.3 Phone 1

	1	2	3	4	5	
Annoying	24	23	23	15	15	Pleasing
Easy to use	37	29	15	10	9	Difficult to use
Value-for-money	26	32	17	13	12	Expensive
Attractive	38	21	29	8	4	Unattractive
Secure	43	22	19	12	4	Not secure
Helpful	51	19	16	12	2	Unhelpful
Hi-tech	28	12	30	18	12	Lo-tech
Robust	46	23	10	11	10	Fragile
Inefficient	10	6	37	29	18	Efficient
Modern	3	10	45	27	15	Dated

Table 8.4 Phone 2

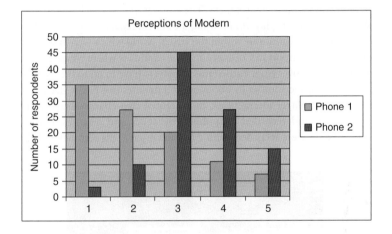

Figure 8.3 A graphical comparison of two smartphone designs according to whether they are perceived as modern or dated

Data logs that capture users' interactions with a system can also be analyzed and represented graphically, thus helping to identify patterns in behavior. Also, more sophisticated manipulations and graphical images can be used to highlight patterns in collected data. Box 8.3 describes how data logs of an online computer game were used to identify patterns of interactions. This example also shows how observational data can be used to interpret quantitative data.

The examples given in this section have largely focused on data sets which have more than 10 records (i.e. respondents or interviewees). If only a small number of records are collected, then it may be more important to analyze the individual records in more depth than to identify trends. In this case, tabulating the data for ease of presentation may be sufficient.

BOX 8.3

Identifying interaction patterns in log data from a massively multiplayer online role-playing game

Massively Multiplayer Online Role-Playing Games (MMORPGs) (e.g. World of Warcraft, EverQuest II, Toontown, etc.) involve hundreds of thousands of players interacting on a daily basis within a virtual world, and working towards achieving certain targets. While the challenges offered by these games are often the same as those in a single-player environment, the attraction of MMORPGs is the ability to join a community of gamers, to gain a reputation within that community, and to share gaming experiences directly. Several games have been designed so that players have to collaborate in order to progress.

Ducheneaut and Moore (2004) wanted to investigate how successful MMORPGs are at encouraging interactivity between players. To do this, they analyzed data logs and video recordings of player-to-player interactions in the game Star Wars Galaxies (SWG), complemented by a three-month ethnography of the same environment. The ethnography was achieved by the researchers joining the SWG community as players and using the system regularly over three months. During this time, they identified two locations within the virtual world which were heavily used by other players – the cantina and starport in Coronet City. The cantina is where entertainers can be found and players often go to recover from battle fatigue; players have to go to the starport in order to travel between locations, and shuttles fly about every 9 minutes (see Figure 8.4).

To collect a log of player interactions, they created two characters, placed one in each location for a month, and recorded all public utterances and gestures at these locations. Twenty-six days of data were recorded, with 21 hours a day. This resulted in 100 MB of data

Figure 8.4 The cantina in SWG's Coronet City

Source: N. Ducheneaut and R.J. Morris (2004): "The social side of gaming: a study of interaction patterns in a massively multiplayer online game" in *Proceedings of CSCW 04.* ©2004 Association for Computing Machinery, Inc. Reprinted by permission.

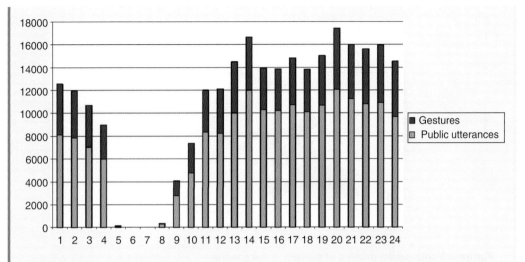

Figure 8.5 Summary of the activity in the cantina over the course of a day. (The gap between 4 a.m. and 7 a.m. is due to a regular server reboot during this time)

Source: N. Ducheneaut and R.J. Morris (2004): "The social side of gaming: a study of interaction patterns in a massively multiplayer online game" in *Proceedings of CSCW 04*. ©2004 Association for Computing Machinery, Inc. Reprinted by permission.

and represented a total of 5493 unique players in the two locations. A purpose-built parser was used to identify who was interacting with whom, in what way (gesture or chat), where, when, and what was the content of the interaction. In this context, a gesture may be a smile, greet, clap, cheer, etc. They then analyzed the data for patterns of behavior. One finding was that a small number of players were frequently present in one location while there were many others who visited for only a short time. The median number of days a player was present was 2, while the average was 3.5; only 2% of the total number of players were present more than half the time. Another aspect they investigated was the activity within the cantina over the course of a day. Figure 8.5 shows a summary graph of activity in the cantina for the 26 days. This shows a fairly even distribution of activity throughout the day, with gestures representing about one-third of the events and public utterances representing two-thirds.

Their analysis of the 10 most popular gestures is summarized in the table below:

Gesture	% of total (cantina)	Gesture	% of total (starport)
Smile	18.13	Thank	15.95
Cheer	9.57	Bow	12.29
Clap	7.77	Wave	9.81
Wave	6.27	Flail	8.17
Wink	4.22	Smile	7.89
Grin	3.72	Nod	7.03
Nod	3.23	Salute	2.48
Bow	3.22	Pet	1.95
Thank	2.51	Puke	1.89
Greet	2.40	Cheer	1.56

(Continued)

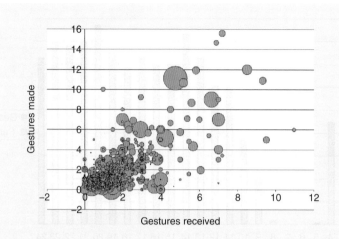

Figure 8.6 Interaction profiles of players in the cantina

Source: N. Ducheneaut and R.J. Morris (2004): "The social side of gaming: a study of interaction patterns in a massively multiplayer online game" in *Proceedings of CSCW 04.* ©2004 Association for Computing Machinery, Inc. Reprinted by permission.

These two kinds of analysis are helpful to get an overview of the different players' interactions but do not indicate the richness of social interaction each player is engaged with. So Ducheneaut and Moore analyzed the interactions on three dimensions for each player: the number of gestures received, the number of gestures made, and the number of public utterances made. Having done so, they concluded that the average player goes into the cantina, makes about one gesture to another player, exchanges about four sentences with him or her, and receives one gesture in return. This conclusion was arrived at from taking averages across the data, but in order to get a clearer view of interactions, they plotted dimensions for each individual set of data on a graph. This is reproduced in Figure 8.6. The *x*-axis represents the number of gestures received, the *y*-axis represents the number of gestures made, and the size of the 'dot' is proportional to the number of public utterances made by the player. This graphical representation illustrated an unexpected finding – that the majority of players do not interact very much. Another set of players make a large number of utterances but make or receive no gestures. Yet another (smaller) set of players gesture and talk a lot, but receive few gestures in return.

The researchers concluded that these last two kinds of behavior are due to the player programming their avatar to repeat actions even when the player is not logged on. This kind of behavior is not truly interactive as it is designed simply to advance the player within the game (one way of gaining points is to repeatedly perform activities related to the avatar's profession). This behavior then affects the social atmosphere of the cantina because other players are unhappy about the false kind of interaction.

Bubbles to the right of this graph represent players who interact a lot – making and receiving gestures, and chatting. These players are engaging in the kind of social interaction that the designers of SWG want to promote.

A similar analysis was performed for the starport (Figure 8.7), but a different pattern of interactions was found. A large number of players made and received no gestures, but made a lot of public utterances. The ethnographic data helped researchers to interpret this finding

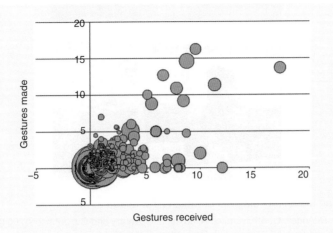

Figure 8.7 Interaction profiles of players in the starport

Source: N. Ducheneaut and R.J. Morris (2004): "The social side of gaming: a study of interaction patterns in a massively multiplayer online game" in *Proceedings of CSCW 04.* ©2004 Association for Computing Machinery, Inc. Reprinted by permission.

too – the starport was a good place to advertise as there were many people gathered waiting for a shuttle. Another set of players at the starport said very little; the researchers believe that these were people looking for trainers to give them a particular skill they needed in order to progress in the game. ■

8.4   Simple Qualitative Analysis

As with quantitative analysis, the first step in qualitative analysis is to gain an overall impression of the data and to start looking for patterns. Some patterns will have emerged during the data gathering itself, and so you may already have some idea of the kinds of pattern to look for, but it is important to confirm and re-confirm findings to make sure that initial impressions are not biasing analysis. For observation data, the guiding framework will have given some structure to the data. For example, the practitioner's framework for observation introduced in Chapter 7 will have resulted in a focus on who, where, and what, while using Robson's more detailed framework will result in patterns relating to physical objects, people's goals, sequences of events, and so on.

There are three simple types of qualitative analysis that we discuss here: identifying recurring patterns and themes, categorizing data, and analyzing critical incidents. These are not mutually exclusive and can be used in combination.

8.4.1   Identifying Recurring Patterns or Themes

As you become more familiar with the data, possible themes or patterns will emerge. An example might be noticing that people visiting TripAdviser.com look for reviews for a hotel that are rated 'terrible' first. Any initial impressions must be confirmed and refined with more

Figure 8.8 Building the affinity diagram of Indian ATM usage

Source: Figure 1, A. DeAngeli, U. Athavamker, A. Joshi, L. Coventry and G.I. Johnson (2004) "Introducing ATMs in India: a contextual inquiry", *Interacting with Computers* 16(1), 29–44. Reproduced with permission.

rigorous analysis, seeking both confirming and disconfirming evidence in the data. Sometimes the refined patterns or themes form the primary set of findings for the analysis and sometimes they are just the starting point for different analyses.

The study goals provide an orienting focus for the formulation of themes. For example, consider a survey to evaluate whether the information displayed on a train travel website is appropriate and sufficient. Several of the respondents suggest that the station stops in between the origin and destination stations should be displayed. This theme is relevant to the study goals and would be reported as a main theme. In another part of the survey, under further comments you might notice that several respondents say the company's logo is distracting. Although this too is a theme in the data, it is not directly relevant to the study's goals and may be reported only as a minor theme.

There are different techniques for identifying themes in qualitative data (e.g. Braun and Clarke, 2006). The affinity diagram, which is used in contextual design (Beyer and Holtzblatt, 1998; Holtzblatt, 2001) is one common technique used in qualitative analysis. It aims to organize individual ideas and insights into a hierarchy showing common structures and themes. Notes are grouped together because they are similar in some fashion. The groups are not predefined, but emerge from the data. The process was originally introduced into the software quality community from Japan, where it is regarded as one of the seven quality processes. The affinity diagram is built by a process of induction. One note is put up first, and then the team searches for other notes that are related in some way. For example, De Angeli *et al* (2004) collected data through field observations and semi-structued interviews to investigate the use of ATMs (automated teller machines) in Mumbai, India. As part of their data analysis they used affinity diagrams to cluster issues into themes (see Figure 8.8).

Note that patterns and themes in your data may relate to a variety of aspects: to behavior, to your user group, to places or situations where certain events happen, and so on. Each of these kinds of theme may be relevant to your goals. For example, descriptions of typical users (personas) may be an outcome of data analysis that focuses on patterns of participant characteristics. Although we include thematic analysis under qualitative analysis, patterns and themes may also emerge from quantitative data.

8.4.2 Categorizing Data

Transcripts of meetings, interviews, or think-aloud protocols can be analyzed at a high level of detail, such as identifying stories or themes, or at a fine level of detail in which each word, phrase, utterance, or gesture is analyzed. Either way, elements identified in the data are usually categorized first using a categorization scheme. The categorization scheme may arise from the data itself, if the investigation is exploratory, as it might be in the requirements activity, or it might originate elsewhere in a well-recognized categorization scheme, or a combination of these two approaches may be used. The principle here is that the data is divided up into elements and each element is then categorized.

Which categories to use is largely determined by the goal of the study. One of the most challenging aspects is determining meaningful categories that are orthogonal (i.e. do not overlap). Another is deciding on the appropriate granularity for the categories (e.g. at word, phrase, sentence, or paragraph level); this is also dependent on the goal of the study and the data being analyzed.

The categorization scheme used must be reliable so that the analysis can be replicated. This can be demonstrated by training a second person to use the categories. When training is complete, both people analyze the same data sample. If there is a large discrepancy between the two analyses, either training was inadequate or the categorization is not working and needs to be refined. When a high level of reliability is reached, it can be quantified by calculating the inter-rater reliability. This is the percentage of agreement between the two researchers, defined as the number of items that both people categorized in the same way, expressed as a percentage of the total number of items examined. An alternative measure where two raters have been used is Cohen's kappa (κ), which takes into account the possibility that agreement has occurred due to chance (Cohen, 1960).

To illustrate categorization, we present an example derived from a set of studies looking at the use of different navigation aids in an online educational setting (Ursula Armitage, 2004). These studies involved observing users working through some online educational material (about evaluation methods), using the think-aloud technique. The think-aloud protocol was recorded and then transcribed before being analyzed from various perspectives, one of which was to identify usability problems that the participants were having with the online environment known as Nestor Navigator (Zeiliger *et al*, 1997). An excerpt from the transcription is shown in Figure 8.9.

This excerpt was analyzed using a categorization scheme derived from a set of negative effects of a system on a user (van Rens, 1997) and was iteratively extended to accommodate the specific kinds of interaction observed in these studies. The categorization scheme is shown in Figure 8.10.

This scheme developed and evolved as the transcripts were analyzed. Figure 8.11 shows the excerpt above coded using this categorization scheme. Note that the transcript is divided up using square brackets to indicate which element is being identified as showing a particular usability problem.

A rigid categorization scheme means that the data is structured only according to the prespecified categories. However, where a significant set of data cannot be categorized, the scheme can be extended. In this case the categorization scheme and the categorization itself develop in parallel, with the scheme evolving as more analysis is done.

Having categorized the data, the results can be used to answer the study goals. In the example above, the study allowed the researchers to be able to quantify the number of usability problems encountered overall by participants, the mean number of problems per participant for each of the test conditions, and the number of unique problems of each type per participant. This also helped to identify patterns of behavior and recurring problems. Having the think-aloud protocol meant that the overall view of the usability problems could take context into account.

I'm thinking that it's just a lot of information to absorb from the screen. I just I don't concentrate very well when I'm looking at the screen. I have a very clear idea of what I've read so far . . . but it's because of the headings I know OK this is another kind of evaluation now and before it was about evaluation which wasn't anyone can test and here it's about experts so it's like it's nice that I'm clicking every now and then coz it just sort of organises the thoughts. But it would still be nice to see it on a piece of paper because it's a lot of text to read.

Am I supposed to, just one question, am supposed to say something about what I'm reading and what I think about it the conditions as well or how I feel reading it from the screen, what is the best thing really?

Observer – What you think about the information that you are reading on the screen . . . you don't need to give me comments . . . if you think this bit fits together.

There's so much reference to all those previously said like I'm like I've already forgotten the name of the other evaluation so it said unlike the other evaluation this one like, there really is not much contrast with the other it just says what it is may be . . . so I think I think of . . .

May be it would be nice to have other evaluations listed to see other evaluations you know here, to have the names of other evaluations other evaluations just to, because now when I click previous I have to click it several times so it would be nice to have this navigation, extra links.

Figure 8.9 Excerpt from a transcript of a think-aloud protocol when using an online educational environment. Note the prompt from the observer about half way through

Source: Excerpts reproduced with permission from Ursula Armitage (2004) Navigation and learning in electronic texts. PhD thesis, Centre for HCI Design, City University London.

1. Interface Problems

1.1. Verbalizations show evidence of dissatisfaction about an aspect of the interface.
1.2. Verbalizations show evidence of confusion/uncertainty about an aspect of the interface.
1.3. Verbalizations show evidence of confusion/surprise at the outcome of an action.
1.4. Verbalizations show evidence of physical discomfort.
1.5. Verbalizations show evidence of fatigue.

Figure 8.10 Criteria for identifying usability problems from verbal protocol transcriptions

Source: Excerpts reproduced with permission from Ursula Armitage (2004) Navigation and learning in electronic texts. PhD thesis, Centre for HCI Design, City University London.

1.6. Verbalizations show evidence of difficulty in seeing particular aspects of the interface.
1.7. Verbalizations show evidence that they are having problems achieving a goal that they have set themselves, or the overall task goal.
1.8. Verbalizations show evidence that the user has made an error.
1.9. The participant is unable to recover from error without external help from the experimenter.
1.10. The participant makes a suggestion for redesign of the interface of the electronic texts.

2. Content Problems

2.1. Verbalizations show evidence of dissatisfaction about aspects of the content of the electronic text.
2.2. Verbalizations show evidence of confusion/uncertainty about aspects of the content of the electronic text.
2.3. Verbalizations show evidence of a misunderstanding of the electronic text content (the user may not have noticed this immediately).
2.4. The participant makes a suggestion for re-writing the electronic text content.

Identified problems should be coded as [UP, << problem no. >>].

Figure 8.10 Continued

[I'm thinking that it's just a lot of information to absorb from the screen. UP 1.1]
[I just I don't concentrate very well when I'm looking at the screen UP 1.1]. I have a very clear idea of what I've read so far . . . [but it's because of the headings UP 1.1] I know OK this is another kind of evaluation now and before it was about evaluation which wasn't anyone can test and here it's about experts so it's like it's nice that I'm clicking every now and then coz it just sort of organises the thoughts. [But it would still be nice to see it on a piece of paper UP 1.10] [because it's a lot of text to read UP 1.1].

Am I supposed to, just one question, am supposed to say something about what I'm reading and what I think about it the conditions as well or how I feel reading it from the screen, what is the best thing really?

Observer – What you think about the information that you are reading on the screen . . . you don't need to give me comments . . . if you think this bit fits together.

[There's so much reference to all those previously said UP2.1] [like I'm like I've already forgotten the name of the other evaluation so it said unlike the other evaluation this one like, there really is not much contrast with the other it just says what it is may be . . . so I think I think of . . . UP 2.2]

[May be it would be nice to have other evaluations listed to see other evaluations you know here, to have the names of other evaluations other evaluations UP 1.10] just to, [because now when I click previous I have to click it several times UP 1.1, 1.7] [so it would be nice to have this navigation, extra links UP 1.10].

Figure 8.11 The excerpt in Figure 8.9 coded using the categorization scheme in Figure 8.10

Source: Excerpts reproduced with permission from Ursula Armitage (2004) Navigation and learning in electronic texts. PhD thesis, Centre for HCI Design, City University London.

ACTIVITY 8.2

The following is another think-aloud extract from the same study. Using the categorization scheme in Figure 8.10, code this extract for usability problems. It is useful to put brackets around the complete element of the extract that you are coding.

Well, looking at the map, again there's no obvious start point, there should be something highlighted that says 'start here.'

Ok, the next keyword that's highlighted is evaluating, but I'm not sure that's where I want to go straight away, so I'm just going to go back to the introduction.

Yeah, so I probably want to read about usability problems before I start looking at evaluation. So, I, yeah. I would have thought that the links in each one of the pages would take you to the next logical point, but my logic might be different to other people's. Just going to go and have a look at usability problems.

Ok, again I'm going to flip back to the introduction. I'm just thinking if I was going to do this myself I would still have a link back to the introduction, but I would take people through the logical sequence of each one of these bits that fans out, rather than expecting them to go back all the time.

Going back . . . to the introduction. Look at the types. Observation, didn't really want to go there. What's this bit [pointing to Types of UE on map]? Going straight to types of . . .

Ok, right, yeah, I've already been there before. We've already looked at usability problems, yep that's ok, so we'll have a look at these references.

I clicked on the map rather than going back via introduction, to be honest I get fed up going back to introduction all the time.

Comment

Coding transcripts is not easy, and you may have had some difficulties doing this, but this activity will have given you an idea of the kinds of decision that need to be taken. As with much data analysis, it gets easier with practice. Our coded extract is below:

[Well, looking at the map, again there's no obvious start point **UP 1.2, 2.2**], [there should be something highlighted that says 'start here' **UP 1.1, 1.10**].

Ok, the next keyword that's highlighted is evaluating, but [I'm not sure that's where I want to go straight away **UP 2.2**], so I'm just going to go back to the introduction.

Yeah, so I probably want to read about usability problems before I start looking at evaluation. So, I, yeah. [I would have thought that the links in each one of the pages would take you to the next logical point, but my logic might be different to other people's **UP 1.3**]. Just going to go and have a look at usability problems.

Ok, again I'm going to flip back to the introduction. [I'm just thinking if I was going to do this myself I would still have a link back to the introduction, but I would take people through the logical sequence of each one of these bits that fans out, rather than expecting them to go back all the time **UP 1.10**].

Going back . . . to the introduction. [Look at the types. Observation, didn't really want to go there. What's this bit [pointing to Types of UE on map]? **UP 2.2**] Going straight to types of . . .

Ok, right, yeah, I've already been there before. We've already looked at usability problems, yep that's ok, so we'll have a look at these references.

I clicked on the map rather than going back via introduction, [to be honest I get fed up going back to introduction all the time. **UP 1.1**]. ■

The example above used a form of content analysis (Krippendorff, 2013). Content analysis typically involves categorizing the data and then studying the frequency of category occurrences. The technique may be used for any text, where 'text' refers to a range of media including video, newspapers, adverts, and so on. For example, Blythe and Cairns (2009) analyzed 100 videos from a YouTube search by relevance for 'iPhone 3G' using content analysis. They categorized the videos into seven categories: review, reportage, 'unboxing,' demonstration, satire, advertisement, and vlog commentaries (e.g. complaints about queues).

Another way of analyzing a transcript is to use discourse analysis. Discourse analysis focuses on the dialog, i.e. the meaning of what is said, and how words are used to convey meaning. Discourse analysis is strongly interpretive, pays great attention to context, and views language not only as reflecting psychological and social aspects but also as constructing them (Coyle, 1995). An underlying assumption of discourse analysis is that there is no objective scientific truth. Language is a form of social reality that is open to interpretation from different perspectives. In this sense, the underlying philosophy of discourse analysis is similar to that of ethnography. Language is viewed as a constructive tool and discourse analysis provides a way of focusing on how people use language to construct versions of their worlds (Fiske, 1994).

Small changes in wording can change meaning, as the following excerpts indicate (Coyle, 1995):

> *Discourse analysis is what you do when you are saying that you are doing discourse analysis . . .*

> *According to Coyle, discourse analysis is what you do when you are saying that you are doing discourse analysis . . .*

By adding just three words, 'According to Coyle,' the sense of authority changes, depending on what the reader knows about Coyle's work and reputation.

Conversation analysis is a very fine-grained form of discourse analysis (Jupp, 2006). In conversation analysis the semantics of the discourse are examined in fine detail, and the focus is on how conversations are conducted. This technique is used in sociological studies and examines how conversations start, how turn-taking is structured, and other rules of conversation. This analysis technique has been used to analyze interactions in a range of settings, and has influenced designers' understanding about users' needs in these environments. It can also be used to compare conversations that take place through different media, e.g. face-to-face versus email.

8.4.3 Looking for Critical Incidents

Data gathering sessions can often result in a lot of data. Analyzing all of that data in any detail is very time-consuming, and often not necessary. We have already suggested that themes, patterns, and categories can be used to identify areas where detailed analysis is appropriate. Another approach is to use the critical incident technique (Grison *et al*, 2013).

The critical incident technique is a set of principles that emerged from work carried out in the United States Army Air Forces where the goal was to identify the critical requirements of good and bad performance by pilots (Flanagan, 1954). It has two basic principles: "(a) reporting facts regarding behavior is preferable to the collection of interpretations, ratings, and opinions based on general impressions; (b) reporting should be limited to those behaviors which, according to competent observers, make a significant contribution to the activity" (Flanagan, 1954, p. 355). In the interaction design context, the use of well-planned observation sessions, as discussed in Chapter 7, satisfies the first principle. The second principle is referring to critical incidents, i.e. incidents that are significant or pivotal to the activity being observed, in either a desirable or an undesirable way.

In interaction design, critical incident analysis has been used in a variety of ways, but the main focus is to identify specific incidents that are significant, and then to focus on these and analyze them in detail, using the rest of the data collected as context to inform interpretation. These may be identified by the users during a retrospective discussion of a recent event, or by an observer either through studying video footage, or in real time. For example, in an evaluation study, a critical incident may be signaled by times when users were obviously stuck – usually marked by a comment, silence, looks of puzzlement, and so on.

In a study by Curzon et al (2002), they identified a set of critical incidents through field trials of an in-car navigation device. One example incident in this context was "On one journey, the system gave directions to turn right when the destination was to the left. Its route was to go round the block to go in the other direction. A car following ignored this turn and went the more obvious way, arriving first." In another study, Grison et al (2013) used the critical incident technique to investigate specific factors that influence travelers' choices of transport mode in Paris in order to adapt new tools and services for mobility, such as dynamic route planners. Participants were asked to report on positive and negative real events they experienced in the context of their route to work or study, and whether they regretted or were satisfied with this choice of transport. Their findings included that contextual factors have a great influence on choice, that people were more likely to choose an alternative route to return home than when setting out, and that emotional state is important when planning a route.

Link to read more on critical incident analysis in HCI, at **www.usabilitynet.org**

It is common practice to employ more than one complementary data analysis approach. For example, following a critical incident analysis, themes may be identified around the circumstances that caused the incident to occur, and then discourse analysis may be conducted to understand the detail. Analyzing video material frequently employs several methods and can be challenging (see Box 8.4).

ACTIVITY 8.3

Set yourself or a friend the task of identifying the next available theater or cinema performance you'd like to attend in your local area. As you perform this task, or watch your friend do it, make a note of critical incidents associated with the activity. Remember that a critical incident may be a positive or a negative event.

Comment

In my local area, information about entertainment is available through the local paper, the Internet, ringing up local cinemas or theaters, or by visiting the local library where they stock leaflets about the entertainment available in the area. When I asked my daughter to attempt this task, I noticed several critical incidents including the following:

1. After searching around the house for a while, she found a copy of the local paper for the correct week.
2. The local paper she had found did not have details of the cinema that she wanted to visit.
3. When trying to book the cinema tickets by phone she discovered that she needed a credit card, which she doesn't have, and so she had to give me the phone! ■

BOX 8.4

Analyzing video material

A good way to start a video analysis is to watch what has been recorded all the way through while writing a high-level narrative of what happens, noting down where in the video there are any potentially interesting events. How you decide which is an interesting event will depend on what is being observed. For example, if you are studying the interruptions that occur in an open plan office, you would include each time a person breaks off from an ongoing activity, e.g. phone rings, someone walks into their cubicle, email arrives. If it is a study of how pairs of students use a collaborative learning tool then activities such as turn-taking, sharing of input device/s, speaking over one another, and fighting over shared objects would be appropriate to record.

Chronological and video times are used to index events. These may not be the same, since recordings can run at different speeds to real time. Labels for certain routine events are also used, e.g. lunchtime, coffee break, staff meeting, doctor's round. Spreadsheets are used to record the classification and description of events, together with annotations and notes of how the events began, how they unfold, and how they end.

Video can be augmented with captured screens or logged data of people's interactions with a computer display. There are various logging and screen capture tools available for this purpose that enable you to play back the interactions as a movie, showing screen objects

(Continued)

being opened, moved, selected, and so on. These can then be played in parallel with the video to provide different perspectives on the talk, physical interactions, and the system's responses that occur. Having a combination of data streams can enable more detailed and fine-grained patterns of behavior to be interpreted (Heath *et al*, 2010). ∎

8.5   Tools to Support Data Analysis

It would be possible to analyze even large data sets using only manual techniques, however most people would agree that it is quicker, easier, and more accurate to use a software tool of some kind, particularly for 'big data.' We introduced the idea of using a simple spreadsheet application in Section 8.3, but there are other more sophisticated tools available – some of which support the organization and manipulation of the data, and some of which are focused on performing statistical tests. For example, Box 8.5 discusses the analysis and presentation of thousands of data points captured in a study on digital library usage.

New tools are developed and existing ones are enhanced on a regular basis, so we do not attempt to provide a comprehensive survey of this area. Instead, we discuss the kind of support available, and describe briefly some of the more popular tools used in interaction design.

Tools to support the organization and manipulation of data include facilities for categorization, theme-based analysis, and quantitative analysis. These typically provide facilities to associate labels (categories, themes, and so on) with sections of data, search the data for key words or phrases, investigate the relationships between different themes or categories, and help to develop the coding scheme further; some tools can also generate graphical representations. In addition, some provide help with techniques such as content analysis and sometimes very sophisticated mechanisms to show the occurrence and co-occurrence of words or phrases. In addition, searching, coding, project management, writing and annotating, and report generation facilities are common.

More detail regarding software tools to support the analysis of qualitative data can be found through the CAQDAS Networking Project, based at the University of Surrey (http://caqdas.soc.surrey.ac.uk/).

Two well-known tools that support some of these data analysis activities are Nvivo and Atlas.ti. Nvivo, for example, supports the annotation and coding of data including PDF documents, photos, and video and audio files. Using Nvivo, field notes can be searched for key words or phrases to support coding or content analysis; codes and data can be explored, merged, and manipulated in several ways. The information can also be printed in a variety of forms such as a list of every occasion a word or phrase is used in the data, and a tree structure showing the relationships between codes. Like all software packages, Nvivo has advantages and disadvantages, but it is particularly powerful for handling very large sets of data and it can generate output for statistical packages such as SPSS.

SPSS (Statistical Package for the Social Sciences) is one of the more popular quantitative analysis packages that supports the use of statistical tests. It is a sophisticated package offering a wide range of statistical tests such as frequency distributions, rank correlations (to determine statistical significance), regression analysis, and cluster analysis. SPSS assumes that the user knows and understands statistical analysis.

BOX 8.5

Web analytics for digital libraries – presenting session length data

Khoo *et al* (2008) discuss four case studies focused on different digital libraries, each of which investigated the use of session length as a useful metric in their context. Associated with session length are various terms including a visit (the sequential viewing of one or more pages from the same IP address), page views (number of times a page is accessed during a visit), and hit (request for a page or page element). One of the problems faced by users of web analytic software is that these elements are measured differently by different tools – hence the need to investigate how best to make use of session length data.

The four digital libraries presented in their article are the Library of Congress, Teachers' Domain of the National Science Digital Library (NSDL), the NSDL itself, and The Instructional Architect. Each of these had different technical and organizational concerns but several common themes emerged from the investigations including the need to identify suitable tools and reconcile differences in metric definitions, and the need to triangulate web metrics with other research.

Of particular interest are the different visualizations used to present the web metrics data for interpretation and discussion (in the article) and other reports mentioned as influencing the conclusions. Data from the NSDL was presented as a heat map (Figure 8.12a) and as timeframes (Figure 8.12b); data from the Library of Congress was presented in a statistical table (Figure 8.12c) and data from the Teachers Domain was presented as a comparison

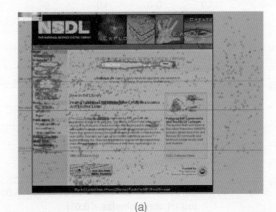

(a)

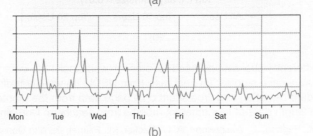

Mon   Tue   Wed   Thu   Fri   Sat   Sun

(b)

(Continued)

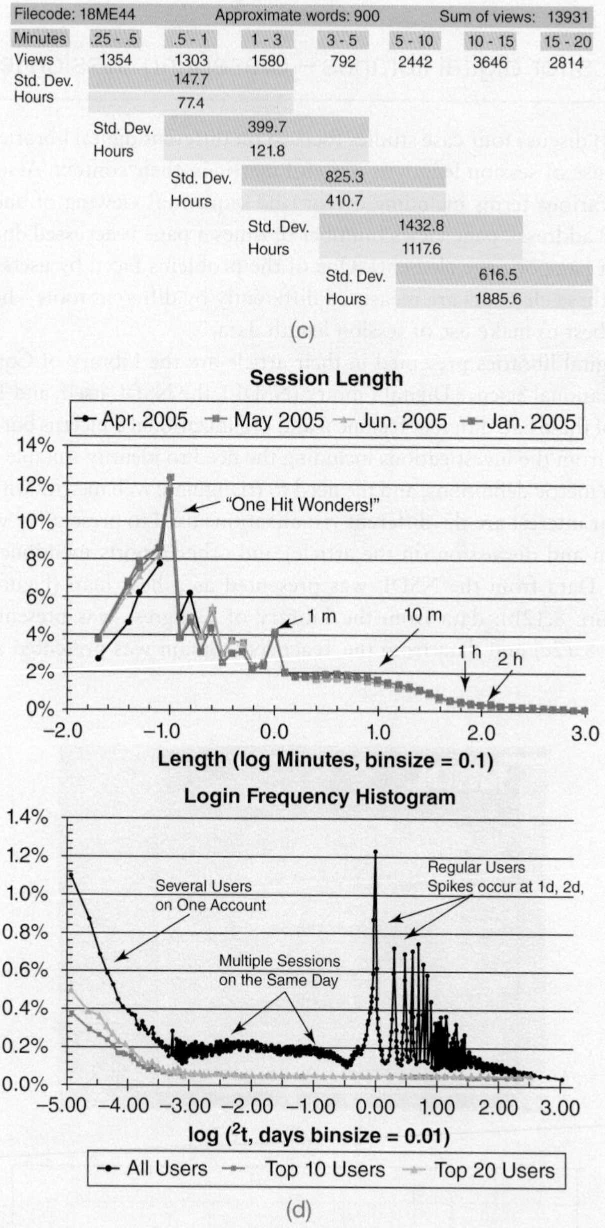
Filecode: 18ME44
Approximate words: 900
Sum of views: 13931
Minutes .25 - .5 .5 - 1 1 - 3 3 - 5 5 - 10 10 - 15 15 - 20
Views 1354 1303 1580 792 2442 3646 2814
Std. Dev. 147.7
Hours 77.4
Std. Dev. 399.7
Hours 121.8
Std. Dev. 825.3
Hours 410.7
Std. Dev. 1432.8
Hours 1117.6
Std. Dev. 616.5
Hours 1885.6
(c)
Session Length
Apr. 2005
May 2005
Jun. 2005
Jan. 2005
"One Hit Wonders!"
1 m
10 m
1 h
2 h
Length (log Minutes, binsize = 0.1)
Login Frequency Histogram
Several Users on One Account
Multiple Sessions on the Same Day
Regular Users Spikes occur at 1d, 2d,
log (²t, days binsize = 0.01)
All Users
Top 10 Users
Top 20 Users
(d)

Figure 8.12 Different visualizations used to present web analytical data from three different digital library case studies: (a) heat map from NSDL; (b) weekly traffic timeline from NSDL; (c) standard deviation and time spent on a page data from the Library of Congress; and (d) session length data of four different months from Teachers' Domain (NSDL)

Source: Khoo, M., Pagano, J., Washington, A. L., Recker, M., Palmer, B., and Donahue, R. A. (2008) Using web metrics to analyze digital libraries. *Proceedings of Joint Conference on Digital Libraries*, Pittsburgh, June 16–20. ©2008 Association for Computing Machinery, Inc. Reprinted by permission.

between several months' figures, on one graph (Figure 8.12d). The Instructional Architect investigations used Google Analytics software. The researchers used a range of reports including users' geographical location, where users were before arriving at the library site, the ratio of student login paths to teacher login paths, and session time (as time on site and pages viewed per visit). ∎

8.6 Using Theoretical Frameworks

Structuring the analysis of qualitative data around a theoretical framework can lead to additional insights that go beyond the results found from the simple techniques introduced earlier. However, these frameworks are quite sophisticated and using them requires investment to make sure that the framework is understood and applied appropriately. This section discusses three frameworks that are commonly used in interaction design to structure the analysis of data gathered in the field, such as observational and interview data: grounded theory, distributed cognition, and activity theory.

8.6.1 Grounded Theory

Grounded theory is an approach to qualitative data analysis that aims to develop theory from the systematic analysis and interpretation of empirical data, i.e. the theory derived is grounded in the data. In this respect it is a bottom-up development of theory since the data is needed to develop the theory. This contrasts with some types of analysis in which the theory (or previous published research) provides the categories used for the analysis of the data. The approach was originally developed by Glaser and Strauss (1967) and since has been adopted by several researchers, with some adaptations to different circumstances. In particular, Glaser and Strauss have individually (and with others) developed grounded theory in slightly different ways, but the aim of this approach remains the same. Glaser (1992) provides further information about the differences and areas of controversy.

The aim of grounded theory is to develop a theory that fits a set of collected data. In this context, theory is: "a set of well-developed concepts related through statements of relationship, which together constitute an integrated framework that can be used to explain or predict phenomena" (Strauss and Corbin, 1998). Development of a 'grounded' theory progresses through alternating data collection and data analysis: first data is collected and analyzed to identify categories, then that analysis may lead to further data collection and analysis to extend and refine the categories and so on; during this cycle, parts of the data may be reanalyzed in more detail. Data gathering and subsequent analysis are hence driven by the emerging theory. This approach continues until no new insights emerge and the theory is well-developed. During this process, the researcher needs to maintain a balance between objectivity and sensitivity. Objectivity is needed to maintain accurate and impartial interpretation of events; sensitivity is required to notice the subtleties in the data and identify relationships between concepts.

The thrust of the analysis undertaken is to identify and define the properties and dimensions of relevant categories and then to use these as the basis for constructing a theory. Category identification and definition is achieved by coding the data, i.e. marking it up according to the emerging categories. According to Corbin and Strauss (2014), this coding has three aspects, which are iteratively performed through the cycle of data collection and analysis:

1. Open coding is the process through which categories, their properties, and dimensions are discovered in the data. This process is similar to our discussion of categorization above, including the question of granularity of coding (at the word, line, sentence, conversation level, and so on).
2. Axial coding is the process of systematically fleshing out categories and relating them to their subcategories.
3. Selective coding is the process of refining and integrating categories to form a larger theoretical scheme. The categories are organized around one central category that forms the backbone of the theory. Initially, the theory will contain only an outline of the categories but as more data is collected, they are refined and developed further.

Early books on grounded theory say little about what data collection techniques should be used, but focus instead on the analysis. Some later books place more emphasis on data collection. For example, Charmaz (2014) discusses interviewing techniques, and collection and analysis of documents for grounded theory analysis. When analyzing data, Corbin and Strauss (2014) encourage the use of written records of analysis and diagrammatic representations of categories (which they call memos and diagrams). These memos and diagrams evolve as data analysis progresses. Some researchers also look to digital tools such as spreadsheets and diagramming tools, but many like to develop their own physical code books such as the one Rotman et al (2014) constructed in a study to understand the motivations of citizens to contribute to citizen science projects. The data that she analyzed was from in-depth semi-structured interviews of 33 citizen scientists and 11 scientists from the USA, India, and Costa Rica (see Figure 8.13).

The following analytic tools are used to help stimulate the analyst's thinking and identify and characterize relevant categories:

- The use of questioning (not questioning your participants, but questioning the data): questions can help an analyst to generate ideas or consider different ways of looking at the data. It can be useful to ask questions when analysis appears to be in a rut.
- Analysis of a word, phrase, or sentence: considering in detail the meaning of an utterance can also help to trigger different perspectives on the data.
- Further analysis through comparisons: comparisons may be made between objects or between abstract categories. In either case, comparing one with the other brings alternative interpretations. Sharp et al (2005) take this idea further and use metaphor as an analysis technique with qualitative data.

One thing that distinguishes a grounded theory approach to data gathering and analysis from ethnographic approaches is that researchers are encouraged to draw on their own theoretical backgrounds to help inform the study, provided that they are alert to the possibility of unintentional bias.

Performing a Grounded Theory Analysis

Sarker et al (2001) used the grounded theory approach to develop a model of collaboration in virtual teams. The virtual teams used in the study were made up of students from two universities – one in Canada and one in the United States of America. Each team consisted of four to five members from each university. Each team was given the task of studying a business

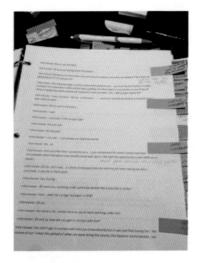

Figure 8.13 Code book used in a grounded theory analysis of citizens' motivations to contribute to citizen science

Source: Rotman, D. *et al* (2014). Does motivation in citizen science change with time and culture? In *Proceedings of the companion publication of the 17th ACM conference on Computer supported cooperative work & social computing (CSCW Companion '14).* ACM, New York, NY, USA, 229–232. ©2014 Association for Computing Machinery, Inc. Reprinted by permission.

systems problem, producing a systems design for it, and developing a working prototype. The projects themselves lasted about 14 weeks and a total of 12 teams participated in the study. The team members could communicate directly with each other using various technologies such as email, videoconferencing, telephone, and fax. The main communication channel, however, was Webboard, a collaborative message board tool supporting threaded discussions, email discussions, chat rooms, instant messaging, calendar, whiteboard, blogging, and so on. Using Webboard meant that communication was more public, and could be recorded more easily.

All communication data through Webboard was automatically saved, minutes of any videoconferences, telephone calls, or Internet chat sessions undertaken were posted on Webboard, and the team members were also asked to provide any additional emails they received or sent to other team members. In addition to this data, the team's final project reports, individual team members' reflections on the lessons learned through the project, feedback on fellow team members' performance, and comments on the virtual project itself were all collected and used as data for the study.

As soon as the teams were formed, informal data analysis began and two of the researchers became participant observers in the project teams, developing sensitivity to the project and its goals. They also began to reflect on their own backgrounds to see what theoretical frameworks they could draw on.

Open coding. This was done initially on a line-by-line basis, but later coding was done at the message level, while other documents such as reports and reflections were coded at document level. Over 200 categories were generated, and as these were refined, some informal axial coding was also done. Table 8.5 shows two messages posted at the beginning of a project, and illustrates how these messages were coded during the open coding process.

Message	Post date, week #, time	Sample codes generated (underlined) and notes
Hi there in UB, I'm Henry. I just wanted to say hello and provide you with the rest of our group members' email address. [Names and email addresses] Well, I guess we'll see each other on Saturday at the videoconference.	1/22/98, week 1, 1:41:52 PM	1. Leadership – initiative to represent. 2. Establishing team's co-presence on the Internet. 3. Implying preference for communication technology (email). 4. Implying technology (VC) can bridge the time and space gap.
Hello UB. Just letting you know that you are free to email us anytime. I might be getting an ICQ account going so that if any of you are into real-time chat and wish to communicate that way, it might be something to try . . .	1/26/98, week 1, 2:56:37 PM	1. UB members' identity viewed at an aggregate level (as in msg. #1). 2. Collapsing/bridging across time boundaries. 3. Invitation. 4. Implying preference for communication technology. 5. Properties of communication technology/medium (real-time, synchronous?). 6. Novelty of technology, recognizing the need to try/explore.

Table 8.5 An illustration of open coding

Sarker *et al* note that codes emerged and continued to be refined over the life of the project. Also, a significant number of the codes that were ultimately used in the theory building were recurrent; for example, preference for technology and time gaps/boundaries. Finally, some of the key categories were identified when considering messages as one unit and looking at comparable strips in other data segments.

Through constant comparison of data across categories, the names of categories were refined, merged, and changed over time.

Axial coding. Sarker *et al* found the suggestions in Corbin and Strauss about how to relate subcategories too constraining. They instead used a two-step process for axial coding:

1. The major categories, e.g. technology, norms, social practices, stages of team development, and frames of reference, were hierarchically related to subcategories. For example, the category technology was linked to the subcategories purpose of technology, nature of ownership, accessibility (by time, location, cost, awareness), future potential, degree of novelty, and interconnectedness. At the next level, purpose of technology was linked to information sharing, triggering, and so on (see Figure 8.14). During this process, the researchers returned to open coding and refined categories further.
2. For each major category, researchers created a description (called a memo) that attempted to integrate as many of the categories and subcategories as possible. These memos also evolved as analysis progressed. Figure 8.15 contains an excerpt from an early draft memo for the technology category.

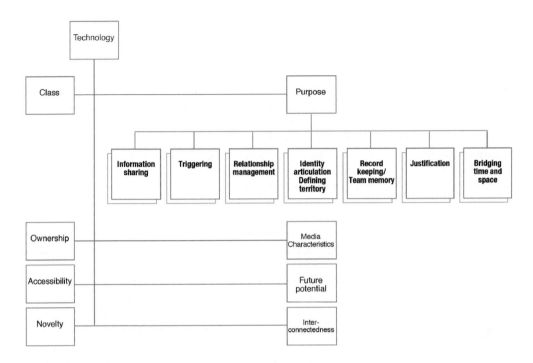

Figure 8.14 Axial coding for the technology category

Source: S. Sarker, F. Lau and S. Sahay (2001): "Using an adapted grounded theory approach for inductivetheory building about virtual team development". *The Data Base for Advances in Information Systems,* 32(1), pp. 38–56 ©2001 Association for Computing Machinery, Inc. Reprinted by permission.

Collaboration across time and space requires mediation by technology for both symbolic and substantive purposes. Substantive purposes include sharing information, record-keeping, managing relationships, pacing and triggering of activities in collaboration. Some symbolic uses of technology involve the articulation of the self and group identity and legitimizing different courses of action by appealing to the use of technology.

Different classes of technology provide different capabilities, some of them different to the features of technology as defined from the designers' or the implementers' point of view. For example, we wanted Webboard to be a public record . . . students have extended this use by creating a local enclave for information exchange with local members in a domain traditionally thought of as being public. The Webboard has also become a project archive, conserving team memory through the documentation of agendas, minutes, project steps, and deliverables.

Figure 8.15 An excerpt from an early draft of an integrative memo for the technology category

Source: Excerpt from S. Sarker, F. Lau and S. Sahay (2001): "Using an adapted grounded theory approach for inductive theory building about virtual team development". *The Data Base for Advances in Information Systems,* 32(1), pp. 38–56.

Selective coding. This stage of coding involves linking the categories and subcategories into a theory, and as theory building is quite complex, we only present an overview of the process here.

Sarker *et al* wanted to develop a theory of virtual teams, and so they used two approaches from their background to help them. One of these approaches (Couch, 1996) emphasizes the concepts that a theory of human conduct must use. The other focuses on social structure (Giddens, 1984). Using these two approaches, the category 'stages of team development' was chosen as the core category for the grounded theory to be built from this data set, and other categories were linked around it. This theory was further elaborated upon through discussions and reading of theory, and evolved into a theory of how virtual teams develop over time. More details can be found in Sarker and Sahay (2003).

8.6.2   Distributed Cognition

We introduced the distributed cognition approach in Chapter 3, as a theoretical account of the distributed nature of cognitive phenomena across individuals, artifacts, and internal and external representations (Hutchins, 1995).

Typically, a distributed cognition analysis results in an event-driven description which emphasizes information and its propagation through the cognitive system under study. The cognitive system under study might be one person's use of a computational tool, such as a calculator, two people's joint activities when designing the layout for the front page of a newspaper, using a shared authoring tool, or, more widely, a large team of software developers, examining how they coordinate their work with one another, using a variety of mediating artifacts, such as schedules, clocks, to-do lists, and shared files.

The granularity of analysis varies depending on the activities and cognitive system being observed and the research or design questions being asked. For example, if the goal is to examine how a team of pilots fly a plane – with a view to improving communication between them – then the focus will be on the interactions and communications that take place between them and their instruments, at a fine level of granularity. If the goal is to understand how pilots learn how to fly – with a view to developing new training materials – then the focus will be at a coarser grain of analysis, taking into account the cultural, historical, and learning aspects involved in becoming a pilot.

The description produced may cover a period of a day, an hour, or only minutes, depending on the study's focus. For the longer periods, verbal descriptions are primarily used. For the shorter periods, micro-level analyses of the cognitive processes are meticulously plotted using diagrammatic forms and other graphical representations. The rationale for performing the finer levels of analysis is to reveal practices and discrepancies that would go unnoticed using coarser grain analysis, but which reveal themselves as critical to the work activity.

Ed Hutchins (1995) emphasizes that an important part of doing a distributed cognition analysis is to have a deep understanding of the work domain that is being studied. He recommends, where possible, that the investigators learn the trade under study. This can take a team of researchers several months and even years to accomplish and in most cases this is impractical for a research or design team to do.

Alternatively, it is possible to spend a few weeks immersed in the culture and setting of a specific team to learn enough about the organization and its work practices to conduct a focused analysis of a particular cognitive system. For example, I spent six weeks with an engineering team, where I was able to learn enough about their work practice to gain a good understanding of how they worked together on projects, how they coordinated their work with each other, and how the technologies that were used mediated their work activities. I was then able to document and analyze a number of problems they were experiencing through the introduction of new networking technology. Using the distributed cognition framework, I described how seemingly simple communication problems led to large delays and recommended how the situation could be improved (Rogers, 1993, 1994).

More recently, distributed cognition has been applied to studying medical teams. For example, Rajkomar and Blandford (2012) examined how healthcare technologies are used; specifically they examined the use of infusion pumps by nurses in an intensive care unit (ICU). They gathered data through ethnographic observations and interviews, which they analysed by constructing representational models that focused on information flows, physical layouts, social structures, and artifacts. They note that "the findings showed that there was significant distribution of cognition in the ICU: socially, among nurses; physically, through the material environment; and through technological artefacts." Based on the results of this study, they were able to suggest changes that would improve the safety and efficiency of the nurses' interactions with the infusion technology.

Performing a Distributed Cognition Analysis

It should be stressed that there is not one single way of doing a distributed cognition analysis, nor is there an off-the-shelf manual that can be followed. A good way to begin analyzing and interpreting the data collected is to describe the official work practices, in terms of the routines and procedures followed, and the work-arounds that teams develop when coping with the various demands placed upon them at different times during their work. In so doing, any breakdowns, incidents, or unusual happenings should be highlighted, especially where it was discovered that excessive time was being spent doing something, errors were made using a system, or a piece of information was passed on incorrectly to someone else or misheard. While writing these observations down it is good to start posing specific research questions related to them (e.g. 'Why did X not let Y know the printer was broken when he came back from his break?') and to contemplate further (e.g. 'Was it a communication failure, a problem with being overloaded at the time, or a technology problem?').

It is at this point that knowledge of the theory of distributed cognition can help in interpreting and representing the observations of a work setting (see Chapter 3 and Hutchins, 1995). It provides an analytic framework and a set of concepts to describe what is happening at a higher level of abstraction. Problems can be described in terms of the communication pathways that are being hindered or the breakdowns arising due to information not propagating effectively from one representational state to another (see Box 8.6). The framework can reveal where information is being distorted, resulting in poor communication or inefficiency. Conversely, it can show when different technologies and the representations displayed via them are effective at mediating certain work activities and how well they are coordinated.

Performing a detailed distributed cognition analysis enables researchers and designers to explore the trade-offs and likely outcomes of potential solutions and in so doing suggest a more grounded set of cognitive requirements, e.g. types of information resources that

BOX 8.6

Distributed cognition concepts

A distributed cognition analysis involves producing a detailed description of the domain area at varying levels of granularity. At the micro-level, a small set of cognitive terms are used to depict the representations employed in a cognitive activity and the processes acting upon them. The terms are intended to steer the analysis towards conceptualizing problems in terms of distributed information and representations. This level of description can also directly lead to recommendations, suggesting how to change or redesign an aspect of the cognitive system, such as a display or a socially mediated practice. The main terms used are:

- *The cognitive system* – the interactions among people, the artifacts they use, and the environment they are working in.
- *The communicative pathways* – the channels by which information is passed between people (e.g. phone, email, physical gesture).
- *Propagation of representational states* – how information is transformed across different media. Media refers to external artifacts (e.g. instruments, maps, paper notes) and internal representations (e.g. human memory). These can be socially mediated (e.g. passing on a message verbally), technologically mediated (e.g. pressing a key on a computer), or mentally mediated (e.g. reading the time on a clock). ■

are considered suitable for specific kinds of activities, and those that could be dealt with by an automated system. Clearly, such a painstaking level of analysis and the expertise required in the interpretation are very costly. In the commercial world, where deadlines and budgets are always looming, it is unlikely to be practical. However, in large-scale and safety-critical projects, where more time and resources are available, it can be a valuable analytic tool to use.

Furniss and Blandford (2006) applied distributed cognition to an emergency medical dispatch setting (ambulance control). They identified 22 principles underlying the literature on distributed cognition, and used diagrams from Contextual Design (Beyer and Holtzblatt, 1998) to capture relevant aspects of activity they observed. The analysis resulted in suggestions for improving the dispatch room operation. The resulting method for applying distributed cognition, called DiCOT (distributed cognition for teamwork, Blandford and Furniss (2006)), has subsequently been used to understand software team interactions (Sharp and Robinson, 2008), mobile healthcare settings (McKnight and Doherty, 2008), and the use of infusion pumps by nurses (Rajkomar and Blandford, 2012).

8.6.3   Activity Theory

Activity theory (AT) is a product of Soviet psychology that explains human behavior in terms of our practical activity with the world. It originated as part of the attempt to produce a Marxist psychology, an enterprise usually associated with Vygotsky (e.g. 1926/1962) and later Leontiev (e.g. 1978, 1989). In the last 20–30 years, versions of AT have become popular elsewhere, particularly in Scandinavia and Germany, and interest is now growing in the USA and UK. The newer versions of AT have been popular in research investigating applied problems, particularly those to do with work, technology, and education.

Activity theory provides a framework that focuses analysis around the concept of an activity and helps to identify tensions between the different elements of the system. For example, in what is now viewed as a classic study of the use of AT in HCI, Mackay *et al* (2000) analyzed a 4-minute excerpt from a video of users working with a new software tool. They identified 19 shifts in attention between different parts of the tool interface and the task at hand. In fact, some users spent so much time engaged in these shifts that they lost track of their original task. Using the theory helped evaluators to focus on relevant incidents.

AT outlines two key framings: the individual model that constitutes an activity and one that models the mediating role of artifacts.

The Individual Model

AT models activities in a hierarchical way. At the bottom level are operations, routinized behaviors that require little conscious attention (e.g. rapid typing). At an intermediate level are actions, behavior that is characterized by conscious planning, e.g. producing a glossary. The top level is the activity, and that provides a minimum meaningful context for understanding the individual actions, e.g. writing an essay (see Figure 8.16). There may be many different operations capable of fulfilling an action, and many actions capable of serving the same activity.

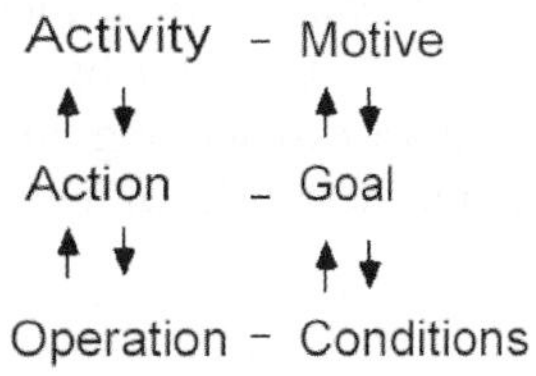

```
Activity  –  Motive
   ↑ ↓         ↑ ↓
 Action    _  Goal
   ↑ ↓         ↑ ↓
Operation  –  Conditions
```

Figure 8.16 The original activity theory model

Activities can be identified on the basis of the motives that elicit them, actions on the basis of conscious goals that guide them, and operations by the conditions necessary to attain the goals. However, there is an intimate and fluid link between levels. Actions can become operations as they become more automatic and operations can become actions when an operation encounters an obstacle, thus requiring conscious planning. Similarly there is no strict demarcation between action and activity. If the motive changes, then an activity can become an action. It is also important to realize that activities are not self-contained. Activities relate to others while actions may be part of different activities, and so on.

The Role of Artifacts

Artifacts can be physical, such as a book or a stone, or they can be abstract, such as a system of symbols or a set of rules. Physical artifacts have physical properties that cause humans to respond to them as direct objects to be acted upon. They also embody a set of social practices, their design reflecting a history of particular use. Leontiev describes the process of learning what these inherent properties are as one of appropriation, signifying the active nature of the learning that is needed. The kind of learning involved is one of identifying and participating in the activity appropriate to the artifact. Consider an infant learning to feed with a spoon. Leontiev (1981) observed that, at first, the infant carries the spoon to its mouth as though it were handling any other object, not considering the need to hold it horizontal. Over time, with adult guidance, the spoon is shaped in the way it is because of the social practice – the activity – of feeding. In turn, the infant's task is to learn that relationship – to discover what practice(s) the object embodies. By contrast a spoon dropped into the cage of a mouse, say, will only ever have the status of just another physical object – no different from that of a stone.

The idea of abstract artifacts follows from the idea of mediation, i.e. a fundamental characteristic of human development is the change from a direct mode of acting on the world to one that is mediated by something else. In AT, the artifacts involved in an activity mediate between the elements of it.

AT also emphasizes the social context of an activity. Even when apparently working alone, an individual is still engaged in activities that are given meaning by a wider set of practices.

The classic view of an activity has a subject (who performs the activity) and an object (on which the activity is performed). Engeström (e.g. 1999) and Nardi and Kaptelinin (2012) have widened the focus from the individual triangle of a single activity (subject, activity, and object) to include supra-individual concepts – tools, rules, community, and division of labor. By tool is meant the artifacts, signs, and means that mediate the subject and object; by community is meant those who share the same object; by rules is meant a set of agreed conventions and policies covering what it means to be a member of that community (set by laws, parents, managers, boards, and so forth); and by division of labor is meant the primary means of classifying the labor in a workplace (e.g. manager, engineer, receptionist). The extended versions allow consideration of networks of interrelated activities – forming an activity system (see Figure 8.17).

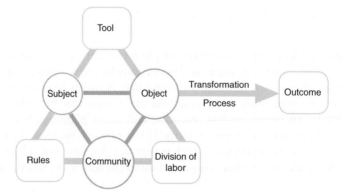

Figure 8.17 Engeström's (1999) activity system model. The tool element is sometimes referred to as the mediating artifact

Source: Reproduced from Engeström, Y. (1999) *Perspectives on Activity Theory,* CUP.

Performing an Analysis Driven by Activity Theory

AT does not present a clear methodological prescription for the description or analysis of behavior as a set of procedures to be followed. The model shown in Figure 8.16 is the main framework that is used to describe levels within an activity. This means that identifying elements will be highly dependent on individual interpretation. Christiansen (1996, p. 177) summarizes: "Methodologically . . . the ideal data for an application of AT consist of longitudinal ethnographic observation, interviews and discussion in real-life settings, supplemented by experiments." She continues that you "cannot interview people directly through rote questions but must interpret their actions and opinions after some careful reflection," which is a difficult process. Nevertheless, the original and later versions of the AT framework have become popular amongst researchers and some practitioners as a way of identifying needs for new tools and to analyze problems that are present in a work or other setting. For example, Saguna and Chakraborty (2013) point out that AT has much to offer in the development of mobile applications where analyzing users' activities and particularly changes in activities can inform design. However, they also point out that there is a lack of a unifying theoretical framework which fully addresses all aspects of the activity and activity domain.

One of the biggest problems with doing an AT analysis is working out when something should be described as a top-level activity and when something is better described as a lower-level action.

Performing an AT analysis enables researchers and designers to identify the tensions in a workplace leading to specific needs for new technological tools; it is also used in evaluation studies. It can be difficult, however, getting to grips with the concepts and being able to determine how to label the points raised in the interviews. Expertise and a good background in the Soviet version of activity theory are recommended to become competent in AT. Similar to the distributed cognition approach in the commercial world, where deadlines and budgets are always looming, it is unlikely to be practical. Where more time and resources are available, it can be a valuable analytic tool.

ACTIVITY 8.4

How does activity theory (AT) analysis differ from and how is it similar to distributed cognition (DC) analysis?

Comment
1. AT focuses on describing the tensions between parts of the AT system, using quotes to back them up, whereas a DC analysis focuses on drilling down on the way representations and technologies are used for a given distributed activity.
2. AT provides a set of concepts by which to label and instantiate specific observations for an activity system, whereas DC represents the sequence of events (often in a diagrammatic form), making explicit how the various media support the way information is propagated across different representational states.
3. Both AT and DC analyses reveal problems with existing technologies. ■

For those interested in exploring activity theory and distributed cognition further, Baumer and Thomlinson (2011) provide a comparison of them, including examples of the use of these theories in video analysis.

8.7   Presenting the Findings

The best way to present findings depends on the audience, and the original goals of the study. However, it also is dependent on the data gathering and analysis techniques used.

In the previous sections of this chapter, you met many different ways of presenting findings – as numbers, through various graphical devices, in tables, in textual descriptions, as a set of themes or categories, and so on. These representations may be used directly to report your findings, provided they are appropriate for your audience and your purpose, or they may be used as background evidence for a different form of representation.

Broadly speaking, data gathering and analysis in interaction design are carried out for one of two purposes: to derive requirements for an interactive product, or to evaluate an interactive product under development. These two purposes have their own needs in terms of the notations to use and the information to be highlighted, but they also have similarities in terms of the choices to be made for presentation. For example, they usually involve reporting findings to a technical design team who will act on the findings.

In this section, we discuss three kinds of presentation style that we have not focused on as yet: using rigorous notations, using stories, and summarizing. There are other ways of presenting findings, but these are representative of the main options; they are not mutually exclusive and are often used in combination.

8.7.1   Rigorous Notations

A number of rigorous notations have been developed to analyze, capture, and present information for interaction design. The term rigorous is not intended to imply formality or rigidity, but simply to say that the notations have clear syntax and semantics. For example, the work models promoted in contextual design (Beyer and Holtzblatt, 1998) use simple but clear conventions for representing flows, breakdowns, individual roles, and so on. The modeling language UML (Unified Modeling Language) has stricter and more precise syntax to be followed and is more often used to specify internal software designs (although it has also been used and extended in the context of user interface design, e.g. Van den Bergh and Coninx, 2005).

Advantages of using a rigorous notation are that it gives you clear guidance on what to look for in the findings and what to highlight, and that it forces you to be precise. Disadvantages include that by highlighting specific elements, it inevitably also downplays or ignores other aspects, and that the precision expressed by the notation may be lost on an audience if they don't know the notation well. Producing diagrams in these notations inevitably requires further analysis of the findings in order to identify the specific characteristics and properties that the notation highlights.

To overcome their disadvantages, rigorous notations are usually used in combination with stories or other more easily accessible formats.

8.7.2   Using Stories

Storytelling is an easy and intuitive approach for people to communicate ideas and experiences. It is not surprising then that stories (also called narratives) are used extensively in interaction design, both to communicate findings of investigative studies, and as the basis for further development such as product design or system enhancements.

Storytelling may be employed in three different ways. First, participants (i.e. interviewees, questionnaire respondents, and those you have observed) may have told stories of their own during data gathering. These stories can be extracted, compared, and may be used to communicate findings to others (e.g. as anecdotes to bring a summary report to life).

Second, stories about participants may be employed. For example, in reporting her findings about European culture, Bell (2001) presents general themes and overall findings, but then illustrates these with specific stories about participants she observed. For example, one of the themes from her observations was that food shopping is important in European cultures. To illustrate the importance of the local market in France, she tells the following story:

> *Patrice lives with her husband Frederico and their two small children in a tiny village in Brittany. In her early 30s, Patrice has retired from working in the company she and her husband started. She now runs her household and looks after her kids and husband. Like many other European women we interviewed, she expressed serious reservations about catalog shopping, saying "I like to touch and see things before I buy them." And although she lives just a five-minute drive from a town with a large supermarket, Patrice chooses to shop in the local produce markets, which cycle through southern Brittany. It is important to buy what is locally seasonally available: "It just tastes better," Patrice says.*

Including these kinds of specific stories gives credibility and adds weight to the summary. Making a multimedia presentation of the story by adding video or audio excerpts and photographs will illustrate the story further. This kind of approach can be particularly effective if presenting data from an evaluation study that involves observation, as it is hard to contest well-chosen video excerpts of users interacting with technology or anecdotes from interview transcripts.

Third, stories may be constructed from smaller anecdotes or repeated patterns that are found in the data. In this case, stories provide a way of rationalizing and collating data to form a representative account of a product's use or a certain type of event.

Any stories collected through data gathering may be used as the basis for constructing scenarios. Scenarios are hypothesized stories about people and their daily life. They are a powerful technique for interaction design and can be used throughout the lifecycle. See Chapters 10 and 11 for more information on scenarios.

8.7.3 Summarizing the Findings

Clearly written reports with an overview at the beginning and a detailed content list make for easy reading and a good reference document. Including anecdotes, quotations, pictures, and video clips helps to bring the study to life, stimulate interest, and make the written description more meaningful. Some teams emphasize quantitative data, but its value depends on the type of study. Often both qualitative and quantitative data analysis are used because they provide alternative perspectives.

Some audiences are likely to be more interested in the headline findings than in the details of stories or precise specifications. These may be high-level managers, the set of users who acted as participants in studies, or product designers who want to use the results to develop a new product. Whoever they are, being able to present a summary of the findings is important. This is where numbers and statistical values (if you have any) can be really powerful. However, in these summaries it is important not to overstate your findings – if 8 out of 10 users preferred design A over design B, this does not mean that design A is 80% more attractive than design B. If you found 800 out of 1000 users preferred design A then you have more evidence to suggest that design A is better, but there are still other factors to take into account. In general, be wary of using words such as 'most,' 'all,' 'majority,' 'none,' and be careful when writing justifications to ensure that they reflect the data.

ACTIVITY 8.5

Consider each of the findings below and the associated summary statement about it. For each one, comment on whether the finding supports the statement.

1. Finding: Two out of four people who filled in the questionnaire ticked the box that said they prefer not to use the ring-back facility on their cell phone.
   Statement: Half of the users don't use the ring-back facility.
2. Finding: Joan who works in the design department was observed one day walking for 10 minutes to collect printout from the high-quality colour printer.
   Statement: Significant time is wasted by designers who have to walk a long distance to collect printout.
3. Finding: A data log of 1000 hours of interaction with a website recorded during January, February, and March records 8 hours spent looking at the helpfiles.
   Statement: The website's helpfiles were used less than 1% of the time during the first quarter of the year.

Comment

1. The questionnaire didn't ask if they use the ring-back, just whether they preferred to use the ring-back facility. In addition, two users out of four is a very small number of participants and it would be better to state the actual numbers.
2. Observing one designer on one day having to walk to get printout does not mean that this is a general problem. There may be other reasons why this happened on this day, and other information is needed to make a clear statement.
3. This statement is justified as the log was recorded for a significant period of time, and using percentages to represent this finding is appropriate as the numbers are so large. ∎

Assignment

The aim of this assignment is for you to practice data analysis and presentation. Assume that you are to present the findings of your data gathering assignment from Chapter 7 to a group of peers, e.g. through a seminar.

(a) Review the data you have gathered and identify any qualitative data and any quantitative data in your data set.

(b) Is there any qualitative data that could sensibly and helpfully be translated into quantitative measures? If so, do the translation and add this data to your quantitative set.

(c) Consider your quantitative data.

- Decide how best to enter your quantitative data into your spreadsheet software. For example, you need to consider how to handle answers to closed questions. Then enter the data and generate some graphical representations. As you are likely to have very few records, i.e. respondents or interviewees, in your data set, you will have to think carefully about what, if any, graphical representations will provide meaningful summaries of your findings.
- Is there any data for which simple measures such as percentages or averages will be helpful? If so, calculate the three different types of average.

(d) Consider your qualitative data.

- Based on your refinement of the study question 'improving the product,' identify some themes from your qualitative data, e.g. what features of the product cause people difficulties, did any of your participants suggest alternative designs or solutions? Refine your themes and collate extracts of data which support the theme.
- Identify any critical incidents in your data. These may arise from interview or questionnaire responses, or from observation. Describe these incidents carefully and choose one or two to analyze in more depth, focusing on the context in which they occurred.

(e) Collate your findings as a presentation and deliver them to a group of your peers.

(f) Review your presentation and any questions you received from your peers and consider where your analysis and presentation could be improved.

Summary

This chapter has described in detail the difference between qualitative and quantitative data and between qualitative and quantitative analysis.

Quantitative and qualitative data can be analyzed for patterns and trends using simple techniques and graphical representations. Qualitative data may be analyzed using a variety of approaches including identifying categories or themes, and using theoretical frameworks, such as grounded theory, distributed cognition, and activity theory.

It was noted that presenting the results is just as important as analyzing the data, hence it is important to make sure that any summary or claim arising from the analysis is carefully contextualized, and can be justified by the data.

Key points
- The kind of data analysis that can be done depends on the data gathering techniques used.
- Qualitative and quantitative data may be collected from any of the main data gathering techniques: interviews, questionnaires, and observation.

- Quantitative data analysis for interaction design usually involves calculating percentages and averages.
- There are three different kinds of average: mean, mode, and median.
- Graphical representations of quantitative data help in identifying patterns, outliers, and the overall view of the data.
- Qualitative data analysis may be framed by theories. Three such theories are grounded theory, activity theory, and distributed cognition.

Further Reading

CHARMAZ, K. (2014) *Constructing Grounded Theory* (2nd edn). Sage Publications. This popular book also provides a useful account of how to actually do grounded theory.

CORBIN, J. M. and STRAUSS, A. (2014) *Basics of Qualitative Research: Techniques and procedures for developing grounded theory*. Sage. This presents a readable and practical account of applying the grounded theory approach. It is not tailored specifically to interaction design and therefore requires some interpretation. It is a good discussion of the basic approach.

HUFF, D. (1991) *How to Lie with Statistics*. Penguin. This wonderful little book illustrates the many ways in which numbers can be misrepresented. Unlike some (many) books on statistics, the text is easy to read and amusing.

KUUTTI, K. (1996) Activity theory as a potential framework for human–computer interaction. In B. A. Nardi (ed.) *Context and Consciousness*. MIT Press, pp. 17–44. This provides a digestible description of activity theory and how it can be applied in HCI.

LAZAR, J., FENG, J. H. and HOCHHEISER, H. (2010) *Research Methods in Human–Computer Interaction*. John Wiley & Sons Ltd. This is a good resource for a more detailed discussion of data gathering and analysis in interaction design.

ROGERS, Y. (2006) Distributed cognition and communication. In K. Brown (ed.) *The Encyclopedia of Language and Linguistics* (2nd edn). Elsevier, pp. 731–733. (A version can also be downloaded from Yvonne Rogers' website.) This chapter provides a readable introduction to the background and application of distributed cognition.

Chapter 9

THE PROCESS OF INTERACTION DESIGN

9.1 Introduction

9.2 What Is Involved in Interaction Design?

9.3 Some Practical Issues

Objectives

The main aims of this chapter are to:

- Consider what doing interaction design involves.
- Explain some advantages of involving users in development.
- Explain the main principles of a user-centered approach.
- Present a simple lifecycle model of interaction design.
- Ask and provide answers for some important questions about the interaction design process.
- Consider how interaction design activities can be integrated into the wider product development lifecycle.

9.1 Introduction

Design is a practical and creative activity with the aim of developing a product that helps its users achieve their goals. In previous chapters, we looked at different kinds of interactive products, issues that need to be taken into account when doing interaction design, some of the theoretical bases for the field, and techniques for gathering and analyzing data to understand users' goals. In this chapter we start to explore how we can design and build interactive products.

Chapter 1 defined interaction design as being concerned with 'designing interactive products to support the way people communicate and interact in their everyday and working lives.' But how do you go about doing this? Developing a product must begin with gaining some understanding of what is required of it, but where do these requirements come from? Whom do you ask about them? Underlying good interaction design is the philosophy of user-centered design, i.e. involving users throughout development, but who are the users? Will they know what they want or need even if we can find them to ask? For an innovative product, users are unlikely to be able to envision what is possible, so where do these ideas come from?

In this chapter, we raise and answer these kinds of questions, discuss user-centered design, and revisit the four basic activities of the interaction design process that were introduced in Chapter 1. We also introduce a lifecycle model of interaction design that captures these activities.

9.2 What Is Involved in Interaction Design?

The previous chapters have introduced you to many exciting ideas, approaches, theories, and opinions about interaction design, but what does it mean to actually do interaction design? The following activity is intended to start you thinking about this by asking you to produce an initial design for an interactive product.

ACTIVITY 9.1

Imagine that you want to design a travel planner for yourself. You might use this system to plan your route, check visa requirements, book flights or train tickets, investigate the facilities at your destination, and so on. Assume that the system is destined to run on a tablet for the purposes of this activity.

1. Make a list of the user experience and usability goals for the system.
2. Outline the initial screen or two for this system, showing its main functionality and its general look and feel. Spend about 10 minutes on this.
3. Having produced an outline, spend 5 minutes reflecting on how you went about tackling this activity. What did you do first? Did you have any particular artifacts or experience to base your design upon? What process did you go through?

Comment

1. The three main usability goals I would like for my system are efficiency, effectiveness, and safety. I'm not so bothered about whether the system is easy to learn or memorable as I am likely to use it regularly, and I am prepared to put the time in to learn something that supports me well. From the list of user experience goals, there are definitely some that I don't wish to be associated with my travel organizer, such as annoying, frustrating, and challenging! I want it to be helpful and satisfying. Being fun or engaging would be additional bonuses, as the main purpose of using the system is to plan my travel.

2. The initial screens I produced are shown in Figure 9.1. The first screen prompts me for the four main items of information I usually have at the top of my mind: where am I going, when am I going there, how do I want to get there, and do I need to organize accommodation? The second screen then shows the kind of response I would like the system to give if I'm trying to go to York by train: it gives me train times from my local station on the specified date (straight-through trains only, as I prefer that), and the range of accommodation available in York. I can then find out more about the trains and the accommodation by drilling down further.

3. The first thing that came into my head when I started doing this was the myriad of resources I currently use to plan my travel. For example, travel agents will arrange accommodation, visas, guided tours, and so on. I can look at paper-based or electronic timetables for journey routes and times, ring up automated timetable readers, talk to embassies who will give me travel advice about their own country, search websites to identify cheap flights,

Figure 9.1 Initial sketches of the travel organizer

and so on. There is a long list. I then thought it would be good to combine the advantages of all of these into one system that could be tailored to me. For example, tailored so that the first airline offered for any flights is my favorite airline, and the starting point for my journey is defaulted to my normal train station or airport.

The next thing I focused on was the dialog I would have with the system. Hence, my sketches focus on questions the system might ask me and my responses. As I was producing this sketch it occurred to me that the location I need to enter and the kind of help I need will depend on the kind of transport I choose. On the other hand, I would want the system to know that I am unlikely to want to drive to Hong Kong, which is several thousand miles away, so it should automatically default to 'travel by air' for some destinations.

On reviewing my sketches, the 'look and feel' seemed very bland, and I realized that I had been subconsciously focusing on business travel. If I was planning travel for a vacation, I would want pictures of the destination and descriptions of local activities, restaurants, historic sites, and so on. This led me to reconsider (although not redraw) my ideas.

The exact steps taken to create a product will vary from designer to designer, from product to product, and from organization to organization (see Box 9.1). In this activity, you may have started by thinking about what such a system could do for you, or you may have been thinking about existing resources. Sketching something or writing down concrete lines, squiggles, and words, helps to focus the mind on what you are designing and the details of the interaction. All the time you were doing this, you will have been making choices between alternatives, exploring requirements in more detail, and refining your ideas about what you would like a travel organizer to do. ■

BOX 9.1

Four approaches to interaction design

Saffer (2010) suggests four main approaches to interaction design, each of which is based on a distinct underlying philosophy: user-centered design, activity-centered design, systems design, and genius design. He acknowledges that the purest form of any of these is unlikely to be realized, and takes an extreme view of each in order to distinguish between them. In user-centered design, the user knows best and is the only guide to the designer; the designer's role is to translate the users' needs and goals into a design solution. Activity-centered design focuses on the behavior surrounding particular tasks. Users still play a significant role but it is their behavior rather than their goals and needs that are important. Systems design is a structured, rigorous, and holistic design approach that focuses on context and is particularly appropriate for complex problems. In systems design it is the system (i.e. the people, computers, objects, devices, and so on) that are the center of attention while the users' role is to set the goals of the system.

Finally, genius design is different from the other three approaches because it relies solely on the experience and creative flair of a designer. Jim Leftwich, an experienced interaction designer interviewed in Saffer (2010, pp. 44–5) prefers the term 'rapid expert design.' In this approach the users' role is to validate ideas generated by the designer, and users are not involved during the design process itself. Saffer points out that this is not necessarily by choice, but may be due to limited or no resources for user involvement. Apple, for example, does very little user research or testing, yet the Apple iPod is acknowledged as a significant design achievement.

Different design problems lend themselves more easily to different approaches, and different designers will tend to gravitate towards using the approach that suits them best. Although an individual designer may prefer a particular approach, it is important that the approach for any one design problem is chosen with that design problem in mind. ■

There are many fields of design; for example, graphic design, architectural design, industrial and software design, and although each discipline has its own interpretation of 'designing,' there are three fundamental activities that are recognized in all design: understanding the requirements, producing a design that satisfies those requirements, and evaluating the design. Interaction design also involves these activities, and in addition we focus attention very clearly on users and their goals. For example, we investigate the artifact's use and target domain by taking a user-centered approach to development, we seek users' opinions and reactions to early designs, and we involve users appropriately in the development process itself. This means that users' concerns direct the development rather than just technical concerns, and for interaction design, the three fundamental activities of design listed above are extended to include an activity of prototyping so that users can interact with the design.

So design involves work on requirements, designing a solution, producing an interactive version of the solution, and evaluating it. But design is also about trade-offs, about balancing conflicting requirements. One common form of trade-off when developing a system to offer advice is deciding how much choice will be given to the user and how much direction the system should offer. Often the division will depend on the purpose of the system, e.g. for business travel or for vacations. Getting the balance right requires experience, but it also requires the development and evaluation of alternative solutions.

Generating alternatives is a key principle in most design disciplines, and one that should be encouraged in interaction design. Linus Pauling, twice a Nobel Prize winner, once said: "The best way to get a good idea, is to get lots of ideas." This is not necessarily easy, however, and unlike many design disciplines, interaction designers are not generally trained to generate alternative designs. The good news is that the ability to brainstorm and contribute alternative ideas can be learned. For example, Kelley (2008) describes seven secrets for better brainstorms, including sharpen the focus (have a well-honed problem statement), playful rules (to encourage ideas), and get physical (use visual props). He also discusses six ways to kill a brainstorm, including do it off-site and write everything down.

Involving users and others in the design process means that the designs and potential solutions will need to be communicated to people other than the original designer. This requires the design to be captured and expressed in some suitable form that allows review, revision, and improvement. There are many ways of doing this, one of the simplest being to produce a series of sketches. Other common approaches are to write a description in natural language, to draw a series of diagrams, and to build prototypes. A combination of these techniques is likely to be the most effective. When users are involved, capturing and expressing a design in a suitable format is especially important since they are unlikely to understand jargon or specialist notations. In fact, a form that users can interact with is most effective, and building prototypes is an extremely powerful approach (see Box 9.2 and Chapter 11 for more on prototyping).

In the rest of this section, we explore in more depth the significance and practicality of involving users in design, i.e. using a user-centered approach, and consider again the four activities of interaction design that were introduced in Chapter 1.

BOX 9.2

The value of prototyping

I learned the value of prototyping through a very effective role-playing exercise. I was on a course designed to introduce new graduates to different possible careers in industry. One of the themes was production and manufacturing and the aim of one group exercise was to produce a book. Each group was told that it had 30 minutes to deliver 10 books to the person in charge. Groups were given various pieces of paper, scissors, sticky tape, staples, etc., and told to organize ourselves as best we could. So in my group we set to work organizing ourselves into a production line, with one of us cutting up the paper, another stapling the pages together, another sealing the binding with the sticky tape, and so on. One person was even in charge of quality assurance. It took us less than 10 minutes to produce the 10 books, and we rushed off with our delivery. When we showed the person in charge, he replied, 'That's not what I wanted; I need it bigger than that.' Of course, the size of the notebook wasn't specified in the description of the task, so we found out how big he wanted it, got some more materials, and scooted back to produce 10 more books. Again, we set up our production line and

(Continued)

produced 10 books to the correct size. On delivery, we were again told that it was not what was required: he wanted the binding down the other edge. This time we got as many of the requirements as we could and went back, developed one book, and took that back for further feedback and refinement before producing the 10 required.

If we had used prototyping as a way of exploring our ideas and checking requirements in the first place, we could have saved so much effort and resource! ∎

9.2.1   The Importance of Involving Users

The description above emphasizes the need to involve users in interaction design, but why is it important? Before the impact that user involvement can have on project success was recognized, it was common for developers to talk to managers or to proxy users, i.e. people who role-played as users, when eliciting requirements, or even to use their own judgment without reference to anyone else. While a proxy user can provide useful information, they will not have the same perspective as someone who performs the task every day, or who will use the intended product on a regular basis. For example, several years ago, I was involved with a system to process and record financial transactions from the foreign exchange (forex) dealers in a large international bank. The users of this system took the handwritten transaction records completed by the forex dealers and entered the details into the system. The system then validated the transaction and communicated a confirmation to the relevant parties. When the requirements for this system were developed, no one from the development team spoke to the end-users of the system; the requirements were identified by higher level managers. Although the system was successfully used to support the task, the end-users had developed several work-arounds and crib sheets. For example, each desk had a sheet of paper with lists of buyer codes and names. The system required both buyer code and buyer name to be entered, but it was quite common for the dealers to write only the buyer name on the transaction record. The list of names and codes was used to identify the codes manually.

The best way to ensure that development continues to take users' activities into account is to involve real users throughout development. In this way, developers can gain a better understanding of users' goals, leading to a more appropriate, more usable product. However, two other aspects that have nothing to do with functionality are equally as important if the product is to be usable and used: expectation management and ownership.

Expectation management is the process of making sure that the users' expectations of the new product are realistic. The purpose of expectation management is to ensure that there are no surprises for users when the product arrives. If users feel they have been cheated by promises that have not been fulfilled, then this will cause resistance and even rejection. Marketing of the new arrival must be careful not to misrepresent the product, although it may be particularly difficult to achieve with a large and complex system (Nevo and Wade, 2007). How many times have you seen an advert for something you thought would be really good to have, but when you see one, discover that the marketing hype was a little exaggerated? I expect you felt quite disappointed and let down. This is the kind of feeling that expectation management tries to avoid.

It is better to exceed users' expectations than to fall below them. This does not mean adding more features, but that the product supports the users' goals more effectively than they expect. Involving users throughout development helps with expectation management because they can see from an early stage what the product's capabilities are. They will also understand better how it will affect their jobs and lives, and why the features are designed that way. Adequate and timely training is another technique for managing expectations. If users have the chance to work with the product before it is released, through training or hands-on demonstrations of a pre-release version, then they will understand better what to expect when the final product is available.

A second reason for user involvement is ownership. Users who are involved and feel that they have contributed to a product's development are more likely to feel a sense of ownership towards it and support its use.

9.2.2 Degrees of User Involvement

Different degrees of user involvement may be implemented in order to manage expectations and to create a feeling of ownership. At one end of the spectrum, users may be co-opted to the design team so that they are major contributors. For any one user, this may be on a full-time basis or a part-time basis, and it may be for the duration of the project or for a limited time only. There are advantages and disadvantages to each situation. If a user is co-opted full-time for the whole project, their input will be consistent and they will become very familiar with the product and its rationale. However, if the project takes many years, they may lose touch with the rest of the user group, making their input less valuable. If a user is co-opted part-time for the whole project, she will offer consistent input to development while remaining in touch with other users. Depending on the situation, this will need careful management as the user will be trying to learn new jargon and handle unfamiliar material as a member of the design team, yet concurrently trying to fulfill the demands of her original job. This can become very stressful for the individuals. If a number of users from each user group are co-opted part-time for a limited period, input is not necessarily consistent across the whole project, but careful coordination between users can alleviate this problem. In this case, one user may be part of the design team for 6 months, then another takes over for the next 6 months, and so on.

At the other end of the spectrum, users may simply be kept informed through regular newsletters or other channels of communication. Provided they are able to influence the development process through workshops or similar events, this can be an effective approach to expectation management and ownership. In a situation with hundreds or even thousands of users, it would not be feasible to involve them all as members of the team, and so this might be the only viable option. In this case a compromise situation is probably the best. Representatives from each user group may be co-opted onto the team on a full-time basis, while other users are involved through design workshops, evaluation sessions, and other data-gathering activities.

The individual circumstances of the project affect what is realistic and appropriate. If your end-user groups are identifiable, e.g. you are developing a product for a particular company, then it is easier to involve them. If, however, you are developing a product for the open market, it is unlikely that you will be able to co-opt a user to your design team, and so alternative approaches are needed. Box 9.3 outlines an alternative way to obtain user input.

How actively users should be involved is a matter for debate. Some studies have shown that too much user involvement can lead to problems. This issue is discussed in the next Dilemma box.

BOX 9.3

Ongoing user involvement after a product is released

Once a product has been released and the focus of development moves to future versions, a different kind of user involvement is possible – one that captures data about the real use of the product. This may be obtained in a number of ways, e.g. through interaction between users and customer service agents, or through automated error reporting systems. For example, Microsoft has millions of customers around the world, about 30% of whom call their customer support lines with problems and frustrations resulting from poor features or software errors. This data about customer behavior and their problems with the products is fed back into product development and improvement (Cusumano and Selby, 1995).

Error reporting systems (ERS, also called online crashing analysis) automatically collect information from users (with their permission), which is used to improve applications in the longer term. Figure 9.2 shows two typical dialog boxes for the Windows error reporting system that is built into Microsoft operating systems (Glerum et al., 2009). ∎

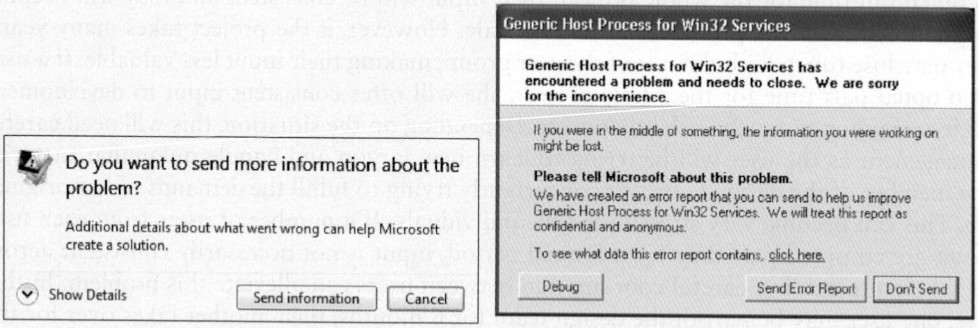

Generic Host Process for Win32 Services

Generic Host Process for Win32 Services has encountered a problem and needs to close. We are sorry for the inconvenience.

If you were in the middle of something, the information you were working on might be lost.

Please tell Microsoft about this problem.

We have created an error report that you can send to help us improve Generic Host Process for Win32 Services. We will treat this report as confidential and anonymous.

To see what data this error report contains, click here.

Debug   Send Error Report   Don't Send

Do you want to send more information about the problem?

Additional details about what went wrong can help Microsoft create a solution.

⌄ Show Details   Send information   Cancel

Figure 9.2 Two typical dialog boxes from the Windows error reporting system. This kind of reporting can have a significant effect on the quality of applications: for example, 29% of the errors fixed by the Windows XP (Service Pack 1) team were based on information collected through their ERS

DILEMMA

Too much of a good thing?

Involving users in development is a good thing. Or is it? And how much should they become involved? In what role(s)? Are users qualified to lead a technical development project? Or is it more appropriate for their role to be confined to evaluating prototypes? Involving users to

(Continued)

any degree incurs costs, so what evidence is there that user involvement is productive, or that it is worth putting the required level of resources into it?

Research by Keil and Carmel (1995) indicates that the more successful projects have direct links to users and customers, while Kujala and Mäntylä (2000) concluded that user studies conducted early in development produce benefits that outweigh the costs of conducting them. Subrayaman *et al* (2010) found a mixed result. They investigated the impact of user participation on the satisfaction with the product by both developers and users. They found that for new products, developer satisfaction increased as user participation increased, while user satisfaction was higher where participation was low, but satisfaction dropped as participation increased. For maintenance projects, both developers and users were most satisfied with a moderate level of participation (approximately 20% of overall project development time). If we focus just on the user satisfaction as an indication of project success, then it seems that low user participation is most beneficial.

According to some research, a low level of user involvement is beneficial whereas too much can lead to problems. For example, Heinbokel *et al* (1996) found that high user involvement projects tended to run less smoothly. Subrayaman *et al* (2010) also identified that high levels of user involvement can generate unnecessary conflicts and increased reworking.

The kind of product being developed, the kind of user involvement possible, and the application domain all influence the impact that users can have on a project. Scaife *et al* (1997) suggest that involving different kinds of user at different stages of design yields positive results, while Wagner and Piccoli (2007) provide evidence that user involvement is most effective when the product becomes salient to their daily lives, which is often close to or even after deployment.

Abelein *et al* (2013) performed a detailed review of the literature in this area and concluded that, overall, the evidence indicates user involvement has a positive effect on user satisfaction and system use. However, they also found that even though the data clearly indicates this positive effect, some links have a large variation, suggesting that there is still no clear conceptual model to measure the effects consistently. In addition, they found that most studies with negative correlations involving users and system success were published over a decade ago.

While user involvement is widely acclaimed as beneficial, there are still many dimensions that need to be considered and balanced. ■

9.2.3 What Is a User-Centered Approach?

Throughout this book, we emphasize the need for a user-centered approach to development. By this we mean that the real users and their goals, not just technology, are the driving force behind product development. As a consequence, a well-designed system will make the most of human skill and judgment, will be directly relevant to the activity in hand, and will support rather than constrain the user. This is less of a technique and more of a philosophy.

In 1985, Gould and Lewis (1985) laid down three principles they believed would lead to a 'useful and easy to use computer system':

1. *Early focus on users and tasks*. This means first understanding who the users will be by directly studying their cognitive, behavioral, anthropomorphic, and attitudinal

characteristics. This requires observing users doing their normal tasks, studying the nature of those tasks, and then involving users in the design process.

2. *Empirical measurement.* Early in development, the reactions and performance of intended users to printed scenarios, manuals, etc., are observed and measured. Later on, users interact with simulations and prototypes and their performance and reactions are observed, recorded, and analyzed.

3. *Iterative design.* When problems are found in user testing, they are fixed and then more tests and observations are carried out to see the effects of the fixes. This means that design and development is iterative, with cycles of design–test–measure–redesign being repeated as often as necessary.

These three principles are now accepted as the basis for a user-centered approach (e.g. see Mao *et al*, 2005) but when Gould and Lewis wrote their paper, they were not accepted by most developers. In fact, they remark in their paper that when they started recommending these to designers, the designers' reactions implied that these principles were obvious. However, when they asked designers at a human factors symposium for the major steps in software design, most of them did not cite many of the principles – in fact, only 2% mentioned all of them. So maybe they had obvious merit, but they were not so easy to put into practice. The Olympic Messaging System (OMS) (Gould *et al*, 1987) was the first reported large computer-based system to be developed using these three principles. Here a combination of techniques was used to elicit users' reactions to designs, from the earliest prototypes through to the final product. In this case, users were mainly involved in evaluating designs. Below, we discuss these principles in more detail.

Early Focus on Users and Tasks
This principle can be expanded and clarified through the following five further principles:

1. Users' tasks and goals are the driving force behind the development.
   In a user-centered approach to design, while technology will inform design options and choices, it should not be the driving force. Instead of saying 'Where can we deploy this new technology?' say 'What technologies are available to provide better support for users' goals?'

2. Users' behavior and context of use are studied and the system is designed to support them.
   This is about more than just capturing the tasks and the users' goals. How people perform their tasks is also significant. Understanding behavior highlights priorities, preferences, and implicit intentions. One argument against studying current behavior is that we are looking to improve work, not to capture bad habits in automation. The implication is that exposing designers to users is likely to stifle innovation and creativity, but experience tells us that the opposite is true (Beyer and Holtzblatt, 1998). In addition, if something is designed to support an activity with little understanding of the real work involved, it is likely to be incompatible with current practice, and users don't like to deviate from their learned habits if operating a new device with similar properties (Norman, 2013).

3. Users' characteristics are captured and designed for.
   When things go wrong with technology, we often say that it is our fault. But as humans, we are prone to making errors and we have certain limitations, both cognitive and physical. Products designed to support humans should take these limitations into account and should limit the mistakes we make. Cognitive aspects such as attention, memory, and

perception issues were introduced in Chapter 3. Physical aspects include height, mobility, and strength. Some characteristics are general, such as about one man in 12 has some form of color blindness, but some characteristics may be associated more with the job or particular task at hand. So, as well as general characteristics, we need to capture those specific to the intended user group.

4. Users are consulted throughout development from earliest phases to the latest and their input is seriously taken into account. As discussed above, there are different levels of user involvement and there are different ways in which to consult users. However involvement is organized, it is important that users are respected by designers.

5. All design decisions are taken within the context of the users, their work, and their environment. This does not necessarily mean that users are actively involved in design decisions. As long as designers remain aware of the users while making their decisions, then this principle will be upheld. Keeping this context in mind can be difficult, but using personas is one way to achieve this (see Chapter 10); an easily accessible collection of gathered data is another. Some design teams set up a specific design room for the project where data and informal records of brainstorming sessions are pinned on the walls or left on the table.

ACTIVITY 9.2

Assume that you are involved in developing a novel online experience for buying garden plants. Although several websites exist for buying plants online, you want to produce a distinct experience to increase the organization's market share. Suggest ways of applying the above principles in this task.

Comment
To address the first three principles, you would need to find out about the tasks and goals, behavior, and characteristics of potential users of the new experience, together with any different contexts of use. Studying current users of existing online plant shops will provide some information, and will also identify some challenges to be addressed in the new experience. However, as you want to increase the organization's market share, consulting existing users alone would not be enough. Alternative avenues for investigation include physical shopping situations – for example, shopping at the market, in the local corner shop, and so on. These alternatives will help you find advantages and disadvantages of buying plants in different settings and you will observe different behaviors. By looking at these, a new set of potential users and contexts can be identified.

For the fourth principle, the set of new users will emerge as investigations progress, but people who are representative of the user group may be accessible from the beginning. Workshops or evaluation sessions could be run with them, possibly in one of the alternative shopping environments such as the market. The last principle could be supported through the creation of a design room that houses all the data collected, and is a place where the development team can go to find out more about the users and the product goals. ■

Empirical Measurement

Specific usability and user experience goals should be identified, clearly documented, and agreed upon at the beginning of the project. They can help designers to choose between alternative designs and to check on progress as the product is developed. Identifying specific goals up front means that the product can be empirically evaluated at regular stages as it is developed.

Iterative Design

Iteration allows designs to be refined based on feedback. As users and designers engage with the domain and start to discuss requirements, needs, hopes, and aspirations, then different insights into what is needed, what will help, and what is feasible will emerge. This leads to a need for iteration, for the activities to inform each other and to be repeated. However good the designers are and however clear the users may think their vision is of the required artifact, it will be necessary to revise ideas in light of feedback, several times. This is particularly true when trying to innovate. Innovation rarely emerges whole and ready to go. It takes time, evolution, trial and error, and a great deal of patience. Iteration is inevitable because designers never get the solution right the first time (Gould and Lewis, 1985).

9.2.4   Four Basic Activities of Interaction Design

Four basic activities for interaction design were introduced in Chapter 1, some of which you will have engaged in when doing Activity 9.1. These are: establishing requirements for the user experience, designing alternatives that meet those requirements, prototyping the alternative designs so that they can be communicated and assessed, and evaluating what is being built throughout the process and the user experience it offers. They are fairly generic activities and can be found in other design disciplines too, such as graphic design, architectural design, and product design.

Establishing Requirements

In order to design something to support people, we must know who our target users are and what kind of support an interactive product could usefully provide. These needs form the basis of the product's requirements and underpin subsequent design and development. This activity is fundamental to a user-centered approach, and is very important in interaction design. Understanding these needs is gleaned through data gathering and analysis, which are discussed in Chapters 7 and 8. The requirements activity is discussed further in Chapter 10.

Designing Alternatives

This is the core activity of designing: actually suggesting ideas for meeting the requirements. This activity can be viewed as two sub-activities: conceptual design and concrete design. Conceptual design involves producing the conceptual model for the product, and a conceptual model describes an abstraction outlining what people can do with a product and what concepts are needed to understand how to interact with it. Concrete design considers the detail of the product including the colors, sounds, and images to use, menu design, and icon design. Alternatives are considered at every point. You met some of the ideas for conceptual design in Chapter 2, and some more design issues for specific interface types in Chapter 6; we go into more detail about how to design an interactive product in Chapter 11.

Prototyping
Interaction design involves designing interactive products. The most sensible way for users to evaluate such designs is to interact with them, and this can be achieved through prototyping. This does not necessarily mean a piece of software is required. There are different prototyping techniques, not all of which require a working piece of software. For example, paper-based prototypes are very quick and cheap to build and are very effective for identifying problems in the early stages of design, and through role-playing users can get a real sense of what it will be like to interact with the product. Prototyping is also covered in Chapter 11.

Evaluating
Evaluation is the process of determining the usability and acceptability of the product or design that is measured in terms of a variety of usability and user experience criteria. Interaction design requires a high level of user involvement throughout development, and this enhances the chances of an acceptable product being delivered. Evaluation does not replace the activities concerned with quality assurance and testing to make sure that the final product is fit for purpose, but it complements and enhances them. We devote Chapters 13 to 15 to evaluation.

The activities of establishing requirements, designing alternatives, building prototypes, and evaluating them are intertwined: alternatives are evaluated through the prototypes and the results are fed back into further design or might identify missing requirements. This iteration is one of the key characteristics of a user-centered approach.

9.2.5   A Simple Lifecycle Model for Interaction Design
Understanding what activities are involved in interaction design is the first step to being able to do it, but it is also important to consider how the activities are related to one another so that the full development process can be seen. The term lifecycle model is used to represent a model that captures a set of activities and how they are related. Software engineering has spawned many lifecycle models including the waterfall, spiral, and RAD (rapid applications development) models (Sommerville, 2010). One lifecycle model that was not widely used, but which was intended to capture the iterative nature of software development, was called the fountain lifecycle model (Henderson-Sellers and Edwards, 1993). The field of HCI has also been associated with several lifecycle models such as the Star (Hartson and Hix, 1989) and an international standard model ISO 9241-210.

Existing models have varying levels of sophistication and complexity. For projects involving only a few experienced developers, a simple process would probably be adequate. However, for larger systems involving tens or hundreds of developers with hundreds or thousands of users, a simple process just isn't enough to provide the management structure and discipline necessary to engineer a usable product. So something is needed that will provide more formality and more discipline (described in Box 9.1 as the systems design approach to interaction design). Note that this does not necessarily mean that innovation is lost or that creativity is stifled, just that a structured process is used to provide a more stable framework for creativity.

However simple or complex it appears, any lifecycle model is a simplified version of reality. It is intended as an abstraction and, as with any good abstraction, only the amount of detail required for the task at hand will be included. Any organization wishing to put a lifecycle model into practice will need to add detail specific to its particular circumstances and culture.

The activities of interaction design are related as shown in Figure 9.3. This model incorporates the four activities of interaction design and the three principles of user-centered design discussed above. Depending on the kind of product being developed, it may not be possible or appropriate to follow this model for every aspect, and more detail would be required to put the lifecycle into practice in a real project. We have not specified outputs from each activity, although measurable usability and user experience criteria would be specified early on and referred to across all the activities.

The model is not intended to be prescriptive; that is, we are not suggesting that this is how all interactive products are or should be developed. It is based on our observations of interaction design and on information we have gleaned in the research for this book. It has its roots in the software engineering and HCI lifecycle models mentioned above and it represents what we believe is practiced in the field.

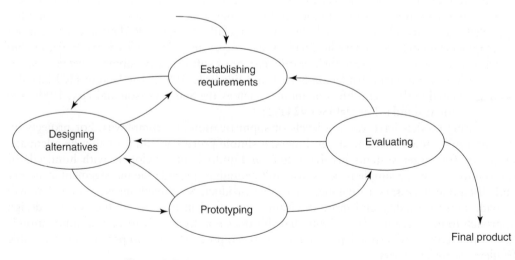

Figure 9.3 A simple interaction design lifecyle model

Most projects start by establishing requirements. The project may have arisen because of some evaluation that has been done, but the lifecycle of the new (or modified) product can be thought of as starting at this point. From this activity, some alternative designs are generated in an attempt to meet the requirements that have been identified. Then prototype versions of the designs are developed and evaluated. Based on the feedback from the evaluations, the team may need to return to identify more needs or refine requirements, or it may go straight into redesigning. It may be that more than one alternative design follows this iterative cycle in parallel with others, or it may be that one alternative at a time is considered. Implicit in this cycle is that the final product will emerge in an evolutionary fashion from a rough initial idea through to the finished product. Exactly how this evolution happens may vary from project to project, and we return to this issue in Chapter 11. The only factor limiting the number of times through the cycle is the resources available, but whatever the number is, development ends with an evaluation activity that ensures the final product meets the prescribed user experience and usability criteria.

9.3 Some Practical Issues

The discussion so far has highlighted some issues about the practical application of user-centered design and the simple lifecycle of interaction design that we have introduced. These issues must be addressed in order to be able to do interaction design in practice. We capture these issues in the following questions:

- Who are the users?
- What do we mean by needs?
- How do you generate alternative designs?
- How do you choose among alternatives?
- How do you integrate interaction design activities with other lifecycle models?

9.3.1 Who Are the Users?
With all this emphasis on users and user involvement in the interaction design process, a fairly basic question to ask is 'Who are the users?'.

Identifying the users may seem like a straightforward activity, but in fact there are many interpretations of the term 'user,' and involving the right users is crucial to successful user-centered design. The most obvious definition is those people who interact directly with the product to achieve a task. Most people would agree with this definition; however, there are others who can also be thought of as users. For example, Holtzblatt and Jones (1993) include in their definition of users those who manage direct users, those who receive products from the system, those who test the system, those who make the purchasing decision, and those who use competitive products. Eason (1987) identifies three categories of user: primary, secondary, and tertiary. Primary users are those likely to be frequent hands-on users of the system; secondary users are occasional users or those who use the system through an intermediary; and tertiary users are those affected by the introduction of the system or who will influence its purchase.

The trouble is that there is a surprisingly wide collection of people who all have a stake in the development of a successful product. These people are called stakeholders. Stakeholders are "people or organizations who will be affected by the system and who have a direct or indirect influence on the system requirements" (Kotonya and Sommerville, 1998). Dix *et al* (2004) make an observation that is very pertinent to a user-centered view of development:

"It will frequently be the case that the formal 'client' who orders the system falls very low on the list of those affected. Be very wary of changes which take power, influence or control from some stakeholders without returning something tangible in its place."

The group of stakeholders for a particular product will be larger than the group of people normally thought of as users, although it will of course include users. Using the definition above, the group of stakeholders includes the development team itself as well as its managers, the direct users and their managers, recipients of the product's output, people who may lose their jobs because of the introduction of the new product, and so on (Sharp *et al*, 1999).

For example, consider again the travel planner in Activity 9.1. According to the description we gave you, the user group for the system has just one member: you. However, the stakeholders for the system would also include the people you are going to visit, the airlines you book flights with, staff in the hotels you might stay at, a wide selection of companies and staff members who have an interest to make sure that any information you are given is correct, and even the restaurants on the route chosen for your journey, since the route suggested by the system will determine whether or not you drive past those restaurants.

Identifying the stakeholders for your project means that you can make an informed decision about who should be involved and to what degree, but how to make sure that you include stakeholders who are relevant is more complex. Alexander and Robertson (2004) suggest using an onion diagram to model stakeholders and their involvement. This diagram shows concentric circles of stakeholder zones with the product being developed sitting in the middle. Lim *et al* (2010) developed a process and supporting tool called StakeNet which relies on recommendations through social networking to identify and prioritize relevant stakeholders. Ellen Gottesdiener expands on the role of stakeholders in her interview at the end of this chapter.

ACTIVITY 9.3

Who are the stakeholders for an automated check-out system of a large supermarket?

Comment

First, there are the customers. Their stake in the success and usability of the system is fairly clear and direct. Customers want the system to work properly so that they are charged the right amount for the goods, receive the correct receipt, and can purchase their goods quickly and efficiently without any frustrations. Then there are the check-out assistants. These are the people who are available to help customers if they have any problems. Check-out assistants want the customers to be satisfied and happy so that they don't have to deal with anyone grumpy. Outside of this group are supermarket managers and supermarket owners, who also want the assistants to be happy and the customers to be satisfied and not complaining. They also don't want to lose money because the system can't handle the payments correctly. Other people who will be affected by the success of the system include other supermarket employees such as warehouse staff, supermarket suppliers, supermarket owners' families, and local shop owners whose business would be affected by the success or failure of the system. We wouldn't suggest that you should ask the local shop owner about requirements for the supermarket check-out system. However, you might want to talk to warehouse staff, especially if the system links in with stock control or other functions. ◼

9.3.2   What Do We Mean by 'Needs'?

If you had asked someone in the street in the late 1990s what she needed, I doubt that the answer would have included interactive television, or a ski jacket with integrated MP3 player, or a robot pet. If you presented the same person with these possibilities and asked whether she would buy them if they were available, then the answer may have been more positive. When we talk about identifying needs, it is not simply a question of asking people, 'What do you need?' and then supplying it, because people don't necessarily know what is possible. Robertson and Robertson (2013) refer to 'un-dreamed-of' needs, which are those that users are unaware they could have. Instead, we have to approach it by understanding the characteristics and capabilities of the users, what they are trying to achieve, how they achieve it currently, and whether they would achieve their goals more effectively and have a more enjoyable experience if they were supported differently.

There are many dimensions along which a user's characteristics and capabilities may vary, and that will have an impact on the product's design. You have met some of the cognitive ones in Chapter 3. A person's physical characteristics may also affect the design: size of hands may affect the size and positioning of input buttons, and motor abilities may affect the suitability of certain input and output devices; height is relevant in designing a physical kiosk, for example; and strength in designing a child's toy – a toy should not require too much strength to operate, but may require strength greater than expected for the target age group to change batteries or perform other operations suitable only for an adult. Cultural diversity and experience may affect the terminology the intended user group is used to, or how nervous about technology a set of users may be, or how a facility is used (we discuss user requirements in more detail in Chapter 10).

If a product is a new invention, then it can be difficult to identify the users and representative tasks for them, e.g. before in-car navigation systems were first developed, there were no users to consult about requirements and there were no representative tasks to identify. Those developing the system had to imagine who might want to use it and what they might want to do with it.

It may be tempting for designers simply to design what they would like to use themselves, but their ideas would not necessarily coincide with those of the target user group, because they have different experiences and expectations. It is imperative that representative users from the real target group be consulted. For example, Netpliance developed a new product that would seamlessly integrate all the services necessary for the user to achieve a specific task on the Internet (Isensee et al, 2000). They took a user-centered approach and employed focus group studies and surveys to understand their customers' needs, but developers observed the focus groups to learn more about their intended user group. Isensee et al (p. 60) comment that, "It is always tempting for developers to create products they would want to use or similar to what they have done before."

Whether the product is a new invention or not, it is always useful to start by understanding similar behavior that is already established. Introducing something new into people's lives, especially a new everyday item, requires a culture change in the target user population, and it takes a long time to effect a culture change.

Focusing on people's goals and on usability and user experience goals is a more promising approach to interaction design than focusing on people's needs and expecting them to be able to tell us the requirements for a product. Techniques for data gathering to investigate these goals and to establish requirements are discussed more in Chapters 7 and 10.

9.3.3   How Do You Generate Alternative Designs?

A common human tendency is to stick with something that we know works. We recognize that a better solution may exist out there somewhere, but it is very easy to accept this one because we know it works – it is 'good enough.' Settling for a solution that is good enough is not necessarily bad, but it may be undesirable because good alternatives may never be considered, and considering alternative solutions is a crucial step in the process of design. But where do these alternative ideas come from?

One answer to this question is that they come from the individual designer's flair and creativity (the genius design described in Box 9.1). Although it is certainly true that some people are able to produce wonderfully inspired designs while others struggle to come up with any ideas at all, very little in this world is completely new. For example, if you think of something commonly believed to be an invention, such as the steam engine, this was in fact inspired by the observation that the steam from a kettle boiling on the stove lifted the lid. Clearly there was an amount of creativity and engineering involved in making the jump from a boiling kettle to a steam engine, but the kettle provided the inspiration to translate experience gained in one context into a set of principles that could be applied in another. Innovations usually arise through cross-fertilization of ideas from different perspectives, individuals, and contexts; the evolution of an existing product through use and observation; or straightforward copying of other, similar products.

Cross-fertilization may result by discussing ideas with other designers, while Buxton (2007) reports that different perspectives from users generated original ideas about alternative designs. As an example of evolution, consider the word processor. The capabilities of suites of office software have gradually increased from the time they first appeared. Initially, a word processor was just an electronic version of a typewriter, but gradually other capabilities, including the spell-checker, thesaurus, style sheets, graphical capabilities, and so on, were added.

Although creativity and invention are often wrapped in mystique, we do understand something of the process and of how creativity can be enhanced or inspired. We know, for instance, that browsing a collection of designs will inspire designers to consider alternative perspectives, and hence alternative solutions. The field of case-based reasoning (Maher and Pu, 1997) emerged from the observation that designers solve new problems by drawing on knowledge gained from solving previous similar problems. As Schank (1982, p. 22) puts it, "An expert is someone who gets reminded of just the right prior experience to help him in processing his current experiences." And while those experiences may be the designer's own, they can equally well be others'.

Another approach to creativity has been taken by Maiden *et al* (2007a). They have been running creativity workshops to generate innovative requirements in an air traffic management (ATM) application domain. Their idea is to introduce experts in different fields into the workshop, and then invite stakeholders to identify analogies between their own field and this new one. For example, they have invited an Indian textile expert, a musician, a TV program scheduler, and a museum exhibit designer. Although not all obviously analogical domains, they sparked creative ideas for the air traffic management application. For example, participants reported that one textile design was elegant, i.e. simple, beautiful, and symmetrical. They then transferred these properties to a key area of the ATM domain – that of aircraft conflict resolution. They explored the meaning of elegance within this context, and realized that elegance is perceived differently by different controllers. From this they generated the requirement that the system should be able to accommodate different air traffic controller styles during conflict resolution.

A more pragmatic answer to this question, then, is that alternatives come from seeking different perspectives and looking at other designs. The process of inspiration and creativity can be enhanced by prompting a designer's own experience and studying others' ideas and suggestions. Deliberately seeking out suitable sources of inspiration is a valuable step in any design process. These sources may be very close to the intended new product, such as competitors' products, or they may be earlier versions of similar systems, or something completely different.

Having said this, under some circumstances the scope to consider alternative designs may be limited. Design is a process of balancing constraints and constantly trading off one set of requirements with another, and the constraints may be such that there are very few viable alternatives available. For example, if you are designing a software system to run under the Windows operating system, then elements of the design will be prescribed because you must conform to the Windows look and feel, and to other constraints intended to make Windows programs consistent for the user. If you are producing an upgrade to an existing system, then you may want to keep the familiar elements of it and retain basically the same user experience.

ACTIVITY 9.4

Consider again the travel planner introduced at the beginning of the chapter. Reflecting on the process again, what do you think inspired your outline design? See if you can identify any elements within it that you believe are truly innovative.

Comment
For my design, I was heavily influenced by existing sources of travel information, and what I see as the flaws in them. For example, having to always enter my home train station when I go to the online timetable (and never remembering that there are two different stations that have to be distinguished) is a hassle. I thought it would be good if the system remembered that piece of information, together with other personal details, such as always ordering a vegetarian meal on a flight.

Some of the things you might have been thinking about include your existing timetables, brochures, and tickets. Maybe you regularly use a website to book flights or accommodation; there are many different kinds available. I'm not sure how innovative my ideas were, but the key thing for me was to have the application tailor its advice to me and my habits. There are probably other aspects that make your design unique to you and which may be innovative to a greater or lesser degree. ■

BOX 9.4

A box full of ideas

The innovative product design company IDEO was introduced in Chapter 1. Underlying some of their creative flair is a collection of weird and wonderful engineering housed in a large flatbed filing cabinet called the TechBox (see Figure 9.4). The TechBox holds hundreds of gizmos and interesting materials, divided into categories such as: Amazing Materials, Cool Mechanisms, Interesting Manufacturing Processes, Electronic Technologies, and Thermal and Optical. Each item has been placed in the box because it represents a neat idea or a new process. Staff at IDEO take along a selection of items from the TechBox to brainstorming meetings. The items may be chosen because they provide useful visual props or possible solutions to a particular issue, or simply to provide some light relief.

Each item is clearly labeled with its name and category, but further information can be found by accessing the TechBox's online catalog. Each item has its own page detailing what the item is, why it is interesting, where it came from, and who has used it or knows more about it. Items in the box include an example of metal-coated wood, and materials with and without holes that stretch, bend, and change shape or color at different temperatures.

Each of IDEO's offices has a TechBox and each TechBox has its own curator who is responsible for maintaining and cataloging the items and for promoting its use within the office. Anyone can submit a new item for consideration, and as items become commonplace they are removed from the TechBox to make way for the next generation of fascinating curios. ∎

Figure 9.4 The TechBox at IDEO

Source: Reproduced by permission of IDEO. Photo by Jorge Davies.

DILEMMA
Copying for inspiration: Is it legal?

Designers draw on their experience of design when approaching a new project. This includes the use of previous designs that they know work, both designs they have created themselves and those that others have created. Others' creations often spark inspiration that also leads to new ideas and innovation. This is well known and understood. However, the expression of an idea is protected by copyright, and people who infringe that copyright can be taken to court and prosecuted. Note that copyright covers the expression of an idea and not the idea itself. This means, for example, that while there are numerous MP3 players all with similar functionality, this does not represent an infringement of copyright as the idea has been expressed in different ways, and it is the expression that has been copyrighted. Copyright is free and is automatically invested in the author of something, e.g. the writer of a book or a programmer who develops a program, unless he signs the copyright over to someone else. People who produce something through their employment, such as programs or products, may have in their employment contract a statement saying that the copyright relating to anything produced in the course of that employment is automatically assigned to the employer and does not remain with the employee.

Patenting is an alternative to copyright that does protect the idea rather than the expression. There are various forms of patenting, each of which is designed to allow the inventor the chance to capitalize on an idea. It is unusual for software to be patented, since it is a long, slow, and expensive process, although there have been some examples of patenting business processes. For example, Amazon has patented its one-click purchasing process, which allows regular users simply to choose a purchase and buy it with one mouse click (US Patent No. 5960411, September 29, 1999). This is possible because the system stores its customers' details and recognizes them when they access the Amazon site again.

In recent years, the creative commons community (creativecommons.org) has suggested more flexible licensing arrangements that allow others to reuse and extend a piece of created work, thereby supporting collaboration. In the Open Source software development movement, for example, software code is freely distributed and can be modified, incorporated into other software, and redistributed under the same open source conditions. No royalty fees are payable on any use of open source code. These movements do not replace copyright or patent law, but they provide an alternative route for the dissemination of ideas.

So the dilemma comes in knowing when it is OK to use someone else's work as a source of inspiration and when you are infringing copyright or patent law. The issues around this question are complex and detailed, and well beyond the scope of this book, but up-to-date information and examples of law cases that have been brought successfully and unsuccessfully can be found in Bainbridge (2014). ■

9.3.4 How Do You Choose Among Alternative Designs?

Choosing among alternatives is about making design decisions: Will the device use keyboard entry or a touch screen? Will the product provide an automatic memory function or not? These decisions will be informed by the information gathered about users and their tasks, and by the technical feasibility of an idea. Broadly speaking, though, the decisions fall into two categories: those that are about externally visible and measurable features, and those that are about characteristics internal to the system that cannot be observed or measured without dissecting it. For example, in a photocopier, externally visible and measurable factors include the physical size of the machine, the speed and quality of copying, the different sizes of paper it can use, and so on. Underlying each of these factors are other considerations that cannot be observed or studied without dissecting the machine. For example, the choice of materials used in a photocopier may depend on its friction rating and how much it deforms under certain conditions.

In an interactive product there are similar factors that are externally visible and measurable and those that are hidden from the users' view. For example, exactly why it takes 30 seconds for a web page to load, or why it takes an hour for a cell phone text message to arrive, will be influenced by technical decisions made when the web page or cell phone software was constructed. From the users' viewpoint the important observation is the fact that it does take 30 seconds to load or an hour to arrive.

In interaction design, the way in which the users interact with the product is considered the driving force behind the design and so we concentrate on the externally visible and measurable behavior. Detailed internal workings are still important to the extent that they affect external behavior or features.

One answer to the question posed above is that we choose between alternative designs by letting users and stakeholders interact with them and by discussing their experiences, preferences, and suggestions for improvement. This is fundamental to a user-centered approach to development. This in turn means that the designs must be available in a form that can be reasonably evaluated with users, not in technical jargon or notation that seems impenetrable to them.

One form traditionally used for communicating a design is documentation, e.g. a description of how something will work or a diagram showing its components. The trouble is that a static description cannot easily capture the dynamics of behavior, and for an interactive product we need to communicate to the users what it will be like to actually operate it.

In many design disciplines, prototyping is used to overcome potential client misunderstandings and to test the technical feasibility of a suggested design and its production. Prototyping involves producing a limited version of the product with the purpose of answering specific questions about the design's feasibility or appropriateness. Prototypes give a better impression of the user experience than simple descriptions, and there are different kinds of prototyping that are suitable for different stages of development and for eliciting different kinds of information. Prototyping is discussed in detail in Chapter 11.

Another basis on which to choose between alternatives is quality, but this requires a clear understanding of what quality means. People's views of what is a quality product vary. Whenever we use anything we have some notion of the level of quality we are expecting, wanting, or needing. Whether this level of quality is expressed formally or informally does not matter. The point is that it exists and we use it consciously or subconsciously to evaluate alternative items. For example, if you have to wait too long to download a web page, then you are likely to give up and try a different site – you are applying a certain measure of quality associated with the time taken to download the web page. If one smartphone makes it easy to access your favorite music channel while another involves several complicated key sequences, then you are likely to buy the former rather than the latter. Here, you are applying a quality criterion concerned with efficiency.

If you are the only user of a product, then you don't necessarily have to express your definition of quality since you don't have to communicate it to anyone else. However, as we have seen, most projects involve many different stakeholder groups, and you will find that each of them has a different definition of quality and different acceptable limits for it. For example, although all stakeholders may agree on targets such as 'response time will be fast' or 'the menu structure will be easy to use,' exactly what each of them means by this is likely to vary. Disputes are inevitable when, later in development, it transpires that 'fast' to one set of stakeholders meant 'under a second' while to another it meant 'between 2 and 3 seconds.' Capturing these different views in clear unambiguous language early in development takes you halfway to producing a product that will be well-regarded by all your stakeholders. It helps to clarify expectations, provides a benchmark against which products of the development process can be measured, and gives you a basis on which to choose among alternatives.

The process of writing down formal, verifiable – and hence measurable – usability criteria is a key characteristic of an approach to interaction design called usability engineering. This has emerged over many years and with various proponents (Whiteside *et al*, 1988; Nielsen, 1993). Usability engineering involves specifying quantifiable measures of product performance, documenting them in a usability specification, and assessing the product against them. One way in which this approach is used is to make changes to subsequent versions of a system based on feedback from carefully documented results of usability tests for the earlier version.

ACTIVITY 9.5

Consider the travel planner that you designed in Activity 9.1. Suggest some usability criteria that you could use to determine the planner's quality. Use the usability goals introduced in Chapter 1: effectiveness, efficiency, safety, utility, learnability, and memorability. Be as specific as possible. Check your criteria by considering exactly what you would measure and how you would measure its performance.

Then try to do the same thing for some of the user experience goals introduced in Chapter 1 (these relate to whether a system is satisfying, enjoyable, motivating, rewarding, and so on).

Comment
Finding measurable characteristics for some of these is not easy. Here are some suggestions, but you may have found others. Where possible, criteria must be measurable and specific.

- Effectiveness: Identifying measurable criteria for this goal is particularly difficult since it is a combination of the other goals. For example, does the system support you in traveling to places, booking accommodation, and so on? In other words, is the planner used?
- Efficiency: When you ask for recommendations from the planner, what is the response time for identifying a suitable hotel or flight details?
- Safety: How often does data get lost or do you choose the wrong option? This may be measured, for example, as the number of times this happens per hour of use.

(Continued)

- Utility: How many functions offered by the planner are used every week, how many every month, how many every two months? How many tasks are difficult to complete in a reasonable time because functionality is missing or the planner doesn't support the right subtasks?
- Learnability: How long does it take for a novice user to be able to do a series of set tasks, e.g. book a hotel room in Paris for a particular date, identify appropriate flights from Sydney to Wellington, find out whether you need a visa to go to China?
- Memorability: If the planner isn't used for a month, how many functions can you remember how to perform? How long does it take you to remember how to perform your most frequent task?

Finding measurable characteristics for the user experience criteria is harder. How do you measure satisfaction, fun, motivation, or aesthetics? What is entertaining to one person may be boring to another; these kinds of criteria are subjective, and so cannot be measured as objectively. ■

9.3.5   How Do You Integrate Interaction Design Activities with Other Lifecycle Models?

There are several lifecycle models associated with other disciplines that contribute to interaction design (see Figure 1.4). Prominent among these lifecycle models are those associated with software engineering. Discussion about how best to integrate user-centered design and software engineering, and how to raise awareness of user-centered techniques with software engineers has been ongoing for several years, e.g. see Seffah *et al* (2005).

The latest, and some would argue the most promising, attempts at integration focus on a relatively recent trend in software engineering, called agile software development. Agile methods began to emerge in the late 1990s. The most well known of these are eXtreme Programming (Beck and Andres, 2005), Crystal (Cockburn, 2005), Scrum (Schwaber and Beedle, 2002), and Adaptive Software Development (ASD) (Highsmith, 2000). Dynamic Systems Development Method (DSDM) (DSDM, 2014), although established before the current agile movement, also belongs to the agile family as it adheres to the agile manifesto (reproduced below). These methods differ, but they all stress the importance of iteration, early and repeated user feedback, being able to handle emergent requirements, and striking a good balance between flexibility and structure. They also all emphasize collaboration, face-to-face communication, streamlined processes to avoid unnecessary activities, and the importance of practice over process, i.e. of getting work done.

The opening statement for the *Manifesto for Agile Software Development* (www.agilemanifesto.org/) is:

> *We are uncovering better ways of developing software by doing it and helping others do it. Through this work we have come to value:*
>
> *Individuals and interactions over processes and tools*
> *Working software over comprehensive documentation*
> *Customer collaboration over contract negotiation*
> *Responding to change over following a plan*

This manifesto is underpinned by a series of principles, which range from communication with the business through to excellence of coding and maximizing the amount of work done. The agile approach to development is particularly interesting from the point of view of interaction design because it incorporates tight iterations and feedback, and collaboration with the customer (e.g. Armitage, 2004; Sharp *et al*, 2006). For example, in eXtreme[1] Programming (XP), each iteration is between one and three weeks, with a product of value being delivered at the end of each iteration. Also, XP stipulates that the customer should be on site with developers. In practice, the customer role is usually taken by a team rather than one person (Martin *et al*, 2009), and integration is far from straightforward (Ferreira *et al*, 2012). Several companies have integrated agile methods with interaction design practices to produce better quality products. Chapter 12 discusses this aspect in more detail.

One of the main proponents for integrating user-centered design and agile development in practice, Jeff Patton, has articulated several patterns of common behaviors for successful agile product development, including the importance of designers being part of the team, using parallel tracks with user research, doing just enough user research, modeling and design up front, buying design time when developers are working on complex engineering stories, and cultivating a user group for continuous user validation. Although they first appeared a while ago, these still represent good and practical advice.

> **Link** to see Jeff Patton's common behaviours for successful agile product development at **http://tinyurl.com/3rfnm2**

These recommendations are echoed in a report from the Nielsen Norman Group (Nielsen Norman Group, 2014) who conducted a study of agile projects, investigating case studies in depth from 16 organizations who care about user experience and who have also embraced an agile approach to development. They make two main recommendations for success: have development and design running in separate tracks (as described in Figure 12.2 in Chapter 12) and maintain a coherent vision of the interface architecture (also see Kollmann *et al*, 2009).

Assignment

Nowadays, timepieces (such as clocks, wristwatches, etc.) have a variety of functions. They not only tell the time and date but they can speak to you, remind you when it's time to do something, and provide a light in the dark, among other things. Mostly, the interface for these devices, however, shows the time in one of two basic ways: as a digital number such as 23:40 or through an analog display with two or three hands – one to represent the hour, one for the minutes, and one for the seconds.

In this assignment, we want you to design an innovative timepiece for your own use. This could be in the form of a wristwatch, a mantelpiece clock, an electronic clock, or any other

(Continued)

---

[1]The method is called 'extreme' because it pushes a key set of good practices to the limit, i.e. it is good practice to test often, so in XP the development is test-driven and a complete set of tests is executed many times a day; it is good practice to talk to people about their requirements, so rather than having weighty documentation, XP reduces documentation to a minimum, thus forcing communication, and so on.

kind of timepiece you fancy. Your goal is to be inventive and exploratory. We have broken this assignment down into the following steps to make it clearer:

(a) Think about the interactive product you are designing: what do you want it to do for you? Find three to five potential users and ask them what they would want. Write a list of requirements for the clock, together with some usability criteria and user experience criteria based on the definitions in Chapter 1.

(b) Look around for similar devices and seek out other sources of inspiration that you might find helpful. Make a note of any findings that are interesting, useful, or insightful.

(c) Sketch out some initial designs for the timepiece. Try to develop at least two distinct alternatives that both meet your set of requirements.

(d) Evaluate the two designs, using your usability criteria and by role playing an interaction with your sketches. Involve potential users in the evaluation, if possible. Does it do what you want? Is the time or other information being displayed always clear? Design is iterative, so you may want to return to earlier elements of the process before you choose one of your alternatives.

Summary

In this chapter, we have looked at user-centered design and the process of interaction design, i.e. what is user-centered design, what activities are required in order to design an interactive product, and how are these activities related. A simple interaction design lifecycle model consisting of four activities was introduced and issues surrounding the involvement and identification of users, generating alternative designs, evaluating designs, and integrating user-centered concerns with other lifecycles were discussed.

Key points

- The interaction design process consists of four basic activities: establishing requirements, designing alternatives that meet those requirements, prototyping the designs so that they can be communicated and assessed, and evaluating them.
- User-centered design rests on three principles: early focus on users and tasks, empirical measurement, and iterative design. These principles are also key for interaction design.
- Involving users in the design process helps with expectation management and feelings of ownership, but how and when to involve users is a matter of dispute.
- Before you can begin to establish requirements, you must understand who the users are and what their goals are in using the product.
- Looking at others' designs and involving other people in design provides useful inspiration and encourages designers to consider alternative design solutions, which is key to effective design.
- Usability criteria, technical feasibility, and users' feedback on prototypes can all be used to choose among alternatives.
- Prototyping is a useful technique for facilitating user feedback on designs at all stages.
- Integrating interaction design activities with other lifecycle models requires careful planning.

Further Reading

GREENBAUM, J. and KYNG, M. (eds) (1991) *Design at Work: Co-operative design of computer systems*. Lawrence Erlbaum. This classic book is a good collection of papers about the co-design of software systems: both why it is worthwhile and early experiences of how to do it.

HIGHSMITH, J. (2002) *Agile Software Development Ecosystems*. Addison-Wesley. This book introduces the main agile methods and their proponents. Highsmith explains the motivation behind the agile approach to development and extracts some common themes. The book includes some case studies, and how you the reader can go about developing your own agile method that suits your own particular environment.

KELLEY, T., with LITTMAN, J. (2004) *The Art of Innovation*. Profile Books. Tom Kelley is general manager of IDEO. In this book, Kelley explains some of the innovative techniques used at IDEO, but more importantly he talks about the culture and philosophy underlying IDEO's success. There are some useful practical hints in here as well as an informative story about building and maintaining a successful design company.

NIELSEN, J. (1993) *Usability Engineering*. Morgan Kaufmann. This is a seminal book on usability engineering. If you want to find out more about the philosophy, intent, history, or pragmatics of usability engineering, then this is the main text.

SEFFAH, A., GULLIKSEN, J. and DESMARAIS, M. C. (2005) *Human-Centered Software Engineering*. Springer. This book is an edited collection of papers focusing on issues relating to the integration of user-centered design and software engineering. It is split into five parts: introduction; requirements, scenarios, and use cases; principles, myths, and challenges; user-centered design, unified, and agile processes; and user-centered design knowledge and UI design patterns. If you want to pursue the thorny issue of how to bring these two communities together, then this is a good starting point.

SOMMERVILLE, I. (2010) *Software Engineering* (9th edn). Addison-Wesley. If you are interested in pursuing the software engineering aspects of the lifecycle models section, then this book provides a useful overview of the main models and their purpose.

INTERVIEW
with Ellen Gottesdiener

Ellen Gottesdiener, EBG Consulting CEO/ Principal, helps organizations discover and deliver the right product at the right time. Ellen is an internationally recognized leader in the collaborative convergence of requirements management + product management + project management. In addition to working with clients, Ellen presents, writes, and trains globally. She is the author of three acclaimed books: *Discover to Deliver: Product Planning and Analysis* – co-authored with Mary Gorman (2012), *Requirements by Collaboration* (Addison-Wesley, 2002), and *The Software Requirements Memory Jogger* (Goal/QPC, 2005). Visit these websites for resources and more: www.ebgconsulting .com and www.DiscoverToDeliver.com

What are requirements?
Product requirements are needs that *must* be satisfied to achieve a goal, solve a problem, or take advantage of an opportunity. The word 'requirement' literally means something that is absolutely, positively, without question, necessary. Product requirements need to be defined in sufficient detail for planning and development. But before going to that effort and expense, are you sure they are not only must-haves but also the right and relevant requirements?

To arrive at this level of certainty, stakeholders ideally start by exploring the product's *options*. An option represents a potential characteristic, facet, or quality of the product. Stakeholders, who I like to refer to as product partners, use expansive thinking to surface a range of options that could fulfill the vision. Then they collaboratively analyze the options and collectively select options, based on value.

Every product has multiple dimensions, seven in fact. Discovering options for each of the 7 Product Dimensions yields a comprehensive, realistic view of the product. They are as follows.

Product dimension	Description
User	Users interact with the product
Interface	The product connects users, systems, and devices
Action	The product provides capabilities to users
Data	The product includes a repository of data and useful information
Control	The product enforces constraints
Environment	The product conforms to physical properties and technical platforms
Quality attribute	The product has certain properties that qualify its operation and development

(You can view and download an image here: http://tinyurl.com/m59lo9x

You want to engage diverse stakeholders across the full product lifecycle, from birth to retirement and demise.

So how do you know who the stakeholders are?

Successful teams work hand in hand with their stakeholders as *product partners*, defining value and then actively discovering – and delivering – high-value solutions. This goes beyond feature requests and requirements documents – beyond user stories and product backlogs – beyond the push-pull of competing interests. It's a partnership where the ideas, perspectives and experiences of three different stakeholder groups converge. The result? Product partners who collaborate to discover and deliver value.

A product partnership includes people from three realms: customer, business, and technology. Each offers a unique perspective and has its own ideas of what is valuable.

The *customer* partners represent users, buyers, and advisers – people or systems that interface with the product, choose to buy it, or influence others to buy it. They tend to value improved productivity, heightened efficiency, greater speed, entertainment, and similar benefits.

Business partners represent the people in your organization who authorize, champion, or support the product or who provide subject matter expertise. They find value in improving market position, complying with regulations, achieving a business case, reducing overhead costs, enhancing internal performance, and so on.

Technology partners (your delivery team, internal or third parties) design, deliver, test, and support the product or advise those who do. They may value building a high-quality product, offering smooth, continual delivery, adopting a stable architecture, and the like.

This mix of partners and perspectives is essential, no matter what kind of delivery method you adopt (agile, traditional, hybrid, or another approach). For the partnership to work, these three disparate groups must collaborate to reach their shared goal: discover and deliver value.

How do you go about identifying requirements?

Requirements discovery is highly proactive, interactive, and, well, sometimes hyperactive! You are engaged in eliciting, analyzing, specifying, prototyping, and testing. And in the best practices we've been involved in, you are constantly discovering (a.k.a. identifying) product needs. It's not a 'one-and-done' activity.

Elicitation includes interviews, existing documentation study, exploratory prototypes, facilitated workshops, focus groups, observation (including apprenticing, contextual inquiry, and ethnography), surveys (and other research-based techniques), and user task analysis (including storyboarding and scenario analysis). There are a number of specific techniques within each of these general categories, and some techniques overlap. Analyzing involves using lightweight models, often combined with specifications, which are often in the form of acceptance tests or prototypes or both.

It's not enough to get the right people together and ask the right questions. To communicate efficiently and effectively about how to deliver, product partners need a focused way to communicate and make decisions together.

What we've found in our work is that the most efficient and effective discovery mechanism is a collaborative approach called the 'structured conversation.' In a structured conversation, the product partners first *explore* possible requirements (options) for their next increment. They do this within and across the 7 Product Dimensions. This enables product partners to collaboratively and creatively explore a range of possibilities. This expansive thinking opens up product innovation, experimentation, and mutual learning.

They then *evaluate* these many options in terms of value. This means having shared understanding of what value really means at that point in time. Once they have narrowed the list of options through the evaluation process, they *confirm* how they will verify and validate these candidate solutions with unambiguous acceptance criteria. The validation includes how to test that they delivered the right requirements, and that they achieved the anticipated value from each delivery.

How do you know when you have collected enough requirements to go on to the next step?

I often get asked by clients how I know when I have a complete set of requirements. I think it's more important to ask whether you are going after the *right* requirements.

I characterize a 'right requirement' as one that is:

1. **Just in time, just enough.** It is essential for achieving the business objectives, in this time period.
2. **Realistic.** It is capable of being delivered with the available resources.
3. **Clearly and unambiguously defined.** Acceptance criteria exist that all partners understand and will use to verify and validate the product.
4. **Valuable.** It is indispensable for achieving the anticipated outcomes for the next delivery cycle.

What's the hardest thing about establishing requirements?

People.

Seriously.

We humans are non-linear creatures. We are unpredictable, fickle, and (as adults) often inflexible. As requirements seekers, we swim in a stew of complex, ever-evolving human systems that interoperate as we do our requirements work.

To top that off, most products' requirements are fraught with complexity and interdependency; there are truly wicked problems, whereby the problem space overlaps with solution space. As Frederick Brooks said [in his essay *No Silver Bullet*], "the hardest single part of building a software system is deciding precisely what to build."

You can't make those decisions without trust. And trust is not an easy thing to build.

Do you have any other tips for establishing requirements?

Employ small, tightly wound cycles of requirements-build-release. Use interactive and incremental (a.k.a. agile) practices to get feedback early and often on the smallest viable releases.

For successful requirements discovery, you need to keep the focus on value – the *why* behind the product and the value considerations of the product partners. During discovery work, some people view a specific option as a 'requirement' for the next delivery cycle, whereas others consider it a 'wish list' item for a future release.

Such was the case in a recent release planning workshop. The team wrestled with a particular option, questioning if it could deliver enough value to justify the cost to develop it. The product champion explained why the option was a requirement – without it the organization was at risk for regulatory noncompliance. Once the others understood this, they all agreed it would be included in the release.

In the end, requirements work is human-centric, and central to successful product delivery. At the same time, the subject matter and content of product requirements is complex. Thus, requirements work is the hardest part of software and will always be.

To be successful with requirements, engineer collaboration into requirements work.

Personally, I'm excited and grateful for the growing recognition of the value of collaboration and the explosion in interest in collaborative practices in the product and software development community – because: collaboration works! ∎

Chapter 10

ESTABLISHING REQUIREMENTS

Objectives

The main aims of this chapter are to:

- Describe different kinds of requirements.
- Enable you to identify different kinds of requirements from a simple description.
- Explain how different data gathering techniques (those introduced in Chapter 7 and others) may be used during the requirements activity.
- Enable you to develop a scenario, a use case, and an essential use case from a simple description.
- Enable you to perform hierarchical task analysis on a simple description.

10.1   Introduction

An interaction design project may aim to replace or update an established system, or it may aim to develop a totally innovative product with no obvious precedent. There may be an initial set of requirements, or the project may have to begin by producing a set of requirements from scratch. Whatever the initial situation and whatever the aim of the project, the users' needs, requirements, aspirations, and expectations have to be discussed, refined, clarified, and probably re-scoped. This requires an understanding of, among other things, the users and their capabilities, their current tasks and goals, the conditions under which the product will be used, and constraints on the product's performance.

Establishing requirements is not simply writing a wish list of features. Given the iterative nature of interaction design, isolating requirements activities from design activities and from evaluation activities is a little artificial, since in practice they are all intertwined: some design will take place while requirements are being established, and the design will evolve through a series of evaluation–redesign cycles. However, each of these activities can be distinguished by its own emphasis and its own techniques.

This chapter provides a more detailed overview of establishing requirements. We introduce different kinds of requirements and explain some useful techniques.

10.2   What, How, and Why?

10.2.1   What Are We Trying to Achieve in the Requirements Activity?

There are two aims. One aim is to understand as much as possible about the users, their activities, and the context of that activity, so the system under development can support them in achieving their goals. Building on this, our second aim is to produce a set of stable requirements that form a sound basis to start designing. This is not necessarily a major document, nor a set of rigid prescriptions, but it must not change radically in the time it takes to do some design and get feedback on the ideas. Because the end goal is to produce this set of requirements, we shall sometimes refer to this as the requirements activity.

10.2.2   How Can We Achieve This?

At the beginning of the requirements activity, there is a lot to find out and to clarify. At the end of the activity we will have a set of stable requirements that can be the basis of the design activity. In the middle, there are activities concerned with data gathering, analysis, interpretation, and presentation, with the aim of expressing the findings as requirements. Broadly speaking, these activities progress in a sequential manner: first gather some data, then analyze and interpret it, and then extract some requirements from it. But it gets a lot messier than this, and the activities influence one another as the process iterates. Once you start data analysis, you will need to gather more data to clarify or confirm your findings. Also, the way in which requirements are presented may affect your analysis, since it will enable you to identify and express some aspects more easily than others (as discussed in Section 8.7). For example, using a notation which emphasizes the data characteristics of a situation will lead the analysis to focus on this aspect rather than, for example, on task structure. Chapter 7 emphasized that it is valuable to use a complementary set of data gathering and analysis techniques. As we discuss below, there are different kinds of requirements, and each can be emphasized or de-emphasized by different techniques.

Establishing requirements is itself an iterative activity in which the subactivities inform and refine one another. It does not last for a set number of weeks or months and then finish. In practice, requirements evolve and develop as the stakeholders interact with designs and see what is possible and how certain facilities can help them. And as shown in the lifecycle model in Chapter 9, the activity itself will be repeatedly revisited.

10.2.3   Why Bother? The Importance of Getting it Right

Much has been written about the significant cost of fixing errors late in the software development cycle rather than early, during the requirements activity. For example, Davis

(1995) identifies insufficient user communication, poor specifications, and insufficient analysis as contributors to poor cost estimation. Boehm and Basili (2001) present a top ten list of software defect reduction findings, the first of which states that "finding and fixing a software problem after delivery is often 100 times more expensive than finding and fixing it during the requirements and design phase."

The cartoon below illustrates very well what can go wrong if requirements are not clearly articulated.

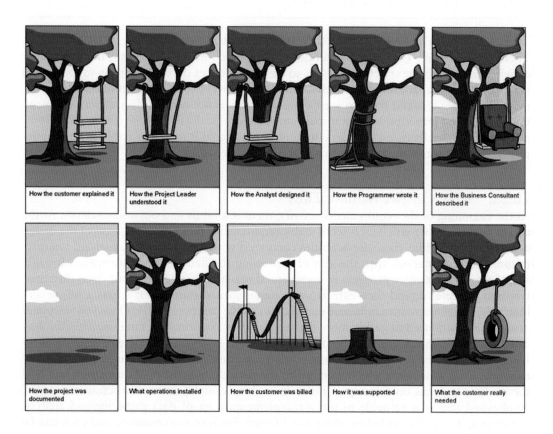

10.2.4 Why 'Establish' Requirements?

The activity of understanding what a product should do has been given various labels – for example, requirements gathering, requirements capture, requirements elicitation, requirements analysis, and requirements engineering. The first two imply that requirements exist out there and we simply need to pick them up or catch them. Elicitation implies that others (presumably the clients or users) know the requirements and we have to get them to tell us. Requirements, however, are not that easy to identify. You might argue that, in some cases, customers must know what the requirements are because they know the tasks that need supporting. However, they may not have articulated requirements as yet, and even if they have an initial set, they probably have not explored them in sufficient detail for development to begin.

The term requirements analysis is normally used to describe the activity of investigating and analyzing an initial set of requirements that have been gathered, elicited, or captured. Analyzing the information gathered is an important step, since it is this interpretation of the facts, rather than the facts themselves, that inspires the design. Requirements engineering is a better term than the others because it recognizes that developing a set of requirements is an iterative process of evolution and negotiation, and one that needs to be carefully managed and controlled.

We chose the term establishing requirements to represent the fact that requirements have been established from a sound understanding of the users' needs and that they can be justified by and related back to the data collected. Current concerns with cross-cultural design have highlighted the importance of understanding who you are designing for, their specific circumstances, and how to enrich their lifestyles (Chavan *et al*, 2009).

10.3   What Are Requirements?

A requirement is a statement about an intended product that specifies what it should do or how it should perform. One of the aims of the requirements activity is to make the requirements as specific, unambiguous, and clear as possible. For example, a requirement for a smartwatch GPS app might be that the time to load a map is less than half a second. Another, less precise, example might be that teenagers should find the smartwatch appealing. In the case of this latter example, further investigation would be necessary to explore exactly what teenagers would find appealing. Requirements come in many different forms and at many different levels of abstraction, but we need to make sure that the requirements are as clear as possible and that we understand how to tell when they have been fulfilled. The example requirement shown in Figure 10.1 is expressed using a format called an atomic requirements shell from the Volere process (Robertson and Robertson, 2013). This shell requires quite a bit of information about the requirement itself, including something called a fit criterion, which is a way of measuring when the solution meets the requirement. In Chapter 9 we emphasized the need to establish specific usability criteria for a product early on in development, and this part of the shell encourages this.

10.3.1   Different Kinds of Requirements

In software engineering, two different kinds of requirements have traditionally been identified: functional requirements, which say what the system should do, and non-functional requirements, which say what constraints there are on the system and its development. For example, a functional requirement for a new video game may be that it should be challenging for a range of user abilities. This requirement might then be decomposed into more specific requirements detailing the structure of challenges, e.g. hierarchical levels, hidden tips and tricks, magical objects, and so on. A non-functional requirement for this same game might

Requirement #: 75   Requirement Type: 9   Event/use case #: 6

Description: The product shall issue an alert if a weather station fails to transmit readings.

Rationale: Failure to transmit readings might indicate that the weather station is faulty and needs maintenance, and that the data used to predict freezing roads may be incomplete.

Source: Road Engineers

Fit Criterion: For each weather station the product shall communicate to the user when the recorded number of each type of reading per hour is not within the manufacturer's specified range of the expected number of readings per hour.

Customer Satisfaction: 3   Customer Dissatisfaction: 5

Dependencies: None   Conflicts: None

Supporting Materials: Specification of Rosa Weather Station

History: Raised by GBS, 28 July 99   Volere

Copyright © Atlantic Systems Guild

Figure 10.1 An example requirement using the Volere shell

Source: An example requirement using the Volere shell, taken from Robertson and Robertson: "Mastering the Requirements Process" 2013 Addison Wesley. © Atlantic Systems Guild.

be that it can run on a variety of platforms such as Xbox, PlayStation, and Wii consoles. A different kind of non-functional requirement would be that it must be delivered in 6 months' time. This represents a constraint on the development activity itself rather than on the product being developed.

Different interactive products will be associated with different constraints. For example, a telecare system designed to monitor an elderly person's movements and alert relevant care staff will be constrained by the type and size of sensors that can be easily worn by the users as they go about their normal activities. Wearable interfaces need to be light, small, fashionable, preferably hidden, and not get in the way. A desirable characteristic of both an online shopping site and a robotic companion is that they should be trustworthy, but this attribute leads to different non-functional requirements: in the former we'd be focused on security of information while in the latter we'd be looking for behavioral norms.

Interaction design involves understanding the functionality required and the constraints under which the product must operate or be developed, hence we are concerned with a wide range of requirements. We will look at some of these in more detail below; Table 10.1 provides an alternative (and long) list of requirements that might be considered.

Functional requirements capture what the product should do. For example, a functional requirement for a robot working in a car assembly plant might be that it should be able to accurately place and weld together the correct pieces of metal. Understanding the functional requirements for an interactive product is fundamental.

Data requirements capture the type, volatility, size/amount, persistence, accuracy, and value of the required data. All interactive products have to handle some data. For example, if the system under consideration is a share-dealing application, then the data must be up-to-date and accurate, and is likely to change many times a day. In the personal banking domain, data must be accurate, must persist over many months and probably years, and there is likely to be a lot of it.

PROJECT DRIVERS	13. Operational and Environmental Requirements
1. The Purpose of the Product	14. Maintainability and Support
2. The Stakeholders	Requirements
PROJECT CONSTRAINTS	15. Security Requirements
3. Mandated Constraints	16. Cultural and Political Requirements
4. Naming Conventions and Definitions	17. Legal Requirements
5. Relevant Facts and Assumptions	PROJECT ISSUES
FUNCTIONAL REQUIREMENTS	18. Open Issues
6. The Scope of the Work	19. Off-the-Shelf Solutions
7. Business Data Model and Data Dictionary	20. New Problems
8. The Scope of the Product	21. Tasks
9. Functional and Data Requirements	22. Migration to the New Product
	23. Risks
NON-FUNCTIONAL REQUIREMENTS	24. Costs
10. Look and Feel Requirements	25. User Documentation and Training
11. Usability and Humanity Requirements	26. Waiting Room
12. Performance Requirements	27. Ideas for Solutions

Table 10.1 The Volere Requirements Specification Template

Source: The Volere Requirements Specification Template version 15 ©Atlantic Systems Guild. The full version of the template may be downloaded from http://www.volere.co.uk/template.htm.

Environmental requirements – or context of use – refer to the circumstances in which the interactive product will operate. Four aspects of the environment must be considered when establishing requirements. First is the physical environment, such as how much lighting, noise, movement, and dust is expected in the operational environment. Will users need to wear protective clothing, such as large gloves or headgear that might affect the choice of interface type? How crowded is the environment? For example, an ATM operates in a very public physical environment – using a speech interface is therefore likely to be problematic. Box 10.1 illustrates interactive products in a different kind of environment.

The second aspect of the environment is the social environment. The issues raised in Chapter 4 regarding the social aspects of interaction design, such as collaboration and coordination, need to be explored. For example, will data need to be shared? If so, does the sharing have to be synchronous (e.g. does everyone need to be viewing the data at once?) or asynchronous (e.g. two people authoring a report take turns in editing it)? Other factors include the physical location of fellow team members, e.g. do collaborators need to communicate across great distances?

The third aspect is the organizational environment, e.g. how good is user support likely to be, how easily can it be obtained, and are there facilities or resources for training? How efficient or stable is the communications infrastructure? And so on.

Finally, the technical environment will need to be established: for example, what technologies will the product run on or need to be compatible with, and what technological limitations might be relevant?

BOX 10.1

Environmental requirements: Underwater computing

Developing a computer for divers to take underwater has one major environmental factor: it is surrounded by water! However, the interface presented more challenges than waterproofing to the designers of WetPC, an underwater wearable computer (see Figure 10.2a). A miniature personal computer is mounted on the diver's air tank; a mask-mounted head-up display presents the diver with a floating display; and a five-button chordic graphical user interface Kord® Pad is attached to the diver's belt or chest (see Figure 10.2b).

Divers typically have only one hand free to operate the computer, and are likely to be swimming and moving up and down in the water at the same time. So a traditional interface

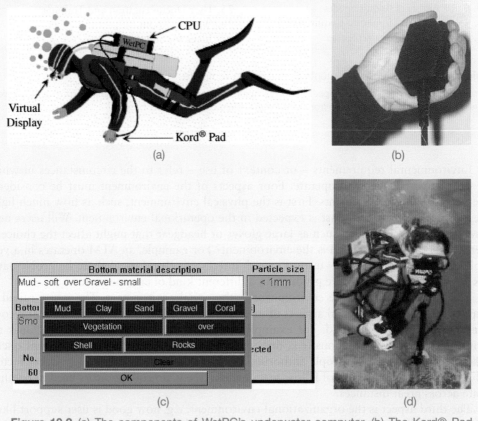

Figure 10.2 (a) The components of WetPC's underwater computer. (b) The Kord® Pad chordic keypad. (c) The floating display 'what you see is what you press.' (d) The Kord® Pad in use underwater

Source: Reproduced by permission of WetPC Pty Ltd. http://www.wetpc.com.au/WetPC.

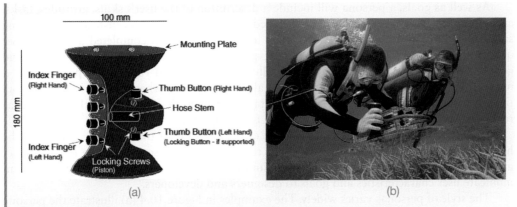

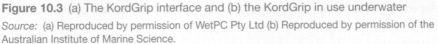

Figure 10.3 (a) The KordGrip interface and (b) the KordGrip in use underwater

Source: (a) Reproduced by permission of WetPC Pty Ltd (b) Reproduced by permission of the Australian Institute of Marine Science.

design is no good. The Kord Pad (see Figure 10.2b) has five keys which can be pressed in different combinations to choose different menu items. It is supported by the floating display interface (see Figure 10.2c) which tells the divers which keys to press for which actions.

WetPC have also designed SeaSlate which is operated by a six-button keypad called KordGrip (see Figure 10.3a). SeaSlate can be used to search areas of the sea bottom. Divers can perform operations such as controlling a camera and sending messages. The system is also linked to a GPS device that tells the divers where they are, which facilitates marking the location of mines and other underwater discoveries. ■

User characteristics capture the key attributes of the intended user group. In Chapter 9 we mentioned the relevance of a user's abilities and skills, and these are an important aspect of user characteristics. Other characteristics that may affect the design are: the users' nationality, educational background, preferences, personal circumstances, physical or mental disabilities, and so on. In addition, a user may be a novice, an expert, a casual, or a frequent user. This affects the ways in which interaction is designed. For example, a novice user will require step-by-step instructions, probably with prompting, and a constrained interaction backed up with clear information. An expert, on the other hand, will require a flexible interaction with more wide-ranging powers of control. The collection of characteristics for a typical user is called a user profile. Any one product may have several different user profiles.

In order to bring user profiles to life, they are often transformed into a number of personas (Cooper, 1999). Personas are rich descriptions of typical users of the product under development that the designers can focus on and design the product for. They don't describe real people, but are realistic rather than idealized. Any one persona usually represents a synthesis from a number of real users who have been involved in data gathering. Each persona is characterized by a unique set of goals relating to the particular product under development, rather than a job description or job role. This is because goals often differ between people within the same job role, and people with very different job roles may have the same goals.

As well as goals, a persona will include a description of the user's skills, attitudes, tasks, and environment. These items are all specified in some detail, and so instead of describing someone simply as a competent sailor, they include that he has completed a Day Skipper qualification, has over 100 hours of sailing experience in and around European waters, and gets irritated by other sailors who don't follow the navigation rules. Each persona has a name, often a photograph, and some personal details such as what they do in their leisure time. It is the addition of precise, credible details that helps designers to see the personas as real potential users, and hence as people they can design for.

Usually a product will require a small set of personas rather than just one and it may be helpful to choose one primary persona who represents a large section of the intended user group. Personas are used widely in industry, and have proved to be a powerful way to communicate user characteristics and goals to designers and developers.

The style of personas varies widely. The examples in Figure 10.4 (a) illustrate the persona format developed and used by the company in Box 10.2, and have quite a compact and eye-catching layout.

BOX 10.2

Persona-driven development in the City of London

Caplin Systems is based in the City of London and provides a framework to investment banks that enables them to quickly build, or enhance, their single-dealer offering, or to create a single-dealer platform for the first time.

The company was drawn to use personas to increase the customer focus of their products by better understanding who they were developing their system for. Personas were seen as a way to provide a unified view of their users, and to start building more customer-focused products.

The first step was to run a workshop for the whole company, to introduce personas, show how other companies were using them, and for employees to experience the benefits

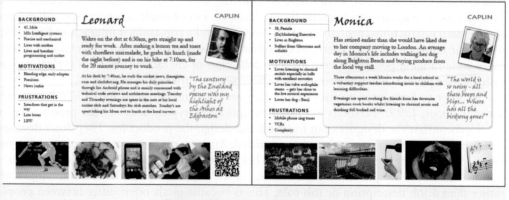

Figure 10.4 (a) Example personas

Figure 10.4 (b) The narrative journey maps – sad faces show pain points for the persona
Source: Caplin Systems.

of using personas first hand through some simple team exercises. The proposition was then put forward: 'Should we adopt personas and persona-driven development?' The response was a resounding 'YES!' This was a good thing to do. Gaining this 'buy in' was fundamentally important to ensure everyone was behind the use of personas and committed to the change.

Everyone got excited and work began to define the way forward. Further workshops were run to refine the first persona, though in hindsight the Caplin team think too long was spent trying to get the first persona perfect. Now they are much more agile about persona creation.

Eighteen months after the persona breakthrough workshop, the main persona for Caplin Trader, Jack, and his 'pain points' were the focus of development, design decisions, and team discussions. Ongoing persona development is focusing on end-users of the software built with Caplin's technology, and Narrative Journey Maps capture their interactions and help define goals/motivations and pain points (see Figure 10.4b). ■

Usability goals and user experience goals were described in Chapter 1. These are another kind of requirement, and should be captured together with appropriate measures. Chapter 9 introduced the idea of usability engineering, an approach in which specific measures for the usability goals of the product are agreed upon early in the development process and used to track progress as development proceeds. This both ensures that usability is given due priority and facilitates progress tracking. If we are to follow the philosophy of usability engineering and meet the usability goals, then appropriate requirements need to be identified. The same is true for user experience goals. Although it is harder to identify quantifiable measures that track these qualities, an understanding of their importance should be obtained during the requirements activity.

There are different perspectives that can be taken when identifying measures for usability and user experience goals – some focus on objective measures of the user's performance while others focus on the user's perceptions of the interaction. This difference is discussed further in Chapters 13–15.

ACTIVITY 10.1

Suggest some key requirements in each category above (functional, data, environmental, user characteristics, usability goals, and user experience goals) for each of the following situations:

1. An interactive product for use in a university's self-service cafeteria that allows users to pay for their food using a contactless card or smartphone.
2. An interactive product to control the functioning of a nuclear power station.

Comment

You may have come up with alternative suggestions; these are indicative of the kinds of answer we might expect.

1. Functional: the product will calculate the total cost of purchases.

   Data: the product must have access to the price of products in the cafeteria.

   Environmental: cafeteria users will be carrying a tray and will most likely be in a reasonable rush. The physical environment will be noisy and busy, and users may be talking with friends and colleagues while using the product.

   User characteristics: the majority of users are likely to be under 25 and comfortable dealing with technology.

   Usability goals: the product needs to be easy to learn so that new users can use it immediately, and memorable for more frequent users. Users won't want to wait around for the system to finish processing, so it needs to be efficient and safe to use, i.e. able to deal easily with user errors.

   User experience goals: of the user experience goals listed in Chapter 1, those most likely to be relevant here are satisfying, helpful, and enhancing sociability. The last of these may be difficult to implement in this kind of environment, but a cafeteria is a sociable place, and so a system that enhances that would be welcome. While some of the other goals may be appropriate, it is not essential for this product to, for example, be cognitively stimulating.

2. Functional: the product will be able to monitor the temperature of the reactors.

   Data: the product will need access to temperature readings.

   Environmental: the physical environment is likely to be uncluttered and to impose few restrictions on the console itself unless there is a need to wear protective clothing (depending on where the console is to be located).

   User characteristics: the user is likely to be a well-trained engineer or scientist who is competent to handle technology.

   Usability goals: the system needs to exhibit all of the usability goals. You wouldn't want a safety-critical system like this being anything other than effective, efficient, safe, easy to learn and remember how to use, and with good utility. For example, outputs from the system, especially warning signals and gauges, must be clear and unambiguous.

   User experience goals: on the other hand, none of the user experience goals is particularly relevant here. You certainly wouldn't want the product to be surprising, provocative, or challenging, although there's nothing wrong with it being aesthetically pleasing or enjoyable. ∎

10.4 Data Gathering for Requirements

The overall purpose of data gathering in the requirements activity is to collect sufficient, relevant, and appropriate data so that a set of stable requirements can be produced. Even if a set of initial requirements exists, data gathering will be required to expand, clarify, and confirm those initial requirements. Data gathering needs to cover a wide spectrum of issues: the tasks that users currently perform and their associated goals, the context in which the tasks are performed, and the rationale for the current situation.

You met three common forms of data gathering in Chapter 7: interviews, questionnaires, and observation. Below, we first consider how these three techniques are used in the requirements activity, and then we introduce two other techniques – studying documentation and researching similar products – and their use in establishing requirements. Box 10.3 describes an approach aimed at prompting inspiration rather than simple data gathering.

BOX 10.3

Using probes for inspiration

The Presence Project (Gaver *et al*, 1999) looked at novel interaction techniques to increase the presence of elderly people in their local community. The project studied groups in Oslo, Norway, near Amsterdam, the Netherlands, and near Pisa, Italy. Rather than take a more traditional approach of questionnaires, interviews, or ethnographic studies, this project used a novel technique called cultural probes. These probes consisted of a wallet containing a variety of items: eight to ten postcards, about seven maps, a disposable camera, a photo album, and a media diary (see Figure 10.5). Recipients were asked to answer questions associated with certain items in the wallet, then to return them directly to the researchers. For example, the postcards had pictures on the front and questions on the back, and were pre-addressed and stamped so that they could be easily returned. Questions included 'Please tell us a piece of advice or insight that has been important to you,' 'What place does art have in your life?' and 'Tell us about your favorite device.' The maps and associated inquiries were designed to find out about the participants' attitudes towards their environment. They were printed on various textured papers and were in the form of folding envelopes, also to facilitate their return. On local maps, participants were asked to mark sites where they would go to meet people, to be alone, to daydream, and where they would like to go, but couldn't. On a map of the world, they were asked to mark places where they had been.

Participants were asked to use the camera to take pictures of their home, what they will wear today (whenever 'today' was), the first person they see today, something desirable, and something boring. In the photo album they were asked to tell the researchers their story in pictures. The media diary was to record their use of television and radio.

"What we learned about the elders is only half the story, however. The other half is what the elders learned from the probes. They provoked the groups to think about the roles they

(Continued)

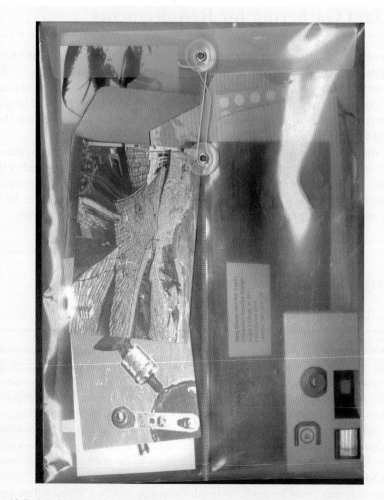

Figure 10.5 A cultural probe package

Source: B. Gaver, T. Dunne and E. Pacenti (1999): "Cultural Probes" from *Interactions* 6(1) pp.21–29. ©1999 Association for Computing Machinery, Inc. Reprinted by permission.

play and the pleasures they experience, hinting to them that our designs might suggest new roles and new experiences" (Gaver *et al*, 1999, p. 29).

The probe idea has been adapted and adopted since its beginnings for various settings (Boehner *et al*, 2007, Wallace *et al*, 2013). Extending this idea to toolkits and technology probes, such as Lego Mindstorms or the SenseBoard (Richards and Woodthorpe, 2009), users themselves have been inspired to directly develop innovative and unexpected products (Rogers *et al*, 2014). ∎

Interviews. Interviews are good for exploring issues, and semi-structured or unstructured interviews are often used early on to elicit scenarios (see Section 10.6.1). In the context of establishing requirements, it is equally important for development team members to meet stakeholders and for users to feel involved. This on its own may be sufficient motivation to arrange interviews.

Focus groups. Focus groups are good for gaining a consensus view and highlighting areas of conflict and disagreement during the requirements activity. On a social level it also helps for stakeholders to meet designers and each other, and to express their views in public. It is not uncommon for one set of stakeholders to be unaware that their understanding of an issue or a process is different from another's, even though they are in the same organization.

The generic idea of a focus group has been tailored for use within the requirements activity and requirements workshops have grown in popularity. Each workshop is carefully planned, attendees are carefully chosen, and specific deliverables are produced. Gottesdiener (2002) suggests a very useful, practical approach to requirements workshops that emphasizes planning and deliverables but also collaboration and facilitation.

Questionnaires. Questionnaires may be used for getting initial responses that can then be analyzed to choose people to interview or to get a wider perspective on particular issues that have arisen elsewhere. For example, a questionnaire might be used in order to gauge whether a new university online help service would be welcomed by students. This questionnaire could ask for impressions and opinions about current support services and whether the respondent is prepared to be interviewed further. Or the questionnaire might be used to get opinions and views about specific suggestions for the kind of help that would be most appreciated.

Direct observation. In the requirements activity, observation of participants in their natural setting is used to understand the nature of the tasks and the context in which they are performed. Sometimes the observation is carried out by trained observers who record their findings and report them back to the design team, and sometimes the observation is carried out by or with a member of the design team.

Indirect observation. Diaries and interaction logging are used less often within the requirements activity where a new product is under development. However, if a product is being developed iteratively or is evolving from an existing product, indirect observation and experience sampling are very valuable. Interaction logging together with sophisticated web analytics are particularly useful for improving websites.

Studying documentation. Manuals and other documentation are a good source of data about the steps involved in an activity and any regulations governing a task. Documentation should not be used as the only source, however, as everyday practices may augment it. Taking a user-centered view of development means being interested in everyday practices rather than an idealized account.

Studying documentation is good for understanding legislation and getting some background information on the work. It also doesn't involve stakeholder time, which is a limiting factor on the other techniques.

Researching similar products. In Chapter 9 we talk about looking at similar products in order to generate alternative designs. Another reason to look at similar products is to help prompt requirements. For example, when developing an image editor for a mobile device,

Kangas and Kinnunen (2005) report that they looked at PC image editing software in order to gain an understanding of the kinds of features and interaction that such a package might offer. Similarly, Chisnell and Brown (2004) evaluated competitors' health plan websites when redeveloping their own.

The choice of data gathering techniques for the requirements activity is influenced by several factors including the nature of the task, the participants, the analyst, and the resources available (see Chapter 7 for a more detailed discussion of these factors). It is usual for more than one data gathering technique to be used in order to provide different perspectives. For example, observation to understand the context of task performance, interviews to target specific user groups, questionnaires to reach a wider population, and focus groups to build a consensus view. There is no right choice or combination as this will depend on the specific circumstances and resources. Many different combinations are used in practice. Box 10.4 includes some examples of the different combinations used. Note that the example from Shaer et al (2012) also illustrates the development of an interactive product for a specialist domain, where users join the development team to help them understand the domain complexities. Also note that evaluating prototypes may be included as part of the requirements activity. This serves to highlight the close relationship between requirements, design, and evaluation, as illustrated in our interaction design process in Chapter 9 – the distinction between these phases is blurred and depends mainly on emphasis.

BOX 10.4

Combining data gathering in requirements activities

Diary and interviews: Dearman et al (2008) were investigating the types of information people need and share in their everyday lives. They conducted a four-week diary study with 20 participants. Each participant was given a paper diary with predefined forms and was asked to complete a form every time they needed some information or shared information. Participants were sent a text message (or email message) twice a day to remind them to keep these entries up to date, and were interviewed each week to elicit further details, hand over the diary for the week, and collect a new diary for the next week. At the end of the study exit interviews were conducted with each participant to understand their overall experience.

Ethnographic study, interviews, usability tests, and user participation: Shaer et al (2012) report on the design of a multi-touch tabletop user interface for collaborative exploration of genomic data (see Figure 10.6). In-depth interviews were conducted with 38 molecular and computational biologists to understand the current work practices, needs, and workflow of small research groups. A small team of nine researchers investigating gene interaction in Tuberculosis was studied for eight weeks using an ethnographic approach, and other labs were also observed. Because the application area was specialized, the design team needed to be comfortable with the domain concepts. To achieve this, biologists were integrated into the development team, and other members of the design team regularly visited biology research group partners, attended courses to teach them relevant domain concepts, and had frequent usability tests with users.

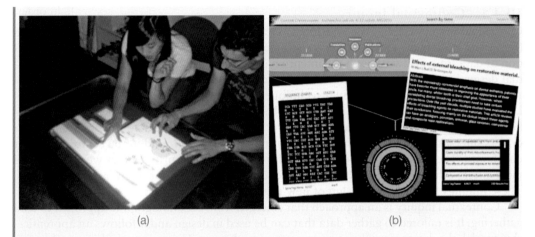

(a)   (b)

Figure 10.6 (a) Exploring mouse gene expression using G-nome Surfer 2.0 (b) G-nome Surfer Pro displaying the chromosome visualizations, an aligned sequence, and publications

Source: Shaer *et al* (2012) The design, development, and deployment of a tabletop interface for collaborative exploration of genomic data, *International Journal of Human–Computer Interaction* 70, 746–764. ©2012 Association for Computing Machinery, Inc. Reprinted by permission.

The result of this two-year effort was a set of five main requirements which were used as the basis of development: alleviating data explosion; lowering the threshold for using advanced bioinformatics tools; facilitating an integrated and flexible workflow; supporting multiple forms of evidence; and fostering collaboration and reflection.

Documentation, interview, online survey, group discussion: Oostveen and van den Besselaar (2004) describe the development of a smart-card-based system that would support mobile European citizens in achieving various administrative transactions between countries. For example, moving from one country to another requires a set of bureaucratic operations to be performed, largely concerned with exchanging documentation. This system would enable the citizen to download the required information onto a smart card and use this electronic document in the new country. In-depth interviews with expatriates from different countries allowed them to catalog the problems mobile Europeans encounter. Interviews with civil servants and various intermediaries whose jobs involve helping such people were also held. In order to check the relevance of the interview results to a wider set of potential users, they then set up an online survey. The administrative processes were investigated through group discussions which were held in different countries between technology designers and administrative experts; potential solutions were also discussed in these workshops. Documentation was studied to underpin the other requirements activities.

Focus groups, interviews, and evaluations: Liu *et al* (2005) report on some research into expanding the use of ATMs in China. This study was conducted in order to identify factors that might affect requirements for ATM design, identify problems or issues with current ATMs in China, and identify appropriate ways in which to increase adoption. They used three different approaches to data gathering: focus groups were used to share good and bad experiences of ATM use, interviews were carried out in a shopping center with 100 participants to find out how widely applicable the findings were from the focus groups, and evaluations of existing ATMs were conducted to uncover confusions and error rates. ■

10.4.1   Contextual Inquiry

Contextual inquiry (Holtzblatt and Jones, 1993) is one of seven parts of contextual design (Beyer and Holtzblatt, 1998), which is a structured approach to the collection and interpretation of data from fieldwork with the intention of building a software-based product. Contextual design involves the production of five different models of work.

Contextual inquiry is a popular technique for uncovering requirements, and in particular in uncovering requirements relating to the context of use. For example Meschtscherjakov *et al* (2011) used contextual inquiry over a period of six weeks to investigate how car drivers interact with the multi-function rotating button often found in the centre of the car dashboard. The study highlighted that comfort, safety, and security factors were mentioned most often, while visual and haptic aesthetics were not mentioned by any participants. These findings informed the design of new in-vehicle information systems.

Contextual inquiry is an approach that emerged from the ethnographic approach to data gathering. It is tailored to gather data that can be used in design and it follows an apprenticeship model: the designer works as an apprentice to the user. The most typical format for contextual inquiry is a contextual interview, which is a combination of observation, discussion, and reconstruction of past events. Contextual inquiry rests on four main principles: context, partnership, interpretation, and focus.

The context principle emphasizes the importance of going to the workplace and seeing what happens. The partnership principle states that the developer and the user should collaborate in understanding the work; in a traditional interviewing or workshop situation, the interviewer or workshop leader is in control, but in contextual inquiry the spirit of partnership means that the understanding is developed through cooperation.

The interpretation principle says that the observations must be interpreted in order to be used in design, and this interpretation should also be developed in cooperation between the user and the developer. For example, I have a set of paper notes stuck above my desk at work; some list telephone numbers and some list commands for the software I use. Someone coming into my office might interpret these facts in a number of ways: that I don't have access to a staff directory; that I don't have a user manual for my software; that I use the software infrequently; that the commands are particularly difficult to remember. The best way to interpret these observations is to discuss them with me. In fact, I do have access to a staff directory, but I would need to log on to a different network than my usual one, which is distracting and takes time. The commands are there because I often forget them and waste time searching through menu structures.

The fourth principle, the focus principle, is related to our discussions in Chapter 7 about keeping the data gathering focused on your goals. In contextual inquiry, as in an unstructured interview, for example, it is easy for the discussion to wander off target. To help avoid this, a project focus is established to guide the interviewer, which will then be augmented by the individual's own focus that arises from their perspective and background.

Normally, each member of the team developing the interactive product conducts at least one contextual inquiry session. Data is collected in the form of notes and perhaps audio and video recording, but a lot of information is in the observer's head. It is important to review the experience and to start documenting the findings as soon as possible after the session. Contextual inquiry is usually followed by an interpretation session in which a number of models are generated: an affinity diagram, the work flow model, the sequence model, the artifact model, the cultural model, and the physical model. More detail about these models and how to generate them is in Beyer and Holtzblatt (1998).

Contextual inquiry has been adapted for use in a remote setting (Rampoldi-Hnilo and English, 2004) and contextual design has been adapted for use with a shortened product cycle (Holtzblatt *et al*, 2004).

ACTIVITY 10.2

How does the contextual inquiry interview compare with the interviews introduced in Chapter 7?

Comment

Structured, unstructured, and semi-structured interviews were introduced in Chapter 7. Contextual inquiry could be viewed as an unstructured interview, but it has other characteristics not normal for an unstructured interview. A contextual inquiry interview is conducted at the interviewee's place of work, while normal work continues. Contextual inquiry specifically incorporates other data gathering techniques as well, such as observation, and the relationship of the interviewer to interviewee is as an apprentice. ∎

10.4.2   Data Gathering Guidelines for Requirements

General advice for data gathering is given in Chapter 7, but here are a few more specific guidelines worthy of note when gathering data for requirements:

- Focus on identifying the stakeholders' needs. This may be achieved by studying their existing behavior and support tools, or by looking at other products, such as a competitor's product or an earlier release of your product under development.
- Involve all the stakeholder groups. It is very important to make sure that you get the views of all the right people. This may seem an obvious comment, but it is easy to overlook certain sections of the stakeholder population if you're not careful. We were told about one case where a large distribution and logistics company reimplemented their software systems and were very careful to involve all the clerical, managerial, and warehouse staff in their development process, but on the day the system went live, the productivity of the operation fell by 50%. On investigation it was found that the bottleneck was not in their own company, but in the suppliers' warehouses that had to interact with the new system. No one had asked them how they worked, and the new system was incompatible with their working routines.
- Involving only one representative from each stakeholder group is not enough, especially if the group is large. Everyone you involve in data gathering will have their own perspective on the situation, the task, their job, and how others interact with them. If you only involve one representative stakeholder then you will only get a narrow view.
- Support the data gathering sessions with suitable props, such as task descriptions and prototypes if available. Since the requirements activity is iterative, prototypes or descriptions

generated during one session may be reused or revisited in another with the same or a different set of stakeholders. Using props will help to jog people's memories and act as a focus for discussions. Maiden *et al* (2007b) recommend the use of mobile technologies and dedicated requirements applications to support the requirements activity.

10.5   Data Analysis, Interpretation, and Presentation

Methods and approaches for analysis, interpretation, and presentation of data are discussed in Chapter 8. These are applicable during the requirements activity to structure and record descriptions of requirements. Using a format such as the Volere shell (Figure 10.7) highlights the kinds of information to look for and is a good first step in data analysis for requirements. Note that many of the entries are concerned with traceability. For example, who raised the requirement and where can more information about it be found? This information may be captured in documents or in diagrams drawn during analysis.

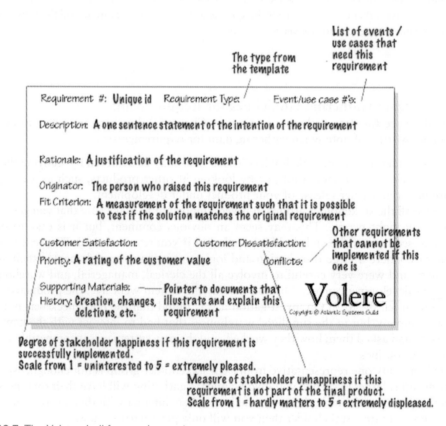

Figure 10.7 The Volere shell for requirements

Source: © Atlantic Systems Guild.

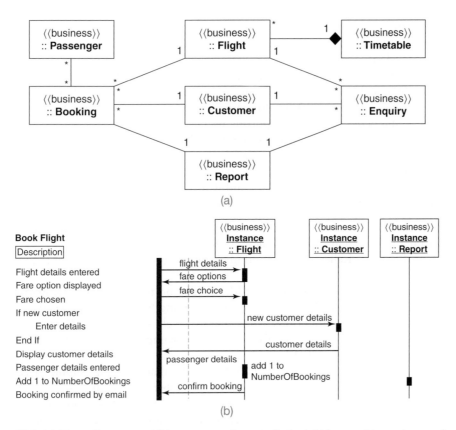

Figure 10.8 (a) Class diagram and (b) sequence diagram that might be used to analyze and capture static structure and dynamic behavior (respectively)

Some kinds of requirements are best investigated using more formal techniques and notations. For example, functional requirements may be analyzed and documented using class diagrams, state charts, and sequence diagrams, among others. Data requirements can be expressed using entity-relationship diagrams, and so on. Examples of two such diagrams representing a portion of a flight booking system are given in Figure 10.8. These diagrams can be linked to the requirements through the Event/use case field in the shell in Figure 10.7.

We don't go into the detail of how specialized diagrams such as these might be developed, as whole books are dedicated to them. Instead, we describe four techniques that have a user-centered focus and are used to understand users' goals and tasks: scenarios (Section 10.6.1), use cases (Section 10.6.2), essential use cases (or task cases) (Section 10.6.3), and task analysis (Section 10.7). All of them may be produced as a result of a data gathering session, and their output used as props in subsequent data gathering sessions.

The requirements activity is iterated a number of times before a stable set of requirements evolves. As more analysis techniques are applied, a deeper understanding of requirements will emerge and the requirements descriptions will expand and clarify.

10.5.1 Brainstorming for Innovation

So far we have focused on how requirements may emerge directly from the data gathered. However, establishing a suitable set of requirements is likely to also involve innovation. Brainstorming is not a technique specific to interaction design, or to any other discipline, and is a generic technique used to generate, refine, and develop ideas. It is widely used in interaction design specifically for generating alternative designs (as discussed in Chapter 9) or for suggesting new and better ideas for supporting users.

Various rules have been suggested for making a brainstorming session successful, some of which we list below. For requirements, two key success factors are firstly that the participants should know the users' goals that the product is to support, and secondly that no ideas should be criticized or debated (Robertson and Robertson, 2013; Kelley, 2008). Some other suggestions for successful requirements brainstorms are:

1. Include participants from a wide range of disciplines, with a broad range of experience (Robertson and Robertson, 2013; Kelley, 2008).
2. Don't ban silly stuff (Kelley, 2008). Wild ideas often turn into really useful requirements (Robertson and Robertson, 2013).
3. Use catalysts for further inspiration. Build one idea on top of another (Robertson and Robertson, 2013). Kelley (2008) also suggests jumping back to an earlier idea, or considering alternative interpretations when energy levels start to flag. If you get stuck, use a word pulled randomly from a dictionary to prompt ideas related to the product (Robertson and Robertson, 2013).
4. Keep records. Robertson and Robertson (2013) suggest that every idea should be captured, without censoring. Kelley (2008) suggests that you number them so that you can refer back to ideas more easily. He also suggests that the walls and tables in the room be covered in paper and that participants be encouraged to sketch, mind-map, and diagram ideas, including keeping the flow of ideas, as spatial memory is very strong and this can facilitate recall.
5. Sharpen the focus (Kelley, 2008). Start the brainstorm with a well-honed problem. This will get the brainstorm off to a good start and makes it easier to pull people back to the main topic if the session wanders.
6. Use warm-up exercises and make the session fun (Robertson and Robertson, 2013). The group will require warming up if they haven't worked together before, most of the group don't brainstorm regularly, or the group is distracted by other pressures (Kelley, 2008). Warm-up exercises might take the form of word games, or the exploration of physical items related or unrelated with the problem at hand. For example, see the description of the TechBox in Chapter 9.

10.6 Task Description

Descriptions of business tasks have been used within software development for many years. During the 1970s and 1980s, business scenarios were commonly used as the basis for acceptance testing, i.e. the last testing stage before the customer paid the final fee installment and accepted the system. In more recent years, due to the emphasis on involving users earlier in the development lifecycle and the large number of new interactive products now being developed, task descriptions are used throughout development, from early requirements activities through prototyping, evaluation, and testing. Consequently, more time and effort has been put into understanding how best to structure and use them.

As shown by Alexander and Maiden's (2004) collection of scenarios, stories, and use cases, there are many different flavors of task description, and they can be used for different purposes, emphasizing different elements of the product being developed. For example, Alexander and Maiden use a structuring framework that distinguishes task descriptions according to four views which are made up of nine facets including method of description (e.g. text, graphics, image or prototype, and formal, informal, or semi-formal notation), context (e.g. organizational environment and system interaction), and role (descriptive, exploratory, or explanatory).

We shall introduce three of the more common description types here: scenarios, use cases, and essential use cases (sometimes referred to as task cases). Each of these may be used to describe either existing tasks or envisioned tasks with a new product. They are not mutually exclusive and are often used in combination to capture different perspectives or to document different stages during the development lifecycle.

In this section and the next, we use two main examples to illustrate the application of techniques. These are a movie rental subscription service and a shared travel organizer. The movie rental service allows subscribers to rent movies of their choice; the shared travel organizer supports a group of people who are exploring vacation possibilities.

10.6.1 Scenarios

A scenario is an 'informal narrative description' (Carroll, 2000). It describes human activities or tasks in a story that allows exploration and discussion of contexts, needs, and requirements. It does not necessarily describe the use of software or other technological support to achieve a task. Using the vocabulary and phrasing of users means that scenarios can be understood by the stakeholders, and they are able to participate fully in the development process. In fact, the construction of scenarios by stakeholders is often the first step in establishing requirements.

Imagine that you have just been invited along to talk to a group of users who perform data entry for a university admissions office. You walk in, and are greeted by Sandy, the supervisor, who starts by saying something like:

> *Well, this is where we process admissions forms. We receive about 50 a day during the peak application period. Brian here checks the applications to see that they are complete, that is, that all the information and supporting evidence has been included. You see, we require evidence of relevant school exam results or work experience before we can process the application. Depending on the result of this initial inspection, the applications are sent on to . . .*

Telling stories is a natural way for people to explain what they are doing or how to achieve something. It is therefore something that stakeholders can easily relate to. The focus of such stories is also naturally likely to be about what the users are trying to achieve, i.e. their goals. Understanding why people do things as they do and what they are trying to achieve in the process allows us to concentrate on the human activity rather than interaction with technology.

This is not to preserve existing behavior in the new product, but to understand current behavior and explore the constraints, contexts, irritations, facilitators, and so on under which people operate. It also allows us to identify the stakeholders and the artifacts involved in an activity. Repeated reference to a particular app, book, behavior, or location indicates that this is somehow central to the activity being performed and that we should take care to understand what it is and the role it plays.

A scenario that might be generated by potential users of an online movie rental subscription service is given below:

> *Say I want to find a movie directed by Martin Scorsese. I don't remember the title but I know it came out in the cinemas around 2006 or 2007. I go to the service website and choose the director option. A huge list of directors is displayed – I had no idea there were so many directors with surnames beginning with S! After scrolling through the list I find Martin Scorsese and choose to see further details about him. Another long list of movies eventually leads me to the movie I was looking for – The Departed. As an existing subscriber, I need to log in to be able to rent the movie. Once my login has been confirmed, I can choose the rental period and payment method. I have my preferences already registered in the system, so I just choose the defaults and download my movie.*

In this limited scenario of existing system use, there are some things of note: the long lists of names and movies that the user has to scroll through, the lack of detailed search possibilities, the importance of choice around rental period, and the usefulness of having default settings chosen by regular users. These are all indicators of potential design choices for the new system. The scenario also tells us one (possibly common) use of the system: to search for a movie by a specific director when we don't know the title.

The level of detail present in a scenario varies depending on where in the development process they are being used. During requirements it is a good idea for scenarios to emphasize the context, the usability and user experience goals, and the tasks the user is performing. When used in combination with detailed personas, this kind of scenario can improve the developers' appreciation of the user experience.

Often scenarios are generated during workshop, interview, or brainstorming sessions to help explain or discuss some aspect of the user's goals. They can be used to imagine potential uses of a product as well as to capture existing behavior. They are not intended to capture a full set of requirements, but are a very personalized account, offering only one perspective.

The following scenario for the shared travel organizer was elicited in an informal interview. This describes how one function of the system might work: to identify potential vacation options. Note that this scenario includes details about some typical users and their needs. This is the kind of information that you might glean from a requirements interview.

> *The Thomson family enjoy outdoor activities and want to try their hand at sailing this year. There are four family members: Sky (10 years old), Eamonn (15 years old), Claire (35), and Will (40). One evening after dinner they decide to start exploring the possibilities. They all gather around the travel organizer and enter their initial set of requirements – a sailing trip for four novices in the Mediterranean. The console is designed so that all members of the family can interact easily and comfortably with it. The system's initial suggestion is a flotilla, where several crews (with various levels of experience) sail together on separate boats. Sky and Eamonn aren't very happy at the idea of going on vacation with a group of other people, even though the Thomsons would have their own boat. The travel organizer shows them descriptions of flotillas from other children their ages and they are all very positive, so eventually, everyone agrees to explore flotilla opportunities. Will confirms this recommendation and asks for detailed options. As it's getting late, he asks for the details to be saved so everyone can consider them tomorrow. The travel organizer emails them a summary of the different options available.*

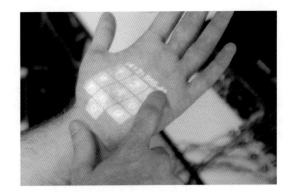

Figure 10.9 How skinput might be used

Source: Reproduced by permission of Chris Harrison, Dan Morris, Desney Tan - Microsoft Research & Carnegie Mellon University.

Scenarios may also be constructed to describe an envisioned situation in the future. An example of a futuristic scenario showing how the skin can be used for input is shown below and the technology is illustrated in Figure 10.9. The technology for such input has been developed and tested (Harrison *et al*, 2010), and the scenario illustrates how it may be used commercially.

> *Bramat has just finished his daily 4 mile run. He likes listening to music while he exercises, and has been playing his favorite pieces. This new skinput technology is great as he can focus on the running while scrolling through the available tracks, skipping through them with a simple tap of his fingers. He comes in exhausted and flops down on his favorite seat. With a flick of his fingers he turns off his music player and opens the palm of his hand to reveal the television remote control panel, graphically projected on his skin. He taps on a button to choose the station for the program he wants, adjusts the volume with a few more taps, and sits back to watch. Feeling hungry, he walks to his kitchen, opens his palm once again and sees a list of recipes possible given the items in his fridge. With another hand gesture, his palm turns into a telephone keypad, from where he can invite a friend over for dinner.*

Video about skinput at **http://youtu.be/g3XPUdW9Ryg**

In this chapter, we refer to scenarios only in their role of helping to establish requirements. They have a continuing role in the design process that we shall return to in Chapter 11. Indeed, as Alexander and Maiden (2004) show, scenarios have a role to play throughout the lifecycle, and Rosson and Carroll (2002) explain an approach called scenario-based usability engineering that illustrates the use of scenarios within a usability engineering framework.

Capturing scenarios of existing behavior and goals helps in determining new scenarios and hence in gathering data useful for establishing the new requirements. The next activity is intended to help you appreciate how a scenario of existing activity can help identify the requirements for a future application to support the same user goal.

ACTIVITY 10.3

Write a scenario of how you would currently go about choosing a new car. This should be a brand new car, not a second-hand car. Having written it, think about the important aspects of the task: your priorities and preferences. Then imagine a new interactive product that supports you in your goal and takes account of these issues. Write a futuristic scenario showing how this product would support you.

Comment
The following example is a fairly generic view of this process. Yours will be different, but you may have identified similar concerns and priorities.

The first thing I would do is to observe cars on the road and identify ones that I like the look of. This may take some weeks. I would also try to identify any consumer reports that will include an assessment of car performance. Hopefully, these initial activities will result in me identifying a likely car to buy. The next stage will be to visit a car showroom and see at first hand what the car looks like, and how comfortable it is to sit in. If I still feel positive about the car, then I'll ask for a test drive. Even a short test drive helps me to understand how well the car handles, how noisy the engine is, how smooth the gear changes are, and so on. Once I've driven the car myself, I can usually tell whether I would like to own it or not.

From this scenario, it seems that there are broadly two stages involved in the task: researching the different cars available, and gaining first-hand experience of potential purchases. In the former, observing cars on the road and getting expert evaluations of them are highlighted. In the latter, the test drive has quite a lot of significance.

For many people buying a new car, the smell and touch of the car's exterior and interior, and the driving experience itself are the most influential factors in choosing a particular model. Other attributes such as fuel consumption, amount of room inside, colors available, and price may rule out certain makes and models, but at the end of the day, cars are often chosen according to how easy they are to handle and how comfortable they are inside. This makes the test drive a vital part of the process of choosing a new car.

Taking these comments into account, we've come up with the following scenario describing how a new 'one-stop shop' for new cars might operate. This product makes use of immersive virtual reality technology that is already used for other applications such as designing buildings and training bomb disposal experts.

I want to buy a new car, so I go down the street to the local 'one-stop car shop.' The shop has a number of booths in it, and when I go in I'm directed to an empty booth. Inside there's a large seat that reminds me of a racing car seat, and in front of that a large display screen. As I sit down, the display jumps into life. It offers me the options of browsing through video clips of new cars which have been released in the last two years, or of searching through video clips of cars by make, by model, or by year. I can choose as many of these as I like. I also have the option of searching through consumer reports that have been produced about the cars I'm interested in. I spend about an hour looking through materials and deciding that I'd like to experience a couple that look promising.

I can of course go away and come back later, but I'd like to have a go with some of those I've found. By flicking a switch in my armrest, I can call up the options for virtual reality simulations for any of the cars I'm interested in. These are really great as they allow me to take the car for a test drive, simulating everything about the driving experience in this car, from road holding, to windscreen display, and front pedal pressure to dashboard layout. It even recreates the atmosphere of being inside the car.

Note that the product includes support for the two research activities mentioned in the original scenario, as well as the important test drive facility. This would be only a first cut scenario, which would then be refined through discussion and further investigation. ▪

BOX 10.5
Scenarios and personas

The difference between personas and scenarios can be difficult to grasp at first. Although reading about it may seem clear, it is a common confusion to end up combining the two. A scenario describes one use of a product or one example of achieving a goal, while a persona characterizes a typical user of the product. Figure 10.10 captures this difference graphically.

Note that this figure introduces the notion of a scenario goal. Thinking about the persona's goal for the scenario helps to scope the scenario to one use of the product. ▪

1. Persona

Defines who the story is about. This main character has attitudes, motivations, goals, and pain points, etc.

3. Goal

Defines what the persona wants or needs to fulfill. The goal is the motivation of why the persona is taking action. When that goal is reached, the scenario ends.

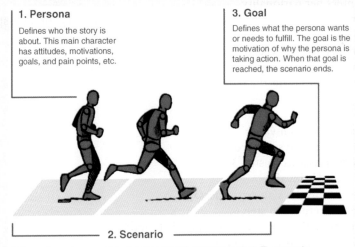

2. Scenario

Defines when, where, and how the story of the persona takes place. The scenario is the narrative that describes how the persona behaves as a sequence of events.

Figure 10.10 The relationship between a scenario and its associated persona

Source: http://www.smashingmagazine.com/2014/08/06/a-closer-look-at-personas-part-1/

10.6.2   Use Cases

Use cases also focus on user goals, but the emphasis here is on a user–system interaction rather than the user's task itself. They were originally introduced through the object-oriented community in the book *Object-Oriented Software Engineering* (Jacobson *et al*, 1992). Although their focus is specifically on the interaction between the user (called an actor) and a software system, the stress is still very much on the user's perspective, not the system's. The term scenario is also used in the context of use cases. In this context, it represents one path through the use case, i.e. one particular set of conditions. This meaning is consistent with the definition given above in that they both represent one specific example of behavior.

A use case is associated with an actor, and it is the actor's goal in using the system that the use case wants to capture. In this technique, the main use case describes what is called the normal course, i.e. the set of actions that the analyst believes to be most commonly performed. So, for example, if through data gathering we have found that most subscribers to the movie rental service know the title of the movie they want to rent, then the normal course for the use case would include the steps necessary to find the movie by title. Other possible sequences, called alternative courses, are then listed at the bottom of the use case.

A use case for retrieving the visa requirements using the travel organizer, with the normal course being that information about the visa requirements is available, might be:

1. The system displays options for investigating visa and vaccination requirements.
2. The user chooses the option to find out about visa requirements.
3. The system prompts the user for the name of the destination country.
4. The user enters the country's name.
5. The system checks that the country is valid.
6. The system prompts the user for her nationality.
7. The user enters her nationality.
8. The system checks the visa requirements of the entered country for a passport holder of her nationality.
9. The system displays the visa requirements.
10. The system displays the option to print out the visa requirements.
11. The user chooses to print the requirements.

Alternative courses:

6. If the country name is invalid:
    6.1 The system displays an error message.
    6.2 The system returns to step 3.
8. If the nationality is invalid:
    8.1 The system displays an error message.
    8.2 The system returns to step 6.
9. If no information about visa requirements is found:
    9.1 The system displays a suitable message.
    9.2 The system returns to step 1.

Note that the number associated with the alternative course indicates the step in the normal course that is replaced by this action or set of actions. Also note how specific the use case is about how the user and the system will interact.

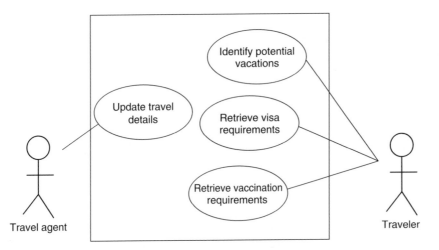

Figure 10.11 Use case diagram for the travel organizer showing four use cases and two actors

Use cases may be described graphically. Figure 10.11 shows the use case diagram for the travel organizer. The Travel agent actor is associated with the use case 'Update travel details.' Another actor for the travel organizer is Traveler, such as the Thomson family. Actors may be associated with more than one use case, so, for example, Traveler is associated with a use case 'Identify potential vacations' as well as the 'Retrieve visa requirements' use case. Each use case may also be associated with more than one actor. Note that an actor represents a role, so when Jasmine, who works for the travel agency, is booking a trip for herself, she adopts the role of the Traveler actor, but when she is working for the travel agent she will adopt the role of Travel agent.

This kind of description has a different style and a different focus from the scenarios described in Section 10.6.1. The layout is more formal, and the structure of good use cases has been discussed by many (e.g. Bittner and Spence, 2002; Alexander and Maiden, 2004). The description also focuses on the user–system interaction rather than on the user's activities; thus a use case presupposes that technology is being used. This kind of detail is more useful at conceptual design stage than during requirements or data gathering, but use cases have been found to help some stakeholders express their views on how existing systems are used and how a new system might work.

To develop a use case, first identify the actors, i.e. the people or other systems that will be interacting with the system under development. Then examine these actors and identify their goal or goals in using the system. Each of these will be a use case.

ACTIVITY 10.4

Consider the example of the movie rental service. One use case is 'Rent movie,' and this would be associated with the Subscriber actor.
1. Identify one other main actor and an associated use case, and draw a use case diagram for the movie rental service.

(Continued)

2. Write out the use case for 'Rent movie' including the normal and some alternative courses. You may assume that the normal course is for users to go to the website to find a movie by director.

Comment

1. One other main actor is the person who is responsible for updating the movie listings, who might be called Movie manager. A use case for this actor might then be 'Update movie collection.' Figure 10.12 is the associated use case diagram. There are other use cases you may have identified.

2. The use case for 'Rent movie' might be something like this:
   1. The system displays a menu of choices.
   2. The user chooses to see a list of movies by director.
   3. The system displays a list of directors.
   4. The user looks through the list to locate required director.
   5. The system displays a list of movies directed by named director.
   6. The user chooses the required movie.
   7. The system prompts for user name and password.
   8. The user enters her user name and password.
   9. The system verifies the user's password.
   10. The system displays the user's default rental and payment options.
   11. The user confirms the default options.
   12. The system provides a link for downloading the movie.

Alternative courses:
   2. If the user knows the movie title:
      2.1 The user identifies movie title.
      2.2 The system displays movie details.
      2.3 The user confirms choice.
      2.4 The system goes to step 7.
   10. If the user password is not valid:
      10.1 The system displays error message.
      10.2 The system returns to step 7. ■

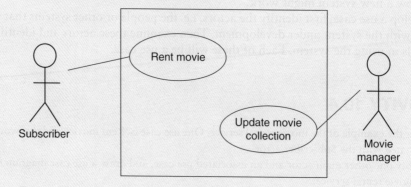

Figure 10.12 Use case diagram for the movie rental subscription service

10.6.3   Essential Use Cases

Essential use cases were developed by Constantine and Lockwood (1999) to combat what they see as the limitations of both scenarios and use cases as described above. Scenarios are concrete stories that concentrate on realistic and specific activities. They therefore can obscure broader issues concerned with the wider organizational view. On the other hand, traditional use cases contain certain assumptions, including the fact that there is a piece of technology to interact with, and also assumptions about the user interface and the kind of interaction to be designed.

Essential use cases (also referred to sometimes as task cases) represent abstractions from scenarios, i.e. they represent a more general case than a scenario embodies, and try to avoid the assumptions of a traditional use case. An essential use case is a structured narrative consisting of three parts: a name that expresses the overall user intention, a stepped description of user actions, and a stepped description of system responsibilities. This division between user and system responsibilities can be very helpful during conceptual design when considering task allocation and system scope, i.e. what the user is responsible for and what the system is to do.

An example essential use case based on the visa requirements example given above is shown in Figure 10.13. Note that the steps are more generalized than those in the use case in Section 10.6.2, while they are more structured than the scenario in Section 10.6.1. For example, the second user intention does not say anything about choosing options or system prompts; it simply states that the user supplies the required information. This could be achieved in a variety of ways including scanning a passport, accessing a database of personal information based on fingerprint recognition, and so on. The point is that at the time of creating this essential use case, there is no commitment to a particular interaction design. Essential use cases would normally be developed before the more detailed use case.

Instead of actors, essential use cases are associated with user roles. An actor could be another system, whereas a user role is a role that a number of different people may play when using the system, so it's not a particular person, and not another system. As with use cases, producing an essential use case begins with identifying user roles.

| retrieveVisa | |
USER INTENTION	SYSTEM RESPONSIBILITY
find visa requirements	request destination and nationality
supply required information	obtain appropriate visa information
obtain a personal copy of visa information	offer information in different formats
choose suitable format	provide information in chosen format

Figure 10.13 An essential use case for retrieving visa requirements in the travel organizer

ACTIVITY 10.5

Construct an essential use case 'rentMovie' for the user role 'Subscriber' of the movie rental subscription service discussed in Activity 10.4.

Comment

Note here that we don't talk about passwords, but merely state that the users need to identify themselves. This could be done using fingerprinting, or retinal scanning, or any other suitable technology. The essential use case does not commit to any particular technology at this point. Neither does it specify listing options or details of how to choose alternatives. ■

rentMovie

USER INTENTION	SYSTEM RESPONSIBILITY
specify director name	
	offer relevant movie titles
identify required movie	
identify self	
	verify identity
	ascertain rental period
	take payment
	provide correct movie

10.7 Task Analysis

Task analysis is used mainly to investigate an existing situation, not to envision new products. It is used to analyze the underlying rationale and purpose of what people are doing: what are they trying to achieve, why are they trying to achieve it, and how are they going about it? The information gleaned from task analysis establishes a foundation of existing practices on which to build new requirements or design new tasks.

Task analysis is an umbrella term that covers techniques for investigating cognitive processes and physical actions, at a high level of abstraction and in minute detail. In practice, task analysis techniques have had a mixed reception. The most widely used version is Hierarchical Task Analysis, and this is the technique introduced in this chapter.

10.7.1 Hierarchical Task Analysis

Hierarchical Task Analysis (HTA) was originally designed to identify training needs (Annett and Duncan, 1967). It involves breaking a task down into subtasks and then into sub-subtasks and so on. These are then grouped together as plans that specify how the tasks might be performed in a real situation. HTA focuses on the physical and observable actions that are performed, and includes looking at actions that are not related to software or an interactive product at all. The starting point is a user goal. This is then examined and the main tasks

0. In order to buy a DVD
1. locate DVD
2. add DVD to shopping basket
3. enter payment details
4. complete address
5. confirm order

plan 0: If regular user do 1-2-5. If new user do 1-2-3-4-5.

Figure 10.14 An HTA for buying a DVD

associated with achieving that goal are identified. Where appropriate, these tasks are subdivided into subtasks, and then subtasks can be divided further – down to low-level steps of the interaction which may be represented in a screen sketch.

Consider the task of buying a DVD (based on Hornsby, 2010). This task can be decomposed into the subtasks: locate DVD; add DVD to shopping basket; enter payment details; complete address; and confirm order. Some of these subtasks might not be performed if the user is a regular user – entering payment and address details may not be performed in this case. This can be captured through plans. Figure 10.14 shows the subtasks for buying a DVD and one plan showing two alternative paths through those subtasks.

An alternative expression of an HTA is a graphical box-and-line notation. Figure 10.15 shows the graphical version of the HTA in Figure 10.14. Here the subtasks are represented by named boxes with identifying numbers. The hierarchical relationship between tasks is shown using a vertical line. If a task is not decomposed any further then a thick horizontal line is drawn underneath the corresponding box. Plans are also shown in this graphical form. They are written alongside the vertical line emitting from the task being decomposed.

Use of HTA has been controversial, with both its supporters and its detractors. There are two main problems with using it on real problems:

1. Real tasks are very complex, and task analysis does not scale very well. The notation soon becomes unwieldy, making it difficult to follow.
2. Task analysis is limited in the kinds of task it can model. For example, it cannot model tasks that are overlapping or in parallel, nor can it model interruptions. Most people work through interruptions of various kinds, and many significant tasks happen in parallel.

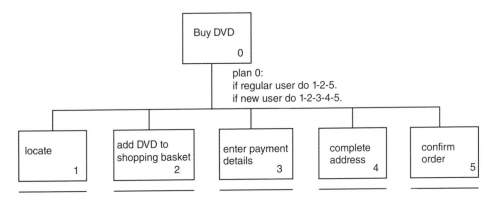

Figure 10.15 A graphical representation of the task analysis for buying a DVD

On the other hand, benefits of task analysis include (Hornsby, 2010):

1. It lets you objectively compare alternative designs, based on a user's planned tasks and subtasks.
2. It provides a good understanding of the interaction at whichever level of abstraction is appropriate. This facilitates good design.
3. It supports design reuse – again at different levels of abstraction.

ACTIVITY 10.6

Consider the travel organizer again and perform hierarchical task analysis for the goal of identifying a vacation. Include all plans in your answer. Express the task analysis textually and graphically.

Comment

The main tasks involved in this activity are to compile a set of initial criteria (e.g. a sailing trip for novices), find out any constraints on the vacation, such as possible dates and facilities required at the destination (e.g. child crèche), identify potential options that fit the criteria (e.g. a flotilla experience around the Greek Islands with BoatsRUs), decide on the preferred vacation, and book it. Identifying potential vacations can be decomposed into other tasks such as looking for suitable destinations, looking at a destination's facilities, identifying travel companies who operate to the chosen destination, and checking availability of potential vacation on preferred dates. At any point while identifying potential vacations, the options can be saved. Figure 10.16 shows the corresponding graphical representation. The textual version of the HTA is shown below. ■

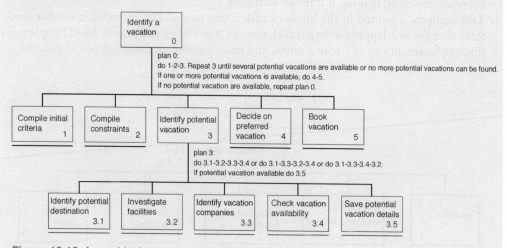

Figure 10.16 A graphical representation of the vacation HTA

0. In order to identify potential vacations:
1. Compile a set of initial criteria.
2. Compile a set of constraints.
3. Identify potential vacation.
    3.1 Identify potential destinations.
    3.2 Investigate facilities at potential destination.
    3.3 Identify travel companies operating at potential destinations.
    3.4 Check availability of potential vacation.
    3.5 Save vacation details.
4. Decide on preferred vacation.
5. Book vacation.

plan 0: do 1-2-3. Repeat 3 until several potential vacations are available or
no more potential vacations can be found. If one or more potential vacations
are available, do 4–5. If no potential vacations are available, repeat plan 0.
plan 3: do 3.1-3.2-3.3-3.4 or do 3.1-3.3-3.2-3.4 or do 3.1-3.3-3.4-3.2. If
potential vacation available, do 3.5.

Assignment

*This assignment is the first of five assignments that together take you through the complete
development lifecycle for an interactive product. This assignment requires you to use techniques described in this chapter for establishing requirements. You will also need to draw on
techniques from Chapters 7 and 8. The further four assignments are at the end of Chapters
11, 12, 14, and 15.*

*The overall assignment is for you to design and evaluate an interactive product for book-
ing tickets online for events like concerts, the theater, and the cinema. Most venues have an
online booking facility already, but it can be awkward and frustrating to identify and book
the seats you want.*

For this assignment, you should:

(a) Identify users' needs for this online facility. You could do this in a number of ways. For
example, you could observe people using ticket agents, think about your own experience
of purchasing tickets, look at websites for booking tickets, interview friends and family
about their experiences, and so on. Record your data carefully.

(b) Based on your user requirements, choose two different user profiles and produce one
persona and one main scenario for each, capturing how the user is expected to interact
with the product.

(c) Perform a task analysis on the main task associated with the ticket booking system, i.e.
booking a ticket.

(d) Based on this analysis, produce a use case for the main task of booking a ticket.

(e) Using the data gathered in part (a) and your subsequent analysis, identify different kinds
of requirements for the product, according to the headings introduced in Section 10.3.
Write up the requirements in the style of the Volere shell.

Summary

In this chapter, we have looked in more detail at the importance of the requirements activity, and how to establish requirements for interaction design. The data gathering techniques introduced in Chapter 7 can be used in various combinations to gather requirements data. In addition, contextual inquiry, studying documentation, and researching similar products are commonly used techniques. Scenarios, use cases, and essential use cases are helpful techniques for documenting the findings from data gathering sessions. Task analysis is a little more structured, but does not scale well.

Key points
- Getting the requirements right is crucial to the success of the interactive product.
- There are different kinds of requirements: functional, data, environmental (context of use), user characteristics, usability goals, and user experience goals. Every product will have requirements under each of these headings.
- The most commonly used data gathering techniques for this activity are: questionnaires, interviews, focus groups, direct observation, indirect observation, studying documentation, researching similar products, and contextual inquiry.
- Descriptions of user tasks such as scenarios, use cases, and essential use cases help users to articulate existing work practices. They also help to express envisioned use for new products.
- Task analysis techniques help to investigate existing systems and current practices.

Further Reading

DIAPER, D. and STANTON, N. (2004) *The Handbook of Task Analysis for Human–Computer Interaction*. Lawrence Erlbaum Associates. This collection of articles covers the wide diversity of task analysis, including the foundations of task analysis, cognitive approaches, formal notations, and industry experiences. This is not a book to read cover to cover, but is more of a reference book.

GOTTESDIENER, E. (2005) *The Software Requirements Memory Jogger*. Goal/QPC. This handy little book is an excellent practical resource for developing and managing requirements. It is written in a direct and informative style that provides specific guidance including tips, warnings, and factors to consider.

PRUITT, J. and ADLIN, T. (2006) *The Persona Lifecycle: Keeping people in mind throughout product design*. Morgan Kaufmann. This book explains how to use personas in practice – how to integrate them into a product lifecycle, stories from the field, and bright ideas – as well as many example personas. It also includes five guest chapters that place personas in the context of other product design concerns.

ROBERTSON, S. and ROBERTSON, J. (2013) *Mastering the Requirements Process* (3rd edn). Pearson Education. In this book, Robertson and Robertson provide a very practical and useful framework for software requirements work.

Chapter 11

DESIGN, PROTOTYPING, AND CONSTRUCTION

Objectives

The main aims of this chapter are to:

- Describe prototyping and different types of prototyping activities.
- Enable you to produce simple prototypes from the models developed during the requirements activity.
- Enable you to produce a conceptual model for a product and justify your choices.
- Explain the use of scenarios and prototypes in design.
- Introduce physical computing kits and software development kits, and their role in construction.

11.1 Introduction

Design activities begin once some requirements have been established. The design emerges iteratively, through repeated design–evaluation–redesign cycles involving users. Broadly speaking, there are two types of design: conceptual and concrete. The former is concerned with developing a conceptual model that captures what the product will do and how it will behave, while the latter is concerned with details of the design such as menu structures, haptic feedback, physical widgets, and graphics. As design cycles become shorter, the distinction between these two becomes blurred, but they are worth distinguishing because each emphasizes a different set of design concerns.

For users to evaluate the design of an interactive product effectively, designers must prototype their ideas. In the early stages of development, these prototypes may be made of paper and cardboard, or ready-made components pulled together to allow evaluation, while as design progresses, they become more polished, compact, and robust so that they resemble the final product.

Broadly speaking, the design process may start from two distinct situations: when starting from scratch or when modifying an existing product. Much of design comes from the latter, and it is tempting to think that additional features can be added, or existing ones tweaked, without extensive investigation, prototyping, or evaluation. Although prototyping and evaluation activities can be reduced if changes are not significant, they are still valuable and should not be skipped.

In Chapter 10, we discussed some ways to identify user needs and establish requirements. In this chapter, we look at the activities involved in progressing a set of requirements through the cycles of prototyping to construction. We begin by explaining the role and techniques of prototyping and then explain how prototypes may be used in the design process. We end with an exploration of physical computing and software development kits (SDKs) that provide a basis for construction.

11.2 Prototyping

It is often said that users can't tell you what they want, but when they see something and get to use it, they soon know what they don't want. Having established some requirements, the next step is to try out design ideas through prototyping and evaluation cycles.

11.2.1 What Is a Prototype?

A prototype is one manifestation of a design that allows stakeholders to interact with it and to explore its suitability; it is limited in that a prototype will usually emphasize one set of product characteristics and de-emphasize others. When you hear the term prototype, you may imagine a scale model of a building or a bridge, or a piece of software that crashes every few minutes. A prototype can also be a paper-based outline of a display, a collection of wires and ready-made components, an electronic picture, a video simulation, a complex piece of software and hardware, or a three-dimensional mockup of a workstation.

In fact, a prototype can be anything from a paper-based storyboard through to a complex piece of software, and from a cardboard mockup to a molded or pressed piece of metal. For example, when the idea for the PalmPilot was being developed, Jeff Hawkin (founder of the company) carved up a piece of wood about the size and shape of the device he had imagined. He used to carry this piece of wood around with him and pretend to enter information into it, just to see what it would be like to own such a device (Bergman and Haitani, 2000). This is an example of a very simple (some might even say bizarre) prototype, but it served its purpose of simulating scenarios of use. Advances in 3D printer technologies, coupled with reducing prices, have increased their use in design. It is now possible to take a 3D model from a software package and print a prototype. Even soft toys and chocolate may be 'printed' in this way (see Figure 11.1).

> **Video** showing a teddy bear being 'printed' is available at
> **http://www.disneyresearch.com/project/printed-teddy-bears/**

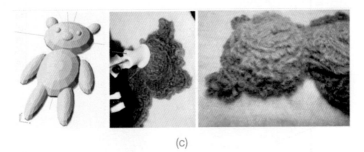

Figure 11.1 (a) Color output from a 3D printer: all the gears and rods in this model were 'printed' in one pass from bottom to top, and when one gear is turned, the others turn too. (b) James Bond's Aston Martin in Skyfall was in fact a 3D-printed model (http://www.telegraph.co.uk/technology/news/9712435/The-names-Printing-3D-Printing.html). (c) A teddy bear 'printed' from a wireframe design http://www.disneyresearch.com/project/printed-teddy-bears/

Source: (a) The Computer Language Company, Inc., courtesy of Alan Freedman (b) Courtesy of voxeljet and Propshop Modelmakers Ltd (c) Courtesy of Scott Hudson, Human–Computer Interaction Institute, Carnegie Mellon University.

11.2.2 Why Prototype?

Prototypes are useful when discussing or evaluating ideas with stakeholders; they are a communication device among team members, and an effective way for designers to explore design ideas. The activity of building prototypes encourages reflection in design, as described by Schön (1983) and is recognized by designers from many disciplines as an important aspect of design.

Prototypes answer questions and support designers in choosing between alternatives. Hence, they serve a variety of purposes: for example, to test out the technical feasibility of an idea, to clarify some vague requirements, to do some user testing and evaluation, or to check that a certain design direction is compatible with the rest of product development. The purpose of your prototype will influence the kind of prototype you build. So, for example, if you want to clarify how users might perform a set of tasks and whether your proposed

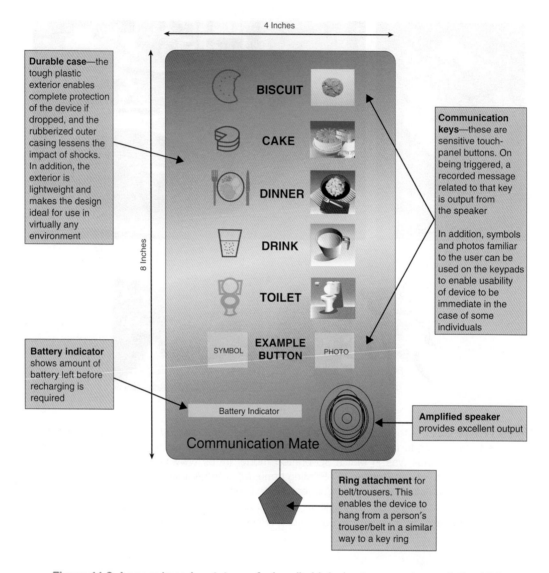

Figure 11.2 A paper-based prototype of a handheld device to support an autistic child
Source: Reprinted by permission of Sigil Khwaja.

design would support them in this, you might produce a paper-based mockup. Figure 11.2 shows a paper-based prototype of a handheld device to help an autistic child communicate. This prototype shows the intended functions and buttons, their positioning and labeling, and the overall shape of the device, but none of the buttons actually work. This kind of prototype is sufficient to investigate scenarios of use and to decide, for example, whether the button images and labels are appropriate and the functions sufficient, but not to test whether the speech is loud enough or the response fast enough. In the development of SITU, a smart food nutrition scale and tablet application, a range of prototypes and representations were used from initial idea to final product. These included screen sketches, paper and cardboard mock-ups, wireframes, and many post-its.

> **Link** to see the full story of SITU at
> **https://www.kickstarter.com/projects/situ/situ-smart-food-nutrition-scale**

Saffer (2010) distinguishes between a product prototype and a service prototype, where the latter involves role playing and people as an integral part of the prototype as well as the product itself. Service prototypes are sometimes captured as video scenarios and used in a similar way to the scenarios introduced in Chapter 10.

11.2.3   Low-Fidelity Prototyping

A low-fidelity prototype does not look very much like the final product and does not provide the same functionality. For example, it may use very different materials, such as paper and cardboard rather than electronic screens and metal, it may perform only a limited set of functions, or it may only represent the functions and not perform any of them. The lump of wood used to prototype the PalmPilot described above is a low-fidelity prototype.

Low-fidelity prototypes are useful because they tend to be simple, cheap, and quick to produce. This also means that they are simple, cheap, and quick to modify so they support the exploration of alternative designs and ideas. This is particularly important in early stages of development, during conceptual design for example, because prototypes that are used for exploring ideas should be flexible and encourage exploration and modification. Low-fidelity prototypes are not meant to be kept and integrated into the final product. They are for exploration only.

Storyboarding. Storyboarding is one example of low-fidelity prototyping that is often used in conjunction with scenarios, as described in Chapter 10. A storyboard consists of a series of sketches showing how a user might progress through a task using the product under development. It can be a series of screen sketches or a series of scenes showing how a user can perform a task using an interactive device. When used in conjunction with a scenario, the storyboard provides more detail and offers stakeholders a chance to role-play with a prototype, interacting with it by stepping through the scenario. The example storyboard shown in Figure 11.3 depicts a person (Christina) using a new mobile device for exploring historical sites. This example shows the context of use for this device and how it might support Christina in her quest for information about the pottery trade at The Acropolis in Ancient Greece.

Sketching. Low-fidelity prototyping often relies on hand-drawn sketches, and many people find it difficult to engage in this activity because they are inhibited about the quality of their drawing, but as Greenberg *et al* (2012) put it, "Sketching is not about drawing. Rather, it is about design" (p. 7). You can get over any inhibition by devising your own symbols and icons and practicing them – referred to by Greenberg *et al* as a 'sketching vocabulary' (p. 85). They don't have to be anything more than simple boxes, stick figures, and stars. Elements you might require in a storyboard sketch, for example, include digital devices, people, emotions, tables, books, etc., and actions such as give, find, transfer, and write. If you are sketching an interface design, then you might need to draw various icons, dialog boxes, and so on. Some simple examples are shown in Figure 11.4. The next activity requires other sketching symbols, but they can still be drawn quite simply. Baskinger (2008) provides further tips for those new to sketching.

Christina walks up hill; the product gives her information about the site

Christina adjusts the preferences to find information about the pottery trade in Ancient Greece

Christina scrambles to the highest point

Christina stores information about the pottery trader's way of life in Ancient Greece

Christina takes a photograph of the location of the pottery market

Figure 11.3 An example storyboard for a mobile device to explore ancient sites such as The Acropolis

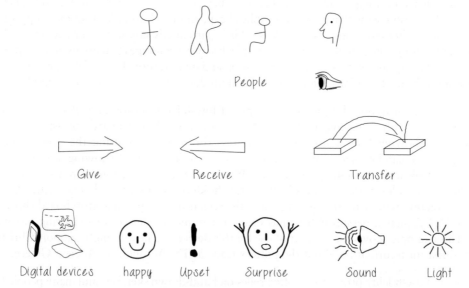

Figure 11.4 Some simple sketches for low-fidelity prototyping

Prototyping with index cards. Using index cards (small pieces of cardboard about 3×5 inches) is a successful and simple way to prototype an interaction, and is used often when developing websites. Each card represents a screen or one element of the interaction. In user evaluations, the user can step through the cards, pretending to perform the task while interacting with the cards. A more detailed example of this kind of prototyping is given in Section 11.6.2.

ACTIVITY 11.1

Produce a storyboard that depicts how to fill a car with gas (petrol).

Comment
Our attempt is shown in Figure 11.5. ∎

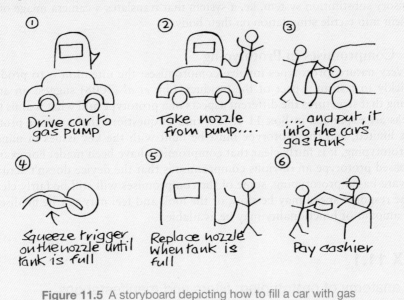

Figure 11.5 A storyboard depicting how to fill a car with gas

Wizard of Oz. Another low-fidelity prototyping method called Wizard of Oz assumes that you have a software-based prototype. In this technique, the user interacts with the software as though interacting with the product. In fact, however, a human operator simulates the software's response to the user. The method takes its name from the classic story of the little girl who is swept away in a storm and finds herself in the Land of Oz (Baum and Denslow, 1900). The Wizard of Oz is a small shy man who operates a large artificial image of himself from behind a screen where no one can see him. The Wizard of Oz style of prototyping has been used successfully for various applications, including PinTrace, a robotic system that helps surgeons to position orthopedic pins accurately during the surgery of hip fractures (Molin, 2004), and to identify gestures for full body interaction with digital games (Norton *et al*, 2010).

11.2.4 High-Fidelity Prototyping

A high-fidelity prototype looks like the final product and/or provides more functionality than a low-fidelity prototype. For example, a prototype of a software system developed in Visual Basic is higher fidelity than a paper-based mockup; a molded piece of plastic with a dummy keyboard is a higher-fidelity prototype of the PalmPilot than the lump of wood. High-fidelity prototyping is useful for selling ideas to people and for testing out technical issues.

High-fidelity prototypes can be developed by modifying and integrating existing components – both hardware and software. In robotics this approach has been called tinkering (Hendriks-Jansen, 1996) while in software development it has been referred to as Opportunistic System Development (Ncube *et al*, 2008). Banzi (2009) comments that: "Reusing existing technology is one of the best ways of tinkering. Getting cheap toys or old discarded equipment and hacking them to make them do something new is one of the best ways to get great results." Bird *et al* (2009) describe how they used this approach to develop a tactile vision sensory substitution system, i.e. a system that translates a camera image of the user's environment into tactile stimulation on their body.

11.2.5 Compromises in Prototyping

By their very nature, prototypes involve compromises: the intention is to produce something quickly to test an aspect of the product. Lim *et al* (2008) suggest an anatomy of prototyping that structures the different aspects of a prototype and what it aims to achieve. Their ideas are expanded in Box 11.1. The kind of questions that any one prototype can answer is limited, and the prototype must be built with the key issues in mind. In low-fidelity prototyping, it is fairly clear that compromises have been made. For example, with a paper-based prototype an obvious compromise is that the device doesn't actually work! For software-based prototyping, some of the compromises will still be fairly clear; for example, the response speed may be slow, or the look and feel may not be finalised, or only a limited amount of functionality may be available.

BOX 11.1

The anatomy of prototyping: filters and manifestations

Lim *et al* (2008) propose a view of prototypes which focuses on their role as filters, i.e. to emphasize specific aspects of a product being explored by the prototype, and as manifestations of designs, i.e. as tools to help designers develop their design ideas through external representations.

They suggest three key principles in their view of the anatomy of prototypes:

1. Fundamental prototyping principle: Prototyping is an activity with the purpose of creating a manifestation that, in its simplest form, filters the qualities in which designers are interested, without distorting the understanding of the whole.

2. Economic principle of prototyping: The best prototype is one that, in the simplest and the most efficient way, makes the possibilities and limitations of a design idea visible and measurable.

3. Anatomy of prototypes: Prototypes are filters that traverse a design space and are manifestations of design ideas that concretize and externalize conceptual ideas.

Lim *et al* identify several dimensions of filtering and of manifestation that may be considered when developing a prototype, although they point out that these dimensions are not complete but provide a useful starting point for consideration of prototype development. These are shown in Tables 11.1 and 11.2. ■

Filtering dimension	Example variables
Appearance	size; color; shape; margin; form; weight; texture; proportion; hardness; transparency; gradation; haptic; sound
Data	data size; data type (e.g. number; string; media); data use; privacy type; hierarchy; organization
Functionality	system function; users' functionality need
Interactivity	input behavior; output behavior; feedback behavior; information behavior
Spatial structure	arrangement of interface or information elements; relationship among interface or information elements – which can be either two- or three-dimensional, intangible or tangible, or mixed

Table 11.1 Example variables of each filtering dimension

Manifestation dimension	Definition	Example variables
Material	Medium (either visible or invisible) used to form a prototype	Physical media, e.g. paper, wood, and plastic; tools for manipulating physical matters, e.g. knife, scissors, pen, and sandpaper; computational prototyping tools, e.g. Macromedia Flash and Visual Basic; physical computing tools, e.g. Phidgets and Basic Stamps; available existing artifacts, e.g. a beeper to simulate a heart attack
Resolution	Level of detail or sophistication of what is manifested (corresponding to fidelity)	Accuracy of performance, e.g. feedback time responding to an input by a user (giving user feedback in a paper prototype is slower than in a computer-based one); appearance details; interactivity details; realistic versus faked data
Scope	Range of what is covered to be manifested	Level of contextualization, e.g. website color scheme testing with only color scheme charts or color schemes placed in a website layout structure; book search navigation usability testing with only the book search related interface or the whole navigation interface

Table 11.2 The definition and variables of each manifestation dimension

Two common compromises that often must be traded against each other are breadth of functionality provided versus depth. These two kinds of prototyping are called horizontal prototyping (providing a wide range of functions but with little detail) and vertical prototyping (providing a lot of detail for only a few functions).

Other compromises won't be obvious to a user of the system. For example, the internal structure of the product may not have been carefully designed, and the prototype may contain spaghetti code or be badly partitioned. One of the dangers of producing functional prototypes, i.e. ones that users can interact with automatically, is that the prototype can appear to be the final product. Another is that developers may consider fewer alternatives because the prototype works and users like it. However, the compromises made in order to produce the prototype must not be ignored, particularly those that are less obvious from the outside. For a good-quality product, good engineering principles must be adhered to.

"THEN IN HERE WE DO A CLAY MOCK-UP
OF THE COMPUTER MODEL"

BOX 11.2

When to use high fidelity and when to use low fidelity prototypes

Table 11.3 summarizes proclaimed advantages and disadvantages of high- and low-fidelity prototyping. Component kits and pattern libraries for interface components (see Section 11.7 and Chapter 12) make it quite easy to develop polished functional prototypes quickly, but there is a strong case for the value of low-fidelity prototypes, such as paper-based sketches, sticky note designs, and storyboarding, to explore initial ideas. Paper prototyping, for example, is used in game design (Gibson, 2014), website development, and product design (Case study 11.1). Both high- and low-fidelity prototypes provide useful feedback during evaluation and design iterations. For example, Dhillon et al (2011) found that a low-fidelity video prototype elicited comparable user feedback as a high-fidelity one, but was quicker and cheaper to produce. In the context of usability testing, most studies have found that there is no difference between the low- and high-fidelity approach in terms of user feedback (Sauer and Sonderegger, 2009), although they present some evidence that medium-fidelity prototypes are viewed as being less attractive than high- or low-fidelity ones. When exploring issues of content and structure, low-fidelity prototyping is preferable simply on the basis of cost, with the caveat that designers must be careful not to design technically infeasible capabilities on paper (Holmquist, 2005). The overriding consideration is the purpose of the prototype, and what level of fidelity is needed in order to get useful feedback. ∎

Type	Advantages	Disadvantages
Low-fidelity prototype	Lower development cost Evaluates multiple design concepts Useful communication device Addresses screen layout issues Useful for identifying market requirements Proof of concept	Limited error checking Poor detailed specification to code to Facilitator-driven Limited utility after requirements established Limited usefulness for usability tests Navigational and flow limitations
High-fidelity prototype	Complete functionality Fully interactive User-driven Clearly defines navigational scheme Use for exploration and test Look and feel of final product Serves as a living specification Marketing and sales tool	More resource-intensive to develop Time-consuming to create Inefficient for proof-of-concept designs Not effective for requirements gathering

Table 11.3 Advantages and disadvantages of low- and high-fidelity prototypes

Case Study 11.1

Paper prototyping as a core tool in the design of cell phone user interfaces

Paper prototyping is being used by cell phone and tablet companies as a core part of their design process (see Figure 11.6). There is much competition in the industry, demanding ever more new concepts. Mobile devices are feature-rich. They include mega-pixel cameras, music players, media galleries, downloaded applications, and more. This requires designing

(Continued)

Figure 11.6 Prototype developed for cell phone user interface

interactions that are complex, but are clear to learn and use. Paper prototyping offers a rapid way to work through every detail of the interaction design across multiple applications.

Mobile device projects involve a range of disciplines – all with their own viewpoint on what the product should be. A typical project may include programmers, project managers, marketing experts, commercial managers, handset manufacturers, user experience specialists, visual designers, content managers, and network specialists. Paper prototyping provides a vehicle for everyone involved to be part of the design process – considering the design from multiple angles in a collaborative way.

The case study on the website describes the benefits of using paper prototyping from the designer's viewpoint, while considering the bigger picture of its impact across the entire project lifecycle. It starts by explaining the problem space and how paper prototyping is used as an integrated part of user interface design projects for European and US-based mobile operator companies. The case study uses project examples to illustrate the approach and explains step by step how the method can be used to include a range of stakeholders in the design process – regardless of their skill set or background. The case study offers exercises so you can experiment with the approach yourself. ∎

Although prototypes will have undergone extensive user evaluation, they will not necessarily have been subjected to rigorous quality testing for other characteristics such as robustness and error-free operation. Building a product to be used by thousands or millions of people running on various platforms and under a wide range of circumstances requires a different testing regime than producing a quick prototype to answer specific questions.

The next Dilemma box discusses two different development philosophies. In evolutionary prototyping, a prototype evolves into the final product. Throwaway prototyping uses the prototypes as stepping stones towards the final design. In this case, the prototypes are thrown away and the final product is built from scratch. If an evolutionary prototyping approach is to be taken, the prototypes should be subjected to rigorous testing along the way; for throwaway prototyping such testing is not necessary.

Low-fidelity prototypes are not integrated into the final product. In contrast, high-fidelity prototypes can be and so present developers with a dilemma. They can choose to either build the prototype with the intention of throwing it away after it has fulfilled its immediate purpose, or build a prototype with the intention of evolving it into the final product.

The compromises made when producing a prototype must not be ignored – whatever those compromises were. However, when a project team is under pressure, it can become tempting to pull together a set of existing prototypes as the final product. After all, many hours of development will have been spent developing them, and evaluation with the client has gone well, so isn't it a waste to throw it all away? Basing the final product on prototypes in this way will simply store up testing and maintenance problems for later on: in short, this is likely to compromise the quality of the product.

Evolving the prototype into the final product through a defined process of engineering can lead to a robust final product, but this must be clearly planned from the beginning.

On the other hand, if the device is an innovation, then being first to market with a 'good enough' product may be more important for securing your market position than having a very high-quality product that reaches the market two months after your competitors'. ∎

11.3   Conceptual Design

Conceptual design is concerned with transforming requirements into a conceptual model. Designing the conceptual model is fundamental to interaction design, yet the idea of a conceptual model can be difficult to grasp. One of the reasons for this is that conceptual models take many different forms and it is not possible to provide a definitive detailed characterization of one. Instead, conceptual design is best understood by exploring and experiencing different approaches to it, and the purpose of this section is to provide you with some concrete suggestions about how to go about doing this.

A conceptual model is an outline of what people can do with a product and what concepts are needed to understand how to interact with it. The former will emerge from the current functional requirements; possibly it will be a subset of them, possibly all of them, and possibly an extended version of them. The concepts needed to understand how to interact with the product depend on a variety of issues related to who the user will be, what kind of interaction will be used, what kind of interface will be used, terminology, metaphors, application domain, and so on. The first step in getting a concrete view of the conceptual model is to steep yourself in the data you have gathered about your users and their goals and try to empathize with them. From this, a picture of what you want the

Figure 11.7 An example mood board
Source: Image courtesy of The Blog Studio www.theblogstudio.com.

users' experience to be when using the new product will emerge and become more concrete. This process is helped by considering the issues in this section, and by using scenarios and prototypes to capture and experiment with ideas. Mood boards (traditionally used in fashion and interior design) may be used to capture the desired feel of a new product (see Figure 11.7). This is informed by results from the requirements activity and considered in the context of technological feasibility.

There are different ways to achieve empathy with users. For example, Beyer and Holtzblatt (1998), in their method *Contextual Design*, recommend holding review meetings within the team to get different peoples' perspectives on the data and what they observed. This helps to deepen understanding and to expose the whole team to different aspects. Ideas will emerge as this extended understanding of the requirements is established, and these can be tested against other data and scenarios, discussed with other design team members, and prototyped for testing with users. Other ways to understand the users' experience are described in Box 11.3.

Key guiding principles of conceptual design are:

- Keep an open mind but never forget the users and their context.
- Discuss ideas with other stakeholders as much as possible.
- Use prototyping to get rapid feedback.
- Iterate, iterate, and iterate.

11.3.1 Developing an Initial Conceptual Model

Some elements of a conceptual model will derive from the requirements for the product. For example, the requirements activity will have provided information about the concepts involved in a task and their relationships, e.g. through task descriptions and analysis. Immersion in the data and attempting to empathize with the users as described above will, together with the requirements, provide information about the product's user experience goals, and give you a good understanding of what the product should be like. In this section we discuss

BOX 11.3

How to really understand the users' experience

Some design teams go to great lengths to ensure that they come to empathize with the users' experience. This box introduces two examples of this approach.

Buchenau and Suri (2000) describe experience prototyping, which is intended to give designers some insight into a user's experience that can only come from first-hand knowledge. They describe a team designing a chest-implanted automatic defibrillator. A defibrillator is used with victims of cardiac arrest when their heart muscle goes into a chaotic arrhythmia and fails to pump blood, a state called fibrillation. A defibrillator delivers an electric shock to the heart, often through paddle electrodes applied externally through the chest wall; an implanted defibrillator does this through leads that connect directly to the heart muscle. In either case, it's a big electric shock intended to restore the heart muscle to its regular rhythm that can be powerful enough to knock people off their feet.

This kind of event is completely outside most people's experience, and so it is difficult for designers to gain the insight they need to understand the user's experience. You can't fit a prototype pacemaker to each member of the design team and simulate fibrillation in them! However, you can simulate some critical aspects of the experience, one of which is the random occurrence of a defibrillating shock. To achieve this, each team member was given a pager to take home over the weekend (see Figure 11.8). The pager message simulated the occurrence of a defibrillating shock. Messages were sent at random, and team members were asked to record where they were, who they were with, what they were doing, and what they thought

Figure 11.8 The patient kit for experience prototyping

Source: Buchenau, M. and Suri, J. F. (2000) Experience prototyping. In *Proceedings of DIS 2000, Design Interactive Systems: Processes, Practices, Methods, Techniques*, pp. 17–19.

(Continued)

Figure 11.9 The Third Age empathy suit helps designers experience the loss of mobility and sensory perception
Source: Ford Motor Co.

and felt knowing that this represented a shock. Experiences were shared the following week, and example insights ranged from anxiety around everyday happenings such as holding a child and operating power tools, to being in social situations and at a loss how to communicate to onlookers what was happening. This first-hand experience brought new insights to the design effort.

Another instance is the Third Age suit, an empathy suit designed so that car designers can experience what it is like for people with some loss of mobility or declining sensory perception to drive their cars. The suit restricts movement in the neck, arms, legs, and ankles. Originally developed by Ford Motor Company and Loughborough University (see Figure 11.9) it has been used to raise awareness within groups of car designers, architects, and other product designers. ∎

approaches which help in pulling together an initial conceptual model. In particular, we consider:

- Which interface metaphors would be suitable to help users understand the product?
- Which interaction type(s) would best support the users' activities?
- Do different interface types suggest alternative design insights or options?

It is not the case that one way of approaching a conceptual design is right for one situation and wrong for another; all of these approaches provide different ways of thinking about the product and help in generating potential conceptual models.

Interface metaphors. Interface metaphors combine familiar knowledge with new knowledge in a way that will help the user understand the product. Choosing suitable metaphors and combining new and familiar concepts requires a careful balance between utility and fun, and is based on a sound understanding of the users and their context. For example, consider an educational system to teach 6-year-olds mathematics. One possible metaphor is a classroom with a teacher standing at the blackboard. But if you consider the users of the system and what is likely to engage them, a metaphor that reminds the children of something they enjoy would be more suitable, such as a ball game, the circus, a playroom, and so on.

Erickson (1990) suggests a three-step process for choosing a good interface metaphor. The first step is to understand what the system will do, i.e. identifying the functional requirements. Developing partial conceptual models and trying them out may be part of the process. The second step is to understand which bits of the product are likely to cause users problems, i.e. which tasks or subtasks cause problems, are complicated, or are critical. A metaphor is only a partial mapping between the software and the real thing upon which the metaphor is based. Understanding areas in which users are likely to have difficulties means that the metaphor can be chosen to support those aspects. The third step is to generate metaphors. Looking for metaphors in the users' description of the tasks is a good starting point. Also, any metaphors used in the application domain with which the users may be familiar may be suitable.

When suitable metaphors have been generated, they need to be evaluated. Erickson (1990) suggests five questions to ask.

1. How much structure does the metaphor provide? A good metaphor will provide structure, and preferably familiar structure.
2. How much of the metaphor is relevant to the problem? One of the difficulties of using metaphors is that users may think they understand more than they do and start applying inappropriate elements of the metaphor to the product, leading to confusion or false expectations.
3. Is the interface metaphor easy to represent? A good metaphor will be associated with particular visual and audio elements, as well as words.
4. Will your audience understand the metaphor?
5. How extensible is the metaphor? Does it have extra aspects that may be useful later on?

For the shared travel organizer introduced in Chapter 10, one metaphor we could use is a printed travel brochure, which is commonly found in travel agents. This familiarity could be combined with facilities suitable for an electronic brochure such as videos of locations, and searching. To evaluate this metaphor, apply the five questions listed above.

1. Does it supply structure? Yes, it supplies structure based on the familiar paper-based brochure. This is a book and therefore has pages, a cover, some kind of binding to hold the pages together, an index, and table of contents. Travel brochures are often structured around destinations but are also sometimes structured around activities, particularly when the company specializes in adventure trips. However, a traditional brochure focuses on the details of the vacation and accommodation and has little structure to support visa or vaccination information (both of which change regularly and are therefore not suitable to include in a printed document).
2. How much of the metaphor is relevant? Having details of the accommodation, facilities available, map of the area, and supporting illustrations is relevant for the travel organizer, so the content of the brochure is relevant. Also, structuring that information around types of vacation and destinations is relevant, and preferably both sets of grouping could be offered. But the physical nature of the brochure, such as page turning, is less relevant. The travel organizer can be more flexible than the brochure and should not try to

emulate its book nature. Finally, the brochure is printed maybe once a year and cannot be kept up-to-date with the latest changes whereas the travel organizer should be capable of offering the most recent information.

3. Is the metaphor easy to represent? Yes. The vacation information could be a set of brochure-like pages. Note that this is not the same as saying that the navigation through the pages will be limited to page-turning.
4. Will your audience understand the metaphor? Yes.
5. How extensible is the metaphor? The functionality of a paper-based brochure is fairly limited. However, it is also a book, and we could borrow facilities from ebooks (which are also familiar objects to most of our audience), so yes, it can be extended.

ACTIVITY 11.2

Another possible interface metaphor for the travel organizer is the travel consultant. A travel consultant takes a set of requirements and tailors the vacation accordingly, offering maybe two or three alternatives, but making most of the decisions on the travelers' behalf. Ask the five questions above of this metaphor.

Comment

1. Does the travel consultant metaphor supply structure? Yes, it supplies structure because the key characteristic of this metaphor is that the travelers specify what they want and the consultant researches it. It relies on the travelers being able to give the consultant sufficient information to be able to search sensibly rather than leaving him to make key decisions.
2. How much of the metaphor is relevant? The idea of handing over responsibility to someone else to search for suitable vacations may be appealing to some users, but might feel uncomfortable to others. On the other hand, having no help at all in sifting through potential options could become very tedious and dispiriting. So maybe this metaphor is relevant to an extent.
3. Is the metaphor easy to represent? Yes, it could be represented by a software agent, or by having a sophisticated database entry and search facility. But the question is: would users like this approach?
4. Will your audience understand the metaphor? Yes.
5. How extensible is the metaphor? The wonderful thing about people is that they are flexible, hence the metaphor of the travel consultant is also pretty flexible. For example, the consultant could be asked to refine their vacation recommendations according to as many different criteria as the travelers require. ∎

Interaction types. Chapter 2 introduced four different types of interaction: instructing, conversing, manipulating, and exploring. Which is best suited to the current design depends on the application domain and the kind of product being developed. For example, a computer game is most likely to suit a manipulating style, while a drawing package has aspects of instructing and conversing.

Most conceptual models will include a combination of interaction types, and it is necessary to associate different parts of the interaction with different types. For example, in the travel organizer, one of the user tasks is to find out the visa regulations for a particular destination. This will require an instructing approach to interaction as no dialog is necessary for the system to show the regulations. The user simply has to enter a predefined set of information, e.g. country issuing the passport and destination. On the other hand, trying to identify a vacation for a group of people may be conducted more like a conversation. For example, the user may begin by selecting some characteristics of the destination and some time constraints and preferences, then the organizer will respond with several options, and the user will provide more information or preferences and so on. (You may like to refer back to the scenario of this task in Chapter 10 and consider how well it matches this type of interaction.) Alternatively, for users who don't have any clear requirements yet, they might prefer to explore availability before asking for specific options.

Interface types. Considering different interfaces at this stage may seem premature, but it has both a design and a practical purpose. When thinking about the conceptual model for a product, it is important not to be unduly influenced by a predetermined interface type. Different interface types prompt and support different perspectives on the product under development and suggest different possible behaviors. Therefore considering the effect of different interfaces on the product at this stage is one way to prompt alternatives.

Before the product can be prototyped, some candidate alternative interfaces will need to have been chosen. These decisions will depend on the product constraints, arising from the requirements you have established. For example, input and output devices will be influenced particularly by user and environmental requirements. Therefore, considering interfaces here also takes one step towards producing practical prototypes.

To illustrate this, we consider a subset of the interfaces introduced in Chapter 6, and the different perspectives they bring to the travel organizer:

- Shareable interface. The travel organizer has to be shareable as it is intended to be used by a group of people, and it should be exciting and fun. The design issues for shareable interfaces which were introduced in Chapter 6 will need to be considered for this system. For example how best (whether) to use the individuals' own devices such as smartphones in conjunction with a shared interface.
- Tangible interface. Tangible interfaces are a form of sensor-based interaction, where blocks or other physical objects are moved around. Thinking about a travel organizer in this way conjures up an interesting image of people collaborating, maybe with the physical objects representing themselves traveling, but there are practical problems of having this kind of interface, as the objects may be lost or damaged.
- Augmented and mixed reality. The travel organizer is not the kind of product that is usually designed for an augmented or mixed reality interface. The question is what would the physical object be in this case, that the virtual element could enhance? One possibility might be to enhance the physical brochure to provide more dynamic and easily changed information.

ACTIVITY 11.3

Consider the movie rental subscription service introduced in Chapter 10.

1. Identify tasks associated with this product that would best be supported by each of the interaction types instructing, conversing, manipulating, and exploring.
2. Pick out two interface types from Chapter 6 that might provide a different perspective on the design.

Comment

1. Here are some suggestions. You may have identified others:
   - Instructing: the user wants to see details of a particular movie, such as script writer and shoot locations.
   - Conversing: the user wants to identify a movie on a particular topic but doesn't know exactly which one.
   - Manipulating: the movies might be represented as icons (maybe still images from the movie) that could be interrogated for information or manipulated to represent the movie being downloaded or tagged for later viewing.
   - Exploring: the user is looking for interesting movies, with no particular topic or actor in mind.
2. Movie rental services tend to be web-based, so it is worth exploring other styles to see what insights they may bring. We had the following thoughts, but you may have had others.

   The movie rental subscription service could be used anywhere – at home, on a boat, in the park – wherever a subscriber might want to view a movie. If the movie has to be viewed through the same interface as the rental is booked then this would limit the suitability of small mobile devices or wearables, but would make shareable interfaces appropriate. Ideally, the movie would be rentable through a wide range of interfaces, and viewable through a more limited set. A multimodal interface would offer the opportunity of experiencing movie clips and trailers (and indeed the movie itself) in different ways – especially with 3D movies, and future promise of successful smell-o-vision, in which odors are released from a TV screen. ∎

11.3.2   Expanding the Initial Conceptual Model

Considering the issues in the previous section helps the designer to produce a set of initial conceptual model ideas. These ideas must be thought through in more detail and expanded before being prototyped or tested with users. For example, concrete suggestions of the concepts to be communicated between the user and the product and how they are to be structured, related, and presented are needed. This means deciding which functions the product will perform (and which the user will perform), how those functions are related, and what information is required to support them. These decisions will be made initially only tentatively and may change after prototyping and evaluation.

What functions will the product perform? Understanding the tasks the product will support is a fundamental aspect of developing the conceptual model, but it is also important to consider which elements of the task will be the responsibility of the user and which will be carried out by the product. For example, the travel organizer may suggest specific vacation options for a given set of people, but is that as much as it should do? Should it automatically reserve the booking, or wait until it is told that this travel arrangement is suitable? Developing scenarios, essential use cases, and use cases will help clarify the answers to these questions. Deciding what the system will do and the user will do is sometimes called task allocation. This trade-off has cognitive implications (see Chapter 3), and is linked to social aspects of collaboration (see Chapter 4). If the cognitive load is too high for the user, then the device may be too stressful to use. On the other hand, if the product has too much control and is too inflexible, then it may not be used at all.

Another decision is which functions to hard-wire into the product and which to leave under software control, and thereby indirectly in the control of the human user.

How are the functions related to each other? Functions may be related temporally, e.g. one must be performed before another, or two can be performed in parallel. They may also be related through any number of possible categorizations, e.g. all functions relating to privacy on a smartphone, or all options for viewing photographs in a social networking site. The relationships between tasks may constrain use or may indicate suitable task structures within the product. For example, if one task depends on another, the order in which tasks can be completed may need to be restricted.

If task analysis has been performed, the breakdown will support these kinds of decision. For example, in the travel organizer example, the task analysis performed in Section 10.7 shows the subtasks involved and the order in which the subtasks can be performed. Thus, the system could allow potential travel companies to be found before or after investigating the destination's facilities. It is, however, important to identify the potential travel companies before looking for availability.

What information is needed? What data is required to perform a task? How is this data to be transformed by the system? Data is one of the categories of requirements identified and captured through the requirements activity. During conceptual design, these requirements are considered to ensure that the model provides the information necessary to perform the task. Detailed issues of structure and display, such as whether to use an analog display or a digital display, will more likely be dealt with during the concrete design activity, but implications arising from the type of data to be displayed may impact conceptual design issues.

For example, identifying potential vacations for a set of people using the travel organizer requires the following information: what kind of vacation is required; available budget; preferred destinations (if any); preferred dates and duration (if any); how many people it is for; and any special requirements (such as disability) that this group has. In order to perform the function, the system needs this information and must have access to detailed vacation and destination descriptions, booking availability, facilities, restrictions, and so on.

Initial conceptual models may be captured in wireframes – a set of documents that show structure, content, and controls. Wireframes may be constructed at varying levels of abstraction, and may show a part of the product or a complete overview. Case Study 11.2 and Chapter 12 include more information and some examples.

11.4 Concrete Design

Conceptual design and concrete design are closely related. The difference between them is rather a matter of changing emphasis: during design, conceptual issues will sometimes be highlighted and at other times, concrete detail will be stressed. Producing a prototype inevitably means making some concrete decisions, albeit tentatively, and since interaction design is iterative, some detailed issues will come up during conceptual design, and vice versa.

Designers need to balance the range of environmental, user, data, usability, and user experience requirements with functional requirements. These are sometimes in conflict. For example, the functionality of a wearable interactive product will be restricted by the activities the user wishes to perform while wearing it; a computer game may need to be learnable but also challenging.

There are many aspects to the concrete design of interactive products: visual appearance such as color and graphics, icon design, button design, interface layout, choice of interaction devices, and so on. Chapter 6 introduces several interface types and their associated design issues; these issues represent the kinds of decision that need to be made during concrete design. Case study 11.2 illustrates the impact that different-sized devices may have on the same application, and the need to explicitly design for different form factors. Chapter 6 also introduces some guidelines, principles, and rules for different interface types to help designers ensure that their products meet usability and user experience goals.

Case Study 11.2

Designing mobile applications for multiple form factors

Trutap is a social networking service designed for more than 350 different models of mobile device, which was built for a UK startup between 2007 and 2009. It aggregates online blogging, instant messaging, and social services like Facebook, allowing its users to interact with them (see Figures 11.10 and 11.11). The design of the Trutap application, which took place over two major releases, posed significant challenges in terms of how to integrate disparate sources of data onto small-screen devices, and produce a design which would scale between form factors, i.e. different physical handset designs.

The product was designed with a clear goal: teenagers and young adults were spending much of their social lives online. Trutap would help them keep connected, wherever they were.

Two versions of the product were launched: Trutap 1.0 offered its own mechanisms for managing people's contacts and communicating with them, and tied into a range of existing instant messaging networks (Yahoo!, MSN, AOL, and the like). Launched in 2008, this version saw far greater take-up in India and Indonesia than with its original target audience of UK students.

| Multiple services, aggregated vertically | Carousel for inter-service navigation, contextual options menus |

Figure 11.10 Trutap: version 2.0 design concepts

Source: © Trutap, Reproduced with permission.

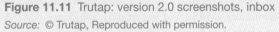

| 128 x 160 screen size | 176 x 220 screen size | 240 x 320 screen size |

Figure 11.11 Trutap: version 2.0 screenshots, inbox

Source: © Trutap, Reproduced with permission.

This take-up, combined with the successful launch of the iPhone in July 2008 and the increasing prominence of Facebook as the dominant site for personal social networking, led to a change in emphasis for the 2.0 release of Trutap. Launched a year after 1.0, and technically an evolution rather than a reworking, release 2.0 emphasized the aggregation of existing online services, tying into Facebook, weblogging software, and photo management, and extending the number of instant messaging services covered. Publicly, the product was presented as a means for aspirational middle classes in the developing world to experience many of the same benefits that the iPhone promised, but on their conventional mobile devices.

This case study, by Tom Hume, Johanna Hunt, Bryan Rieger, and Devi Lozdan from Future Platforms Ltd, explores the impact that different form factors had on the design of Trutap. ■

Concrete design also deals with issues related to user characteristics and context, and two aspects that have drawn particular attention for concrete design are accessibility and national culture. Accessibility was discussed in Box 1.2. Researchers, designers, and evaluators have investigated a range of techniques, toolkits, and interaction devices to support individuals with different accessibility needs. More recently, there has been a reaction to this approach that challenges the 'rhetoric of compassion' in favor of a 'rhetoric of engagement', and suggests that users be empowered rather than designed for (Rogers and Marsden, 2013).

Aspects of cross-cultural design include use of appropriate language(s), colors, icons and images, navigation, and information architecture (Rau *et al*, 2013). Example design guidelines include ensuring that the product supports different formats for dates, times, numbers, measurements, and currencies, and that generic icons are designed where possible (Esselink, 2000). However, Marsden *et al* (2008) warn of the problems in seeing a user's need and attempting to meet that need without first asking the community if they, too, recognize that need (see also Case Study 11.3 and Gary Marsden's interview at the end of this chapter).

Guidelines, although seemingly attractive, can be misguided. One of the most well-known sets of guidelines for cultural web design was proposed by Marcus and Gould (2000), building on the cultural dimensions proposed by Hofstede (1994). However, Hofstede's work, and its application in interaction design, has been challenged (see Box 11.4), and designing for a cross-cultural audience is now recognized as more than a translation exercise. As Carlson (1992, p. 175) has put it, successful products "are not just bundles

BOX 11.4

Using Hofstede's dimensions in interaction design

One of the most influential pieces of work on characterizing national culture differences was carried out by a management theorist called Geert Hofstede around 1970. He was given access to responses from a survey of IBM employees in over 50 countries worldwide and from this he identified four dimensions of national culture: power distance (PD), individualism (IND), masculinity–femininity (MAS), and uncertainty avoidance (UA). As a result of work done in Hong Kong at a later date by a Canadian, Michael Bond, a fifth dimension was added that deals with time orientation.

Although influential, Hofstede's work does have limitations. For example, he admits that the people involved in designing the original questionnaire were all from Western cultures. In addition, his studies have been discussed and challenged over the intervening years: e.g. Oyserman *et al* (2002) challenged his finding that European Americans are more individualistic than people from other ethnic groups. The application of his ideas in interaction design has also been challenged – e.g. work by Oshlyansky (2007) found that Hofstede's model does not help explain cultural differences in affordance; nor does it seem to apply to technology acceptance. So, although popular, Hofstede's dimensions may not be the best approach to accommodating national culture differences in interaction design. ■

of technical solutions; they are also bundles of social solutions. Inventors succeed in a particular culture because they understand the values, institutional arrangements, and economic notions of that culture."

11.5 Using Scenarios

Scenarios are informal stories about user tasks and activities. Scenarios can be used to model existing work situations, but they are more commonly used for expressing proposed or imagined situations to help in conceptual design. Often, stakeholders are actively involved in producing and checking through scenarios for a product. Bødker suggests four roles (Bødker, 2000, p. 63):

1. As a basis for the overall design.
2. For technical implementation.
3. As a means of cooperation within design teams.
4. As a means of cooperation across professional boundaries, i.e. as a basis of communication in a multidisciplinary team.

In any one project, scenarios may be used for any or all of these. More specifically, scenarios have been used as scripts for user evaluation of prototypes, as the basis of storyboard creation (see Section 11.6.1), and to build a shared understanding among team members. Scenarios are good at selling ideas to users, managers, and potential customers.

Bødker proposes the notion of plus and minus scenarios. These attempt to capture the most positive and the most negative consequences of a particular proposed design solution (see Figure 11.12), thereby helping designers to gain a more comprehensive view of the proposal. This idea has been extended by Mancini *et al* (2010) who use positive and negative video scenarios to explore futuristic technology.

11.6 Generating Prototypes

In this section we illustrate how prototypes may be used in design, and demonstrate one way in which prototypes may be generated from the output of the requirements activity: producing a storyboard from a scenario and a card-based prototype from a use case. Both of these are low-fidelity prototypes and they may be used as the basis to develop more detailed interface designs and higher-fidelity prototypes as development progresses.

11.6.1 Generating Storyboards from Scenarios

A storyboard represents a sequence of actions or events that the user and the product go through to achieve a task. A scenario is one story about how a product may be used to achieve the task. It is therefore possible to generate a storyboard from a scenario by breaking the scenario into a series of steps which focus on interaction, and creating one scene in the storyboard for each step. The purpose for doing this is two-fold: first, to produce a storyboard that can be used to get feedback from users and colleagues; second, to prompt the design team to consider the scenario and the product's use in more detail. For example, consider

Scenario 3: Hyper-wonderland

This scenario addresses the positive aspects of how a hypermedia solution will work.

The setting is the Lindholm construction site sometime in the future.

Kurt has access to a portable PC. The portables are hooked up to the computer at the site office via a wireless modem connection, through which the supervisors run the hypermedia application.

Action: During inspection of one of the caissons[1] Kurt takes his portable PC, switches it on and places the cursor on the required information. He clicks the mouse button and gets the master file index together with an overview of links. He chooses the links of relevance for the caisson he is inspecting.

Kurt is pleased that he no longer needs to plan his inspections in advance. This is a great help because due to the 'event-driven' nature of inspection, constructors never know where and when an inspection is taking place. Moreover, it has become much easier to keep track of personal notes, reports etc. because they can be entered directly on the spot.

The access via the construction site interface does not force him to deal with complicated keywords either. Instead, he can access the relevant information right away, literally from where he is standing.

A positive side-effect concerns his reachability. As long as he has logged in on the computer, he is within reach of the secretaries and can be contacted when guests arrive or when he is needed somewhere else on the site. Moreover, he can see at a glance where his colleagues are working and get in touch with them when he needs their help or advice.

All in all, Kurt feels that the new computer application has put him more in control of things.

[1] Used in building to hold water back during construction.

Scenario 4: Panopticon

This scenario addresses the negative aspects of how a hypermedia solution will work.

The setting is the Lindholm construction site sometime in the future.

Kurt has access to a portable PC. The portables are hooked up to the computer at the site office via a wireless modem connection, through which the supervisors run the hypermedia application.

Action: During inspecting one of the caissons Kurt starts talking to one of the builders about some reinforcement problem. They argue about the recent lab tests, and he takes out his portable PC in order to provide some data which justify his arguments. It takes quite a while before he finds a spot where he can place the PC: either there is too much light, or there is no level surface at a suitable height. Finally, he puts the laptop on a big box and switches it on. He positions the cursor on the caisson he is currently inspecting and clicks the mouse to get into the master file. The table of contents pops up and from the overview of links he chooses those of relevance – but no lab test appears on the screen. Obviously, the file has not been updated as planned.

Kurt is rather upset. This loss of prestige in front of a contractor engineer would not have happened if he had planned his inspection as he had in the old days.

Sometimes. he feels like a hunted fox especially in situations where he is drifting around thinking about what kind of action to take in a particular case. If he has forgotten to log out, he suddenly has a secretary on the phone: "I see you are right at caisson 39, so could you not just drop by and take a message?"

All in all Kurt feels that the new computer application has put him under control.

Figure 11.12 Example plus and minus scenarios

Source: S. Bødker (2000) Scenarios in user-centered design – setting the stage for reflection and action. Interacting with Computers, 13(1), Fig. 2, p. 70.

ACTIVITY 11.4

Consider an augmented reality in-car navigation system that takes information from a GPS and displays routes and traffic information directly onto the car windscreen. Suggest one plus and one minus scenario. For the plus scenario, think of the possible benefits of the system. For the minus scenario, imagine what could go wrong.

Figure 11.13 An example car-navigation system based on augmented reality
Source: The Aeon Project, courtesy of Michaël Harboun

Comment

Plus Scenario. This plus scenario shows some potential positive aspects of an augmented reality in-car navigation system.

Beth is on her way to her friend's new house. She hasn't been there before so she's following the directions from her new in-car navigation system. While waiting in a traffic light queue she brings up the overview map of her route and projects it on the windscreen. From this view she sees that there is a traffic jam on the original recommended route and tells the system to recalculate the route in order to avoid the jam. The display automatically reverts to normal driving mode.

Once through the traffic lights, there is quite a complicated set of road changes and intersections. By projecting arrows and route boundaries directly on her windscreen, the navigation system guides her through the road junction. Beth is surprised at how easy it is to follow the system's directions, and as she avoids the traffic jams she arrives at her friend's house on time.

Minus Scenario. This minus scenario shows some potential negative aspects of an augmented reality in-car navigation system.

Beth is on her way to her friend's new house. She hasn't been there before so she's following the directions from her new in-car navigation system. It was quite difficult to set up the route she wants to take because although the system can tell her about traffic jams, she has to manually agree every section of her route and this took a long time because she doesn't know the roads. Finally, she chose to have an 'overview' map of her route displayed as well as local directions for the next turn and other landmarks. At last she set out in the right direction.

Despite being in the bottom corner of her windscreen, the overview map is very distracting as it is constantly changing and flashing information. Her directions are also displayed on her

(Continued)

windscreen but are quite difficult to interpret. Suddenly a large arrow appears right in her line of sight highlighting an upcoming speed camera. This makes her jump and she swerves, narrowly missing the car in front. Feeling quite flustered and nervous, Beth turns off the system and telephones her friend for directions. ∎

the scenario for the travel organizer developed in Chapter 10. This can be broken down into five main steps:

1. The Thomson family gather around the organizer and enter a set of initial requirements.
2. The system's initial suggestion is that they consider a flotilla trip but Sky and Eamonn aren't happy.
3. The travel organizer shows them some descriptions of the flotillas written by young people.
4. Will confirms this recommendation and asks for details.
5. The travel organizer emails the details.

The first thing to notice about this set of steps is that it does not have the detail of a use case but identifies the key events or activities associated with the scenario. The second thing to notice is that some of these events are focused solely on the travel organizer's screen and some are concerned with the environment. For example, the first one talks about the family gathering around the organizer, while the third and fifth are focused on the travel organizer. We therefore could produce a storyboard that focuses on the screens or one that is focused on the environment. Either way, sketching out the storyboard will prompt us to think about design issues.

For example, the scenario says nothing about the kind of input and output devices that the system might use, but drawing the organizer forces you to think about these things. There is some information about the environment within which the system will operate, but again drawing the scene makes you stop and think about where the organizer will be. You don't

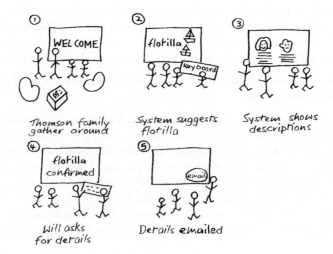

Figure 11.14 The storyboard for the travel organizer focusing on environmental issues

have to make any decisions about, e.g. using a trackball, or a touch screen, or whatever, but you are forced to think about it. When focusing on the screens, the designer is prompted to consider issues including what information needs to be available and what information needs to be output. This all helps to explore design decisions and alternatives, but is also made more explicit because of the drawing act.

We chose to draw a storyboard that focuses on the environment of the travel organizer, and it is shown in Figure 11.14. While drawing this, various questions relating to the environment came to mind such as how can the interaction be designed for all the family? Will they sit or stand? How confidential should the interaction be? What kind of documentation or help needs to be available? What physical components does the travel organizer need? And so on. In this exercise, the questions it prompts are just as important as the end product.

Note that although we have used the scenario as the main driver for producing the storyboard, there is other information from the requirements activity that also informs development.

ACTIVITY 11.5

Activity 10.3 asked you to develop a futuristic scenario for the one-stop car shop. Using this scenario, develop a storyboard that focuses on the environment of the user. As you are drawing this storyboard, write down the design issues you are prompted to consider.

Comment
We used the scenario in the comment for Activity 10.3. This scenario breaks down into five main steps: the user arrives at the one-stop car shop; the user is directed into an empty booth; the user sits down in the racing car seat and the display comes alive; the user can view reports; the user can take a virtual reality drive in their chosen car. The storyboard is shown in Figure 11.15. Issues that occurred to me as I drew this storyboard included how to display the reports, what kind of virtual reality equipment is needed, what input devices are needed: a keyboard or touch screen, a steering wheel, clutch, accelerator and brake pedals? How like the car controls do the input devices need to be? You may have thought of other issues. ∎

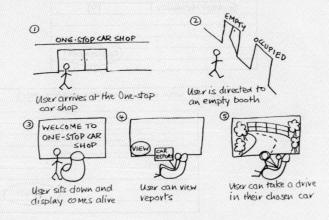

Figure 11.15 The storyboard generated from the one-stop car shop scenario in Section 10.3

11.6.2   Generating Card-Based Prototypes from Use Cases

The value of a card-based prototype lies in the fact that the screens or interaction elements can be manipulated and moved around in order to simulate interaction with a user or to explore the user's end-to-end experience. Where a storyboard focusing on the screens has been developed, this can be translated into a card-based prototype and used in this way. Another way to produce a card-based prototype is to generate one from a use case output from the requirements activity.

For example, consider the use case generated for the travel organizer in Section 10.6.2. This focused on the visa requirements part of the system. For each step in the use case, the travel organizer will need to have an interaction component to deal with it, e.g. a button or menu option, or a display. By stepping through the use case, it is possible to build up a card-based prototype to cover the required behavior. For example, the cards in Figure 11.16 were developed by considering each of the steps in the use case. Card one covers step 1; card two covers steps 2, 3, 4, 5, 6, and 7; and card three covers steps 8, 9, 10, and 11 (notice the print button that is drawn into card three to allow for steps 10 and 11). As with the storyboards, drawing concrete elements of the interface like this forces the designer to think about detailed

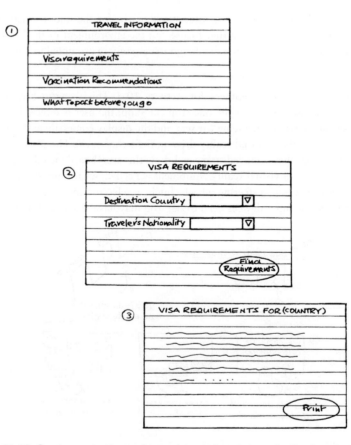

Figure 11.16 Cards one to three of a card-based prototype for the travel organizer

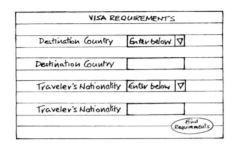

Figure 11.17 Card four of a card-based prototype for the travel organizer

issues so that the user can interact with the prototype. In card two you will see that I chose to use a drop-down menu for the country and nationality. This is to avoid mistakes. However, the flaw in this is that I may not catch all of the countries in my list, and so an alternative design could also be incorporated where the user can choose an 'enter below' option and then type in the country or nationality (see Figure 11.17).

These cards can then be shown to potential users of the system or fellow designers to get informal feedback. In this case, I showed these cards to a colleague, and through discussion of the application and the cards, concluded that although the cards represent one interpretation of the use case, they focus too much on an interaction model that assumes a WIMP/GUI interface. Our discussion was informed by several things including the storyboard and the scenario. One alternative would be to have a map of the world, and users can indicate their destination and nationality by choosing one of the countries on the map; another might be based around national flags. These alternatives could be prototyped using cards and further feedback obtained.

A set of card-based prototypes that cover a scenario from beginning to end may be the basis of a more detailed prototype, such as an interface or screen sketch, or it may be used in conjunction with personas to explore the user's end-to-end experience. This latter purpose is achieved by creating a visual representation of the user's experience. These representations

ACTIVITY 11.6

Produce a card-based prototype for the movie rental subscription service and the task of renting a movie as described by the use case in Activity 10.4. You may also like to ask one of your peers to act as a user and step through the task using the prototype.

Comment
Three of the cards from our prototype are shown in Figure 11.18. Note that these cards do not include any images. Thumbnails from the movie would make the screens attractive, and could be added here or at the next stage. ∎

(*Continued*)

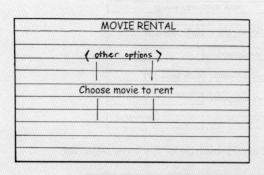

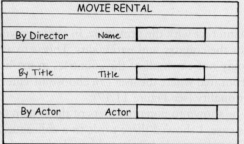

Figure 11.18 A card-based prototype for renting a movie from the movie rental subscription service

are variably called a design map (Adlin and Pruitt, 2010) or a customer journey map (Ratcliffe and McNeill, 2012), or an experience map. They illustrate a user's path or journey through the product or service, and are usually created for a particular persona, hence giving the journey sufficient context and detail to bring the discussions to life. They support designers in considering the user's overall experience when achieving a particular goal and are used to explore and question the designed experience and to identify issues that have not been considered so far. They may be used to analyze existing products and to collate design issues, or as part of the design process.

There are many different types of representation, of varying complexities. Two main ones are: the wheel and the timeline. The wheel representation is used when an interaction phase is more important than an interaction point, e.g. for a flight (see Figure 11.19(a) for an example). The timeline is used where a service is being provided that has a recognizable beginning and end point, such as purchasing an item through a website (an example of a timeline representation is in Figure 10.4(b)). Figure 11.19(b) illustrates the structure of a timeline and how different kinds of issues may be captured, e.g. questions, comments, and ideas.

To generate one of these representations, take one persona and two or three scenarios. Draw a timeline for the scenario and identify the interaction points for the user. Then use this as a discussion tool with colleagues to identify any issues or questions that may arise. Some people consider the user's mood and identify pain points, sometimes the focus will be on technical issues, and sometimes this can be used to identify missing functionality or areas of under-designed interaction.

Video illustrating the benefits of experience mapping using a timeline at **http://youtu.be/eLT_Q8sRpyl**

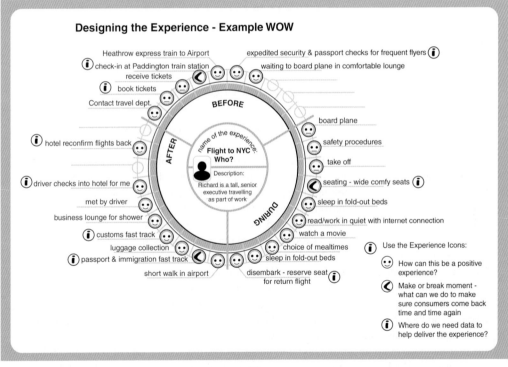

(a)

Figure 11.19 (a) An experience map using a wheel representation. (b) An example timeline design map illustrating how to capture different issues.

Source: (a) http://www.ux-lady.com/experience-maps-user-journey-and-more-exp-map-layout/ (b) Adlin, T. and Pruitt, J. (2010) *The Essential Persona Lifecycle: Your guide to building and using personas.* Morgan Kaufmann p. 134.

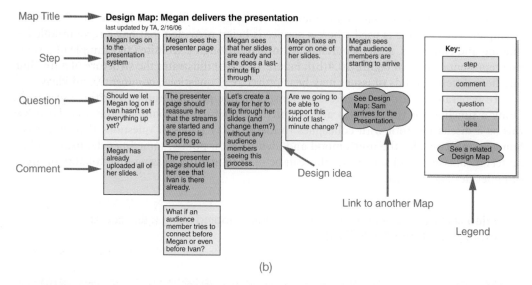

(b)

Figure 11.19 Continued

BOX 11.5

Involving users in design: participatory design

The idea of participatory design emerged in Scandinavia in the late 1960s and early 1970s. There were two influences on this early work: the desire to be able to communicate information about complex systems, and the labor union movement pushing for workers to have democratic control over changes in their work. In the 1970s, new laws gave workers the right to have a say in how their working environment was changed, and such laws are still in force today. A fuller history of the movement is given in Ehn (1989) and Nygaard (1990).

Several projects at this time attempted to involve users in design and focus on work rather than on simply producing a product. One of the most discussed is the UTOPIA project, a cooperative effort between the Nordic Graphics Workers Union and research institutions in Denmark and Sweden to design computer-based tools for text and image processing.

Involving users in design decisions is not simple, however. Cultural differences can become acute when users and designers are asked to work together to produce a specification for a system. Bødker *et al* (1991) recount the following scene from the UTOPIA project: "Late one afternoon, when the designers were almost through with a long presentation of a proposal for the user interface of an integrated text and image processing system, one of the typographers commented on the lack of information about typographical code-structure. He didn't think that it was a big error (he was a polite person), but he just wanted to point out that the computer scientists who had prepared the proposal had forgotten to specify how the codes were to be presented on the screen. Would it read '<bf/' or perhaps just '\b' when the text that followed was to be printed in boldface?"

In fact, the system being described by the designers was a WYSIWYG (what you see is what you get) system, and so text that needed to be in bold typeface would appear as bold (although most typographic systems at that time did require such codes). The typographer was unable to link his knowledge and experience with what he was being told. In response to this kind of problem, the project started using mockups. Simulating the working situation helped workers to draw on their experience and tacit knowledge, and designers to get a better understanding of the actual work typographers needed to do.

Case Study 11.3 describes an extension to the participatory design idea, called community-based design. ■

Case Study 11.3

Deaf telephony

This case study by Edwin Blake, William Tucker, Meryl Glaser, and Adinda Freudenthal discusses their experiences of community-based design in South Africa. The process of community-based co-design is one that explores various solution configurations in a multidimensional design space whose axes are the different dimensions of requirements and the various dimensions of designer skills and technological capabilities. The bits of this space that one can 'see' are determined by one's knowledge of the user needs and one's own skills. Co-design is a way of exploring that space in a way that alleviates the myopia of one's own viewpoint and bias. As this space is traversed, a trajectory is traced according to one's skills and learning, and according to the users' expressed requirements and their learning.

The project team set out to assist South African deaf people to communicate with each other, with hearing people, and with public services. The team has been working for many

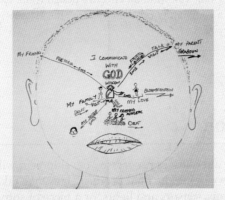

Figure 11.20 One participant's view of communication
Source: Copyright Edwin Blake *et al.*

(Continued)

Figure 11.21 Participants discussing design in sign language

years with a deaf community that has been disadvantaged due to both poverty and hearing impairment. The story of this wide-ranging design has been one of continual fertile (and on occasion frustrating) co-design with this community. The team's long-term involvement has meant they have transformed aspects of the community and that they have themselves been changed in what they view as important and in how they approach design.

Deaf users in this community started out knowing essentially nothing about computers. Their first language is South African Sign Language (SASL) and this use of SASL is a proud sign of their identity as a people. Many are also illiterate or semi-literate. There are a large number of deaf people using SASL; in fact there are more than some of the smaller official languages. Since the advent of democracy in 1994, there has been an increasing empowerment of deaf people and it is accepted as a distinct language in its own right.

In this case study, a brief historical overview of the project and the various prototypes that formed nodes in a design trajectory are presented. The methodology of Action Research and its cyclical approach to homing in on an effective implementation is reviewed. An important aspect of the method is how it facilitates learning by both the researchers and the user community so that together they can form an effective design team. Lastly, such a long-term intimate involvement with a community raises important ethical issues, which are fundamentally concerns of reciprocity. ∎

11.7 Construction

As prototyping and building alternatives progresses, development will focus more on putting together components and developing the final product. This may take the form of a physical product, such as a set of alarms, sensors and lights, or a piece of software, or both. Whatever the final form, it is very unlikely that you will develop anything from scratch as there are many useful (in some cases essential) resources to support development. Here we introduce two kinds of resource: physical computing kits and software development kits (SDKs).

11.7.1 Physical Computing

Physical computing is concerned with how to build and code prototypes and devices using electronics. Specifically, it is the activity of "creating physical artifacts and giving them behaviors through a combination of building with physical materials, computer programming and circuit building"(Gubbels and Froehlich, 2014). Typically, it involves designing things, using a printed circuit board (PCB), sensors (e.g. accelerometers, infrared, temperature) to detect states, and actuators (e.g. motors, valves) that cause some effect. An example is a 'friend or foe' cat detector that senses, via an accelerometer, any cat (or anything else for that matter) that tries to push through a family's catflap. The movement triggers an actuator to take a photo of what came through the catflap using a webcam positioned on the back door. The photo is uploaded to a website that alerts the owner if there are cats or other objects that do not match their own cat's image.

A number of physical computing toolkits have been developed for educational and prototyping purposes. One of the earliest is Arduino (see Banzi, 2009). The aim was to enable artists and designers to learn how to make and code physical prototypes using electronics in a couple of days, having attended a workshop. The toolkit is composed of two parts: the Arduino board (see Figure 11.22), which is the piece of hardware that is used to build objects, and the Arduino IDE (integrated development environment), which is a piece of software that makes it easy to program and upload a sketch (Arduino's name for a unit of code) to the board. A sketch, for example, might turn on an LED when a sensor detects a change in the light level. The Arduino board is a small circuit that contains a tiny chip (the microcontroller). It has a number of protruding 'legs' that provide input and output pins – which the sensors and actuators are connected to. Sketches are written in the IDE using a simple processing language, then uploaded to the board and translated into the 'C' programming language.

There are other toolkits that have been developed, based on the basic Arduino kit. The most well known is the LilyPad, which was co-developed by Leah Beuchley (see Figure 11.23 and her interview at the end of Chapter 6). It is a set of sewable electronic components for building fashionable clothing and other textiles. The Engduino® is a teaching tool based on the Arduino LilyPad; it has 16 multicolour LEDs and a button, which can be used to provide visual feedback, and simple user input. It also has a thermistor (that senses temperature), a

Figure 11.22 The Arduino board
Source: Courtesy of Nicolai Marquardt

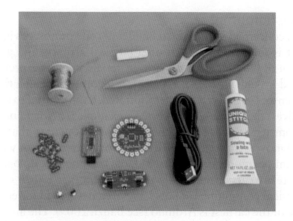

Figure 11.23 The Lilypad Arduino kit

Source: Photo courtesy of Leah Buechley
http://web.media.mit.edu/~leah/LilyPad/build/turn_signal_jacket.html.

3D accelerometer (that measures accelerations), and an infrared transmitter/receiver that can be used to transmit messages from one Engduino® to another.

Video introducing MakeMe (Marquardt *et al*, 2015), a novel toolkit that is assembled from a flat electronic sheet, where six sides are snapped out then slotted together to become an interactive cube that lights up in different colors, depending on how vigorously it is shaken. Intended to encourage children to learn, share, and fire their imagination to come up with new games and other uses, see it in action at **http://www.codeme.io/**

Other kinds of easy-to-use and quick-to-get-started physical toolkits – intended to provide new opportunities for people to be inventive and creative with – are Senseboard (Richards and Woodthorpe, 2009), LittleBits, and MaKey MaKey (Silver and Rosenbaum, 2012). The MaKey MaKey toolkit comprises a printed circuit board with an Arduino microcontroller, alligator clips, and a USB cable (see Figure 11.24). It communicates with a computer to send key presses, mouse clicks, and mouse movements. There are six inputs (the four arrow keys, the space bar, and a mouse click) positioned on the front of the board that alligator clips are clipped onto in order to connect with a computer via the USB cable. The other ends of the clips can be attached to any non-insulating object, such as a vegetable or piece of fruit. Thus, instead of using the computer keyboard buttons to interact with the computer, external objects such as bananas are used. The computer thinks MaKey MaKey is just like a keyboard or mouse. An example is to play a digital piano app using bananas as keys rather than keys on the computer keyboard. When they are touched, they make a connection to the board and MaKey MaKey sends the computer a keyboard message.

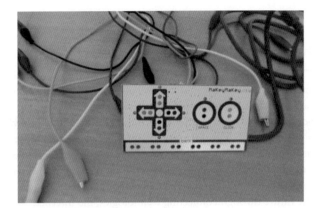

Figure 11.24 The MaKey MaKey toolkit

So far, physical toolkits have been aimed at children or designers to enable them to start programming through rapid creation of small electronic gadgets and digital tools (e.g. Hodges *et al*, 2013). However, Rogers *et al* (2014) demonstrated how retired people were equally able to be creative using the kit, turning "everyday objects into touchpads." They ran a series of workshops where small groups of retired friends, aged between early 60s and late 80s, assembled and played with the MaKey MaKey toolkit (see Figure 11.25). After playing music using fruit and vegetables as input, they saw many new possibilities for innovative design. Making and playing together, however childlike it might seem at first, can be a catalyst for imagining, free thinking, and exploring. People are sometimes cautious to volunteer their ideas, fearing that they are easily squashed, but in a positive environment they can flourish. The right kind of shared experience can create a positive and relaxed atmosphere, in which people from all walks of life can freely bounce ideas around.

Figure 11.25 A group of retired friends playing with a MaKey MaKey toolkit

BOX 11.6

The rise of the Maker Movement

The Maker Movement emerged in the mid 2000s. Following in the footsteps of the computer revolution and the Internet, it is viewed as the next big revolution that will transform manufacturing and production (Hatch, 2014). Whereas the explosion of the web was all about what it could do for us virtually, with a proliferation of apps, social media, and services, the Maker Movement is transforming how we make, buy, consume, and recycle things, from houses to clothes and food to bicycles. At its core is DIY – crafting physical things using a diversity of machines, tools, and methods collaboratively in workshops and makespaces. In a nutshell, it is about inventing the future through connecting technologies, the Internet, and physical things.

While there have always been hobbyists tinkering away making radios, clocks, and other devices, the world of DIY making has been opened up to many more people. Affordable, powerful, and easy-to-use tools, coupled with a renewed focus on locally sourced products and community-based activities, and a desire for sustainable, authentic, and ethically produced products, has led to a ground swell in interest in how to make. Fablabs (fabrication laboratories) first started appearing in cities throughout the world, offering a large physical space containing electronics and manufacturing equipment, including 3D printers, CNC milling machines, and laser cutters. Individuals bring their digital files to print and make things – which would have been impossible for them to do previously – such as large 3D models, furniture, and installations. Then smaller makerspaces started appearing in their thousands across the world, from Shanghai to rural India, again sharing production facilities for all to use and make. While some are small, for example sharing the use of a 3D printer, others are much larger and well resourced, offering an array of manufacturing machines, tools, and workspaces to make in.

Another development has been to build and program e-textiles using sewing machines and electronic thread. E-textiles comprise fabrics that are embedded with electronics, such as sensors, LEDs, and motors that are stitched together using conductive thread and conductive fabrics (Buechley and Qiu, 2014). An early example is the turn-signal biking jacket (developed by Leah Buechley and illustrated in Figure 1.3). Other e-textiles include interactive soft toys, wallpaper that sings when touched, and fashion clothing that reacts to the environment or events.

A central part of the Maker Movement involves tinkering (as discussed in Section 11.2.4) and the sharing of knowledge, skills, know-how, and what you have made. The Instructables .com website is for anyone to explore, document, and share their DIY creations. Go to the Instructables site and take a look at a few of the projects that have been uploaded by makers. How many of them are a combination of electronics, physical materials, and pure invention? Are they fun, useful, or gadgety? How are they presented? Do they inspire you to make? Another site, Etsy.com, is a popular online marketplace for people who make things to sell their crafts and other handmade items. It is designed to be easy for makers to use and set up their store to sell to family, friends, and strangers across the world. Unlike the corporate online sites, (e.g. Amazon, eBay), it is a place for craft makers to reach others and to show off their wares in ways they feel best fit what they have made.

In essence, the Maker Movement is about taking the DIY movement online to make it public and, in doing so, massively increase who can take part and how it is shared (Anderson, 2013). ■

ACTIVITY 11.7

Watch the video of Lady Gaga in the Voltanis, the first flying dress, developed by the e-textile company XO. What do you think of this fusion of fashion and state-of-the-art electronics and technology?

> **Video** of Lady Gaga in the Voltanis at **http://vimeo.com/91916514**

Comment
The Voltanis is a carbon fibre bodice that is also a remote-controlled vehicle. When Lady Gaga puts on this flying dress, she is then flown around the stage by a trained pilot – a bit like it was foreseen in early science fiction movies, with people wearing flatpacks. The emphasis on fashion has turned what is often seen as a geeky vision of the future into one that can engage fans and people from all over the world. Imagine Lady Gaga (or another famous singer) inviting a random fan from across the globe to move her around the stage for a minute (with the aid of the pilot). That beats getting your tweet retweeted by Justin Bieber. ■

11.7.2   SDKs: Software Development Kits

A software development kit (SDK) is a package of programming tools and components that supports the development of applications for a specific platform, e.g. for iOS on iPad, iPhone, and iPod touch, for the Kinect device, and for the Windows phone. Typically an SDK includes an IDE (integrated development environment), documentation, drivers, and sample programming code to illustrate how to use the SDK components. Some also include icons and buttons that can easily be incorporated into the design. While it is possible to develop applications without using an SDK, it is so much easier using such a powerful resource, and so much more can be achieved.

For example, the availability of Microsoft's Kinect SDK makes the device's powerful gesture recognition and body motion tracking capabilities accessible. This has led to the exploration of, for example, motion tracking in immersive games (Manuel *et al*, 2012), user identification using body lengths (Hayashi *et al*, 2014), and robot control (Wang *et al*, 2013).

An SDK will include a set of application programming interfaces (APIs) that allows control of the components without knowing the intricacies of how they work. In some cases, access to the API alone is sufficient to allow significant work to be udertaken, e.g. Hayashi *et al* (2014) only needed access to the APIs. The difference between APIs and SDKs is explored in Box 11.7.

BOX 11.7

APIs and SDKs

SDKs (software development kits) consist of a set of programming tools and components while an API (application programming interface) is the set of inputs and outputs, i.e. the technical interface to those components. To explain this further, an API allows different-shaped

(Continued)

building blocks of a child's puzzle to be joined together, while an SDK provides a workshop where all of the development tools are available to create whatever size and shape blocks you fancy, rather than using pre-shaped building blocks. An API therefore allows the use of pre-existing building blocks, while an SDK removes this restriction and allows new blocks to be created, or even to build something without blocks at all. An SDK for any platform will include all the relevant APIs, but it adds programming tools, documentation, and other development support as well. ∎

Assignment

This assignment continues work on the online booking facility introduced at the end of Chapter 10. The work will be continued in the assignments for Chapters 12, 14, and 15.

(a) Based on the information gleaned from the assignment in Chapter 10, suggest three different conceptual models for this system. You should consider each of the aspects of a conceptual model discussed in this chapter: interface metaphor, interaction type, interface type, activities it will support, functions, relationships between functions, and information requirements. Of these conceptual models, decide which one seems most appropriate and articulate the reasons why.

(b) Produce the following prototypes for your chosen conceptual model:

(i) Using the scenarios generated for the online booking facility, produce a storyboard for the task of booking a ticket for one of your conceptual models. Show it to two or three potential users and get some informal feedback.

(ii) Now develop a card-based prototype from the use case for the task of booking a ticket, also incorporating feedback from part (i). Show this new prototype to a different set of potential users and get some more informal feedback.

(c) Consider your product's concrete design. Sketch out the application's landing page. Consider the layout, use of colors, navigation, audio, animation, etc. While doing this, use the three main questions introduced in Chapter 6 as guidance: Where am I? What's here? Where can I go? Write one or two sentences explaining your choices, and consider whether the choice is a usability consideration or a user experience consideration.

(d) Sketch out an experience map for your product. Use the scenarios and personas you have already generated to explore the user's experience. In particular, identify any new interaction issues that you had not considered before, and suggest what you could do to address them.

(e) How does your product differ from applications that typically might emerge from the Maker Movement? Do software development kits have a role? If so, what is that role? If not, why do you think not?

Summary

This chapter has explored the activities of design, prototyping, and construction. Prototyping and scenarios are used throughout the design process to test out ideas for feasibility and user acceptance. We have looked at different forms of prototyping, and the activities have encouraged you to think about and apply prototyping techniques in the design process.

Key points
- Prototyping may be low fidelity (such as paper-based) or high fidelity (such as software-based).
- High-fidelity prototypes may be vertical or horizontal.
- Low-fidelity prototypes are quick and easy to produce and modify and are used in the early stages of design.
- Ready-made software and hardware components support the creation of prototypes.
- There are two aspects to the design activity: conceptual design and concrete design.
- Conceptual design develops an outline of what people can do with a product and what concepts are needed to understand how to interact with it, while concrete design specifies the details of the design such as layout and navigation.
- We have explored three approaches to help you develop an initial conceptual model: interface metaphors, interaction styles, and interface styles.
- An initial conceptual model may be expanded by considering which functions the product will perform (and which the user will perform), how those functions are related, and what information is required to support them.
- Scenarios and prototypes can be used effectively in design to explore ideas.
- Physical computing kits and software development kits facilitate the transition from design to construction.

Further Reading

BANZI, M. and SHILOH, M. (2014) *Getting started with Arduino* (3rd edn). Maker Media Inc. This hands-on book provides an illustrated step-by-step guide to learning about Arduino with lots of ideas for projects to work on. It outlines what physical computing is in relation to interaction design and the basics of electricity, electronics, and prototyping using the Arduino hardware and software environment.

CARROLL, J. M. (ed.) (1995) *Scenario-based Design*. John Wiley & Sons, Inc. This volume is an edited collection of papers arising from a three-day workshop on use-oriented design. The book contains a variety of papers including case studies of scenario use within design, and techniques for using them with object-oriented development, task models, and usability engineering. This is a good place to get a broad understanding of this form of development.

GREENBERG, S., CARPENDALE, S., MARQUARDT, N. and BUXTON, B. (2012) *Sketching User Experiences*. Morgan Kaufman. This is a practical introduction to sketching. It explains why sketching is important and provides very useful tips to get the reader into the habit of sketching. It is a companion book to Buxton, B. (2007) *Sketching User Experiences*. Morgan Kauffman, San Francisco.

LAZAR, J. (ed.) (2007) *Universal Usability: Designing information systems for diverse user populations*. John Wiley & Sons Ltd. This book provides an interesting selection of case studies that demonstrate how developers can design for diverse populations to ensure universal usability.

INTERVIEW
with the late Gary Marsden

Gary Marsden died suddenly and unexpectedly in December 2013. He was only 43. He was a professor in the Computer Science Department at the University of Cape Town. His research interests spanned mobile interaction, computer science, design and ICT for Development. He is a co-author of a book published in 2015, with Matt Jones and Simon Robinson, entitled, *There's Not an App for That: Mobile User Experience Design for Life*. He was also a co-author of *Mobile Interaction Design*, which was published in 2006. He won the 2007 ACM SIGCHI Social Impact Award for his research in using mobile technology in the developing world. He made a big impression on the HCI world. We have decided to keep his interview from the 3rd edition.

Gary, can you tell us about your research and why you do it?
My work involves creating digital technology for people living in Africa. Most of this work is based on designing software and interfaces for mobile cellular handsets as this is currently the most prevalent digital technology within Africa.

Because the technology is deployed in Africa, we work within a different design space than those working in more developed parts of the world. For instance, we assume that users have no access to personal computers or high-speed Internet connections. We must also take into account different literacy levels in our users and the cultures from which they come. Not only does this affect the technology we create, but the methods we use to create it.

As a computer science professional, I want to understand how to create digital systems that are relevant and usable by the people purchasing them. For many people here, buying a cellular handset is a significant investment and I want to make sure that the discipline of interaction design is able to help deliver a product which maximizes the purchaser's investment.

How do you know if the systems that you build are what people want and need?
This is currently a hotly debated topic in the field and it is only recently that there has been sufficient work from which to draw conclusions.

The first challenge crops up in designing a system for people who have very little exposure to technology. For many of our users, they have no experience of digital technology beyond using a simple cellular handset. Therefore, participatory techniques, where users are asked to become co-designers, can be problematic as they have no abstract notions of basic ideas like the separation between hardware and software. To overcome this, we often take a technology probe approach, allowing users to comment on a high-fidelity prototype rather than require them to make abstract decisions about a series of paper sketches.

For many of the systems we build, we are interested in more than simple measures of efficiency and effectiveness. Sure, it is important that technology is usable, but in the resource-constrained environment, it is critical that the technology is useful; money is too scarce to spend on something that does not significantly improve livelihood.

To measure impact on people and communities we often borrow from the literature on development and measure issues like domestification – the extent to which a technology is appropriated into someone's day-to-day living. In a lot of our work we also partner with non- governmental organizations (NGOs) who are based in a community and are looking for research partners to provide digital solutions to problems they meet – for instance, we have worked with a voter education NGO that wanted to use digital technology to better inform voters about their choices in an upcoming election. In that project we would adopt the goals of the NGO (how much people understand their voting choices) as part of the success criteria for our project. Often NGOs have sophisticated instruments to measure the impact they are having, as their funding relies on it. We can use those instruments to measure our impact.

To understand how our participants truly feel about a system, we use 'poly-phonic' assessment, as reported by Bill Gaver. The method employs unbiased journalists who interview users and report their assessment of the system. We have adopted this approach in our work and found it to be highly effective in gaining feedback on our systems. Furthermore, it overcomes a strong Hawthorne effect experienced by researchers who work in resource poor environments – users are so grateful for the attention and resources being given them, they rate any system highly in an attempt to please the researchers and keep them investing in that community.

At present, there is no clear consensus about how best to evaluate technology deployments in developing world communities, but it is clear that the technology cannot be evaluated solely on a human–computer interaction level, but needs to be considered on a livelihoods and community impact level.

Have you encountered any big surprises in your work?

My work seems to be endlessly surprising which, as a researcher, is highly stimulating. The first surprise when I moved here 12 years ago, was the penetration of mobile handsets. In an era when handsets were considered a luxury in Europe (1999), I saw people living in shacks talking on their mobile handsets. Clearly domestification was not an issue for cellular technology.

When I started to run research projects in Africa, I was surprised by the extent to which much HCI research and methods incorporated assumptions based in the developed world – for example, the issue I mentioned earlier around participatory design. Also, the early HCI literature I read on the internationalization of interfaces did not stand me in good stead. For example, my colleague, Marion Walton, built one interface consisting of a single button on a screen. We asked participants to click on the button, but one participant was unable to do this. When we pointed out the button to him, he said, 'That is not a button, that is a picture of a button.' Of course, he was correct and we learnt something valuable that day about visual culture.

Finally, the environment in Africa leads to surprises. The strangest problem I have had was trying to fix a computer in rural Zambia that had suddenly stopped working. On taking the casing off, I discovered white ants had eaten the green resin out of the circuit board and used it to build a nest over the power supply (where it was warm). Although it now looked like a beautiful lace, the motherboard could not be salvaged.

What are your hopes for the future?
My hope and my passion are to create a new generation of African computer scientists who create technology for their continent. Whilst the work I am engaged in may be helping to some small degree, it is not sustainable for outside people or teams to create new technology for everyone who lives in the developing world. As an educator, I believe the solution is to teach interaction design in African universities and empower Africans to create the technology that is most appropriate to them and their environment. ■

Chapter 12

INTERACTION DESIGN IN PRACTICE

12.1 Introduction

12.2 AgileUX

12.3 Design Patterns

12.4 Open Source Resources

12.5 Tools for Interaction Design

Objectives

The main aims of this chapter are to:

- Describe some of the key trends in practice related to interaction design.
- Enable you to discuss the place of UX design in agile development projects.
- Enable you to identify and critique interaction design patterns.
- Explain how open source and ready-made components can support interaction design.
- Explain how tools can support interaction design activities.

12.1 Introduction

The goal of interaction design is to produce interactive products that are of benefit to their users. This means that all the principles, techniques, and approaches introduced in other chapters of this book for designing products need to be translated into practice, i.e. into real situations with real sets of users. When placed in the wider world of commerce and business, interaction designers face a range of pressures, including time and resource pressures, and they need to work with a wide range of other roles and stakeholders. Many different names may be given to a practitioner conducting interaction design activities, including interface designer, information architect, experience designer, usability engineer, and user experience designer. In this chapter we refer to user experience (UX) designer and user experience (UX) design because these are the labels found most commonly in industry to describe someone who performs the range of interaction design tasks such as interface design, user evaluations, information architecture design, visual design, persona development, and prototyping.

From previous reading of this book, you may have got the impression that designers create their designs from scratch, with little or no help from anyone except users and immediate colleagues, but this is far from the truth. Four main areas of support impact on the job of UX designers in practice. First, working with software and product development teams operating an agile model of development (introduced in Chapter 9) has led to technique and process adaptation, resulting in AgileUX approaches. Second, reusing existing designs and concepts is valuable and time-saving. Interaction design and UX design patterns provide the blueprint for successful designs, utilizing previous work and saving time by avoiding 'reinventing the wheel'. Third, reusable components – from screen widgets and source code libraries to full systems, and from motors and sensors to complete robots – can be modified and integrated to generate prototypes or full products. Design patterns embody an interaction idea, but reusable components provide implemented chunks of code or widgets. Finally, there is a wide range of tools and development environments available to support designers in developing visual designs, wireframes, interface sketches, interactive prototypes, and more. This chapter provides an introduction to each of these four areas.

12.2 AgileUX

Since the rise of agile software development during the 2000s, UX designers have been concerned about the impact that it will have on their own work (Sharp *et al*, 2006), and the debate is ongoing (Holtzblatt *et al*, 2014). AgileUX is the collective label given to efforts that aim to resolve these concerns by integrating techniques and processes from interaction design and those from agile methods. While agile software development and UX design have some characteristics in common, such as iteration, a focus on measurable completion criteria, and user involvement, AgileUX requires a change in mindset compared to UX design.

In a waterfall-style software development process, requirements are specified as completely as possible before any implementation begins. In an agile software development process, requirements are specified only in enough detail for implementation to begin. Requirements are then elaborated as implementation proceeds, according to a set of priorities that change on a regular basis in response to changing business needs. Design also needs to progress in a similar fashion. Re-prioritization may happen as frequently as every two weeks, at the beginning of each iterative cycle. The shift from developing complete requirements upfront to 'just-in-time' or just enough requirements aims to reduce wasted effort, but it means that UX designers (along with their software engineer colleagues) have had to rethink their approach. All the techniques and principles that UX designers use are just as relevant, but how much of each activity needs to be completed at what point in the iterative cycle and how the results of those activities feed into implementation need to be adjusted in an agile development context. This can be unsettling for designers as the design artifacts are their main deliverable, and hence may be viewed as finished, while for agile software engineers they are consumables, and will need to change as implementation progresses and requirements become elaborated.

Consider the travel organizer example introduced in Chapter 10, and assume that at the beginning of the project, the main goal of the product is identified as to support users in choosing a vacation. In Figure 10.10, three other areas of the product are identified: update travel details, retrieve visa requirements, and retrieve vaccination requirements. In terms of agile prioritization, the main goal of the system will be top priority and so this will be the focus of requirements, design, and implementation activities initially. To allow users to choose a vacation, travel details will need to be updated and so this is also likely to be prioritized. Establishing the detailed requirements and the design of the other two areas will be postponed until after a product that allows users to choose a vacation has been delivered. Indeed, once this product is delivered, the customer may decide that offering help for vaccinations and visas does not result in sufficient business value for it to be included at all. In this case, referring users to other, more authoritative, sources of information may be preferable.

Conducting UX activities within an agile framework requires a flexible point of view that focuses more on the product as the deliverable than the design artifacts as deliverables. It also requires cross-functional teams where specialists from a range of disciplines, including UX design and engineering, work closely together to evolve an understanding of both the users and their context, and the technical capabilities and practicalities of the technology. In particular, AgileUX requires attention to three practical areas: (i) what user research to conduct, how much, and when; (ii) how to align UX design and agile working practices; and (iii) what documentation to produce, how much, and when.

"Enough storyboarding. Let's shoot something."

Source: Courtesy of Condé Nast Licensing

12.2.1   User Research

The term 'user research' refers to the data collection and analysis activities necessary to characterize the users, their tasks, and the context of use before product development begins. Field studies and ethnography are often used in these investigations, and are regarded as the most important element of user-centered design (Mao *et al*, 2005), but agile development works on short 'timeboxes' of activity (up to four weeks in length and often only two weeks in length), and hence does not support long periods of user research. (Different names are given by different agile methods to the 'iteration', the most common being sprint, timebox, and cycle.) Even a month to develop a set of personas or to conduct a detailed investigation into how travelers currently choose between vacations (for example) is too long for some agile development cycles. User-focused activities evaluating elements of the design, or interviews to clarify requirements or task context, can be done alongside technical development (see the parallel tracks approach below), but there is no time to conduct extensive user research once iterative development starts.

One way to address this is for user research to be conducted before the project begins, or indeed before it is announced (Norman, 2006), hence avoiding the constraints caused by limited timeboxes. This period is often called iteration zero, and it is used to achieve a range of upfront activities including technical architecture design as well as user research.

Another approach to conducting user research for each project is to have an ongoing program of user research that revises and refines a company's knowledge of their users over a longer timespan. For example, Microsoft actively recruits users of their software to sign up and take part in user research that is used to inform future developments. In this case, the specific data gathering and analysis needed for one project would be conducted during iteration zero, but done in the context of a wider understanding of users and their goals.

ACTIVITY 12.1

Consider the 'one-stop car shop' introduced in Activity 10.3. What kind of user research do you think it would be helpful to conduct before iterative development begins? Of these areas, which would be useful to conduct in an ongoing program?

Comment
Characterizing car drivers and the driving experience would be appropriate user research before iterative development begins. Although many people drive, the driving experience is very different depending on the car itself, and according to the individual's capabilities. Collecting and analyzing suitable data to inform the product's development is likely to take longer than the timebox constraints would allow. Such user research could develop a set of personas (maybe one set for each class of car) and a deeper understanding of the driving experience.

Car performance and handling is constantly evolving, however, and so an understanding of the driving experience would benefit from ongoing user research. ■

Lean UX (see Box 12.1) takes a different approach to user research by focusing on getting products into the market and capturing user feedback on products that are in the marketplace. It specifically focuses on designing and developing innovative products.

12.2.2 Aligning Work Practices
If requirements are specified before implementation begins, there is a tendency for designers to develop complete UX designs at the beginning of a project in order to ensure a coherent design throughout. In agile terms, this is referred to as 'big design upfront' (BDUF), and this is an anathema to agile working. Agile development emphasizes regular delivery of working software through evolutionary development, and the elaboration of requirements as implementation

BOX 12.1

Lean UX (Gothelf, 2013)

Lean UX is designed to create and deploy innovative products quickly. It is linked to AgileUX because agile software development is one of its underlying philosophies, and it champions the importance of providing a good user experience. Lean UX builds upon agile software development, design thinking, and the Lean Startup ideas (Ries, 2011). All three perspectives emphasize iterative development, collaboration between all stakeholders, and cross-functional teams. Design thinking focuses on understanding what people want and what technology can deliver. It is derived from professional design practice and takes a holistic view of the context and product, while evolving a solution through prototyping, evaluation, and learning.

Lean UX is based on tight iterations of build-measure-learn, a concept central to the Lean Startup idea, which in turn was inspired by the lean manufacturing process from Japan. The Lean UX process is illustrated in Figure 12.1. It emphasizes waste reduction, the importance of experimentation to learn, and the need to articulate assumptions about a planned product, as discussed in Chapter 2. Assumptions can be expressed as hypotheses and put to the test through research or by building a minimal viable product (MVP) that can be released to the user group. Testing assumptions is done through experimentation, but before undertaking experimentation, the evidence required to confirm or refute each assumption needs to be characterized. An MVP is the smallest product that can be built that allows assumptions to be tested by giving it to a user group and seeing what happens. Experimentation and the evidence collected are therefore based on actual use of the product. For example, Gothelf (2013, pp. 56–7) describes an example of a company that wanted to launch a monthly newsletter. Their assumption was that a monthly newsletter would be attractive to their customers. To test this assumption, they put a sign-up form on their website and collected evidence in the

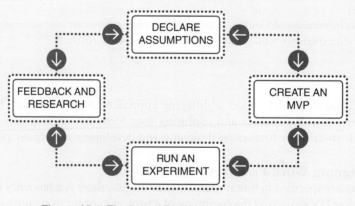

Figure 12.1 The Lean UX process
Source: Gothelf, J. with J. Seiden (2013) *Lean UX*, O'Reilly.

form of the number of sign-ups received. This form was an MVP that allowed them to collect evidence to support or refute their assumption, i.e. that a monthly newsletter would be attractive to their customers. ■

Video where Laura Klein explains Lean UX, is available at
http://youtu.be/7NkMm5WefBA

proceeds. In this context, BDUF leads to practical problems, since the re-prioritization of requirements means that interaction elements (features, workflows, options) may no longer be needed or may require redesigning. The organization of UX design activities hence needs to be spliced into agile iterations.

In response to this, Miller (2006) and Sy (2007) proposed that UX design work is done one iteration ahead of development work, in parallel tracks (see Figure 12.2). The parallel tracks approach to integrating UX design and agile processes originated at Alias – now part of Autodesk. Note that in this diagram, iteration is referred to as Cycle. The principle of parallel tracks development is quite simple: that design activity and user data collection for Cycle n+1 is performed during Cycle n. This enables the design work to be completed just ahead of development work, yet be tightly coupled to it as the product evolves.

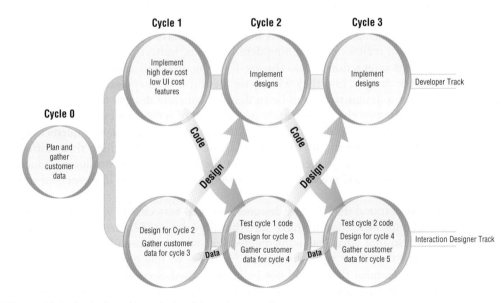

Figure 12.2 Cycle 0 and its relationship to later cycles

Source: Sy, D. (2007) Adapting usability investigations for development, *Journal of Usability Studies* 2(3), May, 112–130. User Experience Professionals Association.

Cycle 0 and Cycle 1 are different from subsequent cycles. Before evolutionary development can begin, the product vision needs to be created. This is handled in different ways in different agile methods, but all agree that there needs to be some kind of work done upfront to understand the product, its scope, and its overall design (both technical and UX). As discussed above, some user research may have been conducted before Cycle 0, but the vision and overall design is completed for the current project by the end of Cycle 0. The work required will depend on the nature of the product: whether it is a new version of an existing product, a new product, or a completely new experience.

One of the originators of the parallel tracks development idea, Desiree Sy (2007), explained this in the context of two different products. The first product is SketchBook Pro v2.0 – a sophisticated sketching, annotating, and presentation tool to support digital artists – and the second is Autodesk's Showcase – a real-time automotive 3D visualization product. For SketchBook Pro v2.0, the team conducted a survey of users who had downloaded v1.0 (a free trial version) but had not purchased v2.0. The results of the survey helped the team to refine 100 features into five major work streams, and this information informed development and prioritization throughout the development. For Showcase, during Cycle 0 the team interviewed potential purchasers who performed work that the tool was going to be designed to support. This data formed the foundation for the design principles of the product as well as prioritization and design decisions as development progressed.

Cycle 1 usually involves technical setting-up activities in the developer track, which allows the UX designers to get started on the design and user activities for Cycle 2. For subsequent cycles, the team gets into a rhythm of design and user activities in Cycle n−1 and corresponding technical activity in Cycle n.

For example, imagine that development of the travel organizer is in Cycle n, and that Cycle n is scheduled to work on capturing vacation reviews (remember that the scenario in Section 10.6.1 mentioned Sky and Eamonn looking at descriptions of flotilla holidays written by children). During Cycle n−1, UX designers will have produced concrete designs for capturing vacation reviews by designing detailed icons, buttons, or other graphics, and prototyping different interaction types. During Cycle n they will answer specific queries about these concrete designs, and they will revise them if necessary based on implementation feedback. Cycle n design work will be to develop concrete designs for the next Cycle, which might be focusing on the identification and display of reviews relevant to the current vacation being considered. Also during Cycle n, UX designers will evaluate implementation coming out of Cycle n−1. So in any one cycle, UX designers are handling three different types of activity: evaluating implementations from the previous cycle, producing concrete designs for the next cycle, and answering queries on the designs being implemented in the current cycle.

The team at Alias found that the UX designers worked very closely with the developers during design and implementation to make sure that they designed something that could be implemented and also that what was implemented was what had been designed. The interaction designers felt that there were three big advantages to this process. First, no design time was wasted on features that would not be implemented. Second, usability testing (for one set of features) and contextual inquiry (for the next set) could be done on the same customer visit, thus saving time. Third, the interaction designers received timely feedback from all sides – both users and developers. More importantly, they had time to react to that feedback because of the agile way of working. For example, the schedule could be changed if something was going to take longer to develop than first thought, or a feature could be dropped if it became apparent from the users that something else had higher priority. In summary, "Agile user-centered design resulted in better-designed software than waterfall user-centered design" (Sy, 2007, p. 130).

These advantages have been realized by others too, and this parallel tracks way of working has become a popular way to implement AgileUX. Sometimes the UX designers work two iterations ahead, depending on the work to be done, the length of the iteration, and external factors such as time required to obtain appropriate user input. Working in this way does not diminish the need for UX designers and other team members to collaborate closely together, and although the tracks are parallel, they should not be seen as separate processes. This does, however, raise a dilemma, as discussed in the Dilemma box.

DILEMMA

To co-locate or not to co-locate, that is the question

UX designers in most large organizations are not numerous enough to have one UX designer for every team, so where should the UX designer be located (physically or virtually)? Agile working emphasizes regular communication and the importance of being aware about the project as it evolves, and hence it would be good for the UX designer to be located with the rest of their team. But which team? Maybe a different agile team every day? Or each team for one iteration? Some organizations, however, believe that it is better for UX designers to sit together in order to provide discipline coherence: "UX designers work best when they are separated from the issues of software construction because these issues hamper creativity" (Ferreira *et al*, 2011). Indeed, this view is shared by some UX designers as well. If you were part of several agile teams, needing to engage with each of them, where would you prefer to be located? Or maybe you'd prefer to use a social awareness tool such as Sococo, introduced in Chapter 4? ∎

Video describing some case studies on the UX techniques used by Android within agile iterations, is available at **http://youtu.be/6MOeVNbh9cY**

ACTIVITY 12.2

Compare Lean UX, AgileUX, and evolutionary prototyping introduced in Chapter 11. In what ways are they similar and how do they differ?

(Continued)

Comment

Lean UX produces a minimum viable product (MVP) to test assumptions by releasing it to users as a finished product, and collecting evidence of users' reactions. This evidence is then used to evolve subsequent (larger) products based on the results of this experimentation. In this sense, Lean UX is a form of evolutionary development, and has similarities with evolutionary prototyping. However, not all the MVPs developed to test assumptions may be incorporated into the final product, just the results of the experiment.

AgileUX is an umbrella term for all efforts that focus on integrating UX design with agile development. Agile software development is an evolutionary approach to development and hence AgileUX is also evolutionary. Additionally, AgileUX projects can employ prototyping to answer questions and test ideas as with any other approach, as described in Chapter 11. ∎

12.2.3   Documentation

The most common way for UX designers to capture and communicate their design has been through documentation, e.g. user research results and resulting personas, detailed interface sketches, and wireframes. Because UX designers' deliverable is the design, a key indicator that their work can be signed off is if there is sufficient documentation to show that their goals have been achieved. Other forms of design capture, such as prototypes and simulations, are valuable, but documentation is still the most common. Agile development encourages only minimal documentation so that more time can be spent on design, thus producing value to the user via a working product.

Minimal documentation does not mean 'no documentation' and some documentation is desirable in most projects. However, a key principle in AgileUX is that documentation should not replace communication and collaboration. To help identify the right level of documentation, Ratcliffe and McNeill (2012, p. 29) suggest asking a set of questions of any documentation process:

1. How much time do you spend on documentation? Try to decrease the amount of time spent on documentation and increase design time.
2. Who uses the documentation?
3. What is the minimum that customers need from the documentation?
4. How efficient is your sign-off process? How much time is spent waiting for documentation to be approved? What impact does this have on the project?
5. What evidence is there of document duplication? Are different parts of the business documenting the same things?
6. If documentation is only for the purpose of communication or development, how polished does it need to be?

They also use the example in Figure 12.3 to illustrate the points. Both images capture a user journey, i.e. one path a user might take through the product. The sketch in Figure 12.3(a) is constructed with sticky notes and string, and was generated by all the team members during a discussion. The sketch in Figure 12.3(b) took hours of designer time to draw up and polish. It looks good, but that time could have been used to design the product rather than the user journey sketch.

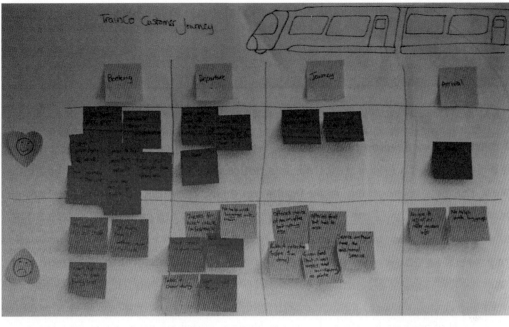

(a)

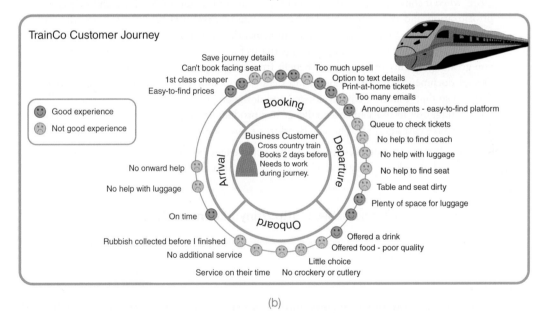

(b)

Figure 12.3 (a) A low-fidelity user journey (b) A high-fidelity user journey

Source: Ratcliffe, L. and McNeill, M. (2012) *Agile Experience Design*. New Riders.

Case Study 12.1

Integrating UX design into a DSDM project: challenges, working practices, and lessons learned

This case study presents a chapter from the story of one organization's journey to integrate UX design into one agile software development approach: the DSDM (dynamic systems development method) framework (see dsdm.org for more details). It describes the difficulties they faced, working practices adopted, and the lessons learned from their experiences of integrating UX designers into their DSDM agile process.

LShift is a hi-tech software development company that works across a broad range of industries, languages, and platforms. They faced four main challenges while integrating UX design into the DSDM framework:

1. Communication between developers and UX designers: what the relevant information is that needs to be communicated, how to best communicate it, how to keep communication channels open, and how to keep the emerging design implementation visible for feedback. Difficulties in these areas can cause frustration, problems with the technical feasibility of design solutions, and mistaken expectations by the client.

2. Level of precision in upfront design: developers suggested five main reasons why 'less is more' when it comes to design documentation ready for the start of developer involvement: prioritization and de-scoping can lead to a waste of pixel-perfect designs; some design issues will only be found once you start implementing; pixel-perfect designs may increase resistance to making design changes; it is better to focus on functionality first and design as you go along; quality of designs can benefit from early input by developers.

3. Design documentation: the amount and detail of documentation needs to be discussed early on so that it meets both developers' and designers' requirements.

4. User testing: user testing can be a challenge in a product development setting if the business does not have customers yet. This can be addressed using personas and user representatives.

This case study describes the background to these challenges, provides more detail about these challenges, and introduces some practices that the company used to address them.

> **Case study** in full is available at **http://tinyurl.com/neehnbk**

The question of how much documentation is needed in an agile project is not limited to AgileUX, however, and Scott Ambler (Ambler, 2002) also provides a detailed description of best practices for agile documentation. These support the production of 'good enough' documentation in an efficient way, and are intended to determine what documentation is needed. He proposes questions such as "what is the purpose of the documentation," "who is the customer of the documentation," and "when should documents be updated."

12.3 Design Patterns

Design patterns capture design experience, but they have a different structure and a different philosophy from other forms of guidance or specific methods. One of the intentions of the patterns community is to create a vocabulary, based on the names of the patterns that designers can use to communicate with one another and with users. Another is to produce literature in the field that documents experience in a compelling form.

The idea of patterns was first proposed by Christopher Alexander, a British architect who described patterns in architecture (Alexander, 1979). His hope was to capture the 'quality without a name' that is recognizable in something when you know it is good.

But what is a design pattern? One simple definition is that it is a solution to a problem in a context, i.e. a pattern describes a problem, a solution, and where this solution has been found to work. Users of the pattern can therefore not only see the problem and solution, but also understand the circumstances under which the idea has worked before and access a rationale for why it worked. A key characteristic of design patterns is that they are generative, i.e. they can be instantiated or implemented in many different ways. Patterns on their own are interesting, but they are not as powerful as a pattern language. A pattern language is a network of patterns that reference one another and work together to create a complete structure.

The application of patterns to interaction design has grown steadily since the late 1990s (e.g. Borchers, 2001; Tidwell, 2006; Crumlish and Malone, 2009). Pattern languages are not very common in this area, but there are several pattern collections. Patterns are attractive to designers because they are tried and tested solutions to common problems. It is common (although not obligatory) for pattern collections to be associated with software components that can be used with little modification, and as they are common solutions, many users are already familiar with them, which is a great advantage for a new app or product on the market. See Box 12.3 for an example pattern – Swiss Army Knife Navigation.

BOX 12.3

Swiss Army Knife Navigation: an example design pattern for mobiles (Nudelman, 2013)

The principle behind the Swiss Army Knife Navigation design pattern is to maximize productive use of the screen space and keep users engaged in the content of what they are doing. For example, in a game design, the user does not want to be side-tracked by navigation bars and menu pop-ups. Having a mechanism that allows the controls to fade in and out of view is a much more engaging design.

This design pattern is commonly instantiated as 'off canvas' or 'side drawer' navigation (Neil, 2014), where the control bar slides in, overlaying the main screen contents. It is useful because it is a 'transient' navigation bar, i.e. it can be swiped in over the top of the main app screen and then swiped back once the user has finished the action. It is good from an interaction design point of view because it supports the use of both text and icons to represent

(Continued)

actions. It is also good from the point of view of screen layout because it only takes up space when the menu is needed. It can also be used for interactions other than navigation (Peatt, 2014). One of the reasons it is a good example to include in this book is that it is a common design pattern, yet is also evolving in a range of different directions.

Exactly how this navigation bar is implemented varies with different platforms. ■

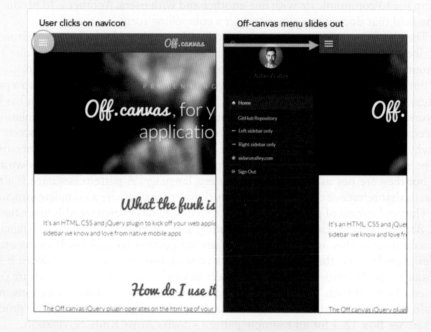

Figure 12.4 Example of Swiss Army Knife Navigation pattern, instantiated as off canvas navigation. In the left-hand image, the menu is represented as a list of lines in the top left of the screen, while in the right-hand image, the menu items have pushed the user view to the right.
Source: Courtesy of Aidan Zealley.

Link to platform guidelines and pattern libraries plus downloadable collections of screen elements, at
http://dev.windows.com/en-us/design/interaction-ux (for Windows)
http://developer.android.com/design/patterns/index.html (for Android)

Pattern collections, libraries, and galleries relevant to interaction design are commonly used in practice (e.g. Nudelman, 2013), and are often accompanied by snippets of code available through open source repositories such as Github (see below) or through platform websites such as http://dev.windows.com/en-us/design/interaction-ux for Windows or https://developer.apple.com/library/iOS/documentation/userexperience/conceptual/mobilehig/ for iOS on an iPhone. Patterns are a work in progress and they continue to evolve as more

ACTIVITY 12.3

One design pattern for mobile devices that is deprecated by some and not others is the Carousel navigation pattern, in which the user is presented with several images (e.g. of products) horizontally across the screen, or one at a time in the same screen location. Swiping (or clicking) left or right displays other images, just like a carousel.

This design pattern has provoked different reactions by different designers. Search for information on this design pattern using your favorite browser and read at least two articles or blog posts about it: one arguing that it should be deprecated and one that explains how it can be used successfully. Decide for yourself whether the Carousel pattern should be labeled outdated or kept alive.

Comment

The Nielsen Norman Group has two articles about the carousel on its website (see URLs at the end of this paragraph). One presents evidence from a usability trial with one user that shows carousels can fail, and the other presents a balanced view of how to design a good carousel. This second article focuses on the version of the carousel where several images are displayed at the same location on the screen, one at a time. They identify the greatest advantages as being the good use of screen space (because several elements occupy the same space),

(a)

(Continued)

(b)

Figure 12.5 Two example carousel navigation styles (a) showing pictures of a house for sale. Note the arrows to the left and right of the row of photos at the bottom. (b) A weather application for a mobile phone that can be swiped left and right for other locations. Note the line of dashes in the bottom middle of the screen that indicate there are other screens.

and having information at the top of the screen means that visitors are more likely to see it. Disadvantages include that users often navigate past the carousel and that even if users do see the image, it is usually only the first one. The article does suggest using an alternative design, but goes on to provide some very useful examples and guidelines for good carousels. See the following websites for more details http://www.nngroup.com/articles/designing-effective-carousels/ and http://www.nngroup.com/articles/auto-forwarding/

There is a thread of posts and articles arguing that the carousel should not be used. These also point to evidence that users rarely use the carousel, but if they do then they focus only on the first image. However, there seems to be no solid set of data to support or refute the usability of the carousel in all its various forms.

On balance, it seems that some forms of carousel meet the product's goals more readily than others, e.g. because only the first image in a series is viewed by most users. Assuming appropriate design and, maybe more importantly, an evaluation with potential users and your content, it seems that the carousel navigation pattern is not yet ready to be deprecated. ■

Link to other sites providing interesting food for thought at
http://yorkwebteam.blogspot.co.uk/2013/03/are-homepage-carousels-effective-aka.html
http://weedygarden.net/2013/07/carousel-interaction-stats/

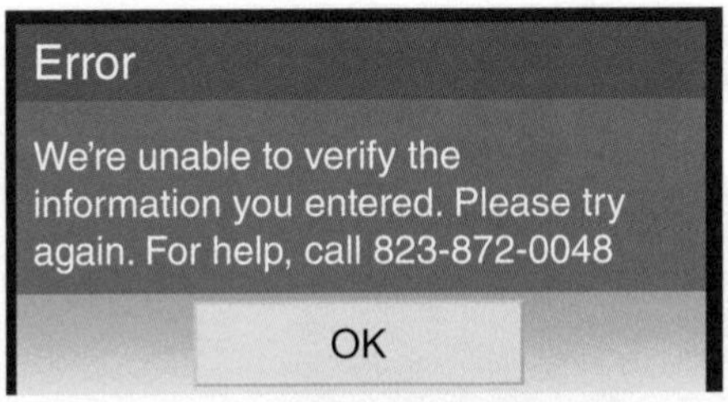

Figure 12.6 An untappable phone number for help when smartphone installation goes wrong

people use them, experience increases, and users' preferences change. Patterns can continue to evolve for some time, but they can also be 'deprecated', i.e. become outdated and no longer considered good interaction design. Reusing ideas that have proved to be successful in the past is a good strategy in general, but should not be used blindly. As with many areas of design, there is disagreement about which patterns are current and which are outdated.

Design patterns are a distillation of previous common practice, but one of the problems with common practice is that it is not necessarily good practice. Design approaches that represent poor practice are referred to as anti-patterns. The quality of interaction design and user experience in general has improved immensely since the first edition of this book in 2002, so why are anti-patterns still a problem? Basically because the technology is changing and design solutions that work on one platform don't necessarily work on another. A common source of anti-patterns for mobile devices is where websites or other software have been migrated from a large screen, such as a laptop, to a smartphone. One example of this is the untappable phone number that displays on a smartphone when an operating system upgrade goes wrong (see Figure 12.6).

Another form of pattern that was introduced in Chapter 1 (see Figure 1.10) is the dark pattern. Dark patterns are not necessarily poor design, but they have been designed carefully in order to trick people. Some apparent dark patterns are just mistakes, in which case they should be corrected relatively quickly, but patterns that are truly dark are used deliberately to trick users into, for example, signing up for email alerts.

12.4 Open Source Resources

Open source software refers to source code for components, frameworks, or whole systems that is available for reuse or modification free of charge. Open source development is a community-driven endeavor in which individuals produce, maintain, and enhance code, which is then given back to the community through an open source repository for further development and use. The community of open source committers, i.e. those who write and maintain this software, are mostly software developers who give their time for free. The components are available for (re)use under software licenses that allow anyone to use and modify the software for their own requirements without the standard copyright restrictions.

Many large pieces of software underlying our global digital infrastructure are powered by open source projects. For example, the operating system Linux, the development environment Eclipse, and the NetBeans development tools are all examples of open source software.

More interestingly, maybe, for interaction designers is that there is a growing proportion of open source software available for designing good user experiences. The design pattern

Figure 12.7 An example website built using the Bootstrap framework http://www.sfarts.org.
Source: Didier Garcia/Larson Associates.

Link to see an up-to-date gallery of recent Bootstrap examples at
http://expo.getbootstrap.com

implementation libraries introduced in Section 12.3 are one example of how open source software is affecting user experience design. Another example is the Bootstrap framework for front-end web development, released as open source in August 2011. This framework contains reusable code snippets, a screen layout grid that supports multiple screen sizes, and pattern libraries that include predefined sets of navigational patterns, typefaces, buttons, tabs, and so on. The framework and documentation are available through Github (https://github.com/twbs/bootstrap#community), currently the fastest-growing open source repository.

The Github repository itself may look a little daunting for those who first come across it, but there is a community of developers behind it who are happy to help and support newcomers.

12.5   Tools for Interaction Design

Many types of automated tool are used in practice by UX designers. These tools support creative thinking, design sketching, simulation, video capture, automatic consistency checking, brainstorming, library search, mindmapping – in fact any aspect of the design process will have at least one associated support tool. For example, Visio© and Omnigraffle© support the creation of a wide range of drawings and screen layouts; while FreeMind is an open source mindmapping tool. In themselves these tools provide significant support for UX design, but they can also work together to speed up the process of creating prototypes of various levels of fidelity.

We have emphasized elsewhere in this book the value of low-fidelity prototyping, and its use in getting user feedback. But as with any prototype, paper-based prototypes have their limitations, and they do not support user-driven interaction (e.g. Lim *et al*, 2006). In recognition of this, developing interactive, low-fidelity prototypes has been investigated through research for many years (e.g. Lin *et al*, 2000), and research into translating sketches into interactive prototypes continues (e.g. Segura *et al*, 2012).

Commercial packages that support the quick and easy development of interactive wireframes, or mockups, are widely used in practice for demonstration and evaluation. Two commonly used tools are Balsamiq© (www.balsamiq.com) and Axure© (www.axure.com). Both of their websites have quick introduction videos that give an introduction to how they work (balsamiq.com for Balsamiq and http://www.axure.com/learn/core/getting-started for Axure). Activity 12.4 invites you to try out one or more of the tools available to create a simple prototype.

> **Link** to an overview of Balsamiq and its use to create mockups quickly and easily at **http://www.disruptware.com/business/wireframe-balsamiq/** You can have a go yourself at **http://webdemo.balsamiq.com**

Having created an interactive wireframe using one of these tools, it is then possible to generate a higher-fidelity prototype by implementing the next prototype using a ready-made pattern library or framework, like those introduced in Sections 12.3 and 12.4, to give a coherent look and feel. This means going from a low-fidelity mockup to a working, styled prototype in one step. Other open source resources can also be adopted to give a wider choice of interface elements or design components with which to create the product.

Paper-based prototypes are also not very good if technical performance issues such as component interfaces need to be prototyped – software-based prototypes are better. For example, Gosper *et al* (2011) describes how, at SAP, they often use a drawing or graphics package to mock up key use cases and their interface, interactions, and task flows, and then output that to PowerPoint. This creates a set of slides that can be flicked through to give an overall sense of a user session. However, when they developed a business intelligence tool with key performance and 'back end' implications, this form of prototyping was not sufficient for them to assess their product goals. Instead, the UX designer worked with a developer who prototyped some of the elements in Java.

ACTIVITY 12.4

Choose one of the commercially available tools that supports the generation of interactive wireframes or low-fidelity prototypes. Generate a wireframe of your movie rental subscription service from Activity 11.6. Unless you have a license for the tools, you may not have access to all the facilities, e.g. the demo version of Balsamiq does not allow images to be included or uploaded.

Comment
We used the Balsamiq web demo at http://webdemo.balsamiq.com to create the screen in Figure 12.8, drawing on the card-based prototype in Activity 11.6.

(Continued)

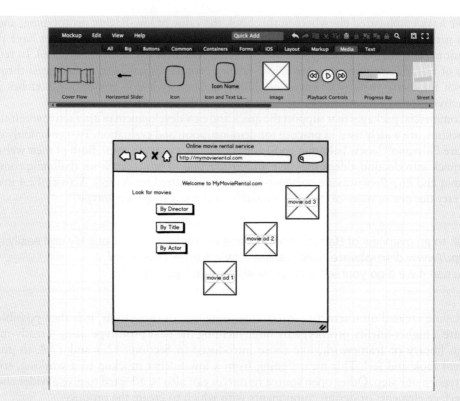

Figure 12.8 A screenshot of our interactive wireframe for the movie rental service, generated using Balsamiq http://www.disruptware.com/business/wireframe-balsamiq/

Assignment

This assignment continues work on the online booking facility introduced at the end of Chapter 10. The work will be continued in the assignments for Chapters 14 and 15.

(a) Assume that you will produce your online booking facility using an agile approach.

   (i) Suggest the kind of user research you would like to conduct for your product before iteration cycles begin.

   (ii) Prioritize the requirements for your product according to business value, i.e. which requirements are likely to provide the greatest business benefit, and sketch out the UX design work you would expect to undertake during the first four iteration cycles, i.e. Cycle 0, and Cycles 1 to 3.

(b) Using one of the mockup tools introduced above, generate a mockup of your product's landing page, as developed in the assignment for Chapter 11.

(c) Using one of the patterns websites listed previously, identify suitable interaction patterns for elements of your product, and develop a software-based prototype that incorporates all the feedback and the results of the user experience mapping achieved at the end of Chapter 11. If you do not have experience in using any of these, create a few HTML web pages to represent the basic structure of your website.

Summary

This chapter has explored some of the issues faced when interaction design is carried out in practice. The move towards agile development has led to a rethinking of UX design, and how relevant techniques and methods may be integrated into Agile's tight timeboxes. The existence of pattern and code libraries, together with open source components and automated tools, means that interactive prototypes with a coherent and consistent design can be generated quickly and easily ready for demonstration and evaluation.

Key points

- AgileUX refers to approaches that integrate UX design activities with an agile approach to product development.
- A move to AgileUX requires a change in mindset, due to repeated re-prioritization of requirements and short timeboxed implementation, which aims to avoid wasted effort.
- AgileUX requires a rethinking of UX design activities: when to perform them, how much detail to undertake, and how to feed back results into implementation cycles.
- Design patterns present a solution to a problem in a context, and there are many UX design pattern libraries available.
- Open source resources such as those on Github make the development of standard applications easier and quicker.
- A range of automated tools to support interaction design in practice is available.

Further Reading

NEIL, T. (2014) *Mobile Design Pattern Gallery* (2nd edn). O'Reilly. This book is packed with color images that illustrate a wide range of patterns (and some anti-patterns) that are used in mobile interaction design, including the 'side drawer' (Box 12.3), and includes some additional comments about their use. It brings the patterns alive and presents them in useful categories, although it does not use a pattern format. Remember that patterns are a work in progress and always evolving.

NUDELMAN, G. (2013) *Android Design Patterns*. John Wiley. Focusing specifically on Android apps, this book provides 58 Android app patterns and 12 anti-patterns. It is supported by a website, http://www.androiddesignbook.com.

RAYMOND, E.S. (2001) *The Cathedral & the Bazaar*. O'Reilly. This classic book is a set of essays introducing the open source movement.

SANDERS, L. and STAPPERS, P. J. (2014) From Designing to Co-Designing to Collective Dreaming: Three Slices in Time, *interactions*, Nov–Dec, p. 25–33. This provides a fascinating account of the changes in design practice over the last 30 years, a reflection on what design practice is like in 2014, and then a projection into the future to see what design practice may be like 30 years from now. It considers the role of the customer and the designer, and how the object being designed emerges from the design process.

SY, D. (2007) Adapting usability investigations for development, *Journal of Usability Studies* 2(3), May, 112–130. This short paper is a very good introduction to some of the key issues faced when trying to perform UX design alongside an agile project.

Chapter 13

INTRODUCING EVALUATION

Objectives

The specific aims of this chapter are to:

- Explain the key concepts and terms used in evaluation.
- Introduce a range of different types of evaluation methods.
- Show how different evaluation methods are used for different purposes at different stages of the design process and in different contexts of use.
- Show how evaluators mix and modify methods to meet the demands of evaluating novel systems.
- Discuss some of the practical challenges that evaluators have to consider when doing evaluation.
- Illustrate through short case studies how methods discussed in more depth in Chapters 7 and 8 are used in evaluation and describe some methods that are specific to evaluation.

13.1 Introduction

Imagine you have designed an app for teenagers to share music, gossip, and photos. You have prototyped your first design and implemented the core functionality. How would you find out whether it would appeal to them and if they will use it? You would need to evaluate it – but how? This chapter presents an introduction to the main types of evaluation and the methods you can use.

Evaluation is integral to the design process. Evaluators collect information about users' or potential users' experiences when interacting with a prototype, an app, a computer system, a component of a computer system, an application, or a design artifact such as a screen sketch. They do this in order to improve its design. Evaluation focuses on both the usability of the system (e.g. how easy it is to learn and to use) and on the users' experience when interacting with it (e.g. how satisfying, enjoyable, or motivating the interaction is).

Devices like smartphones, iPods, iPads, and e-readers have heightened awareness about usability, but many designers still assume that if they and their colleagues can use a product and find it attractive, others will, too. The problem with this assumption is that designers may design only for themselves. Evaluation enables them to check that their design is appropriate and acceptable for the wider user population.

There are many different evaluation methods. Which to use depends on the goals of the evaluation. Evaluations can occur in a range of places such as laboratories, people's homes, outdoors, and work settings. Evaluations usually involve observing participants and measuring their performance – in usability testing, experiments, or field studies. There are other methods, however, that do not involve participants, such as modeling user behavior. These tend to be approximations of what users might do when interacting with an interface, often done as a quick and cheap way of assessing different interface configurations. The level of control on what is evaluated varies; sometimes there is none, such as in field studies, and in others there is considerable control over which tasks are performed and the context, such as in experiments.

In this chapter we discuss why evaluation is important, what needs to be evaluated, where evaluation should take place, and when in the product lifecycle evaluation is needed. The different types are then illustrated by short case studies.

13.2   The Why, What, Where, and When of Evaluation

Conducting evaluations involves understanding not only why evaluation is important but also what aspects to evaluate, where evaluation should take place, and when to evaluate.

13.2.1   Why Evaluate?

Nowadays users expect much more than just a usable system; they also look for a pleasing and engaging experience. This means it is even more important to carry out an evaluation. As the Nielsen Norman Group (www.nngroup.com) notes, "User experience encompasses all aspects of the end-user's interaction . . . the first requirement for an exemplary user experience is to meet the exact needs of the customer, without fuss or bother. Next come simplicity and elegance, which produce products that are a joy to own, a joy to use."

© 1999 Randy Glasbergen.

"it's the latest innovation in office safety.
When your computer crashes, an air bag is activated
so you won't bang your head in frustration."

From a business and marketing perspective, well-designed products sell. Hence, there are good reasons for companies investing in evaluation. Designers can focus on real problems and the needs of different user groups rather than debating what each other likes or dislikes. It also enables problems to be fixed before the product goes on sale.

ACTIVITY 13.1

Identify one adult and one teenager prepared to talk with you about their Facebook usage (these may be family members or friends). Ask them questions such as: How often do you look at Facebook each day? How many photos do you post? What kind of photos do you have in your albums? What photo do you have as your profile picture? How often do you change it? How many friends have you got? What books and music do you list? Are you a member of any groups?

Comment
You are likely to have found some different patterns between the adult and the teenager. Typically, teenagers are avid Facebook users; they will access it wherever they are and upload photos of places they have just visited. They often use it to coordinate their social activities. Many teenagers like games so they download games. Many adults are also on Facebook but may not use it as frequently and they may use it for different reasons such as showing family members where they went on vacation, or posting pictures of children and grandchildren.∎

13.2.2 What to Evaluate

What to evaluate ranges from low-tech prototypes to complete systems; a particular screen function to the whole workflow; and from aesthetic design to safety features. For example, developers of a new web browser may want to know if users find items faster with their product, whereas developers of an ambient display may be interested in whether it changes people's behavior, and game app developers will want to know how engaging and fun their games are and how long users will play them for. Government authorities may ask if a computerized system for controlling traffic lights results in fewer accidents or if a website complies with the standards required for users with disabilities. Makers of a toy may ask if 6-year-olds can manipulate the controls and whether they are engaged by its furry case, and whether the toy is safe for them to play with. A company that develops personal, digital music players may want to know if the size, color, and shape of the casing are liked by people from different age groups living in different countries. A software company may want to assess market reaction to its new homepage design.

ACTIVITY 13.2

What aspects would you want to evaluate for the following systems:
1. a personal music player (e.g. a smartphone app)?
2. a website for selling clothes?

Comment
1. You would need to discover how well they can select tracks from potentially thousands, whether people think it feels and looks good, and whether they can easily add and store new music.
2. Navigation would be a core concern, especially the ability to quickly move between looking at the clothes, comparing them, and purchasing them. In addition, do the clothes look attractive enough to buy? Other core aspects include how trustworthy and how secure the procedure is for taking customer credit card details. ■

13.2.3   Where to Evaluate

Where evaluation takes place depends on what is being evaluated. Some characteristics, such as web accessibility, are generally evaluated in a laboratory, because it provides the control necessary to systematically investigate whether all requirements are met. This is also true for design choices, such as choosing the size and layout of keys for a smartphone. User experience aspects, such as whether children enjoy playing with a new toy and for how long before they get bored, can be evaluated more effectively in natural settings which are often referred to as 'in the wild studies'. Remote studies of online behavior, such as social networking, can be conducted to evaluate natural interactions for a lot of participants in their own homes, cheaply and quickly. Living laboratories have also been built which are somewhere in between labs and in the wild settings; providing the setting of being in an environment, such as the home, while also giving the ability to control, measure, and record activities.

ACTIVITY 13.3

A company is developing a new car seat to monitor if a person starts to fall asleep when driving and to provide a wake-up call using olfactory and haptic feedback. Where would you evaluate it?

Comment
It would be important initially to conduct lab-based experiments using a car simulator to see how effective the new kind of feedback is – i.e. in a safe setting! You would need to find a way of trying to get the participants to fall asleep at the wheel. Once established as an effective mechanism, you would then need to test it in a more natural setting – such as a racing track or airfield – which can be controlled by the experimenter using a dual-control car. ■

13.2.4   When to Evaluate

At what stage in the product lifecycle evaluation takes place depends on the type of product. For example, the product being developed could be a brand-new concept or it could be an upgrade of an existing product. If the product is new, then considerable time is usually invested in market research and establishing user requirements. Once these requirements have been established, they are used to create initial sketches, a storyboard, a series of screens, or a prototype of the design ideas. These are then evaluated to see if the designers have interpreted the users' requirements correctly and embodied them in their designs appropriately. The designs will be modified according to the evaluation feedback and new prototypes developed and subsequently evaluated.

When evaluations are done during design to check that a product continues to meet users' needs, they are known as formative evaluations. Formative evaluations cover a broad range of design processes, from the development of early sketches and prototypes through to tweaking and perfecting an almost finished design.

Evaluations that are done to assess the success of a finished product are known as summative evaluations. If the product is being upgraded then the evaluation may not focus on establishing a set of requirements, but may evaluate the existing product to ascertain what needs improving. Features are then often added, which can result in new usability problems. Other times, attention is focused on improving specific aspects, such as enhanced navigation.

Many agencies such as the National Institute of Standards and Technology (NIST) in the USA, the International Standards Organization (ISO), and the British Standards Institute (BSI) set standards by which particular types of products, such as aircraft navigation systems and consumer products that have safety implications for users, have to be evaluated.

13.3   Types of Evaluation

We classify evaluations into three broad categories, depending on the setting, user involvement, and level of control. These are:

1. *Controlled settings involving users* (examples are laboratories and living labs): users' activities are controlled in order to test hypotheses and measure or observe certain behaviors. The main methods are usability testing and experiments.
2. *Natural settings involving users* (examples are online communities and products that are used in public places): there is little or no control of users' activities in order to determine how the product would be used in the real world. The main method used is field studies.
3. *Any settings not involving users*: consultants and researchers critique, predict, and model aspects of the interface in order to identify the most obvious usability problems. The range of methods includes inspections, heuristics, walkthroughs, models, and analytics.

There are pros and cons of each type. For example, lab-based studies are good at revealing usability problems but poor at capturing context of use; field studies are good at demonstrating how people use technologies in their intended setting but are expensive and difficult to conduct (Rogers *et al*, 2007, Rogers *et al*, 2013); and modeling and predicting approaches are cheap and quick to perform but can miss unpredictable usability problems and subtle aspects of the user experience.

A key concern for deciding on which approach to use is how much control is needed in order to find out how an interface or device is used. For the example of the teenager music app mentioned earlier, we would need to find out how teenagers use it, whether they like it, what problems they experience with the functions, and so on. This requires determining how they carry out various tasks using the interface operations, which will involve a degree of control in designing the evaluation study to ensure they try out all the tasks and operations the app has been designed for.

13.3.1 Controlled Settings Involving Users

Controlled settings enable evaluators to control what users do, when they do it, and for how long. They also enable evaluators to reduce outside influences and distractions, such as friends or colleagues talking. The approach has been extensively and successfully used to evaluate software applications running on PCs and other technologies where participants can be seated in front of them to perform a set of tasks.

Usability testing. Typically this approach to evaluating user interfaces involves collecting data using a combination of methods – i.e. experiments, observation, interviews, and question- naires – in a controlled setting. It is generally done in laboratories although increasingly it is being done remotely or in natural settings. The primary goal is to determine whether an interface is usable by the intended user population to carry out the tasks for which it was designed. This involves investigating how typical users perform on typical tasks. By typical we mean the users for whom the system is designed (e.g. teenagers) and the things that it is designed for them to be able to do (e.g. buy the latest fashions). It often involves comparing the number and kinds of errors that the users make and recording the time that it takes them to complete the task. As users perform the tasks, they may be recorded on video; their interac- tions with the software may also be recorded, usually by logging software. User satisfaction questionnaires and interviews can also be used to elicit users' opinions about how they found the experience of using the system. It can be supplemented by observation at product sites to collect evidence about how the product is being used in work or other environments.

Observing users' reactions to an interactive product has helped developers understand usability issues that would be extremely difficult for them to glean simply through reading reports, or listening to presentations. For many years usability testing has been a staple of HCI, being used in the development of standard products that go through many generations, such as word processing systems, databases, and spreadsheets (Johnson, 2014; Krug, 2014; Redish, 2012; Koyani *et al*, 2004). The findings from the usability testing are often summarized in a usability specification that enabled developers to test future prototypes or versions of the product against it. Optimal performance levels and minimal levels of acceptance are generally specified and current levels noted. Changes in the design can then be implemented, such as navigation structure, use of terms, and how the system responds to the user.

Madrigal and McClain (2010) provide practical guidance including a list of the dos and don'ts of doing usability testing. They also point out how "usability testing is one of the least glamorous, but most important aspects of user experience research."

Experiments are typically conducted in research labs in universities or industry to test hypotheses. They are the most controlled setting, where researchers try to remove any extra- neous variables that may interfere with the participant's performance. The reason for this is so that they can reliably say that the findings arising from the experiment are due to the particular interface feature being measured. For example, an experiment comparing which is the best way for users to enter text when using a tablet interface would control all other aspects of the setting to ensure they do not affect the performance. These include providing the same instructions to the participants, using the same tablet interface, and asking the participants to do the same tasks. The conditions that might be compared could be: typing using a virtual keyboard, typing using a physical keyboard, and swiping using a virtual keyboard (sliding across the keys to select letters, see Chapter 6). The aim of the experiment would be to test whether one is better than the other in terms of speed of typing and number of errors. A number of participants would be brought into the lab separately to carry out a predefined set of text entry tasks and their performance measured in terms of time taken and any errors made, e.g. selecting the wrong letter. The data collected would then be analyzed to determine if the scores for each condition were significantly different. If the performance measures obtained for the virtual keyboard were significantly faster than the other two and had the least number of errors, it could be possible to say that this method of text entry is the best.

BOX 13.1

Living labs

Living labs have been developed to evaluate people's everyday lives – that would be simply difficult to assess in usability labs. For example, research has been conducted to investigate people's habits and routines over a period of several months. An early example of a living lab was the Aware Home, which was a technology-rich, experimental house that enabled research into people's lives to be conducted in an authentic yet experimental setting (Abowd et al, 2000). The house was embedded with a complex network of sensors and audio/video recording devices that recorded their movements throughout the house and their use of technology. This enabled the occupants' behavior to be monitored and analyzed e.g. their routines and deviations.

A primary motivation was to evaluate how real families would respond and adapt to such a setup, over a period of several months. However, it has proved difficult to get participant families to agree to leave their own homes and live in a living lab home for a period of time. Nowadays, many Living Labs have become more like commercial enterprises, which offer facilities, infrastructure, and access to participating communities, bringing together users, developers, researchers, and other stakeholders. For example, MIT's Living Labs "brings together interdisciplinary experts to develop, deploy and test – in actual living environments – new technologies and strategies for design that respond to the changing world" (livinglabs. mit.edu). This enables researchers and companies to observe and record a number of activities related to health, energy, and the environment. The lab is set up to simulate a setting (e.g. a home, a dance floor, a classroom) and fully functional prototypes are installed in order to let users experience future product and service ideas in these experimental authentic settings. Ambient assisted living homes have also been developed where a network of sensors is embedded throughout someone's home rather than in a special house. The rationale is to enable disabled and elderly people to lead safe and independent lives by providing a non-intrusive system that can remotely monitor and provide alerts to caregivers in the event of an accident, illness, or unusual activities (e.g. Fernández-Luque et al, 2009). The term 'living lab' is also used to describe innovation networks in which people gather in person and virtually to explore and form commercial research and development collaborations. ■

DILEMMA
Is a living lab really a lab?

The concept of a living lab differs from a traditional view of a laboratory insofar as it is trying to be both natural and experimental, and where the goal is to bring the lab into the home (or other natural setting). The dilemma is how artificial do you make the more natural setting; where does the balance lie in setting it up to enable the right level of control to conduct evaluation without losing the sense of it being natural? ■

13.3.2 Natural Settings Involving Users

The aim of field studies is to evaluate people in their natural settings. They are used primarily to: (i) help identify opportunities for new technology; (ii) establish the requirements for a new design; and (iii) facilitate the introduction of technology, or inform deployment of existing technology in new contexts. Methods that are typically used are observation, interviews and focus groups, and interaction logging (see Chapter 7). The data takes the form of events and conversations that are recorded by the researchers as notes, or by audio or video recording, or by the participants, as diaries and notes. A goal is to be unobtrusive and not to affect what people do during the evaluation. However, it is inevitable that some methods will influence how people behave. For example, diary studies require people to document their activities or feelings at certain times and this can make them reflect on and possibly change their behavior.

More recently, there has been a trend towards conducting in the wild studies in HCI and ubiquitous computing. These are essentially field studies that look at how new technologies or prototypes have been deployed and used by people in various settings, such as the outdoors, public places, and homes. In moving into the wild, researchers inevitably have to give up control of what is being evaluated in order to observe how people approach and use, or don't use technologies in their everyday lives. For example, a researcher might be interested in observing how a new mobile navigation device will be used in urban environments. To conduct the study they would need to recruit people who are willing to use the device for a few weeks or months in their natural surroundings. They might then tell the participants what they can do with the device. Other than that, it is up to the participants to decide how to use it and when, as they move between their work or school, home, and other places.

The downside of handing over control is that it makes it difficult to anticipate what is going to happen and to be present when something interesting does happen. This is in contrast to usability testing where there is always an investigator or camera at hand to record events (Rogers *et al*, 2013). Instead, the researcher has to rely on the participants recording and reflecting how they use it, by writing up their experiences in diaries, filling in online forms, and/or taking part in intermittent interviews. The participants, however, may get too busy to do this reliably or forget certain events when they come to doing it. In addition, the participants may not try out the full range of functions provided by the device – meaning that the researcher has no idea as to whether they are useful or usable. However, the fact that the participants do not use them can be equally revealing.

Field studies can also be virtual, where observations take place in multiuser games such as World of Warcraft, online communities, chat rooms, and so on (e.g. Bainbridge, 2010). A goal of this kind of field study is to examine the kinds of social processes that occur in them, such as collaboration, confrontation, and cooperation. The researcher typically becomes a participant and does not control the interactions (see Chapters 7 and 8). Similar to in the wild studies, which are a form of field study, it can be difficult to anticipate what is going to happen and where.

13.3.3   Any Settings Not Involving Users

Evaluations that take place without involving users are conducted in settings where the researcher has to imagine or model how an interface is likely to be used. Inspection methods are commonly employed to predict user behavior and to identify usability problems, based on knowledge of usability, users' behavior, the contexts in which the system will be used, and the kinds of activities that users undertake. Examples include heuristic evaluation that applies knowledge of typical users guided by rules of thumb and walkthroughs that involve stepping through a scenario or answering a set of questions for a detailed prototype. Other techniques include analytics and models.

The original heuristics used in heuristic evaluation were for screen-based applications (Nielsen and Mack, 1994; Nielsen and Tahir, 2002). These have been adapted to develop new sets of heuristics for evaluating web-based products, mobile systems, collaborative technologies, computerized toys, and other new types of systems. One of the problems of using heuristics is that designers can sometimes be led astray by findings that are not as accurate as they appeared to be at first (Cockton *et al*, 2002; Tomlin, 2010 and for an overview see: http://www.nngroup.com/topic/heuristic-evaluation/).

Cognitive walkthroughs, which were the first walkthroughs developed, involve simulating a user's problem-solving process at each step in the human–computer dialog, and checking to see how users progress from step to step in these interactions (see Wharton *et al*, 1994 in Nielsen and Mack, 1994). A key feature of cognitive walkthroughs is that they focus on evaluating designs for ease of learning.

As discussed in Chapters 7 and 8, analytics is a technique for logging data either at a customer's site or remotely. Web analytics is the measurement, collection, analysis, and reporting of Internet data in order to understand and optimize web usage (Arikan, 2008). For example, Google provides a commonly used approach for collecting analytics data (http://www.google.com/analytics/). The kind of data collected depends on the reasons why the evaluation is being conducted. Analytics is a particularly useful method for evaluating design features of a website. For example, a company may want to evaluate its audience potential or the buzz (comments) that are happening about the products described on its website. Using specially developed tools, transactions on the website can be analyzed from log files of interaction data (also now called big data). Analysis of which web pages are visited (i.e. page hits) can also be analyzed, and so can direct mail campaign data, sales and lead information, and user performance data. Using a variety of automated analysis tools, including statistical analysis and data visualization, variations in web traffic can be identified and so can the most popular pages and products. Recently, with an increased focus on web-based learning through Massive Open Online Courses (MOOCs) and other forms of distance learning, there is more focus on learning analytics to see how well people really do learn using online technology.

Models have been used primarily for comparing the efficacy of different interfaces for the same application, for example, the optimal arrangement and location of features. A well-known approach uses Fitts' Law to predict the time it takes to reach a target using a pointing device (MacKenzie, 1995).

13.3.4 Choosing and Combining Methods

The three broad categories identified above provide a general framework to guide the selection of evaluation methods. Often combinations of methods are used across the categories to obtain a richer understanding. For example, sometimes usability testing in labs is combined with observations in natural settings to identify the range of usability problems and find out how users typically use a product. Figure 13.1 illustrates one way in which laboratory-based usability testing and field studies in natural settings can be combined to evaluate a mobile application – e.g. for a smartphone.

How do you choose between using a controlled and uncontrolled setting? There are obviously pros and cons for each one. The benefits of controlled settings include being able to test hypotheses about specific features of the interface, where the results can be generalized to the wider population. A benefit of uncontrolled settings is that unexpected data can be obtained that provides quite different insights into people's perceptions and their experiences of using, interacting, or communicating through the new technologies in the context of their everyday and working lives.

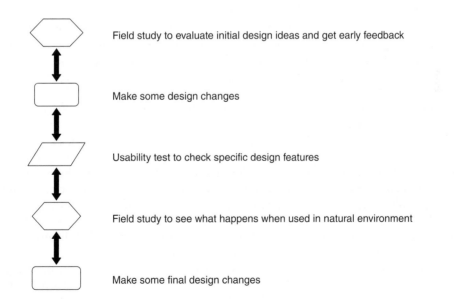

Figure 13.1 Example of the way laboratory-based usability testing and field studies can complement each other

13.3.5   Opportunistic Evaluations

Evaluations may be detailed, planned studies or opportunistic explorations. The latter are generally done early in the design process to provide designers with feedback quickly about a design idea. Getting this kind of feedback early in the design process is important because it confirms whether it is worth proceeding to develop an idea into a prototype. Typically, these early evaluations are informal and do not require many resources. For example, the designers may recruit a few local users and ask their opinions. Getting feedback this early in design can help save time and money if an idea needs to be modified or abandoned. Opportunistic evaluations with users can also be conducted in addition to more formal evaluations.

13.4   Evaluation Case Studies

Two contrasting case studies are described below to illustrate how evaluations can take place in different settings with different amounts of control over users' activities. The first case study (Section 13.4.1) describes an experiment that tested whether it was more exciting playing against a computer versus playing against a friend for a collaborative computer game (Mandryk and Inkpen, 2004). The focus was on how to measure user experience, which they note is more difficult to achieve than traditional usability measures. The second case study (Section 13.4.2) describes an in the wild evaluation of skiers (Jambon and Meillon, 2009) that used a combination of methods to assess how a mobile device providing personal feedback, on how well users are doing, helped improve their performance. The focus of the evaluation was whether and how often the participants consulted the feedback.

13.4.1   Case Study 1: An Experiment Investigating a Computer Game

For games to be successful they must engage and challenge users. Ways of evaluating this aspect of the user experience are therefore needed and, in this case study (Mandryk and Inkpen, 2004), physiological responses were used to evaluate users' experiences when playing against a friend and when playing alone against the computer. The researchers conjectured that physiological indicators could be an effective way of measuring a player's experience. Specifically, they designed an experiment to evaluate the participants' experience of playing an online ice-hockey game.

Ten participants, who were experienced game players, took part in the experiment. During the experiment sensors were placed on the participants to collect physiological data. These included measures of the moisture produced by sweat glands in the hands and feet, and changes in heart rate and breathing rate. In addition, they videoed participants and asked them to complete user satisfaction questionnaires at the end of the experiment. In order to reduce the effects of learning, half of the participants played first against a friend and then against the computer, and the other half played against the computer first. Figure 13.2 shows the setup for recording data while the participants were playing the game.

Results from the user satisfaction questionnaire revealed that the mean ratings on a 1–5 scale for each item indicated that playing against a friend was the favored experience (Table 13.1). Data recorded from the physiological responses was compared for the two conditions and in general revealed higher levels of excitement when participants played against a friend than when they played against the computer. The physiological recordings were also

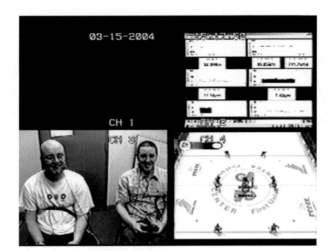

Figure 13.2 The display shows the physiological data (top right), two participants, and a screen of the game they played

Source: Mandryk and Inkpen (2004) Physiological Indicators for the Evaluation of Co-located Collaborative Play, *CSCW'2004*, pp. 102–111. ©2004 Association for Computing Machinery, Inc. Reprinted by permission.

compared across participants and, in general, indicated the same trend. Figure 13.3 shows a comparison for two participants.

Because of individual differences in physiological data, it was not possible to directly compare the means of the two sets of data collected: subjective questionnaires and physiological

	Playing against computer		Playing against friend	
	Mean	St. Dev.	Mean	St. Dev.
Boring	2.3	0.949	1.7	0.949
Challenging	3.6	1.08	3.9	0.994
Easy	2.7	0.823	2.5	0.850
Engaging	3.8	0.422	4.3	0.675
Exciting	3.5	0.527	4.1	0.568
Frustrating	2.8	1.14	2.5	0.850
Fun	3.9	0.738	4.6	0.699

Table 13.1 Mean subjective ratings given on a user satisfaction questionnaire using a five-point scale, in which 1 is lowest and 5 is highest for the 10 players. Identifying strongly with an experience state is indicated by a higher mean. The standard deviation indicates the spread of the results around the mean. Low values indicate little variation in participants' responses, high values indicate more variation

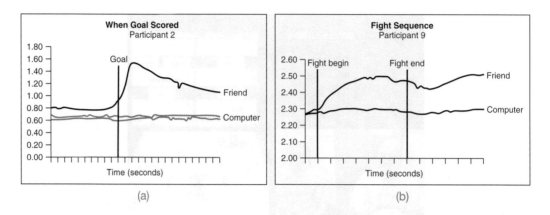

Figure 13.3 (a) A participant's skin response when scoring a goal against a friend versus against the computer and (b) another participant's response when engaging in a hockey fight against a friend versus against the computer

Source: Mandryk and Inkpen (2004) Physiological Indicators for the Evaluation of Co-located Collaborative Play, *CSCW'2004*, pp. 102–111. ©2004 Association for Computing Machinery, Inc. Reprinted by permission.

measures. However, by normalizing the results it was possible to correlate the results across individuals. This indicated that the physiological data gathering and analysis methods were effective for evaluating levels of challenge and engagement. Although not perfect, these two kinds of measures offer a way of going beyond traditional usability testing in an experimental setting to get a deeper understanding of user experience goals.

ACTIVITY 13.4

1. What kind of setting was used in this experiment?
2. How much control did the evaluators exert?
3. Which methods were recorded and when?

Comment

1. The experiment took place in a research laboratory, which is a controlled setting.
2. The evaluation was strongly controlled by the evaluators. They specified which of the two gaming conditions was assigned to each participant. The participants also had sensors placed on them to collect physiological data as they played the game (e.g. change in heart rate and breathing).
3. Physiological measures of the participants while playing the game were collected together with data collected afterwards using a user experience questionnaire that asked questions about how satisfied they were with the game and how much they enjoyed it. ■

(a)   (b)

Figure 13.4 (a) A skier wearing a helmet with an accelerometer (dark red box) and a mini-camera (black cylinder) placed on it for assessing the skier's performance and (b) the smartphone that provides feedback to the skier in the form of visualizations

Source: Jambon and Meillon (2009) User experience in the wild. In: *Proceedings of CHI '09, ACM Press*, New York, p. 4070.

13.4.2   Case Study 2: In the Wild Study of Skiers

Jambon and Meillon (2009) carried out an in the wild study to evaluate whether and how skiers might use a mobile device the authors designed to help skiers improve their performance. Each skier wore a helmet that had an accelerometer and a mini-camera on top of it (Figure 13.4a). These were used to gather data that could be used to provide feedback of the skiers' performance, which were displayed on a smartphone (Figure 13.4b). The skiers had access to the smartphones while on the slopes – which they kept in their pockets.

The study examined how the mobile system was used by the participants while skiing. A series of trials were run in which skiers descended the mountain. Video clips from the mini-camera and data from the accelerometers were collected for each skier's descent. The skiers were then asked to enter a chalet where the research team downloaded this data. The skiers then received SMS messages telling them that their data could be viewed on their smartphones. This included: maps of their ski runs, distance covered, duration of descent, maximum speed, and the video recorded. Figure 13.5 shows how the different components were linked together.

When and how often the skiers consulted their smartphones for feedback was logged. To the great surprise of the evaluators, the skiers did not check their performance on the slopes. Instead they preferred to wait and review it in the bar during breaks. This shows how in the wild studies can reveal unexpected findings.

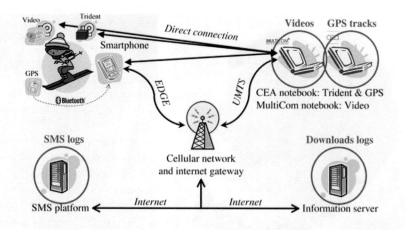

Figure 13.5 Components of the e-skiing system. Back arrows indicate the data transfers between devices, servers, and linking systems. Arrow shapes indicate different types of communications and the red circles indicate the data collection points

Source: Jambon *et al* (2009) User experience in the wild. In: *Proceedings of CHI '09, ACM* Press, New York, p. 4070.

Approximately a week after the ski trials, the evaluators ran a focus group with the skiers in order to learn how they felt about the system. This was organized as an informal dinner at which the skiers confirmed that they preferred to get their feedback after skiing on the slopes, so that their time on the slopes was not interrupted. The skiers also discussed the problems associated with using the equipment on the slopes. For example, the Bluetooth links between the GPS system and the smartphones were not reliable and there were other technical problems too.

ACTIVITY 13.5

1. What kind of setting was used in this evaluation?
2. How much control did the evaluators exert?
3. Which types of data were collected?

Comment
1. The evaluation took place in a natural setting.
2. The evaluators imposed less control on the participants than in the previous case study. The skiers were free to go where they wished on the mountain. However, the participants did have to agree to have cameras, GPS, and other tracking devices strapped to them.
3. The skiers' movements when going down the slopes were collected using video and accelerometers. In addition, a focus group was run in order to learn more about what the skiers thought about the system: what they liked or did not like, and what problems they experienced with the system. ∎

BOX 13.2

Crowdsourcing

Imagine having access to hundreds of thousands of participants who will perform tasks or provide feedback on a design or experimental task quickly and almost immediately. The service Mechanical Turk, hosted by Amazon, has thousands of people registered (known as Turkers), who have volunteered to take part by performing various activities, online, known as human intelligence tasks (HITs) for a very small reward. HITs are submitted by researchers or companies who pay from $0.01 for simple tasks (such as tagging pictures) to a few dollars (for taking part in an experiment). An advantage of using crowdsourcing in HCI is that it can be less expensive to run than traditional lab studies (where typically a participant is paid between $15 and $30, depending on the length of the experiment). Another benefit is that potentially many more participants can be recruited.

Heer and Bostock (2010) used crowdsourcing to determine how reliable it was to conduct an experiment in this way, i.e. asking random people over the Internet to take part. Using Mechanical Turk, they asked the Turkers signed up to the service to take part in a series of perception tasks using different visual display techniques. A large number agreed, enabling them to analyze their results statistically and generalize from their findings. They also developed a short set of test questions which generated 2880 responses. They then compared their findings from using crowdsourcing with those reported in published lab-based experiments. They found that while the results from their study using Turkers showed wider variance than in the reported study, the overall results across the studies were the same. They also found that the total cost of their experiment was a sixth of the cost of a typical laboratory study involving the same number of people. Crowdsourcing has become popular in a wide variety of applications ranging from planned experiments like Heer and Bostock's study (2010) to collecting design ideas and data from visitors at a nature park (Maher *et al*, 2014). ■

13.5 What Did We Learn from the Case Studies?

The case studies provide examples of how different evaluation methods are used in a variety of physical settings that involve users in different ways to answer various kinds of questions. They demonstrate how evaluators exercise control in different settings and also how they need to be creative when working with innovative systems and dealing with constraints created by the evaluation setting, and the robustness of the technology being evaluated. In addition, the case studies demonstrated:

- How to observe users in natural settings.
- Unexpected findings resulting from in the wild studies.
- Having to develop different data collection and analysis techniques to evaluate user experience goals such as challenge and engagement.
- The ability to run experiments on the Internet that are quick and inexpensive using crowdsourcing.
- How to recruit a large number of participants using Mechanical Turk.

BOX 13.3

The language of evaluation

Sometimes terms describing evaluation are used interchangeably and have different meanings. In order to avoid confusion we define some of these terms below in alphabetical order. (You may find that other texts use different terms).

Analytics: Data analytics refers to examining large volumes of raw data with the purpose of drawing inferences about that information. Web analytics is commonly used to measure website traffic through analyzing users' click data.

Analytical evaluation: Evaluation methods that model and predict user behavior. This term has been used to refer to heuristic evaluation, walkthroughs, modeling, and analytics.

Bias: The results of an evaluation are distorted. This can happen for several reasons. For example, selecting a population of users that has already had experience with the new system and describing their performance as if they were new users.

Controlled experiment: A study that is conducted to test hypotheses about some aspect of an interface or other dimension. Aspects that are controlled typically include the task that participants are asked to perform, the amount of time available to complete the tasks, and the environment in which the evaluation study occurs.

Crowdsourcing: A web-based method that provides the opportunity to enable potentially hundreds, thousands, or even millions of people to evaluate a product or take part in an experiment. The crowd may be asked to perform a particular evaluation task using a new product, or to rate or comment on the product.

Ecological validity: A particular kind of validity that concerns how the environment in which an evaluation is conducted influences or even distorts the results.

Expert review or crit: An evaluation method in which one or more people with usability expertise and knowledge of the user population review a product looking for potential problems.

Field study: An evaluation study that is done in a natural environment such as in a person's home, or in a work or leisure place.

Formative evaluation: An evaluation that is done during design to check that the product fulfills requirements and continues to meet users' needs.

Heuristic evaluation: An evaluation method in which knowledge of typical users is applied, often guided by heuristics, to identify usability problems.

Informed consent form: A form describing what a participant in an evaluation study will be asked to do, what will happen to the data collected about them, and their rights while involved in the study.

In the wild study: A field study in which users are observed using products or prototypes within their everyday context.

Living laboratory: A place that is configured to measure and record people's everyday activities in a natural setting, such as the home.

Predictive evaluation: Evaluation methods in which theoretically based models are used to predict user performance.

Reliability: The reliability or consistency of a method is how well it produces the same results on separate occasions under the same circumstances.

Scope: Refers to how much the findings from an evaluation can be generalized.

Summative evaluation: An evaluation that is done when the design is complete.

Usability laboratory: A laboratory that is specially designed for usability testing.

Usability testing: Involves measuring users' performance on various tasks.

User studies: A generic term that covers a range of evaluations involving users, including field studies and experiments.

Users or participants: These terms are used interchangeably to refer to the people who take part in evaluation studies.

Validity: Validity is concerned with whether the evaluation method measures what it is intended to measure. ■

13.6 Other Issues to Consider when Doing Evaluation

When reading the case studies, you probably thought of other issues, such as the importance of asking a good question to focus the evaluation and help you to decide on the best approach and methods to use. You may also have wondered about how to find suitable participants and, having found them, how to approach them. Can you just ask children in a café to participate or do you need permission from their parents? What do you have to tell participants and what if they decide part way through the study that they don't want to continue? Can they stop or do they have to continue? These and other issues are discussed on the ID-Book 4th Edition website but two things for you to think about now are: informing participants about their rights, and making sure that you take account of biases and other influences that impact how you describe your evaluation findings.

13.6.1 Informing Participants about Their Rights and Getting Their Consent
Most professional societies, universities, government, and other research offices require researchers to provide information about activities in which human participants will be involved. They do this to protect participants by ensuring that they are not endangered physically (e.g. in medical studies) or emotionally and that their right to privacy is protected. This documentation is reviewed by a panel and the researchers are notified whether their plan of work, particularly the details about how human participants and data collected about them will be treated, is acceptable. Drawing up such an agreement is mandatory in

many universities and major organizations. Indeed, special review boards generally prescribe the format required and many provide a detailed form that must be completed. Once the details are accepted, the review board checks periodically in order to oversee compliance. In American universities these are known as Institutional Review Boards (IRB). Other countries use different names and different forms for similar processes. Over the years IRB forms have become increasingly detailed, particularly now that much research involves the Internet and people's interaction via communication technologies. Several lawsuits at prominent universities have heightened attention to IRB compliance to the extent that it sometimes takes several months and multiple amendments to get IRB acceptance. IRB reviewers are not only interested in the more obvious issues of how participants will be treated and what they will be asked to do; they also want to know how the data will be analyzed and stored. For example, data about subjects must be coded and stored to prevent linking participants' names with that data. This means that names must be replaced by codes or pseudonyms that must be stored separately from the data and stored in a secure location.

Participants in evaluation studies have to be told what they will be asked to do, the conditions under which data will be collected, and what will happen to their data when they finish the task. Participants are told their rights, e.g. that they may withdraw from the study at any time if they wish. As discussed in Chapter 7, this information is usually presented in a form that the participant reads and signs before the study starts. This form is often called an informed consent form.

13.6.2   Some Things that Influence how You Interpret Data

Decisions have to be made about what data is needed to answer the study questions, how the data will be analyzed, and how the findings will be presented (see Chapter 8). To a great extent the method used determines the type of data collected, but there are still some choices. For example, should the data be treated statistically? Some general questions also need to be asked. Is the method reliable? Will the method measure what is intended, i.e. what is the validity of the method and the data collected? Will the evaluation study be ecologically valid or is the fundamental nature of the process being changed by studying it? Are biases creeping in that will distort the results? Will the results be generalizable, i.e. what is their scope?

Reliability

The reliability or consistency of a method is how well it produces the same results on separate occasions under the same circumstances. Another evaluator or researcher who follows exactly the same procedure should get similar results. Different evaluation methods have different degrees of reliability. For example, a carefully controlled experiment will have high reliability, whereas observing users in their natural setting will be variable. An unstructured interview will have low reliability: it would be difficult if not impossible to repeat exactly the same discussion.

Validity

Validity is concerned with whether the evaluation method measures what it is intended to measure. This encompasses both the method itself and the way it is implemented. If, for example, the goal of an evaluation study is to find out how users use a new product in their homes, then it is not appropriate to plan a laboratory experiment. An ethnographic study in users' homes would be more appropriate. If the goal is to find average performance times for completing a task, then a method that only recorded the number of user errors would be invalid.

Ecological Validity

Ecological validity is a particular kind of validity that concerns how the environment in which an evaluation is conducted influences or even distorts the results. For example, laboratory experiments are controlled, so what the participants do and how they behave is quite different from what happens naturally in their workplace, at home, or in leisure environments. Laboratory experiments therefore have low ecological validity because the results are unlikely to represent what happens in the real world. In contrast, ethnographic studies do not impact the participants or the study location as much, so they have high ecological validity.

Ecological validity is also affected when participants are aware of being studied. This is sometimes called the Hawthorne effect after a series of experiments at the Western Electric Company's Hawthorne factory in the USA in the 1920s and 1930s. The studies investigated changes in length of working day, heating, lighting, and so on; however, eventually it was discovered that the workers were reacting positively to being given special treatment rather than just to the experimental conditions. Similar findings sometimes occur in medical trials. Patients given the placebo dose (a false dose in which no drug is administered) show improvement that is due to receiving extra attention that makes them feel good.

Biases

Bias occurs when the results are distorted. For example, expert evaluators performing a heuristic evaluation may be more sensitive to certain kinds of design flaws than others, and this will be reflected in the results. Evaluators collecting observational data may consistently fail to notice certain types of behavior because they do not deem them important. Put another way, they may selectively gather data that they think is important. Interviewers may unconsciously influence responses from interviewees by their tone of voice, their facial expressions, or the way questions are phrased, so it is important to be sensitive to the possibility of biases.

Scope

The scope of an evaluation study refers to how much its findings can be generalized. For example, some modeling methods, like Fitts' Law (discussed in Chapter 15) which is used to evaluate keypad design, have a narrow, precise scope. (The problems of overstating results are discussed in Chapter 8).

Assignment

In this assignment, think about the case studies and reflect on the evaluation methods used.

1. For the case studies think about the role of evaluation in the design of the system and note the artifacts that were evaluated, *when* during the design they were evaluated, *which* methods were used, and *what* was learned from the evaluations. Note any issues of particular interest. You may find that constructing a table like the one that follows is a helpful approach.

Name of the study or artifact evaluated	When during the design the evaluation occurred	How controlled was the study and what role did users have	Which methods were used	What kind of data was collected and how was it analyzed	What was learned from the study	Notable issues

2. What were the main constraints that influenced the evaluation?

3. How did the use of different methods build on and complement each other to give a broader picture of the evaluation?

4. Which parts of the evaluation were directed at usability goals and which at user experience goals?

Summary

The aim of this chapter was to introduce the main approaches to evaluation and the methods typically used. These will be revisited in more detail in the next two chapters. This chapter stressed how evaluation is done throughout design; collecting information about users' or potential users' experiences when interacting with a prototype, a computer system, a component of a computer system, or a design artifact (e.g. screen sketch) in order to improve its design.

The pros and cons of running lab-based versus in the wild studies were outlined, in terms of cost, effort, constraints, and the types of results that can be elicited. Choosing which approach to use will depend on the aims of the evaluation, and the researcher's or evaluator's expectations and the resources available to them. Crowdsourcing was presented as a creative, and sometimes cost-saving evaluation approach. Finally we briefly mentioned the ethical issues concerned with how evaluation participants are treated and their rights to privacy. We also raised questions about data interpretation including the need to be aware of biases, reliability, data and ecological validity, and the scope of the study.

Key points
• Evaluation and design are very closely integrated.
• Some of the same data gathering methods are used in evaluation as for establishing requirements and identifying users' needs, e.g. observation, interviews, and questionnaires.
• Evaluations can be done in controlled settings such as laboratories, less controlled field settings, or where users are not present.
• Usability testing and experiments enable the evaluator to have a high level of control over what gets tested, whereas evaluators typically impose little or no control on participants in field studies.

- Different methods are usually combined to provide different perspectives within a study.
- Participants are made aware of their rights through an informed consent form.
- It is important not to over-generalize findings from an evaluation.

Further Reading

ALBERT, B., TULLIS, T. and TEDESCO, D. (2010) *Beyond the Usability Lab*. Morgan Kaufmann. This book describes methods that can be used to plan, organize, conduct, and analyze specifically large-scale online user experience studies targeted at the professional UX market.

LAZAR, J., FENG, J. H. and HOCHHEISER, H. (2010) *Research Methods in Human–Computer Interaction*. John Wiley & Sons Ltd, Chichester, UK. This book provides a useful overview of qualitative and quantitative methods. Chapter 14, 'Working with Human Subjects,' discusses ethical issues of working with human participants.

ROGERS, Y., YUILL, N. and MARSHALL, P. (2013) Contrasting Lab-Based and In-the-Wild Studies For Evaluating Multi-User Technologies. In B. Price (2013) *The SAGE Handbook on Digital Technology Research*. SAGE Publications: 359–173. This chapter explores the pros and cons of lab-based and in-the-wild evaluation studies with reference to different types of technology platforms including tabletops and large wall displays.

SHNEIDERMAN, B. and PLAISANT, C. (2010) *Designing the User Interface: Strategies for effective human–computer interaction* (5th edn). Addison-Wesley. This text provides an alternative way of categorizing evaluation methods and offers a useful overview.

TULLIS, T. and ALBERT, B. (2008) *Measuring the User Experience*. Morgan Kaufmann. This book provides a more general treatment of usability testing.

WHITESIDE, J., BENNETT, J. and HOLTZBLATT, K. (1988) Usability engineering: our experience and evolution. In M. Helander (ed.) *Handbook of Human–Computer Interaction*. North Holland, pp. 791–817. Though written many years ago, this seminal article reviews the strengths and weaknesses of usability engineering and explains why ethnographic techniques can provide a valuable alternative, or supplement, in some circumstances.

Chapter 14

EVALUATION STUDIES: FROM CONTROLLED TO NATURAL SETTINGS

Objectives

The main aims of this chapter are to:

- Explain how to do usability testing.
- Outline the basics of experimental design.
- Describe how to do field studies.

14.1 Introduction

Imagine you have designed a new shared web space intended for advertising second-hand goods. How would you find out whether householders would be able to use it to find what they wanted and whether it was a reliable and effective service? What evaluation methods would you employ?

In this chapter we describe evaluation studies that take place in a spectrum of settings, from controlled laboratories to natural settings. Within this spectrum we focus on usability testing which takes place in usability labs; experiments which take place in research labs; and field studies which take place in natural settings such as people's homes, schools, work, and leisure environments.

14.2 Usability Testing

The usability of products has traditionally been tested in controlled laboratory settings. This approach emphasizes how usable a product is. It has been most commonly used to evaluate desktop applications, such as websites, word processors, and search tools. Doing usability testing in a laboratory, or a temporarily assigned controlled environment, enables evaluators to control what users do and to control environmental and social influences that might impact the users' performance. The goal is to test whether the product being developed is usable by the intended user population to achieve the tasks for which it was designed.

14.2.1 Methods, Tasks, and Users

Collecting data about users' performance on predefined tasks is a central component of usability testing. As mentioned in Chapter 13, a combination of methods is often used to collect data. The data includes video recordings of the users including their facial expressions and logged keystrokes and mouse movements. Sometimes participants are asked to think aloud while carrying out tasks, as a way of revealing what they are thinking and planning (see Section 14.2.3). In addition, a user satisfaction questionnaire is used to find out how users actually feel about using the product, by asking them to rate it along a number of scales, after interacting with it. Structured or semi-structured interviews may also be conducted with users to collect additional information about what they liked and did not like about the product. Sometimes evaluators also collect data about how the product is used in the field.

Examples of the tasks that are given to users include searching for information, reading different typefaces (e.g. Helvetica and Times), and navigating through different menus. Performance times and numbers are the two main performance measures used, in terms of the time it takes typical users to complete a task, such as finding a website, and the number of errors that participants make, such as selecting wrong menu options when creating a spreadsheet. The quantitative performance measures that are obtained during the tests produce the following types of data (Wixon and Wilson, 1997):

- Time to complete a task.
- Time to complete a task after a specified time away from the product.
- Number and type of errors per task.
- Number of errors per unit of time.
- Number of navigations to online help or manuals.
- Number of users making a particular error.
- Number of users completing a task successfully.

In the early days of usability testing, tests were conducted to investigate specific features of an interface. For example, a team of scientists from Xerox Corporation ran a series of tests to determine what was the optimal number of buttons to put on a mouse, how many items to put in a menu, and how to design icons, as part of their Xerox Star office workstation system (Bewley *et al*, 1990). In total, over 15 tests were performed involving over 200 users, lasting over 400 hours. The results of the various tests were then fed back into the design of the interface.

A key concern is the number of users that should be involved in a usability study: five to twelve is considered an acceptable number (Dumas and Redish, 1999), but sometimes it is possible to use fewer when there are budget and schedule constraints. For instance, quick feedback about a design idea, such as the initial placement of a logo on a website, can be obtained from only two or three users.

14.2.2 Labs and Equipment

Many companies, such as Microsoft and IBM, used to test their products in custom-built usability labs (Lund, 1994). These facilities comprise a main testing laboratory, with recording equipment and the product being tested, and an observation room where the evaluators watch what is going on and analyze the data. There may also be a reception area for testers, a storage area, and a viewing room for observers. The space may be arranged to superficially mimic features of the real world. For example, if the product is an office product or for use in a hotel reception area, the laboratory can be set up to look like those environments. Soundproofing and lack of windows, telephones, co-workers, and other workplace and social artifacts eliminate most of the normal sources of distraction so that the users can concentrate on the tasks set for them to perform.

Typically there are two to three wall-mounted video cameras that record the users' behavior, such as hand movements, facial expression, and general body language. Microphones are also placed near where the participants will be sitting to record their utterances. Video and other data is fed through to monitors in the observation room. The observation room is usually separated from the main laboratory or workroom by a one-way mirror so that evaluators can watch participants being tested but testers cannot see them. It can be a small auditorium with rows of seats at different levels or, more simply, a small backroom consisting of a row of chairs facing the monitors. They are designed so that evaluators and others can watch the tests while ongoing, both on the monitors and through the mirror. Figure 14.1 shows a typical arrangement.

Sometimes, modifications may have to be made to the room set up to test different types of applications. For example, Nodder and his colleagues at Microsoft had to partition the space into two rooms when they were testing NetMeeting, an early videoconferencing product, in the mid-1990s, as Figure 14.2 shows (Nodder *et al*, 1999). This allowed users in both rooms to be observed when conducting a meeting via the videoconference system.

Usability labs can be very expensive and labor-intensive to run and maintain. A less expensive alternative, that started to become more popular in the early and mid-90s, is the use of mobile usability testing equipment. Video cameras, laptops, and other measuring equipment are temporarily set up in an office or other space, converting it into a makeshift usability laboratory. Another advantage is that equipment can be taken into work settings, enabling testing to be done on site, making it less artificial and more convenient for the participants.

Figure 14.1 A usability laboratory in which evaluators watch participants on a monitor and through a one-way mirror

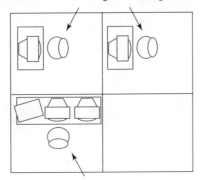

Evaluation: Participants communicating with each other using NetMeeting

Usability engineer uses another PC to become the third participant

Figure 14.2 The testing arrangement used for NetMeeting, an early videoconferencing product

There is an increasing number of products that are specifically designed for mobile evaluation. Some are referred to as lab-in-a-box or lab-in-a-suitcase because they pack away neatly into a convenient carrying case. One example is the Tracksys portable lab that costs under $5000 depending on exactly what equipment is included (Figure 14.3). It is composed of off-the-shelf components that plug into a PC and can record video direct to hard disk

Figure 14.3 The Tracksys lab-in-a-box system, which comprises components that pack into a heavy duty padded flight case plus a PC system

Source: Courtesy of Harry Brignull.

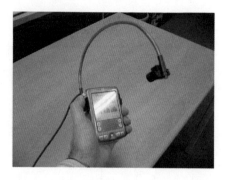

Figure 14.4 The Tracksys system being used with a mobile device camera that attaches to a flexible arm, which mounts on a mobile device, and is tethered to the lab

Source: Courtesy of Harry Brignull.

(Figure 14.4). Some recent additions to Tracksys include: a system called the GoToMeeting package, an easier remote control system including a remote eye-tracker, and a mobile head-mounted eye-tracker. The latter is fitted to a helmet or lightweight cap so that the system offers complete portability for research in sports, usability studies, and a variety of other disciplines (Figure 14.5). There are also mobile eye-tracking and eye-gaze systems available that can be used.

Another trend has been to conduct remote usability testing, where users perform a set of tasks with a product in their own setting and their interactions with the software are logged remotely. An advantage of this approach is that many users can be tested at the same time and the logged data automatically compiled into statistical packages for data analysis. For example, the number of clicks per page and the tracking of clicks when searching websites for specified tasks can be readily obtained.

Figure 14.5 The mobile head-mounted eye-tracker

Source: Picture courtesy of SensoMotoric Instruments (SMI), copyright 2010.

14.2.3 An Example of Usability Testing: The iPad

Usability specialists Budiu and Nielsen (2010) from the Nielsen Norman Group conducted a usability test of the websites and apps specific to the iPad. They wanted to understand how the interactions with the device affected people and to get feedback to their clients and developers as well as those who were eager to know if the iPad lived up to the hype – which was being reported at the time it came to market. They used two methods: usability testing with think-aloud in which users said what they were doing and thinking as they did it, and an expert review. Here we describe the usability testing they conducted. A key question they asked was: 'Are user expectations different for the iPad compared with the iPhone?' A previous study of the iPhone showed people preferred using apps than browsing the web because the latter was slow and cumbersome at that time. Would this be the same for the iPad, where the screen was larger and web pages were more similar to how they appeared on the laptops or desktop computers that most people were used to using? Budiu and Nielsen also hoped that their study would be able to address the question that many companies were considering at that time: whether it was worth developing specific websites for the iPad (in the way some companies were doing for smartphones) or would the desktop versions be acceptable when interacted with using the iPad multitouch interface.

The usability testing was carried out in two cities in the United States: Fremont, California, and Chicago. The test sessions were similar; the aim of both was to understand the typical usability issues that people encounter when using applications and accessing websites on the iPad. Seven participants were recruited: all were experienced iPhone users who had owned their phones for at least 3 months and who had used a variety of apps. One participant was also an iPad owner. One reason for selecting participants who used iPhones was because they would have previous experience of using apps and the web with a similar interaction style to the iPad.

The participants were considered typical users. They varied in age and occupation. Two participants were in their 20s, three were in their 30s, one in their 50s, and one in their 60s. Their occupations were: food server, paralegal, medical assistant, retired food driver, account rep, and homemaker. Three were males and four were females.

Before taking part, the participants were asked to read and sign an informed consent form agreeing to the terms and conditions of the study. This form described:

- what the participant would be asked to do;
- the length of time needed for the study;
- the compensation that would be offered for participating;
- the participants' right to withdraw from the study at any time;
- a promise that the person's identity would not be disclosed; and
- an agreement that the data collected would be confidential and would not be made available to marketers or anyone other than the evaluators.

The Tests

The session started with participants being invited to explore any application they found interesting on the iPad. They were asked to comment on what they were looking for or reading, what they liked and disliked about a site, and what made it easy or difficult to carry out a task. A moderator sat next to each participant and observed and took notes. The sessions were video recorded and lasted about 90 minutes. Participants worked on their own.

After exploring the iPad they were asked by the evaluator to open specific apps or websites and to explore them, then carry out one or more tasks as they would if they were

App or website	Task
iBook	Download a free copy of *Alice's Adventures in Wonderland* and read through the first few pages.
Craigslist	Find some free mulch for your garden.
eBay	You want to buy a new iPad on eBay. Find one that you could buy from a reputable seller.
Time Magazine	Browse through the magazine and find the best pictures of the week.
Epicurious	You want to make an apple pie for tonight. Find a recipe and see what you need to buy in order to prepare it.
Kayak	You are planning a trip to Death Valley in May this year. Find a hotel located in the park or close to the park.

Table 14.1 Examples of some of the tests used in the iPad evaluation (adapted from Budiu and Nielsen, 2010).

Source: Copyright Nielsen Norman Group, from report available at http://www.nngroup.com/reports/.

on their own. Each was assigned the tasks in a randomized order. All the apps that were tested were designed specifically for the iPad, but for some tasks the users were asked to do the same task on a website that was not specifically designed for the iPad. For these tasks the evaluators took care to balance the presentation order so that the app would be first for some participants and the website would be first for others. Over 60 tasks were chosen from over 32 different sites. Examples are shown in Table 14.1.

ACTIVITY 14.1

1. What was the main purpose of this study?
2. What aspects are considered to be important for good usability and user experience?
3. How representative are the tasks outlined in Table 14.1 of what a typical iPad user might do?

Comment
1. To find out how participants interacted with apps and websites on the iPad. The findings were intended to help developers determine whether specific websites need to be developed for the iPad.
2. Our definition of usability suggests that the iPad should be: efficient, effective, safe, easy to learn, easy to remember, and have good utility (i.e. good usability). It should also support creativity and be motivating, helpful, and satisfying to use (i.e. good user experience). The iPad is designed for the general public so the range of users is broad in terms of age and experience with technology.
3. The tasks are a small sample of the total set prepared by the evaluators. They cover shopping, reading, planning, and finding a recipe – which are common activities people engage in during their everyday lives. ∎

Figure 14.6 The setup used in the Chicago usability testing sessions

Source: Copyright Nielsen Norman Group, from report available at http://www.nngroup.com/reports/.

The Equipment

The testing was done using a setup similar to the mobile usability kit shown in Figure 14.6. A camera recorded the participant's interactions and gestures when using the iPad and streamed the recording to a laptop computer. A webcam was also used to record the expressions on the participants' faces and their think-aloud commentary. The laptop ran software called Morae, which synchronized these two data streams. Up to three observers (including the moderator sitting next to the participant) watched the video streams (rather than observing the participant directly) on their laptops situated on the table – meaning they did not have to invade the participants' personal space.

Usability Problems

The main findings from the study showed that the participants were able to interact with websites on the iPad but that it was not optimal. For example, links on the pages were often too small to tap on reliably and the fonts were sometimes difficult to read. The various usability problems identified in the study were classified according to a number of well-known interaction design principles and concepts, including: mental models, navigation, the quality of images, problems of using a touch screen with small target areas, lack of affordances, getting lost in the application, the effects of changing orientations, working memory, and the feedback that they received.

An example of a navigation problem identified during the evaluation was that when the cover of *Time* magazine appeared on the iPad, it didn't contain any hyperlinks. The contents page did but it was not easily accessible. In order to access it, users first had to tap the screen to reveal the controls at the bottom, then select the Contents button to display the contents carousel, and then select the contents page in the carousel.

Another problem they identified was that the participants sometimes did not know where to tap on the iPad to select options such as buttons and menus. It should be obvious from the affordances of an interface as to where they are and how to select them.

However, the evaluators found that in many cases the participants repeatedly tapped the iPad interface in order to initiate an action, such as when trying to select an option from a menu.

Getting lost in an application is an old but important problem for designers of digital products and some participants got lost because they tapped the iPad too much and could not find a back button and could not get themselves back to the home page. One participant said " . . . I like having everything there [on the home page]. That's just how my brain works" (Budiu and Nielsen, 2010, p. 58). Other problems arose because applications appeared differently in the two views possible on the iPad: portrait and landscape. More information was provided by some app developers in the horizontal (landscape) view than in the vertical (portrait) view, which caused problems for some participants.

Interpreting and Presenting the Data

Based on the findings of their study, Budiu and Nielsen made a number of recommendations, including supporting standard navigation. The results of the study were written up as a report that was made publically available to app developers and the general public (it is available from www.nngroup.com). It provided a summary of key findings for the general public as well as specific details of the problems the participants had with the iPad, so that developers could decide whether to make specific websites and apps for the iPad.

While being revealing about how usable websites and apps are on the iPad, the usability testing was not able to reveal how it will be used in people's everyday lives. This would require an in the wild study where observations are made of how people use them in their own homes and when traveling.

ACTIVITY 14.2

1. Was the selection of participants for the iPad study appropriate? Justify your comments.
2. What might have been the problems with asking participants to think out loud as they completed the tasks?

Comments

1. The evaluator tried to get a representative set of participants across an age range with similar skill levels – i.e. they had used an iPhone or iPad. Ideally, it would have been good to have had more participants to see if the findings were more generalizable. However, it was important to do the study as quickly as possible and get the results out to developers and the general public.
2. The think-aloud technique was used to record verbally what the participants were doing, trying to do, and thinking. If a person is concentrating hard on a task, however, it can be difficult to talk at the same time. This can often be at exactly the time when it is most interesting to hear the participants' comments – i.e. when the task is difficult, the person goes quiet. ∎

Video produced in 2010 by Blue Duck Labs illustrates some special considerations that evaluators need to know and include when testing systems with young children. It describes having a young child test a paper prototype of a potential coloring program for kids – see it at **http://youtu.be/9wQkLthhHKA**

When more rigorous testing is needed, a set of standards can be used for guidance – such an approach is described in Box 14.1 for the development of the US Government's Recovery.gov website. For this large website, several methods were used including: usability testing, expert reviews (discussed in Chapter 15), and focus groups.

BOX 14.1

Ensuring Accessibility and Section 508 Compliance for the Recovery.gov Website (Lazar *et al*, 2010b)

The American Recovery and Reinvestment Act (informally known as 'the Stimulus Bill') became law on February 17, 2009, with the intention of infusing $787 billion into the US economy to create jobs and improve economic conditions. The Act established an independent board, the Recovery Accountability and Transparency Board, to oversee the spending and detect, mitigate, and minimize any waste, fraud, or abuse. The law required the Board to establish a website to provide the public with information on the progress of the recovery effort. A simple website was launched the day that the Act was signed into law, but one of the immediate goals of the Board was to create a more detailed website, with data, geospatial features, and Web 2.0 functionality, including data on every contract related to the Act. The goal was to provide political transparency at a scale not seen before in the US federal government so that citizens could see how money was being spent.

A major goal in the development of the Recovery.gov website was meeting the requirement that it be accessible to those with disabilities, such as perceptual (visual, hearing) and motor impairments. It had to comply with guidelines specified in Section 508 of the Rehabilitation Act (see the id-book.com website for details). At a broad level, three main approaches were used to ensure compliance:

- Usability testing with individual users, including those with perceptual and motor impairments.
- Routine testing for compliance with Section 508 of the Rehabilitation Act, done every 3 months, using screenreaders such as JAWS, and automated testing tools such as Watchfire.

(Continued)

- Providing an online feedback loop, listening to users, and rapidly responding to accessibility problems.

During development, ten 2-hour focus groups with users were convened in five cities. An expert panel was also convened with four interface design experts, and usability testing was performed, specifically involving 11 users with various impairments. Several weeks before the launch of Recovery.gov 2.0, the development team visited the Department of Defense Computer Accommodations Technology Evaluation Center (CAPTEC) to get hands-on experience with various assistive technology devices (such as head-pointing devices) which otherwise would not be available to the Recovery Accountability and Transparency Board in their own offices.

Approaches were developed to meet each compliance standard, including situations where existing regulations don't provide clear guidance, such as with PDF files. A large number of PDF files are posted each month on Recovery.gov, and those files also undergo Section 508 compliance testing. The files undergo automated accessibility inspections using Adobe PDF accessibility tools, and if there are minor clarifications needed, the recovery.gov web managers make the changes; but if major changes are needed, the PDF file is returned to the agency generating the PDF file, along with the Adobe-generated accessibility report. The PDF file is not posted until it passes the Adobe automated accessibility evaluation. Furthermore, no new modules or features are added to the Recovery.gov site until they have been evaluated for accessibility using both expert evaluations and automated evaluations. Because of the large number of visitors to the Recovery.gov website (an estimated 1.5 million monthly visitors), ensuring accessible, usable interfaces is a high priority. The full case study is available on www.id-book.com. Since the original Act was passed, it has since been amended in 2013 so that it now includes aid victims of Hurricane Sandy, a particularly devastating hurricane that destroyed thousands of homes and businesses along the north east coast of the USA. ∎

14.3 Conducting Experiments

In research contexts, specific hypotheses are tested that make a prediction about the way users will perform with an interface. The benefits are more rigor and confidence that one interface feature is easier to understand or faster to use than another. An example of a hypothesis is: context menus (i.e. menus that provide options related to the context determined by the users' previous choices) are an easier to select option compared with cascading menus. Hypotheses are often based on a theory, such as Fitts' Law (see next chapter), or previous research findings. Specific measurements provide a way of testing the hypothesis. In the above example, the accuracy of selecting menu options could be compared by counting the number of errors made by participants for each menu type.

Hypotheses Testing
Typically, a hypothesis involves examining a relationship between two things, called variables. Variables can be independent or dependent. An independent variable is what the investigator

manipulates (i.e. selects), and in the above example it is the different menu types. The other variable is called the dependent variable, and, in our example, this is the time taken to select an option. It is a measure of the user performance and, if our hypothesis is correct, will vary depending on the different types of menu.

When setting up a hypothesis to test the effect of the independent variable(s) on the dependent variable, it is usual to derive a null hypothesis and an alternative one. The null hypothesis in our example would state that there is no difference in the time it takes users to find items (i.e. selection time) between context and cascading menus. The alternative hypothesis would state that there is a difference between the two on selection time. When a difference is specified but not what it will be, it is called a two-tailed hypothesis. This is because it can be interpreted in two ways: either the context menu or the cascading menu is faster to select options from. Alternatively, the hypothesis can be stated in terms of one effect. This is called a one-tailed hypothesis and would state that context menus are faster to select items from, or vice versa. A one-tailed hypothesis would be made if there was a strong reason to believe it to be the case. A two-tailed hypothesis would be chosen if there was no reason or theory that could be used to support the case that the predicted effect would go one way or the other.

You might ask why you need a null hypothesis, since it seems the opposite of what the experimenter wants to find out. It is put forward so that the data can reject a statement without necessarily supporting the opposite statement. If the experimental data shows a big difference between selection times for the two menu types, then the null hypothesis that menu type has no effect on selection time can be rejected, which is different from saying that there is an effect. Conversely, if there is no difference between the two, then the null hypothesis cannot be rejected (i.e. the claim that context menus are faster to select options from is not supported).

In order to test a hypothesis, the experimenter has to set up the conditions and find ways to keep other variables constant, to prevent them from influencing the findings. This is called the experimental design. Examples of other variables that need to be kept constant for both types of menus might include size and screen resolution. For example, if the text is in 10 pt font size in one condition and 14 pt font size in the other then it could be this difference that causes the effect (i.e. differences in selection speed are due to font size). More than one condition can also be compared with the control, for example:

Condition 1 = Context menu
Condition 2 = Cascading menu
Condition 3 = Scrolling

Sometimes an experimenter might want to investigate the relationship between two independent variables: for example, age and educational background. A hypothesis might be that young people are faster at searching on the web than older people and that those with a scientific background are more effective at searching on the web. An experiment would be set up to measure the time it takes to complete the task and the number of searches carried out. The analysis of the data would focus on both the effects of the main variables (age and background) and also look for any interactions among them.

Hypothesis testing can also be extended to include even more variables, but it makes the experimental design more complex. An example is testing the effects of age and educational background on user performance for two methods of web searching: one using a search engine and the other a browser. Again, the goal is to test the effects of the main variables (age, educational background, web searching method) and to look for any interactions among them. However, as the number of variables increases in an experimental design, it makes it more difficult to work out from the data what is causing the results.

Experimental Design

A concern in experimental design is to determine which participants to involve for which conditions in an experiment. The experience of participating in one condition will affect the performance of those participants if asked to participate in another condition. For example, having learned about the way the heart works using multimedia, if one group of participants was exposed to the same learning material via another medium, e.g. virtual reality, and another group of participants was not, the participants who had the additional exposure to the material would have an unfair advantage. Furthermore, it would create bias if the participants in one condition within the same experiment had seen the content and others had not. The reason for this is that those who had the additional exposure to the content would have had more time to learn about the topic and this would increase their chances of answering more questions correctly. In some experimental designs, however, it is possible to use the same participants for all conditions without letting such training effects bias the results.

The names given for the different designs are: different-participant design, same-participant design, and matched-pairs design. In different-participant design, a single group of participants is allocated randomly to each of the experimental conditions, so that different participants perform in different conditions. Another term used for this experimental design is between-subjects design. An advantage is that there are no ordering or training effects caused by the influence of participants' experience of one set of tasks on their performance in the next, as each participant only ever performs in one condition. A disadvantage is that large numbers of participants are needed so that the effect of any individual differences among participants, such as differences in experience and expertise, is minimized. Randomly allocating the participants and pre-testing to identify any participants that differ strongly from the others can help.

In same-participant design (also called within subjects design), all participants perform in all conditions so only half the number of participants is needed; the main reason for this design is to lessen the impact of individual differences and to see how performance varies across conditions for each participant. It is important to ensure that the order in which participants perform tasks for this set up does not bias the results. For example, if there are two tasks, A and B, half the participants should do task A followed by task B and the other half should do task B followed by task A. This is known as counterbalancing. Counterbalancing neutralizes possible unfair effects of learning from the first task, known as the order effect.

In matched-participant design (also known as pair-wise design), participants are matched in pairs based on certain user characteristics such as expertise and gender. Each pair is then randomly allocated to each experimental condition. A problem with this arrangement

Design	Advantages	Disadvantages
Different participants	No order effects	Many participants needed. Individual differences among participants are a problem. Can be offset to some extent by randomly assigning to groups
Same participants	Eliminates individual differences between experimental conditions	Need to counterbalance to avoid ordering effects
Matched participants	Same as different participants, but the effects of individual differences are reduced	Can never be sure that subjects are matched across variables that might affect performance

Table 14.2 The advantages and disadvantages of different allocations of participants to conditions

is that other important variables that have not been taken into account may influence the results. For example, experience in using the web could influence the results of tests to evaluate the navigability of a website. So web expertise would be a good criterion for matching participants. The advantages and disadvantages of using different experimental designs are summarized in Table 14.2.

The data collected to measure user performance on the tasks set in an experiment usually includes response times for subtasks, total times to complete a task, and number of errors per task. Analyzing the data involves comparing the performance data obtained across the different conditions. The response times, errors, etc. are averaged across conditions to see if there are any marked differences. Statistical tests are then used, such as *t*-tests that statistically compare the differences between the conditions, to reveal if these are significant. For example, a *t*-test will reveal whether context or cascading menus are faster to select options from.

Statistics: t-tests

There are many types of statistics that can be used to test the probability of a result occurring by chance but *t*-tests are the most widely used statistical test in HCI and related fields, such as psychology. The scores, e.g. time taken for each participant to select items from a menu in each condition (i.e. context and cascading menus), are used to compute the means ($\bar{x}$) and standard deviations (SDs). The standard deviation is a statistical measure of the spread or variability around the mean. The *t*-test uses a simple equation to test the significance of the difference between the means for the two conditions. If they are significantly different from each other, we can reject the null hypothesis and in so doing infer that the alternative hypothesis holds. A typical *t*-test result that compared menu selection times for two groups with 9 and 12 participants each might be: $t = 4.53$, $p < 0.05$, df $= 19$. The *t*-value of 4.53 is the score derived from applying the *t*-test; df stands for degrees of freedom, which represents the number of values in the conditions that are free to vary. This is a complex concept that we will not explain here other than to mention how it is derived and that it is always written as part of the result of a *t*-test. The dfs are calculated by summing the number of participants in one condition minus one and the number of participants in the other condition minus one. It is calculated as $df = (N_a - 1) + (N_b - 1)$, where N_a is the number of participants in one condition and N_b is the number of participants in the other condition. In our example, $df = (9 - 1) + (12 - 1) = 19$. *p* is the probability that the effect found did not occur by chance. So, when $p < 0.05$, it means that the effect found is probably not due to chance and that there is only a 5% chance that it could be by chance. In other words there most likely is a difference between the two conditions. Typically, a value of $p < 0.05$ is considered good enough to reject the null hypothesis, although lower levels of *p* are more convincing, e.g. $p < 0.01$ where the effect found is even less likely to be due to chance, there being only a 1% chance of that being the case.

14.4   Field Studies

Increasingly, more evaluation studies are being done in natural settings with either little or no control imposed on participants' activities. This change is largely a response to technologies being developed for use outside office settings. For example, mobile, ambient, and other technologies are now available for use in the home, outdoors, and in public places. Typically, field studies are conducted to evaluate these user experiences.

As mentioned in Chapter 13, evaluations conducted in natural settings are very different from those in controlled environments, where tasks are set and completed in an orderly way. In contrast, studies in natural settings tend to be messy in the sense that activities often overlap and are constantly interrupted. This follows the way people interact with products in their everyday messy worlds, which is generally different from how they perform on set tasks in a laboratory setting. By evaluating how people think about, interact, and integrate products within the settings they will ultimately be used in, we can get a better sense of how successful the products will be in the real world. The trade-off is that we cannot test specific hypotheses about an interface nor account, with the same degree of certainty, for how people react to or use a product – as we can do in controlled settings like laboratories. This makes it more difficult to determine what causes a particular type of behavior or what is problematic about the usability of a product. Instead, qualitative accounts and descriptions of people's behavior and activities are obtained that reveal how they used the product and reacted to its design.

Field studies can range in time from just a few minutes to a period of several months or even years. Data is collected primarily by observing and interviewing people; collecting video, audio, and field notes to record what occurs in the chosen setting. In addition, participants may be asked to fill out paper-based or electronic diaries, which run on cell phones or other handheld devices, at particular points during the day, such as when they are interrupted during their ongoing activity or when they encounter a problem when interacting with a product or when they are in a particular location (Figure 14.7). This technique is based on the experience sampling method (ESM) discussed in Chapter 7, which is often used in healthcare

Figure 14.7 An example of a context-aware experience sampling tool running on a mobile device

Source: From Cogdill, K. (1999) "MedlinePlus Interface Evaluation: Final Report". Reproduced by permission of Prof. Keith Cogdill.

(Csikszentmihalyhi and Larson, 1987). Data on the frequency and patterns of certain daily activities, such as the monitoring of eating and drinking habits, or social interactions like phone and face-to-face conversations, are recorded. Software running on the smartphones triggers messages to study participants at certain intervals, requesting them to answer questions or fill out dynamic forms and checklists. These might include recording what they are doing, what they are feeling like at a particular time, where they are, or how many conversations they have had in the last hour.

When conducting a field study, deciding whether to tell the people being observed, or asked to record information, that they are being studied and how long the study or session will take is more difficult than in a laboratory situation. For example, when studying people's interactions with an ambient display, telling them that they are part of a study will likely change the way they behave. Similarly, if people are using an online street map while walking in a city, their interactions may only take a few seconds and so informing them that they are being studied would disrupt their behavior.

It is important to ensure the privacy of participants in field studies. For example, photographs should not be included in reports without the participant's permission. Participants in field studies that run over a period of weeks or months, such as an investigation into how they use a type of remote control device in their homes, should be informed about the study and asked to sign an informed consent form in the usual way as mentioned in Chapter 13. In situations like this, the evaluators will need to work out and agree with the participants what part of the activity is to be recorded and how. For example, if the evaluators want to set up cameras, they need to be situated unobtrusively and participants need to be informed in advance about where the cameras will be and when they will be recording their activities. The evaluators will also need to work out in advance what to do if the prototype or product breaks down. Can the participants be instructed to fix the problem themselves or will the evaluators need to be called in? Security arrangements will also need to be made if expensive or precious equipment is being evaluated in a public place. Other practical issues may also need to be taken into account depending on the location, product being evaluated, and the participants in the study.

The system for helping skiers to improve their performance (discussed in Chapter 13) was evaluated with skiers on the mountains to see how they used it and whether they thought it really did help them to improve their ski performance. A wide range of other studies have explored how new technologies have been appropriated by people in their own cultures and settings. By appropriated we mean how the participants use, integrate, and adapt the technology to suit their needs, desires, and ways of living. For example, the Opinionizer system mentioned in Chapter 4 was designed as part of a social space where people could share their opinions visually and anonymously, via a public display. The Opinionizer was intended to encourage and facilitate conversations with strangers at a party or other social gatherings. Observations of it being interacted with at a number of parties showed a honey-pot effect: as the number of people in the immediate vicinity of the system increased, a sociable buzz was created, where a variety of conversations were started between the strangers. The findings from these and other studies in natural settings are typically reported in the form of vignettes, excerpts, critical incidents, patterns, and narratives to show how the products are being appropriated and integrated into their surroundings.

14.4.1   In the Wild Studies

For several years now it has become increasingly popular to conduct in the wild studies to determine how people use and persist in using a range of new technologies or prototypes in situ. The case study in Chapter 13 (Section 13.4.2) is an example of an in the wild study in which the researchers wanted to gather feedback about how a new system designed to help skiers improve their performance actually did help them and whether the skiers liked it. As mentioned previously, the term 'in the wild' reflects the context of the study – where the new technologies are created, deployed, and evaluated in situ (Rogers, 2011). The evaluation takes place in a natural setting in which the researchers release their prototype technology and observe from a distance how it is approached and used by people in their own homes, and elsewhere. Instead of developing solutions that fit in with existing practices, researchers often explore new technological possibilities that can change and even disrupt behavior. Opportunities are created, interventions installed, and different ways of behaving are encouraged. A key concern is how people react, change, and integrate the technology into their everyday lives. The outcome of conducting in the wild studies for different periods and at different intervals can be most revealing – demonstrating quite different results from those arising out of lab studies. Comparisons of findings from lab studies and in the wild studies have revealed that while many usability issues can be uncovered in a lab study, actual use aspects are more difficult to discern. These aspects include how users approach the new technology, the kinds of benefits that they could derive from it, how they appropriate it in the context of everyday activity, and its sustained use over time (Rogers *et al*, 2013; Kjeldskov and Skov, 2014).

An In the Wild Study: The UbiFit Garden

Another early example of an in the wild study was the UbiFit Garden project (Consolvo *et al*, 2008), which evaluated activity sensing in the wild to address the growing problem of people's sedentary lifestyles. A mobile device was designed to encourage physical activity that used on-body sensing and activity inferencing. The personal mobile display had three components: a fitness device that monitored different types of fitness activities, an interactive application that kept detailed information, including a journal of the

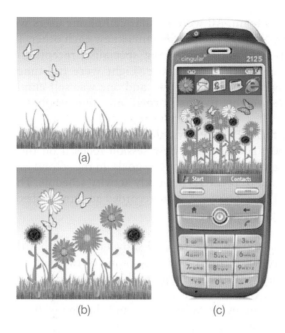

Figure 14.8 UbiFit Garden's glanceable display: (a) at the beginning of the week (small butterflies indicate recent goal attainments; the absence of flowers means no activity this week); (b) a garden with workout variety; (c) the display on a mobile phone (the large butterfly indicates this week's goal was met)

Source: From Consolvo, S., McDonald, D.W., Toscos, T. *et al* (2008) "Activity sensing in the wild: a field trial of UbiFit garden". In: *Proceedings of CHI 2008*, ACM Press, New York, p. 1799.

individual's activities, and a glanceable display that ran on cell phones. The system worked by inferring what the wearer was doing, in terms of walking, running, cycling, and using gym equipment based on data detected from accelerometer and barometer sensors. The sensor data was processed and then communicated to the cell phone using Bluetooth. The data was analyzed and used as input for the glanceable display that depicted the UbiFit Garden (see Figure 14.8). The display depicted a garden that bloomed throughout the week as the user carried out the various physical activities. A healthy regime of physical exercise was indicated by a healthy garden full of flowers and butterflies. Conversely, an unhealthy garden with not much growth or butterflies indicated an unhealthy lifestyle.

Data collection and participants. Two evaluation methods were used in this study: an in the wild field study over 3 weeks with 12 participants and a survey with 75 respondents from 13 states across the USA that covered a range of attitudes and behaviors with mobile devices and physical activity. The goals of the in the wild study were to identify usability problems and to see how this technology fitted into the everyday lives of the six men and six women, aged 25–35, who volunteered to participate in the study. Eleven of these people were recruited by a market research firm and the twelfth was recruited by a member of the research team. All were regular cell phone users who wanted to increase their physical activity. None of the participants knew each other. They came from a wide range of occupations, including marketing specialist, receptionist, elementary school employee, musician, copywriter, and more. Eight were full-time employed, two were homemakers, one was employed part time, and one was self-employed. Six participants were classified as overweight, five as normal, and one as obese, based on body mass calculations.

The study lasted for 21 to 25 days, during which the participants were interviewed individually three times. The first interview session focused on their attitudes to physical activity and included setting their own activity goals. In the second interview sessions (day 7) participants were allowed to revise their weekly activity schedule. The last interview session took place on day 21. These interviews were recorded and transcribed. The participants were compensated for their participation.

Data analysis and presentation. Figure 14.9 shows the data that the evaluators collected for each participant for the various exercises. Some of the data was inferred by the system, some was manually written up in a journal, and some was a combination of the two. The way in which they were recorded over time and participant varied (the participants are represented by numbers in the vertical axis and the day of the study is represented by the horizontal axis). The reason for this is that sometimes the system inferred activities incorrectly which the participants then changed. An example was housework, which was inferred as bicycling. Manually written up activities (described as 'journaled' in the figure) included such things as swimming and weightlifting, which the system could not or was not trained to record.

From the interviews, the researchers learned about the users' reactions to the usability of UbiFit Garden, how they felt when it went wrong, and how they felt about it in general as

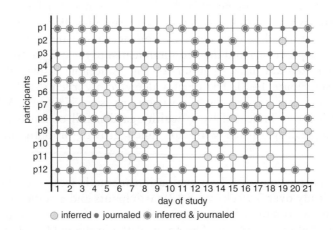

Figure 14.9 Frequency of performed activities and how they were recorded for each participant
Source: From Consolvo, S., McDonald, D.W., Toscos, T. *et al* (2008) "Activity sensing in the wild: a field trial of UbiFit garden". In: Proceedings of CHI 2008, ACM Press, New York, p. 1802.

a support for helping them to be fitter. Seven types of error with the system were reported. These included: making an error with the start time, making an error with the duration, confusing activities in various ways, failing to detect an activity, and detecting an activity when none occurred. These were coded into categories backed up by quotes taken from the participants' discussions during the focus groups. Two examples are:

> *What was really funny was, um, I did, I did some, um a bunch of housework one night. And boom, boom , boom, I'm getting all these little pink flowers. Like, ooh, that was very satisfying to get those.* (P9, Consolvo *et al*, 2008, p. 1803)

> *. . . it's not the end of the world, [but] it's a little disappointing when you do an activity and it* [the fitness device] *doesn't log it* [the activity] *. . . and then I think, 'am I doing something wrong?'* (P2, Consolvo *et al*, 2008, p. 1803)

An example of a general comment was:

> *The silly flowers work, you know? . . . It's right there on your wallpaper so every time you pick up your phone you are seeing it and you're like, 'Oh, look at this. I have all those flowers. I want more flowers.' It's remarkable, for me it was remarkably like, 'Oh well, if I walk there it's just 10 minutes. I might get another flower. So, sure, I'll just walk.'* (P5, Consolvo *et al*, 2008, p. 1804)

Overall the study showed that participants liked the system (i.e. the user experience). Some participants even commented about how the system motivated them to exercise. However, there were also technical and usability problems that needed to be improved, especially concerning the accuracy of activity recording.

ACTIVITY 14.3

1. Why was UbiFit Garden evaluated in the wild rather than in a controlled laboratory setting?
2. Two types of data are presented from the field study. What does each contribute to our understanding of the study?

Comment
1. The researchers wanted to find out how UbiFit Garden would be used in people's everyday lives, what they felt about it, and what problems they experienced over a long period of use. A controlled setting, even a living lab, would have imposed too many restrictions on the participants to achieve this.
2. Figure 14.9 provides a visualization of the activity data collected for each participant, showing how it was collected and recorded. The anecdotal quotes provide information about how the participants felt about their experiences. ∎

14.4.2   Other Perspectives

Field studies may be conducted where a behavior of interest to the researchers only reveals itself after a long time of using a tool. For example, the expected changes in user problem-solving strategies using a sophisticated visualization tool for knowledge discovery may only emerge after days or weeks of active use (Shneiderman and Plaisant, 2006). To evaluate the efficacy of such tools, users are best studied in realistic settings of their own workplaces, dealing with their own data, and setting their own agenda for extracting insights relevant to their professional goals. An initial interview conducted by the researchers is usually carried out to ensure the participant has a problem to work on, available data, and a schedule for completion. Then the participant will get an introductory training session, followed by 2–4 weeks of novice usage, followed by 2–4 weeks of mature usage, leading to a semi-structured exit interview. Additional assistance may be provided by the researcher as needed, thereby reducing the traditional separation between researcher and participant, but this close connection enables the researcher to develop a deeper understanding of the users' struggles and successes with the tools. More data such as daily diaries, automated logs of usage, structured questionnaires, and interviews can also be used to provide a multidimensional understanding of weaknesses and strengths of the tool.

Sometimes, a particular conceptual or theoretical framework is adopted to guide how the evaluation is performed or how the data collected from the evaluation is analyzed (see Chapter 8). This enables the data to be explained at a more general level in terms of specific cognitive processes, or social practices such as learning, or conversational or linguistic interactions. For example, Activity Theory was used as a framework to analyze how a family learned to use a new TV and video system in their own home (Petersen *et al*, 2002). Another example of theory use is semiotic engineering (de Souza, 2005), which is based on semiotic theory. In semiotic engineering, the study of signs aids designers in analyzing communication between designers and users.

> **Video** discussing the design of scalable games by Brazilian children, aided by their teachers, using concepts from semiotic engineering, at **http://youtu.be/CYTi0bXjzYU**

Typically, studies in the field, particularly those done in the wild, are useful when evaluators want to discover how new products and prototypes will be used within their intended social and physical context of use. Routines and other types of activities are analyzed as they unfold in their natural settings, describing and conceptualizing the ways artifacts are used and appropriated. Interventions by evaluators are limited, other than the placement of the prototype or product in the setting, and questions and/or probes to discover how the system is learned, used, and adopted. In contrast, evaluations in laboratories tend to focus on usability and how users perform on predefined tasks.

With the development of a wide variety of mobile, ambient, wearable, and other kinds of systems during the past few years, evaluators have to be creative in adapting the methods that they use to meet the challenges of participants on the move and in unusual environments.

DILEMMA

How many users should I include in my evaluation study?

A question students always ask is how many users do I need to include in my study? Deciding on how many to involve in a usability study is partly a logistical issue that depends on schedules, budgets, representative users, and the facilities available. Many professionals recommend that 5–12 testers is enough for many types of studies such as those conducted in controlled or partially controlled settings (Dumas and Redish, 1999), although a handful of users can provide useful feedback at early stages of a design. Others say that as soon as the same kinds of problems start being revealed and there is nothing new, it is time to stop. The more participants there are, the more representative the findings will be across the user population, but the study will also be more expensive and time-consuming, so there is a trade-off to be made.

For field studies the number of people being studied will vary, depending on what is of interest: it may be a family at home, a software team in an engineering firm, children in a playground. The problem with field studies is that they may not be representative of how other groups would act. However, the detailed findings gleaned from these studies about how participants learn to use a technology and appropriate it over time can be very revealing. ∎

Assignment

This assignment continues work on the online booking facility introduced at the end of Chapter 10 and continued in Chapter 11. Using any of the prototypes you have developed to represent the basic structure of your product, follow the instructions below to evaluate your prototype:

(a) Based on your knowledge of the requirements for this system, develop a standard task (e.g. booking two seats for a particular performance).

(b) Consider the relationship between yourself and your participants. Do you need to use an informed consent form? If so, prepare a suitable informed consent form. Justify your decision.

(c) Select three typical users, who can be friends or colleagues, and ask them to do the task using your prototype.

(d) Note the problems that each user encounters. If you can, time their performance. (If you happen to have a camera or a smartphone with a camera, you could film each participant.)

(e) Since the system is not actually implemented, you cannot study it in typical settings of use. However, imagine that you are planning a controlled usability study or a field study. How would you do it? What kinds of things would you need to take into account? What sort of data would you collect and how would you analyze it?

(f) What are the main benefits and problems with doing a controlled study versus studying the product in a natural setting?

Summary

This chapter described evaluation studies in different settings. It focused on controlled laboratory studies, experiments, and field studies in natural settings. A study of the iPad when it first came out was presented as an example of usability testing. This testing was done in an office environment; this was controlled to avoid outside influences affecting the testing. The participants were also asked to conduct predefined tasks that the evaluators were interested in investigating. Experimental design was then discussed that involves testing a hypothesis in a controlled research lab. The chapter ended with a discussion of field studies in which participants use new technologies in natural settings. The UbiFit Garden example involved evaluating how participants used a mobile fitness system designed to encourage people to do daily exercise. The goal of the evaluation was to examine how participants used the system in their daily lives, what kinds of problems they encountered, and whether they liked the system.

Key differences between usability testing, experiments, and field studies include the location of the study – usability or makeshift usability lab, research lab, or natural environment – and how much control is imposed. At one end of the spectrum is laboratory testing and at the other are in the wild studies. Most studies use a combination of different methods and evaluators often have to adapt their methods to cope with unusual new circumstances created by the new systems being developed.

Key points

- Usability testing takes place in usability labs or temporary makeshift labs. These labs enable evaluators to control the test setting.
- Usability testing focuses on performance measures such as how long and how many errors are made, when completing a set of predefined tasks. Indirect observation (video and keystroke logging) is conducted and supplemented by user satisfaction questionnaires and interviews.
- Remote testing systems have been developed that are more affordable than usability labs and also more portable. Many contain mobile eye-tracking and other devices.
- Experiments aim to test a hypothesis by manipulating certain variables while keeping others constant.
- The experimenter controls independent variable(s) in order to measure dependent variable(s).
- Field studies are evaluation studies that are carried out in natural settings; they aim to discover how people interact with technology in the real world.
- Field studies that involve the deployment of prototypes or technologies in natural settings may also be referred to as 'in the wild'.
- Sometimes the findings of a field study are unexpected, especially for in the wild studies in which the aim is usually to explore how novel technologies are used by participants in their own homes, places of work, or outside.

Further Reading

BUDIU, R. and NIELSEN, J. (2012) *Mobile Usability.* New Riders Press. This book asks and attempts to answer the question of how we create usability and a satisfying user experience on smartphones, tablets, and other mobile devices.

CRABTREE, A., CHAMBERLAIN, A., GRINTER, R.E., JONES, M., RODDEN, T. and ROGERS, Y. (2013) Introduction to the special issue of "The Turn to The Wild" *ACM Transactions on Computer-Human Interaction (TOCHI)*, 20 (3). This collection of articles provides in-depth case studies of projects that were conducted in the wild over many years, from the widespread uptake of children's story-telling mobile apps to the adoption of online community technologies.

DUMAS, J. S. and REDISH, J. C. (1999) *A Practical Guide to Usability Testing.* Intellect. Many books have been written about usability testing, but though now old, this one is useful because it describes the process in detail and provides many examples.

KRUG, S. (2014) *Don't Make Me Think, Revisited: A Common Sense Approach to Web Usability (3rd edn).* Morgan Kaufmann. This revised book provides many common-sense suggestions for doing usability testing.

LAZAR, J., FENG, J. and HOCHHEISER, H. (2010) *Research Methods in Human–Computer Interaction.* John Wiley & Sons Ltd. This book discusses experimental design in detail as well as other research methods such as surveys.

ROBSON, C. (1994, 2011) *Experimental Design and Statistics in Psychology.* Penguin Psychology. Though now old, this book provides a useful introduction to experimental design and basic statistics. Another useful book by the same author is *Real World Research* (3rd edn), published in 2011 by Blackwell Publishing.

SHNEIDERMAN, B. and PLAISANT. C. (2010) *Designing the User Interface: Strategies for effective human–computer interaction* (5th edn). Addison-Wesley. Chapter 4 provides a good overview of all the main evaluation techniques used in HCI.

INTERVIEW
with danah boyd

danah boyd is a principal researcher at Microsoft Research, a research assistant professor at New York University, and the founder and president of the Data & Society Research Institute. In her research, danah examines the intersection of technology and society. Lately, she has been focused on issues related to privacy, publicity, visibility, and the 'big data' phenomenon. In 2014, she published *It's Complicated: The Social Lives of Networked Teens,* which examines teens' engagement with social media. She blogs at http://www.zephoria.org/thoughts/ and tweets at @zephoria.

danah, can you tell us a bit about your research and what motivates you?
I am an ethnographer who examines the interplay between technology and society. For almost a decade, I researched different aspects of social media, most notably how American teens integrate social media into their daily practices. Because of this, I've followed the rise of many popular social media services – MySpace, Facebook, YouTube, Twitter, Instagram, Snapchat, etc. I examined what teens do on these services, but I also consider how these technologies fit into teens' lives more generally. Thus, I spent a lot of time driving around the United States talking to teens and their parents, educators and youth ministers,

law enforcement, and social workers, trying to get a sense of what teens' lives look like and where technology fits in.

More recently, I've been concerned with understanding the 'big data' phenomenon, focusing specifically on the different ways in which data are used to reinforce structural divisions that have long existed. I'm particularly interested in how we construct our understanding of fairness when deploying algorithms that can be fundamentally discriminatory. As Melvin Kranzberg once said, "technology is neither good nor bad; nor is it neutral." I'm trying to figure out how technological decisions intersect with cultural practices, who is affected and in what ways, and what the right points of intervention are to help construct a society that we want to live in. To do this requires moving between disciplines, sectors, and frames to get at the complexity that we've created.

Fundamentally, I'm a social scientist invested in understanding the social world. Technology inflects social dynamics, providing a fascinating vantage point for understanding cultural practices.

How would you characterize good ethnography? (Please include example(s) from your own work.)
Ethnography is about mapping culture. To do this successfully, it's important to dive

deep into the cultural practices of a particular population or community and try to understand them on their own terms. The next stage is to try to ground what one observes in a broader discourse of theory and ideas, in order to provide a framework for understanding cultural dynamics.

Many people ask me why I bother driving around the United States talking to teens when I can see everything that they do online. Unfortunately, what's visible online is only a small fraction of what they do and it's easy to misinterpret why teens do something simply by looking at the traces of their actions. Getting into their lives, understanding their logic, and seeing how technology connects with daily practice is critically important, especially because teens don't have distinct 'online' vs. 'offline' lives. It's all intertwined so it's necessary to see what's going on from different angles. Of course, this is just the data collection process. I tend to also confuse people because I document a lot of my thinking and findings as I go, highlighting what I learned publicly for anyone to disagree with me. I find that my blog provides a valuable feedback loop and I'm especially fond of the teen commenters who challenge me on things. I've hired many of them.

I know you have encountered some surprises – or maybe even a revelation – in your work on Facebook and MySpace. Would you tell us about it please?
From 2006–2007, I was talking with teens in different parts of the country and I started noticing that some teens were talking about MySpace and some teens were talking about Facebook. In Massachusetts, I met a young woman who uncomfortably told me that the black kids in her school were on MySpace while the white kids were on Facebook. She described MySpace as "like ghetto." I didn't enter into this project expecting to analyze race and class dynamics in the United States but, after her comments, I couldn't avoid them. I started diving into my data, realizing that race and class could explain the difference between which teens preferred which sites. Uncomfortable with this and totally afar from my intellectual strengths, I wrote a really awkward blog post about what I was observing. For better or worse, the BBC picked this up as a "formal report from UC Berkeley" and I received over 10,000 messages over the next week. Some were hugely critical, with some making assumptions about me and my intentions. But the teens who wrote consistently agreed. And then two teens starting pointing out to me that it wasn't just an issue of choice, but an issue of movement, with some teens moving from MySpace to Facebook because MySpace was less desirable and Facebook was 'safe.' Anyhow, recognizing the racist and classist roots of this, I spent a lot of time trying to unpack the different language that teens used when talking about these sites in a paper called "White Flight in Networked Publics? How Race and Class Shaped American Teen Engagement with MySpace and Facebook." ∎

Chapter 15

EVALUATION: INSPECTIONS, ANALYTICS, AND MODELS

15.1 Introduction

15.2 Inspections: Heuristic Evaluation and Walkthroughs

15.3 Analytics

15.4 Predictive Models

Objectives

The main aims of this chapter are to:

- Describe the key concepts associated with inspection methods.
- Explain how to do heuristic evaluation and walkthroughs.
- Explain the role of analytics in evaluation.
- Describe how to use Fitts' Law – a predictive model.

15.1 Introduction

The evaluation methods described so far in this book have involved interaction with, or direct observation of, users. In this chapter we introduce methods that are based on understanding users through knowledge codified in heuristics, or data collected remotely, or models that predict users' performance. None of these methods requires users to be present during the evaluation. Inspection methods typically involve an expert role-playing the users for whom the product is designed, analyzing aspects of an interface, and identifying any potential usability problems by using a set of guidelines. The most well known are heuristic evaluation and walkthroughs. Analytics involves user interaction logging, which is usually done remotely. Predictive models involve analyzing the various physical and mental operations that are needed to perform particular tasks at the interface and operationalizing them as quantitative measures. One of the most commonly used predictive models is Fitts' Law.

15.2 Inspections: Heuristic Evaluation and Walkthroughs

Sometimes users are not easily accessible, or involving them is too expensive or it takes too long. In such circumstances other people, usually referred to as experts, can provide feedback.

These are people who are knowledgeable about both interaction design and the needs and typical behavior of users. Various inspection methods were developed as alternatives to usability testing in the early 1990s, drawing on software engineering practice where code and other types of inspections are commonly used. Inspection methods for interaction design include heuristic evaluations, and walkthroughs, in which experts examine the interface of an interactive product, often role-playing typical users, and suggest problems users would likely have when interacting with it. One of the attractions of these methods is that they can be used at any stage of a design project. They can also be used to complement user testing.

15.2.1 Heuristic Evaluation

Heuristic evaluation is a usability inspection method that was developed by Nielsen and his colleagues (Nielsen and Mohlich, 1990; Nielsen, 1994a) and others (Hollingshead and Novick, 2007), and later modified by other researchers for evaluating specific types of systems (e.g. Mankoff *et al*, 2003; Pinelle *et al*, 2009). In heuristic evaluation, experts, guided by a set of usability principles known as heuristics, evaluate whether user-interface elements, such as dialog boxes, menus, navigation structure, online help, and so on, conform to tried and tested principles. These heuristics closely resemble high-level design principles (e.g. making designs consistent, reducing memory load, and using terms that users understand). The original set of heuristics for HCI evaluation was developed by Jakob Nielsen and his colleagues who derived them empirically from an analysis of 249 usability problems (Nielsen, 1994b); a revised version of these heuristics is listed below (Nielsen, 2014: useit.com):

- **Visibility of system status**
  The system should always keep users informed about what is going on, through appropriate feedback within reasonable time.
- **Match between system and the real world**
  The system should speak the users' language, with words, phrases, and concepts familiar to the user, rather than system-oriented terms. Follow real-world conventions, making information appear in a natural and logical order.
- **User control and freedom**
  Users often choose system functions by mistake and will need a clearly marked emergency exit to leave the unwanted state without having to go through an extended dialog. Support undo and redo.
- **Consistency and standards**
  Users should not have to wonder whether different words, situations, or actions mean the same thing. Follow platform conventions.
- **Error prevention**
  Even better than good error messages is a careful design that prevents a problem from occurring in the first place. Either eliminate error-prone conditions or check for them and present users with a confirmation option before they commit to the action.
- **Recognition rather than recall**
  Minimize the user's memory load by making objects, actions, and options visible. The user should not have to remember information from one part of the dialog to another. Instructions for use of the system should be visible or easily retrievable whenever appropriate.

- **Flexibility and efficiency of use**
  Accelerators – unseen by the novice user – may often speed up the interaction for the expert user such that the system can cater to both inexperienced and experienced users. Allow users to tailor frequent actions.
- **Aesthetic and minimalist design**
  Dialogs should not contain information that is irrelevant or rarely needed. Every extra unit of information in a dialog competes with the relevant units of information and diminishes their relative visibility.
- **Help users recognize, diagnose, and recover from errors**
  Error messages should be expressed in plain language (no codes), precisely indicate the problem, and constructively suggest a solution.
- **Help and documentation**
  Even though it is better if the system can be used without documentation, it may be necessary to provide help and documentation. Any such information should be easy to search, focused on the user's task, list concrete steps to be carried out, and not be too large. Before reading on, watch the YouTube video developed by David Lazarus.

Video developed by David Lazarus, which aims to provide insight into Jakob Nielsen's 10 Usability Heuristics for Interface Design, is available at **http://youtu.be/hWc0Fd2AS3s**

These heuristics are intended to be used by judging aspects of the interface against them. For example, if a new social networking system is being evaluated, the evaluator might consider how a user would find out how to add friends to her network. The evaluator is meant to go through the interface several times, inspecting the various interaction elements and comparing them with the list of usability principles, i.e. the heuristics. At each iteration, usability problems will be identified or their diagnosis will be refined, until she is satisfied that the majority of them are clear.

Although many heuristics apply to most products (e.g. be consistent and provide meaningful feedback), some of the core heuristics are too general for evaluating products that have come onto the market since Nielsen and Mohlich first developed the method, such as smartphones and other mobile devices, digital toys, online communities, ambient devices, and new web services. Nielsen suggests developing category-specific heuristics that apply to a specific class of product as a supplement to the general heuristics. Evaluators and researchers have therefore typically developed their own heuristics by tailoring Nielsen's heuristics with other design guidelines, market research, and requirements documents. Exactly which heuristics are appropriate and how many are needed for different products is debatable and depends on the goals of the evaluation, but most sets of heuristics have between five and ten items. This number provides a good range of usability criteria by which to judge the various aspects of an interface. More than ten becomes difficult for evaluators to remember; fewer than five tends not to be sufficiently discriminating.

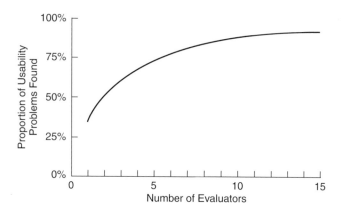

Figure 15.1 Curve showing the proportion of usability problems in an interface found by heuristic evaluation using various numbers of evaluators. The curve represents the average of six case studies of heuristic evaluation

Source: Usability Inspection Methods, J. Nielson & R.L. Mack ©1994. Reproduced with permission of John Wiley & Sons Inc.

A key question that is frequently asked is how many evaluators are needed to carry out a thorough heuristic evaluation. While one evaluator can identify a large number of problems, she may not catch all of them. She may also have a tendency to concentrate more on one aspect at the expense of missing others. For example, in a study of heuristic evaluation where 19 evaluators were asked to find 16 usability problems in a voice response system allowing customers access to their bank accounts, Nielsen (1992) found a substantial difference between the number and type of usability problems found by the different evaluators. He also notes that while some usability problems are very easy to find by all evaluators, there are some problems that are found by very few experts. Therefore, he argues that it is important to involve multiple evaluators in any heuristic evaluation and recommends between three and five evaluators. His findings suggest that they can typically identify around 75% of the total usability problems, as shown in Figure 15.1 (Nielsen, 1994a).

However, employing multiple experts can be costly. Skillful experts can capture many of the usability problems by themselves and some consultancies now use this technique as the basis for critiquing interactive products – a process that has become known as an expert critique or expert crit in some countries. But using only one or two experts to conduct a heuristic evaluation can be problematic since research has challenged Nielsen's findings and questioned whether even three to five evaluators is adequate. For example, Cockton and Woolrych (2001) and Woolrych and Cockton (2001) point out that the number of experts needed to find 75% of problems depends on the nature of the problems. Their analysis of problem frequency and severity suggests that highly misleading findings can result.

The conclusion from this is that more is better, but more is also more expensive. However, because users and special facilities are not needed for heuristic evaluation and it is comparatively inexpensive and quick, it is popular with developers and is often known as discount evaluation. For a quick evaluation of an early design, one or two experts can probably identify most potential usability problems, but if a thorough evaluation of a fully working prototype is needed then having a team of experts conducting the evaluation and comparing their findings would be advisable.

Heuristic Evaluation for Websites

In recent years, considerable attention has been focused on the web, mobile apps, and other digital technologies. Heuristics for evaluating websites have become increasingly important and several slightly different sets of heuristics have been developed. Box 15.1 contains an extract from a version compiled by web developer Andy Budd that places a stronger emphasis on information content than Nielsen's original heuristics.

BOX 15.1

Extract from the heuristics developed by Budd (2007) that emphasize web design issues

Clarity

Make the system as clear, concise, and meaningful as possible for the intended audience.

- Write clear, concise copy
- Only use technical language for a technical audience
- Write clear and meaningful labels
- Use meaningful icons.

Minimize unnecessary complexity and cognitive load

Make the system as simple as possible for users to accomplish their tasks.

- Remove unnecessary functionality, process steps, and visual clutter
- Use progressive disclosure to hide advanced features
- Break down complicated processes into multiple steps
- Prioritize using size, shape, color, alignment, and proximity.

Provide users with context

Interfaces should provide users with a sense of context in time and space.

- Provide a clear site name and purpose
- Highlight the current section in the navigation
- Provide a breadcrumb trail
- Use appropriate feedback messages
- Show number of steps in a process
- Reduce perception of latency by providing visual cues (e.g. progress indicator) or by allowing users to complete other tasks while waiting.

Promote a pleasurable and positive user experience

The user should be treated with respect and the design should be aesthetically pleasing and promote a pleasurable and rewarding experience.

- Create a pleasurable and attractive design
- Provide easily attainable goals
- Provide rewards for usage and progression. ■

ACTIVITY 15.1

1. Select a website that you regularly visit and evaluate it using the heuristics in Box 15.1. Do these heuristics help you to identify important usability and user experience issues?
2. Does being aware of the heuristics influence how you interact with the website in any way?

Comment

1. The heuristics focus on key usability criteria such as whether the interface seemed unnecessarily complex and how color was used. Budd's heuristics also encourage consideration of how the user feels about the experience of interacting with the website.
2. Being aware of the heuristics leads to a stronger focus on the design and the interaction, and raises awareness of what the user is trying to do and how the website is responding. ■

A similar approach to Budd's is also taken by Leigh Howells in her web article entitled "A guide to heuristic website reviews" (Howells, 2011). Howells' approach goes one step further and suggests a way of quantifying the heuristics and consequently also the heuristic evaluation, which can then be presented using various types of visual diagrams.

Turning Design Guidelines into Heuristics

There is a strong relationship between design guidelines and the heuristics used in heuristic evaluation. So another approach to developing heuristics for evaluating the many different types of systems now available – mobile, tabletop, online communities, ambient, etc. – is to convert design guidelines into heuristics for evaluation. As a first step, evaluators sometimes translate design guidelines into questions for use in heuristic evaluation. This practice has become quite widespread for addressing usability and user experience concerns for specific types of interactive product. For example Väänänen-Vainio-Mattila and Waljas (2009) from the University of Tempere in Finland took this approach when developing heuristics for a web service user experience. They tried to identify what they called 'hedonic heuristics,' which was a new kind of heuristic that directly addressed how users feel about their interactions. These were based on design guidelines concerning whether the user feels that the web service provides a lively place where it is enjoyable to spend time, and whether it satisfies the user's curiosity by frequently offering interesting content. When stated as questions these become: Is the service a lively place where it is enjoyable to spend time? Does the service satisfy users' curiosity by frequently offering interesting content?

ACTIVITY 15.2

Consider the following design guidelines for information design and for each one suggest a question that could be used in heuristic evaluation:

1. Good graphical design is important. Reading long sentences, paragraphs, and documents is difficult on screen, so break material into discrete, meaningful chunks to give the website structure (Horton, 2005).

(Continued)

2. Avoid excessive use of color. Color is useful for indicating different kinds of information, i.e. cueing (Koyani *et al*, 2004).
3. Avoid gratuitous use of graphics and animation. In addition to increasing download time, graphics and animation soon become boring and annoying.
4. Download time for smartphone apps must be short.

Comment

We suggest the following questions; you may have identified others:

1. Good graphical design is important. Is the page layout structured meaningfully? Is there too much text on each page?
2. Avoid excessive use of color. How is color used? Is it used as a form of coding? Is it used to make the site bright and cheerful? Is it excessive and garish? Does it have an impact on the user's enjoyment (i.e. user's experience)?
3. Avoid gratuitous use of graphics and animation. Are there any flashing banners? Are there complex introduction sequences? Can they be short-circuited? Do the graphics add to the site and improve the user's experience?
4. Avoid multiple server calls when downloading content to smartphone apps. Is all the content really needed? Can versions be provided that are quick to download? Increasingly, users expect fast delivery of content and responses from mobile devices. ■

Another important issue when designing and evaluating web pages and other types of system is their accessibility to a broad range of users. In the USA, a requirement known as Section 508 of the Rehabilitation Act came into effect in 2001. The act requires that all federally funded IT systems be accessible for people with disabilities. The guidelines provided by this Act can be used as heuristics to check that systems comply with it (see Case Study 14.1). Mankoff *et al* (2005) also used guidelines as heuristics to evaluate specific kinds of usability. They discovered that developers doing a heuristic evaluation using a screen reader found 50% of known usability problems – which was more successful than user testing directly with blind users.

Heuristic evaluation has also been used to evaluate abstract aesthetic peripheral displays that portray non-critical information at the periphery of the user's attention (Mankoff *et al*, 2003). Since these devices are not designed for task performance, the researchers had to develop a set of heuristics that took this into account. They did this by developing two ambient displays: one indicated how close a bus is to the bus-stop by showing its number move upwards on a screen; the other indicated how light or dark it was outside by lightening or darkening a light display (see Figure 15.2). Then they modified Nielsen's heuristics to address the characteristics of ambient displays and asked groups of experts to evaluate the displays using them.

The heuristics that they developed included some that were specifically geared towards ambient systems such as:

• Visibility of state: The state of the display should be clear when it is placed in the intended setting.
• Peripherality of display: The display should be unobtrusive and remain so unless it requires the user's attention. Users should be able to easily monitor the display.

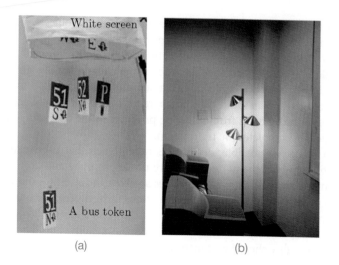

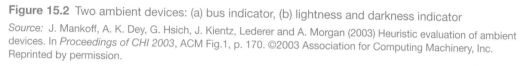

(a)   (b)

Figure 15.2 Two ambient devices: (a) bus indicator, (b) lightness and darkness indicator
Source: J. Mankoff, A. K. Dey, G. Hsieh, J. Kientz, Lederer and A. Morgan (2003) Heuristic evaluation of ambient devices. In *Proceedings of CHI 2003*, ACM Fig.1, p. 170. ©2003 Association for Computing Machinery, Inc. Reprinted by permission.

In this study the researchers found that three to five evaluators were able to identify 40–60% of known usability issues. In a follow-up study, different researchers used the same heuristics with different ambient applications (Consolvo and Towle, 2005). They found 75% of known usability problems with eight evaluators and 35–55% were found with three to five evaluators, suggesting that the more evaluators you have, the more accurate the results will be – as other researchers have also reported.

Heuristics for other products, adapted from Nielsen's original heuristics, have continued to be developed and include heuristics for evaluating shared groupware (Baker *et al*, 2002), video games (Pinelle *et al*, 2008), multi-player games (Pinelle *et al*, 2009), online communities (Preece and Shneiderman, 2009), and information visualization (Forsell and Johansson, 2010). Shneiderman's eight golden rules, a set of guidelines first developed in the mid-1980s, are also frequently adapted for use with different types of systems and environments and used as heuristics for identifying usability problems (Shneiderman and Plaisant, 2010; http://www.cs.umd.edu/~ben/goldenrules.html):

1. *Strive for consistency.* Consistent sequences of actions should be required in similar situations: identical terminology should be used in prompts, menus, and help screens; and consistent color, layout, capitalization, fonts, and so on should be employed throughout. Exceptions, such as required confirmation of the delete command or no echoing of passwords, should be comprehensible and limited in number.

2. *Cater to universal usability.* Recognize the needs of diverse users and design for plasticity, facilitating transformation of content. Novice to expert differences, age ranges, disabilities, and technological diversity each enrich the spectrum of requirements that guides design. Adding features for novices, such as explanations, and features for experts, such as shortcuts and faster pacing, can enrich the interface design and improve perceived system quality.

3. *Offer informative feedback.* For every user action, there should be system feedback. For frequent and minor actions, the response can be modest, whereas for infrequent and major actions, the

response should be more substantial. Visual presentation of the objects of interest provides a convenient environment for showing changes explicitly.

4. *Design dialogs to yield closure.* Sequences of actions should be organized into groups with a beginning, middle, and end. Informative feedback at the completion of a group of actions gives operators the satisfaction of accomplishment, a sense of relief, a signal to drop contingency plans from their minds, and an indicator to prepare for the next group of actions. For example, e-commerce websites move users from selecting products to the checkout, ending with a clear confirmation page that completes the transaction.

5. *Prevent errors.* As much as possible, design the system such that users cannot make serious errors; for example, gray out menu items that are not appropriate and do not allow alphabetic characters in numeric entry fields. If a user makes an error, the interface should detect the error and offer simple, constructive, and specific instructions for recovery. For example, users should not have to retype an entire name-address form if they enter an invalid zip code, but rather should be guided to repair only the faulty part. Erroneous actions should leave the system state unchanged, or the interface should give instructions about restoring the state.

6. *Permit easy reversal of actions.* As much as possible, actions should be reversible. This feature relieves anxiety, since the user knows that errors can be undone, and encourages exploration of unfamiliar options. The units of reversibility may be a single action, a data-entry task, or a complete group of actions, such as entry of a name-address block.

7. *Support internal locus of control.* Experienced users strongly desire the sense that they are in charge of the interface and that the interface responds to their actions. They don't want surprises or changes in familiar behavior, and they are annoyed by tedious data-entry sequences, difficulty in obtaining necessary information, and inability to produce their desired result.

8. *Reduce short-term memory load.* Humans' limited capacity for information processing in short-term memory (the rule of thumb is that we can remember 'seven plus or minus two chunks' of information) requires that designers avoid interfaces in which users must remember information from one screen and then use that information on another screen. It means that smartphones should not require re-entry of phone numbers, website locations should remain visible, multiple-page displays should be consolidated, and sufficient training time should be allotted for complex sequences of actions.

Doing Heuristic Evaluation

Heuristic evaluation has three stages:

1. The briefing session, in which the experts are told what to do. A prepared script is useful as a guide and to ensure each person receives the same briefing.

2. The evaluation period, in which each expert typically spends 1–2 hours independently inspecting the product, using the heuristics for guidance. The experts need to take at least two passes through the interface. The first pass gives a feel for the flow of the interaction and the product's scope. The second pass allows the evaluator to focus on specific interface elements in the context of the whole product, and to identify potential usability problems.

   If the evaluation is for a functioning product, the evaluators need to have some specific user tasks in mind so that exploration is focused. Suggesting tasks may be helpful but many experts suggest their own tasks. However, this approach is less easy if the evaluation is done early in design when there are only screen mockups or a specification; the approach needs to be adapted to the evaluation circumstances. While working through the interface, specification, or mockups, a second person may record the problems identified, or the

evaluator may think aloud. Alternatively, she may take notes herself. Evaluators should be encouraged to be as specific as possible and to record each problem clearly.
3. The debriefing session, in which the evaluators come together to discuss their findings and to prioritize the problems they found and suggest solutions.

The heuristics focus the evaluators' attention on particular issues, so selecting appropriate heuristics is critically important. Even so, there is sometimes less agreement among evaluators than is desirable, as discussed in the next Dilemma.

There are fewer practical and ethical issues in heuristic evaluation than for other methods because users are not involved. A week is often cited as the time needed to train evaluators (Nielsen and Mack, 1994), but this depends on the person's initial expertise. Typical users can be taught to do heuristic evaluation, although there have been claims that this approach is not very successful (Nielsen, 1994a). A variation of this method is to take a team approach that may also involve users.

ACTIVITY 15.3

Look at the Nielsen (2014) heuristics and consider how you would use them to evaluate a website for purchasing clothes (e.g. www.rei.com, which has a homepage similar to that in Figure 15.3).
1. Do the heuristics help you focus on the website more intently than if you were not using them?
2. Might fewer heuristics be better? Which might be combined and what are the trade-offs?
3. If you did this activity using a smartphone, were all the heuristics relevant and useful?

Figure 15.3 Part of the homepage of rei.com
Source: www.rei.com.

(*Continued*)

Comment

1. Most people find that using the heuristics encourages them to focus on the design more than when they are not using them.
2. Some heuristics can be combined and given a more general description. For example, 'the system should speak the users' language' and 'always keep users informed' could be replaced with 'help users to develop a good mental model,' but this is a more abstract statement and some evaluators might not know what is packed into it. An argument for keeping the detail is that it reminds evaluators of the issues to consider.
3. REI has developed a home page for the small screens of smartphones such as my iPhone. This works well and as a casual user I was able to quickly review a variety of camping and other equipment that REI assumed would be of particular interest to casual users during the summer. However, it was more difficult to explore the clothes I might need or want and took much longer than I expected. Therefore, for me, the design did not support 'flexibility and efficiency of use' as well as I had hoped.

DILEMMA

Classic problems or false alarms?

You might have the impression that heuristic evaluation is a panacea for designers, and that it can reveal all that is wrong with a design. However, it has problems. Shortly after heuristic evaluation was developed, several independent studies compared heuristic evaluation with other methods, particularly user testing. They found that the different approaches often identify different problems and that sometimes heuristic evaluation misses severe problems (Karat, 1994). This argues for using complementary methods. Furthermore, heuristic evaluation should not be thought of as a replacement for user testing.

Another problem concerns experts reporting problems that don't exist. In other words, some of the experts' predictions are wrong (Bailey, 2001). Bailey cites analyses from three published sources showing that only around 33% of the problems reported were real usability problems, some of which were serious, others trivial. However, the heuristic evaluators missed about 21% of users' problems. Furthermore, about 43% of the problems identified by the experts were not problems at all; they were false alarms! Bailey points out that this means only about half the problems identified are true problems: "More specifically, for every true usability problem identified, there will be a little over one false alarm (1.2) and about one half of one missed problem (0.6). If this analysis is true, heuristic evaluators tend to identify more false alarms and miss more problems than they have true hits."

How can the number of false alarms or missed serious problems be reduced? Checking that experts really have the expertise that they claim would help, but how can this be done? One way to overcome these problems is to have several evaluators. This helps to reduce the impact of one person's experience or poor performance. Using heuristic evaluation along with user testing and other methods is also a good idea. ■

While heuristic evaluation has proven to be very useful and used by many usability experts over the years, the guidelines were designed to be applied to PC-based applications that were being developed in the 1980s. Given the range of current technologies (e.g. smartphones and various other mobile devices, tablets, tabletops, and ambient systems) that have been developed since Nielsen devised his original set of heuristics – it raises the question of whether they can continue to be of use to test the usability and user experience of new products. For example, how useful will they be for evaluating wearable technologies, such as smartwatches and augmented glasses? What other heuristics might be needed? There is also overlap between how evaluation heuristics and other kinds of design guidelines are used. Design guidelines are often converted into heuristics so it is possible to use these instead or in combination with heuristic evaluation.

15.2.2 Walkthroughs

Walkthroughs have been used by system developers for many years for inspecting code and the concept offers an alternative approach to heuristic evaluation for predicting users' problems without doing user testing. As the name suggests, walkthroughs involve walking through a task with the product and noting problematic usability features. Most walkthrough methods do not involve users. Others, such as pluralistic walkthroughs, involve a team that may include users, as well as developers, and usability specialists.

In this section we consider cognitive and pluralistic walkthroughs. Both were originally developed for desktop systems but, as with heuristic evaluation, they can be adapted to web-based systems, smartphones and mobile devices, tabletops, and products such as DVD players.

Cognitive Walkthroughs

"Cognitive walkthroughs involve simulating a user's problem-solving process at each step in the human–computer dialog, checking to see if the user's goals and memory for actions can be assumed to lead to the next correct action" (Nielsen and Mack, 1994, p. 6). The defining feature is that they focus on evaluating designs for ease of learning – a focus that is motivated by observations that users learn by exploration (Wharton *et al*, 1994). The steps involved in cognitive walkthroughs are:

1. The characteristics of typical users are identified and documented and sample tasks are developed that focus on the aspects of the design to be evaluated. A description, mockup, or prototype of the interface to be developed is also produced, along with a clear sequence of the actions needed for the users to complete the task.
2. A designer and one or more expert evaluators come together to do the analysis.
3. The evaluators walk through the action sequences for each task, placing it within the context of a typical scenario, and as they do this they try to answer the following questions:
   - Will the correct action be sufficiently evident to the user? (Will the user know what to do to achieve the task?)
   - Will the user notice that the correct action is available? (Can users see the button or menu item that they should use for the next action? Is it apparent when it is needed?)
   - Will the user associate and interpret the response from the action correctly? (Will users know from the feedback that they have made a correct or incorrect choice of action?)
     In other words: will users know what to do, see how to do it, and understand from feedback whether the action was correct or not?

4. As the walkthrough is being done, a record of critical information is compiled in which:
   - The assumptions about what would cause problems and why are identified.
   - Notes about side issues and design changes are made.
   - A summary of the results is compiled.
5. The design is then revised to fix the problems presented.

   As with heuristic and other evaluation methods, developers and researchers can modify the method to meet their own needs more closely, or adapt the process so that it applies to particular features of mobile or other new technologies.

When doing a cognitive walkthrough it is important to document the process, keeping account of what works and what doesn't. A standardized feedback form can be used in which answers are recorded to each question. Any negative answers are carefully documented on a separate form, along with details of the system, its version number, the date of the evaluation, and the evaluators' names. It is also useful to document the severity of the problems: for example, how likely a problem is to occur and how serious it will be for users. The form can also record the process details outlined in points 1 to 4 as well as the date of the evaluation.

Compared with heuristic evaluation, this technique focuses more closely on identifying specific user problems at a high level of detail. Hence, it has a narrow focus that is useful for focusing on certain types of system rather than for evaluating whole systems. In particular, it can be useful for applications involving complex cognitive operations. However, it is very time-consuming and laborious to do and evaluators need a good understanding of the cognitive processes involved.

ACTIVITY 15.4

Conduct a cognitive walkthrough to find a copy of this book to buy as an ebook at www.amazon.com or www.wiley.com.

Comment

   Task: to buy an ebook version of this book from www.amazon.com or www.wiley.com
   Typical users: students who use the web regularly

(Note that the interface for www.amazon.com or www.wiley.com may have changed since we did our evaluation.)
Selecting the search box on the home page and typing in the title or author/s of the book.

Q: Will users know what to do?
Answer: Yes, they know that they must find books and the search box is a good place to start.

Q: Will users see how to do it?
Answer: Yes, they have seen one before and will know to type in the appropriate term and to click on the 'go' or the search icon.

Q: Will users understand from the feedback whether the action was correct or not?
Answer: Yes, their action should take them to a page that shows them the cover of the book. They need to click on this or an icon 'buy' next to the cover of the book.

Q: Will users understand from the feedback whether the action was correct or not?
Answer: Yes they have probably done this before and will be able to continue to purchase the book.

ACTIVITY 15.5

Activity 15.3 asked you to do a heuristic evaluation of www.rei.com or a similar online retail site. Now go back to that site and do a cognitive walkthrough to buy some clothing. When you have completed the evaluation, compare your findings from the cognitive walkthrough with those from heuristic evaluation.

Comment
The cognitive walkthrough probably took longer than the heuristic evaluation for evaluating the same part of the site because it examines each step of a task. Consequently, you probably did not see as much of the website. It is also likely that the cognitive walkthrough resulted in more detailed findings. Cognitive walkthrough is a useful method for examining a small part of a system in detail, whereas heuristic evaluation is useful for examining a whole system or large parts of systems. As the name indicates, the cognitive walkthrough focuses on the cognitive aspects of interacting with the system. It was developed before there was much emphasis on aesthetic design and other user experience goals. ∎

Another variation of cognitive walkthrough was developed by Rick Spencer of Microsoft, to overcome some problems that he encountered when using the original form of cognitive walkthrough (Spencer, 2000). The first problem was that answering the three questions in step 3 and discussing the answers took too long. Second, designers tended to be defensive, often invoking long explanations of cognitive theory to justify their designs. This second problem was particularly difficult because it undermined the efficacy of the method and the social relationships of team members. In order to cope with these problems, Rick Spencer adapted the method by reducing the number of questions and curtailing discussion. This meant that the analysis was more coarse-grained but could be completed in about 2.5 hours. He also identified a leader, the usability specialist, and set strong ground rules for the session, including a ban on defending a design, debating cognitive theory, or doing designs on the fly.

These adaptations made the method more usable, despite losing some of the detail from the analysis. Perhaps most important of all, Spencer directed the social interactions of the design team so that they achieved their goals.

> **Link** to an up-to-date discussion on the value of the cognitive walkthrough method for evaluating various devices, at
> **http://www.userfocus.co.uk/articles/cogwalk.html**

Pluralistic Walkthroughs

"Pluralistic walkthroughs are another type of walkthrough in which users, developers and usability experts work together to step through a [task] scenario, discussing usability issues associated with dialog elements involved in the scenario steps" (Nielsen and Mack, 1994, p. 5). In a pluralistic walkthrough, each of the evaluators is asked to assume the role of a typical user. Scenarios of use, consisting of a few prototype screens, are given to each evaluator who writes down the sequence of actions they would take to move from one screen to another, without conferring with fellow panelists. Then the panelists discuss the actions they each suggested before moving on to the next round of screens. This process continues until all the scenarios have been evaluated (Bias, 1994).

The benefits of pluralistic walkthroughs include a strong focus on users' tasks at a detailed level, i.e. looking at the steps taken. This level of analysis can be invaluable for certain kinds of systems, such as safety-critical ones, where a usability problem identified for a single step could be critical to its safety or efficiency. The approach lends itself well to participatory design practices by involving a multidisciplinary team in which users play a key role. Furthermore, the group brings a variety of expertise and opinions for interpreting each stage of an interaction. Limitations include having to get all the experts together at once and then proceed at the rate of the slowest. Furthermore, only a limited number of scenarios, and hence paths through the interface, can usually be explored because of time constraints.

15.3   Analytics

Analytics is a method for evaluating user traffic through a system (discussed in Chapters 7, 8, and 13) – mostly such systems involve selling a product or service so knowing what customers do and want is important for improving the product or service, but analytics are also being used for evaluating non-transactional systems (e.g. Sleeper *et al*, 2014). When used to examine traffic on a website or part of a website as mentioned in Chapter 7, the analytics are known as web analytics. Web analytics can be collected locally or remotely across the Internet by logging user activity, counting and analyzing the data in order to understand what parts of the website are being used and when. Although analytics are a form of evaluation that is particularly useful for evaluating the usability of a website, they are also valuable for business planning including the business of online education. Recently, analytics have been applied to understand how learners in massive open online courses (MOOCs) and other web-based education courses interact with these systems (e.g. Oviatt *et al*, 2013).

For example, the developers of these systems are interested in such questions as: Why do learners enroll in these systems and at what point do learners tend to drop out and why? What are the characteristics of learners who complete the course compared with those who do not complete it?

Video of Simon Buckingham Shum's 2014 keynote presentation at the EdMedia 2014 Conference which provides an introduction to learning analytics, and how analytics are used to answer key questions in a world where people are dealing with large volumes of digital data — see it at **http://people.kmi.open.ac.uk/sbs/2014/06/edmedia2014-keynote/**

Many companies are developing their own analytics tools; others use the services of companies such as Google and VisiStat, which specialize in providing analytics and the analysis necessary to understand large volumes of data. Typically these companies present their analysis in forms that are easy for developers and website managers to understand – e.g. as graphs, tables, and other types of data visualizations. The home page of VisiStat (VisiStat.com) contains a short promotional video describing the kinds of services that the company offers and why these services are important to businesses. An example of how web analytics can be used to analyze and help developers to improve website performance is provided by VisiStat's analysis of Mountain Wines' website (VisiStat, 2010).

Mountain Wines, located in Saratoga, California, aims to create memorable experiences for guests who visit the vineyard. Following on the tradition started by Paul Masson, world famous wine maker, Mountain Wines offers a beautiful venue for a variety of events including weddings, corporate meetings, dinner parties, birthdays, concerts, and vacations. Mountain Wines uses a variety of advertising media to attract customers to its website and in 2010 invested about $10 000 a month in advertising. However, the website has remained unchanged for several years because the company didn't have a way of evaluating its effectiveness and could not decide whether to increase or decrease investment in it. They then decided to employ VisiStat, to use their web analytics tool. Prior to enlisting this company, the only record that Mountain Wines had of the effectiveness of its advertising came from its front-desk employees who were instructed to ask visitors 'How did you hear about Mountain Wines?'

VisiStat provided Mountain Wines with data showing how their website was being used by potential customers, e.g. data like that shown in Figures 15.4 to 15.6. Figure 15.4 provides an overview of the number of page views of the website per day. Figure 15.5 provides additional details and shows the hour-by-hour traffic. Clicking on the first icon for more detail shows where the IP addresses of the traffic are located (Figure 15.6). VisiStat can also provide information about such things as which visitors are new to the site, which are returners, and which other pages visitors came from.

Using this data and other data provided by VisiStat, Mountain Wines could see visitor totals, traffic averages, traffic sources, visitor activity, and more. They discovered the importance of visibility for their top search words; they could pinpoint where guests were going on their website; and they could see where their guests were geographically located.

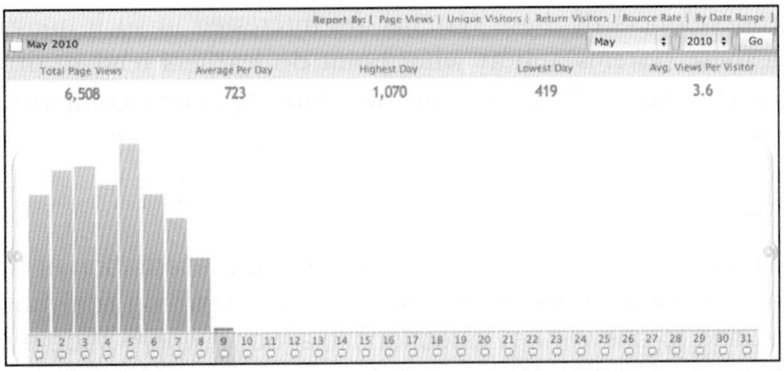

Figure 15. 4 A general view of the kind of data provided by VisiStat

Source: http://www.visistat.com/tracking/monthly-page-views.php

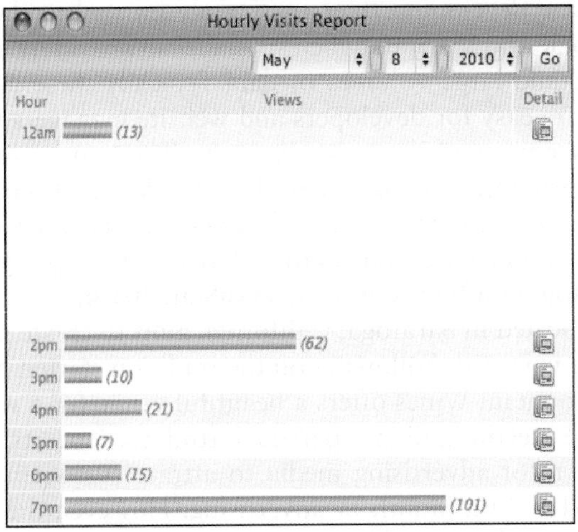

Figure 15.5 Clicking on May 8 provides an hourly report from midnight until 10.00 p.m. (only midnight and 2.00 p.m.–7.00 p.m. shown)

Source: http://www.visistat.com/tracking/monthly-page-views.php

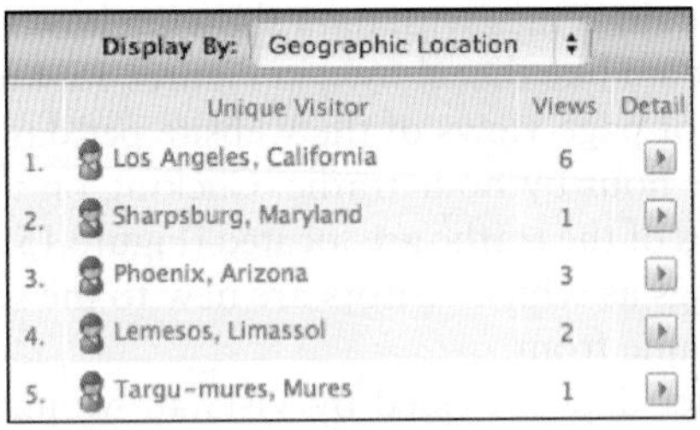

Figure 15.6 Clicking on the icon for the first hour in Figure 15.5 shows where the IP addresses of the 13 visitors to the website are located

Source: http://www.visistat.com/tracking/monthly-page-views.php

ACTIVITY 15.6

1. How were users involved in the Mountain Wines website evaluation?
2. From the information described above, how might Mountain Wines have used the results of the analysis to improve its website?
3. Where was the evaluation carried out?

Comment

1. Users were not directly involved but their behavior on the website was tracked.
2. Mountain Wines may have changed its keywords. By tracking the way visitors traveled through the website, web navigation and content layout could be improved to make searching and browsing more effective and pleasurable. The company also may have added information to attract visitors from other regions.
3. We are not told where the evaluation was carried out. VisiStat may have installed its software at Mountain Wines (the most likely option) or they may have collected and analyzed the data remotely. ∎

More recently, other types of specialist analytics have also been developed such as visual analytics, in which thousands and sometimes millions of data points are displayed and manipulated visually, such as Hansen *et al*'s (2011) social network analysis (see Figure 15.7).

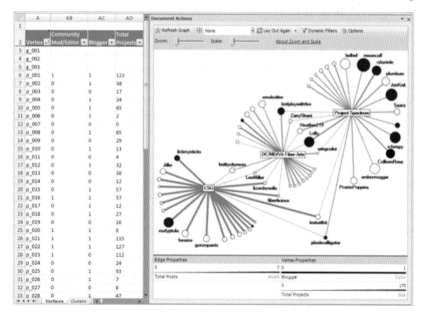

Figure 15.7 Social network analysis showing clusters and the relationships between the entities and the clusters

Source: Perer, A. and Shneiderman, B. (2008) Integrating Statistics and Visualization: Case Studies of Gaining Clarity during Exploratory Data Analysis. *CHI 2008 Proceedings*. Visual Synthesis April 5–10, 2008, 265–274. ©2008 Association for Computing Machinery, Inc. Reprinted by permission.

Lifelogging is another interesting variation that can be used for evaluation as well as for sharing information with friends, family, and colleagues. Typically, lifelogging involves recording GPS location data and personal interaction data on smartphones. In an evaluation context this can raise privacy concerns. Even though users tend to get used to being logged, they generally want to remain in control of the logging (Kärkkäinen *et al*, 2010).

DILEMMA

Analyzing workers' social networking behavior – an invasion of privacy?

Some analytics software can be used by IT administrators to track workers' behavior on social networking sites during working hours. The data collected can be used to determine who is collaborating with whom, and to inform developers about how much their applications are being used – a concept often referred to as stickiness. While these reasons for tracking users appear to be bona fide, is this a threat to personal privacy? ■

15.4   Predictive Models

Similar to inspection methods and analytics, predictive models evaluate a system without users being present. Rather than involving expert evaluators role-playing users as in inspections, or tracking their behavior as in analytics, predictive models use formulas to derive various measures of user performance. Predictive modeling provides estimates of the efficiency of different systems for various kinds of task. For example, a smartphone designer might choose to use a predictive model because it can enable her to determine accurately which is the optimal layout of keys on the phone for allowing common operations to be performed.

Two types of predictive models have been particularly influential in HCI and interaction design over the years: Fitts' Law, which we discuss in more detail below, and the GOMS family of models (Card *et al*, 1983), which are rarely used now as the tools were designed in the early 1980s, primarily for comparing PC-based interfaces for tasks that were highly predictable (now archived from the 3rd edition of this book on the ID-Book.com website).

15.4.1   Fitts' Law

Fitts' Law (Fitts, 1954) predicts the time it takes to reach a target using a pointing device. It was originally used in human factors research to model the relationship between speed and accuracy when moving towards a target on a display. In interaction design, it has been used to describe the time it takes to point at a target, based on the size of the object and the distance to the object. Specifically, it is used to model the time it takes to select objects on a screen, such as alphanumerics, for different spatial configurations. One of its main benefits is that it can help designers decide where to locate physical or digital buttons, what size they should be, and how close together they should be on a touch display or a physical device. To begin with, it was most useful for designing physical laptop/PC keyboard layouts and the placement of physical keys on mobile devices, such as phones, watches, and remote controls. Since then, it has been used more for designing the layout of digital input displays for touch screen interfaces, especially, for considering the effectiveness of new ways of single-digit typing such as using finger swiping (see Chapter 6).

Fitts' Law states that:

$$T = k \log_2(D/S + 1.0)$$

where

$T =$ time to move the pointer to a target
$D =$ distance between the pointer and the target
$S =$ size of the target
k is a constant of approximately 200 ms/bit

In a nutshell, the bigger the target, the easier and quicker it is to reach it. This is why interfaces that have big buttons are easier to use than interfaces that present lots of tiny buttons crammed together. Fitts' Law also predicts that the most quickly accessed targets on any computer display are the four corners of the screen. This is because of their pinning action, i.e. the sides of the display constrain the user from over-stepping the target. However, as pointed out by Tog on his AskTog.com website, corners seem strangely to be avoided at all costs by designers.

Fitts' Law can be useful for evaluating systems where the time to physically locate an object is critical to the task at hand. In particular, it can help designers think about where to locate objects on the screen in relation to each other. This is especially useful for mobile devices, where there is limited space for placing icons and buttons on the screen. For example, in a study carried out by Nokia, Fitts' Law was used to predict expert text entry rates for several input methods on a 12-key cell phone keypad (Silverberg *et al*, 2000). The study helped the designers make decisions about the size of keys, their positioning, and the sequences of presses to perform common tasks. Trade-offs between the size of a device and accuracy of using it were made with the help of calculations from this model. Fitts' Law has also been used to compare eye-tracking input with manual input for visual targets (Vertegaal, 2008); to compare different ways of mapping Chinese characters to the keypad of cell phones (Liu and Räihä, 2010); to investigate the effect of the size of the physical gap between displays and the proximity of targets in multiple-display environments (Hutchings, 2012); and to evaluate tilt as an input method for devices with built-in accelerometers, such as touch screen phones and tablet computers (MacKenzie and Teather, 2012). The AskTog.com website also discusses the application of Fitts' Law to smartphones and other new technologies with limited screen real estate.

ACTIVITY 15.7

Microsoft toolbars provide the user with the option of displaying a label below each tool. Give a reason why labeled tools may be accessed faster. (Assume that the user knows the tool and does not need the label to identify it.)

(Continued)

Comment

The label becomes part of the target and hence the target gets bigger. As we mentioned earlier, bigger targets can be accessed more quickly.

Furthermore, tool icons that don't have labels are likely to be placed closer together so they are more crowded. Spreading the icons further apart creates buffer zones of space around the icons so that if users accidentally go past the target they will be less likely to select the wrong icon. When the icons are crowded together, the user is at greater risk of accidentally overshooting and selecting the wrong icon. The same is true of menus where the items are closely bunched together. ■

Assignment

This assignment continues the work you did on the new interactive product for booking tickets online at the end of Chapters 10, 11, and 14. The aim of this assignment is to evaluate the prototypes produced in the assignment of Chapter 11 using heuristic evaluation.

(a) Decide on an appropriate set of heuristics and perform a heuristic evaluation of one of the prototypes you designed in Chapter 11.

(b) Based on this evaluation, redesign the prototype to overcome the problems you encountered.

(c) Compare the findings from this evaluation with those from the usability testing in the previous chapter. What differences do you observe? Which evaluation approach do you prefer and why?

Summary

This chapter presented inspection evaluation methods, focusing on heuristic evaluation and walkthroughs which are usually done by specialists (usually referred to as experts), who role-play users' interactions with designs, prototypes, and specifications using their substantial knowledge of the kinds of problems that users typically encounter and then offer their opinions. Heuristic evaluation and walkthroughs offer the evaluator a structure to guide the evaluation process.

Analytics, in which user interaction are logged, are often performed remotely and without users being aware that their interactions are being tracked. Very large volumes of data are collected, anonymized, and statistically analyzed using specially developed software services. The analysis provides information about how a system is used, e.g. how different versions of a website or prototype perform, or which parts of a website are seldom used – possibly due to poor usability design or lack of appeal. Data are often presented visually so that it is easier to see trends and interpret the results.

Fitts' Law is an example of a technique that can be used to predict user performance by determining whether a proposed interface, system, or keypad layout will be optimal. Typically Fitts' Law is used to compare different design layouts for virtual or physical objects, such as buttons on a device or screen, for a small sequence of frequently performed tasks.

Evaluators typically find that they have to modify this method for evaluations with the wide range of products that have come onto the market since Fitts' Law was originally developed; this is similar to the other methods discussed in earlier chapters, which frequently also have to be modified.

Key points
- Inspections can be used for evaluating a range of representations including requirements, mockups, functional prototypes, or systems.
- User testing and heuristic evaluation often reveal different usability problems.
- Other types of inspections used in interaction design include pluralistic and cognitive walkthroughs.
- Walkthroughs are very focused and so are suitable for evaluating small parts of a product.
- Analytics involves collecting data about the interactions of users in order to identify which parts of a website or prototype are underused.
- When applied to websites, analytics are often referred to as 'web analytics.' Similarly, when applied to learning systems, they are referred to as 'learning analytics.'
- Fitts' Law is an example of a predictive model that can be used to predict performance involving the selection of virtual or physical objects.
- Predictive models require neither users nor usability experts to be present, but the evaluators must be skilled in applying the models.
- Predictive models like Fitts' Law are used to evaluate systems with limited, clearly defined, functionality such as data entry applications, and key-press sequences for smartphones and other handheld devices.

Further Reading

BUDIU, R. and NIELSEN, J. (2012) *Mobile Usability*. New Riders Press. This book discusses why designing for mobile devices is different from designing for other systems. It describes how to evaluate these systems, including doing expert reviews, and provides many examples.

MACKENZIE, I. S. (1992) Fitts' Law as a research and design tool in human–computer interaction. *Human–Computer Interaction*, 7, 91–139. This early paper by Scott Mackenzie, an expert in the use of Fitts' Law, provides a detailed discussion of how it can be used in HCI.

MACKENZIE, I. S. and SOUKOREFF, R. W. (2002) Text entry for mobile computing: models and methods, theory and practice. *Human–Computer Interaction*, 17, 147–198. This paper provides a useful survey of mobile text-entry techniques and discusses how Fitts' Law can inform their design.

MANKOFF, J., DEY, A. K., HSICH, G., KIENTZ, J. and LEDERER, M. A. (2003) Heuristic evaluation of ambient devices. *Proceedings of CHI 2003, ACM*, 5(1), 169–176. More recent papers are available on this topic but we recommend this paper because it describes how to derive rigorous heuristics for new kinds of applications. It illustrates how different heuristics are needed for different applications.

References

Abelein, U., Sharp, H., and Paech, B. (2013) Does Involving Users in Software Development Really Influence System Success?, *IEEE Software*, Nov/Dec 2013, 13–19.

Abowd, G. and Mynatt, E. (2000) Charting past, present, and future research in ubiquitous computing, *ACM Transactions on Computer–Human Interaction* 7(1), 29–58.

Abowd, G. D., Atkeson, C. G., Bobick, A. F., Essa, I. A., MacIntyre, B., Mynatt, E. D. and Starner, T. E. (2000) Living laboratories: the future computing environments group at the Georgia Institute of Technology. In *CHI '00 Extended Abstracts on Human Factors in Computing Systems* (The Hague, Netherlands, April 1–6, 2000). CHI 2000, ACM, New York, pp. 215–216.

ACM SIGCHI (1992) The Association for Computing Machinery Special Interest Group on Computer–Human Interaction (www.sigchi.org/) (accessed February 7, 2011).

Adlin, T. and Pruitt, J. (2010) *The Essential Persona Lifecycle: Your guide to building and using personas*. Morgan Kaufmann.

Ahn, J., Clegg, T., Yip, J., Bonsignore, E., Pauw, D., Gubbels, M., Lewittes, B. and Rhodes, E. (2014, forthcoming). Seeing the Unseen Learner: Designing and Using Social Media to Recognize Children's Science Dispositions in Action. Submitted to *Learning Media and Technology Special Issue on Digital Media and Data: Using and designing technologies to support learning in practice*. DOI:10 .1080/17439884.2014.964254

Albert, B., Tullis, T. and Tedesco, D. (2010) *Beyond the Usability Lab*. Morgan Kaufmann.

Alexander, C. (1979) *A Pattern Language: Towns, Buildings, Construction*. Oxford University Press.

Alexander, I. F. and Maiden, N. (2004) *Scenarios, Stories and Use Cases*. John Wiley & Sons Inc., New York.

Alexander I. and Robertson, S. (2004) Understanding project sociology by modeling stakeholders, *IEEE Software* **21**(1), 23–27.

Allanwood, G. and Beare, P. (2014) *User Experience Design*. Fairchild Books.

Allison, D., Wills, B., Bowman, D., Wineman, J. and Hodges, L. (1997) The virtual reality gorilla exhibit, *IEEE Computer Graphics and Applications*, 30–38.

Alty, J. L. (1991) Multimedia – what is it and how do we exploit it? In D. Diaper and N. Hammond (eds) *People and Computers IV*. Cambridge University Press, Cambridge.

Ambler, S. (2002) *Agile modeling*. John Wiley. Also at http://www.agilemodeling.com/essays/ agileDocumentationBestPractices.htm.

Anderson, C. (2013) *Makers*. Random House Business Books.

Andrews, D., Nonnecke, B. and Preece, J. (2003) Electronic survey methodology: A case study in reaching hard-to-involve internet users. *International Journal of Human–Computer Interaction* **16**(2), 185–210.

Annett, J. and Duncan, K. D. (1967) Task analysis and training design. *Occupational Psychology* **41**, 211–221.

Antle, A. N., Corness, G. and Droumeva, M. (2009) Human–Computer-Intuition? Exploring the cognitive basis for intuition in embodied interaction. *International Journal of Arts and Technology* **2**, 3, 235–254.

Arikan, A. (2008) *Multichannel Marketing. Metrics and methods for on- and offline success*. Sybex.

Armitage, J. (2004) Are agile methods good for design? *ACM Interactions*, January/February, 14–23.

Armitage, U. (2004) Navigation and learning in electronic texts. PhD thesis, Centre for HCI Design, City University London.

Arroyo, E., Bonnanni, L. and Selker, T. (2005) WaterBot: exploring feedback and persuasive techniques at the sink. In *Proceedings of CHI 2005*. ACM Press, New York, pp. 631–639.

Bachour, K., Kaplan, F. and Dillenbourg, P. (2008) Reflect: An interactive table for regulating face-to-face collaborative learning. *Proceedings of the 3rd European Conference on Technology Enhanced Learning: Times of Convergence: Technologies Across Learning Contexts*. In P. Dillenbourg and M. Specht (eds) Lecture Notes in Computer Science, 5192. Springer-Verlag, Berlin, Heidelberg, pp. 39–48.

Bachour, K., Seiied Alavi, H., Kaplan, F. and Dillenbourg, P. (2010) Low-resolution ambient awareness tools for educational support. *Proceedings of CHI 2010 Workshop: The Future of HCI and Education*.

Bailey, B. (2000) How to improve design decisions by reducing reliance on superstition. Let's start with Miller's 'Magic 7.' Human Factors International, Inc. www.humanfactors.com (accessed December 16, 2010).

Bailey, R. W. (2001) Insights from Human Factors International Inc. (HFI). Providing consulting and training in software ergonomics. January (www.humanfactors.com/home).

Bainbridge, D. (2014) *Information Technology and Intellectual Property Law* (6th edn). Bloomsbury Professional.

Bainbridge, W. S. (2010) *The Warcraft Civilization: Social science in a virtual world*. MIT Press, Cambridge, MA.

Baker, K., Greenberg, S. and Gutwin, C. (2002) Empirical development of a heuristic evaluation methodology for shared workspace groupware. *ACM Proceedings of CSCW'02 Conference*.

Baker, M., Casey, R., Keyes, B. and Yanco, H. A. (2004) Improved interfaces for human–robot interaction in urban search and rescue. In *Proceedings of the IEEE Conference on Systems, Man and Cybernetics*, October.

Ballmer, S. (2010) CES 2010: A transforming trend – the natural user interface, *The Huffington Post*, January 12, 2010. Downloaded from www.huffingtonpost.com/steve-ballmer/ces-2010-a-transforming-t_b_416598.html (retrieved December 16, 2010).

Banzi, M. (2009) *Getting Started with Arduino*. O'Reilly Media Inc.

Barnard, P. J., Hammond, N., Maclean, A. and Morten, J. (1982) Learning and remembering interactive commands in a text editing task, *Behavior and Information Technology* 1, 347–358.

Baskinger, M. (2008) Pencils before pixels: A primer in hand-generated sketching, *interactions*, March–April, 28–36.

Baum, F. L. and Denslow, W. (1900) *The Wizard of Oz*. Random House, New York.

Baumeister, R.F. Vohs, K.D., DeWall, C.N. and Zhang, L. (2007) How emotion shapes behavior: Feedback, anticipation, and reflection, rather than direct causation. *Personality and Social Psychology Review*, **11**(2), 167–203.

Baumer, E. P. S. and Thomlinson, B. (2011) Comparing Activity Theory with Distributed Cognition for Video Analysis: Beyond Kicking the Tyres. *ACM Proceedings of CHI'11*, 133–142.

Beck, K. and Andres, C. (2005) *Extreme Programming Explained: Embrace change* (2nd edn). Addison-Wesley.

Bederson, B. B. and Shneiderman, B. (eds) (2003) *The Craft of Information Visualization: Readings and Reflections.* Morgan Kaufmann, San Francisco, CA.

Bekker, M., Beusmans, J., Keyson, D. and Lloyd, P. (2003) KidReporter: A user requirements gathering technique for designing with children, *Interacting with Computers* 15(3), 187–202.

Bell, G. (2001) Looking across the Atlantic, *Intel Technical Journal* 5(3), August.

Bell, G. (2003) Other homes: Alternate visions of culturally situated technologies for the home. In *Proceedings of CHI 2003.* ACM, New York.

Bell, G., Blythe, M. and Sengers, P. (2005) Making by making strange: Defamiliarization and the design of domestic technologies, *ACM Transactions on Computer–Human Interaction* 12(2), 149–173.

Bergman, E. and Haitani, R. (2000) Designing the PalmPilot: a conversation with Rob Haitani. In *Information Appliances.* Morgan Kaufmann, San Francisco.

Bewley, W. L., Roberts, T. L., Schroit, D. and Verplank, W. (1990) Human factors testing in the design of Xerox's 8010 'Star' office workstation. In J. Preece and L. Keller (eds) *Human–Computer Interaction: A Reader.* Prentice Hall, Hemel Hempstead, pp. 368–382.

Beyer, H. and Holtzblatt, K. (1998) *Contextual Design: Defining customer-centered systems.* Morgan Kauffman, San Francisco.

Bias, R. G. (1994) The pluralistic usability walk-through – coordinated empathoes. In J. Nielsen and R. L. Mack (eds) *Usability Inspection Methods.* John Wiley & Sons Inc., New York.

Bird, J. and Rogers, Y. (2010) The Pulse of Tidy Street: Measuring and Publicly Displaying Domestic Electricity Consumption. *Workshop on Energy Awareness and Conservation through Pervasive Applications, Pervasive 2010 Conference.* Downloaded from http://www.changeproject.info/projects .html (retrieved September 2014).

Bird, J., Marshall, P. and Rogers Y. (2009) Low-fi skin vision: A case study in rapid prototyping a sensory substitution system. In *Proceedings of HCI 2009.* ACM, New York.

Bittner, K. and Spence, I. (2002) *Use Case Modelling.* Addison-Wesley, Harlow, Essex.

Blandford, A. and Furniss, D. (2006) DiCoT: A methodology for applying distributed cognition to the design of team working systems. In S. W. Gilroy and M. D. Harrison (eds) *Interactive Systems: 12th International Workshop, DSVIS 2005,* Lecture Notes in Computer Science, 3941 Springer-Verlag, Berlin, Heidelberg, pp. 26–38.

Blythe M. and Cairns, P. (2009) Critical methods and user generated content: The iPhone on YouTube. In *Proceedings of CHI 2009.* ACM, pp. 1467–1476.

Bødker, S. (2000) Scenarios in user-centered design—setting the stage for reflection and action, *Interacting with Computers* 13(1), 61–76.

Bødker, S., Greenbaum, J. and Kyng, M. (1991) Setting the stage for design as action. In J. Greenbaum and M. Kyng (eds) *Design at Work: Cooperative design of computer systems.* Lawrence Earlbaum Associates, Hillsdale, NJ, pp. 139–154.

Boehm, B. and Basili, V.R. (2001) Software defect reduction Top 10 list, *IEEE Computer* 34(1), 135–137.

Boehner, K., Janet Vertesi, J., Sengers, P., and Dourish, P. (2007) How HCI Interprets the Probes. In *Proceedings of CHI 2007.* ACM, pp. 1077–1086.

Borchers, J. (2001) *A Pattern Approach to Interaction Design.* Wiley.

Borovoy, R., Martin, F., Vemuri, S., Resnick, M., Silverman, B. and Hancock, C. (1998) Meme tags and community mirrors: moving from conferences to collaboration. In *Proceedings of CSCW '98*. ACM Press, New York, pp. 159–168.

Bouchet, J. and Nigay, L. (2004) ICARE: a component-based approach for the design and development of multimodal interfaces. In *Proceedings of CHI 2004*. ACM, pp. 1325–1328.

Boyd, D. (2014) *It's Complicated: the social lives of networked teens*. Yale.

Braun, V. and Clarke, V. (2006) Using thematic analysis in psychology. *Qualitative Research in Psychology*, **3**(2). pp. 77–101, ISSN1478-0887.

Breazeal, C. (1999) Kismet: A robot for social interactions with humans: www.ai.mit.edu/projects/kismet/ (accessed December 16, 2010).

Breazeal, C. (2005) Socially intelligent robots, *interactions* **12**, 19–21.

Brereton, M. and McGarry, B. (2000) An observational study of how objects support engineering design thinking and communication: Implications for the design of tangible media. In *Proceedings of CHI 2000*. ACM, pp. 217–224.

Brignull, H. and Rogers, Y. (2003) Enticing people to interact with large public displays in public spaces. In *Proceedings of INTERACT 2003*, Zurich, pp. 17–24.

Brignull, H., Izadi, S., Fitzpatrick, G., Rogers, Y. and Rodden, T. (2004) The introduction of a shared interactive surface into a communal space. In *Proceedings of the 2004 Conference on Computer Supported Cooperative Work, CSCW 2004*. ACM Press, New York, pp. 49–58.

Buchenau, M. and Suri, J. F. (2000) Experience prototyping. In *Proceedings of DIS 2000, Design Interactive Systems: Processes, Practices, Methods, Techniques*, pp. 17–19.

Budd, A. (2007) *Web Heuristics*. Available at: www.andybudd.com/archives/2007/01/heuristics_for_modern_web_application_development/ (accessed September 2010).

Budiu, R. and Nielsen, J. (2010) *Usability of iPad Apps and Websites. First research findings*. Nielsen Norman Group. Downloaded from www.nngroup.com/reports/mobile/ipad/ (retrieved August, 2010).

Budiu, R. and Nielsen, J. (2012) *Mobile Usability*. New Riders Press.

Buechley, L. and Qiu, K. (2014) *Sew Electric. A Collection of DIY projects that combine fabric, electronics, and programming*. HLT Press.

Burak, A. and Sharon, T. (2004) Usage patterns of FriendZone—mobile location-based community services. In *Proceedings of 3rd International Conference on Mobile and Ubiquitous Computing*. ACM Press, New York, pp. 93–100.

Buxton, B. (2007) *Sketching User Experiences*. Morgan Kauffman, San Francisco.

Callahan, E. (2005) Interface design and culture. *Annual Review of Information Science and Technology* **39**, 257–310.

Card, S. K., Mackinley, J. D. and Shneiderman, B. (eds) (1999) *Readings in Information Visualization: Using vision to think*. Morgan Kaufmann, San Francisco.

Card, S. K., Moran, T. P. and Newell, A. (1983) *The Psychology of Human–Computer Interaction*. Lawrence Earlbaum Associates, Hillsdale, NJ.

Carlson, W. B. (1992). *Shaping Technology/Building Society: Studies in sociotechnical change*. MIT Press, Cambridge, MA.

Carroll, J. M. (ed.) (1995) *Scenario-based Design*. John Wiley & Sons, Inc., New York.

Carroll J. M. (2000) Introduction to the Special Issue on Scenario-Based Systems Development, *Interacting with Computers* **13**(1), 41–42.

Carroll, J. M. (ed.) (2003) *HCI Models, Theories and Frameworks: Towards a multidisciplinary science*. Morgan Kaufmann, San Francisco.

Carroll, J. M. (2004) Beyond fun, *interactions* **11**(5), 38–40.

Carter, S. and Mankoff, J. (2005) When participants do the capturing: The role of media in diary studies. In *Proceedings of CHI 2005*. ACM, pp. 899–908.

Cassell, J. (2000) Embodied conversational interface agents, *Communications of the ACM* **43**(3), 70–79.

Cawood, S. and Fiala, M. (2008) *Augmented Reality: A practical guide*. Pragmatic Bookshelf.

Chang, T. (2004) The results of student ratings: paper vs online, *Journal of Taiwan Normal University: Education* **49**(1), 171–186.

Chapman, N. and Chapman, J. (2004) *Digital Multimedia* (2nd edn). John Wiley & Sons Inc., New York.

Charmaz, K. (2014) *Constructing Grounded Theory* (2nd edn). Sage Publications.

Chavan, A. L., Gorney, D., Prabhu, B. and Arora, S. (2009) The washing machine that ate my sari – mistakes in cross-cultural design, *interactions*, January/February, **xvi**(1), 26–31.

Chen, C. (2004) *Information Visualization: Beyond the horizon* (2nd edn). Springer-Verlag, Berlin.

Chisnell, D. and Brown, M. (2004) Matching user and business goals. In *Proceedings of CHI2004*, April 24–29, Vienna, Austria, pp. 943–958.

Christiansen, E. (1996) Tamed by a rose: Computers as tools in human activity. In B. A. Nardi (ed.) *Context and Consciousness*. MIT Press, Cambridge, MA, pp. 175–198.

Churchill, E. F., Nelson, L. and Denoue, L. (2003) Multimedia fliers: Informal information sharing with digital community bulletin boards. In *Proceedings of Communities and Technologies*, Amsterdam.

Clark, A. (2003) *Natural Born Cyborgs: Minds, technologies, and the future of human intelligence*. Oxford University Press.

Clegg, T., Bonsignore, E., Ahn, J., Yip, J., Pauw, D., Gubbels, M., Lewittes, B., and Rhodes, E. (2014). Capturing Personal and Social Science: Technology for Integrating the Building Blocks of Disposition. Paper presented at the *International Conference of the Learning Sciences*. Boulder, CO.

Clemmensen, T., Hertzum, M., Hornbaek, K., Shi, Q. and Yammiyavar, P. (2008) Cultural Cognition in the Thinking-Aloud Method for Usability Evaluation. In *Proceedings of Twenty Ninth International Conference on Information Systems*. Paris, 2008, Paper 189.

Cobb, S., Beardon, L., Eastgate, R., Glover, T., Kerr, S., Neale, H., Parsons, S., Benford, S., Hopkins, E., Mitchell, P., Reynard, G. and Wilson, J. (2002) Applied virtual environments to support learning of social interaction skills in users with Asperger's Syndrome, *Digital Creativity* **13**(1), N-22.

Cockburn, A. (2005) *Crystal Clear: A human-powered methodology for small teams*. Addison-Wesley, Harlow, Essex.

Cockton, G., Lavery, D. and Woolrych, A. (2002) Inspection-based evaluation. In J. Jacko and A Sears (eds) *The Human–Computer Interaction Handbook: Fundamentals, emerging technologies, and emerging applications*. Lawrence Earlbaum Associates, Mahwah, NJ, pp. 1118–1138.

Cockton, G. and Woolrych, A. (2001) Understanding inspection methods: lessons from an assessment of heuristic evaluation. In A. Blandford and J. Vanderdonckt (eds), *People & Computers XV*. Springer-Verlag, Berlin, pp. 171–191.

Cohen, J. (1960). A coefficient of agreement for nominal scales. *Educational and Psychological Measurement* **20**(1), 37–46.

Cohen, M., Giangola, J. P. and Balogh, J. (2004) *Voice User Interface Design*. Addison-Wesley, Harlow, Essex.

Consolvo, S. and Towle, J. (2005) Evaluating an ambient display for the home. In *Proceedings of CHI 2005, Late Breaking Results: Posters*. ACM, pp. 1304–1307.

Consolvo, S., McDonald, D. W., Toscos, T., Chen, M. Y., Froehlich, J., Harrison, B. L., Klasnja, P. V., LaMarca, A., LeGrand, L., Libby, R., Smith, I. E. and Landay, J. A. (2008) Activity sensing in the wild: A field trial of UbiFit Garden. In *Proceedings of CHI 2008*. ACM, pp. 1797–1806.

Constantine, L. L. and Lockwood, L. A. D. (1999) *Software for Use*. Addison-Wesley, Harlow, Essex.

Cooper, A. (1999) *The Inmates are Running the Asylum*. SAMS, Indianapolis.

Cooper, A., Reimann, R., Cronin, D. and Noessel, C. (2014) *About Face: The essentials of interaction design* (4th edn). John Wiley & Sons Inc., New York.

Corbin, J. M. and Strauss, A. (2014) *Basics of Qualitative Research: Techniques and Procedures for Developing Grounded Theory*. Sage Publications.

Couch, C. J. (1996) In D. R. Maines and S. Chen (eds) *Information Technologies and Social Orders*. Aldine de Gruyter, New York.

Coyle, A. (1995) Discourse analysis. In G. M. Breakwell, S. Hammond and C. Fife-Schaw (eds) *Research Methods in Psychology*. Sage, London.

Crabtree, A. (2003) *Designing Collaborative Systems: A practical guide to ethnography*. Springer-Verlag, Berlin.

Crabtree, A., Chamberlain, A., Grinter, R. E., Jones, M., Rodden, T. and Rogers, Y. (2013) Introduction to the special issue of "The Turn to The Wild" *ACM Transactions on Computer-Human Interaction (TOCHI)*, **20**(3).

Crabtree, A., Rodden, T., Tolmie, P. and Button, G. (2009) Ethnography considered harmful. In *Proceedings of CHI 2009*. ACM.

Craik, K. J. W. (1943) *The Nature of Explanation*. Cambridge University Press, Cambridge.

Crampton Smith, G. (1995) The hand that rocks the cradle. *ID Magazine* May/June, 60–65.

Crumlish, C. and Malone, E. (2009) *Designing Social Interfaces: Principles, patterns and practices for improving the user experience*, O'Reilly.

Csikszentmihalyi, M. (1996) *Wired* interview. Go with the flow. www.wired.com/wired/archive/4.09/czik.html (retrieved May 6, 2005).

Csikszentmihalyi, M. (1997) *Finding Flow: The psychology of engagement with everyday life*. Basic Books, New York.

Csikszentmihalyhi, M. and Larson, R. (1987) Validity and reliability of the experience-sampling method, *Journal of Nervous and Mental Disease* **175**, 526–536.

Curzon, P., Blandford, A., Butterworth, R. and Bhogal, R. (2002) Interaction design issues for car navigation systems. In *Proceedings of HCI 2002*, Vol. 2.

Cusumano, M. A. and Selby, R. W. (1995) *Microsoft Secrets*. Harper-Collins Business, London.

CuteCircuit (2010) CuteCircuit's Hug Shirt. Downloaded from www.cutecircuit.com (retrieved June 25, 2010).

Davis, A. M. (1995) *201 Principles of Software Development*. McGraw-Hill, New York.

De Angeli, A., Athavankar, U., Joshi, A., Coventry, L. and Johnson, G. I. (2004) Introducing ATMs in India: A contextual inquiry, *Interacting with Computers* **16**(1), 29–44.

De Angeli, A., Coventry, L., Johnson, G. and Renaud, K. (2005) Is a picture worth a thousand words? Exploring the feasibility of graphical authentication systems, *International Journal of Human Computer Studies* **63**, 128–152.

De Choudhury, M., Gamon, M., Hoff, A. and Roseway, A. (2013) "Moon Phrases": a social media faciliated tool for emotional reflection and wellness. In *Proceedings of PervasiveHealth*'13, 41–44.

Dearman, D. Kellar, M., Truong, K. N. (2008) An examination of daily information needs and sharing opportunities. In *Proceedings of CSCW 2008*, November 8–12, San Diego, CA, pp. 679–688.

Deng, L. and Huang, X. (2004) Challenges in adopting speech recognition, *Communications of the ACM* **47**(1), 69–75.

De Souza, S. C. (2005) *The Semiotic Engineering of Human–Computer Interaction*. MIT Press, Cambridge, MA.

Denzin, N. (2006). *Sociological Methods: A Sourcebook*. Aldine Transaction (5th edn), ISBN 9780-202308401.

Denzin, N. K. and Lincoln, Y. S. (2011) *The Sage Handbook of Qualitative Research*. Sage Publications.

Dewey, J. (1934) *Art as Experience*. Perigee Trade.

Dhillon, B., Banach, P., Hocielnik, R., Emparanza, J.P., Politis, I., Paczewska, A. and Markopoulos, P. (2011) Visual fidelity of video prototypes and user feedback: a case study, in *Proceedings of BCS-HCI*.

Diaper, D. and Stanton, N. (2004) *The Handbook of Task Analysis for Human–Computer Interaction*. Lawrence Earlbaum Associates.

Diaz de Rada, V. and Dominguez-Alvarez, J. A. (2014) Response Quality of Self-Administered Questions: A Comparison Between Paper and Web. *Social Science Computer Review*, 32, 2, Sage Publications.

Dietz, P. H. and Leigh, D. L. (2001) DiamondTouch: A multi-user touch technology. In *Symposium on User Interface Software and Technology (UIST)*. ACM Press, New York, pp. 219–226.

Dindler, C., Eriksson, E., Iversen, O. S., Lykke-Olesen, A. and Ludvigsen, M. (2005) Mission from Mars – A method for exploring user requirements for children in a narrative space. In *Proceedings of Interaction Design and Children, IDC 2005*, pp. 40–47.

DiSalvo, C., Sengers, P. and Brynjarsdottir, H. (2010) Mapping the landscape of sustainable HCI. In *Proceedings of CHI 2010*. ACM, pp. 1975–1984.

Dix, A., Finlay, J., Abowd, G. and Beale, R. (2004) *Human–Computer Interaction* (3rd edn). Pearson Education, Harlow, Essex.

Dourish, P. (2001) *Where the Action Is: The foundations of embodied interaction*. MIT Press, Cambridge, MA.

Dourish, P. and Bly, S. (1992) Portholes: Supporting awareness in a distributed work group. In *Proceedings of CHI '92*. ACM, pp. 541–547.

Drascic, D. and Milgram, P. (1996) Perceptual issues in augmented reality. In M. T. Bolas, S. S. Fisher and J. O. Merritt (eds) *SPIE Volume 2653: Stereoscopic Displays and Virtual Reality Systems III*. SPIE, San Jose, CA, pp. 123–134.

Druin, A. (2002) The role of children in the design of new technology, *Behaviour and Information Technology* **21**(1), 1–25.

DSDM (2014) *The DSDM Agile Project Framework Handbook*, DSDM Consortium, Kent, UK, ISBN 978-0-9544832-9-6.

Dubois, L. (2014) *11 Best Web Analytics Tools*. Retrieved from http://www.inc.com/guides/12/2010/11-best-web-analytics-tools.html.

Ducheneaut, N. and Moore, R. J. (2004) The social side of gaming: A study of interaction patterns in a massively multiplayer online game. In *Proceedings of CSCW 2004*, November 6–10, Chicago.

Dumas, J. S. and Redish, J. C. (1999) *A Practical Guide to Usability Testing* (rev. edn). Intellect, Exeter.

Dumas, B., Lalanne, D. and Oviatt, S. (2009) Multimodal Interfaces: A Survey of Principles, Models and Frameworks. Human Machine Interaction Lecture Notes in *Computer Science*, **5440**, 3–26.

Duveskog, M., Bednarik, R., Kemppainen, K. and Sutlinen, E. (2009) Designing a story-based platform for HIV and AIDS counselling with Tanzanian children. In *Proceedings of Interaction Design and Children, IDC 2009*, June, Como Italy, pp. 27–35.

Eason, K. (1987) *Information Technology and Organizational Change*. Taylor and Francis, London.

Edwards, A. D. N. (1992) Graphical user interfaces and blind people. In *Proceedings of ICCHP '92*, Austrian Computer Society, Vienna, pp. 114–119.

Ehn, P. (1989) *Word-Oriented Design of Computer Artifacts* (2nd edn). Lawrence Earlbaum Associates, Hillsdale, NJ.

Eliot, C. and Woolf, B. (1994) Reasoning about the user within a simulation-based real-time training system. In *Proceedings of 4th International Conference on User Modeling*, Mitre Corp., Bedford, MA.

Elrod, S., Bruce, R., Gold, R., Goldberg, D., Halasz, F., Janssen, W., Lee, D., McCall, K., Pedersen, E., Pier, K., Tang, J. and Welch, B. (1992) Liveboard: A large interactive display supporting group meetings, presentations and remote collaboration. In *Proceedings of CHI '92*. ACM Press, New York, pp. 599–607.

Empson, R. (2012). *Google Biz Chief: Over 10M Websites Now Using Google Analytics*. Retrieved from http://techcrunch.com/2012/04/12/google-analytics-officially-at-10m/.

Engeström, Y. (1999) *Perspectives on Activity Theory*. Cambridge University Press, Cambridge.

Erickson, T. D. (1990) Working with interface metaphors. In B. Laurel (ed.) *The Art of Human–Computer Interface Design*. Addison-Wesley, Boston.

Erickson, T. and Kellogg, W. A. (2000) Social translucence: an approach to designing systems that support social processes, *Transactions of Computer-Human Interaction* 7(1), 59–83.

Erickson, T. D. and McDonald, D. W. (2008) *HCI Remixed: Reflections on works that have influenced the HCI community*. MIT Press, Cambridge, MA.

Erickson, T. D. and Simon, H. A. (1985) *Protocol Analysis: Verbal reports as data*. MIT Press, Cambridge, MA.

Erickson, T. D., Smith, D. N., Kellogg, W. A., Laff, M., Richards, J. T. and Bradner, E. (1999) Socially translucent systems: Social proxies, persistent conversation and the design of 'Babble.' In *Proceedings of CHI '99*, pp. 72–79.

Esselink, B. (2000) *A Practical Guide to Localisation*. John Benjamins, Amsterdam.

Fekete, J.-D. and Plaisant, C. (2002) Interactive information visualization of a million items. In *Proceedings of IEEE Symposium on Information Visualization 2002 (InfoVis 2002)*, Boston.

Fernaeus, Y. and Tholander, J. (2006) Finding design qualities in a tangible programming space. In *Proceedings of CHI 2006*. ACM, pp. 447–456.

Fernández-Luque, F., Zapata, J., Ruiz, R., and Iborra, E. (2009) A wireless sensor network for assisted living at home of elderly people, *Lecture Notes In Computer Science*, 5602. Springer-Verlag, Berlin, Heidelberg, pp. 65–74.

Ferreira, J., Sharp, H. and Robinson, H.M. (2011) User Experience Design and Agile Development: Managing cooperation through articulation work. In: *Software Practice and Experience*, **41**(9), 963–974.

Ferreira, J., Sharp, H. and Robinson, H. (2012) Agile Development and User Experience Design Integration as an On-going Achievement in Practice. In *Proceedings of Agile 2012*, Dallas, Texas.

Fetterman, D. M. (2010) *Ethnography: Step by Step* (3rd edn). Applied Social Research Methods Series, Vol. 17. Sage.

Few, S. (2013) *Information Dashboard Design* (2nd edn). Analytics Press, Burlingame, California.

Fish, R. S. (1989) Cruiser: A multimedia system for social browsing. *SIGGRAPH Video Review* (video cassette), Issue 45, Item 6.

Fishkin, K. P. (2004) A taxonomy for and analysis of tangible interfaces, *Personal and Ubiquitous Computing* **8**, 347–358.

Fiske, J. (1994) Audiencing: Cultural practice and cultural studies. In N. K. Denzin and Y. S. Lincoln (eds) *Handbook of Qualitative Research*. Sage, Thousand Oaks, CA, pp. 189–198.

Fitts, P. M. (1954) The information capacity of the human motor system in controlling amplitude of movement, *Journal of Experimental Psychology* **47**, 381–391.

Flanagan, J. C. (1954) The critical incident technique, *Psychological Bulletin* **51**, 327–358.

Fogg, B. J. (2003) *Persuasive Technology: Using computers to change what we think and do*. Morgan Kaufmann, San Francisco.

Folmer, E., Yuan, B., Carr, D., and Sapre, M. (2009) TextSL: A command-based virtual world interface for the visually impaired. In *Proceedings 11th international ACM SIGACCESS Conference on Computers and Accessibility*, pp. 59–66.

Fontana, A. and Frey, J. H. (2005). The interview: From neutral stance to political involvement. In N. K. Denzin & Y. S. Lincoln (eds) *The Sage Handbook of Qualitative Research* (3rd edn), pp. 695–727. Thousand Oaks, CA: Sage.

Forsell, C. and Johansson, J. (2010) An heuristic set for evaluation in information visualization. In *Proceedings of the Conference on Advanced Visual Interfaces, AVI 2010*.

Froehlich, J., Findlater, L. and Landay, J. (2010) The design of eco-feedback technology. In *Proceedings of CHI '10*, ACM, pp. 1999–2008.

Frohlich, D. and Murphy, R. (1999) Getting physical: what is fun computing in tangible form? In *Computers and Fun 2, Workshop*, 20 December, York.

Fulton Suri, J. (2005) *Thoughtless Acts?* Chronicle Books, San Francisco.

Funke, F., Reips, U-D. and Thomas, R. K. (2011) Sliders for the Smart: Type of Rating Scale on the Web Interacts with Educational Level. *Social Science Computer Review*, 29, 2, Sage Publications.

Furniss, D. and Blandford, A. (2006) Understanding Emergency Dispatch in terms of distributed cognition: a case study, *Ergonomics* **49**(12/13), October, pp. 1174–1203.

Gabrielli, S., Rogers, Y. and Scaife, M. (2000) Young children's spatial representations developed through exploration of a desktop virtual reality scene, *Education and Information Technologies* 5(4), 251–262.

Galitz, W. O. (1997) *The Essential Guide to User Interface Design*. John Wiley & Sons Inc., New York.

Gao, Y., Bianchi-Berthouze, N. and Meng, H. (2012) What Does Touch Tell Us about Emotions in Touchscreen-Based Gameplay? *ACM Trans. Comput.-Hum. Interact.* **19**(4), Article 31, 30 pages.

Gardner, H. and Davis, K. (2013) *The App Generation: how today's youth navigate identity, intimacy, and imagination in a digital world*. Yale.

Garrett, J. J. (2010) *The Elements of User Experience: User-centered design for the web and beyond* (2nd edn). New Riders Press.

Gaver, B., Dunne, T. and Pacenti, E. (1999) Cultural probes, *ACM Interactions Magazine* January/February, 21–29.

Gibson, J. (2014) *Introduction to Game Design, Prototyping, and Development*. Addison Wesley.

Giddens, A. (1984) *The Constitution of Society: Outline of the Theory of Structure*. University of California Press.

Gigante, M. A. (1993) Virtual reality: enabling technologies. In R. A. Earnshaw, M. A. Gigante and H. Jones (eds) *Virtual Reality Systems*. Academic Press, London, pp. 15–25.

Gigerenzer, G. (2008) *Gut Feelings*. Penguin.

Gigerenzer, G., Todd, P., and the ABC Research Group (1999) *Simple Heuristics that Make Us Smart*. Oxford University Press, New York.

Glaser, B. G. (1992) *Basics of Grounded Theory: Emergence vs Forcing*. Sociology Press.

Glaser, B. G. and Strauss, A. (1967) *Discovery of Grounded Theory*. Aldine, London.

Glerum, K., Kinshumann, K., Greenberg, S., Aul, G., Orgovan, V., Nichols, G., Grant, D., Loihle, G. and Hunt, G. (2009) Debugging in the (Very) Large: Ten Years of Implementation and Experience, *SOSP '09*.

Golbeck, J. (2013). *Homework 10,000* [course assignment]. Retrieved from http://www.cs.umd .edu/~golbeck/LBSC708L/hw10K.shtml.

Golsteijn, C., Gallacher, S., Koeman, L., Wall, L., Andberg, S., Rogers, Y. and Capra, L. (2015) VoxBox: a Tangible Machine that Gathers Opinions from the Public at Events. In *Proc. of TEI 2015*. ACM.

Google (2014) *Material Design*. http://www.google.com/design/spec/material-design/introduction.html.

Gosper, J., Agathos, J-L., Rutter, R. and Coatta, T. (2011) Case Study: UX Design and Agile: A Natural Fit? *Communications of the ACM*, **54**(1), 54–60.

Gothelf, J. with Seiden, J. (2013) *Lean UX*. O'Reilly.

Gottesdiener, E. (2002) *Requirements by Collaboration: Workshops for defining needs*. Addison-Wesley, Harlow, Essex.

Gottesdiener, E. (2005) *The Software Requirements Memory Jogger*. Goal/QPC.

Gottesdiener, E. and Gorman, M. (2012) *Discover to Deliver: Product Planning and Analysis*. EBG Consulting, Inc.

Gould, J. D. and Lewis, C. H. (1985) Designing for usability: Key principles and what designers think, *Communications of the ACM* **28**(3), 300–311.

Gould, J. D., Boies, S. J., Levy, S., Richards, J. T. and Schoonard, J. (1987) The 1984 Olympic Message System: A test of behavioral principles of system design, *Communications of the ACM* **30**(9), 758–769.

Greenbaum, J. and Kyng, M. (eds) (1991) *Design at Work: Co-operative design of computer systems*. Lawrence Earlbaum Associates.

Greenberg, S. and Rounding, M. (2001) The Notification Collage: Posting information to public and personal displays, *CHI Letters* 3(1), 515–521.

Greenberg, S., Carpendale, S., Marquardt, N. and Buxton, B. (2012) *Sketching User Experiences*. Morgan Kaufman.

Greenfield, A. (2006) *Everyware: The dawning age of ubiquitous computing*. New Riders Press.

Greif, I. (1988) *Computer Supported Cooperative Work: A book of readings*. Morgan Kaufmann, San Francisco.

Griffiths, A. (2014) How Paro the robot seal is being used to help UK dementia patients. Downloaded from: http://www.theguardian.com/society/2014/jul/08/paro-robot-seal-dementia-patients-nhs-japan.

Grison, E., Gyselinck, V., and Burkhardt, J-M. (2013) Using the critical incidents technique to explore variables related to users' experience of public transport modes. In *Proceedings of ECCE '13 Proceedings of the 31st European Conference on Cognitive Ergonomics*, Article No. 21, ACM.

Grudin, J. (1989) The case against user interface consistency, *Communications of the ACM* 32(10), 1164–1173.

Gubbels, M. and Froehlich, J. (2014) Physically Computing Physical Computing: Creative Tools for Building with Physical Materials and Computation. *IDC '14 Extended Abstracts*.

Guha, M. L. ,Druin, A. and Fails, J.A. (2013). Cooperative Inquiry revisited: Reflections of the past and guidelines for the future of intergenerational co-design. *International Journal of Child-Computer Interaction*, 1(1), 14–23.

Gunther, V. A., Burns, D. J. and Payne, D. J. (1986) Text editing performance as a function of training with command terms of differing lengths and frequencies, *SIGCHI Bulletin* 18, 57–59.

Gutwin, C. and Greenberg, S. (2002) A descriptive framework of workspace awareness for real-time groupware, *Computer Supported Cooperative Work* 11(3), 411–446.

Hansen, D., Schneiderman, B. and Smith , M. (2011) *Analyzing Social Media Networks with NodeXL: Insights from a Connected World*. Elsevier/Morgan-Kaufman: Boston, MA.

Harper, R., Rodden, T., Rogers, Y. and Sellen, A. (2008) *Being Human: HCI in the year 2020*. Microsoft (free copies from: http://research.microsoft.com/en-us/um/cambridge/projects/hci2020/).

Harrison, C., Tan, D. and Morris, D. (2010) Skinput: Appropriating the body as an input surface. In *Proceedings of the 28th International Conference on Human Factors in Computing Systems, CHI 2010*. ACM, New York, NY, pp. 453–462.

Harrison, E. (ed.) (2009) *Media Space 20+ Years of Mediated Life*. Springer.

Hartson, H. R. and Hix, D. (1989) Toward empirically derived methodologies and tools for human–computer interface development, *International Journal of Man–Machine Studies* 31, 477–494.

Hatch, M. (2014) *The Maker Movement Manifesto*. McGraw Hill.

Hayashi, E., Maas, M. and Hong, J.I. (2014) Wave to Me: User Identification Using Body Lengths and Natural Gestures, in *Proceedings of CHI 14*, pp. 3453–3462.

Hazas, M., Bernheim Brush, A.J. and Scott, J. (2012) Sustainability does not begin with the individual. *Interactions* 19(5), 14–17.

Hazlewood, W., Dalton, N. S., Rogers, Y., Marshall, P. and Hertrich, S. (2010) Bricolage and Consultation: A case study to inform the development of large-scale prototypes for HCI research. In *Proceedings of Designing Interactive Systems, DIS 2010*. ACM, pp. 380–388.

Heath, C., Hindmarsh, J. and Luff, P. (2010) *Video in Qualitative Research*. Sage.

Heath, C. and Luff, P. (1992) Collaboration and control: crisis management and multimedia technology in London Underground line control rooms. In *Proceedings of CSCW '92* 1(1&2), 69–94.

Heer, J. and Bostock, M. (2010) Crowdsourcing graphical perception: Using Mechanical Turk to assess visualization design. In *Proceedings of CHI 2010*. ACM, New York, pp. 203–212.

Heinbokel, T., Sonnentag, S., Frese, M., Stolte, W. and Brodbeck, F. C. (1996) Don't underestimate the problems of user centredness in software development projects—there are many! *Behaviour and Information Technology* 15(4), 226–236.

Hektner, J. M., Schmidt, J. A. and Csikszentmihalyi, M. (2006) *Experience Sampling Method: Measuring the quality of everyday life*. Sage.

Henderson-Sellers, B. and Edwards, J. M. (1993) The Fountain Model for object-oriented system development, *Object Magazine* July–August, 71–79.

Hendriks-Jansen, H. (1996) *Catching Ourselves in the Act: Situated activity, interactive emergence, evolution, and human thought*. MIT Press, Cambridge, MA.

Henkel, L. A. (2014) Point-and-Shoot Memories The Influence of Taking Photos on Memory for a Museum Tour. *Psychological science*, 25.2, 396–402.

Hicks, J. (2012) *The Icon Handbook*. Five Simple Steps Publishing Ltd.

Highsmith, J. (2000) *Adaptive Software Development: A collaborative approach to managing complex systems*. Dorset House.

Highsmith, J. (2002) *Agile Software Development Ecosystems*. Addison-Wesley.

Hine, C. (2000) *Virtual Ethnography*. Sage.

Hodges, S., Scott, J., Sentance, S., Miller, C., Villar, N., Schwiderski-Grosche, S., Hammil, K. and Johnston, S. (2013) .NETGadgeteer: A New Platform for K-12 Computer Science Education. In *Proc. SIGCSE '13*, ACM, 391–396.

Hodges, S., Williams, L., Berry, E., Izadi, S., Srinivasan, J., Butler, A., Smyth, G., Kapur, N. and Wood, K. (2006) SenseCam: A retrospective memory aid. In P. Dourish and A. Friday (eds) *Ubicomp 2006*, LNCS 4206. Springer-Verlag, pp. 177–193.

Hofstede, G. (1994) *Cultures and Organisations, Intercultural Cooperation and its Importance for Survival*. Harper-Collins, London.

Hollingshead, T. and Novick, D. G. (2007) Usability inspection methods after 15 years of research and practice. *SIGDOC 2007*, pp. 249–255.

Holmquist, L. E. (2005) Prototyping: Generating ideas or cargo cult designs? *interactions* March/April, 48–54.

Holtzblatt, K. (2001) *Contextual Design: Experience in Real Life*. Mensch & Computer.

Holtzblatt, K. and Jones, S. (1993) Contextual inquiry: A participatory technique for systems design. In D. Schuler and A. Namioka (eds) *Participatory Design: Principles and practice*. Lawrence Earlbaum Associates, Hillsdale, NJ, pp. 177–210.

Holtzblatt, K., Wendell, J. B. and Wood, S. (2004) *Rapid Contextual Design: A how-to guide to key techniques for user-centered design*. Morgan Kauffman.

Holtzblatt, K., Koskinen, I., Kumar, J., Rondeau, D. and Zimmerman, J. (2014) Design methods for the future that is now: have disruptive technologies disrupted our design methodologies? In *Proc. of CHI 2014 Extended Abstracts*, ACM, 1063–1068.

Höök, K. (2008) Knowing, communicating, and experiencing through body and emotion, *IEEE Transactions on Learning Technologies* **1**(4), pp. 248–259.

Hornecker, E. (2005) A design theme for tangible interaction: Embodied facilitation. In *Proceedings of the 9th European Conference on Computer Supported Cooperative Work*, *ECSCW '05*, 18–22 September, Paris. Kluwer/Springer, pp. 23–43.

Hornsby, P. (2010) Hierarchical Task Analysis, UX matters website: www.uxmatters.com/mt/archives/2010/02/hierarchical-task-analysis.php (accessed December 16, 2010).

Horton, S. (2005) *Access by Design: A guide to universal usability for web designers*. New Riders Press, Indianapolis, IN.

Howells, L. (2011). *A guide to heuristic website reviews* http://www.smashingmagazine.com/2011/12/16/a-guide-to-heuristic-website-reviews/ (accessed August, 2014).

Huff, D. (1991) *How to Lie with Statistics*. Penguin.

Hurtienne, J. (2009) Cognition in HCI: An ongoing story, *Human Technology* **5**(1), 12–28.

Hutchings, D. (2012) An Investigation of Fitts' Law in a multiple-display environment. *ACM Proceedings CHI'12*.

Hutchings, D., Smith, G., Meyers, B., Czerwinski, M. and Robertson, G. (2004) Display space usage and window management operation comparisons between single monitor and multiple monitor users. In *Proceedings of the Working Conference on Advanced Visual Interfaces*, *AVI 2004*, pp. 32–39.

Hutchins, E. (1995) *Cognition in the Wild*. MIT Press, Cambridge, MA.

Hutchins, E., Holan, J. D. and Norman, D. (1986) Direct manipulation interfaces. In D. Norman and S. W. Draper (eds) *User Centered System Design*. Lawrence Earlbaum Associates, Hillsdale, NJ, pp. 87–124.

Isaacs, E., Konrad, A., Walendowski, A., Lennig, T., Hollis, V. and Whittaker, S. (2013) Echoes from the past: how technology mediated reflection improves well-being. In *Proceedings of CHI '13*, ACM, 1071–1080.

Isensee, S., Kalinoski, K. and Vochatzer, K. (2000) Designing Internet appliances at Netpliance. In E. Bergman (ed.) *Information Appliances and Beyond*. Morgan Kaufmann, San Francisco.

Ishii, H., Kobayashi, M. and Grudin, J. (1993) Integration of interpersonal space and shared work-space: clearboard design and experiments. *ACM Transactions on Information Systems* **11**(4), 349–375.

Ishii, H. and Ullmer, B. (1997) Tangible bits: Towards seamless interfaces between people, bits and atoms. In *Proceedings CHI 1997*. ACM Press, New York, pp. 234–241.

Izadi, S., Brignull, H., Rodden, T., Rogers, Y. and Underwood, M. (2003) Dynamo: A public interactive surface supporting the cooperative sharing and exchange of media. In *Proceedings of UIST 2003*, *Symposium on User Interface Software and Technology*, November 2–5, Vancouver. ACM Press, New York, pp. 159–168.

Jacko, J. (ed.) (2012) *The Human–Computer Interaction Handbook: Fundamentals, evolving technologies and emerging applications* (3rd edn). CRC Press.

Jacko, J. and Sears, A. (eds) (2007) *The Human–Computer Interaction Handbook: Fundamentals, evolving technologies and emerging applications* (2nd edn). Lawrence Earlbaum Associates.

Jacob, R. J. K. (1996) A visual language for non-WIMP user interfaces. In *Proceedings IEEE Symposium on Visual Languages*. IEEE Computer Society Press, pp. 231–238.

Jacobson, I., Christerson, M., Jonsson, P. and Overgaard, G. (1992) *Object-Oriented Software Engineering—A use case driven approach*. Addison-Wesley, Harlow, Essex.

Jambon, F. and Meillon, B. (2009) User experience in the wild. In *Proceedings of CHI 2009*. ACM, New York, pp. 4069–4074.

Johnson, J. (2007) *GUI Bloopers. 2.0: Common user interface design don'ts and dos* (2nd edn). Morgan Kaufmann.

Johnson, J. (2014) *Designing with the Mind in Mind: Simple Guide to Understanding User Interface Design Rules*. Morgan Kaufmann.

Johnson, J. and Henderson, A. (2002) Conceptual models: Begin by designing what to design, *interactions* January/February, 25–32.

Johnson, J. and Henderson, A. (2012) *Conceptual Models: Core to Good Design*. Morgan and Claypool Publishers.

Johnson, R., Van der Linden, J. and Rogers, Y. (2010). To buzz or not to buzz: Improving awareness of posture through vibrotactile feedback. In *Whole Body Interaction Workshop, CHI 2010*. ACM.

Johnson-Laird, P. N. (1983) *Mental Models*. Cambridge University Press, Cambridge.

Jones, L. A. and Sarter, N. B. (2008) Tactile displays: Guidance for their design and application, *Human Factors: The Journal of the Human Factors and Ergonomics Society* 50, 90–111.

Jones, M. and Marsden G. (2006) *Mobile Interaction Design*. John Wiley & Sons Ltd, Chichester, UK.

Jones, Q., Grandhi, S. A., Whitakker, S., Chivakula, K. and Terveen, L. (2004) Putting systems into place: A qualitative study of design requirements for location-aware community systems. In *Proceedings of CSCW 2004*, Chicago, IL, pp. 202–211.

Jordà, S., Kaltenbrunner, M., Geiger, G. and Bencina, R. (2005) The Reactable. In *Proceedings of the International Computer Music Conference, ICM 2005*.

Jordan, P. W. (2000) *Designing Pleasurable Products*. Taylor & Francis/Morgan Kaufmann, San Francisco.

Jouppi, N. P. (2002) First steps towards mutually-immersive mobile telepresence. In *Proceedings of the 2002 ACM Conference on Computer Supported Cooperative Work, CSCW '02*. ACM Press, New York, pp. 354–363.

Jouppi, N. P., Iyer, S., Thomas, S., and Slayden, A. (2004) BiReality: Mutually-immersive telepresence. In *Proceedings of MULTIMEDIA '04*. ACM, New York, pp. 860–867.

Jupp, V. (ed.) (2006) *The Sage Dictionary of Social Research Methods*. Sage.

Kahn, R. and Cannell, C. (1957) *The Dynamics of Interviewing*. John Wiley & Sons Inc., New York.

Kahneman, D. (2011) *Thinking, fast and slow*. Penguin.

Kalawsky, R. S. (1993) *The Science of Virtual Reality and Virtual Environments*. Addison-Wesley, New York.

Kangas, E. and Kinnunen, T. (2005) Applying user-centred design to mobile application development, *Communications of the ACM* 48(7), 55–59.

Karapanos, E., Martensi, J.-B. and Hassenzahl, M. (2009) Accounting for diversity in subjective judgments. In *Proceedings of CHI 2009*. ACM, New York, pp. 639–648.

Karat, C.-M. (1994) A comparison of user interface evaluation methods. In J. Nielsen and R. L. Mack (eds) *Usability Inspection Methods*. John Wiley & Sons Inc., New York.

Kärkkäinen, T., Vaittinin, T. and Väänänen-Vainio-Mattila, K. (2010) I don't mind being logged, but want to remain in control: A field study of mobile activity and context logging. In *CHI 2010, Privacy Awareness and Attitudes*, ACM, pp. 163–172.

Keil, M. and Carmel, E. (1995) Customer–developer links in software development, *Communications of the ACM* 38(5), 33–44.

Kelley, T. with Littman, J. (2004) *The Art of Innovation*. Profile Books, Croydon, Surrey.

Kelley, T. with Littman, J. (2008) *The Ten Faces of Innovation*. Profile Books, Croydon, Surrey.

Kempton, W. (1986) Two theories of home heat control, *Cognitive Science* 10, 75–90.

Khoo, M., Pagano, J., Washington, A. L., Recker, M., Palmer, B. and Donahue, R. A. (2008) Using web metrics to analyze digital libraries. In *Proceedings of Joint Conference on Digital Libraries*, Pittsburgh, June 16–20.

Kim, S. (1990) Interdisciplinary cooperation. In B. Laurel (ed.) *The Art of Human–Computer Interface Design*. Addison-Wesley, Reading, MA.

Kirk, D. S., Rodden, T. and Stanton-Fraser, D. (2007) Turn it this way: Grounding collaborative action with remote gestures. In *Proceedings of CHI 2007*. ACM, New York, pp. 1039–1048.

Kirkham, R., Mellor, S., Green, D., Lin, J-S., Ladha, K., Ladha, C., Jackson, D., Olivier, P., Wright, P. and Ploetz, T. (2013) The break-time barometer: an exploratory system for workplace break-time social awareness. In *Proc. of the 2013 ACM international joint conference on Pervasive and ubiquitous computing (UbiComp '13)*. ACM, 73–82.

Kirsh, D. (2010) Thinking with external representations, *AI & Soc.* Online version: downloaded from www.springerlink.com/content/5913082573146k68/ (retrieved May 1, 2010).

Kjeldskov, J. and Skov, M. (2014) Was it Worth the Hassle? Ten Years of Mobile HCI Research Discussions on Lab and Field Evaluations. In ACM *Proceedings of MobileHCI*. Toronto, Canada, September 23–26.

Klemmer, S. R., Hartmann, B. and Takayama, L. (2006) How bodies matter: Five themes for interaction design. In *Proceedings of the 6th Conference on Designing Interactive Systems, DIS 2006*. ACM, New York, pp. 140–149.

Klemmer, S. R., Newman, M. W., Farrell, R., Bilezikjian, M. and Landay, J. A. (2001) The designer's outpost: A tangible interface for collaborative website design. In *Symposium on User Interface Software and Technology*. ACM Press, New York, pp. 1–10.

Kollman, J., Sharp, H. and Blandford, A. (2009) The role of user experience practitioners on agile project. In *Proceedings of the 2009 Agile Conference*, IEEE Computer Society, Washington DC.

Kotonya, G. and Sommerville, I. (1998) *Requirements Engineering: Processes and techniques*. John Wiley & Sons Ltd, Chichester, UK.

Koyani, S. J., Bailey, R. W. and Nall, J. R. (2004) *Research-Based Web Design and Usability Heuristics*. General Services Administration, Washington, DC.

Kozinets, V. (2010) *Netnography*. Sage.

Kraut, R., Fish, R., Root, R. and Chalfonte, B. (1990) Informal communications in organizations: Form, function and technology. In S. Oskamp and S. Krug (eds) *Don't Make Me Think*. New Riders/Peachpit.

Krippendorff, K. (2013) *Content Analysis: An Introduction to Its Methodology* (3rd edn). Sage Publications.

Krug, S. (2014) *Don't Make Me Think, Revisited: A Common Sense Approach to Web Usability* (3rd edn). Pearson.

Kuhn, T. S. (1972/1962) *The Structure of Scientific Revolutions* (2nd edn). University of Chicago Press, Chicago.

Kujala, S. and Mäntylä, M. (2000) Is user involvement harmful or useful in the early stages of product development? In *CHI 2000 Extended Abstracts*. ACM Press, New York, pp. 285–286.

Kuutti, K. (1996) Activity theory as a potential framework for human–computer interaction. In B. A. Nardi (ed.) *Context and Consciousness*. MIT Press, Cambridge, MA, pp. 17–44.

Lakoff, G. and Johnson, M. (1980) *Metaphors We Live By*. University of Chicago Press, Chicago.

Lambourne, R., Feiz, K. and Rigot, B. (1997) Social trends and product opportunities: Philips' Vision of the Future Project. In *Proceedings of CHI '97*. ACM Press, New York, pp. 494–501.

Lansdale, M. and Edmonds, E. (1992) Using memory for events in the design of personal filing systems, *International Journal of Human–Computer Studies* **26**, 97–126.

Law, E. L., Roto, V., Hassenzahl, M., Vermeeren, A. P., and Kort, J. (2009) Understanding, scoping and defining user experience: a survey approach. In *Proceedings of the 27th International Conference on Human Factors in Computing Systems, CHI 2009*. ACM, New York, pp. 719–728.

Lazar, J. (ed.) (2007) *Universal Usability: Designing information systems for diverse user populations*. John Wiley & Sons Ltd, Chichester, UK.

Lazar, J., Feng, J. H. and Hochheiser, H. (2010a) *Research Methods in Human–Computer Interaction*. John Wiley & Sons Ltd, Chichester, UK.

Lazar, J., Green, D. Fuchs, T. Siempelkamp, A. and Wood, M. (2010b) *Evaluating a Large Government Website for Usability and Standards Compliance*, www.id-book.com.

Ledgard, H., Singer, A. and Whiteside, J. (1981) Directions in human factors for interactive systems. In G. Goos and J. Hartmanis (eds) *Lecture Notes in Computer Science*, 103. Springer-Verlag, Berlin.

Ledoux, J. E. (1998) *The Emotional Brain: The mysterious underpinnings of emotional life*. Simon & Schuster.

Leontiev, A. N. (1978) *Activity, Consciousness and Personality*. Prentice Hall, Englewood Cliffs, NJ.

Leontiev, A. N. (1981) *Problems of the Development of Mind*. Progress, Moscow.

Leontiev, A. N. (1989) The problem of activity in the history of Soviet psychology, *Soviet Psychology* **27**(1), 22–39.

Lidwell, W., Holden, K. and Butler, J. (2003) *Universal Principles of Design*. Rockport Publishers, Inc.

Lim, S. L., Quercia. D. and Finkelstein, A. (2010) StakeNet: Using social networks to analyze the stakeholders of large-scale software projects, In *Proceedings of ICSE 2010*, pp. 295–304.

Lim, Y.-K., Stolterman, E. and Tenenburg, J. (2008) The anatomy of prototypes: Prototypes as filters, prototypes as manifestations of design ideas, *ACM Transactions on Computer–Human Interaction* **15**(2).

Lim, Y-K., Pangam, A., Periyasami, S., and Aneja, S. (2006) Comparative Analysis of High- and Low-fidelity Prototypes for More Valid Usability Evaluations of Mobile Devices. In *Proc of NordiCHI '06*, 291–300.

Lin, J., Newman, M.W., Hong, J.I. and Landay, J.A. (2000) DENIM: finding a tighter fit between tools and practice for Website design. In *Proc. of CHI '00*, 510–517.

Liu, Y. and Räihä, K.-J. (2010) Predicting Chinese text entry speeds on mobile phones. In *Proceedings of CHI 2010: HCI in China*, April 10–15, Atlanta, GA, pp. 2183–2192.

Liu, Z., Coventry, L., White, R., Wu, H. and Johnson, G. (2005) Self-service technology in China: Exploring usability and consumer issues. In *Proceedings of HCI 2005*, Vol. 2, pp. 173–178.

Lopuck, L. (1996) *Designing Multimedia*. Peachpit Press, Berkeley, CA.

Lowgren, J. and Stolterman, E. (2004) *Thoughtful Interaction Design: A design perspective on information technology*. MIT Press, Cambridge, MA.

Luce, K. H., Winzelberg, A. J., Das, S., Osborn, M. I., Bryson, S. W. and Taylor, C. B. (2003) Reliability of self-report: paper versus online administration, *Computers in Human Behavior* (accessed online January 20, 2005).

Lund, A. M. (1994) Ameritech's usability laboratory: From prototype to final design, *Behaviour and Information Technology* **13**(1&2), 67–80.

Mackay, W. (1999) Media spaces: Environments for informal multimedia interaction. In C. Beaudouin-Lafon (ed.) *Computer Supported Cooperative Work*. John Wiley & Sons Inc., New York.

Mackay, W. E., Ratzer, A. V. and Janecek, P. (2000) Video artifacts for design: bridging the gap between abstraction and detail. In *Proceedings of DIS 2000*, pp. 72–82.

Mackenzie, I. S. (1992) Fitts' law as a research and design tool in human–computer interaction, *Human–Computer Interaction* **7**, 91–139.

Mackenzie, I. S. (1995). Movement time prediction in human-computer interfaces. In R. M. Baecker, W. A. S. Buxton, J. Grudin, & S. Greenberg (eds.), *Readings in Human-Computer Interaction* (2nd edn) (pp. 483–493). Los Altos, CA: Kaufmann.

Mackenzie, I. S. and Soukoreff, R. W. (2002) Text entry for mobile computing: Models and methods, theory and practice, *Human–Computer Interaction* **17**, 147–198.

MacKenzie, I. S. and Teather, R. J. (2012) Fitts Tilt: The Application of Fitts' Law to Tilt-based Interaction. *ACM Proceedings of NordiCHI'2012*.

Madrigal, D. and McClain, B. (2010) Do's and don'ts of usability testing. Downloaded from www.uxmatters.com/mt/archives/2010/03/dos-and-donts-of-usability-testing.php (retrieved May 1, 2010).

Maglio, P. P., Matlock, T., Raphaely, D., Chernicky, B. and Kirsh, D. (1999) Interactive skill in Scrabble. In *Proceedings of Twenty-first Annual Conference of the Cognitive Science Society*. Lawrence Earlbaum Associates, Mahwah, NJ.

Maher, M. L. and Pu, P. (1997) *Issues and Applications of Case-Based Reasoning in Design*. Lawrence Earlbaum Associates, Hillsdale, NJ.

Maher, M. L., Preece, J., Yeh, T., Boston, C., Grace, K., Pasupuleti, A. and Stangl, A. (2014) NatureNet: A model for crowdsourcing the design of citizen science systems. In *Proceedings of the Companion Publication of the 17th ACM Conference on Computer Supported Cooperative Work & Social Computing (CSCW Companion '14)* pp. 201–204. New York: ACM.

Maiden, N. A. M., Ncube, C. and Robertson, S. (2007a) Can requirements be creative? Experiences with an enhanced air space management system. In *Proceedings of ICSE '07*.

Maiden, N. A. M., Otojare, O., Seyff, N., Grünbacher, P., and Mitteregger. K. (2007b) Determining stakeholder needs in the workplace: How mobile technologies can help, *IEEE Software*, March/April, 46–52.

Mancini, C., Thomas, K., Rogers, Y., Price, B. A., Jedrzejczyk, L., Bandara, A. K., Joinson, A. N., and Nuseibeh, B. (2009) From spaces to places: Emerging contexts in mobile privacy, *UbiComp 2009*, September 30–October 3.

Mancini, C., Rogers, Y., Bandara, A. K., Coe, T., Jedrzejczyk, L., Joinson, A. N., Price, B. A., Thomas, K., and Nuseibeh, B. (2010) ContraVision: Exploring users' reactions to futuristic technology. In *Proceedings of CHI 2010*. ACM, New York, pp. 153–162.

Mandryk, R. and Inkpen, K. (2004) Physiological indicators for the evaluation of co-located collaborative play. In *CSCW 2004*. ACM Press, New York, pp. 102–111.

Mankoff, J., Dey, A. K., Hsich, G., Kientz, J. and Lederer, M. A. (2003) Heuristic evaluation of ambient devices. In *Proceedings of CHI 2003*. ACM Press, New York, pp. 169–176.

Mankoff, J., Fait, H. and Tran, T. (2005) Is your web page accessible? A comparative study of methods for assessing web page accessibility for the blind. In *Proceedings of CHI 2003*. ACM Press, New York, pp. 41–50.

Mankoff, J., Kravets, R. and Blevis, E. (2008) Some computer science issues in creating a sustainable world, *Computer* **41**(8), 102–105.

Mann, S. (1997) An historical account of the 'WearComp' and 'WearCam' inventions developed for applications in personal imaging. In *The First International Symposium on Wearable Computers: Digest of Papers*. IEEE Computer Society, pp. 66–73.

Manuel, D., Moore, D. and Charissis, V. (2012) An Investigation into Immersion in Games Through Motion Control and Stereo Audio Reproduction, September 26–28 *AM '12: Proceedings of the 7th Audio Mostly Conference: A Conference on Interaction with Sound* pp. 124–129.

Mao, J.-Y., Vredenburg, K., Smith, P. W. and Carey, T. (2005) The state of user-centered design practice, *Communications of the ACM* **48**(3), 105–109.

Marcus, A. and Gould, W. E. (2000) Crosscurrents: Cultural dimensions and global Web user-interface design, *interactions* **7**(4), 32–46.

Marquardt, N., Shum, V., Rogers, Y., Balestrini, M., Baker, H. and Davies, M. (2015) Rethinking Making: Engaging Young Children in Playful Maker Explorations with Electronics, Sensors and Lights (under review).

Marsden, G., Maunder, A. and Parker, M. (2008) People are people, but technology is not technology, *Philosophical Transactions of the Royal Society* **366**, 3795–3804.

Marshall, P., Price, S. and Rogers, Y. (2003) Conceptualizing tangibles to support learning. In *Proceedings of Interaction Design and Children, IDC 2003*. ACM Press, New York, p. 101–109.

Martin, A., Biddle, R. and Noble, J. (2009) XP Customer Practice: A grounded theory. In *Proceedings of the 2009 Agile Conference*, IEEE Computer Society, Washington DC.

McCarthy, J. and Wright, P. (2004) *Technology as Experience*. MIT Press, Cambridge, MA.

McCullough, M. (2004) *Digital Ground: Architecture, pervasive computing and environmental knowing*. MIT Press, Cambridge, MA.

McKnight, J. and Doherty, G. (2008) Distributed cognition and mobile healthcare work. In *People and Computers XXII: Culture Creativity Interaction, Proceedings of HCI 2008*, The 22nd British HCI Group Annual Conference.

Meschtscherjakov, A., Wilfinger, D., Gridling, N., Neureiter, K., and Tscheligi, M. (2011) Capture the Car! Qualitative In-situ Methods to Grasp the Automotive Context. In *Proceedings of AutomotiveUI 2011*, Nov. 30–Dec. 2, Salzburg, Austria, ACM.

Miller, G. (1956) The magical number seven, plus or minus two: Some limits on our capacity for processing information, *Psychological Review* **63**, 81–97.

Miller, L. (2006) Interaction Designers and Agile Development: A Partnership. *Proceedings of UPA 2006*. Denver/Broomfield: Usability Professionals' Association.

Miller, L. H. and Johnson, J. (1996) The Xerox Star: An influential user interface design. In M. Rudisill, C. Lewis, P. G. Polson and T. D. McKay (eds) *Human–Computer Interface Design*. Morgan Kaufmann, San Francisco.

Miyake, N. (1986) Constructive interaction and the iterative process of understanding. *Cognitive Science* 10(2) pp. 151–177.

Molin, L. (2004) Wizard-of-Oz prototyping for cooperative interaction design of graphical user interfaces. In *Proceedings of NordiCHI 2004*, October 23–27, Tampere, Finland, pp. 425–428.

Morikawa, O. and Maesako, T. (1998) HyperMirror: Towards pleasant-to-use video mediated communication system. In *Proceedings of CSCW '98*, pp. 149–158.

Morville, P. (2005) *Ambient Findability*. O'Reilly Media Inc.

Müller-Tomfelde, C. (ed.) (2010) *Tabletops: Horizontal Interactive Displays*. Springer.

Mullet, K. and Sano, D. (1995) *Designing Visual Interfaces*. Prentice Hall, Mountain View, CA.

Myers, B. (1988) Window interfaces: a taxonomy of window manager user interfaces. *IEEE Computer Graphics and Applications* 8(5), 65–84.

Nardi, B. A. (ed.) (1996) *Context and Consciousness*. MIT Press, Cambridge, MA.

Nardi, B. and Kaptelinin, V. (2012) *Activity Theory in HCI: Fundamentals and Reflections*. Morgan & Claypool.

Ncube, C., Oberndorf, P. and Kark, A. W. (2008) Opportunistic software development: Making systems from what's available, *IEEE Software* 25(6), 38–41.

Neil, T. (2014) *Mobile Design Pattern Gallery* (2nd edn). O'Reilly.

Nevo, D. and Wade, M. R. (2007) How to avoid disappointment by design, *Communications of the ACM* 50(4), 43–48.

Newell, A. (2003) Design for all: An inclusive approach to digital TV, *Consumer Policy Review* 13(1), 2–6.

Nielsen, J. (1992) Finding usability problems through heuristic evaluation. In *Proceedings of CHI '92*. ACM, New York, pp. 373–800.

Nielsen, J. (1993) *Usability Engineering*. Morgan Kaufmann, San Francisco.

Nielsen, J. (1994a) Heuristic evaluation. In J. Nielsen and R. L. Mack (eds) *Usability Inspection Methods*. John Wiley & Sons Inc., New York.

Nielsen, J. (1994b) Enhancing the explanatory power of usability heuristics. In *Proceedings of CHI '94*. ACM, New York, pp. 152–158.

Nielsen, J. (2000) *Designing Web Usability*. New Riders Press, Indianapolis, IN.

Nielsen, J. (2010) Ten Usability Heuristics, www.useit.com/papers/heuristic/heuristic_list.html (accessed September 2010).

Nielsen (2014) www.useit.com.

Nielsen, J. and Loranger, H. (2006) *Prioritizing Web Usability*. New Riders Press.

Nielsen, J. and Mack, R.L. (eds) (1994) *Usability Inspection Methods*. John Wiley & Sons Inc., New York.

Nielsen, J. and Mohlich, R. (1990) Heuristic evaluation of user interfaces. In *Proceedings of CHI '90*. ACM, New York.

Nielsen, J. and Norman, D. (2014) The Definition of User Experience, www.nngroup.com/articles/definition-user-experience/ (accessed July 2, 2014).

Nielsen, J. and Tahir, M. (2002) Homepage Usability: 50 websites deconstructed. New Riders Press.

Nielsen Norman Group (2014) Agile Development that Incorporates User Experience Practices, Nielsen Norman Group, www.nngroup.com/reports/agile (accessed November 6, 2014).

Nodder, C., Williams, G. and Dubrow, D. (1999) Evaluating the usability of an evolving collaborative product—changes in user type, tasks and evaluation methods over time. In *Proceedings of GROUP '99*, pp. 150–159.

Norman, D. (1983) Some observations on mental models. In D. Gentner and A. L. Stevens (eds) *Mental Models*. Lawrence Earlbaum Associates, Hillsdale, NJ.

Norman, D. (1986) Cognitive engineering. In D. Norman and S. W. Draper (eds) *User Centered System Design*. Lawrence Earlbaum Associates, Hillsdale, NJ, pp. 31–62.

Norman, D. (1988) *The Design of Everyday Things*. Basic Books, New York.

Norman, D. (1990) Four (more) issues for cognitive science, *Cognitive Science Technical Report No. 9001*, Department of Cognitive Science, UCSD, USA.

Norman, D. (1993) *Things That Make Us Smart*. Addison-Wesley, Reading, MA.

Norman, D. (1999) Affordances, conventions and design, *ACM Interactions Magazine*, May/June, 38–42.

Norman, D. (2004) Beauty, Goodness, and Usability/Change Blindness. *Human–Computer Interaction*, **19**(4), 311–318.

Norman, D. (2005) *Emotional Design: Why we love (or hate) everyday things*. Basic Books, New York.

Norman, D. (2006) Why doing user observations first is wrong, *interactions*, July/Aug, 50.

Norman, D. (2010) Natural interfaces are not natural, *interactions*, May/June, 6–10.

Norman, D. (2013) *The Design of Everyday Things*. The MIT Press, Cambridge, Massachusetts.

Norton, J., Wingrave, C. A., LaViola Jr., J. J. (2010) Exploring strategies and guidelines for developing full body video game interfaces. In *Proceedings of FDG (Foundations of Digital Games) 2010*, pp. 155–162.

Norton, M. I., Di Micco, J. M., Caneel, R. and Ariely, D. (2004) AntiGroupWare and Second Messenger, *BT Technology Journal* **22**(4), 83–88.

Nudelman, G. (2013) *Android Design Patterns*. John Wiley.

Nygaard, K. (1990) The origins of the Scandinavian school, why and how? *Participatory Design Conference 1990 Transcript*. Computer Professionals for Social Responsibility.

O'Connaill, B., Whittaker, S. and Wilbur, S. (1993) Conversations over video conferences: An evaluation of the spoken aspects of video-mediated communication, *Human–Computer Interaction* **8**, 389–428.

O'Hara, K., Glancy, M. and Robertshaw, S. (2008) Understanding collective play in an urban screen game. In *Proceedings of the 2008 ACM Conference on Computer Supported Cooperative Work, CSCW 2008*. ACM, New York, pp. 67–76.

O'Hara, K., Perry, M., Churchill, E. and Russell, D. (eds) (2003) *Public and Situated Displays*. Kluwer Publishers, Dordrecht.

O'Hara, K., Gonzalez, G., Sellen, A., Penney, G., Varnavas, A. Mentis, H., Criminisi, A., Corish, R., Rouncefield, M., Dastur, N. and Carrell, T. (2013) Touchless Interaction in Surgery, *Communications of the ACM*, **57**(1)70–77.

Obama for America uses Google Analytics to democratize rapid, data-driven decision making [PDF document]. Retrieved from http://static.googleusercontent.com/media/www.google.com/en/us/analytics/customers/pdfs/obama-2012.pdf.

Olson, J. S. and Kellogg, W. A. (eds) (2014) *Ways of Knowing in HCI*. Springer.

Olson, J. S. and Moran, T. P. (1996) Mapping the method muddle: Guidance in using methods for user interface design. In M. Rudisill, C. Lewis, P. B. Polson and T. D. McKay (eds) *Human–Computer Interface Design: Success stories, emerging methods, real-world context*. Morgan Kaufmann, San Francisco, pp. 269–300.

Oostveen, A.-M. and van den Besselaar, P. (2004) From small scale to large scale user participation: A case study of participatory design in e-government systems. In *Proceedings of the Participatory Design Conference 2004*, Toronto, Canada, pp. 173–182.

Ophir, E., Nass, C. I. and Wagner, A. D. (2009) Cognitive control in media multitaskers, *Proc Natl Acad Sci USA* 106:15583–15587.

Oppenheim, A.N. (1998) *Questionnaire Design, Interviewing and Attitude Measurement*. Pinter Publishers.

Ortony, A., Norman, D. A. and Revelle, W. (2005) Affect and proto-affect in effective functioning. In J. M. Fellous and M. A. Arbib (eds) *Who Needs Emotions? The brain meets the machine*. New York: Oxford University Press, pp. 173–202.

Oshlyansky, L. (2007) Cultural Models in HCI: Hofstede, Affordance and Technology Acceptance, PhD dissertation, Swansea University.

Oviatt, S. (2002) Multimodal interfaces. In J. Jacko and A. Sears (eds) *Handbook of Human–Computer Interaction*. Lawrence Earlbaum Associates, New Jersey.

Oviatt, S., Cohen, A. and Weibel, N. (2013) Multimodal learning analytics: Description of Math Data Corpus of ICMI Grand Challenge Workshop. *ICMI '13: Proceedings of the 15th ACM International Conference on Multimodal Interaction*.

Oyserman, D., Coon, H. M. and Kemmelmeier, M. (2002) Rethinking individualism and collectivism: Evaluation of theoretical assumptions and meta-analyses, *Psychological Bulletin* **128**, 3–72.

Palen, L. and Salzman, M. (2002) Voice-mail diary study for naturalistic data capture under conditions. *ACM Proceedings of CSCW'02 Conference*.

Park, S.J., MacDonald, C.M. and Khoo, M. (2012) Do you care if a computer says sorry?: user experience design through affective messages. In *Proceedings of DIS'12*. ACM, 731–740.

Peatt. K. (2014) Off The Beaten Canvas: Exploring The Potential Of The Off-Canvas Pattern downloaded from http://www.smashingmagazine.com/2014/02/24/off-the-beaten-canvas-exploring-the-potential-of-the-off-canvas-pattern/ Sept 2014.

Petersen, M. J., Madsen, K. H. and Kjaer, A. (2002) The usability of everyday technology: Emerging and fading opportunities, *Transactions on Computer–Human Interaction (TOCHI)* **9**(2), 74–105.

Petrie, H., Schlieder, C., Blenkhorn, P., Evans, G., King, A., O'Neill, A.-M., Ioannidis, G. T., Gallagher, B., Crombie, D., Mager, R. and Alafaci, M. (2002) TeDUB: A system for presenting and exploring technical drawings for blind people. In K. Miesenberger, J. Klaus and W. Zagler (eds) *Lecture Notes in Computer Science 239: Computers Helping People with Special Needs*. Springer-Verlag, Berlin.

Pew Research (2014) www.pewresearch.org/fact-tank/2014/02/03/6-new-facts-about-facebook/

Picard, R. W. (1998) *Affective Computing*. MIT Press, Cambridge, MA.

Pinelle, D., Wong, N. and Stach, T. (2008) Heuristic evaluation for games: Usability principles for video games. In *Proceedings of SIGCHI 2008*, Florence, Italy, pp. 1453–1462.

Pinelle, D., Wong, N., Stach, T. and Gutwin, C. (2009) Usability heuristics for networked multiplayer games. *ACM Proceedings of GROUP'09*.

Poulter, N. (2013) 6 Google Analytics Custom Dashboards To Save You Time NOW! Retrieved from http://www.stateofdigital.com/google-analytics-dashboards/.

Preece, J. and Shneiderman, B. (2009) The Reader to Leader Framework: Motivating technology-mediated social participation, *AIS Transactions on Human–Computer Interaction* **1**(1), 13–32.

Pruit, J. and Adlin, T. (2006) *The Persona Lifecycle: Keeping people in mind throughout product design*. Morgan Kaufmann.

Quesenbery, W. (2009) Usable Accessibility: Making web sites work well for people with disabilities. Downloaded from www.uxmatters.com/mt/archives/2009/02/usable-accessibility-making-web-sites-work-well-for-people-with-disabilities.php (retrieved May 1, 2010).

Rajkomar, A. and Blandford, A. (2012) Understanding infusion administration in the ICU through Distributed Cognition. *Journal of Biomedical Informatics*, **45**(3), 580–590.

Rampoldi-Hnilo, L. and English, J. (2004) Remote Contextual Inquiry: A technique to improve enterprise software: available from www.boxesandarrows.com (accessed December 16, 2010).

Raskin, J. (2000) *The Humane Interface*. Addison-Wesley, Harlow, Essex.

Ratcliffe, L. and M. McNeill (2012) *Agile Experience Design*. New Riders.

Rau, P.P., Plocher, T. and Choong, Y. (2013) *Cross-Cultural Design for IT Products and Services*. CRC Press.

Raymond, E. S. (2001) *The Cathedral & the Bazaar*. O'Reilly.

The Reactable Experience (2010) Downloaded from www.reactable.com/products/reactable_experience/ (retrieved June 26, 2010).

Read, J. C. (2005) The usability of digital ink technologies for children and teenagers. In *Proceedings of HCI 2005*. Springer-Verlag, pp. 19–35.

Read, J., Macfarlane, S. and Casey, C. (2002) Endurability, engagement and expectations: Measuring children's fun. In *Proceedings of Interaction Design and Children 2002*, Eindhoven, Amsterdam. ACM, pp. 189–198.

Redish, G. (2012) *Letting Go of the Words: Writing Web Content that Works* (2nd edn). Morgan Kaufmann.

Reeves, B. and Nass, C. (1996) *The Media Equation: How people treat computers, television, and new media like real people and places*. Cambridge University Press, Cambridge.

Reeves, L., Lai, J. C., Larson, J. A., Oviatt, S. L., Balaji, T. S., Buisine, S., Collings, P., Cohen, P. R., Kraal, B., Martin, J.-C., McTear, M. F., Raman, T. V., Stanney, K. M., Su, H. and Wang, Q. Y. (2004) Guidelines for multimodal user interface design, *Communications of the ACM* **47**(1), 57–59.

Reitmayr, G., Eade, E. and Drummond, T. (2005) Localisation and interaction for augmented maps. In *Proceedings IEEE ISMAR '05*, October 5–8, Vienna, Austria.

Richards M. and Woodthorpe J. (2009) Introducing TU100 "My Digital Life": Ubiquitous computing in a distance learning environment. In *Proceedings of UbiComp 2009*, Walt Disney Beach Club Resort, Orlando, Florida.

Ries, E. (2011) *The Lean Startup: How Constant Innovation Creates Radically Successful Businesses*. Portfolio Penguin.

Robertson, S. and Robertson, J. (2013) *Mastering the Requirements Process* (3rd edn). Pearson Education, New Jersey.

Robertson, T. (1997) Cooperative work and lived cognition: A taxonomy of embodied actions. In *Proceedings of the Fifth Conference on European Conference on Computer-Supported Cooperative Work*. Kluwer Academic Publishers, Norwell, MA, pp. 205–220.

Robson, C. (1994) *Experimental Design and Statistics in Psychology*. Penguin Psychology.

Robson, C. (2011) *Real World Research*. John Wiley & Sons.

Robinson, S., Marsden, G. and Jones, M. (2015) *There's Not An App For That: Mobile User Experience Design For Life*. Elsevier.

Rogers, Y. (1989) Icons at the interface: Their usefulness, *Interacting with Computers* 1(1), 105–117.

Rogers, Y. (1993) Coordinating computer-mediated work. *Computer-Supported Cooperative Work* 1, 295–315.

Rogers, Y. (1994) Exploring obstacles: integrating CSCW in evolving organisations. In *CSCW'94 Proceedings*. ACM Press, New York, pp. 67–78.

Rogers, Y. (2006) Moving on from Weiser's vision of calm computing: Engaging UbiComp experiences. In *Proceedings of UbiComp 2006*, LNCS 4206, Springer-Verlag, Berlin, Heidelberg, pp. 404–421.

Rogers, Y. (2011) Interaction design gone wild: striving for wild theory. *interactions*, 18(4): 58–62.

Rogers, Y. (2012) *HCI Theory: Classical, Modern, and Contemporary*. Morgan and Claypool Publishers.

Rogers, Y. and Aldrich, F. (1996) In search of clickable Dons: Learning about HCI through interacting with Norman's CD-ROM, *SIGCHI Bulletin* 28(3).

Rogers, Y., Connelly, K., Tedesco, L., Hazlewood, W., Kurtz, A., Hall, B., Hursey, J. and Toscos, T. (2007) Why it's worth the hassle: The value of in-situ studies when designing UbiComp. In J. Krumm *et al* (eds) *Proceedings of UbiComp 2007*, LNCS 4717. Springer-Verlag, Berlin, Heidelberg, pp. 336–353.

Rogers, Y., Hazlewood, W., Marshall, P., Dalton, N. S. and Hertrich, S. (2010) Ambient influence: Can twinkly lights lure and abstract representations trigger behavioral change? In *Proceedings of Ubicomp 2010*, pp. 261–270.

Rogers, Y., Lim, Y. and Hazlewood, W. (2006) Extending tabletops to support flexible collaborative interactions. In *Proceedings of Tabletop 2006*, Adelaide, Australia, January 5–7. IEEE, pp. 71–78.

Rogers, Y., Lim, Y. Hazlewood, W. and Marshall, P. (2009) Equal opportunities: Do shareable interfaces promote more group participation than single users displays? *Human–Computer Interaction* 24(2), 79–116.

Rogers, Y. and Lindley, S. (2004) Collaborating around vertical and horizontal displays: which way is best? *Interacting With Computers* 16, N33–N52.

Rogers, Y., Payne, S. and Todd, P. (2010) Projecting instant information in situ: can it help us make more informed decisions? In *Ubiprojection 2010: Workshop Proceedings, Pervasive 2010*.

Rogers, Y. and Marsden, G. (2013) Does He Take Sugar? Moving Beyond the Rhetoric of Compassion. *interactions* XX.4 July + August 2013.

Rogers, Y., Paay, J., Brereton, M., Vaisutis, K., Marsden, G. and Vetere, F. (2014) Never Too Old: Engaging Retired People Inventing the Future with MaKey MaKey. In *Proc. CHI 2014*, ACM, 2675–2684.

Rogers, Y., Price, S., Randell, C., Fraser, D.S., Weal, M. and Fitzpatrick, G. (2005) Ubi-learning integrates indoor and outdoor experiences, *CACM* 48(1), 55–59.

Rogers, Y. and Scaife, M. (1998) How can interactive multimedia facilitate learning? In J. Lee (ed.) *Intelligence and Multimodality in Multimedia Interfaces: Research and Applications*. AAAI Press, Menlo Park, CA.

Rogers, Y., Scaife, M., Aldrich, F. and Price, S. (2003) Improving children's understanding of formalisms through interacting with multimedia, *CSRP Technical Report*, No. 559, School of Informatics, University of Sussex, UK.

Rogers, Y., Yuill, N. and Marshall, P. (2013) Contrasting lab-based and in-the-wild studies for evaluating multi-user technologies. In Price, S., Jewitt, C. and Brown, B. (eds.) *SAGE Handbook of Technology Research*. 359–173.

Rønby-Pedersen, E., McCall, K., Moran, T. P. and Halasz, F. G. (1993) Tivoli: An electronic whiteboard for informal workgroup meetings. In *Proceedings of CHI '93*. ACM Press, New York, pp. 391–398.

Rooksby, J., Rost, M., Morrison, A. and Chalmers, M. (2014) Personal tracking as lived informatics. In *Proceedings of CHI'14*, ACM, 1163–1172.

Rosson, M. B. and Carroll, J. M. (2002) *Usability Engineering: Scenario-based development of human–computer interaction*. Morgan Kaufmann, San Francisco.

Roth, I. (1986) An introduction to object perception. In I. Roth and J. B. Frisby (eds) *Perception and Representation: A cognitive approach*. The Open University Press, Milton Keynes, UK.

Rotman, D., Hammock, J., Preece, J., Boston, C. L., Hansen, D. L., Bowser, A. and He, Y. (2014). Does motivation in citizen science change with time and culture? In *Proceedings of the companion publication of the 17th ACM conference on Computer supported cooperative work & social computing* (CSCW Companion '14). ACM, New York, NY, USA, 229–232.

Rotman, D., He, Y., Preece, J. and Druin, A. (2013) Understanding Large Scale Online Environments with Qualitative Methods. *iConference*, February 2012, Texas.

Rotman, D., Preece, J., He, Y. and Druin, A. (2012) Extreme Ethnography: Challenges for Research in Large Scale Online Environments *iConference*, February 7–10, 2012, Toronto, Ontario, Canada.

Ryall, K., Forlines, C., Shen, C. and Ringel-Morris, M. (2004) Exploring the effects of group size and table size on interactions with tabletop shared-display groupware. In *Proceedings of Conference on Computer Supported Cooperative Work (CSCW)*. ACM Press, New York.

Sacks, H., Schegloff, E. and Jefferson, G. (1978) A simplest systematics for the organization of turn-taking for conversation, *Language* 50, 696–735.

Saffer, D. (2010) *Designing for Interaction: Creating smart applications and clever devices* (2nd edn). New Riders Press, Indianapolis, IN.

Sagawa, H., Takeuchi, M. and Ohki, M. (1997) Description and recognition methods for sign language based on gesture components. In *Proceedings of the 2nd International Conference on Intelligent User Interfaces*. ACM Press, New York, pp. 97–104.

Saguna, A., Z. and Chakraborty, D. (2013) Complex Activity Recognition using Context-Driven Activity Theory and Activity Signatures. *ACM Transactions on Computer-Human Interaction* 20(6), Article 32.

Sarker, S. and Sahay, S. (2003) Understanding virtual team development: an interpretive study, *Journal of the Association for Information Systems* 4, 1–38.

Sarker, S., Lau, F. and Sahay, S. (2001) Using an adapted grounded theory approach for inductive theory building about virtual team development, *The Data Base for Advances in Information Systems* 32(1), 38–56.

Sas, C. and Whittaker, S. (2013) Design for forgetting: disposing of digital possessions after a breakup. In *Proceedings of CHI '13*. ACM, pp.1823–1832.

Sauer, J. and Sonderegger, A. (2009) 'The influence of prototype fidelity and aesthetics of design in usability tests: Effects on user behaviour, subjective evaluation and emotion', *Applied Ergonomics*, **40**(4), 670–677.

Sawano, H. and Okada, M. (2005) A car-navigation system based on augmented reality, *SIGGRAPH 2005 Sketches*, article number 115.

Scaife, M. and Rogers, Y. (1996) External cognition: How do graphical representations work? *International Journal of Human–Computer Studies* **45**, 185–213.

Scaife, M., Rogers, Y., Aldrich, F. and Davies, M. (1997) Designing for or designing with? Informant design for interactive learning environments. In *Proceedings of CHI '97*, pp. 343–350.

Scapin, D. L. (1981) Computer commands in restricted natural language: Some aspects of memory of experience, *Human Factors* **23**, 365–375.

Schaffer, E. (2009) Beyond Usability: Designing web sites for persuasion, emotion and trust. Downloaded from www.uxmatters.com/mt/archives/2009/01/beyond-usability-designing-web-sites-for-persuasion-emotion-and-trust.php (retrieved May 1, 2010).

Schank, R. C. (1982) *Dynamic Memory: A theory of learning in computers and people*. Cambridge University Press, Cambridge.

Schegloff, E. (1981) Discourse as an interactional achievement: Some uses of 'uh-huh' and other things that come between sentences. In D. Tannen (ed.) *Analyzing Discourse: Text and talk*. University Press, Georgetown.

Schegloff, E. A. and Sacks, H. (1973) Opening up closings, *Semiotica* **7**, 289–327.

Schilit, B., Adams, N., Gold, R., Tso, M. and Want, R. (1993) The PARCTAB mobile computing system. In *Proceedings of Fourth Workshop on Workstation Operating Systems, WWOS-IV*. IEEE, pp. 34–39.

Schön, D. (1983) *The Reflective Practitioner: How professionals think in action*. Basic Books, New York.

Schuler, R. P., Grandhi, S. A., Mayer, J. M., Ricken, S. T. and Jones, Q. (2014) The doing of doing stuff: understanding the coordination of social group-activities. In *Proc. CHI '14*, ACM, 119–128.

Schultz, P. W., Nolan, J. M., Cialdini, R. B., Goldstein, N.J. and Griskevicius, V. (2007) The constructive, destructive, and reconstructive power of social norms, *Psychological Science* **18**(5), 429–434.

Schwaber, K. and Beedle, M. (2002) *Agile Software Development with Scrum*. Prentice Hall, Englewood Cliffs, NJ.

Scott, S. D., Grant, K. D. and Mandryk, R. L. (2003) System guidelines for co-located, collaborative work on a tabletop display. In *Proceedings of European Conference Computer-Supported Cooperative Work, ECSCW 2003*, September, Helsinki, Finland, pp. 159–178.

Seffah, A., Gulliksen, J. and Desmarais, M. C. (2005) *Human-Centered Software Engineering*. Springer.

Segura, V.C.B., Barbosa, S.D.J. and Simões, F.P. (2012) UISKEI: A Sketch-based Prototyping Tool for Defining and Evaluating User Interface Behavior. In *Proc. of the International Working Conference on Advanced Visual Interfaces*, 18–25.

Sellen, A., Buxton, W. and Arnott, J. (1992) Using spatial cues to improve videoconferencing. In *Proceedings of CHI '92*, pp. 651–652.

Shaer, O. and Hornecker, E. (2010) Tangible user interfaces: Past, present and future directions, *Foundations and Trends in HCI (FnT in HCI)* **3**(1–2), 1–138.

Shaer, O., Strait, M., Valdes, C., Wang, H., Feng, T., Lintz, M., Ferreirae, M., Grote, C., Tempel, K. and Liu, S. (2012) The design, development, and deployment of a tabletop interface for collaborative exploration of genomic data, *International Journal of Human-Computer Interaction* **70**, 746–764.

Sharp, H., Biddle, R., Gray, P. G., Miller, L. and Patton, J. (2006) Agile development: opportunity or fad? Addendum to *Proceedings of CHI 2006*, Montreal.

Sharp, H., Galal, G. H., Finkelstein, A. (1999) Stakeholder identification in the requirements engineering process. In: *Proc. of the Database & Expert System Applications Workshop (DEXA)*, pp. 387–391.

Sharp, H., Hovenden, F. and Woodman, M. (2005) Using metaphor to analyse qualitative data: Vulcans and Humans in software development. *Empirical Software Engineering* **10**(3), 343–365.

Sharp, H. and Robinson, H. (2008) Collaboration and co-ordination in mature eXtreme programming teams, *International Journal of Human–Computer Studies* **66**, 506–518.

Shen, C., Everitt, K. and Ryall, K. (2003) UbiTable: Impromptu face-to-face collaboration on horizontal interactive surfaces. In *Proceedings of Ubicomp 2003*, pp. 281–288.

Shen, C., Lesh, N. B., Vernier, F., Forlines, C. and Frost, J. (2002) Building and sharing digital group histories. In *Proceedings CSCW 2002*. ACM, New York, pp. 324–333.

Shneiderman, B. (1983) Direct manipulation: A step beyond programming languages, *IEEE Computer* **16**(8), 57–69.

Shneiderman, B. (1992) Tree visualization with tree-maps: 2-d space-filling approach. *ACM Trans. Graph.* **11**(1), 92–99.

Shneiderman, B. (1998) *Designing the User Interface: Strategies for effective human–computer interaction* (3rd edn). Addison-Wesley, Reading, MA.

Shneiderman, B. and Plaisant, C. (2006) Strategies for evaluating information visualization tools: Multidimensional in-depth long-term case studies. In *Proceedings Beyond Time and Errors: Novel evaluation methods for information visualization. Workshop of the Advanced Visual Interfaces Conference.*

Shneiderman, B. and Plaisant, C. (2010) *Designing the User Interface: Strategies for effective human–computer interaction*, (5th edn). Addison-Wesley.

Sidner, C. and Lee, C. (2005) Robots as laboratory hosts, *interactions* **12**, 24–26.

Siek, K. A., Rogers, Y. and Connelly, K. H. (2005) Fat finger worries: How older and younger users physically interact with PDAs. In *Proceedings of INTERACT '05*, Rome.

Silver, J. and Rosenbaum, E. (2012). Makey Makey: Improvising Tangible and Nature-Based User Interfaces. In *Adjunct Proc. TEI'12*.

Silverberg, M., MacKenzie, I. S. and Korhonen, P. (2000) Predicting text entry speed on mobile phones. In *Proceedings of CHI 2000*. ACM, New York, pp. 9–16.

Singer, J., Lethbridge, T., Vinson, N. and Anquetil, N. (1997) An examination of software engineering work practices. Paper presented at Centre for Advanced Studies Conference (CASCON), Toronto, Ontario.

Slater, M. and Wilbur, S. (1997) A framework for immersive virtual environments (FIVE): speculations on the role of presence in virtual environments, *Presence: Teleoperators and Virtual Environments* **6**, 603–616.

Slater, M., Pertaub, D. and Steed, A. (1999) Public speaking in virtual reality: Facing an audience of avatars. *IEEE Computer Graphics and Applications* **19**(2), 6–9.

Sleeper, M., Consolvo, S. and Staddon, J. (2014) Exploring the benefits and uses of web analytics tools for non-transactional websites. *ACM Proceedings of the 2014 conference on Designing interactive systems (DIS).*

Smith, A. (2014) 6 new Facts about Facebook. Pew Research. Downloaded from http://www.pewre search.org/fact-tank/2014/02/03/6-new-facts-about-facebook/.

Smith, D., Irby, C., Kimball, R., Verplank, B. and Harslem, E. (1982) Designing the Star user interface, *Byte* 7(4), 242–282.

Smyth, J. D., Dillman, D. A., Christian, L. M. and Stern, M. J. (2004) How visual grouping influences answers to Internet surveys. Technical Report #04-023. Washington State University Social and Economic Sciences Research Center, Pullman, 32 pp.

Smyth, J. D., Dillman, D. A., Christian, L. M. and Stern, M. J. (2005) Comparing check-all and forced-choice question formats in web surveys: The role of satisficing, depth of processing, and acquiescence in explaining differences. Technical Report #05-029. Washington State University Social and Economic Sciences Research Center, Pullman, 30 pp.

Sohn, T., Li, K. A., Griswold, W. G. and Hollan, J. D. (2008) A diary study of mobile information needs. In *Proceedings of CHI 2008*. AMC, New York.

Solovey, E.T., Afergan, D., Peck, E., Hincks, S. and Jacob, R.J.K. (2014) Designing Implicit Interfaces for Physiological Computing: Guidelines and Lessons Learned using fNIRS1. *ACM Transactions on Computer–Human Interactions*, 21(6).

Sommerville, I. (2010) *Software Engineering* (9th edn). Addison-Wesley, Boston.

Sparrow, B., Liu, J. and Wegner, D. M. (2011) Google effects on memory: cognitive consequences of having information at our fingertips. *Science*, 333(6043), 308–314.

Spelmezan, D., Jacobs, M., Hilgers, A. and Borchers, J. (2009) Tactile motion instructions for physical activities. In *Proceedings of the 27th International Conference on Human Factors in Computing Systems, CHI 2009*. ACM, New York, NY, pp. 2243–2252.

Spencer, R. (2000) The streamlined cognitive walkthrough method: Working around social constraints encountered in a software development company. In *Proceedings of CHI 2000*. ACM, pp. 253–359.

Spool, J. M., Scanlon, T., Schroeder, W., Snyder, C. and DeAngelo, T. (1997) *Web Site Usability: A designer's guide*. User Interface Engineering, North Andover, MA.

Spreenberg, P., Salomon, G. and Joe, P. (1995) Interaction design at IDEO product development. In *Proceedings of ACM CHI '95 Conference Companion*. ACM, New York, pp. 164–165.

Starbird, K., Palen, L., Hughes, A. L., and Vieweg, S. (2010) Chatter on the red: What hazards threat reveals about the social life of microblogged information. *Proceedings of the 2010 ACM Conference on Computer Supported Cooperative Work, CSCW 2010*. ACM, pp. 241–250.

Steptoe, W., Julier, J. and Steed, A. (2014) Presence and Discernability in Conventional and Non-Photorealistic/Immersive Augmented Reality. In *Proceedings of International Symposium on Mixed and Augmented Reality (ISMAR 2014)*. Munich, Germany, September 10–12.

Strauss, A. and Corbin, J. (1998) *Basics of Qualitative Research: Techniques and procedures for developing grounded theory* (2nd edn). Sage, London.

Strommen, E. (1998) When the interface is a talking dinosaur: Learning across media with ActiMates Barney. In *Proceedings of CHI '98*. ACM, New York, pp. 288–295.

Subrayaman, R., Weisstein, F. L. and Krishnan, M. S. (2010) User participation in software development projects, *Communications of the ACM* 53(3), 137–141.

Suchman, L. A. (1987) *Plans and Situated Actions*. Cambridge University Press, Cambridge.

Sue, V. M. and Ritter, L. A. (2012) *Conducting Online Surveys*. Sage.

Sutcliffe, A. (2002) *Multimedia and Virtual Reality: Designing multisensory user interfaces*. Lawrence Earlbaum Associates, Hillsdale, NJ.

Sy, D. (2007) Adapting usability investigations for development, *Journal of Usability Studies* **2**(3), May, 112–130.

Thackara, J. (2001) The design challenge of pervasive computing. In *Interactions* May/Jun, 47–52. Thaler, R. H. and Sunstein, C. R. (2008) *Nudge: Improving decisions about health, wealth and happiness*. Penguin.

The People's Bot http://civic.mit.edu/blog/chelseabarabas/the-peoples-bot

Thimbleby, H. (1990) *User Interface Design*. Addison-Wesley, Harlow, Essex.

Tidwell, J. (2006) *Designing Interfaces: Patterns for effective interaction design*. O'Reilly Media Inc.

Tomlin, W. C. (2010) Usability, www.usefulusability.com/ (accessed May 1, 2010).

Tractinsky, N. (1997) Aesthetics and apparent usability: Empirically assessing cultural and methodological issues. *CHI '97 Electronic Publications: Papers,* www.acm.org/sigchi/chi97/proceedings/paper/nt.htm (accessed December 16, 2010).

Tractinsky, N., Shoval-Katz, A. and Ikar, D. (2000) What is beautiful is usable, *Interacting with Computers* **13**(2), 127–145.

Tran, Q., Calcaterra, G. and Mynatt, E. (2005) How an older and a younger adult adopted a cooking memory aid. In *Proceedings of HCII 2005*, York, April 13–15.

Trimble, J., Wales, R. and Gossweiler, R. (2002) NASA position paper for the CSCW 2002 workshop on Public, Community and Situated Displays: MERBoard.

Tsukada, K. and Yasumura, M. (2002) Ubi-Finger: gesture input device for mobile use. In *Proceedings of APCHI 2002*, Vol. 1, pp. 388–400.

Tullis, T. S. (1997) Screen design. In M. Helander, T. K. Landauer and P. Trabhu (eds) *Handbook of Human–Computer Interaction* (2nd edn). Elsevier, New York, pp. 377–411.

Tullis, T. and Albert, B. (2008) *Measuring the User Experience*. Morgan Kaufmann.

Ullmar, B., Ishii, H. and Jacob, R. J. K. (2005) Token + Constraint Systems for tangible interaction with digital information. *TOCHI* **12**(1), 81–N8.

Underkoffler, J. and Ishii, H. (1998) Illuminating light: An optical design tool with a luminous–tangible interface. In *Conference Proceedings on Human Factors in Computing Systems*. ACM Press/Addison-Wesley, pp. 542–549.

Usability Net http://www.usabilitynet.org/tools/criticalincidents.htm.

Väänänen-Vainio-Mattila, K. and Waljas, M. (2009) Development of evaluation heurisitcs for web service user experience. *CHI 2009 Spotlight on Works in Progress, Session 1*, pp. 3679–3684.

Van den Bergh, J. and Coninx, K. (2005) Towards modelling context-sensitive interactive applications: the context-sensitive user interface profile (CUP). In *Proceedings of the 2005 ACM Symposium on Software Visualization*, St Louis.

van den Broek, E.L. (2013) Ubiquitous emotion-aware computing. *Pers. Ubiquit. Comput,* **17**, 53–67.

van der Linden, J., Schoonderwaldt, E., Bird, J. and Johnson, R. (2011) MusicJacket – combining motion capture and vibrotactile feedback to teach violin bowing. *IEEE Transactions on Instrumentation and Measurement,* **60**(1), pp. 104–113.

Van Rens, L. S. (1997) Usability problem classifier. Unpublished Master's Thesis, Virginia Polytechnic Institute and State University, Blacksburg, VA.

Veen, J. (2001) *The Art and Science of Web Design*. New Riders Press, Indianapolis, IN.

Vertegaal, R. (2008) A Fitts' Law comparison of eye tracking and manual input in the selection of visual targets, *ICMI 2008*, October 20–22, Chania, Crete, Greece, pp. 241–248.

VisiStat (2010) *Case Study: The MountainWinery.com*, visistat.com/case-study-mountain-winery.php (accessed September 2010).

von Neumann, J. and Morgenstern, O. (1944) *Theory of Games and Economic Behavior*. Princeton University Press.

Vygotsky, L. S. (1926/1962) *Thought and Language*. MIT Press, Cambridge, MA.

Wagner, E. L. and Piccoli, G. (2007) Moving beyond user participation to achieve successful IS design, *Communications of the ACM* **50**(12) 51–55.

Wallace, J., McCarthy, J., Wright, P. and Olivier, P. (2013) Making Design Probes Work. In *Proceedings of CHI 2013*. ACM, pp. 3441–3450.

Walter, A. (2011) *A Book Apart: Designing for Emotion*. Zeldman, Jeffrey.

Wang, Y., Song, G., Qiao, G., Zhang, Y., Zhang, J. and Wang, W. (2013) Wheeled Robot Control Based on Gesture Recognition Using the Kinect Sensor, in *Proceedings of the IEEE International Conference on Robotics and Biomimetics (ROBIO)*, Shenzhen, China, December 2013, pp. 378–383.

WCAG (Web Content Accessibility Guidelines) Version 1.0 (2006) www.w3.org/TR/WAI-WEBCONTENT/ (retrieved September 1, 2006).

Weiser, M. (1991) The computer for the 21st century, *Scientific American*, 94–104.

Weiss, S. (2002) *Handheld Usability*. John Wiley & Sons Inc., New York.

Weller, D. (2004) The effects of contrast and density on visual web search, *Usability News* **6**(2): http://psychology.wichita.edu/surl/usabilitynews/62/density.htm (retrieved July 11, 2005).

Wellner, P. (1993) Interacting with paper on the DigitalDesk, *Communications of the ACM* **36**(7), 86–96.

Wetzel, R., McCall, R., Braun, A. and Broll, W. (2008) Guidelines for designing augmented reality games. In *Proceedings of the 2008 Conference on Future Play: Research, Play, Share Future Play*. ACM, New York, pp. 173–180.

Wharton, C., Rieman, J., Lewis, C., and Polson, P. (1994) The cognitive walkthrough method: A practitioner's guide. In J. Nielsen and R. L. Mack (eds) *Usability Inspection Methods*. John Wiley & Sons Inc., New York.

Whiteside, J., Bennett, J. and Holtzblatt, K. (1988) Usability engineering: Our experience and evolution. In H. Helander (ed.) *Handbook of Human–Computer Interaction*. Elsevier Science Publishers, Amsterdam, pp. 791–817.

Winograd, T. (1997) From computing machinery to interaction design. In P. Denning and R. Metcalfe (eds) *Beyond Calculation: The next fifty years of computing*. Springer-Verlag, Amsterdam, pp. 149–162.

Winograd, T. and Flores, W. (1986) *Understanding Computers and Cognition: A new foundation for design*. Addison-Wesley, Norwood, NJ.

Winschiers-Theophilus, H. and Bidwell, N. J. (2013) Toward an Afro-Centric Indigenous HCI Paradigm, *International Journal of Human-Computer Interaction*, **29**(4), 243–255.

Winschiers-Theophilus, H., Bidwell, N. J. and Blake, E. (2012) Community Consensus: Design Beyond Participation, *Design Issues*, **28**(3) Summer 2012, 89–100.

Wixon, D. and Wilson, C. (1997) The usability engineering framework for product design and evaluation. In M. G. Helander, T. K. Landauer and P. V. Prabju (eds) *Handbook of Human–Computer Interaction*. Elsevier, Amsterdam, pp. 653–688.

Woolrych, A. and Cockton, G. (2001) Why and when five test users aren't enough. In *Proceedings of IHM-HCI 2001 Conference*, Vol. 2. Cépadèus Éditions, Toulouse, pp. 105–108.

Yip, J., Clegg, T., Bonsigore, E., Gelderblom, H., Rhodes, E., and Druin, A. (2013) Brownies or Bags-of-Stuff? Domain Expertise in Cooperative Inquiry with Children. Paper presented at the *Interaction, Design, and Children Annual Conference*, New York, NY.

Yohanan, S. and MacLean, K. E. (2008) The Haptic Creature Project: Social human-robot interaction through affective touch. In *Proceedings of the AISB 2008 Symposium on the Reign of Catz & Dogs: The Second AISB Symposium on the Role of Virtual Creatures in a Computerized Society*, **1**, 7–11.

Yuill, N. and Rogers, Y. (2012) Mechanisms for collaboration: A design and evaluation framework for multi-user interfaces. *ACM Trans. Comput.-Hum. Interact.* **19**(1), Article 1, 25 pages.

Zeiliger, R., Reggers, T., Baldewyns, L. and Jans, V. (1997) Facilitating web navigation: integrated tools for active and cooperative learners. In *Proceedings of the 5th International Conference on Computers in Education, ICCE '97*, December, Kuching, Sarawak, Malaysia.

Zuckerman, O. and Resnick, M. (2005) Extending tangible interfaces for education: digital Montessori-inspired manipulatives. In *Proceedings of Conference on Human Factors in Computing Systems*. ACM Press, New York, pp. 859–868.

Zufferey, G., Jermann, P., Lucchi, A. and Dillenbourg, P. (2009) TinkerSheets: Using paper forms to control and visualize tangible simulations. In *Proceedings of TEI09*. ACM, New York, pp. 377–384.

Index